FOREWORD

I RECALL CLEARLY my first therapy session with Anne Sexton. Her vivid description was poignant with regard to her total inability to live the life she believed was demanded of her. She felt helpless, unable to function as a wife or mother, and expressed resentment at having her children taken away from her, yet at the same time she recognized that she was truly unable to care for them. In many ways she loved her children and family dearly, but she simply could not cope with the roles required. Although she was trying her best to live up to the 1950s image of the good wife and mother, she found the task completely beyond her.

Since I have always believed that it is at least as important to understand a patient's resources as to determine the amount of psychopathology, I sought to explore Anne's resources and goals. She had married early and had barely finished high school. She particularly regretted her lack of formal education, which contributed to her feelings of inadequacy. It is difficult to communicate fully how pervasive Anne's profound lack of self-worth was and how totally unable she was to think of *any* positive abilities or qualities within herself. When I pressed her to think hard about what she might be able to do, she finally revealed that there was only one thing that she might possibly be capable of doing well — to be a good prostitute and to help men feel sexually powerful. It was clear that in her case, goals were not a place to start to find positive facets to bolster a sense to self.

Early in therapy, I focused on Anne's developing her skills, suggesting among other things that she begin writing about her experiences in order to help other patients. This idea struck a responsive chord in her, and we were able to work on it together without her immediately getting so discouraged as to reject it. Developing the supports for a sense of self that Anne could appreciate was not easy. It took some months, but there finally came a time when we were able to begin to discuss the possibility of her continuing her education. While this was a goal that she was now willing at least to talk about, her fear of strangers left her unwilling to take the necessary steps to attend formal courses. At that point, however, she herself returned to my original, almost offhand comment, "How about writing?" and she began to bring poems to our sessions.

In the beginning, her poems obviously needed much additional work, but they were clearly pieces with a compelling communication and a flair that Anne and I could discuss — a meaningful project on which she could begin to build a foundation. The sheer existence of the task of writing poetry, through which she could describe her pain, her confusion, and her observations, provided the basis for a critical sense of self-esteem. The impetus to go forward with it eventually gave her the strength to follow up by participating in poetry workshop sessions. She was able to obtain and use the necessary criticism and feedback she received in these sessions to improve her work in a way that is very unusual early in an artist's career. Once Anne was assured that she really was able to write poetry, she almost could not stop. Writing poetry became the driving force.

Thus began an incredibly rocky but strengthening period in Anne's life. Little by little, she began to deal with the practical problems of correspondence, of submission and resubmission, of reviewing and rewriting. At last she could connect with peers and teachers, with whom she could for the first time begin to communicate *outside* the therapy setting. Even though Anne was among my first long-term patients, my experience had been, and still is to this day, that the sicker the patient is, the more important it is for the therapist and the patient to work on a task together, so that the patient can develop a stronger sense of self from the work accomplished. If the patient can fully involve herself in a task that takes on its own meaning in her life *outside* the therapy sessions, then resolution of the other problems we need to deal with in the sessions can also carry over to her world outside.

Originally, when Anne sought help following the birth of her second child, she had been diagnosed as having postpartum depression. When I first saw her in therapy in the hospital in August 1956, a year after the birth, her thoughts and behaviors were not really consistent with the presumptive diagnosis. As I began to get to know Anne, I realized that she was showing ideation that one might expect in a patient with a thought disorder. Fortunately, she happened to mention that she was spending a good deal of time with two patients who suffered from a schizophrenic disorder, and thus I became aware of her tendency to take on symptoms that were like those of the people with whom she was currently interacting. Indeed, because of this tendency, I was even more careful not to have Anne stay in a hospital setting any longer than was absolutely necessary, lest she adopt new symptoms from other patients.

As we continued to work together, it became increasingly evident that in addition to her tendency to absorb symptoms and mannerisms from those who impressed her, Anne's core problem was that she suffered from a severe difficulty of memory. While to some extent each of us is selective in what we remember, Anne's selectivity was extreme in the sense that she literally remembered almost nothing of relevance from one session to the next. In short, for this and other reasons, it was clear that she had a condition that traditionally was known as hysteria.

Anne's severe memory problem was eventually to lead to an impasse in her therapy. That is, although within an individual session she was able to work effectively during treatment, it emerged over a period of months that each therapy session had the quality of having a beginning, a middle, and an end — which gave both therapist and patient the feeling that something meaningful was being accomplished. Yet, in looking back over the work of the sessions, I gradually realized that each session was a vignette unto itself, with very little progress being made *across* therapy sessions. In other words, even though Anne was expressing and working with intense feelings, the therapeutic process somehow failed to move forward in the larger sense.

At first I tried to aid Anne's memory by taking more extensive notes myself, so that I could more easily help her recall the important aspects of the previous sessions in order to achieve a much-needed feeling of continuity. After several false starts in this endeavor, I realized that it was necessary for Anne herself to become the one responsible for remembering what we were doing together. In other words, it was not my role to take on the responsibility to remember what occurred in our previous sessions, but hers.

Together we worked toward evolving a procedure to deal with the problem that resulted from Anne's inability to recall what had occurred in previous sessions. I tried to have Anne make extensive notes as an aid to her memory, but performing this task interfered with the process of treatment. I then suggested that we audiotape our sessions and that it would be *her* responsibility to review what had happened in the session. It turned out, however, that simply listening to the audiotape was by no means sufficient to break down Anne's tendency to develop amnesia for the events of the past session. Furthermore, it did not have the consequence of making *her* aware of the difference between what she *remembered* of a session and what actually *occurred* during that session. However, we eventually hit upon a viable procedure.

First we would audiotape the therapy session, and afterward Anne was asked to make extensive notes about everything she could remember from the session. The next day she would come to the office, and my secretary would put the tape on the recorder and leave her alone to listen to the session. She was asked to note particularly the discrepancies between her memories, her notes from the previous day, and what actually happened on the tape. In the beginning, it was necessary for Anne to listen to the audiotape *twice* before she was able to recall on her own what we had dealt with during the session. This tedious approach demanded a great deal of Anne, but its consequences were profound. For the first time in her life, she was able to recall *why* she had been upset about something someone had said, or why she had been angry at me, without knowing the reason. In other words, Anne could really remember and learn about her feelings, whereas in the past she had been unable to recall more than fragments of what occurred — many of which she recalled incorrectly.

The constructive consequences of this audiotaping, listening, and note-taking procedure for increasing memory and for making progress in therapy cannot be overemphasized. Though it is fair to say that the procedure led to some embarrassing moments for me as the therapist — since Anne was able to point to errors in *my* memory of prior sessions — it was a unique experience for Anne to know more about what transpired in her treatment than her therapist did. In many regards, it made the relationship between us far more equal than in the past — a true collaboration, in which Anne could discover important insights and share them with me. Thus, her sense of self had developed to the extent that she could attend to her own behavior as well as to that of others. Whereas the therapist usually holds all the cards, the patient now could know more about what was happening in treatment than the therapist did. Indeed, Anne made a major step forward when she was first able to show me that I was wrong!

By listening to and being able to tolerate her own pain and anger on the audiotapes, and by developing the ability to recall emotional events that mattered to her, Anne was gradually able to deal with these emotions in her poetry. Soon after her poetry began to be published, she found that many troubled individuals sought her guidance and counsel. Indeed, she took great pride in being able to help others with similar pain. She spent an inordinate amount of time answering letters from strangers, and undoubtedly helped many of them. Although she became a professional poet in a remarkably short time,

Anne never stopped recognizing the importance that her poetry might play in the lives of her readers.

When Professor Diane Middlebrook requested an interview to discuss my work with Anne, it was uppermost in my mind how important it had been to Anne always to try to help others, especially in their writing. Although I had many misgivings about discussing any aspects of the therapy, which extended over eight years, I also realized that Anne herself would have wanted to share this process — much as she did in her poetry — so that other patients and therapists might learn from it. After much soul-searching, and after being assured that Anne's family had given their encouragement and approval, I allowed Professor Middlebrook to have access to the audiotapes and my therapy file, including the early unpublished poems Anne brought to therapy. It is in the spirit of helping others that I also offer here a view of what I believe contributed to Anne's untimely death.

There is one aspect of Anne's life that has not been clarified, that is, her tendency to become uncommunicative in a self-induced trance, which could last minutes, hours, or, in a few rare circumstances, even days. Typically, the trance episode could easily be ended by a therapist familiar with the symptom. But in therapy and out, the problem persisted: when Anne was extremely angry, she was given to entering a trance and becoming unresponsive. Treatment helped to decrease these events, but they were never eliminated. Anne also had a remarkable fascination with death, and it seemed likely that she used some of the trance episodes to play the role of dying, which perhaps helped her not to suicide. However, when her relationship with significant others was diminished, and if she was in a period when death seemed attractive, there was always the danger that she would do the deed rather than play the role. Unfortunately, Anne's relationships with a number of significant others, especially her husband, were diminished through a series of events that began with my move from Boston to Philadelphia.

When I made the decision to leave Harvard to come to Pennsylvania to further develop the Institute for Experimental Psychiatry, Anne and I had the opportunity to work together for several months before she transferred to another therapist in Boston. By then she had progressed in treatment in many areas of functioning, though she continued to need therapeutic help. At that time she was already a well-known poet, having published two collections and having written a play. She was also soon to win the Pulitzer Prize and to be accepted by the academic world, which had become a major goal for her. Equally important was the fact that by this time Anne's relationship with her husband, Kayo, had improved significantly, and she was earning sufficient funds from poetry to begin to save toward a safari in Africa, which her husband had long wanted.

It was always clear to me that her husband was a crucial part of Anne's life. This was evident even in the beginning, when Anne described becoming markedly worse whenever Kayo had to go away on business trips. Although many therapeutic gains had been made from 1956 to 1964, I felt that Anne's emotional health still depended heavily on the support she received from her husband and many other people who cared for her. When I left Boston, I arranged to return once a month for several years to see a number of patients for follow-up. It was clearly necessary for Anne to have another therapist on an ongoing basis, but I also saw her during my regular visits to Boston. Although Anne initially did extremely well with another therapist, the therapeutic contract became untenable because of a change in their relationship. Unfortunately, this change also undermined her crucial relationship with her husband, thereby depriving Anne of what had been a vital interpersonal support.

During this difficult time, Anne continued to see me in treatment on follow-up, and I was eventually able to help her in the difficult process of finding yet another therapist. Finally she decided on a female therapist who had been suggested by her previous therapist. Unfortunately, this new therapist decided she could treat Anne *only* if Anne stopped seeing me completely, because in her view, Anne's transference relationship with me would undermine treatment. In this way Anne lost yet another support, which further eroded her ability to withstand a serious therapeutic setback. Not long thereafter, she and her husband were divorced.

Although I felt obligated not to interfere with the guidelines that had been established for Anne's treatment, in the last year of her life, Anne called to say that she would be in Philadelphia to give a reading at the public library and that she hoped she could see me. I expected to see her, but she never made it. Sadly, if in therapy Anne had been encouraged to hold on to the vital supports that had helped her build the innovative career that meant so much to her and others, it is my view that Anne Sexton would be alive today.

MARTIN T. ORNE, M.D., PH.D.
*The Institute of Pennsylvania Hospital
and University of Pennsylvania*

PREFACE

"I don't read poetry, but I read Anne Sexton."
— A fan, 1985

ANNE SEXTON liked to arrive about ten minutes late for her own performances: let the crowd work up a little anticipation. She would saunter to the podium, light a cigarette, kick off her shoes, and in a throaty voice say, "I'm going to read a poem that tells you what kind of a poet I am, what kind of a woman I am, so if you don't like it you can leave." Then she would launch into her signature poem, "Her Kind": "I have gone out, a possessed witch . . . A woman like that is misunderstood . . . I have been her kind."

What kind of woman was she? Spirited, good-looking: tall and lean as a fashion model; a suburban housewife who called herself Ms. Dog; a daughter, a mother; a New England WASP; like Emily Dickinson, "half-crack'd." And what kind of poet? Intimate; confessional; comic; insistently, disruptively female; a word wizard; a performance artist; a crowd pleaser. Those were some of the things you could learn during her first fifteen minutes onstage.

Some people didn't like the Sexton persona. But behind it stood a serious, disciplined artist whose work had been admired from the beginning by distinguished peers. During her eighteen years as a writer, Sexton earned most of the important awards available to American poets. She published eight books of poetry (leaving others in manuscript), and she saw her play *Mercy Street* produced off-Broadway. She was a shrewd businesswoman, and she became a successful teacher; though skimpily educated, she rose to the rank of professor at Boston University, teaching the craft of poetry. She conducted this career in the context of a mental disorder that eluded diagnosis or cure. Suicidal self-hatred led to repeated hospitalizations in mental institutions. She became addicted to alcohol and sleeping pills. By the time she committed suicide in 1974, misery had hollowed her out and drinking had obliterated her creativity. Yet from the rising of Anne Sexton's star in 1960, with the publication of *To Bedlam and Part Way Back*, hers had been an important new voice in American poetry.

Ten years ago, when I was invited by Anne Sexton's elder daughter, Linda Gray Sexton, to write her biography, I counted myself among the people who didn't much like Sexton's public persona. I liked the project, though, because Sexton's career posed big, interesting questions: How did a mad housewife become a star? What connected her madness and her art? Why did her work appeal to poetry-avoiders? As literary executor, Linda Sexton had decided to let the biographer pursue such questions freely, with full access to her mother's private papers and a pledge to cooperate in the development of a complete account without exercising control over its editorial viewpoint. Such an attitude on the part of an artist's family is rare, needless to say, but all these promises were kept.

As I worked through the ample, sometimes harrowing records of Anne Sexton's life, my initial impressions gave way to surprise and fascination, amusement and affection, and finally to understanding. Sexton did some awful things at times, but she was also intelligent, generous, witty, talented, and hard-working; despite her illness, she found ways to get her work done, and she had deep capacities for love and for pleasure. I came to see her eighteen-year career as a successful response to a set of conditions that she could not change very much except by writing about them. Her maladies did not wholly succumb to insight: although psychotherapy helped her dramatically, she stayed sick. Yet her poems invented a self that others valued, and this endowed her real life with opportunities.

Sexton wrote about the social confusions of growing up in a female body and of living as a woman in postwar American society. Thousands of women have shared the mental disorders that disabled her, and hundreds of thousands have shared her dissatisfaction with life as a suburban housewife, but few possess the gift, or summon the discipline and courage, or make the friends, or command the financial resources, or have the well-timed good luck that made Anne Sexton into a serious poet. That is why, in representing the relationship between her illness and her art, I have attempted to avoid the perspective of a pathography. Sexton's life ended in a suicide that was the act of a lonely and despairing alcoholic, but it might have ended silently and much earlier if she had not, almost miraculously, found something else profoundly important to do with it.

Writing this book also clarified for me Sexton's distinctive achievements as an artist. In her first two books, *To Bedlam and Part Way Back* (1960) and *All My Pretty Ones* (1962), she made her debut as a skilled formalist tutored by a cohort of deft technicians: Maxine Kumin, Robert Lowell, W. D. Snodgrass, and George Starbuck. These volumes, combined and lightly edited, were published in England as *Selected Poems* (1964). With her next books, *Live or Die* (1966) and *Love Poems* (1969), she began exploring modes of surrealism she was shown by her mentor James Wright; increasingly, she experimented with "writing from the unconscious" and developed a poetics to account for her practice. With Maxine Kumin, Sexton wrote a number of children's books over the years. She was also interested in writing for the theater. Her unpublished play went through several phases of development before production as *Mercy Street* in New York at the American Place Theater in 1969, and some of her poems read like scripts for a voice; I attribute much of the formal looseness that disturbed her hostile critics to the influence of that genre on her conception of the poem. This skill reached its most effective artistic expression in *Transformations* (1971), long poems adapted from Grimm's fairy tales narrated by a "middle-aged witch"; an opera by Conrad Susa was later based on this book.

Sexton's last poems increasingly concerned religious questions. Though her standing as a popular artist has obscured the originality of her struggles with spiritual themes, in my view she published some of her most vital work in *The Book of Folly* (1972) and *The Death Notebooks* (1974). Her poetry and her health had collapsed by the time she produced her last three books of poems, which were published posthumously: *The Awful Rowing Toward God* (1975), *45 Mercy Street* (1976), and *Words for Dr. Y.* (1978). *Complete Poems* (1981) collected previously unpublished work, and *Selected Poems* followed in 1988. *Anne Sexton: A Self-Portrait in Letters*, edited by Linda Sexton and Lois Ames, appeared in 1977.

Sexton goes on attracting readers. By the end of the 1980s, remarkably, nearly a half-million volumes of her work had been sold in the United States by Houghton Mifflin Company; in Britain, Oxford University Press and then Chatto & Windus brought her work to another responsive audience.

·   ·   ·

This book is based on an unusual range of materials. Anne Sexton was a self-documenting person: from childhood on she kept scrapbooks of treasured moments; from the earliest months of what was to become her professional life she kept carbon copies of her letters; she dated worksheets of poems; she saved correspondence, photographs, clippings. After her death, Linda Sexton transferred ownership of her papers to the Harry Ransom Humanities Research Center at the University of Texas at Austin (HRHRC). During the years that Anne Sexton was making herself into a poet, her psychiatric illnesses also generated numerous records. Linda Sexton helped me acquire hospital records, and also permitted me to use a unique resource: audiotapes of over three hundred psychotherapy sessions with Dr. Martin Orne, Sexton's principal psychiatrist from 1956 to 1964. Dr. Orne began taping their sessions in January 1961, with Sexton's cooperation, as a way to address her inability to remember. Between sessions, Sexton would play back the tapes and make notes on them. Both the poet and her doctor regarded this practice as very productive. It was discontinued only in 1964, when Dr. Orne moved from Boston to Philadelphia and Sexton entered therapy with another psychiatrist.

Since the years of taping coincided with Sexton's maturation as an artist, Linda Sexton decided to place her mother's therapy notebooks at HRHRC, under restriction during the lifetime of family members. I was allowed to use them. After I had written about the period covered by the notebooks, Dr. Orne granted me an interview, and then, with the executor's permission, sent me the incomplete but large collection of tapes that had survived his move from Boston in 1964. I spent the next two years transcribing these tapes; a part of one transcript is included here as an appendix. Though I eventually quoted them sparingly, listening to them changed my view of Anne Sexton very much. I abandoned the book I had been writing and started over.

How might Sexton have viewed this exposure of the doctor-patient relationship? She made no reference to the tapes when writing her will, which dealt very professionally with the disposition of her literary estate. Four tapes were jumbled among her papers at the time of her death, however, and these have become part of the restricted collection of materials at HRHRC. Everything I have learned about her suggests that she would not have held back from the archive of her manuscripts and private papers the full collection of tapes. Sexton was not a person with a strong sense of privacy. She was open and impulsive: many people found her exhibitionistic, and some of the people who lived with her found her outrageously, immorally invasive. But her lack of reserve had a generous side as well, which was, I think, connected to her spirituality. If suffering like hers had any use, she reasoned, it was not to the sufferer. The only way that an individual's pain gained meaning was through its communication to others. I have tried to honor that attitude of Sexton's in writing about her life.

A NOTE ON PUNCTUATION AND NAMES

Sexton and her correspondents frequently used three or more periods as punctuation, which can be mistaken for ellipses. For clarity, I have placed brackets around an ellipsis [. . .] when it signifies my omission from written or printed texts. In quoting from the doctor's notes and from my transcriptions of Anne Sexton's therapy tapes, I completed the syntax for ease of reading, and for the same reason I indicated omissions or other breaks in continuity in the conventional way, with ellipses. In quoting from Sexton's transcriptions and notes in her therapy notebooks, I have followed her punctuation and spelling.

Four pseudonyms have been used in this book: Ollie Zweizung and Constance Chase are not the names of Sexton's psychiatrists; Jerry is not the name of the poet from the workshop with whom Sexton had an affair in 1957; and Brother Dennis is not the name of the priest with whom Sexton corresponded, 1962–1963.

I

BECOMING ANNE SEXTON
1928-1957

1

BEGINNINGS
1928-

ANNE SEXTON BEGAN writing poetry as a teenager, like many of us, then stopped, like most of us. She began writing again when she was a suicidal woman undergoing psychiatric treatment, with two young children of her own. In Anne Sexton's life, psychotherapy constructed a bridge between the girl's creativity and the woman's commitment to a vocation in art.

Sexton spent a good deal of her adult life pursuing associations that led back into childhood, particularly to her years as the "baby" in an affluent extended family. She was drawn again and again to painful, encysted feelings toward her mother, father, and great-aunt, Nana, through which the past survived in her. One thing that became clear to her, since she spent so much time dwelling on it, was that the past exists only in versions, which differ according to our motives at the moment of recall.

Usually Sexton's motive was to tell a good story. After she became famous, interviewers would ask the predictable question, "How did you become a poet?" and she would always give the same details, often repeating whole phrases as if she had them by heart. What she said often evoked the plot of "Snow White." The queen in her story was her impressive mother, the daughter of a writer. The poisoned apple was society's pressure on Anne to lead a conventional life in the suburbs of Boston, caring for her two daughters and helping her husband advance in his career in the wool business. The poison took: she became sick, attempted suicide. The magical transformation came in treatment by a psychiatrist who, something like the prince in the fairy tale, stumbled onto a remedy that woke her into a new life as a poet. Sexton called this awakening her "rebirth at twenty-nine," and added, "When I'm writing, I know I'm doing the thing I was born to do."

Anne Sexton the artist, by her own account, was born at twenty-eight. It was not an easy gestation. She broke down completely as a wife and mother, and for a year and a half she shuttled between extremes of stupefied vacancy and panicky agitation. Her sickness was horrible to her, and often appalling to the people who lived with her. Nonetheless, the seeds of her identity as an important American writer were sown in the rich mess that spilled from her first mental breakdown in 1956. The poet's life starts there.

But there were other storytellers in Anne Sexton's family, too, some of whom survived her to challenge the truthfulness of the dramatic narratives into which Sexton distilled her feelings about the past. Their versions of her history help us to piece together other views of her early life, the years before her "rebirth," which sometimes conflict with her own but also illuminate both her madness and her art.

Anne Gray Harvey was born on 9 November 1928 in Newton, Massachusetts, the third of three daughters: Jane (1923), Blanche (1925), and Anne. Her parents, Ralph and Mary Gray Staples Harvey, were like characters out of a Scott Fitzgerald novel, children of the Roaring Twenties: good-looking, well-to-do, party-loving, and self-indulgent. Ralph Churchill Harvey was born on 7 February 1900 in Chelsea, Massachusetts, but grew up in Wellesley, a prosperous suburb west of Boston. By the time of Anne's birth he was well established in the wool business and about to open his own firm, R. C. Harvey Company. He was a tall man, about six feet, who stood very erect and dressed fastidiously. A successful salesman who frequently traveled long distances throughout New England and upstate New York by car and train, he managed to remain meticulously well-groomed: hair sleek, shoes shined, nails manicured. An air of mostly genial shrewdness marked his demeanor toward others. "You've got to stay on the *qui vive*, girls," he would say to his children.

Ralph's father, Louis Harvey, was a banker and a self-made man. By the time Anne was born, he was a prominent businessman, long-time president of the Wellesley National Bank. But unlike his gregarious son, Louis Harvey was a rather rigid moralist who did not permit drinking or smoking in his presence. His views left a lasting mark on Wellesley: as a member of the town's Advisory Board, he saw to it that the only movie house was built without balconies, to discourage necking. A hardworking man who permitted himself few distractions, he suffered what his family described as a nervous breakdown after one particularly strenuous period of attempting to set up a bank in Puerto Rico. Anne seems to have retained few impressions of him, but the memory of his collapse later influenced Ralph Harvey's concern for his daughter's mental health.

Louis's wife, Elizabeth Anderson, was a sociable, attractive woman rather ill-matched to her husband. "I'm going to put on my boots and have some fun!" she liked to say. She loved shopping and gossip, and would happily join her daughter-in-law for a furtive cocktail in the pantry before Sunday dinner. Anne's father, Ralph, was her first child, and both his parents' favorite. His sister, Frances, born five years later, was the antithesis of her feminine mother, preferring horses to boyfriends. She went to secretarial college and found a job in the bursar's office at Wellesley College, but had a somewhat troubled youth, and in her twenties she attempted suicide. Eventually Fran established herself on a farm in New Hampshire, breeding horses, and late in life she married a fellow horse farmer. Anne's suicide in 1974 affected her profoundly. A year later, she shot herself to death; she was sixty-nine.

Louis Harvey's old-fashioned paternal inflexibility inspired rebellion in young Ralph, who ran away in 1916 to join the army. Louis fetched him home to finish Wellesley High School, but overruled Ralph's intention to go to college. With little education himself, perhaps he considered higher education unnecessary for success in the postwar marketplace. Ralph went directly into business at age seventeen, joining a wool firm as a sample boy (with his first fifty dollars he bought his mother a solid gold bracelet). Demand for blankets and uniforms during World War I had made the Massachusetts wool business a boom industry. Backed by family connections, Ralph rose to road salesman and began making big commissions. By the time he fell in love with Anne's mother, in 1922, he could afford to marry.

Mary Gray Staples — always called Mary Gray — was born on 14 March 1901, when her own mother was thirty-six years old and her father forty-one. An only child, she was raised like a little princess. Members of her family held important social positions as politicians and journalists in the twin cities of Lewiston and Auburn, Maine, and exercised a good deal of local influence as staunch Republicans. The most eminent of Mary Gray's ancestors, Nelson Dingley, Jr., had been governor of Maine and a member of the U.S. Congress, and her grandfather had founded the *Lewiston Evening Journal*, of which her father, Arthur Gray Staples (usually referred to by his initials, A.G.S.), was now editor and publisher. Mary Gray's mother, Jane Dingley Staples, is remembered as devoted to the child born late in her marriage, but it was A.G.S. with whom Mary Gray formed the most intense bond — possibly the most intense of her life. He christened her with his mother's name, Mary Gray, perhaps to stake out space for the two of them in the midst of the mass of Dingleys who surrounded them. People remember the closeness of father and daughter: they looked much alike, and shared such diversions as jokes and books and baseball, listening to the Red Sox broadcasts together on summer afternoons. They also took up the fad for crossword puzzles, new in the 1920s; later, Anne Sexton connected her pleasure in working out tricky rhyme schemes with her mother's competitive zeal for solving crossword puzzles.

A.G.S. was ambitious about Mary Gray's education. He sent her to boarding school at Walnut Hill in Natick, Massachusetts, and then to Wellesley College. She had completed her junior year at Wellesley

Anne's mother and grandfather, Mary Gray Staples and Arthur Gray Staples.

when she met Ralph Harvey at Squirrel Island in Maine, two miles off Boothbay Harbor, where her family had a summer home. A petite, lively, outgoing woman with deep dimples around her smile, Mary Gray was one of the ringleaders of the social set on the island. She and Ralph fell instantly in love, and she decided to quit college and marry him, over her father's protests.

Mary Gray was young when she had her children. Jane was born when she was twenty-two years old; Blanche fifteen months later, and Anne in 1928, when she was twenty-seven. The sisters did not form strong emotional ties with one another; instead, they acquired distinctive characters as individuals, playing very different roles in the family.

As the eldest daughter, Jane became Daddy's girl. She was the only one of the children who took an interest in their father's hobby of raising English bull terriers for show, and she shared Ralph Harvey's passion for cars, learning to drive at age ten. In junior high, fitted out in elaborate gear, she and her girlfriends played sports with the local boys; her favorite possessions were a football and a well-oiled catcher's mitt, which no one else was permitted to touch. By the time she became interested in clothes, Jane had a lean, muscular body on which to show them off.

In contrast, Blanche came to be known in the family as the smart one. She loved to read, and was the only daughter who went to college. Anne later recalled that Blanche also had a phase of political fervor: "Blanche was all fired up about causes and theories of government." As a teenager, Blanche accompanied her mother on regular visits to a nearby convalescent home for children crippled by rheumatic fever; Mary Gray, who had had a severe case of the disease herself at age sixteen, felt that the experience would make her tough and keep her from feeling sorry for herself. Indeed, Blanche was the only Harvey daughter who seemed to gain a legacy of stability from family life; both of her sisters were to commit suicide in middle age.

Anne was the baby of the family, and she loved to be cuddled. A look of shy appeal glows from her face in a picture taken when she was about four years old; it is easy to imagine the emotional claim she made on those whose attention she craved. She remembered being very lonely as a child. One of her most haunting images was of being shut up in her room as a toddler, by a folding gate drawn across the doorway. It was a spacious, high-ceilinged room in the top story of the house, papered with a pattern of red roses. Tall windows looked onto the crowns of trees. Anne's imagination endowed this room with terrors in her late poetry: the roses become blood clots, and all the leaves rustling beyond the windowpanes are tongues urging her to die. "I was a nothing, crouching in the closet!" By the time these memories proved useful to the poet, of course, they were very old and she was very crafty. Yet as symbols they convey her conviction that she was cut off from everyone else in the family, "locked in the wrong house."

The children were sent to Sunday school at the Wellesley Congregational Church in Wellesley Hills — probably out of respect for their grandfather, since their parents kept a sophisticated distance from religious enthusiasm. This was an attitude Anne was to share; she wasn't a joiner. When in later life she concerned herself with spiritual questions, she explored them in the context of friendships, not institutions.

Through the fourth grade, Jane, Blanche, and Anne in turn attended

Anne Gray Harvey, age four or five.

the Brown Elementary School in Wellesley, near their house at 81 Garden Road. At home, their daily routines were supervised by Helen Dealand, a trained nurse who joined the household shortly after Jane's birth and remained in it until Ralph Harvey's death. More like an aunt than like hired help, Helen tended the children with a mixture of Yankee toughness and reserve, seeing to it that they kept to the strict forms of deportment demanded by their father.

Family life at the Harveys' was very formal. Ralph enforced a dress code which he was most punctilious about observing himself; he never sat down at dinner without a jacket and tie — even his underwear was ironed. When the children joined their parents for any kind of social gathering, including dinner, they were expected to check their hems and adjust their clothes beforehand, using the full-length mirrors in each of their rooms. Ralph was particularly fussy about their appearance in public. Despite everyone's efforts to keep the children always on the *qui vive,* Anne was chronically messy, fidgety, and loud. She hated mealtimes and habitually carried food off to her room, where she let it spoil — a habit that continued in later life, as her children commented. Her personal appearance consistently failed to meet her father's expectations. From a very young age, all three girls were sent weekly to the beauty parlor to have their hair washed and set. Anne's hairdo would succumb quickly to her habit of twirling her hair between her fingers into masses of snarls. Her clothes were just as bad: hems trailing, unlikely combinations of scarves and belts donned over mismatched blouses and skirts. She talked irrepressibly, in a loud voice. And she was constantly on the go; someone or other was always begging her to sit still. So she tended to be left out of occasions in which good manners counted. When her sisters moved on from Brown Elementary School to Dana Hall, a private school for girls, they began to take their dinners in the family dining room with their parents, but Anne continued to have all her meals in the breakfast room with Helen until she was eleven years old.

Ralph and Mary Gray Harvey were very close during Anne's early years. Ralph traveled three weeks out of four, selling wool processed in his factory to blanket mills and clothing manufacturers. He liked to be in constant touch with his wife from his office, and they held several phone conversations a day concerning his business affairs. He and Mary Gray went out together almost every night, and occasionally threw big parties. Later, during her psychotherapy, Anne recalled a comment Jane had made: "When Mother and Daddy had people over, they kicked us upstairs until Daddy would come up and say, now turn on the charm — oh, how I used to dread it." Command performances were the rule: "Nobody ever dropped in on our family. If they did, Father ran upstairs: he had to get ready for the performance."

Getting their parents' attention seemed to require ingenious strategies on the children's part. When Ralph and Mary Gray went out for the evening, the girls would write them notes or make drawings to leave under the pillows when the housekeeper went in to turn down the bed. They vied with one another for praise, particularly from their elusive mother.

Ralph Harvey was adopted by his wife's extended family much as A.G.S. had been absorbed into the Dingleys', perhaps for some of the same reasons. He looked up to Mary Gray as a superior person and to A.G.S. as a paragon. Though the Ralph Harveys exchanged weekly visits for Sunday dinner with the Louis Harveys, it was with the Dingley-Staples clan that they celebrated Christmas and spent long summer vacations.

The summer holidays on Squirrel Island gave the big family its most significant experience of intimacy. Until the death of Mary Gray's mother in 1938, Mary Gray and her children left Wellesley every year on the first of June. As the girls grew older, this meant taking them out of school — a departure from the rigorous discipline customary in the Harvey household, but the family encampment took priority. At Squirrel Island Mary Gray and the children and their grandparents and great-aunt Anna and assorted household staff spent the whole summer in two big houses, Dingley Dell and the Aerie, surrounded by trees and with a view of the sea. The Aerie was equipped with miniature bathroom fixtures for the children and housing for Helen Dealand and a nursemaid, Jean Mayo. Most wonderful, it held a theater with a raised stage, footlights, and a real curtain. Anne took this over as her own province when she was a little girl. Family members recalled the skill and hilarity of her theatrics and viewed this gift as the key to her personality: Anne was an actress, and loved playing to an audience. In their experience, this made her an unreliable if entertaining source of information.

A.G.S. kept a typewriter in his study at the Aerie, dispatching his editorials to the *Lewiston Evening Journal* by ferry. He also tended a raspberry patch and led a sociable life with the other elders of the community. A.G.S. was one of the chief citizens of the island, where the Dingleys had set a high tone: their philanthropy established an impressive library, for which they are still remembered. The young Ralph Harveys, however, were ringleaders of a set that went in for boisterous entertainment; for example, one year they hired a producer from New York to oversee the annual variety show that ended the summer season. There were no automobiles on the island, and it was not unusual to see boys pulling their drunken fathers home at night in the wagons that household staff used to carry supplies from the ferry to the big houses. On weekends, Ralph would drive from Wellesley to Boothbay and then take his speedboat from the Yacht Club to Squirrel Island; he is remembered as a hell-raiser. He and Mary Gray were famous for devising theme parties and clever games with other couples: they represented "the end of the flapper era" in the memory of some of the people who knew them when they were young.

The summers at Squirrel Island provided Anne with tender, enduring, happy memories of her mother's family. Particularly important to her were the names that attached the younger generation to the older ones. Anne's oldest sister was named for her grandmother, Jane Dingley, and Blanche was named for her great-aunt Blanche Dingley Mathews, a concert pianist who lived in Denver. Since the elder Blanche was unavailable most of the time, A.G.S. stood in as little Blanche's

Anne's father, Ralph Churchill Harvey, and mother, Mary Gray Harvey, on the ferry dock at Squirrel Island, Maine.

special person. They called each other Comfort, a term of endearment Anne later applied to a poet she loved. A letter A.G.S. wrote to Blanche when she was eight years old shows his grandfatherly concern that she not feel slighted as the middle child, without a namesake near: "You are my chickabiddy and my little rooster. You are my small purp-dog . . . all put together in one sublunary and transcendental prize-winner," he assures her. "For me you yank all the blue ribbons in any prize show of girls of exactly your age. I have a place in my more or less roomy heart for Jane and Anne, believe me, but nobody crowds out the glorious pulchritude of Blanche."

If Blanche was thought lucky to have her amusing grandfather pinch-hit for the elder Blanche, Anne was thought the luckiest of all for having at *her* constant disposal Great-Aunt Anna Ladd Dingley, whom everyone called Nana. An extremely important emotional reference point for Anne after she became a mother herself, Anna Dingley was an interesting person in her own right. As a young woman, she had lived abroad for three years and had written long, newsy letters that the Dingley family bound in leather and eventually passed on to Anne, who used them as the basis for her itinerary the year she went to Europe. Back home in Maine, Anna Dingley took up an unconventional profession for a woman of her time, becoming a reporter for her father's newspaper. (At one point she devised a scheme for getting herself incarcerated in the local mental institution in order to write an inside account, but the family vetoed this project.) Eventually she became part owner of the paper, as well as state and magazine editor. Her obituary mentions that she was active in the Maine Writers' Research Club.

At the same time, she played a wholly conventional family role as a dependent spinster. When her sister Jane married A.G.S., Anna shared their home. After Mary Gray was born, she briefly moved into an apartment nearby, but she was so lonely that she quickly abandoned the experiment and never lived separately again. To Mary Gray and Mary Gray's children she was always Nana, and her absorption in family life was an enormous boon; she was like an extra grandmother in the household. She would hold and cuddle the little girls by the hour, and she gave wonderful back rubs with scented talcum. When Anne was five or so, she confided to Nana that she had a pretend brother named Bobby Pressit, and Nana bought from an antique store a portrait of Bobby to hang in the sitting room where Anne visited her. The two called each other "twins."

.   .   .

Anne's idyllic childhood summers ended in 1940, when A.G.S. died and the houses at Squirrel Island were sold. In that year Ralph Harvey decided to build a new home on a large piece of property at 82 Oxbow Road in nearby Weston. With an architect, he worked out the design to his own specifications: three floors, with a suite of rooms for Nana, who had been left homeless by her brother-in-law's death; a library for Mary Gray; a finished playroom with a garden entrance for the teenagers; a big screened verandah; seven bathrooms; and five garages.

The Harveys had remained prosperous during the years of the Depression, and shortly after the family's move to Oxbow Road in 1941, the war economy lifted profits at the R. C. Harvey Company even higher. Ralph didn't have to pursue business and was on the road far less. He began to drink heavily, sequestering himself in his room. When he did appear, his moods were sometimes ugly; his wife's icy sarcasm, his daughters' table manners, or even the sight of their bad complexions could set him off on a tirade of derision. Mary Gray had a ploy to break the family tension at dinner: "Hands around the table!" she would say, grasping hands on either side of her, and sometimes this restored a mood of affection. Anne later recalled feeling that her mother was a victim of Ralph's unpredictability, but it was Mary Gray's own unpredictability that upset Jane. "Daddy was either drunk or he was sober," Jane said to Anne some years after their parents' deaths. "But you never knew, with Mother, when she was going to be horrible or nice. The minute you thought you knew where you were, she'd turn on you."

A frequent visitor at the Harvey home, Jack McCarthy — Anne's friend and then her boyfriend for several years — observed that the family mainly handled Ralph's drinking by avoiding any reference to it. Once when the Harveys' chauffeur was unavailable, Jack was asked to drive Ralph to the dentist. Stony drunk but extremely dignified, the older man sat in the back seat of his Cadillac in complete silence the whole trip, giving no sign of recognizing Jack.

Mary Gray rarely refused a cocktail, either. In later life Anne identified with the way her mother drank, joking that she would rather be regarded as a drunk than as an alcoholic. Mary Gray, she recalled, "could drink anytime she wanted. My mother drank two drinks every noon and three drinks every night come hell or high water. Once my father stopped drinking she would stand at the sink with a glass and — slosh — pour the whiskey right down. My father would drink on the sly, by the case ... I still have the glasses they had in the

twenties — I thought, my God, this is justice: my parents drank themselves into the grave and now I'm drinking out of the same glasses!"
But Mary Gray regarded herself as a social drinker; it was Ralph who
had the problem.

Anne's father drank heavily for about ten years before entering
Westwood Lodge, a private hospital, for treatment. During those
years he experienced some business setbacks and began borrowing
money, though he continued to spend lavishly on his cars (he bought
a new Cadillac every year) and the three new homes he built between
1940 and 1950. "Fuck the heirs! Let 'em walk" was what he said to
Mary Gray when she questioned his extravagance. Ralph's drinking
was episodic and unpredictable, and he tried several times to bring it
under control before he finally quit, once and for all, in 1950. When
he was drunk the family avoided him, and afterward they forgave
him: he could be so charming, so attentive.

Forgiveness came very hard to Anne. She retained distressing memories of her father's drinking binges, partly because in childhood she
didn't recognize them. "He would just suddenly become very mean,
as if he hated the world," she later told her psychiatrist. "He would sit
and look at you as though you had committed some terrible crime. He
hated everyone! Mostly I remember the expression on his face." It
seemed that he singled her out for verbal abuse when he was drinking,
complaining that her acne disgusted him and that he could not eat at
the same table with her. She felt invaded by his expressions of revul-
sion, and it seemed that no one tried to shield her from these attacks.
His drinking permanently destroyed her trust in his love.

Throughout Anne's childhood, the person who offered a parent's un-
conditional love was her beloved "twin," Nana, who moved to
Wellesley to live with the Harveys when Anne was eleven. For the previous three years Anne had been having difficulties at school. Kept
back to repeat the third grade in one system, she had been skipped to
the fifth grade in another, then made to repeat that grade too, in
1939–1940. That was the year of A.G.S.'s terminal illness, so Mary
Gray spent much of the winter in Maine, nursing her father and leaving the children in the care of household staff. Arthur Gray Staples
died in April 1940, and during the following summer Anne was hospitalized at the Lahey Clinic for severe constipation.

Anne later recalled this as a very traumatic period in her life, remembering her mother routinely inspecting her bowel movements and

threatening her with a colostomy if she didn't cooperate with efforts to regulate her elimination. Although these recollections may have to be taken with a grain of salt, since she tended to exaggerate her childhood grievances in therapy, they do point to difficulty in her relationship with her mother during an influential era when Mary Gray was away from home a great deal. Apparently the Harveys were encouraged to seek psychological counseling for their daughter around this time, advice they did not follow. Later Anne recognized that a pattern began with this important separation from Mary Gray and its timing in family life; the frequent absences of her husband would produce panic that no reasonableness could address.

When Nana arrived in the Harvey household in the midst of this troubled period, she offered Anne a refuge. Anne remembered spending all her time with Nana, playing cards in her room, doing her homework there, eating lunch with her, and going to movies with her after school. The only letter from Anne's childhood that survives — written to her Aunt Frances — contains a charming reference to Nana's place in her day: "Down here [in Weston] I have a regular time for everything. First in the morning I sleep, then I do my work, at 12 o'clock I have my daily cuddle with Nana." Nana's loneliness welcomed Anne's neediness. While they lay together under Nana's blue-bordered quilt, Nana would stroke Anne's back and tell stories or reminisce about the old days.

Anne's intense bond with Nana lasted until she was about thirteen, when she became absorbed in attracting and teasing boys. She began inviting her boyfriends home for long afternoons in the delightful privacy of the playroom. In the evenings she spent hours gossiping on the phone. Gradually she came to spend very little time with Nana. Mary Gray too devoted less time to amusing her aunt; she was preoccupied with worries over Ralph's drinking, and tried as far as possible to conceal his binges, particularly from business associates.

One evening at a performance of the Boston Symphony, Nana dramatically lost her hearing. She had been suffering a toothache, and she suddenly felt her left ear close. Unable to adapt to a hearing aid, she began to subside into herself, walking about the house whispering incessantly, "Mary. Mary Gray." Anne later put it into a formula: "Nana had been my mother in many ways — she got sick and just wanted to be my mother's child." The Harveys hired a live-in companion for her, but she continued to decline. The move from her home in Maine had already circumscribed her life a good deal; now, with her hearing diminished, she withdrew ever more deeply. Anne, visiting her in her room, would often find her distracted and uncomprehending: "You're not Anne!" Nana would cry out. Anne remembered Nana calling her "horrible and disgusting" and once attacking her with a nail file. One night, before Anne's horrified eyes, Nana was carried off to a mental hospital. Electroshock therapy seemed to improve her condition, and she returned home. "She wasn't like someone mad, she was suffering," Anne remembered. "Even when she was sick I kept pretending she was all right. She had been such a wonderful mother and friend."

This was a terrible experience for Anne, and it occurred during another very troubled era in her family's life. Her paternal grandfather, Louis Harvey, had his second breakdown and was hospitalized at Glenside, in Boston. Anne was now fifteen. "My father was drinking every minute, Nana was going crazy, my grandfather was crazy, Jane was having a baby" — the family seemed to be deteriorating all around her. In 1944, Ralph and Mary Gray decided to remove Nana to a small private nursing home nearby, where they could visit easily; she died in 1954, at age eighty-six.

After Anne Sexton's own breakdown, she worried about ending up in a mental institution like Nana. More important, she believed that she had personally caused her great-aunt's breakdown, and that Nana, who condemned her as "not Anne" but a "horrible and disgusting" impostor, had sentenced her to break down as well. Nana's rage took root in Sexton as a frightening symptom, which she described as a "tiny voice" in her head "shouting from far away," telling her she was awful, often taunting her to kill herself. "[I] should never have left Nana. She'd never have gotten sick — then I'd always be just me." By this logic, her illness was a form of loyalty to Nana, useless but compelling: "I'd much rather get back to Nana before she was sick than to get well. That's the entire goal. If I were really sick I could get back to Nana." Losing Nana meant losing the knowledge of who she was. Sexton was convinced that the only good person she had ever been was the Anne that Nana loved.

But disabling psychological problems were to emerge only much later, after she became a mother herself. During her teenage years, Anne bloomed.

2

ROMANCE AND MARRIAGE
1944-

IN JUNIOR HIGH SCHOOL, Anne Harvey emerged from her shyness and became the center of a gang of girlfriends, taking new interest in her appearance. As the little sister in an affluent family full of daughters, she had an early introduction to styles of femininity fashionable in the 1940s. She grew out her black hair to a long pageboy and began experimenting with various forms of padding in her bra. One evening when her sister Jane's husband, Brad Jealous, was home on leave from the navy with some of his friends, Anne made a dramatic entrance in high heels and red lipstick, pausing on the stairs to announce in a husky voice, "I see the navy has landed." She was probably no more than thirteen or fourteen years old at the time.

Anne had her first romance at fourteen, with an English boy, Michael Bearpark, who had been sent to Weston to wait out the war with American relatives. She pasted the corsage he gave her to wear at a "party preceding 1st kiss" in a scrapbook. Both the kiss and the boy had long lives in her memory. In 1964, Michael Bearpark wrote to her from Yorkshire after spotting her portrait on the cover of her *Selected Poems,* which had just been published in England. He told her that he had become a psychiatrist and hadn't married, "never having recovered from the trauma of being rejected by yourself — not true, but I always enjoy a little hysteria." Sexton replied with a teasing letter: "I should have married you right then and there! For one thing, it would have saved me a lot of money to be married to a psychiatrist." She went on to remind him about the kiss: "I do not know if it was *your* first kiss . . . but it was an event in my life that sent me along quite a trail." The kiss was a social triumph, but later, during her treatment for psychological problems, she associated it with Nana's breakdown, condensing the three years of Nana's deterioration into a few nightmarish images.

Anne's house in Weston became a center of social activity. Unlike Blanche and Jane, Anne went to public schools where most of her classmates were not so well-to-do as her own family. One of her best friends, Richard Sherwood, recalled the playroom where they congregated after school: "beautifully furnished, complete with Cokes in the fridge and a Stromberg Carlson that would play *both* sides of about twenty records, for over two hours." The housekeeper, Helen Dealand, firmly disbanded the little group in the playroom well before dinner, but Anne would then go immediately to the telephone and occupy the line almost nonstop until bedtime. Family members compared Anne's junior high school days to scenes in the play *Junior Miss,* a hit on Broadway around that time. Maybe a bit steamier: Sherwood remembered that they were all obsessed with sex. "Anne stole *The Life and Loves of Frank Harris* from her father and loaned it to me. I was barely home before she wanted it back — she was terrified that her father would find out. There was a lot of sexual experimentation, but I would be willing to bet that Anne was a virgin when she married."

Anne had many crushes and flirtations, but one steady boyfriend for five years, from eighth grade on into high school — Jack McCarthy. Michael Bearpark remembered him as a rival: "His father worked in a men's wear department of a Boston department store, and Jack had a collection of rather loud sports jackets unsurpassed by those of his contemporaries." Jack was invited along with the Harveys on a glamorous trip to New York when he and Anne were only fourteen: they stayed at the Waldorf, attended *The Fred Allen Show,* and went nightclubbing at El Morocco and "21." Because Mary Gray and Jack took a special liking to each other, he usually stopped by during his daily visits to Anne to say hello to Mary Gray in her retreat, the family library, where she often talked to him about her adored father. It was hard for Mary Gray to unbend, Jack thought, but he noticed that she was constantly tense over Ralph's drinking. Though Ralph Harvey "did things first rate," Jack sensed between husband and wife what he described as a difference in class: Mary Gray "had a tweedy, Wellesley air" and "came across as something of an intellectual" mated uncomfortably to a prosperous businessman "whose dignity didn't extend to polish."

Almost from the beginning of their friendship, Anne and Jack believed they had fallen permanently in love; they made a pact to marry in five years, when they turned eighteen. They had long talks about religion — Jack was Catholic — and about literature — Jack wrote poetry and wanted to be a novelist. Jack remembers Anne as extraordinary in their social set for her openness about feelings, her freshness and vulnerability. "Anne's best friend was the reigning queen of cool," he said, "but Anne was distinctly uncool, enthusiastic and bouncy."

The depressions Sexton was to associate with her teenage years did not find their way into Jack's memory of her. But he did recall an event that disturbed him deeply at the time. One evening when Anne and Jack were about fifteen years old (Nana had just been hospitalized for the first time), they made a date to go tobogganing on a steep hill behind the Harveys' house. Jack was late. When he arrived, Anne wasn't there, but at the bottom of the hill he could make out, by moonlight, her motionless body in the snow. He ran down to her and found her unconscious, bleeding from her head. After he took her up to the house, he discovered that the blood was mercurochrome: she had been faking unconsciousness, dramatizing her own death. She considered it a good joke on him.

For teenagers, Jack and Anne led a rather sophisticated social life. At sixteen they began going to bars and dances, getting high on Singapore slings — a pace set by older friends, veterans returning from the war. Anne *looked* older: she took up smoking, and had grown tall and slim (she was five feet seven and a half inches tall at maturity, and her weight stayed normally between 115 and 120 pounds). Snapshots show her cultivating a resemblance to Jane Russell, and she tormented Jack by flirting constantly. Noticing what they called her "boy-crazy" behavior, her parents sent her as a remedy to Rogers Hall, a girls' boarding school in Lowell, Massachusetts, in 1945. Anne and Jack wrote to each other faithfully, but the plan to pry them apart worked. Anne began dating boys from nearby Phillips Academy and conducting numerous romantic intrigues by mail.

Apparently both Ralph and Mary Gray hoped Anne really would marry Jack McCarthy. They liked him very much, and thought he would make a trustworthy, steadying husband for her. In fact, during one of Ralph's drinking bouts, he had his chauffeur drive to the McCarthys' home, where he amazed Jack's mother and grandmother by falling to his knees and proposing that Jack and Anne become engaged. This occurred when Anne was seventeen, but shortly thereafter, in their senior year, Jack broke off the relationship. In the heartbroken phase that followed, Anne wrote her first poems ("bleak, depressed, horrific poems" at that, she scoffed later). They drifted apart and lost touch by the time Jack went to Harvard.

Anne's yearbooks from Rogers Hall suggest that she was active and popular, though she always claimed otherwise. She had places on the swimming and basketball teams and was captain of the cheerleaders; she directed one school play and starred in all the others. In her senior year she began writing elaborate formal poetry, some of which was published in the school literary magazine, *Splinters*. Her "Cinquains" show that somewhere along the line — despite her later protestations to the contrary — somebody showed her something about writing:

EVIL
Beware!
It lurks so near,
Green serpent of fiery breath,
That distorts men's souls, warps minds, 'tis
Jealousy.

Perhaps at this time Anne thought she might inherit the mantle of writer in the family, a possibility signaled by the middle name that she shared with her mother and grandfather. Among Mary Gray's prize possessions were bound volumes of personal letters from her father and inscribed copies of his books of essays, compiled from his weekly columns for the *Lewiston Evening Journal*. One such book (*Just Talks on Common Themes*) survives from Anne Sexton's library, with an inscription by Mary Gray: "To the author's youngest grandchild [. . .] from the author's daughter." Mary Gray was not an author herself; she never worked on the family newspaper, and her own contributions to literature consisted of scripts for family skits and verses for family birthdays. Anne once commented dryly that her mother's forte was the beautiful handwriting in which she wrote the girls "elegant excuses" for school absences. Yet among family members, Mary Gray was spoken of as a writer — a social position they idealized. In 1958, when Anne Sexton's poems began appearing occasionally in the *Christian Science Monitor,* Ralph Harvey bought multiple copies to send to his business acquaintances. But he infuriated his daughter by comparing her poems to the wonderful letters Mary Gray had written to him while he was traveling. "We ought to have kept those letters," he said. "None of you girls are as brilliant as your mother. You are creative but she is brilliant."

Anne suffered painfully from his unfeeling remarks, even as a grown-up woman, for conflict with her mother over writing dated back to her school days at Rogers Hall. When her "Cinquains" were accepted for publication in the school yearbook, Mary Gray became suspicious. Jane had been caught plagiarizing from the work of Arthur Gray Staples, turning in one of his "talks on common themes" as her own in an English class, and very recently one of Anne's classmates had been expelled for submitting her father's work as her own. Anne often copied out poems she liked without indicating the author's name. (In fact, poems by Sara Teasdale found among her papers were published as examples of her own early work for just this reason.) Was it possible that she had been tempted by all these bad examples to pilfer from Sara Teasdale or some other *real* poet? Wondering about this, Mary Gray sent a sheaf of Anne's writing to a college professor she knew in New York, for an expert opinion. According to family memories, he told her that the work was probably original and showed a lot of promise. But Anne was devastated, not appeased; she interpreted her mother's action as evidence of a desire to keep "top billing," as she put it later. She wrote no poetry for the next ten years.

Anne did not get particularly good grades at Rogers Hall. She selected the non–college-preparatory curriculum, which suggests that no one expected academic achievements of her. On the evidence of her own record-keeping, her aim in high school was to acquire a fiancé. Into several thick scrapbooks she crammed evidence of a hectic social life: corsages, swizzle sticks, matchbooks, theater programs, and letter after letter commemorating romantic evenings, many of them referring dreamily or thrillingly to marriage. In her senior year, during spring break, she wired to her best friend: "Have fallen in love [. . .], diamond due this summer"; but nothing more is heard of this liaison. From Rogers Hall she went to a finishing school, the Garland School on Commonwealth Avenue in Boston, and sometime that year she actually did become engaged and began planning a big wedding. This worried her family: she didn't know the boy well enough; she was too young; her fiancé seemed immature. But early in the summer, still engaged, Anne met Kayo Sexton, fell in love with him, and eloped.

Alfred Muller Sexton II was nicknamed Kayo as a baby, because, like the cartoon character in the comic strip *Moon Mullins,* he was once put to bed in a dresser drawer. The name stuck; it seemed to suit his boyish good looks well into manhood. Like Anne, Kayo grew up in a big house in a prosperous suburb of Boston. When his parents, Wilhelmine Muller and George Sexton, had married in 1923, they had been presented with a fully furnished mansion on Middlesex Road in Chestnut Hill, with a new Buick in the garage, purchased with profits from the family-owned Sexton Can Company. Caught up in the craze for speculation, however, George overextended himself buying stock on margin. He lost — on paper — two million dollars the first day of the 1929 crash, and the rest of their inheritance soon after. They managed to keep the house, though, and George reestablished himself in a retail liquor business, then in a Buick agency, and then in a wholesale beef and veal business. In 1931, three years after Kayo was born, the Sextons had a second child, Joan. During Kayo's teenage years his father became, like Anne's, a heavy drinker, disappearing for days at a time. Kayo had early training as a family caretaker: he was sent around to the local bars to find his father and bring him home. He escaped some of this burden when he left home for boarding school, and in 1947 he enrolled at Colgate University, in Hamilton, New York, hoping to go on to medical school.

Kayo and Anne met in May 1948 through an exchange of letters. A mutual girlfriend sent him Anne's address, and he wrote a bashful note introducing himself. Anne mailed him a flirtatious reply, a greeting card picturing a cherub on a cloud, printed "Come up and see me sometime"; she described herself as "a woman of mystery," but she did not mention that she was already engaged. Clues to the mystery woman's identity included that "she loves — convertibles (and has one)"; she didn't mention that it was her father's car. They arranged a date at the Longwood Cricket Club in Chestnut Hill in early July. Kayo remembered her as "pretty as hell." Immediate infatuation set in. A program from the performance of Noel Coward's *Design for Living* at the Boston Summer Theater on July 30 carries the note "a riot! — and Kayo talked about diamonds." Daringly, they became lovers. Anne hadn't yet broken her engagement; having lost her virginity to Kayo, she made love guiltily with her fiancé, figuring that she owed it to him.

Invited to Sunday dinner at the Sextons', Anne made a bad impression on Kayo's mother, who remembered being dismayed at her smoking and the brilliant lipstick stains she left on the good linen napkins. By mid-August Anne's menstrual period was distressingly late, however, and Mary Gray advised her daughter to elope. The couple executed a classic escape, climbing out of upper-story windows in the dead of night, yet Anne was well equipped, not only with the convertible, in which they drove to North Carolina where the legal marrying age was eighteen, but also with a Massachusetts premarital health certificate. Later she wrote just such an elopement into a scene for a never-finished novel: "We eloped while underage, you see; but with birth certificates and blood tests and no signs of syphilis, we could marry in that state. We found these facts in the *World Almanac* — a very informative little book."

Anne's period started before they crossed the Virginia state line, but they were crazy about each other: nothing could stop them now. They married in the little town of Sunbury, North Carolina, on 16 August 1948 and spent four nights of their honeymoon in a swank resort hotel at Virginia Beach. There they ran into Richard Sherwood, Anne's pal from junior high in Weston, whom they invited to their room for a drink. Sherwood remembered long afterward the sexual excitement they exuded. "After a short time I was asked to leave temporarily. They just couldn't wait, so I went down to the bar and sat until paged and asked to return. Anne told me about her sex life with Kayo, and I, still a virgin, was absolutely flabbergasted."

Kayo's parents were furious at the elopement, but they had hardly even digested the news in the telegram when Kayo and Anne arrived on their doorstep, intending to move into Kayo's room for the few weeks before he returned to Colgate. Ralph Harvey presented the young couple with the convertible as a wedding gift. He also welcomed the opportunity to give Kayo some advice about how he might support them, "later on when he has more of an idea of what he wants to do."

Kayo had already decided what he wanted to do: continue his pre-med courses at Colgate. The newlyweds found housing off-campus at Reg Scott's dairy farm, on the road to Syracuse. "We lived with Reg and I did the laundry," Anne recalled, "washing the sour milk overalls." Kayo took on an extra load of courses to speed his progress toward graduation, and Anne rejoiced in learning how to cook. "Before I was married I had never washed one dish or seen how you fried an egg or baked a potato," she later claimed. "I can remember Kayo showing me how." That fall they partied with his fraternity brothers, and Anne was named the sweetheart of Sigma Chi. But financial dependence on their families irked Kayo, and medical school began to seem an unrealistic goal for a married man. At Thanksgiving, he decided to drop out of college. Once again the couple moved in with the George Sextons. Kayo found a job with a wool firm, and Anne began to get better acquainted with her new family.

She quickly made friends with her fun-loving sister-in-law Joan, who at seventeen also lived in her parents' home. Shortly after Kayo found his job, the two of them enrolled in a modeling class at the Academie Moderne, "dedicated to the development of a woman's most priceless possession . . . natural femininity." Anne later recalled that she told "dreadful lies" to get a job with the Hart Agency in Boston: "Said I'd modeled throughout the South." She and Joan both worked occasionally as models in department stores and promotional events at local businesses, but according to Anne, her acne scars relegated her to second-class status as a fashion model.

Anne's mother-in-law, Billie, was proud of the girls' modeling appearances, and long after Anne's death she kept outsize, handsomely framed professional photographs of her daughter-in-law in poses suggesting pensive maidenhood. Billie was a handsome woman herself, with a strong, open face and a high forehead, features her son inherited. She also had strong standards of propriety, and many of Anne's

Kayo (below) *and Anne* (opposite) *on their honeymoon, at Virginia Beach.*

habits distressed her. Anne would lie in bed long after Kayo left for work in the morning, then spend a frivolous day reading magazines and gossiping with Joan; she didn't show much interest in learning to manage a home. Billie also noticed that she was impulsive and moody; Anne once shocked her by throwing a tantrum when asked to go to the store for milk. Years later, Billie recalled wistfully that she had hoped for closeness with Kayo's young wife, but it seemed they were too different, from the start.

Anne and Kayo moved back and forth between their parents' homes for almost a year before moving into an apartment of their own in nearby Cochituate. Anne took a job selling lingerie at a small specialty shop in Wellesley for thirty dollars a week, work her mother found for her. She opened a savings account for money to buy a house. They also began spending time with another young couple: a surgeon named Johnny, who was finishing his training at the Harvard Medical

School, and his wife, who had been a friend of Kayo's. Anne and Johnny fell in love, though according to Anne it remained a romance, not an affair, despite passionate feelings on both sides. But apparently she considered leaving her marriage. She later recalled telling her mother that Johnny thought she had a good mind and said that if Anne were with him, she wouldn't have to talk baby-talk to feel feminine.

Mary Gray insisted that Anne stop seeing Johnny and start seeing a psychiatrist. She sent her to Dr. Martha Brunner-Orne, who had treated Ralph for alcoholism. Anne was extremely unhappy about giving up Johnny, and apparently took an overdose of sleeping pills in protest. As she later described the event, it was fraught with melodrama: "I took the pills in their kitchen. [. . .] I made it to my room but before I reached the bed I blacked out. I guess they heard me fall because they came in and kept trying to stand me up. As soon as this happened I was terribly dizzy and started to throw up. Johnny kept making me walk from one side of the room to the other." Dr. Brunner-Orne's notes in the medical records summarize a view that Anne had "difficulty controlling her desire for romance and adventure." Three months of psychotherapy helped change Anne's mind about divorcing Kayo, but Johnny stayed in her heart as a man who encouraged the best in her and might have helped her become a different person.

When the Korean War broke out in 1950, Kayo joined the Naval Reserve, and in November he and Anne moved to Baltimore for his training. He was shipped overseas the following May, and Anne returned to her parents' house. She began working at the Hathaway House bookstore near Wellesley College and also began reading again, for the first time since high school, eagerly discussing books with the clientele.

From the time Kayo left Colgate, he and Anne had been trying without success to start a family. During his first absence overseas, in 1951, Anne was checked out for infertility, as well as for vague complaints of pain and listlessness that she thought might indicate rheumatic fever. Restless and bored, she began dating other men. Exploring this period of her life many years later with her psychiatrist, she connected this first separation from her husband with the development of feelings of wildness that were among the symptoms of her illness. "When he's gone I want to be with someone, I want lights and music and talk. When I say running I don't mean running from something, but something I express by action — people, people, talk, talk, wanting to stay up all night, no way to stop it. I don't really *want* to have an affair with anyone, but I have to; it's the quality of action. I first had this feeling, I suppose, when I was dating, after Kayo went into the service. Pound, pound, pound heart: makes me feel crazy, out of control."

These infidelities, unlike Anne's crush on Johnny, didn't disrupt her marriage, though they landed her in trouble with her mother again. She remembered that Mary Gray guessed she was stepping out. "I had given no indication," she recalled. "But she said, 'You're just like me — and I know!' " When Kayo's ship was sent to San Francisco for overhaul in the fall of 1952, Anne decided to join him. She withdrew all her savings from the bank and equipped herself with five hundred silver dollars to feed the slot machines at Harrah's Club in Reno, hoping for a jackpot that would win them a home of their own. She and a WAVE shared the drive to California in September. Reunited with her husband, she immediately became pregnant. Kayo accompanied her back to Weston for the Christmas holidays; then, when they were all set to return to San Francisco on 7 January, Anne changed her mind and decided to remain behind. She later remarked, "All of my mother's daughters stayed with her during their first pregnancies; I wanted to follow suit."

Anne spent the winter in Weston, being pampered. She shopped and visited with her mother until the first of February, when Ralph and Mary Gray departed for a Florida vacation. During this period she often visited Nana, who was keeping a daily diary. Anna Dingley loved news, and her jottings provide a set of small windows onto Anne Sexton's life the year she became a mother. Nana's diary suggests that she and Anne were affectionate though probably not close during this period. Her charming notes indicate that Anne frequently took her to the hairdresser and on other outings. They whiled away one long snowy afternoon working a jigsaw puzzle of Anne's dream house, and in mid-February Anne dropped by elated with the news that she had felt the baby's "first stirrings." Another day there was a flurry of telephone calls about an airplane accident: Anne's sister-in-law, Joan, was a stewardess on the plane, but escaped injury. ("Wheel collapsed when plane was landing — no casualties," Nana noted professionally.)

Anne hardly recalled this time in Nana's life, for her memories focused on Nana's breakdown in 1943–1944. Yet by 1952 Nana seems to have recovered her sanity, mended her spirits, and reclaimed her involvement in family life. She reported cheerfully the first "grand day" in April that permitted a walk outdoors, she looked forward to a trip to Cape Cod for lunch at the Lobster Bar, she exclaimed over her spin in Ralph's new Cadillac ("a beauty and the last word!"), and she rejoiced in Ralph's gift of a TV set in time to view the Democrats' national convention. Her entries show a journalist's passion for facts, including the pages on which she noted merely, "No one came." This phrase haunted Anne when the book arrived in her keeping after Nana's death, sixteen months later. At some point she made a note of her own at 15 July 1952, where Nana had written, "Present! A television! Ralph brought it — Mary Gray came later — I'm all set! Rah rah rah!" and then, in 1953, had added a new date and a new note: "Nobody came. Blanche dropped in for 5 minutes bringing my laundry." At the bottom of this page Sexton wrote, "Nana, forgive me, forgive me, forgive me." Anne thought Nana felt abandoned, lonely, but although she sounded lonely sometimes, she had not been abandoned. She noted continually, with lively interest, the frequent visits and phone calls that kept her up to date on family news.

On 23 February, Anne joined her parents for a month of sunshine in Sarasota. The vacation was shortened for Ralph Harvey by his mother's illness; on 20 March he flew back to oversee her hospitalization, leaving Mary Gray and Anne to return a few days later by train. During the long trip back to Boston, Anne experienced some contractions and a little bleeding, and feared she would miscarry. Later she recalled for her psychiatrist how her father met them at the station with a crew of porters and took her by ambulance directly to the hospital. Her condition was treated with the drug DES, which was later found to increase the incidence of uterine cancer or malformation and miscarriage in daughters born to women to whom it was administered during pregnancy.

After the miscarriage scare, Anne spent the rest of her pregnancy near home. In June the family watched the coronation of Elizabeth II on television; when Anne went to the hospital a few weeks later with labor pains, her father sent flowers with a little note: "I hope to see you tomorrow with Prince George or Princess Linda." Linda Gray Sexton was born on 21 July 1953. Kayo arrived from San Francisco three days later to take up fatherhood and civilian life. Shortly afterward, with Mary Gray's help, Anne and Kayo bought a house at 40 Clearwater Road in Newton Lower Falls, and Kayo joined the R. C.

Harvey Company as a road salesman. Two years after Linda's birth, they had a second daughter, Joyce Ladd Sexton, born on 4 August 1955; the Ladd commemorated Nana, Anna Ladd Dingley, who had died on 15 July 1954. Kayo and Anne were twenty-seven years old, and their family was now complete.

In later years, Kayo Sexton recognized it had been a mistake to accept a job from his father-in-law. "I was under his thumb. I would hear him tell other people, 'I love to get these sons-in-law in here and kick 'em in the ass.' " Brad Jealous, Jane's husband, had resigned in anger in March 1953 because of Ralph's temper, as Nana noted in her diary. But at the time it seemed logical for Kayo to accept the offer. The R. C. Harvey Company employed seventy workers in its single factory, at Waltham. It was not a big company, but it was doing well, running three shifts a day, six days a week, fifty weeks a year. Interest rates were low, and business was good all over America; in the wool industry there were no imports to contend with and no competing synthetic fibers. Within a year of taking his job, Kayo was promoted and began traveling greater distances. He would go to the Midwest for two weeks, come home for a week and work the local territory — Connecticut, Rhode Island, Massachusetts — then go south for two weeks.

The R. C. Harvey Company was in the garnetting business. The factory bought wool by-products — selvages and loose wool thrown off in the manufacture of cloth — and returned this stuff to a fibrous state for reuse, mainly in blankets. The wool produced by this process was cheaper than virgin wool, because duties were lower. In the 1930s and 1940s, when the company was getting established, the country was full of blanket mills. In the late 1950s, when synthetics began to replace wool as blanket material and as covering fabric for the new electric blankets, R. C. Harvey began selling its garnetted wool to felt mills, and the company underwent another spurt in growth.

Ralph Harvey was a superb salesman and a skillful manager, and his company managed to do pretty well even in lean times. The salesmen were paid minimal salaries, but expected to share the company's prosperity when profits were in. The bonuses were disbursed at Christmas. Shortly after Kayo went to work for Ralph, the company enjoyed one of its best years: everybody was making $20,000 to $25,000 bonuses. This was the year Kayo was put in his place as a son-in-law. "One of my presents was a wallet from Ralph," he later recalled. "I needed a wallet, but I thought he was being cute and had put the bonus inside. As I took it out of the package, he said in a very loud voice, so that everyone could hear, 'Now I want you to look inside and see your Christmas bonus.' There was nothing in it. I didn't know whether to cry or kick him."

Anne shared the feeling of being under the family thumb. She was humiliated by her father's treatment of Kayo, and by constant criticism from both her mother and her mother-in-law. Her closest neighbor, Sandy Robart, recalled that "Anne always dropped ten years or more in her mother's presence. She was overwhelmed — she was awed. I think it was probably an attempt to please. I can see her standing at the phone in the kitchen, talking to her mother, and feeling that Anne had turned into a little girl." Robart thought that Anne was entirely too susceptible to criticism, especially from Billie, whom Anne saw or talked to every day. After Linda was born, Billie was a regular visitor — in Robart's view, intrusively so: "At that time, Anne was a passive, helpless, dependent goody-goody! I think she just got to a stage where her whole feeling was of terrible inadequacy. If she had been a healthier person in general, she would have been able to defend her own turf."

Still, it was hard for Anne to get angry at help offered so willingly and abundantly. Billie loved babies and was devoted to her granddaughters, even though Anne claimed that after Linda's birth her mother-in-law was always around, "hanging over me, wanting to spend every minute looking at my baby." Billie became so attached to Linda that Anne felt a certain relief when Joy arrived two years later. She remembered feeling "Well, you can have the other one; this one's for me."

Now and then Kayo and Anne dreamed of leaving the Boston area, but somehow the right moment never presented itself. Like almost everybody else in the generations of Stapleses and Harveys and Sextons that preceded them, Anne and Kayo lived and worked after marriage under the watchful eyes of their parents, never more than a short distance from their childhood homes.

3

BREAKING DOWN
1955-

ANNE SEXTON LEARNED to love her children deeply after they had
grown up enough to offer care in exchange, but looking after them
during their infancy brought her to the brink of madness. She had a
hard time coping with the physical and psychological demands of Linda's babyhood; the addition of newborn Joy to the household intensified her difficulties.

Shortly after Joy's birth in August 1955, when Linda was two years
old, Sexton began going through what she later described as "terrible
spells of depression." She wasn't just tired and low; she was agitated,
disoriented, and subject to fits of feeling "unreal." She thought the
problem was "hormones," and decided to consult Dr. Martha Brunner-Orne, the psychiatrist she had seen when she had fallen in love
with Johnny. She held pleasant memories of this woman, a queenly
Viennese in her late fifties whose style of address was at once brisk and
motherly. The doctor diagnosed a postpartum depression and prescribed medications. These seemed to help, as did talking about her
disturbances to Dr. Brunner, as Sexton called her.

Sexton's psychological state took a definitive turn for the worse five
months after entering treatment, when she developed a morbid dread
of being alone with her babies. She was able to pinpoint the occasion
on which this fear overtook her: it was in March 1956, near Easter,
when Kayo was away on his first long business trip. In the background
was Sexton's parents' recent move to Annisquam, a fashionable seacoast town forty miles northeast of Boston. Joy was about seven
months old, and had croup. A neighbor sat with the children while
Sexton went to a party with the wife of one of Kayo's business associates. "I came home late and heard Joy choking, like a dog barking. She
couldn't breathe!" Sexton later recalled. "I ran in and turned on the

shower [for steam], then spent the whole night in the bathroom with her, thinking she was going to die."

Joy recovered, but Sexton didn't recover from her fears for the children's safety. From then on, whenever Kayo left home on a trip that would keep him away overnight, she would stop eating and grow weepy, fearful, and listless. Virtually all of her serious difficulties arose during his absences, and only his return released her from them. She began to have other symptoms, such as intense pains in her stomach, for which her internist found no physiological basis. She became prone to attacks of anxiety that left her panting and sweating.

Her self-preoccupation made it hard to pay proper attention to Linda, whom she decided to put in the nursery school run by a next-door neighbor, just a few steps from the Sextons' back door. On Linda's first day Sexton showed her the way, but then she began seeing her off with a wave rather than taking her to nursery school by the hand. It was several days before she discovered that Linda, shy and fearful of strangers, had been hiding in the garage all morning.

Increasingly, Sexton became prone to episodes of blinding rage in

Anne Sexton with baby Linda.

which she would seize Linda and begin choking or slapping her. In later life she recalled with great shame a day she found Linda stuffing her excrement into a toy truck and as punishment picked her up and threw her across the room. She felt she could not control these outbursts, and she began to be afraid that she would kill her children. When she finally confided some of her fears to the family, they rallied. Kayo's parents proposed that Joan stay with her during Kayo's business trips, and George Sexton offered to pay her psychiatrist's fees. Ralph and Mary Gray Harvey began sending their housemaid, Mary LaCrosse, to help with housework twice a week, and Mary Gray also gave her daughter money for doctor's bills.

But Sexton's fears were not allayed by practical help. One night in mid-July, near the anniversary of Nana's death, her anxieties mounted to a crisis. As she described the episode to Dr. Brunner-Orne, Kayo had fallen asleep on the couch after supper, and singlehandedly she had finally got the children to bed. Feeling absurdly alone and desperate, she resolved to kill herself. Out of a special drawer she took a small oval portrait of Nana and the diary Nana had kept in the nursing home, noting again how similar Nana's handwriting was to her own. Out of the medicine chest she took the bottle of pills Dr. Brunner-Orne had prescribed for sleeping. But looking at the doctor's name on the bottle made her hesitate. Dr. Brunner-Orne had been so kind and encouraging: how could she let her down? Sexton sat on the back porch for a long time, with the pills in one hand and Nana's picture in the other. Kayo woke and found her sitting in the dark. They called her psychiatrist.

Sexton hadn't actually taken the pills, yet her actions were significant. From then on, she described her suicide attempts as a means for getting back to "the place" where Nana was ("I want to curl up and sigh, 'Don't leave me,' " as she put it). Taking nightly sleeping pills became a ritual substitute for just such oblivion. At the time, Dr. Brunner-Orne thought the situation was serious enough to warrant hospitalizing Sexton at Westwood Lodge, where in 1950 she had treated Ralph Harvey for alcoholism and where sometime earlier she had treated his sister, Frances, for the same problem. Sexton's parents were shocked by this decision. Ralph Harvey "has no sympathy," Dr. Brunner-Orne noted; "he feels as if it were a personal insult that someone in his family is not able to overcome an emotional condition." But discussion of the family's history of mental illness made Sexton's parents see the importance of taking her symptoms seriously, and she checked into Westwood Lodge for a stay of three weeks. Billie Sexton took the children, but she was having health problems herself, so after a few days Mary Gray took Linda up to stay with her in Annisquam.

At Westwood Lodge Sexton underwent numerous psychological evaluations, including a Rorschach test that suggested to the doctors "rather prevalent psychoneurotic features, not entirely the picture of a true depression." Dr. Brunner-Orne prescribed vitamins and various psychoactive medications and discharged her on 3 August 1956, two days before Joy's first birthday. That month, during Dr. Brunner-Orne's vacation, Sexton was seen by her son, Dr. Martin Orne, whom she knew and liked (he had administered the battery of diagnostic tests at Westwood Lodge). She got on so well with him that she continued to see him after Dr. Brunner-Orne returned, and Dr. Orne continued as her psychiatrist for the next eight years.

Meanwhile, a family council was called. It seemed clear to everyone that Anne was too sick to care for the children. Mary Gray wasn't up to having Linda full-time, so Anne's sister Blanche agreed to have the little girl stay with her big family in Scituate, on the south shore of Boston Bay, less than an hour's drive from the Sextons'. It was yet another hard move for Linda, a shy three-year-old who was deeply pained by the separation from her mother, and the five months she spent in Scituate left an imprint of fear. Baby Joy fared better. She was to remain with her grandmother for the next three years, and for the rest of her life she felt that Billie was a second mother, a real mother.

Summer passed into autumn; Sexton's condition worsened. In November, the day before her twenty-eighth birthday, alone at home while Kayo was away on one of his long trips to the Midwest, she swallowed an overdose of barbiturates — Nembutal, which ever after she called her "kill-me" pills. When the effects began setting in she phoned Billie and was rushed to Newton-Wellesley Hospital. After the medical emergency had been resolved, Dr. Orne transferred her to Glenside, a grim institution for mental patients, where she stayed for two or three weeks. As he later explained, he chose Glenside rather than Westwood Lodge to protect her from her family's anger. "Her family was not very sympathetic about her problems. Seeing her at Glenside, they recognized that things were serious. Moreover, Glenside cost less than Westwood Lodge, and that mattered." Dr. Orne added that Sexton was one of the few patients at this hospital who did not receive electroshock therapy, which the staff doctors favored; instead, he saw her five times a week for psychotherapy.

Recalling these events, Sexton later said, "I was trying my damnedest to lead a conventional life, for that was how I was brought up, and it was what my husband wanted of me. But one can't build little white picket fences to keep nightmares out. The surface cracked when I was about twenty-eight. I had a psychotic break and tried to kill myself." Her summary called "psychotic" and a "break" what had been a bumpy downward course lasting over a year. "Psychotic" was something of a misnomer, for Sexton was probably never as out of touch with reality as psychotic patients are thought to be. But her suicide attempt did mark a break in her family life. She was now officially "sick," quite possibly "insane." She took on the role of patient, which she did not abandon for the rest of her life. The family in turn began to adjust to an illness with symptoms of unpredictable, irresponsible behavior that required long-term treatment, which was both expensive and uncertain of results.

With Billie taking full charge of Joy and a great deal of responsibility for Anne and Kayo's household, Anne's relationship to her mother-in-law grew ever more fraught. Billie had adopted the role played by Helen Dealand in Anne's own childhood home: the nanny who relieved the mother of many child-care duties. Throughout the rest of Anne's life, whether she was well or ill, she accepted Billie's service as her due. But Billie was the Sexton matriarch, and no matter how conciliatory her manner, she exercised considerable authority over the men, children, and other women in her domain. Linda's return home at Christmas normalized life a bit for Anne, restoring some of her role as mother, but it also seems to have enhanced her resentment of her mother-in-law. Billie had the family to dinner every Sunday, and Anne's journal notes suggest that these occasions aroused bitter emotions in both women. Sunday: "Went to Billie's — made me angry interfering with Linda." Monday: "Told Billie wanted Joy back soon — she is fighting me right down the line — I hate her —" Tuesday: "Am ready to take Joy back but not ready to face Billie's anger." Billie saw the situation from another angle. At dinners Anne always seemed withdrawn and aloof, and other family members became tense around her, never knowing when or how she would blow up. It seemed to Billie that Anne was thoroughly disabled emotionally — that she took no interest in Joy. If Billie suggested that she should get the baby ready for bed, she would refuse stiffly. "She wouldn't even kiss Joy goodnight!" Anne's own memory of those nights was equally painful: "I just pretended Joy wasn't mine."

Sexton's deepening breakdown was hard on everyone, especially her husband and children. Kayo remembered the relief with which he would set off for work in the mornings, leaving his wife groggy from the after-effects of her sleeping pills, or weepy and depressed. One day particularly stood out in his memory, comic and sad in retrospect. "I used to leave at five A.M., get up and drive out to upstate New York, past Syracuse. I'd make my calls and drive back. Eight hundred miles of driving, all day. I remember calling Anne from around Albany one night around seven, and I said, 'Put the baked potatoes in, I'll get the rest of it when I get home' — because she was in one of her downers then. When I got home, she hadn't even put the baked potatoes in — she 'didn't know how'! I think I chewed my loafers down about an inch in frustration."

Stupid as it seemed to everyone, that was how Sexton felt when Kayo was gone: that she didn't know how to do anything. Sheets of notes she typed out or wrote by hand for Dr. Orne early in the winter, after more than a year of treatment, provide an inside view of her panic and despair.

I am so alone — nothing seems worth while — I walk from room to room trying to think of something to do — for a while I will do something, make cookies or clean the bathroom — make beds — answer the telephone — but all along I have this almost terrible energy in me and nothing seems to help . . . I sit in a chair and try to read a magazine and I twirl my hair until it is a mass [of] snarls — then as I pass a mirror I see myself and comb it again . . . Then I walk up and down the room — back and forth — and I feel like a caged tiger. [. . .]

Now Kayo is gone — his absence absolutely removes all reason for a day to begin or end . . . I am rudderless with no direction. [. . .] My sexual life is in reality a hideous mess and I don't understand it and furthermore I don't want to discuss it or understand it . . . Here I am so oversexed that I have to struggle not to masturbate most of the day — and I certainly don't want to discuss that — but it's true nevertheless — and when Kayo starts to make love to me I can't concentrate on it —

I had Joy for the weekend and she has gone back today — I love her, she is adorable and winning — but it seems to take so much patience and energy and I was glad to see her go . . . I guess I don't love anyone — that is a terrible statement and now I am crying [. . .] My heart pounds and it's all I can hear — my feeling for my children does not surpass my desire to be free of their demands upon my emotions ... What have I got? Who would want to live feeling that way?

Her bewilderment was justifiable; there were no obvious answers to her questions about the causes of such misery. Her history and her symptoms put her in ambiguous diagnostic territory that is only somewhat clearer today than it was in 1956. An overview of her case would distinguish at least three different possible sources: biological, psychological, and sociological.

At the outset of Sexton's treatment, Dr. Brunner-Orne had noted the possibility that her difficulties derived from a postpartum depression; later notes, however, convey doubts that she had a "true" organically based depression. Yet anecdotal evidence of breakdowns on both sides of her family suggests a genetic predisposition to a biologically based illness, a supposition reinforced by Sexton's extreme physiological symptoms: wildly alternating moods, anorexia, insomnia, waves of suicidal and other impulses, rages, rapid heartbeat. It is possible that biochemical imbalances throughout her life intensified the underlying psychological vulnerabilities that were the primary focus of her psychotherapy.

Whatever the constitutional givens, Sexton's difficulties obviously had much to do with the psychological dynamics into which motherhood thrust her. During treatment, she gained insight into the ways in which most of her intimate relationships provoked feelings associated with her two "mothers," Mary Gray and Nana. At twenty-eight, she was still agonizingly attached to Mary Gray, and subject to outlandish fits of rage when her mother ignored her. As she later told Dr. Orne succinctly, "I know I was dependent — but Mother didn't want to be motherly. I clung to her." Mary Gray seems to have been a vivacious, sociable woman, attractive and strong-willed, absorbed in her own concerns; she demanded attention herself. ("My mother was top billing in our house," as Sexton put it.) She tended to squelch Anne or to compete with her, and she doled out approval parsimoniously — just often enough to keep Anne "dancing the jig."

In contrast, Sexton idealized Nana, whom she remembered as purely receptive and soothing, an uncomplicated white-haired spinster who had nothing to do but cuddle. Kayo, for example, was "a masculine Nana! Pretty wonderful thing, psychologically speaking. I keep telling Kayo to tell me he loves me, that I'm a good girl, hate it when he disapproves of me." When Nana arrived in the Harvey household, Anne's psyche may have been especially burdened by the legacy of her mother's coldness and indifference. Nana arrived like the cavalry at a time when Anne's self-esteem was under heavy attack, and Anne turned to her as to a substitute mother. But Nana was not adequate to the task. Though emotionally available, she did not take a fully adult role in assisting Anne's development, as Dr. Orne was later to do. Instead, the "twins" merged their hungers. Even though Anne was on the brink of adolescence, they continued to delight in childish cuddling and back rubs and in mutual fantasies about Anne's pretend brother. All true love is sometimes childish in its play, but Nana's love seemed to remain constricted, infantilizing, and it did not direct Anne's energies toward accomplishments appropriate to her age or instigate exploration of the world. Significantly, Anne Sexton never mentioned in treatment that Nana had been a writer, nor that she had been something of a rebel. Nana's behavior with Anne, no matter how welcome, may well have been a prelude to the breakdown that was disastrous for Nana and badly timed in Anne's life as well.

Now a mother herself, Sexton was experiencing the process of her

Anne's portrait of her great-aunt, Anna Ladd Dingley ("Nana").

children's developing independence. Linda had been going through the "terrible twos" when Joy was born, testing boundaries and asserting separateness. As her recollections indicate, Sexton had made a powerful emotional investment in Joy's dependence ("This one's for me"). Perhaps Joy's increasing powers of separation and the anniversary of Nana's death were both factors in the timing of Sexton's breakdown in July, echoing a failure of sustaining encouragement in her own childhood. The relatively minor losses she suffered at that time — Kayo's frequent absences and her mother's move to Annisquam, separations that were neither permanent nor unpredictable — seem to have added to an old reservoir of easily aroused nervous alarm until it overflowed in waves of fear and pain. The normal development of Linda and Joy into little beings demanding to be let go and nevertheless to be loved unconditionally may have broken the dam that held such a flood in place. These babies were supposed to provide Sexton's fulfillment as a woman, but instead they made demands on her emotions; rather than feeding her hunger for acceptance, they required her to respond to their separateness. As an adult she was supposed to be able to participate intuitively in this exchange, as intuitively as her children did. But what was involuntarily called into play by their demands was her own neediness. Sexton expressed this conflict at first in bodily suffering, later in plain language to her doctor: "I want to be a child and not a mother, and I feel guilty about this."

Dr. Orne recalled that when he began treating Sexton, "She was very, very sick, but like many interesting patients didn't fit textbook criteria. I did the diagnostic work on her when she was at the hospital, which indicated that she was hysteric in the classic sense: like a chameleon, she could adopt any symptom. She experienced profound dissociation, and she had lesions of memory. Some therapists were convinced that Anne was schizophrenic. I don't doubt that hospitalized in a ward of schizophrenics, she would exhibit their symptoms; that is why I discharged her as soon as possible from Westwood Lodge, where there were schizophrenic patients in treatment. But I never saw evidence in her of loose associations or formal thought disorders, or other major symptoms of schizophrenia. She certainly had a depressive illness for many years, which was never really resolved. One wonders whether the new antidepressant drugs might not have successfully treated the more serious aspects of her depression."

To these biological and psychological interpretations of Sexton's misery, though, must be added a third perspective, the sociological one. After a "boy-crazy" girlhood culminating in early marriage, and especially after the birth of two children, Sexton's life, to outward appearances, was virtually a caricature of the ideal of womanhood promoted in the movies, in women's magazines, and at women's college commencements. One of the magazines she may have been reading as she twirled her hair into snarls that day in January 1957 was *Life*'s "special issue on women" (December 1956), with its glowing reports on the "completely fulfilling" moments of a woman's life: the first prom, the first kiss, the first baby. This was a view Sexton and her friends had ardently shared. As she later told an interviewer, "I wanted to get married from the age of thirteen on. I wanted nothing else. I thought that having children was some kind of answer, then." The glorification of "feminine" roles did not offer insight into the rage and guilt aroused by the behavior of small children — women were supposed to be naturally good at mothering. They were also expected to find their greatest satisfaction in homemaking. Women who weren't and didn't found little validation in social institutions for their "unfeminine" departures from the norm.

Among Sexton's social peers, emotional problems like hers were widespread, partly because in postwar America the concept of woman's place in society had contracted into idealization of the housewife's role. Of course, women found many ways other than becoming ill to counteract some of the limitations placed on them by social conventions: by writing, for example. Women's poetry was to provide a very important form of resistance during the next decades, and much of the most influential was to be written by Sexton and some of her Boston friends: Maxine Kumin, Denise Levertov, Sylvia Plath, and Adrienne Rich.

Obviously, Anne Sexton was not simply a discontented housewife when she wrote to the doctor in January 1957. She was sick, and she needed treatment. Yet something not merely pathological is struggling to get a hearing in these pages: an irrepressible wish for an authentic social presence that was not wife, lover, or mother. Sexton was beginning, tentatively, to release her "terrible energy" not only in symptoms but in writing. Typewriting, at that: her grandfather's work.

4

"THESE ARE MY PEOPLE"
1956-

DR. MARTIN ORNE was barely a year older than Anne Sexton when he became her psychiatrist. At twenty-nine he held an M.D. from Tufts University and was completing his Ph.D. in psychology from Harvard while working as a resident in psychiatry at Massachusetts Mental Health Center. As a clinical psychologist he had been treating patients for several years, but Sexton was among his first long-term psychiatric patients. Their different personal styles proved highly compatible. A tall, big-boned, portly man, Dr. Orne wore a thin mustache and spoke in a low voice inflected slightly by a Viennese accent. His manner, in fact, had something in it of the *Herr Doktor Professor*: kind but judicious, even pedagogical. "We had a relationship which could tolerate my mistakes and could tolerate her being impossible," he said, looking back. "I had a temper, and I lost it with her more than once. I learned from her that it didn't matter what mistakes I made — only what I could do to help her. We were in it together. She was a very difficult patient; she pushed the world of reality away. At the beginning, you had to see deeply into her to know there was someone there."

Despite many setbacks, under Dr. Orne's care Sexton began to emerge from her anguish and attain a sense of purpose that rapidly grew into ambition: she discovered her vocation. It is possible to observe this process at close hand, because about a year after her first suicide attempt, Dr. Orne began keeping extensive records of her treatment, including handwritten notes made during her therapy sessions. Sporadic, incomplete, and full of private abbreviations, these notes nonetheless provide a slow-motion documentary of Sexton's conflicts, dreams, fantasies, manipulations, and, ultimately, her development as a writer. Perhaps the most surprising discovery Dr. Orne's files afford is a large batch of formally ambitious poems, neatly typed and dated, which Sexton began bringing to sessions early in January 1957. Many of them were never printed, but all of them show that early in her therapy with Dr. Orne, Sexton began to regard herself as a poet. How did this happen?

At her first interview with Dr. Orne back in 1956, Sexton had told him that she thought her only talent might be for prostitution: she could help men feel sexually powerful. He countered that his diagnostic tests indicated she had a good deal of undeveloped creative potential, and he later proposed that she might try to do some writing about her experiences in treatment. This might help others with similar difficulties to feel less alone, he suggested.

Sexton subsequently singled out that conversation as the first encouragement she had ever received to think of herself as a capable person. Dr. Orne's judgment carried weight with her, partly because during her hospitalization at Westwood Lodge she had met another of his patients, a talented musician, and she had gathered (mistakenly) that he specialized in treating creative people. She didn't immediately see how she might develop this hypothetical potential. She didn't want to enroll in courses. She had never been a good student, and since her breakdown she had become acutely fearful of mingling with strangers: even the prospect of leaving her house now terrified her. But she found some ingenious ways to apply the doctor's advice; for instance, she bought a new antenna for her television set so she could watch cultural programs on educational television.

One night about a month after her suicide attempt, Sexton tuned in while Professor I. A. Richards of Harvard was lecturing on the sonnet. As Richards talked about its structure of fourteen lines patterned by rhythms and rhymes, she scribbled the formula. "I thought, well I could do that. So I went downstairs and wrote one. Interestingly, I called up my mother to read it to her — she suggested a better image, for one thing. I wrote one another day, and I took them to my doctor. [. . .] He said they were wonderful." This was what she needed to hear. "I kept writing and writing and giving them all to him — just from transference; I kept writing because he was approving."

A few months later Sexton's suicidal thoughts returned, and the little strengths she had been cultivating in therapy withered under renewed onslaughts of self-disgust. On 29 May 1957 she attempted suicide again. Dr. Orne met her at the hospital, Sexton later recalled, and told her, " 'You can't kill yourself, you have something to give. Why, if people read your poems (they were all about how sick I was) they would think, "There's somebody else like me!" They wouldn't feel alone.' " This was the message Sexton called her turning point: "I had found something to *do* with my life."

Dr. Orne did not discuss Sexton's poems with her as sources of insight into psychological problems, much less as works of art, but he did vigorously encourage her to keep writing. It was important, he thought, for the poetry to be something completely *hers*. "Anne had no resources that she could recognize," he explained in retrospect. One goal of psychotherapy was to address the vulnerabilities she carried from childhood by giving her the confirming kind of attention she had needed from her parents in order to develop a secure sense of herself. "She felt parasitic, helpless, profoundly angry. My task was to help her develop any resources within her which allowed her to be a person, and allowed her to form relationships on a healthier basis than before. That was why, later, I taped our sessions — to help her understand what she was doing."

Sexton recognized that her interactions with Dr. Orne drew on very

Martin Orne, M.D., Ph.D., around 1956.

intense feelings toward her parents and Nana, and that her steady relationship with him enabled her to experience these feelings in an environment of understanding and inquiry. "All your life you have been an expert at feeling, but not an expert at knowing what you are feeling," he told her. His most important role was to help her find ways to rechannel her impulses, to analyze — without merely intellectualizing — the private meanings coded in significant gestures and inner states.

Sexton's dissociative mechanisms created some of the greatest obstacles to treatment, Dr. Orne commented later.

It is difficult to describe the profound inability to respond that marked these states of dissociation, which she called trances. Eventually it became clear that she would dissociate when she had not been able to come to the end point of a session. I began to see that the trance was interactional. Often she was annoyed, or she was feeling too much to stop just then, but she could not really verbalize much of what was troubling her. This symptom interfered with treatment. To some extent, she was aware of what she was doing. At times I couldn't help becoming angry about her lack of response. I was able to deal with the problem most of the time by sharing with Anne that I had pressing commitments following her session and couldn't allow her to go on. Anne used a metaphor for the comfort she needed in order to discuss things effectively in treatment: she called this "having room." It helped her a great deal when I adopted this metaphor to describe my own needs. As we worked together on this problem, she began to be able to take into account my reality, and her ability to tolerate difficult material without going into trance improved greatly.

Sexton usually saw Dr. Orne twice a week. She was not undergoing a psychoanalysis, but Dr. Orne was trained during an era in which all psychiatrists were introduced to analytic principles, and these showed up in the language of the insights they reached in the course of treatment. Sexton and her doctor sat face to face, not separated by a desk. Each could observe the other's countenance; awareness of their interplay had an important role in the therapy. Occasionally Dr. Orne prescribed medications. As he later explained, "When Kayo was away, or she was away from treatment, she tended to fall apart. I was quite prepared to give her some medication in the hopes that it would make it easier to bear these absences. She did respond to most medications, for a time."

And writing poetry, in Sexton's case, became part of the therapy. Any work that elicited approval would, quite obviously, assist in the repair of self-esteem, and writing had a special validity in Sexton's family. "Much of our training and evaluation is of people's pathology," Dr. Orne observed later, thinking about Sexton's progress in therapy. "But the patient's pathology matters less than the resources he or she brings into the treatment. If you focus on what's *there*, you can develop wellness in a person." By writing poems, Sexton confirmed her own existence as an able person; by typing them out for her doctor, she entrusted herself ever more deeply to his affirming attention.

With an astonishing sense of purpose given her emotional state, Sexton threw herself into writing. Though she was floundering in self-disgust and confusion — a condition that eludes representation but is well registered in the doctor's notes — between January and December of 1957 she brought Dr. Orne over sixty poems. These were not diary entries or drafts but finished works, carefully typed on white erasable bond paper and usually dated. They were manuscripts.

The doctor's approval would surely not have been sufficient to create the poet if her ambitions had not been spurred by the family tradition coded in the middle name Gray. Sexton claimed this legacy from her reluctant mother in a struggle that intensified and clarified in the period between Christmas 1956, when Sexton wrote her first sonnet, and Christmas 1957, when she presented Mary Gray with a sheaf of poems. As if in dialogue with her daughter's drama, Mary Gray became very sick that year, underwent surgery, and during her recovery began competing with Sexton for the title of family poet.

Anne's problems had brought unwelcome pressures on Mary Gray's way of life, beginning in 1955, when Anne entered treatment. It was partly Mary Gray's money — as the heir of A.G.S., she had her own money — that paid Dr. Orne's bills. During Anne's hospitalization, Mary Gray had helped out by taking Linda to Annisquam, and she had brought Anne there too for several weeks after her release. Among other treats intended to make her daughter feel better, Mary Gray had commissioned a local artist to paint her portrait in a blue off-the-shoulder gown that evoked the sweetheart of Sigma Chi. However, the summer proved only a time-out in the downward spiral that culminated in Anne's first suicide attempt, in November.

When Sexton began feeling well enough to try to act on Dr. Orne's advice about pursuing an education the following February, she did

not receive her mother's support. She was considering enrolling at
Newton Junior College, or perhaps Boston University, and she asked
Mary Gray to pay the fees. She reported her mother's withering reply
to Dr. Orne: "No! Why should I? It seems to me I deserve some fun in
my old age. . . . You could never do the work. You have no idea of
how hard it would be." Shortly after this exchange, a lump Mary Gray
had been trying to ignore in one of her breasts was diagnosed as malig-
nant. Like many of her friends, Mary Gray believed cancer was caused
by stress. Angrily, she attributed her problem to Sexton's breakdown
(so Sexton said). In April she underwent a radical mastectomy, from
which she emerged hopeful. She pampered herself by having her own
portrait painted by the same artist she had commissioned to paint her
daughter. She began dabbling with watercolors a little; then she began
writing poems.

Both Mary Gray's illness and her apparent recovery exacerbated
Sexton's feelings of rivalry and helplessness. "Mother makes me sick

Mary Gray Staples Harvey.

but I love her," she noted in the understated format of her little diary. "Such attraction, dependence." After Mary Gray's prognosis for health seemed secure, Sexton remarked to her doctor, "Mother sort of lost glory, not dying," and Dr. Orne's notes during ensuing months show her both wishing for and dreading her mother's death: "Part of me would be free if she died. It would also be awful — I would dissolve." Her second suicide attempt, in May, occurred about six weeks after her mother's surgery. By that time Sexton had received from Dr. Orne what she regarded as definitive encouragement to become a poet. Apparently around the same time, she received a similar message from Mary Gray.

We have always been a two-way radio, with perhaps one exception — Do *you* suppose subconsciously you feel — that *if* you don't please ME you are losing an anchor? I would not know — but I have a feeling that your love for me and my "sympatica" for you — could be licking you. [. . .]
You — Anne — my sweet daughter find life unattractive — Sometimes I do, *too* — and cry and cry — all full of self-pity and utter misery — So I can understand how you feel — Yet — you have something to give — *a* word — The word — a beautiful appreciation of what life — nature — and human relationship does — *You* are not anyone's baby — *You* are adult in your sense of decency — Granted — trees rot — plants die — we humans fail — *but* we are spirit — It may be BUM spirit — but it's something —

Despite its peculiar blend of empathy and bathos, this letter must have spoken deeply to Sexton's need for recognition from her mother (though Mary Gray was known as a letter writer, this is one of very few communications from her in Sexton's files). It may also help to explain an association Sexton made between her mother and radios. When Mary Gray lay dying of cancer two years after her surgery, Sexton guiltily took a portable radio from her hospital room. Ever after, this radio and its successive incarnations were always playing while she worked at her desk, while she breakfasted, and while she fell asleep at night. "I will die with this radio playing — last sounds," she wrote.

Sexton also saved two poems that Mary Gray wrote after her operation. One of these echoes the feelings of helplessness expressed in her letter, again using a metaphor of damaged trees: "It matters not to me at all / that trees can rise as well as fall / because with you I am a frail / expression of the will to fail." In the other, titled "Misery," Mary Gray describes her emotions on watching Sexton recover from the deathlike state of a drug overdose. Her heartfelt rhyming couplets decidedly resemble the poetry Sexton was producing in 1957 — though unlike her mother, Sexton never wrote out poems by hand. Perhaps the typewriter effaced for her the visual associations of her own handwriting with Nana's diary and the "elegant excuses" Mary Gray wrote so well. In any case, Mary Gray's style is like Sexton's at the time, for example in a verse titled "A Birthday," which Mary Gray almost certainly read:

> I sit upon the floor and play a game —
> "O lunatic ancestor . . . give me another name."
> I sit on this floor and crazily break
> the pieces apart . . . for my children's sake.

Bringing Mary Gray's poetry into a therapy session a year later, Sexton commented on the resemblances. Though she dismissed her mother's work as "horrible," she went on to compare it with her own.

A.S.: Mother probably could be as good as I am if she knew something about it. She uses old language — but I didn't know current language either, when I started out writing poetry. I remember — can't remember well — showing it to Mother. At school I would write in a "school" way.

Dr.: Talk about Mother resenting your writing.

A.S.: I remember at some young age writing stories, remember Mother reading one to a friend. In junior high school won "person with most imagination" — thought it was wonderful — wonder what ever happened to it — somewhere I stopped, I stopped imagining. Now I've lost all this time.

The doctor probed for resentment, but Sexton responded with pride in her youthful creativity. This exchange shows that she had made some gains in struggling free of the "attraction, dependence" that previously kept her begging for Mary Gray's love. She was able to remember her mother in a rare act of giving admiring attention to her written words; whether it was fantasy or memory that supplied the image, Sexton very much needed to reclaim this experience of Mary

Gray. Notably, she associated Mary Gray's ability to learn new skills with her own increasing knowledge.

During her years in therapy with Dr. Orne, Sexton gradually came to see both her ambitions and her achievements as strengths supported by this particular identification with her mother. "I always thought I was Mother's favorite — I was just like her, I had to be: it's a fixed idea," Sexton was later to say to Dr. Orne, "[Mother's] father was a writer and she should have been a writer — I'm my mother, only I did it and she didn't. . . . I think my father was kind of crazy, though not overtly. If you tapped my father he fell apart like a jigsaw puzzle. But my mother was solid and that's what I want to be." Writing poems, even writing them badly, Mary Gray irrefutably validated Sexton's accomplishments; without such a model — and such a competitor — among her primary attachments, Sexton might not have felt entitled to become a poet at all.

Throughout this era of mother-daughter struggle, Dr. Orne continued to encourage Sexton to broaden her horizons. He pressed her to take an IQ test; she had shown herself capable of extraordinary discipline, and he thought her poetry was clever and affecting. He also showed her work to an expert, a young professor of literature at Harvard, who found it promising. Moreover, during her hospitalizations Sexton had demonstrated the powers of a natural therapist, deft at awakening in others what she often could not find in herself: hope and interest. There was much in her personality that could be cultivated in school. Since members of her social set tended to take a college education for granted, it was an obvious goal to propose.

Sexton did not, however, enroll at Boston University or Newton Junior College. Somehow she learned about a poetry workshop that was held evenings at the Boston Center for Adult Education on Commonwealth Avenue. Too shy to call for information, she begged her neighbor Sandy Robart to do it for her. Robart remembered this as a low point in Sexton's life. "She had retreated so that she practically couldn't get herself out of her house. She wanted badly to go to that poetry place — she'd read about it and heard about it. I said, 'All right, I'll make the first call.' I knew it wasn't doing her any good, but I was trying to get a balance — to take the first step so she'd take the second one. I remember we finally arrived at a bargain. I said, 'I'll go the first night.' " Terrifically nervous, Sexton arrived accompanied by Robart and bearing copies of some of the thirty-odd poems that she was already arranging book-fashion in a cardboard folder, with titles such as "The Suicide Note," "Life Again," "In Defense of Not Trying," and "One Life Asks the Question."

The poetry class, which had already been in progress for several weeks, was taught that year by John Holmes, a professor of literature at Tufts. Most of the other class members were regulars at such workshops. Some had poems in print and were already friends with Holmes; Sam Albert, Maxine Kumin, and Ruth Soter belonged to this inner circle. Kumin remembered the strong impression Anne Sexton made when she arrived that evening, wearing earrings and bracelets, perfume, high heels, matching lipstick and fingernail polish, "all intimidating sophistication in the chalk-and-wet-overshoes atmosphere of the Boston Center for Adult Education."

To others Sexton may have seemed an unlikely candidate for the workshop, but she knew at once she had come to the right place. It must have been obvious that her own poems were at least as good as most of what she heard and saw that night, because she decided to enroll in the class. As she later recalled,

> The most important aspect of the class was that I felt I belonged somewhere. When I first got sick and became a displaced person, I thought I was quite alone, but when I went into the mental hospital, I found I wasn't, that there were other people like me. It made me feel better — more real, sane. I felt, "These are my people." Well, at the John Holmes workshop that I attended for two years, I found I belonged to the poets, that I was *real* there, and I had another "These are my people."

Anne Sexton's uninformed decision to join the class was a piece of very good luck. John Holmes was a kind man and an experienced, dedicated teacher. He earned his living as a professor, but poetry was his vocation. He wrote poems, he reviewed books of poetry, he led workshops; more than that, he lived as if poetry were of the greatest importance. He served as president of the New England Poetry Club for many years because no one else would do it, and though the club was a sometimes excruciatingly provincial meeting-ground, it was a meeting-ground, and many promising poets new to Boston first got their names into circulation by reading there. Sexton was invited to join the club that fall, and she was thrilled when she won the prize for best lyric at one of its monthly sessions.

Attending Holmes's class at the Boston Center, Sexton at first felt a bit like a schoolgirl. The participants sat around a long oak table; as Kumin recalled, they all "prayed that our poems would rise to the top of the pile under Professor Holmes's fingers as he alternately fussed with his pipe and shuffled pages, and one of us would thus be divinely elected for scrutiny." The atmosphere was not very academic, however. Sexton described the class as "unlike college," because no one was there "to get a good mark or to learn how to write a poem to satisfy a teacher." She estimated that about half the members were "fugitives from the analyst's couch . . . but so was I."

What Sexton learned when she began studying poetry in 1957 were the tricks — her word — of making smooth, complex stanzas. Her early poems were modeled on magazine verse of the kind regularly published by the *Saturday Evening Post*. They are short, often humorously self-deprecating, and frequently sentimental; rhythm and rhyme are vehicles for the delivery of messages. An example is "Traveler's Wife," enclosed in a letter to Kayo written about the time that Sexton joined Holmes's poetry class.

> Although I lie pressed close to your warm side,
> I know you find me vacant and preoccupied.
> If my thoughts could find one safe walled home
> Then I would let them out to strut and roam.
> I would, indeed pour me out for you to see,
> a wanton soul, somehow delicate and free.

The poem has the bravado of a novice ice skater unsteady on her blades but determined to execute a figure eight, closing up with a strong rhyme after a wobble or two in the middle of a line. It ends effectively, on an image in which the husband and wife exchange glances of shock at her pain on his departure:

> You must not find, in quick surprise,
> one startled ache within my vacant eyes.

The surprising internal rhymes of "ache" with "vacant" and "quick," of "find" and "my" with the end rhyme "surprise" and "eyes," forecast a strength Sexton was soon to learn how to develop very deliberately.

Such poems seemed promising enough for Holmes to suggest that Sexton begin seeking publication in local magazines. It was probably on his advice that she sent a sentimental lyric titled "Eden Revisited" to *The Fiddlehead Review.* It came out in April 1958 — her first real publication, though she never reprinted it. She then began keeping a card file on which she noted dates of submission and return. These indicate that she made a point of sending out a poem almost immediately after writing it; if her manuscript was returned with a rejection slip (in 1957 and 1958 it usually was), she sent it elsewhere within a few days. This practice was remarkably sensible but also unusual in an apprentice poet: most egos bruise too easily to go through the process of resubmitting a poem twelve or fifteen times in one year, which is what Sexton often had to do. She had rapidly acquired the outlook of a professional — another legacy, perhaps, from A.G.S.

In Sexton's first years of treatment, writing reinforced the effects of psychotherapy, and the two activities almost completely interlocked. Her earliest poems in 1957 were about her therapy, directly and descriptively, as some titles indicate: "Appointment Hour," "The End of the Illusion," "One Patient Released Today," "Some Hope," "The Psychosomatic Stomach," "One Way of Avoiding the Issue," "The Poems I Gave You," "A Foggy Adjustment." Around the anniversary of her first suicide attempt, she typed a book-length manuscript for submission to a contest. "I'd rather be doing something productive than sitting around thinking about killing myself — or killing myself," she joked to Dr. Orne. "I put some aggression into something constructive. Cheered me up." This got her thinking about compiling a book of poems about therapy. "Some of them are really good," she commented to Dr. Orne. "I suppose I have a book that the average person in treatment would want to read." Such a book might have to be published anonymously, she speculated. And she might have to write a bit more about institutions. Perhaps after Christmas she could go back to Glenside, or even to a state hospital: "Westwood isn't horrible enough" to be interesting to readers, she said. (Sexton didn't comment on the analogy with Nana's youthful scheme to get herself admitted to a mental institution so she could write it up for the *Lewiston Evening Journal.*) A few months later she wrote two short stories, never published, about psychiatric patients with hysterical symptoms. She told Dr. Orne she was trying for an effect like J. D.

Salinger's, using a first-person narrator to give the "implication of a psychosis."

Early in her work with Dr. Orne, Sexton undertook writing as a form of education, and as her references to psychoanalytic concepts indicate, she used reading as a way to understand her treatment. During the first months of 1957, while she was considering enrolling at Boston University, she was also pressing her psychiatrist to see her in therapy more frequently than twice a week. He agreed to add one extra session per week on the condition that she earn the money to pay for it — a condition that would help her to gain some independence from her mother, he reasoned, and demonstrate her ability to do something difficult on her own behalf. This demand presented Sexton with another problem requiring an ingenious solution. She talked her sister-in-law, Joan, into selling Beauty Counselor cosmetics with her door to door, and Dr. Orne adjusted his fee and his schedule to accommodate her.

In retrospect, this move can be seen as allied with Sexton's efforts to go to college. Though she began reading poetry again that year, to her doctor she talked about reading psychology. She did not pursue a systematic understanding of the subject, in the sense of studying it, but once Dr. Orne became her psychiatrist she began reading both popular and professional literature in the field. "I had been with you only a week when I got all the books on psychiatry. I read them to try to find out what kind of patient to be," she confessed. Another motivation she acknowledged was "to learn what I must avoid doing — if this is a sign of illness I mustn't do it." She appears to have made a friend who directed her to a number of books she mentioned in therapy: Freud on the Oedipus complex, on the theory of the superego, and on "Creative Writers and Daydreaming"; Jung on the notion of the self conversing with the self; a book about women's sexuality; a book arguing in favor of silence on the part of the analyst. "Someone asked me the other day if my doctor is analytical," she told Dr. Orne. "I said, 'No — just me!' "

Sexton's first allusions to psychoanalytic concepts occur in poetry written during late January and early February 1957. One poem, titled "Real Love in Imaginary Wagon," offers a pop-psychology version of Freud's concept of transference: the observation, fundamental to psychoanalytic theory, that the patient's relationship to the analyst recapitulates childhood relationships with parents and other significant figures.

Well Doctor — all my loving poems
write themselves to you.
If I could channel love,
by gum, it's what I'd do.

And never pen another
foolish freudian line
that bleeds across the page
in half assed metered rhyme.
[. . .]
If all this bother and devotion
is not, in truth, for you —
(since you're the expert on emotion)
tell me Doctor — who?

A similar consciousness of psychoanalytic concepts, particularly the theory of transference, invests such poems as "More Than All the Rest," in which the doctor is favorably compared to a father ("He gave the gift of life, but not the gift a child would need / to mark its mind / as the years unwind"), and others with more overtly erotic content, such as "The Poems I Gave You" ("Oh, I have raped my inner soul / And given it, naked, to you, / Since my warm mouth and arms / might love, and frighten you"). As Dr. Orne later commented, "Anne viewed psychotherapy as a kind of fraud, which she called 'the big cheat,' because the powerful feelings aroused could never be consummated. The patient's improvement, rather than the patient's gratification, were the goals of treatment."

Though Dr. Orne did not, apparently, encourage Sexton to read psychology, he didn't discourage the practice either; after all, he had prescribed any kind of educational effort as highly therapeutic in her case. Perhaps she realized another kind of gain as well. Her inexactness about analytic theory indicates that she was not attempting to master it. Was her reading a way of identifying with her doctor, of finding yet another "twin"? In childhood she had had the adored Nana, and she had secured for herself a pretend brother for protection and companionship. Amid the dangers of therapy's artificial childhood, perhaps she sought another such person in Dr. Orne, perhaps even as a strategy for containing the confusing energies released by the therapeutic relationship. Throughout the period of treatment annotated by Dr. Orne, Sexton referred casually and knowledgeably to concepts such as transference, resistance, defense, regression, acting out — all in the course of providing the doctor with "memories" that sound suspiciously like updated versions of Freud and Breuer's *Studies on Hysteria*. It seems likely that by 1958 Sexton had read the case history of the first hysteric in psychoanalytic literature and had found another namesake in the famous patient Freud and Breuer called Anna O. Moreover, Orne and Sexton were both taking notes on her case, he in longhand, she in poetry. As she was to tell him rather grandly later on, "Therapy is a *minor* art, Dr. Orne!"

For whatever reason, a particularly dramatic development in her own case was the emergence during the summer and fall of 1957 of a flamboyantly naughty role she liked to play, called Elizabeth, and of a memory or fantasy, narrated in trance, about an incestuous experience with her father.

Early in Sexton's therapy, the Elizabeth persona began making appearances while Sexton was in a trance by scrawling messages in childlike handwriting across pages torn from a lined notebook. Sexton told Dr. Orne how she had chosen the name. Leaving his office after an episode of automatic writing, she had become very despairing. She had walked for a long time, thinking about suicide and trying to forget herself, and she had begun to be afraid that someone would notice her and ask her name. "Looked (for some reason) at the back of my watch [inherited from Elizabeth Harvey, her father's mother] and the initials E. H. were on it. So thought, 'I must be E. H.' [. . .] To [my] truthful knowledge I had never been 'Elizabeth' before."

By September, she was typing letters which she left unsigned, though "Elizabeth" appeared in the return address on the envelopes. Somewhat comically, the writer claimed that she had to type her introductory letter in the dark so Anne wouldn't read it. "Help me somehow," Elizabeth urges Dr. Orne. "There must be something you can do about this except sit there like a blinking toad." Anne would be more cooperative "if she were less afraid of what you thought. [. . .] I'm the one who'll talk." Elizabeth explains that formerly, Anne "thought of me as a brother that died — she used to think about him all the time — there wasn't really any brother — but she liked to pretend about him — I'm not so different from her but I would tell you what she doesn't dare think — She acts her life away. [. . .] I am part of her sometimes but she is not part of me. [. . .] Nana knew I was not Anne."

Elizabeth wanted Dr. Orne to put Anne under hypnosis during therapy, so that she, Elizabeth, could speak openly: "If you give her time to get dissociated enough she will be willing. . . . I know a lot," she promised. When Dr. Orne wouldn't agree to hypnotize his patient, both Anne and Elizabeth began appealing for a session under sodium pentothal. Together "they" laboriously typed a letter, one line superimposed on another: "Only sometimes do I lie," says one; "it's me that wants pentothal," says the other.

At several points in her therapy, Sexton made an association, while in trance, between the name Elizabeth and "a little bitch," the angry words her father once used when he was drunk and spanked her for some naughtiness. She also associated this phrase with a night, recalled several times in trance at widely spaced intervals, when her father came into her bedroom and fondled her sexually.

A.S.: Father comes in drunk; wakes me up, saying "I just wanted to see where you were — your sister [Jane] is out letting someone feel her." And he says it again. Sits on the bed, takes a bottle out of his pocket and drinks. I asked where Mommy was: gone to bed and locked the door. He says, "Do you like me?"

Dr.: What side of the bed is he sitting on?

A.S.: [Points with finger.] He asks me if anybody ever felt me. I don't know what he means. I lay down and cuddle with Nana. I know that this isn't good, I shouldn't.

Dr.: Shouldn't what?

A.S.: He is holding me. He says to press up against him, sort of wriggles and asks if I like it. And it feels good.

Dr.: Does he say you are a good girl?

A.S.: He puts his hand on me and asks if I — if I ever do this and did I ever do it.

Dr.: What did you tell him?

A.S.: [Shakes head.] He kissed me on the lips and he started to leave and I held on and didn't want him to go. Then he came back, left his bottle on the table.

In later sessions Sexton questioned the status of this memory. As she put it on one occasion,

A.S.: I couldn't make all this up, or I don't exist at all! Or do I make up a trauma to go with my symptoms?

Dr.: There wasn't a simple cause; it's something that happened many times without its necessarily happening just this way. When your father was drinking he was communicating something to you.

A.S.: Disgust.

Dr.: Or attraction.

A.S.: Sitting beside Daddy, his saying I can't eat when she's at the dinner table — I thought pimples were a sign of things inside that were showing.

Dr.: Your feelings about him?

Shortly after Sexton recounted this episode in therapy for the first time, Dr. Orne requested an interview with Mary Gray and asked about Ralph's behavior toward Anne. Mary Gray replied that he had often used nasty language with her when he was drunk. She remembered his saying as Anne left the house one evening on a date that she looked as if she were planning "to get laid." Sexton remembered this too, but she remembered his saying "fucked." She was about seventeen at the time.

Still, abusive remarks are not the same thing as erotic fondling. Was Sexton's report a memory or a fantasy? This question achieved great importance in her therapy, and in her art, but it cannot be answered with certainty. The evidence for its actuality lies chiefly in the vividness and frequency of her descriptions during trance states. Moreover, Sexton's symptoms and behavior — in particular, the dissociative states that were so prominent a feature in her case, her tendency to sexualize significant relationships, and the fluidity of the boundaries she experienced between herself and other people — fit the clinical picture of a woman who has undergone sexual trauma. From a clinical point of view, her doubts about this memory were not evidence that it did not happen.

However, the details of her reports of the scene varied a good deal, most significantly in dating the episode in her life anywhere from age five or six to age twelve or thirteen and in the role attributed to Nana, which changed from guilty point of reference, as above, to actual witness. It is also significant that Sexton's memories arose in therapy when she was reading and writing about incest, especially during several phases of active work on a play with an incestuous episode as its central conflict. As Sexton frequently commented, once she had put a memory into words, the words were what she remembered. Thus she could give dramatic reality to a feeling by letting it generate a scene and putting that scene into words for Dr. Orne while in a trance. Members of her family believe that these "memories" *had* to be a dramatization, and they strongly contest the implication that Ralph

Harvey could have made sexual overtures of any kind to his daughter. Maxine Kumin also doubted Sexton's credibility in this account. Yet several of Sexton's other confidantes were convinced that these were real memories; Lois Ames, a psychiatric social worker who has treated incest survivors and who was very close to Sexton for many years, said unhesitatingly, "I could never believe anything *but* that Anne was a victim of child sexual abuse by both Nana and her father."

Asked for his retrospective view of this issue, Dr. Orne said, "I dealt with it in therapy as a real event, because there were times that it was real to her. Anne, like most patients with this kind of disorder, easily adopted pseudo-memories in treatment which are experienced with great vividness, and their treatment may help the patient even though the events may never have occurred. If you ask me either as a psychiatrist or as a scientist, however, I would have to say I am virtually certain that it never occurred. It's not plausible the way she described it, and it wasn't the father's style when he was drinking. But it fit her feelings about her father having abused her, and since she sexualized everything, it would become the metaphor with which she would deal with it."

Perhaps the question needs to be rephrased: not was the incident fantasy or memory, but what kind of experience was it? For Sexton the artist, the developmentally layered and conflicted love of a girl for her father was a source of insight into the psychological and social complexity of living as a woman. Sexton was to write a number of important works in which she explored this love with great sensitivity: "The Bells" and "The Moss of His Skin," written when her father was still living; after his death, "The Truth the Dead Know," "All My Pretty Ones," "Young," "Ghosts," "The House," "Wallflower," "And One for My Dame," "Flee On Your Donkey," "Consorting with Angels," and "In the Beach House"; many poems in *Transformations*, her sequence based on Grimm's fairy tales; several versions of the play that became *Mercy Street*; and a strong sequence of poems titled "The Death of the Fathers," written near the end of her life. The "truth" of these works of art rests not in their factuality but in their emotional credibility. It would be naive to assume that Sexton could not have written them without having experienced a direct sexual overture from her father. Equally, it seems reasonable to allow that her narratives in trance during psychotherapy were not reports of actual events but explanatory fictions summoned by the power of transference to evoke sexual feelings and fantasies. The way Sexton told Dr. Orne in 1958 about her father's visit to her bedroom communicated, at the very least, her awareness that her father paid aggressive attention to her sexually developing body (and to her sister Jane's) when he was drunk, and that she associated his transgression with Mother's unavailability and with Nana's cuddling.

From the standpoint of Sexton's feelings, at least as important as the father in the foreground of this scene are the maternal figures in its background. As she elaborated the recollection in therapy — and later in *Mercy Street* — there are always two mothers, one who has retreated and locked everyone out and one who is shocked into madness by the spectacle of the girl's exchange with her father. In Sexton's story, it is Nana's horror at witnessing her role in the seduction that explains Anne's phobias and her self-loathing, for this episode shows Nana the sexiness that Anne has been feeling secretly — even while cuddling with Nana.

Sexton was to raise the question of whether she was "normal," by which she meant heterosexual, early in her psychiatric treatment, and later to explore it in the context of sexual intimacy with women. Behind that question were other memories that troubled her self-esteem, focused on genital inspections by her mother. From the earliest period of toilet training, she had to report to her mother daily and show her the stool before flushing it away. This was a common child-rearing practice at the time. But Sexton also recalled another humiliating experience, from about her fourth year: her mother laying her down on the bathroom floor, pulling her legs apart, and inspecting her vulva, "looking at me and saying how we had to keep it clean and mustn't touch — there was something she looked at and it was growing, and I know — I don't remember, I know — I had a little cyst — they had to operate and take it off." As Dr. Orne commented, "In many ways, her mother was the dangerous relationship."

The point is, the veracity of the incest narrative cannot be established historically, but that does not mean that it didn't, in a profound and lasting sense, "happen." It is clear from many sources that Sexton's physical boundaries were repeatedly trespassed by the adults in her family in ways that disturbed her emotional life from girlhood onward. As she put it, "I have frozen that scene in time, made everyone stop moving. I thought I could stop this all from happening. That's what I want to believe — when I'm in that hard place — that's not what I believe now, just when I'm that child in trance. I can't grow up because then all these other things will happen. I want to turn around and start everything going backward."

By 1958, after two years of treatment, all of these issues were finding their way into Sexton's self-account under the influence of her transference to Dr. Orne. During the same months that she was communicating in therapy through Elizabeth, the "little bitch," she was acting out this persona in an affair she referred to as an exciting game. One of her classmates at the Boston Center for Adult Education had taken a shine to her, and they began having drinks together after class, followed by sex in his car. "With Jerry I am different — I don't know what happens to me," she told Dr. Orne. "Jerry is vital, gobbles life up"; she liked "making him fall in love with me — when he is finished with sex and I feel I have won." Jerry admired her poetry, but Sexton did not value his opinion. Nor did she permit the relationship to grow into a friendship. She restricted their involvement to brief sexual encounters over which she exercised control. "Problem of Jerry — he wants to see me — last thing I want to do is get into a sexual fuss with Jerry — like to see him and make him fall in love with me — [. . .] like boy I was engaged to — not appealing to me but don't have to be involved, all I have to do is finish him and he is happy — with Kayo I have to be sexy and just can't — something's wrong."

With Kayo away frequently on business trips, Sexton acted on these impulses fairly often, for about six months. In May, as the poetry course was ending, she decided to abandon the affair, which she was now finding offensive to her pride. "I think it's me *being* sexy that I find horrible," she told Dr. Orne. Yet her ability to fascinate Jerry had in some ways operated as a counterbalance to her sense that she was not making progress in therapy: "I suppose you could say that I have Kayo. But really he makes it worse. He hates me if I am sick. — Or I have the children. Don't you see, all I have is a lot of faces that signify my failure. It is easier, if I am sick, not to have to watch the constant mirror of my daily failure to make anyone happy or pleased with me." Her "Elizabeth" characteristics attracted approval, even though it was approval she didn't wholly respect; and she had now been able to associate these with the poetry class.

But Sexton's desire to give these characteristics a name and a personality signaled what Dr. Orne regarded as a dangerous tendency. Discussing Elizabeth later, he commented that after a brief initial interest in this manifestation, he observed that Sexton was perilously close to developing multiple personality disorder, so he disengaged himself from acknowledging Elizabeth as a person distinct from Anne. "It was helpful to let her play out the fantasy of Elizabeth, to develop aspects of herself that had been held in check. Let me emphasize that this was a fantasy: Anne did not have multiple personality disorder, though she could have been encouraged in that direction," he said. "Once my interest dropped, so did hers, and no doctor ever saw Elizabeth again." As therapy went on, Dr. Orne stressed the positive sides that Sexton expressed through this persona: her charismatic leadership, her sense of fun, her capacity for pleasure, her self-confidence. " 'Elizabeth' expresses a side of your childhood which showed some assets you never really owned," Dr. Orne told her. "The 'magic' you, 'Elizabeth,' is the one who involves people. But you don't view it as *you.*" The focus of therapy as it pertained to Elizabeth was an effort to help Sexton recognize and tolerate the feelings she wanted to split off and act out.

No matter what was going on in therapy, Sexton remained enormously productive as a poet. By spring, when the poetry class ended, she had finished perhaps sixty-five poems. Writing poetry had taken over her life, as the only activity outside therapy that gave value to existence. Once she arrived at this feeling of vocation, she pursued it at the expense of all else. "I feel like begging you to send me away somewhere," she said to Dr. Orne. "It's the only thing I want — enough food to keep alive, go to poetry class — write — rest of world shut off. I don't want to stop treatment because that's the hope I have to solve this." Writing put her into a state similar to a trance, making her dangerously inattentive to her children, she was aware. Being in an institution full-time, she thought, might ease the burden of guilt she felt about ignoring her family. "Only time I am there is when I am thinking about poetry or writing — shuffling between methods of escape — liquor, pills, writing — I don't have anything else."

Just as the act of writing took Sexton out of herself, into what she felt was another identity, so the finished poem conveyed meanings she had no consciousness of intending. As early as November 1957 she began to give Freudian interpretations to her work, uncovering in metaphor and the silence between lines of a poem the unmistakable (to her) presence of father and mother. A poetic image "can't be determined — just appears — not willed," she told Dr. Orne. "I suppose you would be surprised to know how little I understand my own poems." This truth was borne in on her when "Eden Revisited" was published in *The Fiddlehead Review.* Seeing the poem in print, she was horrified to discover it was about her transference to Dr. Orne, displaced into delicate yearnings for spring. "Poems don't lie," she told him. "It seems I have no control over this sort of trance. I had no idea what the poems were communicating — no idea till a year later. That makes me feel better."

Both the reading and the writing Sexton did in therapy bore fruit in the spring of 1958, as she struggled to gain perspective on the veracity of images she had been retrieving under the thrall of transference. In March Dr. Orne told her he would be taking a research leave during the summer: three months, beginning in June. Sexton sulked and worried, but his impending departure brought to a head certain issues that were increasingly urgent in her therapy. At the end of April she told him a story (about being molested by an older man, a family friend, while swimming at Squirrel Island) that she knew she had made up on the spot. Leaving the doctor's office chagrined at having told such an outrageous lie, she vowed to work from then until his departure on a "personal record" that would establish a baseline of truth. She began at once; arriving home, she typed out a long commentary on the problems as she saw them.

> I am nothing, if not an actress off the stage. In fact, it comes down to the terrible truth that there is no true part of me. . . . It is as if I will permit my therapy and think it all very interesting as long as it doesn't touch me. I am a story-maker, a — doesn't it strike him as odd that this "story" is too pat???? I know that often people in analysis will tell these great stories about having intercourse with their father etc. and that they are fictitious but are a childhood fantasy. I have read about this — and also know that they still have some validity — but — but — [. . .]
>
> My reaction was to laugh — when I realized this ridiculous lie that I had told — I mean it was funny to have thought up this nice theory for my symptoms — I am acting the part of a nice case history —

For the next month, spurred by distress over Dr. Orne's plans and the increasing extravagance of what she now called "truth crimes" — "lies" that she had been dealing with as "memories" in trance — Sexton typed about fifteen single-spaced pages of this personal record. "I do not understand why I must do these things — it makes me lose sight of any true me": this was her main theme. "I suspect that I have no self so I produce a different one for different people. I don't believe me, and I seem forced to constantly establish long fake and various personalities." She doubted even the sincerity of her two suicide attempts; these were, she suggested, attention-getting acts. But her worst "truth crime" was the invention of Elizabeth. "I made her up — I think I did. [...] Any element of truth about her is just a certain freedom of expression, a lack of sexual (I guess) repression. I could say 'she feels' but not, o never me." Sexton also admitted having faked the "total amnesia" about Elizabeth she had been professing to Dr. Orne. "I would feel better, less guilty, if I thought Elizabeth were true — I would rather have a double personality than be a total lie."

Actually, Sexton had confessed to virtually the same "truth crimes" six months earlier in one of their sessions face to face. But the written record had purposes other than self-condemnation. Embedded in these pages is an extraordinary progress report on the sense of identity that Sexton had slowly accrued through her months of writing.

> I realize, with guilt, that I am a woman, that it should be the children, or my husband, or my home — not writing. But it is not — I do love my children but am not feminine enough to be all lost in their care. It wears me — I do not have the patience. (How can you really know what I mean — you have never been worn down by a nagging child?) . . . But of course, I am truly neurotic enough so that I don't want intrusion by people — and children are people — every five minutes of the day. I suppose one of my truth confessions was going to be "I am not sick" — and just realized in a way, this is sick.

Yet all that was "sick" or "hysterical" about her behavior in day-to day life could be turned into something valuable through the act of writing poetry. Poetry too required a trancelike state for its disclosures. "Only in that funny trance can I believe myself, or feel my feeling," Sexton observed. If in therapy trance led to lying, at her typewriter it led to art. She could draw a simple equation: in trances she was a channel of lies; at her typewriter she was a channel of poetry. "Think I am a poet? false — someone else writes — I am a person selling poetry."

None of this decreased its value for her, nor her passion to succeed, to become a real poet. "My goals may be unrealistic — but how can I find the limit of what I can do if I am satisfied with mediocrity? In the field I have chosen, to be halfway is to be nothing. There is no point in being half a poet. [. . . My] poetry has got to be so good that people who shrug will read and not forget the feeling of their shrug."

In poetry, Sexton found a true and proper home for her powers of invention. Through "the talking cure," she came to understand that the symptoms of her mental illness were like metaphors, encoding meanings rich with personal history. In pursuit of such meanings during therapy sessions, she learned techniques of rapid association that later proved valuable at her desk, and later still in the classroom. Apparently Sexton's first inklings about figurative language as a mode of thought had come during her initial hospitalization at Westwood Lodge, back in July 1956, when she had met the musician who was also Dr. Orne's patient. She described the experience later to a friend who was a psychiatrist and a writer: "I was thrilled [. . .] to get into the Nut House. At first, of course, I was just scared and crying and very quiet (who me!) but then I found this girl (very crazy of course) (like me I guess) who talked language. What a relief! I mean, well . . . someone! And then later, a while later, and quite a while I found out that Martin [Orne] talked language [. . .] I don't know who else does. I don't use it with everyone. No one of my whole street, suburb neighbors . . ."

Sexton's experience with therapy instructed her in the laws of substitution and displacement, and in the cunning that underlay her physical symptoms and her florid associations. But it was in the poetry workshop that she found what was to be her vocational use of these insights. Poetry, she came to understand, was the *art* of "language." Later she expressed the relation in a metaphor that internalized the doctor as a function of the creative psyche. "It is the split self, it seems to me, that is the mad woman. When writing you make a new reality and become whole. [. . .] It is like lying on the analyst's couch, reenacting a private terror, and the creative mind is the analyst who gives pattern and meaning to what the persona sees as only incoherent experience."

Although Sexton viewed her suicidal depression as a form of "language" — an expressive gesture toward the otherwise inexpressible — she did not identify mental illness with creativity. "Not all language is poetry. Nor is all poetry language." Nonetheless, the two were linked in her origins as a poet, because without the catastrophe of her suicide attempt she probably would have gone on living the life of a depressed housewife, medicated but still functional. The way she formulated the story of becoming a poet, however, conveys nothing less than a sense of destiny in its metaphors of crazing and breakage: "The surface cracked when I was about twenty-eight. I had a psychotic break and tried to kill myself. [. . .] It was a kind of rebirth at twenty-nine." Like a goddess from an egg, motherless and fatherless, the poet bursts into history as a completely new being. Choosing this metaphor, Sexton was signaling not so much a break with her family as an affiliation with another set of progenitors, and another identity, focused on work. Leaving the domestic world composed of infant-parent dynamics, she burst into the cosmos of poetic art.

By the time Sexton told the story of how she had been born again, a number of diagnostic labels had been attached to her disorder — "hysteric," "psychoneurotic," "borderline," and "alcoholic" — but "psychotic" was not among them. For the purposes of her story, however, the term "psychotic break" implied a significant poetic lineage. It connected her not only to such "mad" poets as Robert Lowell, Theodore Roethke, John Berryman, Delmore Schwartz, and Sylvia Plath, but also to T. S. Eliot and Ezra Pound and, before the age of psychiatry, to Rimbaud, Baudelaire, and Coleridge. Sexton was positioning herself among all those poets whose careers had included, in Rimbaud's widely applied phrase, "a lengthy, immense, and systematic derangement of the senses." She made this connection explicit in her claim "I found I belonged to the poets, that I was *real* there, and I had another 'These are my people.' "

This was a decisive change of identity, and she had firmly achieved it by the end of 1957, when she discontinued the practice of submitting her poems for publication under the name Mrs. A. M. Sexton and began signing them "Anne Sexton." Later she would comment, regarding her first book, "By God, I don't think I'm the one who writes the poems! They don't center in my house — I can't write about Kayo, nothing — I was very careful about the picture on my book: didn't want it to look suburban, wanted just to be a face, a person whose life you couldn't define." Renaming herself was a stage in her symbolic reconstitution: she annulled the "Mrs." that indicated her dependent relationship to a husband and stepped forth in a euphonious triad of syllables all her own. Equally significant evidence of this change was the letter she wrote to accompany the carefully typed manuscript she presented at Christmas to Mary Gray: "Here are some forty-odd pages of the first year of Anne Sexton, Poet. You may remember my first sonnet written just after Christmas one year ago. I do not think all of these are good. However, I am not ashamed of them. [. . .] I love you. I don't write for you, but know that one of the reasons I do write is that you are my mother."

A copy of this interesting manuscript has survived: typescripts or carbons of thirty-seven poems, all written by the end of 1957, carefully arranged in a green cardboard folder. In 1973 Sexton wrote on this folder "NEVER TO BE SEEN." She wanted no one to inspect her fumbling beginnings; but it is obvious why she could not bring herself to destroy the manuscript, even in 1973: It was the only proof Mary Gray ever saw that Anne Sexton had become a writer. "This is just a start for me," she asserted in her Christmas letter to Mary Gray. "I hope I am going to continue to improve and if I do I'm going to aim high. And why not."

II

HOUSEWIFE INTO POET
1957–1962

5

FROM *RATS* TO *STAR*
1957–1958

THE MOST IMPORTANT relationship in Anne Sexton's life as a poet was the friendship she formed in 1957 with Maxine Kumin, an extraordinary bond that lasted to the day of her death.

Kumin had kept a wary distance from Sexton during their first term together in John Holmes's class. She had recently lost a friend to suicide and was put off by Sexton's self-dramatizing references to the mental hospital, while Sexton, put off by Kumin's neat little bun of hair, dismissed her as "the most frump of the frumps." But shortly after the new term started at the Boston Center in September, Sexton ran into Kumin at the Newton Free Library. They chatted, and discovered that they were neighbors — Kumin lived in nearby Newton Highlands. Hungry for suggestions about contemporary poetry, Sexton asked for advice. They arranged to commute to the poetry class together, and exchanged telephone numbers.

A few days after that chance encounter, Sexton called Kumin. "I've written something — I don't know whether it's a poem or not. Can I come over?" She took "Music Swims Back to Me" and sat waiting nervously while Kumin read it.

> Wait Mister. Which way is home?
> They turned the light out
> and the dark is moving in the corner.
> There are no sign posts in this room,
> four ladies, over eighty,
> in diapers every one of them.
> La la la, Oh music swims back to me
> and I can feel the tune they played
> the night they left me
> in this private institution on a hill.

Imagine it. A radio playing
and everyone here was crazy.
I liked it and danced in a circle.
Music pours over the sense
and in a funny way
music sees more than I.
I mean it remembers better;
remembers the first night here.
It was the strangled cold of November;
even the stars were strapped in the sky
and that moon too bright
forking through the bars to stick me
with a singing in the head.
I have forgotten all the rest.

They lock me in this chair at eight a.m.
and there are no signs to tell the way,
just the radio beating to itself
and the song that remembers
more than I. Oh, la la la,
this music swims back to me.
The night I came I danced a circle
and was not afraid.
Mister?

Remarkably, Sexton had arrived at the strengths that three years later gained wide praise for her first book, *To Bedlam and Part Way Back*, where "Music Swims Back to Me" appears almost unchanged from the version Maxine Kumin saw in September 1957. What made this a milestone in Sexton's development was the daring representation of the perspective of a madwoman. Some kind of breakdown has exiled her to an asylum. Which way is home? Further into madness. The poem registers desire for the condition Sexton frequently sought and rarely achieved during therapy sessions by falling into trance states — the security of complete delusion. In the poem, this desire is cleverly conveyed in an analogy to the common experience of hearing a banal popular song playing on a radio and being invaded by an intense earlier experience that the music "remembers." (Notably, this is not a "two-way radio" but a voice that drowns out other signals.) In Sexton's metaphor, the music is a former identity that overtakes her: not a memory, but a consciousness that unfolds in the violent imagery of "strangled cold" and "moon too bright / forking through the bars to stick me / with a singing in the head." This condition cannot be remembered, but it can be reentered. The poem is an appeal to a gatekeeper: Mister, which way?

Maxine Kumin marveled that the poem had come to Sexton "almost whole — just occurred on the page, and was still quivering. It was just wonderful." Her response that day was like signing an agreement to become another of Sexton's "twins." There were already striking resemblances, which their long friendship was to enhance. Like Sexton, Kumin was tall, broad-shouldered, and dark, though lean and athletic where Sexton was merely thin. She had been a competitive swimmer and kept fit by working out in a pool; thus Sexton's metaphor held personal resonance for her. Born in 1925, she was thirty-one when they met, Sexton twenty-eight. Kumin too was the mother of young children (Jane, Judy, and Dan, who was Linda's

Anne Sexton and Maxine Kumin at a meeting of the John Holmes workshop.

age). But in other regards she was way, way ahead of Sexton. For one thing, she had been to college and had studied poetry; she knew what was "good." She had graduated from Radcliffe in 1946, married Victor Kumin, and completed a master's degree in history and literature before settling into raising a family. In college she had studied Latin and started Russian, and in graduate seminars she had ventured into the heady intellectual terrain of postwar existentialism, which was just coming into fashion when she finished her master's. She had spent hours learning by heart the formally complex, witty poetry of W. H. Auden, Stephen Spender, Louis MacNeice, Karl Shapiro, and Randall Jarrell; when she wrote poetry, she tried to write like them.

After several years as a mother, Kumin had become restless. "I made a pact with myself that I would sell something before the [third] baby was born," and she did: she published her first poem that year — 1953 — and went on to publish regularly in magazines such as the *Ladies' Home Journal* and the *Saturday Evening Post*. "I had a profitable cottage industry going, writing light verse. But the longing to write serious stuff was still there." Through mutual friends, Kumin learned about John Holmes's poetry class at the Boston Center and decided to attend.

So Kumin was both a serious poet and a writer who had published in magazines that were respected in the suburbs. Not only had she published some poems, she had been paid for them. In comprehending Sexton's work instantly, knowledgeably, warmly — maybe even a bit enviously — she slipped into the space of empathy essential to Sexton's creativity, a position she would occupy permanently. In Dr. Orne, Sexton had found an intelligent and responsive nurturer of her humanity. When Maxine Kumin expressed her admiration of "Music Swims Back to Me," Sexton for the first time received validation from a real poet. While writing poetry remained a therapy in her life, from this time on it was also a vocation. And Kumin's belief in Sexton's gift became both a prop and a comfort as Sexton rose to prominence as an important American writer.

During the autumn and winter of 1957, Kumin and Sexton became a twosome on the poetry scene. They attended poetry readings together: W. S. Merwin at the De Cordova Museum, Marianne Moore at Wellesley College, Robert Graves, Robert Frost. During one of Kayo's business trips, Anne invited Max and her husband to dinner, along with a few other poets and the neighbors Les and Sandy Robart.

She rarely felt like entertaining without Kayo's assistance, but she scheduled this party to leave Kayo out: "Max is Jewish & a poet — with Kayo, that's two strikes against her." By the year's end, she was reporting happily to her doctor, "I think Max likes me; I do like her" and "Max likes me — makes a big difference."

During the early years of their friendship, Sexton was glad to have Kumin's moral support in negotiating her own and her family's view of her writing as more than occupational therapy. It was a particularly sore point with her family that she felt well enough to join a poetry class but not well enough to resume full responsibility for her children. During 1957 and half of 1958, only Linda lived at home; Joy remained with George and Billie Sexton. George, who continued to pay most of Anne's medical bills, decided to address Dr. Orne directly: "It is my personal belief that she is playing us all for a bunch of suckers, and that she has no intention of ever assuming her family responsibilities," he wrote. "It appears to me that we all, you, her husband and I, should now get tough with her."

At her worst moments, Sexton concurred in such harsh opinions. On a typical day, as she described it, she would "take half an hour to clean the house," then rush to the typewriter, not moving until Linda came home from nursery school at lunchtime. "Linda eats, then I put on a record or put her in front of television and go back to my desk. At moments I feel so guilty I read her a story. . . . I'm always willing to cuddle, but I won't bother to prepare food: there I sit." Sexton realized she was being neglectful, but the pressure angered her too. "If I didn't have [Linda] there to reflect my depression it wouldn't be so bad," she told her psychiatrist. "Any demand is too much when I'm like this. I want her to go away, and she knows it." Nothing she was learning about herself in therapy seemed to help her function as a mother, and she struggled with shocking feelings of rage toward Linda. "I've loved Joy, never loved Linda. . . . Something comes between me and Linda. I hate her, and slap her in the face — never for anything naughty; I just seem to be constantly harming her. . . . Wish I didn't have a mother-in-law at my every move. They act as if I were crazy or something when I get angry." Sexton felt as though she were leading two lives, one in treatment and one in the midst of her family. "I *think* a different language than I must practice speaking," she explained. "I am too queer to try to help the children adjust."

Writing seemed the only activity that rewarded her efforts. By mid-

1958, she had established a pattern of single-mindedness about writing poetry that was to become familiar to her family. The house was small, and she had no private work space, so she took over a corner of the tiny dining room, first setting up a card table. To Kayo's annoyance, the room began to look like a messy office, with every flat surface concealed under books and drafts.

Poring over her rhyming dictionary, Sexton would work out elaborate sound patterns and rhyme schemes by hand and then, at her typewriter, fill them slowly to the brim with images, sentences, and phrases that finally turned into poems. Worksheets show that her earliest

A manuscript of "The Operation," showing Sexton's plan for the poem on the page.

poems very often began, like the sonnet inspired by Professor Richards's television lecture, with a formal problem. She would type a phrase or line at the top of a page; from this she would develop a path of end rhymes, an access road to pools of feeling. Feelings in turn begat images, more than she could use; these had to be fit into the boundaries set by the end rhymes, and some boundaries would give way ("Music Swims Back to Me," for instance, is irregularly rhymed). Gradually the channeled flow of images would coalesce into a work of art.

Some of these exercises produced poems that stand among the best Sexton ever wrote. Very inconclusive drafts of "Elizabeth Gone," "The Double Image," and "Unknown Girl in the Maternity Ward" began emerging in January, February, and March of 1958. Other poems Sexton worked over and finished in Holmes's class that term were "For Johnny Pole on the Forgotten Beach," "Torn Down from Glory Daily," "The Moss of His Skin," "What's That," "The Kite," "The Bells," "Hutch," "The Exorcists," "Said the Poet to the Analyst," and "You, Doctor Martin." She worked on others as well, some of which were published in journals but later discarded. Under the influence of the poetry class, she was gradually shaping a preference for the dramatic lyric in place of the moony and moody strains of her "transference" verses from the year before.

By mid-June Sexton probably had sixty poems in circulation, seeking publishers. On 26 June she submitted "The Reading" and "The Balance Wheel" to the *Christian Science Monitor,* which was published in Boston but had a national circulation. The newspaper had the advantage of rapid turnaround; it accepted both poems and published "The Balance Wheel" on 15 July and "The Reading" on 28 July. This was the acceptance that won the respect of her family. "My father was terribly proud. At that point I was getting acceptances from *Harper's, The New Yorker,* that hadn't come out, but the newspaper ones would come out very quickly. My father would get thirty copies of the newspaper and send them to all his customers — all his friends — maybe forty or fifty. After he died, I found all these clippings. . . . He loved celebrities, and I had become his celebrity."

That winter and spring Sexton was taking an antidepressant drug, with good effect: "I really have the feeling I never will be depressed again." She knew it wasn't a cure, "yet here I am, what I think of as well," she told her doctor; "when I am better, better than I used to be — though when I am sick, as sick as always." The drug's benefit lasted only a few months, but it enabled Sexton to work with more focus than she ever had before. During these weeks she consumed the works of psychoanalytic literature that had such impact on her therapy. She also spent hours examining the poems in a book that all her friends in John Holmes's class were reading: *New Poets of England and America,* with a preface by Robert Frost.

This anthology was widely discussed in the poetry world, largely because it assembled so much that was academic and conservative in mainstream American writing. Detractors dismissed it as "gray flannel poetry." But in its pages, sometime in mid-March, Sexton encountered a poem that had a definitive influence on her development: "Heart's Needle," by William DeWitt Snodgrass. Unlike many of the other poems in the anthology, "Heart's Needle" had a personal theme. It was addressed to the poet's three-year-old daughter, separated from him by divorce — a topic that spoke loud and clear to Sexton, whose own toddler still lived with Billie.

In "Heart's Needle," Snodgrass balances images of the Korean War, which began during the winter of his daughter's birth, against images of caretaking. During her visits he and the little girl plant a garden, go bird watching in the marshes, feed animals in the park. He learns to cook so he can fix her supper. The context of the war functions to illuminate the plight of loveless men doomed to banishment and conflict. The divorced father feels as helpless and lonely as the soldiers freezing in a foreign country, longing for home: "I've gone / As men must." The poem's emotional center is Snodgrass's claim that "I am your real mother"; what does a man need to change in himself in order to care for a child? A new marriage gives him a comforting structure for his life, but for instruction in the role of father he visits the Museum of Natural History, where the dioramas of wildlife offer him vignettes of relationship that he takes to heart.

> The bison, here, immense,
> shoves at his calf, brow to brow,
> and looks it in the eye
> to see what it is thinking now.
> I forced you to obedience;
> I don't know why.

The poem ends in the spring, with a visit to the zoo. Nothing is resolved in the ongoing war between the child's parents, but life reasserts itself in new generations. Some bonds are simply given, whether or not they are understood.

> Punished and cared for, behind bars,
> the coons on bread and water
> stretch thin black fingers after ours.
> And you are still my daughter.

"Heart's Needle" engaged issues central in Sexton's therapy; as she later recalled, "I ran up to my mother-in-law's house and brought my daughter home. That's what a poem should do — move people to action. True, I didn't keep my daughter at the time — I wasn't ready. But I was beginning to be ready."

The impact of "Heart's Needle" on the poetry world was also dra-

W. D. Snodgrass.

matic and immediate. In retrospect, this poem can be singled out as the first in what became known as the "confessional" mode of contemporary poetry, mainly because it was emulated by Robert Lowell, the most influential poet in Boston, perhaps in America, at the time. Snodgrass had been a student of Lowell's at the University of Iowa. When "Heart's Needle" came out, Lowell was trying to write about similar domestic and "unpoetic" themes: his early life, his manic-depressive illnesses, his time in jail as a conscientious objector, his second marriage. Snodgrass's poem provided a model of truthfulness that was also carefully artful. "Other poems that are direct that way are slack and have no vibrance," Lowell commented. "[Snodgrass's] experience wouldn't be so interesting and valid if it weren't for the whimsy, the music, the balance, everything revised and placed and pondered. All that gives light to those poems on agonizing subjects comes from the craft."

Reading "Heart's Needle" at her dining room table amid the clutter of her worksheets, with their laborious templates of rhyme and meter, Anne Sexton felt much the same as Robert Lowell. She later told Snodgrass, "When I read your poem, that first time, leafing through the anthology, [. . .] it walked out at me and grew like a bone inside of my heart." His example emboldened her to take a formally elaborate but emotionally direct approach to autobiographical material that was pressing urgently for expression — her separation through mental illness from Joy and Linda — in the poem "Unknown Girl in the Maternity Ward." The speaker is a new mother giving up her illegitimate baby. Sexton avoided melodrama by centering on the mother's brooding amazement at the newborn's animal poise: "I prize/your need [. . .] the wild bee farms / of your nerves." The poem's overriding feeling is a wise sadness over the separations that begin with birth: "I burst empty / of you, letting you learn how the air is so. [. . .] I am a shore / rocking you off." In a deft displacement, Sexton uses the dramatic situation of "Unknown Girl" to affirm a difference between the maternal bond and the maternal role. And though she named only Snodgrass as an influence on this new direction in her work, it is reasonable to assume that the impulse to write about motherhood was reinforced by her strengthening ties to Maxine Kumin, with whom she shared every manuscript.

In April, stabilized on her antidepressant drug and shakily confident in her strengthening powers as a poet, Sexton began bringing Joy home for longer and longer periods: two weeks, then three. In 1957, poetry had saved her life; in 1958, it was restoring her to motherhood. That summer Joy returned to her parents' house for good.

By mid-1958 Sexton had begun to think of herself as a real poet, but her family still thought of her, with good reason, as an unstable person undergoing intensive psychiatric treatment. Her writing craze could easily be mistaken for yet another symptom, to a wary eye. Kayo in particular was not convinced that her obsession with poetry was a sign of health. When Sexton tried to argue that not just writing poetry but being with poets was essential to her well-being, he would become "furious — purple with rage," she told Dr. Orne. And there was a good deal of justice in his attitude, she acknowledged. "In a physical way I am lonely living with him, lonelier now because he bores me. And he hates what I am: he not only doesn't like poetry, he hates poetry. Of course I couldn't have gone on the way I was. It seems as though we could get along if he didn't hate me. He is a good father. But I am physically lonely; and intellectually I go elsewhere. When he gets so martyrish — silly word — it makes me think of his mother. Wish he could let me go to the poetry class and be glad."

Holmes's class at the Boston Center ended in May. Learning that W. D. Snodgrass was scheduled to lead a week-long workshop at the Writers' Conference at Antioch College in Yellow Springs, Ohio, that summer, Sexton wrote to Nolan Miller at *The Antioch Review* inquiring about the possibility of getting a scholarship. The *Review* had just accepted her poem "For Johnny Pole on the Forgotten Beach." She hoped to piggyback acceptance at the conference onto acceptance of her poem, with some financial aid thrown in.

Kayo was distressed when she began thinking out loud about her wish to attend Antioch, or maybe one of the writers' conferences held in New England, during the summer. John Holmes ran one at Tufts; Robert Frost taught at Bread Loaf in Vermont. Then there were the artists' colonies at Yaddo and MacDowell. Sexton's talk of the future increasingly focused on poetry and poets. One Saturday morning she announced that she planned to stay in Boston following her regular appointment with Dr. Orne, to lunch with Maxine Kumin and John Ciardi, poetry editor of the *Saturday Review of Literature*. Kayo blew up. As Sexton described the ensuing quarrel to her doctor, Kayo told her that poetry was an indulgence, just as her psychiatry was an indulgence, and he was tired of trying to explain her selfish behavior to both sides of the family.

He said that all he did now was fight for me with his parents and my parents. I can't remember what I said, but I walked into the dining room, picked up my poetry and tore it up, picked up my typewriter and threw it across the room.

Then we got into the living room and Kayo started hitting me, the usual way we end a fight. After he smacked me down there was nothing left — I told him he'd won, I'd stop going to a psychiatrist and stop writing poetry, then he would love me.

Then I thought, "Okay, we don't get along, we should divorce." But I have no way to get along by myself. And giving up poetry or giving up therapy are about equal in importance. Both are my chance, I think, to be myself.

The typewriter is broken, all my carefully kept records are torn up. I wasn't going to come in here, but he wanted me to. So I got all dressed up, applied the beauty that doesn't exist.

By the time Sexton discussed this episode with Dr. Orne, she and Kayo had established a pattern: a dispute would escalate between them; he would grab her and shake her, and sometimes throw her to the ground and hit her; then he would become very remorseful. They were now used to ending significant quarrels with his blows and her dramatic gestures. The problem was surely enhanced by Sexton's growing independence. First her illness, now her vocation, were thieving from the scarce time the couple could devote to their relationship. But once she had the scholarship that paid her tuition at the Antioch Writers' Conference, Kayo yielded to her wishes. Once again, Billie took the children.

Sexton was afraid to travel alone, so she persuaded Ruth Soter, one of her pals from John Holmes's class, to enroll in the Writers' Conference and accompany her to Ohio in mid-August. Constantly together, they became close friends. Sexton said that Soter could see right through her defenses: "As Ruth advised me on the plane, 'stop thinking that you can avoid people with all your words — or even reach them with your words.' " Sexton went in order to work with Snodgrass, but she also became friends with the other instructors — Nolan Miller, Hollis Summers, Jessamyn West, and James McConkey, who directed the conference — and with Jack Matthews, a fellow participant.

Snodgrass and Sexton hit it off at once. Four or five people in the group were more gifted than Anne Sexton, Snodgrass thought at the time: Jack Matthews was one, Ruth Soter another "by a considerable margin" (years later, Snodgrass still remembered a villanelle Soter had written at Antioch, which he considered to be "within two or three words of being absolutely perfect"). But, he mused, poetry "is a game where talent is cheap and where it is hardly the decisive factor. It seemed clear that Sexton was a person so driven that she would go on and do the work. And indeed that is what happened. At the time she came to Antioch she had published, I suppose, between four and six poems. The following year she published in something like forty different magazines." At Antioch both Sexton and Soter worked on poems that had already made the rounds in John Holmes's class. Eventually the work Sexton showed Snodgrass ended up in her first book. "Everything she wrote had at least a line or two with some striking insight or some marvelous turn of language about it," Snodgrass said. "I felt about them, I think, the way I feel about some of Hardy's poems: almost all of them I am glad to have read once."

Sexton left a strong impression at Antioch. She aggressively sought the attention of instructors, always asking the same question: does this poem have a voice, *my* voice? Nolan Miller remembered her attitude as "Here I am, a little housewife, and suddenly I've turned to poetry and I still don't know what I'm doing." She was also flirtatious: "Bawdy and funny," reminisced Jack Matthews. "Dashing. Flamboyant. Spectacular. A house afire," Nolan Miller remembered. "She appeared to be in a state of exhilaration, [. . .] a constant high." Sexton had a fling with one fellow poet who was working on a torrid verse play about "an insane sexual adventure," which Snodgrass thought was "simply marvelous." This romance continued for several months by mail after they left Antioch, and Sexton's comments make it clear that she considered it a transference relationship in which her partner stood in for the unavailable De Snodgrass (as she called him), whose moustache was like Dr. Orne's. For instructors at writing conferences, thrown together day and night with creative people who had temporarily abandoned their families, flirtations were an occupational hazard. Snodgrass resisted seduction, adopting a mentorly role that stood Sexton's fragile psyche in good stead.

Sexiness was only one ingredient of Sexton's glamour. Thinking about her after nearly thirty years, Snodgrass struggled to identify the qualities that drew him in 1958. She resembled, he decided, poets such as Robert Lowell, Randall Jarrell, and John Berryman, "terribly exciting" people who cultivated around themselves such emotional turbulence that biographical accounts tend to misrepresent their complexity. "It's very much easier to write about their misbehavior when they went bad. I guess I'm finding it hard to re-create the sense of what was good about the relationship [with Anne Sexton]. I guess it was her energy and the sense you got — that was, perhaps, partly misleading — of openness to experience and to insight. She had exciting and interesting things to say, and her letters were a pleasure to read."

The enchantment was mutual. If John Holmes was the professional influence visible in Sexton's early poems, guiding her in the task of speaking through a mask and valuing an air of distance and clever formal effects, it was De Snodgrass who helped her find an authentic first-person voice: her goal in going to Antioch. None of the poems she wrote or revised at the Antioch Writers' Conference — "Where I Live in This Honorable House of the Laurel Tree," "Portrait of an Old Woman on the College Tavern Wall," "The Farmer's Wife" — reflects his influence. But Snodgrass catalyzed in her a talent that had not found encouragement in John Holmes's class but that would become her signature: the talent for making poetry the vehicle of autobiography, of self-analysis.

Home from Antioch, Sexton wrote to Dr. Orne, who was away for the summer, about what she had learned by living for a whole week among writers. The experience had confirmed an insight from therapy: even very personal poetry came from the power of words to radiate meanings beyond the poet's conscious intention.

If I write RATS and discover that rats reads STAR backwards, and amazingly STAR is wonderful and good because I found it in rats, then is star untrue? [. . .] Of course I KNOW that words are just a counting game, I know this until the words start to arrange themselves and write something better than I would ever know. [. . .] I don't really believe the poem, but the name is surely mine so I must belong to the poem. So I must be real. . . . When you say "words mean nothing" then it means that the real me is nothing. All I am is the trick of words writing themselves.

Sexton's tone of humble self-assessment in this letter masks a deep insight into the workings of society: that "poet" is an identity extrapolated from a published poem. The poem's "I" is real because it has become visible in the medium of print and circulated among those who are positioned to recognize it. The better the journal in which the poem appears, the more secure the identity deflected onto its maker. Like other forms of currency, the first-person pronoun has a value established in a cultural marketplace. That value accrues to the poem's author as a side effect of the recognition of her or his work.

In 1958, the market value of an autobiographical "I" in a poem was rising. Literary criticism had devised the term "persona" to reinforce the distinction between the poem's maker and its speaker, and the work of T. S. Eliot and Ezra Pound had helped to strengthen the notion that greatness in art was equivalent to impersonality, sometimes called universality. Snodgrass's and Lowell's poetry in the mid-1950s was driving a wedge into this assumption. The autobiographical or "confessional" mode, no less literary for *seeming* less literary, invited the reader to equate word with person. Sexton's letter zeros in on the gap. The feel of reality is only one of the tricky effects words achieve just by being arranged in certain ways, she observes. Readers are taken in by this. Praising the poem, they create a poet by projection.

But readers are only disposed to praise a poem that carries some guarantee of cultural value. This point was not lost on the daughter and wife of salesmen. Though Sexton noticed that poets and businessmen tended to ridicule one another, she was in a position, after attending the Antioch Writers' Conference, to appreciate their similarities. Antioch had advanced her understanding of the literary marketplace to which she aspired, in which Snodgrass held influence. Partly because she adored him and partly because she knew the value of his good opinion, she began a lively correspondence with him. He was to become her freeway ramp to the fast lane of literary success.

From the end of August 1958 through mid-1959, Sexton wrote to Snodgrass several times a month, gossiping about family life, enclosing poems, and keeping him up-to-date on the trajectory of her career. At moments of crisis in her therapy, she flooded him with long, leaky letters. His responses were steady and warm, like Kumin's. He adopted an avuncular, teasing style of giving her approval, advice, and criticism. Although he addressed his letters to "Annie lover," "Lotus," or "Annie-pants," he did not allow their intimacy to become sexual on more than a metaphorical level, unlike the previous poet-lovers she had attracted.

Snodgrass's tone of familial warmth comforted Sexton as she struggled with family calamities. Mary Gray had recovered physically from her surgery but was depressed by the loss of her breast. To cheer her up, her husband planned a trip to Europe that November — their first trip abroad. But on his way to pick up their tickets from the travel agent, he had a stroke. He slumped against the steering wheel; the blasting horn attracted the attention of a passing motorist, and he was rushed to a Boston hospital for treatment. During his hospitalization, Mary Gray stayed with Anne and Kayo, and sometime during those months her cancer metastasized. The family toppled like dominoes as shock waves spread from one member to the next. In mid-November, Sexton too sought hospitalization, spending two days at Westwood Lodge in a flight from the inner voices she describes in the poem she was writing at the time, "The Double Image": "They tattled / like green witches in my head, letting doom / leak like a broken faucet." A desperately lighthearted letter to Snodgrass indicates how she called on her relation to him as a defense against the ebbing of her parents' lives.

> Dear passionflower tender, I was just looking out the window at the truck that was delivering two bottles of whiskey and it was, yes it was, snowing. I am young. I am younger each year at the first snow. [. . .] I am a good girl and the man left two bottles of booze because my mother is rich and she ordered them. [. . .] My mother keeps telling me that soon I will be rich because they will be dead (she is greedily wordy about this) and I listen to her and think about a poem by you about a mother . . . she is like a star . . . everything MUST center around her.

However, Sexton's continual demands to be told she was a good girl tried the limits of Snodgrass's affection that year, perhaps most dramatically during a visit around the time of her thirtieth birthday. He stayed with the Sexton family after a reading Robert Lowell arranged for him at the Poets' Theater in Cambridge. After his return to Rochester, where he taught, Sexton wrote an embarrassed, self-justifying letter, attempting to account for what must have been seductive behavior, which he must have rebuffed. "I am always saved by men who understand me better than I understand myself," she told him ruefully. Apparently she was right in this case, as Snodgrass's tone in succeeding letters remained unruffled, affectionate, and admiring. He seemed to understand her need for approval from a point of view inflected by some kind of family feeling; during their two or three years of close friendship, he typically spoke in letters to her as to a much younger person, though he was in fact only two years older than she.

What Sexton struggled hardest to preserve in the friendship was Snodgrass's loyalty to her poetry. By mentioning his name in the letters she sent with her poems to various publications, she received closer, perhaps more respectful attention. Even more valuable was Snodgrass's enthusiastic reaction to her work in progress and his encouragement to find her own voice. Particularly important was his influence on the evolution of one of her strongest poems, "The Double Image." In a letter, she confided to him the reasons that "Heart's Needle" had moved her so deeply when she read it back in March: it had touched "the unconscious area of my guilt." She described the family battles over custody of the children — "Everyone said I wasn't good for them" — and her sense of failure. "I do not dare write this true poem," she concluded.

Perhaps writing the story line to Snodgrass in a letter helped her organize the poem in her imagination. "The Double Image," addressed to Joy, explains why Sexton "chose two times/to kill myself" rather than live within the family as Joy's mother. "Why did I let you grow in another place?" she asks. The narrative incorporates many factual details about the period between July 1956, when Joy was sent to live with Billie, and November 1958, when "you stay for good [. . .] You learn my name [. . .] You call me *mother*." It reports that Sexton was hospitalized, attempted suicide, recuperated in her parents' home; that her mother was diagnosed and treated for breast cancer and blamed Sexton for the illness; that Sexton attempted suicide a second time.

Within this factual, chronological account the poet condenses and interprets the emotional dynamic between herself and her mother in the rich metaphor of the poem's title: the double image is the pair of portraits that Mary Gray commissioned in Annisquam.

> I cannot forgive your suicide, my mother said.
> And she never could. She had my portrait
> done instead.
>
> I lived like an angry guest,
> like a partly mended thing, an outgrown child.
> I remember my mother did her best.
> She took me to Boston and had my hair restyled.
> Your smile is like your mother's, the artist said.

The mother had been painted in a pose like the daughter's: "matching smile, matching contour." When, toward the end of the poem, Sexton returns to the question of "why I would rather / die than love," she interprets the symbolism of these portraits:

> In north light, my smile is held in place,
> the shadow marks my bone.
> What could I have been dreaming as I sat there,
> all of me waiting in the eyes, the zone
> of the smile, the young face,
> the foxes' snare.
>
> In south light, her smile is held in place,
> her cheeks wilting like a dry
> orchid; my mocking mirror, my overthrown
> love, my first image. She eyes me from that face,
> that stony head of death
> I had outgrown.
> [. . .]
> And this was the cave of the mirror,
> that double woman who stares
> at herself, as if she were petrified.

Finally, the last lines beautifully extend the implications of the metaphor, as Sexton recognizes that she has now stepped into the mother's position herself.

> I remember we named you Joyce
> so we could call you Joy.
> [. . .]
> I needed you. I didn't want a boy,
> only a girl, a small milky mouse
> of a girl, already loved [. . .]
> I, who was never quite sure
> about being a girl, needed another
> life, another image to remind me.
> And this was my worst guilt; you could not cure
> nor soothe it. I made you to find me.

"The Double Image" has been justly praised as a courageous and moving example of the "confessional" poem. Indeed, Sexton wrote a part of it in the mental institution that autumn — "the 'scaled hotel' helped unblock me on its writing," she told Snodgrass. Within the autobiographical line of the poem, however, is a second network of meaning that broadens its reference, making it an important contribution to the literature of feminine psychology. Sexton pointed to this larger set of meanings herself. "The mother-daughter relationship is more poignant than Romeo and Juliet," she commented once before reading this poem to a radio audience. "Just as Oedipus is more interesting."

It is a provocative analogy. When is the mother-daughter relation like Oedipus? Before the "complex" sets in, in the dawning recognition, for girl as well as boy, that Mother is not hers alone. Successful development requires that the child repress and redirect this erotic attachment ("my overthrown / love, my first image"), replacing Mother and Daughter eventually with some version of Romeo and Juliet. The loss of this earliest love is presumably "more poignant" because it cannot be avoided.

Anne holding a kitten, with Joy, on the back porch in Newton Lower Falls.

Except, of course, through madness, which functions in "The Double Image" to reveal the buried longing for lost joy. Illness infantilizes the speaker and permits a return to Mother. The suicide attempt is thus a shrewd, if unconsciously devised, solution to the problem of having grown up. Sexton's child is taken away (in the poem there is only one child), and the poet is sent home to live again with her mother. Introducing the poem to her radio audience, Sexton said matter-of-factly, "What the poem does for me is it tells of me living with my parents — I'm trying to be a daughter, not have one. . . . Then I get better in the hospital; I get out for good."

But only one parent is important to the kind of health achieved in "The Double Image." Sexton is here concerned exclusively with the nature of the bond a certain type of mother forms with her infant daughter. She identifies the type metaphorically as the unforgiving mother who seeks in her daughter an ideal, or "restyled," female image, one that reflects back to her an ideal self, equally imaginary. This is "the cave of the mirror": a world reduced to a female dyad in which the mother's need for a certain type of daughter ("we named you Joyce / so we could call you Joy") fatefully constricts the daughter's growth as a separate self.

The deep insight in the poem is that within such a mother is buried an infant who was also made the mirror of a mother's need for admiration. A baby's blissful contentment in its mother's presence, a baby's total dependency, make it available to the mother's emotional needs as no other human being will consent to be. The daughter of a woman who does not forgive her for growing out of this mirror-stage of engrossment hungers for restitution of the mirror condition with her own child ("I needed you. I didn't want a boy").

This mirror is a true heirloom, where in "The Double Image" the false selves of at least two generations are reflected. Sexton's gestures first of renouncing motherhood ("I would rather die than love") and later of accepting guilt are acts in a struggle to end the reproduction of the false self that the mother nurtures in her hunger for a daughter who is an image, not a person. Hence, the true healing in the poem takes place not only in the scene of reunion among the generations (the mother takes three-year-old Joy to visit her ailing grandmother) but inwardly, as Sexton acknowledges finding her mother's needs and hungers reflected in herself: "I made you to find me." The history of the poet's relationship to her own mother rearranges itself around the reluctant clarity of these last lines. This guilt, like the guilt of Oedipus, has been uncovered only after a catastrophe revealed its meaning; it is a sphinx's riddle hidden, for Sexton and her mother both, in the mother-daughter bond.

Sexton worked on "The Double Image" for three months, from early September until around Thanksgiving 1958. She was putting the finishing touches on the poem when Mary Gray came to stay in Newton Lower Falls for the holidays. Ralph was still in the hospital, convalescing from his stroke, and Sexton was happy to have her mother in the house. Later, reminiscing about this season, she remembered with humor, "Mother wasn't a Puritan. She liked to drink; she was fun when she was living with us. I ignored her at Thanksgiving, when I was trying to write; she got furious and kept it up and kept it up. . . . Oh, I got mad at her, she made me furious, but that's the way she was if anyone ignored her for a minute. When she used the apparatus of her sarcasm — oh, she knew me! — she could twist me! But I spent my life trying to be with her."

Perhaps it was awareness of the imminence of a permanent separation from Mary Gray that made Sexton avidly productive that autumn; the threat of separation would always be the ally of her deepest work. It is certainly the case that in writing "The Double Image" she made a compelling analysis of the psychological resemblance between herself and her mother that powered both her neurosis and her art: the poet was an entitled daughter, not a mother.

Sexton's letters to Snodgrass invariably contained a note of buoyancy as she began to receive the first benefits of this entitlement. In September, with Snodgrass's encouragement, she had joined Robert Lowell's class in poetry at Boston University, where she was reworking manuscripts drafted at the Boston Center and at Antioch, learning under Lowell's scrutiny "what to leave out." In late October, *Harper's* accepted "The Farmer's Wife." Sexton was jubilant. "You have 'discovered' me in a way," she wrote to the editor, Russell Lynes. "Your letter is pasted up on the wall and I have been feeling 'discovered' all this week." (In fact, Sexton credited several editors with having discovered her that year: Nolan Miller at *The Antioch Review* had been the first.) When, on the next to last day of December, she found a prestigious publisher for "The Double Image," her satisfaction was complete. This was *The Hudson Review,* a respected literary journal in New York. Its editor, Frederick Morgan, wrote to her warmly, "You have real power and strength of feeling in your work, — and at the same time, control. The poem isn't flawless, I think, but what does that matter when it is so strong and true and authentic in its essentials? I have great hopes and expectations of your work." Exactly two years after composing her first poem — the sonnet she scribbled after watching I. A. Richards on television — Sexton had written a major work and received major recognition for it. Yes, she had been discovered.

6

MENTORS
1958-1959

SNODGRASS'S NAME opened the door for Sexton to Robert Lowell's
writing seminar at Boston University in September 1958. With Snodgrass's encouragement, she sent Lowell a sheaf of recent poems. He
responded graciously: "Of course your poems qualify. They move
with ease and are filled with experience, like good prose. I am not very
familiar with them yet, but have been reading them with a good deal
of admiration and envy this morning after combing through pages of
fragments of my own unfinished stuff. You stick to truth and the simple expression of very difficult feelings, and this is the line in poetry
that I am most interested in." Lowell's "unfinished stuff" was the
manuscript of *Life Studies,* which he sent to his publisher only seven
weeks later, on 31 October.

Lowell's writing courses have been so widely memorialized that it is
possible to gain a feeling for what they must have been like when Sexton took her seat among fifteen graduate students every week, listening, fidgeting, and defiantly chain-smoking forbidden cigarettes. The
class met Tuesdays from two to four P.M. Students came prepared
with typed manuscripts to circulate in carbon copies. During the first
hour Lowell would discuss a poem or two from the assigned anthology; he could spend a long time talking about the effects of just one or
two lines by master poets. Then he would turn to the students' poems.
Alan Williamson recalled his magisterial procedure.

> He would listen to the student read the poem once, then read it
> aloud himself, his hand hovering like a divining-rod until he reached
> a particular detail or turn of phrase, then plumping down: "it comes
> to life here." As often as not he would hand the student back a new
> poem, constructed on the spot out of the two or three passages that

"came to life." [. . .] He was often uncannily right as to where the emotional center, the possible originality, lay. He came as near as I can imagine anyone coming to teaching the intuitions — about one's real subject; about diction; about structure — which so often distinguish good, let alone great, poets from journeymen.

Discomfiting his students was a side effect of one of Lowell's most successful teaching techniques: his focus on small but important achievements that were worth studying and admiring in a phrase or line. Sexton had not read much of the published poetry he singled out for admiration. After a month in class, she worried to Snodgrass, "I shall never write a really good poem. I overwrite. I am a reincarnation of Edna St. Vincent . . . I am learning more than you could imagine from Lowell. I am learning what I am not. He didn't say I was like Edna (I do — a secret fear) — also a fear of writing as a woman writes. I wish I were a man — I would rather write the way a man

Robert Lowell talking to Jane Brooks; John Malcolm Brinnin is the shorter man in the background.

writes." In class and in the office hours to which Lowell invited a few privileged younger poets every week, he spent a good deal of time mulling over whether this or that poet was "major" or "minor," and women were almost inevitably categorized as "minor, definitely minor" — though he made an exception of Elizabeth Bishop. Sexton's boarding school models had been Sara Teasdale and Adelaide Crapsey, accomplished lyricists in the vein of Edna St. Vincent Millay — very different from Bishop, definitely minor. Suddenly Sexton was confronting the poetry of Robert Browning, Gerard Manley Hopkins, Hart Crane, and William Carlos Williams and assuming they represented what it meant both to be "major" and to "write like a man."

The ambiguity about the status of women in Lowell's class was enhanced by his reputation as a skirt-chaser. As one of his friends put it, "Cal had to be 'in love.' Poets were always in love"; so women came in for another kind of classification. After Lowell was appointed to the Harvard faculty in 1963, he routinely interviewed the women students — not the men — who signed up for his classes and admitted them on the basis of looks, or so he claimed to friends. There was always "a girl" somewhere in the background of his professional life, and during the manic phases of his mood swings, she was very much in the foreground. Lowell did not cultivate privacy in regard to his erotic adventures.

Sexton wasn't exactly a student, and she didn't engage in a flirtation with Lowell, but she shared the classroom tensions created by what she called his "soft dangerous voice" as he sorted through the poems in front of him, zeroing in on a phrase or line he might characterize as "almost perfect . . . of its *kind*." Until she won praise for her formal skills, she was convinced Lowell didn't like her, and she was irritated by the attitude of reverence that pervaded his classroom. "I am very bitchy acting in class," she complained to Snodgrass. "The class just sits there like little doggies waggling their heads at his every statement." Yet the seminar consolidated Sexton's strengths, probably because she was learning how to analyze particular nuances and sound effects. "Lowell can not have influenced my work with his work as I haven't been reading his stuff . . . just listening to his ideas about other people's work. I do not feel he is influencing me — but teaching me what NOT to write — or mainly," she told Snodgrass in February "I am learning leaps and boundaries." At the end of the term she summed up the experience. "He taught me great. It was as easy as filling an empty vase. After all, I didn't know a damn thing about any poetry really. 2 years ago I had never heard of any poet but Edna St. Vincent . . . and now do know how to walk through lots of people's poetry and pick and pick over."

Lowell may not have influenced the style of Sexton's poems that fall and winter, but he certainly validated the direction her work was taking — and this included "writing as a woman." It was in Lowell's class that Sexton began scheming early drafts of "The Double Image," trying to achieve the effect of a spontaneous-sounding first-person voice within the constraints of a complex rhymed stanza, surefootedly building up a dramatic narrative. She spent over three months on the project. When *The Hudson Review* accepted "The Double Image" at the end of December — all 240 lines — Lowell was impressed.

By early January, most of the poems Sexton was circulating for publication had been accepted. Snodgrass marveled, "Jesus God! You're publishing everywhere!" Now she decided to ask Lowell's advice about publishing a whole manuscript, 122 pages long, with a title drawn from lines in "The Double Image": *To Bedlam and Part Way Back*. The process of selecting and arranging the poems for his scrutiny inaugurated a new phase of creativity, and during the next five months in his class Sexton wrote eight new poems, which strengthened the theme of Bedlam and reduced the number of poems written as formal exercises. Meanwhile, Lowell reviewed the manuscript and passed it on to other readers for advice about placing it with a publisher. Sexton wrote to Snodgrass,

> Lowell is really helping me, De, as kindly as possible and I can't figure it out. I am always so startled by goodness. He likes the looks of my "book," with some critical reservations, and has shown it to Stanley Kunitz and Bill Alfred, who both, he says, agree with his enthusiasm (and his reservations). [. . .] Isn't that something, De . . . I mean, I am — jeepers creepers about it. He means by Sept. that I might get it accepted now, but should still rewrite and work out the poorer stuff and write some new ones to fill their place. I am confused and delighted with this — and time and the publishing market will tell the rest. But, I remind my self's self, I've got to stay sane to do it.

Sanity meant losing herself in trances of writing. She "would willingly push a poem through twenty or more drafts," Maxine Kumin remembered. "She had an unparalleled tenacity in those early days."

Sexton was also assiduous in the business end of poetry, tediously re-typing poems to send out for serial publication before they appeared in book form, and writing personal notes to the editors of journals. Enthusiastic responses led to new affections that winter. Sexton began a correspondence with Carolyn Kizer at *Poetry Northwest,* and her first acceptance at *The New Yorker,* in February, inaugurated what was to become a warm rapport with its poetry editor, Howard Moss. She was elated: she regarded publication in *The New Yorker* as a major debut, for most of the literary journals that accepted her work had circulations under 1000. "Despite many successes," she wrote to Moss, "nothing has been sweeter. (I mean yippee.)"

She was also becoming an active self-promoter. Parties held in honor of visiting poets (often at John Holmes's house) made it clear that success in the poetry business rather resembled success in the wool business, in that the visibility of one's trademark was all-impor-tant and a certain amount of salesmanship was required. "It is politics and as bad as the University itself. See Cal [Lowell] at them, but avoid hanging onto his jacket," she wrote to Snodgrass. "Last week for Dick Wilbur, John Holmes had a party. After most had left (Cal, Stanley Kunitz, John Brinnin, and Isabella Gardner) we sat around and read our poems aloud (dozens of others[;] must have been 50 people there!) . . . Wilbur, Holmes, Dave Ferry, Phil Booth, Maxine, Me, George Starbuck and some others I forget. and that was kind of fun. But still all very political and 'who do *you* know' and 'do you have a new book in process.' "

Sexton liked to hobnob, so she was pleased but nervous when Fred-erick Morgan, editor of *The Hudson Review,* invited her to drop by the journal's offices if she ever came to New York. Arriving late one day in mid-January, she met the whole *Hudson Review* staff — Mor-gan, Joseph Bennett, Mary Emma Elliott — and Morgan's wife, Rose, as well; they spent the evening drinking martinis, and the Morgans persuaded Sexton to stay on so they could all go out to dinner. Mor-gan remembered the occasion vividly. "Anne struck me as someone who had it all ahead of her. She had all the interest, all the spark and the personality, but really didn't have a great deal of culture. She had a very nice laugh, a kind of gusty laugh, and was rather breezy and kind of silly. She was just fun. I took a strong liking to her, and so did my wife." Catching the midnight flight to Boston in a mood of exhil-aration, Sexton wrote a poem to Rose Morgan, which she tucked into the growing manuscript of *Bedlam.* But once home, she wrote in panic to Snodgrass about whether she had behaved properly. "I might have axed myself — but I don't think I did. [. . .] I tried NOT to act suave (as you said) but this was difficult because part of my well-worn mask is being suave . . . I tried to tone down the mask and, as you said, 'be myself.' If there had been time I would have written you back, 'which self????' . . . but there wasn't time . . . Still, I was pretty much my own self's self, booming with enthusiasm about this and that."

Sexton was already beginning to experience her professional persona as a mask, whether in the offices of *The Hudson Review* or onstage. It was during this same winter that she began developing the reading style that eventually made her one of the most memorable performers on the poetry circuit. What she called her first "real" poetry reading took place 1 March at the Poets' Theater in Cambridge, where she appeared with Arthur Freeman, a precocious Harvard undergraduate; Maxine Kumin; George Starbuck, a young poet who had just arrived in Boston; and Harvard professor William Alfred, who performed the introductions. The reading sold out and was repeated the following week. "Most of the really important people came the first time," she told Snodgrass, but "the second reading was a greater success" — both times she drew tears from the audience with her reading of "The Double Image."

At least as important to Sexton's progress as Lowell's class that year was her participation in the private workshop that developed out of John Holmes's poetry course. Sexton, Kumin, Sam Albert, and George Starbuck began meeting in the fall of 1958 for open-ended evening sessions at one or another of their homes. It was a tight little group that only occasionally welcomed drop-ins, since the success of its procedures required intimate knowledge of one another's work and respect for quite different artistic goals.

Holmes and Sexton were polar opposites in this group. She set his teeth on edge; he disliked almost everything about her conduct. When the workshop met in the Holmeses' living room, John's widow, Doris Eyges, remembered, Sexton's strident cries would penetrate to the upstairs study where Doris sat grading English papers. "YOU'VE GOT TO HEAR THIS! IT WORKS! IT WORKS! FANTASTIC!" The loud voice demanded a large share of the collective attention. Photographs from one of the workshop evenings show how Sexton's personal style contrasted with that of the other poets: she sits on the floor, a glamour girl with long legs extended, wearing bright red lipstick, red sweater, and red high-heeled pumps, while nearby, sedate on chair and sofa, sit horn-rimmed George Starbuck in tweed and Maxine Kumin in navy. Holmes would have been allied with the navy blue side of the room.

One night George Starbuck invited a young poet named Joseph DeRoche, one of his colleagues at Houghton Mifflin, the publishers, to attend the workshop. The group met at Sexton's home that evening, and DeRoche noted in his journal that Kayo was a discreet host, pleasantly serving drinks before retiring upstairs, while Anne "held court for us on her living-room sofa, constantly adjusting an electric heating pad for her 'stomach-ache.' " The poets grew increasingly raucous after liberal supplies of bourbon and gin had been poured and

John Holmes.

they began discussing poems. DeRoche noted that he came out "battle-scarred — praised for a semblance of technique, but chided for too little substance."

Returning home on the subway, Starbuck surprised DeRoche by praising Sexton's work and belittling his own for possessing *only* technique. "Technique poems" were a specialty of the John Holmes workshop. As Starbuck recalled, "None of us in this group was the psychiatrist kind of workshop teacher, poem teacher; we didn't try to do the kind of thing Anne later learned to do as a teacher — insistently but noncoercively asking simple little questions about where does this come from, how did you dream this up, how old were you when this first happened to you. I was, and Max was, much more interested in tricks and wordplay. Anne would pick up on that. She'd notice one of us writing an acrostic, and she wrote maybe four acrostic poems addressed to other members of the group. I think one of them snuck into one of her books." (There are no acrostics in Sexton's published books, though the numerous worksheets of "For God While Sleeping" show her working out a double acrostic using Starbuck's name. In one draft the poem had thirty-one lines; the first letter and the last letter of each line, spelled down the page, read

S T A R B U C K S L U S T I S N A U G H T Y A N D S I C K H E
t u c k s h i s t r i c k i n a c a u s t i c a c r o s t i c

But few of these lines survived in the poem that finally emerged from this game.)

Naturally Sexton sought advice from her workshop colleagues about the manuscript she was revising for publication. Holmes wrote her a long commentary that began cautiously: "It's a book, all right, well put together." Next he suggested a change in the title, *To Bedlam and Part Way Back,* for marketing reasons: "I really think booksellers and publishers would be wary." Then he went on to express a view he had been holding silently since their earliest days of working together. "I distrust the very source and subject of a great many of your poems, namely, all those that describe and dwell on your time in the hospital. [. . .] It bothers me that you use poetry this way. It's all a release for you, but what is it for anyone else except a spectacle of someone experiencing release? [. . .] Don't publish it in a book. You'll certainly outgrow it, and become another person, then this record will haunt and hurt you. It will even haunt and hurt your children, years from now."

A manuscript of "For God While Sleeping," showing how Sexton worked out a double acrostic using Starbuck's name.

The result.

Astonished, Sexton hastily drafted a letter she did not send. The letter she did send enclosed a poem titled "For John, Who Begs Me Not to Enquire Further." She knew how to profit from the attention of another poet, but Holmes wasn't saying "Revise," he was saying "Don't publish." Her reply was a defense not only of her manuscript but of the whole genre of poetry that would soon be labeled "confessional."

> I tapped my own head;
> It was glass, an inverted bowl.
> [. . .]
> And if you turn away
> because there is no lesson here
> I will hold my awkward bowl,
> with all its cracked stars shining
> [. . .]
> This is something I would never find
> in a lovelier place, my dear,
> although your fear is anyone's fear,
> like an invisible veil between us all . . .
> and sometimes in private,
> my kitchen, your kitchen,
> my face, your face.

Shrewd as neurotic people often are about the anxieties of others, Sexton proposed in the poem that Holmes's rejection of her poetry was in part a psychological defense. His life had been, as his widow put it, "ragged with horrors." He had been a Jekyll-and-Hyde alcoholic, and his first wife had committed a gruesome suicide, slashing her wrists and bleeding to death over all his papers, which she assembled for that purpose on his desk. "John never got over it, and he feared the suicidal side of Anne," Maxine Kumin said. "He couldn't really blink away her talent — it was so evident — but he had as little to do with her as possible. And here she was desperately trying to make him into her Christian academic Daddy. Anne had such a thing about authority figures. He would have none of that!"

By the late 1950s, Holmes had stopped drinking and was happily remarried; his life was outwardly peaceful and secure. His advice to Sexton was possibly advice he had followed himself: "Don't publish it . . . you will certainly outgrow it and become another person." But Sexton based her work on a different understanding of breakdown. In her imagery, "tapping" the head produces "stars," signs radiant with significance, uniting sufferer and beholder despite the "glass bowl" of mutual difference that shuts them off from other forms of contact. "Anyone's fear" of the sick inhibits this identification; the courage in the poetry of *Bedlam* issues from Sexton's lucidity about how general suffering is, and how it must be experienced as personal but can be grasped and transferred in metaphor. Far from discouraging her, Holmes's reaction gave her insight into her poetry's distinctive characteristics. The title "For John, Who Begs Me Not to Enquire Further" alludes to a letter of Schopenhauer's to Goethe: "Most of us carry in our heart the Jocasta who begs Oedipus for God's sake not to inquire further." A longer quotation from this letter became the epigraph of *To Bedlam and Part Way Back,* and "For John . . ." began Part II, in which Sexton collected her most ambitious and self-revealing poems. Thus she addressed within the book itself the objections these themes were bound to excite.

By February 1959 Mary Gray was in the terminal stages of cancer, suffering terrible pain. This made Ralph Harvey, who was still recovering from his stroke, pathetically sad. "He acts about ten years old, and keeps crying and begging my mother not to die," Sexton told Snodgrass. She was making almost daily visits to the hospital where her mother lay "blown up like a balloon, as if she was having a baby." She explained to Snodgrass, "I feel as if, now, I were taking each one of her bones, separately, and carrying them to a soft basket." Of all the family members, she was most loyal in easing Mary Gray's last months of life; having been in the hospital herself, she understood the lift she could give her mother by making regular, breezy visits. Besides, she had a lot of news she needed desperately to deliver before it was too late. "I go in today and smile and laugh and tell her how Robert Lowell called me and how good he thinks the book is and I show her the book (as if that would help) and she smiles and seems proud, but meanwhile this is her life I'm taking over. How can she smile? Robert Lowell says I will have many of my poems in anthologies, that some are 'great' . . . and mother says, 'I don't know how you did it. I can't believe it.' . . . Mother doesn't think I wrote them still . . . No one does who knows me . . . but she says I'm her most fun visitor."

Sexton's facade cracked briefly in January, and she spent two days in Westwood Lodge (13–15 January); as she reported to Snodgrass, "If I don't watch out I'll be committed for 6 mos." Just as she had done in November, she used Westwood Lodge as a writing retreat, and during this hospitalization she produced a new poem, "Ringing the Bells."

Mary Gray had seen the manuscript of "The Double Image" before going into the hospital and said she liked it. Now that the poem was in galleys, ready for publication, Lowell asked Sexton to present it in class by reading it aloud, and "didn't pick it apart," she reported to Snodgrass. It was as if Sexton and her parents were trading places: Mary Gray and Ralph were diminishing, turning as needy and helpless as little children, metamorphosing into characters in poems, just as Anne was being reborn in print. "I know it's crazy," she wrote to Snodgrass, "but I feel like it is my fault."

Mary Gray Staples Harvey died on 10 March, a few days before her fifty-eighth birthday.

> I wanted to hold her hand, as one holds a child's hand, to take her across, to say "It's all right. I'm here. Don't be afraid." . . . And I did. And then she was gone. She was in the nothingness . . . Without me. Without *herself!* . . . Thus she made the transition from something-ness to nothingness . . . but what good was I? With all that love (longing) I couldn't stop the hours or the pain . . . I couldn't matter. No. Pain mattered more and it was, dear God, pain that rocked her out. Not me. For all my longing and my wanting, not me. And now she is a nothing. Except for me . . . for me she is a big something . . . a something I love and hate and still react and talk to.

Sexton blundered on with her work, moving the process of grieving over into the process of completing the manuscript of *Bedlam,* which she closed with an oddly chilly elegy to her mother, "The Division of Parts."

> I planned to suffer
> and I cannot.
> [. . .]
> Time, that rearranger
> of estates, equips
> me with your garments, but not with grief.
> [. . .]
> my Lady of my first words,
> this is the division of ways.

It was not until October, writing a story called "Dancing the Jig," that she began to undertake the process of reevaluating her daughterhood to this strong, elusive mother, a task that occupied the rest of her life.

That same winter, another regular auditor joined Lowell's writing seminar at Boston University: Sylvia Plath. Twenty-six years old when she moved to Boston with her husband, the British poet Ted Hughes, she was introduced around Boston and Cambridge as Hughes's wife "who also wrote"; at twenty-nine, Hughes had established himself with a prizewinning book, *The Hawk in the Rain*. Plath had just completed a year of teaching at Smith College; during this year she hoped to complete a novel and a book of poems, and the following year to have a baby. She measured her expectations by the achievements of Virginia Woolf. "I shall go better than she," Plath promised in her journal. *"No children until I have done it."* To fulfill this agenda, she imposed on herself a strict schedule of writing, reading, and studying German, but four months into her Boston life she began to feel miserably housebound. In October she took a job in the records office of the psychiatric clinic at Massachusetts General Hospital, and in mid-

Left to right: Herbert Hitchens, Ted Hughes, Sylvia Plath, and Stanley Kunitz, 1959.

December she went back into psychotherapy. In February 1959 she began attending Lowell's poetry class.

Plath hadn't paid much attention to Lowell's work before — her tastes had been formed as a very traditional English major at Smith and then as a Fulbright scholar at Cambridge University in England. Her journal for 5 May 1958 notes that she browsed in Lowell's poetry the evening before he gave a reading at Smith; his "tough, knotty" phrases "blazing with color and fury" stirred her to "excitement, joy, admiration, curiosity to meet and praise." In a fit of exuberance she put on red silk stockings to attend his reading. Going to his class in 1959, like working at the hospital, was a way to give the day "an objective structure" and to dissipate some of the horror of neurotic self-confrontation. Plath despised what she called her "laziness" — "not working for a Ph.D. or on a third book like A.C.R. [Adrienne Cecile Rich, another young Boston poet] or having four children and a profession."

Plath ridiculed herself for such ambitions, but she nonetheless studied the local competition, calculating her chances for success. Particularly she scrutinized the women, with an attitude she described as "the quiet righteous malice of one with better poems than other women's reputations have been made by." Like Lowell, Plath kept a list of great poets, and now and then, especially after a period of frenzied creative activity, she would privately reward herself by adjusting her own position on this list. "Arrogant, I think I have written lines which qualify me to be The Poetess of America (as Ted will be the Poet of England and her dominions). Who rivals? Well, in history Sappho, Elizabeth Barrett Browning, Christina Rossetti, Amy Lowell, Emily Dickinson, Edna St. Vincent Millay — all dead. Now: Edith Sitwell and Marianne Moore, the aging giantesses, and poetic godmother Phyllis McGinley is out — light verse: she's sold herself. Rather: May Swenson, Isabella Gardner, and most close, Adrienne Cecile Rich — who will soon be eclipsed by these eight poems."

Plath no doubt expected to gain some professional visibility by attending Lowell's class, for she knew his good word would help her career along. That winter and spring she was to write a dozen poems that she eventually published in her first book, *The Colossus* (1960). Only a few of them ("The Eye-mote," "Point Shirley," "Electra on Azalea Path") suggest the strengths of the justly famous poems she wrote in England between 1961 and her suicide in 1963. In 1959 it was not Plath's poetry but her literary intelligence that impressed her

classmates, or so they recall: her choice of Wallace Stevens as a "favorite poet," her ability to one-up everybody but Lowell in modish
observations about poetic mannerisms. (" 'Reminds me of Empson,'
she would say through clenched teeth. 'It reminds me of Herbert. Perhaps the early Marianne Moore?' ")

But Plath herself designated Lowell's seminar as a stimulus for
breakthrough in her poetry, partly because of the example of *Life
Studies* and partly because of the example of Anne Sexton. Lowell's
and Sexton's subject matter — "peculiar private and taboo subjects"
such as mental breakdown — influenced her most, she later told an
interviewer: "I think particularly of the poetess Anne Sexton, who
writes also of her experiences as a mother; as a mother who's had a
nervous breakdown, as an extremely emotional and feeling young
woman. And her poems are wonderfully craftsmanlike poems, and yet
they have a kind of emotional and psychological depth which I think
is something perhaps quite new and exciting."

Plath's warm admiration for Sexton developed only gradually that
winter. The class members were too preoccupied with Lowell's teaching to pay much attention to each other. When one of the students in
the class, Kathleen Spivack, later met Roger Rosenblatt, then director
of the National Endowment for the Humanities, they realized that
they had sat opposite each other for a year without introducing themselves, but "eight years later we could still remember each other's
poems and the devastating comments about them." "We orbited
around the class silently," Sexton recalled in a memoir, "letting our
own poems come up, as for a butcher, as for a lover. Both went on.
We kept as quiet as possible in view of the father." Predictably, Sexton
and Plath began to take notice of each other when "the father" began
comparing them, shortly after Sexton's presentation of "The Double
Image" in March. Lowell thought they "might rub off on each other,"
since "Anne was more herself and knew less," he recalled later. "Sylvia learned from Anne." For example, Sexton's poem "My Friend, My
Friend," which was almost certainly critiqued in class, appears to have
provided Plath with rhymes and a theme for one of her most famous
poems, "Daddy."

Lowell's undertaking provoked a meditation in Plath's journal. In
psychotherapy, Plath was trying to clarify her complex feelings for her
father, whose grave she had visited on 9 March, the day before Sexton's mother died and the week after Sexton read "The Double
Image." She was also actively trying to become pregnant. The journal

entry begins with a sad note about menstrual blood signaling another failure, then goes on to make despairing reflections about floundering for insights in therapy and poetry.

> I cry at everything. Simply to spite myself and embarrass myself. Finished two poems, a long one, "Electra on Azalea Path," and "Metaphors for a Pregnant Woman," ironic, nine lines, nine syllables in each. They are never perfect, but I think I have goodnesses. Criticism of 4 of my poems in Lowell's class: criticism of rhetoric. He sets me up with Anne Sexton, an honor, I suppose. Well, about time. She has very good things, and they get better, though there is a lot of loose stuff.
>
> A desire to get my hair cut attractively instead of this mousy ponytail. Will no doubt go out and get a pageboy cut as of old. Is it money keeps me back? Must get fixed up.

"I regress terribly," she comments. "I may have all the answers to my questions in myself, but I need some catalyst to get them into my consciousness."

Yet what couldn't be hauled into consciousness was working productively in the unconscious: "Electra on Azalea Path" displaced the father-quest into a successful narrative, while a primitive sort of magic thinking produced the fertility riddle "Metaphors for a Pregnant Woman." The unconscious, too, glistens in Plath's satisfaction with being compared to Sexton. The associations flow along a buried axis, an identification with Sexton as a poet who struggled directly with issues that evaded Plath in therapy: Sexton as the daughter of a domineering mother; Sexton as a mother; Sexton as a poet Lowell admired; Sexton as a woman who was always "fixed up," with a well-kept hairdo.

In early April, the friendship blossomed. Sexton normally stayed in Boston for several hours after Lowell's class ended, because she had an appointment with her psychiatrist at seven. She and Plath began going out for drinks after class. Sometimes they were accompanied by George Starbuck, who now and then took off from work as a junior editor at Houghton Mifflin to drop in on the seminar. Starbuck wrote witty, jubilantly complicated poems; his boyish exuberance made him something of an anomaly among Lowell's sober attendants, who were involved in "rating and dating." Sexton and Plath enjoyed his sly good humor. "We would pile into the front seat of my old Ford," Sexton recalled, and I would drive quickly through the traffic to, or near, the Ritz. I would park illegally in a LOADING ONLY ZONE telling them gaily, "It's okay, because we are only going to get loaded!" Off we'd go, each on George's arm, into the Ritz and drink three or four or two martinis. George even has a line about this in his first book of poems, *Bone Thoughts.* He wrote, "*I weave with two sweet ladies out of the Ritz.*" [. . .]

Often, very often, Sylvia and I would talk at length about our first suicides; at length, in detail, and in depth between the free potato chips. Suicide is, after all, the opposite of the poem. Sylvia and I often talked opposites. We talked death with burned-up intensity, both of us drawn to it like moths to an electric light bulb. Sucking on it!

"I guess that's as close as I'll ever come to feeling like what they used to call a *cavalier servente,*" George Starbuck recalled, "giving these two talkative ladies an escort while they had their drinks at the Ritz. *Not* martinis: Anne drank stingers at the time — awful stuff — I don't remember what Sylvia drank. They had these hilarious conversations comparing their suicides and talking about their psychiatrists. It was just a few times that I was privileged to eavesdrop on them." He remembered Plath's reserve. "She'd picked up the mannerisms of the ordinary Seven Sisters young lady." Anne, in contrast, was "flamboyant about her reminiscences of mental hospitals and suicides and things like that. Not exaggerating — in fact, she had an American-style comic sense of it: self-deprecating, humor at her own expense. Sylvia was more matter-of-fact. As a result it didn't quite cross my mind that Sylvia's episodes had been as severe as they came out in her writing. She was playful, but not flamboyant. Her journals indicate that she was wary of me, which is odd. Everybody at that age thinks the other people are the lions."

Starbuck was in fact a kind of lion: an editor and scout for poetry manuscripts. Plath knew that he had lobbied at Houghton Mifflin to publish Sexton's book. But she was also in on the secret that Sexton and Starbuck were becoming lovers, a bit of inside knowledge that triggered a good deal of commentary in her journals for several weeks. Perhaps she too had flirted with Starbuck; it went with the territory — "poets were always in love."

Sexton's life every Tuesday proposed to the wickedly parodic Plath the plot of one or two ladies' magazine stories: seminar with famous poet, martinis at the Ritz, love in the afternoon, and an appointment with her psychiatrist in the evening. Plath applied some self-conscious prose to the situation. "I should be turning in [a volume of poems] to Houghton Mifflin this week. But A.S. is there ahead of me, with her lover G.S. writing *New Yorker* odes to her and both of them together: felt our triple-martini afternoons at the Ritz breaking up. That memorable afternoon at G.'s monastic and miserly room on Pinckney: 'You shouldn't have left us': where is responsibility to lie? I left, yet felt like a brown-winged moth around a rather meagre candle flame, drawn. That is over. As Snodgrass would say." She thought gleefully of writing the affair into "a double story, 'August Lighthill and the Other Woman.' . . . Here is horror. And all the details. Get life in spurts in stories, then the novel will come." She sketched the plot in her journal: "An insufferable woman (myself of course)" maliciously tells a man's wife that her husband is having an affair with "Anne," then learns that he *is* having an affair with her. "It becomes nasty busibodiness. THE OLYMPIANS. Poor, married poets in Ritz bar."

Houghton Mifflin accepted Sexton's manuscript of *To Bedlam and Part Way Back* on 19 May, the same month in which Lowell's *Life Studies* was published in the United States (it had been published in England a month earlier). Lowell's book received the National Book Award that year, and in his acceptance speech he offered an explanation of his artistic goals that was later used to account for Anne Sexton's style too. Borrowing a metaphor from the structuralist anthropologist Claude Lévi-Strauss, Lowell distinguished between two "competing" kinds of poetry, "cooked" and "raw." "The cooked, marvelously expert and remote," he said, "seems constructed as a sort of mechanical or catnip mouse for graduate seminars; the raw, jerry-built and forensically deadly, seems often like an unscored libretto by some bearded but vegetarian Castro." "Cooked" was Lowell's way of referring to the poetry of high seriousness and elaborate formal effects that he had abandoned in writing *Life Studies*; at the opposite extreme stood poems like Allen Ginsberg's "Howl" (thus the simile of the libretto by a bearded vegetarian — Lowell had been quite impressed by Ginsberg at a poetry reading in San Francisco). Poetry had taken a turn to the left, and Lowell was throwing in his lot with the new movement — in an aloof, intellectual sort of way.

On the day *Life Studies* was published, however, he was at McLean Hospital in Belmont, Massachusetts, which he had entered in late

April. Lowell was manic-depressive, and his life was punctuated by breakdowns, which were often followed by rich periods of creativity. During his convalescence from a breakdown in 1956, he had rapidly produced much of *Life Studies*; following another severe breakdown in early 1958, he had finished it. With the privilege of hindsight, Lowell's biographer Ian Hamilton has speculated that Lowell treasured the "infancy of madness" he surrendered in periods of stability. "The diagnosed manic-depressive will surely always have a buried yearning for the 'tropical' terrain of his affliction," Hamilton remarked, "and the pursuit of 'health' will in some measure always be more contractual than voluntary."

In what ways was Lowell's mania affiliated with his genius? And to what degree were his manic episodes voluntary? Such questions are bound to emerge in discussions of this era of American culture, when so many celebrated artists were or seemed to be psychologically unstable. Among Lowell's contemporaries, many had spent days or weeks on alcoholic binges, weeks or months in mental institutions, years under psychiatric care. To mention only the poets, these included Randall Jarrell and Theodore Roethke, who like Lowell had manic-depressive illnesses; Delmore Schwartz, exiled from friends and profession alike by paranoia; Elizabeth Bishop, hospitalized a number of times for alcoholism; and John Berryman, whose disorders compounded all of the above.

No one who witnessed an episode of actual breakdown was likely to confuse the poet's sometimes freakish or infantile imaginative freedom with the person's pathetic, often frightening insanity. Yet hypomania during the throes of creation could resemble the behavioral disorganization that marked the onset of illness. Lowell himself remarked on the similarities in a letter to Roethke: "There's a strange fact about the poets of roughly our age, and one that doesn't exactly seem to have always been true. It's this, that to write we seem to have to go at it with such single-minded intensity that we are always on the point of drowning. . . . I feel it's something almost unavoidable, some flaw in the motor."

Lowell's instability made him a somewhat unreliable friend or mentor, but since nerviness and a rather childish self-regard gave riveting immediacy to his teaching, younger poets and students developed a high tolerance for the insecurity his vulnerability inspired. From Sexton, the spectacle of Lowell's breakdown that April elicited both compassion and voyeuristic fascination. Early that month she reported to

Snodgrass that he was squiring a new girl — "(shhh secret)" — recognized by gossips as a symptom of the onset of another episode of his illness. On 1 May she wrote, "Lowell has shifted to a manic phase and it seems so disturbing. He is at MacLean's but only for a short while I hear. But such a change in his manner. A little frightening this way. But I guess he isn't [as] bad as other times." She enclosed, for Snodgrass's eyes only, a poem (which she later added to the manuscript of *Bedlam*):

> In the thin classroom, where your face
> was noble, and your words were all things,
> I find this boily creature in your place;
>
> find you disarranged, squatting on the window sill,
> irrefutably placed up there,
> like a hunk of some big frog
> watching us through the V
> of your woolen legs.
>
> Even so, I must admire your skill.
> You are so gracefully insane.
> We fidget in our plain chairs
> and pretend to catalogue
> our facts for your burly sorcery
>
> or ignore your fat blind eyes
> or the prince you ate yesterday
> who was wise, wise, wise.

Lowell almost certainly would have suggested revision of the slack diction ("all things," "some big," the repeated "place"), if he had been invited to comment. This was not Sexton's best poem, but it helped establish her turf in the poetry world. Lowell, reigning monarch of the kingdom of mad poets, had inadvertently supplied her with an opportunity to cast him in a cameo role: Great Poet as Frog Prince.

Lowell was back at home in Boston by the middle of June, and he and Elizabeth Hardwick, his wife, gave a party. Adrienne Rich and her husband, Alfred Conrad, were among the guests, and as Rich remembered, the party revolved around Anne Sexton's celebrity. "I remember feeling that suddenly there was this *woman* whom Lowell and people around Cambridge were talking about, this woman who was going to publish a book called *To Bedlam and Part Way Back*. I would never have acknowledged it at the time, but I felt threatened, very competitive with her. There was little support for the idea that another woman poet could be a source of strength or mutual engagement. I think I suspected — and not because of some profound character defect in me — that if she was going to take up space, then I was not going to have that space." Meeting Sexton in person gave Rich a shock. "I didn't expect her to be such a knock-out — tall, tan, wearing white, and looking very gorgeous. And I gathered that she didn't think of herself as an educated person, didn't think of herself as an intellectual. It was as if she was thrown into a room full of Harvard types and literary critics and so on: all these super-achieving people."

Rich's mood was inflected by the feeling that she herself had arrived at an impasse as an artist. "I wanted to be a great poet. I had some idea of what that was," she said with a laugh. "I felt I hadn't served a long enough apprenticeship. I also had the very romantic notion, I suppose from Keats, that you could live and write obscurely all your life and then be dead, leaving all these great poems. Maybe that was going to happen to me. I think that in some way I dealt with the fear, and the problems of competing in a literary world, by that notion that someone would come along and recognize me someday. I think that was tied up with my problems with being a woman, too. Competing in the literary establishment felt to me defeminizing."

This impasse was strengthened by Rich's other vocation: marriage and motherhood. It was ironic, she later commented, that the only detail she could remember about conversations with Sylvia Plath that spring was Plath's curiosity about combining motherhood and writing. "I answered something very sage, like 'It can be done, but you'd better think about it really hard.' What I wanted to tell her was 'Don't try,' because I was in such despondency: I'd just had my third child, I was thirty, and I felt that in many ways my life was over, that I would never write again. I couldn't foresee a future different from the past two years of raising children and being almost continuously angry."

Like Lowell, Rich and Plath and Sexton had all been reared under exacting notions of propriety. The mourning over discredited masculinity that resonates in *Life Studies* had its counterpart in the guilty rage toward mothers that was sounding in the women's poetry — for instance, in Plath's "The Disquieting Muses," Rich's "Snapshots of a Daughter-in-Law," and Sexton's "The Double Image." (Maxine Kumin's mother-daughter poetry of this period was more guarded but full of omens.) This generation of privileged female poets was beginning to produce imagery expressing their reluctance to relinquish social entitlement. Layered into their poetry was a protest against the equation of womanhood with motherhood. Few mothers made it onto the list of role models Plath was keeping, for example; why did the choice of motherhood, if or when it was a choice, disallow writing works of genius?

There were — are — no simple answers to this question, but in the 1960s it became territory which the distinguished work of all these women was to open for poetry. Because Lowell had made unidealized domesticity a theme in *Life Studies,* a critical language evolved to assess its seemliness as subject matter for serious art, and this too played a role in making the subject available for women poets. When the critic M. L. Rosenthal expanded his review of Lowell into the thesis of a book on what he dubbed confessional poetry, including evaluations of Plath and Sexton, he endowed this cohort with a movement of their own. Lowell had broken a taboo in *Life Studies.* The two world wars of the century had definitively reduced the scale in which human heroism could be invoked credibly in art, but psychoanalysis, which focused on the childhood origins of adult behavior, could evoke memories of a time when adults loomed very large. The psychoanalytic point of view, paradoxically, legitimized the return, in art, of exorbitant passions and a sense of destiny, understood as an economy of sublimation.

The label "confessional" stuck to this kind of art, but in retrospect it seems to have emphasized the wrong thing, treating the poems as rising from shame, not self-knowledge. The lyric was a wholly appropriate vehicle for exploring Freudian insights into the ways in which family life gave permanent, empowering, and also deforming structure to individual experience. The poetry of Lowell, Plath, Sexton, and Rich inverted the categories "public" and "private." Moreover, these poets mined the discovery that roles established in family life were shaped by what we now call gender ideologies. They "confessed" to feeling overwhelmed by the energy of capacities denied by sexual differentiation and pressures to conform.

In 1963, Adrienne Rich left Boston for New York with her husband, involved herself ever more deeply in political issues, and developed a feminist poetics through which to double back into the torment of feminine sexual and social identity. The beauty and the pathbreaking courage of her work continues to elicit wide if sometimes appalled acknowledgment of its importance.

Plath left Boston with Ted Hughes to live in England, where — under the pressure of caring for two infants and "being almost continuously angry" — she at last fulfilled the aspirations recorded in her Boston journal: to write a poetry of "real situations, behind which the great gods play the drama of blood, lust and death." The work trickled into print after her death, one slim volume at a time over a period of years. It was probably the finality of her brilliant production that won for her the longed-for status her journal forecast, to become "Poetess of America." Plath's *Collected Poems* won the Pulitzer Prize in 1982, recognition conferred as much on the tragic female career as on the indisputable greatness of the work. And in an ironic reversal of position, Plath's *Ariel* set the standard by which Anne Sexton's work came to be measured — by Robert Lowell, among others.

Sexton stayed in the Boston suburbs, where she and Maxine Kumin provided each other with unflagging support as they built what Kumin called their "cottage industry" into successful careers. Of the four, Sexton was the first to tap the constraints women felt in conforming to prevailing feminine stereotypes, perhaps because she was developing her art under the psychological influence of a mother identified not with self-sacrifice but with writing. The last poem Sexton wrote for the manuscript of *Bedlam,* "Her Kind," shows her trying to do just that.

Bedlam was due at the printers on 1 August. At the eleventh hour Sexton was still frantically shuffling poems in and out and worrying about Lowell's advice to supply fifteen or so new ones. In arriving at the final manuscript, she shrewdly discarded work that she had been proud to send out for serial publication just a few months earlier. She also made a policy decision: "not a love lyric in the lot," she wrote to Snodgrass cheerfully. She divided the book into two parts, roughly of early and recent work. That first section worried her, because it lacked a keynote, a dominant image, a theme. Riffling through what she called her "bone pile" of discarded efforts, she picked up a piece of sentimental verse that had started life in December 1957 as "Night Voice on a Broomstick" and that she had sent to literary journals without success. In July 1959 she retitled it "Witch" and reworked it into a sixteen-line quasi-sonnet form. Then she broke those lines up into very short pieces with irregular but striking rhymes; in that thirty-eight-line version, "Witch" ended

> Who see me here
> this ragged apparition
> in their own air
> see a wicked appetite,
> if they dare.

This is the sort of poem Sexton had been writing for workshops throughout her apprenticeship. Like "The Farmer's Wife," "Unknown Girl in the Maternity Ward," "For Johnny Pole on the Forgotten Beach," and "The Moss of His Skin," "Witch" is spoken through a mask by a dramatic persona and offers a psychological portrait of a social type. Sexton polished the poem through several revisions, but something about the short lines bothered her. She lengthened them again, this time trying another structuring principle, punctuating the stanza breaks with a refrain: "I have been her kind." The poem now began this way:

> I have gone out, a possessed witch,
> haunting the black air, braver at night;
> dreaming evil, I have done my hitch
> over the plain houses, light by light:
> lonely thing, twelve-fingered, out of mind.
> A woman like that is not a woman, quite.
> I have been her kind.

Through the use of an undifferentiated but double "I," the poem sets up a single persona identified with madness but separated from it through insight. Two points of view are designated "I" in each stanza. The witch (stanza one), the housewife (stanza two), and the adulteress (stanza three) are those who act, or act out; in the refrain, an "I" steps through the frame of "like that" to witness, interpret, and affirm her alter ego in the same line. The double subjectivity of "Her Kind," as Sexton now called the poem, cleverly finds a way to represent a condition symbolized not in words but in symptoms that yearn to be comprehended. "Her Kind" contains its own perfect reader, its own namesake, "I."

Sexton liked this version. The poem had been through nineteen pages of drafting; as she noted on the final manuscript, "took one week to complete." From that time on, "Her Kind" served as the poem with which she began her readings, telling the audience that it would show them what kind of woman she was, and what kind of poet. It was a most dramatic gesture, and one that Maxine Kumin disliked (she thought Sexton's readings were hammy), but it was the way Sexton stepped from person to persona. The subjectivity in the poem insists on a separation between a kind of woman (mad) and a kind of poet (a woman with magic craft): a doubleness that expressed the paradox of Sexton's creativity. "Her Kind" is not spoken through a mask, nor is it a first-person narrative like "The Double Image." It calls attention to the difference between pain and the representation of pain, between the poet onstage in print — flippant, glamorous, crafty — and the woman whose anguish she knew firsthand. "Her Kind" was Sexton's debut as witch; it made the ideal keynote poem for *To Bedlam and Part Way Back.*

7

DEATHS, DISPLACEMENTS,
AND SUBSTITUTIONS
1959–1960

UNUSED TO SOLITUDE and lonely for Mary Gray, Ralph Harvey now turned for companionship to the other women in his family. During the spring of 1959, still under treatment for high blood pressure and unable to work, he took to dropping in on Anne and Kayo, sometimes spending whole mornings chatting in the kitchen over a cup of coffee. Sexton recalled in interviews later this brief period of contact, more precious because she measured it against a former relationship she described as "almost nil." She was astounded when he confided to her that he had grown suicidally melancholy and that he now understood how she had felt when she tried to kill herself. He also confided about his sexuality, which alarmed and distressed her. "His personality changed after the stroke," she told Dr. Orne. "Just like any old mentally ill person I ever saw, he kept saying the same things over and over."

Ralph paid several visits to his sister, Frances, in New Hampshire that spring as well, and added a codicil to his will increasing his bequest to her tenfold. Then he began courting a neighborly widow. Barely a month after Mary Gray's death, he announced his intention to remarry. This news brought Anne and Jane into a rare sibling alliance. Jane was outraged, and Anne was afraid the Harvey estate would slip into the widow's hands, and together the cunning sisters managed to subvert the wedding plans. Sexton paid for this success with an abundance of guilty feelings that mingled with her still-fresh grief for her mother, and the burden derailed her late in the month of May. She spent three days at Westwood Lodge, returning home with Kayo on the evening of 2 June. The next morning, Ralph Harvey died suddenly of another stroke. Anne and Blanche stayed in the background during the next few days as Jane, who lived in nearby Wellesley, carried out their father's explicit instructions regarding the funeral. Family members recall that when the time came to conduct his body to the crematorium, Jane stepped forward to claim the privilege fiercely: "You can't come, I'm going to do this myself. He was *my* father!" Anne and Blanche seemed too surprised and sad to protest.

The course of settling the estate produced further unpleasant surprises. As the only son-in-law still working for the R. C. Harvey Company, Kayo expected to inherit Ralph Harvey's shares and to succeed his father-in-law as president. But the will revealed that in order to support his lavish way of life, Anne's father had sold all his shares for cash to a silent partner, who now intended to put his own son into management. If Kayo stayed with the company, he was going to stay on as vice president and salesman, continually traveling. Astounded by the bad news, Anne threw her father's picture to the floor and ground her heel in his face.

In addition, she had the sorrow of helping to dismantle the family home in Annisquam. It was not her childhood home, but it was the site of her first struggles to recover from suicidal depression, the house where her portrait hung "in north light" across from the portrait of Mary Gray. Anne, Blanche, and Jane drove to Annisquam, where the executor of their father's estate gave them colored labels to stick on the possessions they wished to claim. Anne took her mother's writing desk and a large collection of books. After they finished this task, she entered the hospital again for two days, fighting suicidal impulses: it was the fifth anniversary of Nana's death, Dr. Orne was out of town, and she badly needed support. As she wrote to Snodgrass, "The trouble with everyone just up and dying like that is that there are no faces left to throw your emotions at: love or hate. What do you do with the emotion? It's still there, though *they* are gone." One thing she did was to have one of Ralph Harvey's rash, extravagant gifts to Mary Gray, a platinum band set with a large ruby and a large diamond, sized to her hand, and from then on she never removed it. And in July she wrote for her father the elegy "All My Pretty Ones," the first of many poems to the dead.

Sexton took her consolation from the second family she had constituted about her: the poets, especially Maxine Kumin and George Starbuck. She and Kumin fell into the habit, about this time, of phoning each other every morning as they changed gears, turning to poetry. Sexton also hung out that summer with Starbuck and with Arthur Freeman, the Harvard student she had met the previous year, in Freeman's rooms at Adams House or at the Grolier Book Shop, which specialized in poetry (the owner, Gordon Cairnie, held court on a decrepit sofa, surrounded by portraits of famous friends). Freeman, young and avid for recognition, recalled that among the poets visible around Harvard Square in those days, "the big ones" were I. A. Richards, Adrienne Rich, and her sister, Cynthia; "on the way up" were John Hollander, Stephen Orgel, Donald Hall, Allen Grossman, and George Starbuck. He remembered Sexton as very attached to Starbuck: "She couldn't cross the street without getting George's advice." Kumin, Holmes, Sexton, and Starbuck continued to hold a workshop every other week, and Starbuck and Sexton stayed in love. Sometime before his book *Bone Thoughts* went to press, he wrote for her its tender dedication:

> To the one with her head out the window, drinking the rain.
> To the one who said me a lullaby over the phone.
> To the one who, divining love in this rocky terrain,
>   has made it her own.

Once, maybe that summer, Sexton put on a red dress and made a picnic they carried to the banks of the Charles; ever after, she always had a red dress and always invested it with romantic wishes. Together Sexton and Starbuck went to the Bread Loaf Writers' Conference (Sexton had been awarded the Robert Frost Fellowship), and later that year they traveled to New York for a reading. Among poets they were not particularly discreet about their liaison. Starbuck was separated from his wife, Kayo was often away, and Billie uncomplainingly took the children, with no questions asked. Sexton's feeling that summer of having a second home with a brotherly lover-husband as its hidden center is memorialized in her poem "Doors, Doors, Doors":

> Climbing the dark halls, I ignore their papers and pails,
> the twelve coats of rubbish of someone else's dim life.
> Tell them need is an excuse for love. Tell them need prevails.
> Tell them I remake and smooth your bed and am your wife.

Gradually the erotic intensity between them diminished to an enduring warmth, but Starbuck remained one of Sexton's most comprehending friends.

Sexton rode the wave of her success on into the fall. In August, *Audience,* the Boston literary journal edited by Firman Houghton, awarded her its annual prize for poems published earlier that year, and accepted five more for its autumn issue. Robert Lowell delighted her by graciously supplying a cover blurb for *Bedlam*. "Mrs. Sexton writes with the now enviable swift lyrical openness of a Romantic Poet," he said. "Yet in her content she is a realist and describes her very personal experience with an almost Russian accuracy and abundance. Her poems stick in my mind. I don't see how they can fail to make the great stir they deserve to make." And in December — almost exactly three years from the day she had tuned her television to I. A. Richards's lecture on poetry — she was invited to give a reading at Harvard, in the series named for the benefactor Morris Gray. This was distinguished recognition; Ted Hughes had given a Morris Gray reading the previous year. Among the members of Sexton's audience that afternoon was probably Professor Richards himself, who made a point of attending poetry readings and who by then had probably heard from Sexton about how his televised lecture on the sonnet had launched her career.

By the end of 1959, Sexton's audience was already growing beyond the circumference of the New England poetry circuit. That fall, one of her readings was recorded for possible release in the Yale Series of Recorded Poets. Carolyn Kizer accepted four poems for *Poetry Northwest* — "Ghost of a Memo," "Funnel," "Said the Poet to the Analyst," and "The Kite" — and in October Sexton read with George Starbuck and Joseph Bennett at the Poetry Center at the 92nd Street YMHA in New York. Despite her severe anxieties about "axing" herself with literary folk, she was never shy around them, and usually left an impression of radiant high spirits. At the party after the Y reading, Sexton charmed the fiction writer Herbert Gold by telling him that his recent story "Love or Like" should be sold in a boxed set with Snodgrass's *Heart's Needle* to people who were getting divorced — or getting married.

Still, with a book in press and no real agenda for study, Sexton felt at loose ends. Occasionally she attended Lowell's seminar, but she agreed with him that there was little to gain in a rerun. As often in her career, new subject matter came to her in the wake of an illness. In September she developed pneumonia, and during treatment her doctor discovered a suspicious mass in her pelvic area, which prompted exploratory surgery. A nonmalignant ovarian cyst was removed, as was her appendix. Sexton recovered rapidly from surgery, in time to keep her precious reading date in New York on 30 October, but the threat of cancer stimulated memories of her mother's illness and, more deeply, conviction that both she and her mother nurtured an "embryo of evil" in their female parts. She had written about this weird doubling a year earlier in the doom-saying "Double Image." Fate seemed to be pressing her again into her mother's death script. But this time Sexton approached the material through her "American-style comic sense." Two new works emerged in October, during her convalescence: a story titled "Dancing the Jig," and "The Operation," a long poem.

In "The Operation," Sexton displaced her identification with her mother into extraordinary imagery, pairing surgical technologies and primitive terror: "I soar in hostile air [. . .] / I plunge down the backstair / calling *mother* at the dying door, / to rush back to my own skin, tied where it was torn." Rhymes and the indignities of hospital routines provide comic inflections, subduing but intensifying the poem's pathos.

"Dancing the Jig" is a brief, eerie narrative situated in the mind of a woman at a party, who hopes to be mistaken for drunk while she tries to control a powerful impulse to leap up and dance like a puppet. She traces her state of mind back to the family dinner table. The core of the memory is fusion with the rhythms of her mother's mouth — chewing, talking, smoking. In memory, Mother keeps up a steady stream of criticism while the daughter tries to chew, talk, and hold her own. The daughter cannot unconfuse their mouths; when she tries to break from this dyad, her mother brings her back with the snap of a sharp fingernail. Here the comedy arises from the juxtaposition of suburban party-going with the surreal permanence of the fantasy that grips the daughter's body.

"Dancing the Jig" immediately found a publisher, and its appearance in *New World Writing* produced an invitation from Sterling Lord, a literary agent in New York, for Sexton to become one of the stable of writers for whom he served as professional go-between. She hoped the agent would help place her fiction in women's magazines; she was also trying to break into the market for children's picture books. This contract marked a new stage in the development of Sexton's career, for poets did not usually publish at an economic level and rate that made them attractive to literary agents.

The following spring, death prodded again at Sexton's emotional security. In March her father-in-law, George Sexton, was killed in an auto accident while vacationing in Florida with Billie. The death toll was now three parents in twelve months. She wrote to Snodgrass, "Kayo's father was more fatherly toward me than my own father ever was. He has, in fact, paid one half of all my psychiatric bills for these past 4 yrs and one time that I tried to kill myself he was the one who stayed at the hospital. They won't let you stay alone if you've tried to kill yourself and they refuse to let any nurse be responsible for you. It has to be a member of your family. Kayo was away and my mother and father said they wouldn't come ... Well, it doesn't matter now ... Just to explain why I mind so much about his being killed."

Then, just a few weeks after George Sexton's burial, Anne discovered she was pregnant. Fearing that Kayo was not the father, she persuaded him that she was not healthy enough to have another baby, though this was not easy: Kayo wanted another child, and losing his father must have intensified that longing. Nonetheless, in early May Billie accompanied her on her visit to a doctor who would perform an illegal abortion.

These new losses precipitated new bouts of despondency, which Sexton battled not by drawing closer to her grieving family but by

Billie and George Sexton.

writing furiously: "Old Dwarf Heart" in March, following George Sexton's death; "Ghosts" in April; "The Starry Night" in May; "The Abortion" and several poems with religious themes — "With Mercy for the Greedy," "For God While Sleeping," "In the Deep Museum" — in early June. Probably around the same time she drafted a short play titled *Ladybug, Fly Away Home,* in which the protagonist is a college girl whose psychiatrist persuades her to seek an abortion. She began keeping a journal as well. "I have, indeed, spent my life turning from myself," it began bravely. "Dostoevsky says 'what filthy things the heart is capable of.' I start this journal full of my own sense of filth. Why else keep a journal, if not to examine your own filth?"

Sexton thought that psychotherapy wasn't helping her much during that bleak winter and spring. "The life of poetry is saving me (I hope) as some things are as bad as I've ever known," she told Snodgrass. "I am sometimes totally lost from the world. Maybe I am crazy and will never get really well. God knows I've been working at it long enough." She began testing anew the possibility that her problems might be better understood in spiritual than in psychiatric terms. Letters from her friend Ruth Soter, who had moved to Japan with her husband and, surprisingly, become a Catholic, intensified Sexton's religious self-questioning. She wrote to Snodgrass about her envy of Soter's conversion. "I certainly don't believe in God," she mused, ". . and that's rather sad of me." "I wish religion would work with me," she added in another letter. "As far as I can see life is just packed with dead people and God knows I keep bumping into them every which way I try to turn."

It was to Soter, never to Snodgrass, that Sexton confided she had had an abortion. Distressed and moved, Soter wrote immediately that she hoped Sexton would seek forgiveness through the sacraments of the Catholic church, and she enclosed in the letter a tooth-marked wooden cross. Sexton's reply was a cleverly structured poem, "With Mercy for the Greedy," in which she expressed the ambivalent outlook on Christianity that remained consistent throughout her lifetime.

The poem is prefaced by an epigraph: "For my friend, Ruth, who urges me to make an appointment for the Sacrament of Confession." In the five stanzas that follow, Sexton sets up two parallel kinds of "mercy": the one available to Ruth through religious practices, and the one she herself achieves through writing poetry. Both derive their power from confession. Ruth's practice has been codified: her rebirth, through the sacrament of baptism, assures that she can gain absolution from sin through the sacrament of confession, and reunite herself with Spirit through the sacrament of communion. This kind of mercy is not — or is not yet — available to Sexton: "I detest my sins and I try to believe / in The Cross. [. . .] But I can't. Need is not quite belief." Nonetheless, she has hung Ruth's cross around her neck: "All morning long / I have worn / your cross, hung with package string around my throat. / It tapped me lightly as a child's heart might, / tapping secondhand, softly waiting to be born."

In what sense is Sexton's practice analogous to Soter's? The last stanza answers, with a riddle:

> My friend, my friend, I was born
> doing reference work in sin, and born
> confessing it. This is what poems are:
> with mercy
> for the greedy,
> they are the tongue's wrangle,
> the world's pottage, the rat's star.

The poem veers from statement to metaphor, requiring quite a different method of reading to get at the meanings "tapping secondhand" in this lineup of analogues ("tongue's wrangle," "world's pottage," "rat's star"). It requires, in fact, the kind of reading that poetry requires: alertness to a multiplicity of connections latent in the signs on the page. Like Soter's cross, Sexton's metaphors are vehicles of Spirit.

To illustrate: this last stanza contains echoes of two early "failed" poems that Soter must have critiqued in the workshops she and Sexton had attended together. "With Mercy for the Greedy" resurrects them in ways that Soter would hear. The vocative "My friend, my friend" is the title of the villanelle Sexton addressed to Maxine Kumin in 1958, expressing envy that she was not "born a Jew." George Starbuck recalled Sexton's fascination with Kumin's Jewishness: "I think Maxine felt at times she was some kind of ethnic village or historic exhibit for Anne, the religion student wanting to know 'What's this Jewishness all about? Who's this Yahweh?' " But Sexton could not *become* a Jew; the point of the villanelle is that Jews are born, not made.

Jews are born, but Christians are born again. In the key term "born," used twice in a rhyme position, Sexton encodes a reference to her abortion — one of the unspecified sins for which she seeks redemption — but also calls attention to the repetition itself as a poetic device for multiplying meanings.

A cue to an important meaning latent in the closure of "Mercy for the Greedy" is its allusion to Sexton's favorite palindrome, "rats live on no evil star." In 1958, possibly during her week at Antioch with Soter, Sexton had produced an awkward little exercise titled "An Obsessive Combination of Ontological Inscape, Trickery and Love," in which she tried for the first time to explain the significance, to her, of this bit of wordplay.

> Busy, with an idea for a code, I write
> signals hurrying from left to right,
> or right to left, by obscure routes,
> for my own reasons; taking a word like "writes"
> down tiers of tries until its secret rites
> make sense; or until, suddenly, RATS
> can amazingly and funnily become STAR
> and right to left that small star
> is mine, for my own liking, to stare
> its five lucky pins inside out, to store
> forever kindly, as if it were a star
> I touched and a miracle I really wrote.

"Rat" was one of Sexton's metaphors for her sick self; in another religious poem she wrote in June 1960, she made rats the agents of Christ's death ("In the Deep Museum"). But back in 1958 she had made the reversal rats / star her example for Dr. Orne of how words used *her* as a vehicle for putting meanings into the world ("Of course I KNOW that words are just a counting game, I know this until the words start to arrange themselves and write something better than *I* would ever know"). This "miracle" inevitably occurred with the use of rhyme, Sexton found; words chosen for one kind of likeness (sound) displayed other kinds once set in place, expressing meanings more abundant than the poet intended. Her poems gave evidence of her psychological health: "I am pretending when I find it, but then I am real when I find it possible. [. . .] I did it so I must be real."

"With Mercy for the Greedy" broadens this insight. The contexts in which meanings occur are communal, not merely personal, it asserts: signs are the world's pottage. In exchange for your cross, I offer my rat's star, my code for the secular redemption I undergo when moved by love or need to the making of poems. The exchange in "Mercy" is at once dyadic, between two friends who have developed a private understanding, and universal — a capacity inherent in language itself.

To Bedlam and Part Way Back was published by Houghton Mifflin on 22 April 1960. For a first book of poems it received rather wide attention; as the *New York Times* critic observed, its theme had "a natural, built-in interest: a mental breakdown, pictured with a pitiless eye and clairvoyant sharpness."

Partly because of Lowell's blurb on the jacket, *Life Studies* was the point of reference by which Sexton's local peers evaluated *Bedlam*. Over at Brandeis University, the distinguished professor of literature Irving Howe passed Sexton's book on to a junior colleague, the poet Allen Grossman, who remembered noticing that the jacket showed a woman in great pain. "Irving Howe said to me about the book, 'Well, there's the real thing.' That's how a lot of people felt, as I remember — people who didn't normally pay attention to poetry, like Irving Howe." Grossman wrote a review of *Bedlam* for the Brandeis newspaper, which he then sent to Sexton. The poems "seem to me incredibly distinguished and compassionate," he told her. "They reach me, and hold me, and give me pleasure." Ironically, this glowing review brought even John Holmes around, or so Sexton reported to Dr. Orne. "John Holmes saw it (don't know where he got it as I didn't show it to him) and he told Maxine that it had changed his mind about my 'bedlam' poetry and that Grossman was right and he (John Holmes) had been wrong."

A hemisphere away from Boston, and from the other side of the fence, Elizabeth Bishop received a review copy from Houghton Mifflin and wrote to Robert Lowell, "She *is* good, in spots — but there is all the difference in the world, I'm afraid, between her kind of simplicity and that of *Life Studies,* her kind of egocentricity that is simply that, and yours that has been — what would be the reverse of *sub*-limated, I wonder — anyway, made intensely *interesting,* and painfully applicable to every reader. I feel I know too much about her. [. . .] I like some of her really mad ones best; those that sound as [though] she'd written them all at once. I think she really must have been in what Lota called the other day the 'Luna bin.' "

At issue in the praise or criticism of these readers is the question of what use Sexton made of the loss of social functioning labeled "madness." Both sides granted the authenticity and skill of her work, but was it interesting or was it embarrassing? Discussion of the quality of Sexton's poetry throughout her career tended to question whether the speaker was the victim or the moral survivor of her illness; that is, it focused on one side or the other of the double consciousness Sexton wrote into "Her Kind."

Elizabeth Bishop was perhaps applying an Aristotelian standard of character in finding Sexton "egocentric" where Lowell was "painfully applicable to every reader." On first reading the poems of *Life Studies,* she had told Lowell that he was "the luckiest poet I know," because owing to his family lineage, nothing about his personal life was quite without historic interest: "All you have to do is put down the names! And the fact that it seems significant, illustrative, American, etc. gives you, I think, the confidence you display about tackling any idea or theme, *seriously,* in both writing and conversation."

For Grossman, in contrast, Sexton's personal voice was ennobled by speaking "from the other side of an enormous *dérèglement,* expressing how much one had to give up in order to attain reconstitution, after a dire reduction of the self." He saw this as quite the opposite of egocentrism: "Anne Sexton was the first major writer who was able to be heard as a voice not concerned with itself" as an artistic ego. Rather, she reflected the recuperation of self in the aftermath of madness and then of medical treatment. Her poetry conveyed "an immediacy such as people sometimes experience when first reading Thomas Hardy — but not very many other writers." Having survived, having endured, was also the "psychological collage" of Lowell's work, but Sexton was less digressive, willing to speak of what really happened in the process of reduction. This is what both Howe and Grossman valued in *Bedlam.*

The review Sexton took most to heart was by James Dickey in *Poetry,* which zeroed in on what was amateur in her work. Sexton told Dr. Orne that she was mortified by Dickey's remark that she wrote like an A student in the typical writing class. "But you've just started to write," her doctor observed. "I lack taste, I haven't had the real foundation," she countered. "This made me very original, because I'm really not up against a lot of things I have to imitate. Writing comes from inside, but you learn how to refine it." Attendance at Lowell's class had given her an appetite for real study. "As a poet, it may be better to be crazy than educated. But I doubt it," she joked.

Bravely trying to overcome this disadvantage, Sexton enrolled that summer at Brandeis's Institute of Literature, where she took two courses on modern writers. "Howe had written me a 'fan letter' about my book," she crowed to Snodgrass, "so I got a fellowship" that covered tuition. Howe was one of the instructors; Philip Rahv, editor of *Partisan Review,* was another; and through them she met the British poet Stephen Spender, who invited her to submit poems to the British journal *Encounter,* which he edited. Sexton and Howe were "a wonderful pair of contraries," said George Starbuck. "I'd like to have seen that class. Howe keeps to an extremely term-paperish, tree-diagram exposition. Whatever he was plodding along systematically doing she wasn't going to slow down to pick up on. She was just feverish and high energy, and had a two-year-old's sense of the passage of time. Weeks and months were immense periods of time for her because of all the things she could have been covering — so she could be very insistent in following up. I'm surprised in retrospect that she didn't put more people off."

Irving Howe's good opinion had conferred on Sexton the equivalent of a bachelor's degree in literature. "It is amazing how much schooling you can skip if you have actually done something in the field," she wrote happily to Dr. Orne as the term began (the other students in the class were studying for graduate degrees). She had just finished reading Dostoevsky's *Crime and Punishment.* "How beautiful and sick and morbid it was. By God, if this is what 'great books' are all about — maybe I could just write like I write anyhow and stop worrying that it would be too 'sick and morbid' a view of life." Other European writers on her summer list were Mann, Brecht, Pirandello, Gide, Rilke, Sartre, and Camus; she also took a course on American writers that included Henry James, T. S. Eliot, Wallace Stevens, Allen Tate, Nathanael West, and William Faulkner. "So I ought to learn a hell of a lot."

Attending classes at Brandeis put Sexton through some predictable anguish. Only her closest friends knew how terrified she was when she opened her car door and stepped away from its protective frame into the midst of strangers. "Walking into places is the worst part," she wrote to Dr. Orne. She feared exposure of every kind; she decided not to take the courses for credit, so she wouldn't have to take exams. "It's very important that *they* don't find out I'm dumb as they think I'm a poetic genius." But even casual exchanges with her teachers could precipitate humiliating betrayals of fear. "Rahv asked me how I liked being a success . . . and I started to shake all over and couldn't even light a cig," she told Snodgrass. On another occasion she was sitting in the cafeteria after the marathon of her morning classes when Irving Howe joined her and began talking about her poems. "Then he walked away, and when I tried to pick up the cup it was like a Charlie Chaplin movie — I just couldn't pick it up! — From then on at Brandeis I couldn't eat — the fork would shake."

But Sexton took what she wanted from her summer at Brandeis: a feeling for such writers as Kafka, Dostoevsky, and Rilke, whose names she had learned from mentors. She complained to Dr. Orne that she seemed incapable of following her professors' lectures on the books, but reading them stimulated her creativity and fed her hunger for knowledge. "After two hours a day of Rahv on Dostoevsky or Kafka etc. I swallowed fire with the excitement . . . and returned home to put my head next to the speaker of the hi-fi and let a sonata bear away the heat, the intensity, or at least ease some of it," she later recalled. "Anne kept on being a wide-eyed, gaga student right up to the end," Starbuck commented.

More important than a college course to Anne Sexton's education that year, however, was her developing friendship with the poet James Wright, and the deep love that prevailed between them while she produced her second book of poems. They had been introduced when Robert Lowell invited Wright to his poetry class during a visit Wright made to Boston. A shy, soft, short, round man, startlingly eloquent, Wright had grown up in Martin's Ferry, Ohio, in a poor working-class family, but had gone on to receive a splendid education at Kenyon College. Later, on a Fulbright scholarship to Vienna, he experienced the peculiar release of an American discovering European culture. Quirkily learned, he was ardent about music and literature. He was also a natural storyteller; his long letters, like his talk, veered self-delightingly between pedantry and comedy. Like Sexton, Wright never lost the awe of a person given a second chance. He was, as Sexton put it, "real."

In February 1960 Sexton impulsively sent Wright a fan letter praising his new book of poems, *Saint Judas,* and this triggered a cascade of correspondence. Over the next eleven months she wrote to and received from him what she described as "several hundred 'faintly scarlet' letters." Most of these disappeared mysteriously after her death, but enough survived to reveal the kind of good luck Sexton had in becoming friends with Wright at just this time. She dubbed him

"Comfort," the pet name by which she had known her grandfather A.G.S. This name signaled the important way in which Wright psychologically mediated Sexton's artistic identification; to her mourning psyche, he felt like a composite of all the parental figures who had provided her with empowering forms of attention, including Mary Gray and Dr. Orne.

Or so Sexton saw it. In one of the long, driftingly narrative letters that streamed from her, she told Wright about spending a day's earnings from selling cosmetics door to door on his book *The Green Wall*, prizewinner in the Yale Younger Poets Series in 1957. "I wasn't poor, but I had to work awfully hard selling face cream to strangers who wouldn't open the door and besides I'd just come out of the booby hatch and I was nervous with strangers, I was even nervous with face cream." This was the job she had taken, at Dr. Orne's insistence, to pay for an extra session of therapy each week. She told Wright that *The Green Wall* was the first book of poetry she ever bought. "I had never heard of you . . . but I had never heard of Yeats either." The next day she had gone to Annisquam to visit her mother and had slipped away to read the book. "I held it in my hand and it moved, not like the sea below me, but like a small mechanical heart might. I say that, extravagant or not, because the book told me who I was, who I could be. The book was more alive than all the ruined sea." Interestingly, Sexton here moved into rhythms — ". . . who I could be. / The book was more alive / than all the ruined sea" — that echo the three-beat iambic of Wright's keynote poem:

> Be glad of the green wall
> You climbed across one day,
> When winter stung with ice
> That vacant paradise.

She mentioned in particular a poem that touchingly idealized the wounded and the sick, then went on to claim that at the moment of reading *The Green Wall*, "I knew that at last I was in contact with my life, my family, my world."

Wright's friendship with Sexton blossomed at a fraught period in his own life. His marriage was deteriorating, and he was bracing for a wrenching separation from his young sons, Franz and Marshall. But he was also embarking on new work far from the lyricism Sexton admired in *The Green Wall*. For almost a year he found in Sexton a muse who reconnected him to inspiration. He called her "Blessing" (sometimes "Bee" or "B."), the title of a much-admired poem he wrote during this period, which describes "two Indian ponies" that "bow shyly as wet swans. They love each other." It ends with the lines "Suddenly I realize / That if I stepped out of my body I would break / Into blossom." Offering Sexton what quickly developed, on paper, into a courtship, Wright answered her hunger for affectionate recognition with a hunger of his own. "My beautiful kind Blessing, my discovered love," he called her. "In the midst of everything you do you can know you are utterly loved. [. . .] I survive by sitting and thinking of you."

Sometimes they wrote each other two or three letters in a single day. Garrulous, gossipy, and warmheartedly pedantic, Wright was eager to develop Sexton's ear for music as well as her knowledge of European literature, and his advice about music came complete with serial numbers of recordings by his favorite conductors. He was translating Neruda at this time, as part of an effort to transform his formal style into a more spare and imagistic poetry, and the flavor of his letters can be sampled in a note introducing Sexton to a pair of translations of Neruda's "Walking Around." Wright thought it useful to tell her that Neruda "is a South American Communist, which is a historically complicated kind of creature. In any case, he is, like, say, Mayakovsky in that his directly *political* poems are so bad as to be, not funny, but distressing, as if you were seeing Sir John Gielgud forget several lines at the very dramatic crisis of *Hamlet*." For many months Wright served as Sexton's avid mentor, typing out poems he admired. Under his tutelage she also began reading the Bible, which he would read aloud by the hour to her over the telephone, as Maxine Kumin remembered.

Just as Wright welcomed Sexton's letters, and her ignorance, he welcomed manuscripts of poems in progress, and was liberal, even prodigal, with advice, writing all over her drafts with a blunt soft lead pencil in tiny script. He had direct influence on several of the poems Sexton wrote in 1960 and 1961. Drafts of "The Truth the Dead Know" and "A Curse Against Elegies" suggest that they may have started out as the same poem, titled "Refusal"; in August 1960 Wright remarked on their similarity to his own poem "The Refusal," observing that Sexton's two versions have different themes and that in following him, she has chosen the "narrower and less powerful" theme. He tried to dissuade her from imitating him. "B. must trust her own imagination: call her own stubbornness to aid," he advised.

But it was not so much Wright's practical advice as his acceptance of her as a peer that mattered to Sexton, helping her to internalize the identity she was rapidly acquiring in the professional world of poetry. He sent her a copy of Rainer Maria Rilke's *Letters to a Young Poet,* with a sybilline inscription: "To Anne Sexton, for whom this book was written — 'Let those who may complain that it was only upon paper remember that only upon paper have humanity yet achieved glory, beauty, truth, knowledge, virtue and abiding love' (G. B. Shaw, on his letters to Ellen Terry) — Jim Wright, Spring 1960." Quoting Shaw, Wright may have been thinking of Rilke's miserable record as a husband and father, much in contrast with the commitment to love and work that he idealizes in *Letters to a Young Poet.* But Sexton received and cherished the book as a sacred object that embodied Wright's soul. She adopted it as a personal manifesto, and reread it whenever she wanted to make emotional contact with Wright.

By midsummer Sexton and Wright had cooked up a way to get together. Wright had been invited to spend five days in late July and early August at Montauk on Long Island, at an estate owned by Hy Sobiloff, a financier who aspired to recognition as a poet. Sobiloff was gregarious and energetic, an entrepreneur who served as chairman of the board of several corporations and had important philanthropic interests in medicine but whose loves were poetry and poetic styles of filmmaking. The gathering at Montauk, which included Oscar Williams, the editor of a popular poetry anthology, was to be a salon seminar on poetry. Wright was invited for an additional purpose: to help Sobiloff finish poems to be published in his third book, *Breathing of First Things.* (Sobiloff's previous books had been worked over by the distinguished poets Conrad Aiken and Allen Tate.)

To her chagrin, Sexton was invited as Wright's girlfriend. Usually cautious about calling attention to her affairs, she might not have accepted; but Kayo was scheduled to be away for two weeks on a business trip, Dr. Orne was out of town, Billie could be talked into taking the children, and Wright was importunate. So on Friday morning the twenty-ninth of July, Sexton took off for Long Island to live in sin with Wright for five days. "I just left, as though I'd taken a freedom pill!"

Once she arrived in Montauk, her nervousness evaporated in the warmth of Hy Sobiloff's personality. He lived "like a king," she thought, and reminded her of her father. While the other poets stayed dutifully indoors, working on manuscripts, she and Hy went fishing on his yacht. "I was the only one who knew how to act around him," she remarked. "Jim, who came from a poor family, didn't." During the cocktail hour she was chagrined to learn that Jim couldn't mix a martini and embarrassed that Jim didn't tuck in his sport shirt; Hy, like her father, would notice such things.

The poetry seminars were held by day in Sobiloff's home, but the participants retired at night to a nearby motel. Jim and Anne shared a room. Nervous as newlyweds, they spent their first night together clasped in each other's arms, too shy to make love. But in the morning, Anne woke full of desire. Wright described this in a letter he later wrote to Dr. Orne: "I was afraid and inhibited; and she made love to me. [. . .] Her powers of femininity and unqualified kindness, as well as her deeply graceful sexuality, were quite beyond anything I had ever known or even imagined in a woman. I have had a good share of fantasies, of course, [. . .] but Anne was different from fantasy."

For these two guilty souls, such happiness required immediate payment of a high price. They started quarreling the next night, after drinking too much — a struggle that had a farcical quality both of them remembered later. The motel's walls were thin, so they had to conduct their fight in whispers and gestures. Wright told Sexton im-

Anne Sexton, Hy Sobiloff, and James Wright at Montauk.

petuously that he wanted her to divorce Kayo and marry him. Sexton said she could never abandon her family. Wright retaliated for this perceived rejection by embarking on a long, abstract, self-pitying monologue ("as is my habit," he confessed) about "old lonely devotions," about how "betrayal was the normal human experience," about how "Anne had 'used' me," meeting for "a tawdry summer-love-affair that would help her while away the time during her husband's annual business trip."

Rapt in his own eloquence, Wright didn't notice that Sexton had passed out until her peculiar silence attracted his attention. She was lying face down on the bed, and remained limp when he lifted her. "The gray world rushed in on me," he recalled. "I am afraid to face even the smallest real problem. I am 32 years old and cannot even drive a car." Not knowing whether she was ill, fearing she might have poisoned herself, he held her in his arms and talked gently to her for a long hour. But when she finally opened her eyes, she couldn't see him; her gaze was fixed on some invisible adversary. Sexton spent this whole night slipping back and forth from deep unconsciousness to spells of hallucination, while Wright watched over her. Awaking the next day, she professed no recollection of what had happened.

Sexton's own most troubling memory of this episode concerned an argument over money. She always felt short of cash, but to Wright she seemed rich. She thought he used his working-class background to make her feel unworthy: "You people don't understand" the value of money, he told her. Then she discovered that Sobiloff was paying him five hundred dollars for the week's work. "I kept paying for everything and he lied to me," she told Dr. Orne. "I found out he was 'taking me.'"

Yet the poems that issued from this meeting mined a rich layer of feeling. Back home in Ohio, Wright inscribed to Sexton a poem titled "Lazy on a Saturday Morning": "Gulls poise on the wet arms / Of a woman who is in love with the sea. / She floats away from the shore on an oak leaf, calling me / By a strange name." In pencil he added, "I think you are beautiful. It's true that I caught no fish, that day in the launch. Still, I caught *you* in the act of loving the waters. As long as the sea lasts, it will remember us. I gave it the clean white handkerchief of your face, dear B." Back home in Boston, Sexton commemorated the emotional dynamics between them in the last section of *All My Pretty Ones*, in three love poems: "Letter Written on a Ferry While

Crossing Long Island Sound," "From the Garden," and "Love Song for K. Owyne." She dedicated this section of the book to "Comfort, who was actually my grandfather."

This intense, self-dramatizing meeting was much influenced on Sexton's side by the absence of Dr. Orne, who had accepted a research fellowship that took him to Australia for the summer months, leaving Sexton in the care of another therapist. In discussing the affair with her later, Dr. Orne suggested that she consider it a form of acting out, in which her real bond with Wright was made to substitute for the symbolic bonds with her parents and Nana, now deeply transferred to Dr. Orne. Sexton partially concurred with this insight. Both she and Wright were self-aware enough to accept that the meeting had taken place more in the realm of dovetailing fantasies than in the world of practical arrangements — and to value the privilege, which Sexton celebrated in "The Black Art."

Sexton recognized very well that her intermittent trances had been symptomatic, hysterical, but she resisted Dr. Orne's evaluation of her love for Wright as sheer transference. By the time *All My Pretty Ones* came out in 1962, she and Wright had abandoned the fantasy of running away together, but Wright's letter about the book reaffirmed her confidence in the reality of their mutual understanding as artists. Wright, like Rilke, was able to sustain intimacy mainly through the medium of words, and Sexton felt uplifted and supported by the transcendental glide of their regular correspondence. Upon receiving his copy of *All My Pretty Ones,* Wright wrote, "My dear Bee, [. . .] I have the book. It is lovely. I am proud to be quoted on the jacket. *You* are lovely. I will write you soon. I was so moved by the page about 'Comfort' that I won't discuss it yet." He told her that he knew from a preceding letter that she was sick, and he consulted Dr. Orne about whether to get in touch with her. "It occurs to me that just about anyone else I know on earth [. . .] would consider you and me worse than crazy [. . .] because, whatever either of us happens to be going through at any given moment, we are still totally unafraid and unguilty about saying or writing or phoning absolutely anything to each other." Showing Dr. Orne this letter, Sexton commented, "It makes transference to you seem like water to wine. He gives me so many gifts, but with both of us it's a 'weird abundance.' Is it my mother — who is it? It doesn't have anything to do with sex [. . .] he's not strong on responsibility — he's a genius — he makes me want to write."

· · ·

The abundant energy Sexton brought to poetry and poets that year was a token of the headway she had made in therapy. July 1960 marked the fourth anniversary of her first hospitalization — the normal length of a college education. What had she gained from this strenuous course? The repetitiousness of her worst behavior always discouraged her, but Dr. Orne constantly challenged her gloomy perspective. Her love for Nana, he argued, had fortified a base in her psyche on which other loves rested securely. "I've never known anyone able to do anything in treatment if they hadn't had a real relationship in the past," he would tell her. "The one way you could continue to own Nana, once she became psychotic, was to take in the sick parts." A principal goal of her therapy was to engage with Dr. Orne in a relationship of trust that would in effect reeducate her emotionally.

Sexton's gains were reinforced by the increasing strength of her relationship to her children. Linda turned seven that summer; Joy, five. Their growing maturity made mothering them easier, more natural, for Sexton, and she felt deep love for them: they too were "real." Though she was not the "good mother" of convention, and though her children were never to experience her as stable and reliable, her capacities for affection and pleasure endowed them with lasting emotional resources. But Sexton's work was poetry; as in Mary Gray's household, the work of child care was delegated.

Fortunately for Linda and Joy, their grandmother seemed to welcome this work, and she *was* a good mother. They felt completely at home in Billie's house — "safe" was the word Joy chose later — and she had a way of making their visits into special occasions by preparing their favorite foods, putting treats by their bedsides, or laying out small gifts. She also looked after their clothing and their appearance. The minute they arrived she would march them to the bathroom for a session with the toothbrush; often she would bathe them and wash their hair, as she found their mother lax in matters of personal hygiene. An accomplished dressmaker, Billie was clever at altering clothes; Joy remembered how she fashioned a little appliqué in the form of a cat to cover a smear of indelible red Magic Marker on a favorite dress.

After the shattering death of George Sexton, Billie and her own daughter, Joan (now in her late twenties), welcomed the presence of the children more than ever. Joan still lived at home, and like a fun big sister had numerous fascinating hobbies, going through infectious enthusiasms for weaving, modeling with clay, and stringing beads, sweeping the girls along with her. She also loved picnics, and would pack huge hampers full of delicious surprises to take to the woods. Thinking back, Linda and Joy both remembered Joan's buoyant spirits fondly, and marveled at her patience. "I used to tease to see how far I could go with her," Joy admitted. "I *once* made her mad enough to yell at me. She never once spanked me."

Anne Sexton was unusually lucky in having Billie's and Joan's unstinting, loving investment in Linda and Joy while she threw herself into developing her art and gaining recognition for it. But it was hard for her to acknowledge this debt generously, because she experienced it as a reproach. Increasingly, the role she let Billie take in her family's life created tension between her and Kayo as her stability waxed and waned.

8

GETTING A HEARING
1961

AFTER DR. ORNE returned from his summer in Australia, in the autumn of 1960, he took a new approach in therapy. Sexton was not getting from treatment what he had hoped. As he put it later, their sessions had the quality of self-contained vignettes with a beginning, middle, and end. Often the material was interesting, the sense of movement lively. But over time, he observed that she was making no progress. "Anne was so busy interacting that she gained no sense of what had been going on," he commented. "She couldn't recall the content of the interactions, or she would misremember them. She was really trying to work, but she was severely handicapped by the inaccuracy of her memory." Moreover, toward the end of her treatment hour she would often fall into a trance state, which lengthened the appointment. Sometimes the trance was so deep that he could not waken her. He occasionally let her sleep it off in the consulting room, but this was not always convenient. These trances further distanced the content of the preceding hour from Sexton's memory.

To address the problem, Dr. Orne asked Sexton to make notes about their transactions immediately after each session. For a few weeks she did so faithfully. These notes reveal that while she knew how she had felt during the treatment hour, she could not remember what had happened to cause the feelings, no matter how intense they were.

Dr. Orne next proposed capturing the feelings of the therapy sessions by recording them on tape. Following each session Sexton was to complete a demanding set of assignments. Immediately she was to make a brief written record of significant issues they had discussed. A day later she was to come back to the office and listen to the tape in a private room, taking notes. This helped her become aware of how little she had retained. Dr. Orne reasoned that listening to the tapes would help preserve the continuity of treatment for her — in effect, it would serve as additional therapy. If the material was very painful, he sometimes held back the tape. Occasionally he sat with her while she listened. The goal was to help her begin to "own" the whole range of feelings and memories that surfaced during therapeutic interactions, only to sink from consciousness when she left the doctor's presence. He hoped that making notes would help her take responsibility for remembering, a responsibility she tried to delegate to him. Her problems with memory, Dr. Orne told her, were "symptoms that some part of you knows a lot about. The tape gives you a tool, enables you to work with that part of yourself." Moreover, it was intended to help Sexton build confidence in her own version of her experience. As he put it later, "It allowed Anne to be on a more equal basis with me. It was now possible for her to say to me, when I got it wrong, 'You got it wrong, Dr. Orne!' "

The new regimen began in January 1961. Sexton's notes express surging confidence that this approach might finally diminish the force of symptoms in her life. Though she had made giant strides in the poetry world, her personal life was still narrowly circumscribed by her ability to "forget" who she was and what she had said. To limit the embarrassment this caused, she kept carbon copies of most letters she wrote, even to friends. But it was the key problem in her family relationships. She continued to suffer exorbitantly during Kayo's absences on business trips; even when life was outwardly calm, though, Sexton tended to panic whenever she had to leave her house for any reason except to see Dr. Orne or to go to the hairdresser, trips that had become utterly routine. She yearned to browse in bookstores and libraries, but couldn't go unless a friend accompanied her. Grocery stores, drugstores, and department stores terrified her, and she refused to enter them unless someone — usually Maxine Kumin — coached her ahead of time and stayed with her while she shopped. "I hate to go to the market because it's full of making up your mind, it's full of decisions and crowds of people," she explained. "Somebody sees me, *and I see myself through them*. Then it's all gone, the whole world falls apart." She would agonize for hours even before placing an order by telephone. The task of buying the children new shoes could absorb three weeks of worry in advance. Most often, it was Billie or Kayo who did the shopping.

Now, for the first time, therapy seemed to hold real promise of freedom from the threats other people exercised just by noticing her.

"I feel as if you and I have declared war on my neurosis — jointly," she told Dr. Orne. "Intellectually, I feel this is really going to do it. Before, I would come in here and spend my time verbally acting out, then just walk away from it." Still, she often found the process of listening to taped transactions with her doctor very disturbing. After one listening session in mid-January she annotated her entry, "Right now I would like to kill this book, which demands remembering and the ugly truth — which means I *will* remember and I *will* get well!"

Listening to the tapes took the time Sexton was used to spending on her poetry: "The time has to come out of your creative effort, not out of your neurotic effort," Dr. Orne acknowledged. She wrote very little that year. Yet because *Bedlam* was attracting rave notices, she was being treated like a star poet, being interviewed, discussed, and scheduled into the college poetry circuit. That January she learned that *Bedlam* was one of thirteen books of poetry nominated for the National Book Award, an unusual honor for a first book. She was invited to New York to read her work and discuss "Poetry as Therapy" on a radio broadcast. In early February Arthur Freeman invited her to Adams House at Harvard to read and discuss her book with visiting scholars and student writers, and later that month she appeared at Amherst College at a poetry weekend, on a program with Louis Simpson, one of her current heroes. Also in February Louis Untermeyer requested permission to print some of her work in a new edition of his poetry anthology, which Lowell had assigned as a textbook. Only a few living poets (including Lowell) were represented in the anthology. Maxine Kumin was elated by the news. "This is the audience we write for: the *vertical* audience," she told Sexton. "Think of the company Hardy and Yeats! Every college has this anthology in its library!" Sexton confided another angle on this honor to Untermeyer: "I have felt sad since your letter came . . . a gripping longing, usually well repressed, to share all this with my parents."

Sexton was also receiving numerous requests for public appearances. In April she served on a panel at Boston College, where her old beau Jack McCarthy was a member of the English Department faculty. Other panel members were John L. Sweeney, from Harvard's Lamont Library, W. D. Snodgrass, and John Holmes — "a mess of father substitutes." Sexton revised her eight-minute comments six times, she claimed. The resulting talk, based on a line from Rilke's *Letters to a Young Poet,* comes across in manuscript as polished but lively and unpretentious; however, the prospect of giving it terrified her so much that she had to brace herself in the car beforehand with two Thermos bottles of martinis.

That same month she read at the Cornell University Arts Festival, along with George Starbuck and Peter Davison, a young poet and an editor at the *Atlantic Monthly*. "Anne read splendidly from both *Bedlam* and newer work," Davison recalled. "I especially admired her long poem 'The Operation.' I wasn't prepared for how extroverted she was. Once the parties started, she was going half the night." He remembered Sexton's striking physical presence at the time, "a combination of awkwardness and grace, long legs and long arms, and smoke, smoke, smoke, smoke, smoke — always smoking. Intense blue eyes with big pupils; blue-black hair; slightly crooked nose. She would sit with her limbs crossed in every direction, leaning forward, with her hand on her chin. She dressed well, carried herself like a model." Coming back from Ithaca, "we drove slowly and she told me a great deal about herself," Davison said. He had been aware of Sexton's stage fright at Cornell, but her anxiety had seemed melodramatic, like an act. "I was tempted to think of it as a joke. But I learned from her it wasn't."

Sexton's own memory of the partying focused on how she managed to drink a lot without exhibiting her shaky hands. "I was scared the whole time — ordered double martinis on the rocks with a long straw, and reached for it only with my arm braced," she told Dr. Orne. "And when I'd light a cigarette, I'd rest my elbow on the chair." She claimed that she only survived the experience at Cornell because she arranged "constantly to have a guardian, and managed not to have an affair with anyone."

Throughout 1961, Sexton was still attending the John Holmes workshop. Four of the five regulars now had books in print that had been wrangled into shape during their semimonthly meetings. Holmes's *The Fortune Teller* came out in March and was nominated for the National Book Award the following year. Starbuck's *Bone Thoughts* had won the Yale prize the preceding year, and Kumin's *Halfway* was up for the Lamont prize. Sexton's *Bedlam* didn't get the National Book Award that year, nor did *All My Pretty Ones* when it was nominated, but the workshop process contributed to the very high quality of finish in all these volumes.

The accolades accruing to Sexton's book did not change John Holmes's opinion of the woman. Her affair with Starbuck had distressed him, and he confided in Kumin: "Why do we stand for her and her fake-or-true love affairs?" Normally a gracious man and always a collegial one, Holmes vented his feelings privately and tried to keep them from interfering with the workshop. But his disapproval boiled up into rage after one session that winter. Ostensibly to comfort Sam Albert, whom he saw as a victim of Sexton's bad behavior, Holmes wrote a letter to each of them, letting off steam. To Sexton he was avuncular, but he got his point across: "You gave Sam an awfully rough time, I felt, too much of it, and hard for a man to take, and he took it like a good sport. [. . .] Also, for the first time I've ever minded, I thought you and Max had too much to drink, and that it took the meaning and responsible thinking away from the poems."

Holmes wanted to conduct the sessions high-mindedly. Sexton liked the atmosphere of a free-for-all. "What kind of workshop is this?" she fumed to him. "Are we mere craftsmen or are we artists! [. . .] I resent the idea that an almost good poem isn't worth any amount of time if we can make it better and first the actual writer has got to be able to HEAR." For Sexton, the unbridled excitement of the group process led frequently to inspired revision. "This is a great strength and a great, but mutual intuitive creative act each time it happens," she argued; to repress the process would be to kill the work. Moreover, she knew the issue was not merely workshop manners. "In the long pull, John, where you might be proud of me, you are ashamed of me. I keep pretending not to notice . . . But then, you remind me of my father (and I KNOW that's not your fault). But there is something else here . . . who do I remind you of?"

Sexton was, of course, hurt by Holmes's dislike, but this exchange of letters provoked a productive insight into her relationship with the whole critical establishment, elaborated in a dream she reported to Dr. Orne.

A.S.: This perfect voice was enunciating very carefully as if to tell me exactly how it was — and yet he was kind and patient about it — very irritated but patient all at once — and this was terrible because whatever he was telling me I was seeing the reverse.

He'd talk reasonably, reasonably, and he wouldn't stop telling me, you know, just nicely . . . It would become so frightening that I would pound on the floor — maybe screaming stop it, stop it — that would be the feeling: LISTEN! and then I'd try something else. PLEASE. Like HE COULDN'T HEAR ME.

Dr.: There is one thing I have trouble understanding; that is, what you wanted when you had to pound on the floor.

A.S.: Well, associate. If you're pounding on the floor then you must be down on the floor — like a child or an animal or someone very afraid. — He keeps telling me what's so and probably he's right but it isn't so for me so I've got to try again to make the same thing so for both of us so we can make sense to each other. Otherwise, I'm crazy. I'm lost.

Dr.: If you can talk to one person, you're not crazy?

A.S.: Right. One sane person, that is.

Implicated in the figure of the male auditor were some of the critical reviews Sexton's book had been receiving, along with the parents — now cleverly dead, beyond appeal — who had not lived long enough to read Anne Harvey Sexton's words in a book nor see the world confirm her as a poet. And at least part of the dream records Sexton's struggle to listen to herself. Among the many internal voices condensed into the heedless voice in her dream is surely that of her taped therapy sessions, going on and on while the living woman crouches in earphones, aghast at "seeing the reverse" in every enunciation of her own words.

Yet Sexton had for some time been making productive use of critical feedback that did not merely censor and craze, first and continuously from Dr. Orne (in his role as good mother), and, as important, from Maxine Kumin. "Max and I say we love each other like sisters — that's kind of a new category [for me]," Sexton commented. With her blood sisters she experienced only rivalry, but with Kumin she knew reciprocity. After Sexton built herself a new study, they both had special phones installed at their desks and used them through the day to check out drafts of poems. "We sometimes connected with a phone call and kept the line linked for hours at a stretch," Kumin remembered. "We whistled into the receiver for each other when we were ready to resume."

Kumin's affectionate fascination made the work real for Sexton. Trying out lines and drafts over the phone defused a little the trance-like state of inspiration she referred to as "milk[ing] the unconscious." Describing the process to an interviewer, Sexton said, "All poets have a little critic in their heads. [. . .] You have to turn off the little critic while you are beginning a poem so that it doesn't inhibit you. Then you have to turn it on again when you are revising and refining." Whistling into the receiver for her friend was a way of engaging an inner critical process through the agency of an external contact, a merging of resources. It was a model of work Sexton made use of throughout her life, as a playwright, as a member of the chamber rock group Anne Sexton and Her Kind, which performed her poems to music, as a teacher, and, of course, in the workshop.

Maxine Kumin rebuked John Holmes for putting her in the middle of his quarrel with Sexton. As a poet, though, she *was* in the middle. Strong on technique and fond of the wordplay that delighted Starbuck and Holmes, Kumin was nonetheless aware that the lovers of technique in her circle tended to lavish it on shallow work. It was Sexton for whom the "tricks" were modes of trimming sail on a vessel laden with precious cargo: imagery that, as Starbuck put it, she brought to class with her on the first day and could never have been taught. Sexton helped Kumin locate the same strengths in herself. Kumin acknowledged this in her poem "For Anne at Passover" in *Halfway,* a moving antiphon to Sexton's "My Friend, My Friend," and Sexton affirmed the connection in her inscription of Kumin's copy of *Bedlam*: "For Max, who encouraged me with all of these poems, and 'halfway' wrote some, and who is all the way my friend, my friend." Their telephone dialogues were, Kumin remembered, marvels of "ongoing, complete encouragement" of whatever piece was to hand. "Does this image work? Does the poem end here? Can I begin like this? What about these rhymes?" But Kumin acknowledged a deeper level of communication as well. "Anne gave me wildness. She pulled me out of my shell. I am very contained, very reticent; she made me see that the cerebral really needed a strong admixture of the visceral."

The visceral was precisely what John Holmes loathed about Sexton's work. He apologized to Kumin for his intemperate letter, but he went on to insist that he was right about Sexton's *artistic* badness. Appealing to Kumin's conscience, he claimed that someone had to make Sexton see the misdirection in her work. "I said way back, that she was going to have a hard time to change subject matter, after the book, and it's true. [. . .] Not that she has two subjects, mental illness and sex, but that she writes so absolutely selfishly, of herself, to bare and shock and confess. Her motives are wrong, artistically, and finally the self-preoccupation comes to be simply damn boring."

Kumin held a different view, which she expressed retrospectively in her foreword to Sexton's *Complete Poems.* Sexton "wrote openly about menstruation, abortion, masturbation, incest, adultery, and drug addiction at a time when the proprieties embraced none of these as proper topics for poetry," she commented. "Today, the remonstrances seem almost quaint. Anne delineated the problematic position of women — the neurotic reality of the time — though she was not able to cope in her own life with the personal trouble it created." At stake for Sexton, and for Kumin as well, was what amounted to ideological conflict over the true nature of poetry. Could poetry be made to express experience that only women could "hear" — the dilemma of women's position?

Back in 1961, such questions were harder to formulate. Yet Kumin and Sexton both were to become the beneficiaries that year of a social experiment involving women. One Sunday the preceding autumn, the *New York Times* had carried a front-page story announcing an experimental new program designed to "harness the talents of 'intellectually displaced women' " whose careers had been interrupted. The program, which was to be called the Radcliffe Institute, was founded by Mary Ingraham Bunting, the recently inaugurated president of Radcliffe, the women's college at Harvard University. Among the first to apply was Anne Sexton, who called Radcliffe for information the Monday morning after the story appeared. Eventually, 2400 women called or wrote to ask about the program, and two hundred applied for the twenty available fellowships, a few of which were allocated specifically for working artists.

President Bunting, who had been a biologist before she became a canny administrator, privately looked on the institute as a kind of laboratory where she could test a hypothesis. She speculated that many well-educated women in the Boston area were ready, after raising families, to return to full-time intellectual or artistic work but struggling for opportunity in a "climate of unexpectation." Men of the same background were usually well established in professions by the time their children were self-sufficient, but women had to break through firmly held cultural beliefs that a woman's choice was either marriage *or* career. The Radcliffe Institute was to be a place where women who had already set their sights on a career path could make up for lost time, using the facilities of the Harvard libraries and laboratories. Perhaps the prestige of renewed recognition of their accomplishments would nudge them into the path of further opportunities. Bunting's idea was radical, but not *too* radical: she had targeted a social group — educated housewives — that represented the probable future of current Radcliffe undergraduates.

Sexton's letter of application contained a characteristic mix of meekness and hubris. "I know my academic background looks anemic and without interest. However it seems to me that I have come a long way alone," she stated. "I feel that I am already an accomplished poet. What I ask for now is the opportunity to be a lasting one." Letters from Philip Rahv, Dudley Fitts, Louis Untermeyer, and John Sweeney supported her application. All of them emphasized her talent, but Rahv also praised her "unusually keen and avid mind, capable of assimilating advanced ideas." He thought she would benefit enormously from a period of sustained reading and writing within the Harvard ambience. "Wow!" was the response of the Harvard committeeman who interviewed her. "We'll know she's around. She has enormous vitality and zest! Her comments on writing are fascinating."

When her letter of appointment arrived — a day after Kumin's — Sexton capered through the neighborhood, "running into the neighbors' houses, leaping up on their counters. I got it, I got it!" She immediately sent Dr. Orne a night letter with a joyful message in doggerel: "Hark Hark the lark / Gadzooks Hear Hear / My I.Q.'s OK this year." Only a few things in her life had ever meant so much to her as receiving the Radcliffe grant, she told him at their next appointment. "This is something *we* did." It was Dr. Orne and his mother who could really appreciate how far she had come. "Both you and Dr. Brunner said I could do this; I'm trying to say you were right even though I didn't think so. If my parents were alive they'd be the ones to tell."

This development "was a real coup"; what kind of opportunity it represented was another question she explored with her doctor. "The Radcliffe thing is for overeducated women who are stuck at home and have lost touch with their field, though they were brilliant once. But Maxine and I are in our field, we're not stuck at home!" When Dr. Orne observed that she might enroll in literature courses at Harvard, Sexton gave a quick no. Philip Rahv might admire her ability to assimilate advanced ideas, but at this point in her life she would rather have lunch with Rahv than hear him lecture. She was through taking courses.

She did hope that the Radcliffe Institute would offer a chance to be tutored by a professional prose writer. So far she had only one story in print, "Dancing the Jig." It had the force of her best poetry: psychological truthfulness and a dramatic situation. But in retrospect, she wished she had hung on to it or published it under a pseudonym.

"There are no guards in prose," she explained: no line endings, no rhythmic intervals, no rhymes to close up a thought. She didn't think "Dancing the Jig" was as good as her best poetry, and now regretted having anything in print that didn't fulfill the highest literary standards. Given her current visibility in the poetry world, editors might be willing to print anything she sent them. "You've got to have a terrific critical sense, and I don't quite have it — and if my friends don't have it for me, things are going to get out that are awfully bad." Maybe through Radcliffe she could find a writer to work with privately. Her appointment would begin in September; then she would see.

In any case, Sexton's preferred mode of learning was apprenticeship to a master who would participate in a melting fusion of souls, as Jim Wright had. That spring, when she met handsome Anthony Hecht, she thought she had found a new soulmate. Hecht was a *Hudson Review* poet, a talented craftsman whose elegant formal verse indicated an ex-

Anthony Hecht.

cellent literary education. Sexton met him on a trip to New York. Recently separated from his wife, he was touched by Sexton's abundant interest in his poetry, in his children, in his divorce, and in his attraction to her. Immediately upon returning to Boston, Sexton began showering him with notes and letters. His cautious replies groped for just the right note of gallantry. "And now, what do I say? I love you? Yes, I guess I do. But I feel sort of foolish writing a love letter to a happily married woman." He sent her a gift of two wineglasses: "I should like you and Kayo to drink a toast to each other first, then one to me. [. . .] You are an astonishingly gifted and accomplished poet, and an unbelievably lovely human being. Everyone who knows you is lucky."

Sexton returned to New York to visit Hecht in May. Apparently she increased the sexual pressure, but he drew a line that he wouldn't be lured across. After putting her on the plane to Boston he wrote her a letter: "I have come to think that the best thing about our relationship is precisely that there is a 'safety factor' and that we really, without ever having told each other any lies about ourselves, managed to maintain a certain privacy." He enclosed a copy of a poem he had been telling her about, by Sir Thomas Wyatt: "Whoso list to hunt, I know where is an hind . . ." Graciously displacing the sentiment from himself onto the Renaissance poet, Hecht excused himself from the chase:

> But as for me, alas, I may no more —
> [. . .]
> There is written her fair neck round about:
> "*Noli me tangere,* for Caesar's I am,
> And wild for to hold, though I seem tame."

Sexton was really fond of Hecht, and she knew he was right to set limits to their intimacy. She was very much afraid that her own impulses would take over, that her competitive spirit would grow more stubborn under his resistance. "It's not that I want to go to bed with him; I want to be sure he loves me. This [wanting] is like pills or drugs but much more complex." Sexton discussed this attraction in therapy because she recognized an underlying pattern; lovers were stand-ins for some inexplicit, unavailable person, such as Dr. Orne himself. "It's not that I'm beautiful; it's just that I can make some men fall in love with me," she explained. "The aura of this thing is more strong than alcohol. Not just sleeping with them: it's a ritual. If I want to push it I just say 'I need you.'. . . . I've been thinking, well, I'm going to die of this, it's a disease; it will destroy the kids, axe my husband and anyone else's opinion of me. Ever since George, ever since my mother died, I want to have the feeling someone's in love with me. From George to Jim. A fine narcotic, having people in love with me."

To reinforce her good intentions, she invited Hecht up to Newton Lower Falls. He came to visit the Sextons several times, and became a family friend. Sexton clung to his affection that summer, it seems, as a substitute for James Wright, who was increasingly out of touch; when Sexton sent him her ardent love poem "Letter Written on a Ferry While Crossing Long Island Sound" as a gift, he responded to it as a draft, advising her to delete the last line, *"good news, good news"* — "As though Oedipus were to be rescued at the last minute — in the nick of time — by Bishop Sheen disguised as the Lone Ranger. [. . .] I will explain why I think it's a superb poem later." (It was a developing pattern in his letters to delay positive responses until "later.")

In July, under the spell of feelings renewed by her bond with Hecht, Sexton wrote a rueful tribute to her complicated attachment with Wright in her poem "The Black Art."

> A woman who writes feels too much,
> those trances and portents!
> As if cycles and children and islands
> weren't enough; as if mourners and gossips
> and vegetables were never enough.
> She thinks she can warn the stars.
> A writer is essentially a spy.
> Dear love, I am that girl.
>
> A man who writes knows too much,
> such spells and fetiches!
> [. . .]
> With used furniture he makes a tree.
> A writer is essentially a crook.
> Dear love, you are that man.

Wright was to be in Manhattan early in September to deliver a paper at a professional meeting, and after much stewing, Sexton worked up the courage to meet him there. He stayed with Tony Hecht's brother, Roger, who had been his Kenyon College classmate.

Sexton joined them in the afternoon for drinks, then they went on to dinner. Roger Hecht remembered the occasion vividly: "A warm-to-hot not quite twilit evening: Jim Wright in suit with short-sleeved white shirt and tie; Anne in black hat, black dress, bare feet, her shoes over a shoulder and held by their straps: Anne almost but not quite leaning into Jim as they walked in Greenwich Village . . . A restaurant: the two of them seated side by side, Jim saying — I think more than once — 'Stop bugging me, Anne.' " Sexton captured her sense of this unhappy evening in "Lament," written immediately after her return home. A push-me-pull-you conflict went on for several days, with Sexton wanting reassurance and Wright wanting to get out of what was perhaps feeling like a messy situation with a married woman. He drank constantly, avoiding her appeals for intimacy; it was a way he had.

Sexton never understood what made James Wright withdraw from her, though as time went on she came to believe that his increasingly close friendship with the poet Robert Bly had something to do with it. ("No matter what Robert Bly thinks about your opinion of me," she wrote to Wright in February 1964, "he doesn't know how much you gave to me as a writer; that you didn't bother to judge me, you were too busy giving.") There was no real break, only a lengthening silence. In a mood of mourning, four months after their meeting in New York, Sexton wrote "Letter Written During a January Northeaster." Each object in the winter landscape is animated by silence, waiting with her; only ghosts are afoot.

> Dearest,
> where are your letters?
> The mailman is an impostor.
> He is actually my grandfather.
> He floats far off in the storm
> with his nicotine mustache and a bagful of nickels.
> His legs stumble through
> baskets of eyelashes.
> Like all the dead
> he picks up his disguise,
> shakes it off and slowly pulls down the shade,
> fading out like an old movie.
> Now he is gone
> as you are gone.
> But he belongs to me like lost baggage.

Loss was Sexton's most reliable muse. In trances of mourning she could move to her desk and, sweeping the drifts of mail off her typewriter keys, let words seethe out through her fingers. Yearning for unattainable "pretty ones" activated the powers of condensation on display in this poem. The connections she draws between her grandfather and James Wright link writer, death, island (Squirrel Island, Montauk, Manhattan), invisible presence of God ("the tree has quietness in it; / quiet as the crucifix"), and cosmic game (in the bagful of nickels with which A.G.S. fed the Squirrel Island slot machine) to produce an elegiac love poem with a consistently effective tone, a surprising blend of pathos and humor.

Sexton ended her next volume of poems with "January Northeaster." These same elements — death, island, God — uncannily recombined later to yield "The Rowing Endeth," which became the last poem in Sexton's last book, *The Awful Rowing Toward God*. She dedicated it to James Wright.

In the fall of 1961, when the first group of Radcliffe Scholars congregated, *Time* put President Bunting on its cover and *Newsweek* ran an article on these "Women of Talent" featuring a photograph of Anne Sexton, feet propped high against a bookcase, with a pen in her hand, an open book in her lap, and a wide smile on her face. It was big news.

As a Radcliffe Scholar, Sexton was awarded an honorarium of $2000, paid in two installments. Since most of the fellowship recipients were married women supported by husbands, the issue of what the money was actually *for* became a major source of commentary in the national press. *Newsweek* was typical in playing up the information that most of the women had used the grant to hire help around the house. One "sent her willing children to summer camp," while another bought a new washing machine and dishwasher "to ease her household chores." Anne and Kayo decided to use some of the money to convert their back porch into a study. Anne was still using the dining room as her workplace, and she liked sitting in the middle of the house, but Kayo hated the clutter.

Sexton used the rest of her Radcliffe grant as the down payment on a swimming pool, which filled up most of the back yard. It was far from opulent; a canvas inset of the sort currently being peddled in the suburbs, it was about fifteen by twenty-five feet, and Anne and Kayo did most of the finishing work and replanting themselves. Yet this apparently frivolous use of the grant scandalized the Yankee director of the institute, and the story that Anne Sexton used her Radcliffe fellow-ship to build a swimming pool is still told in Boston circles. Sexton thought she was entitled to this luxury, and that it would help her as a writer. She hated to leave her house — that was one of the debilitating symptoms of her illness. "I can meet my goals if they are *writing* goals," she commented once, "because writing does not involve going out into the frightening world." Her home was her workplace, and the pool was an extension of the study. The long window in her little room looked across the pool fence to a freight spur that bordered the yard, where trains rumbled by twice a day, and beyond that to a golf course bounded by a tributary of the Charles River; but Sexton would pretend that the pool was a pond, the golf course a field edged by for-est. The Radcliffe Institute fellowship had given her a room of her own at last. Though she went to Cambridge for the group's regular gath-erings, she did all her writing in the new study, surrounded by books. "My books make me happy," she explained to an interviewer. "They sit there and say, 'Well, we got written and you can too.' "

As soon as the Radcliffe Scholars had been selected, they began to be studied. President Bunting appointed Alice Ryerson, who held a doctorate in education from Harvard, to collect information about the social backgrounds and aspirations of a sample of them, and an exit interview was conducted by Dr. Martha White, a psychologist. The interviews Sexton gave these researchers provide an index to the life narrative she was evolving for public consumption, which included not mere information but consciousness about the significance of her transformation from housewife into poet. Though she never affiliated herself with the politics of women's liberation, these interviews indi-cate that she viewed her own development as shaped by economic and social processes that defined women's lives. "Have you ever felt at a disadvantage in your profession because of being a woman?" Ryerson asked. "That's a very big subject. Oh terrific. Yes. Definitely" was Sex-ton's emphatic reply. "There are so many lady poets and they're al-most all so bad. [. . .] There are whole clubs of women poets: it's all right to be a poet if you're a woman. Therefore you can be a bad one. [. . .] Women don't strive to make anything real out of it. They just dabble in it." The difference between a dabbler and a professional? "Money helps: it's the only thing — in the society I live in."

Sexton had already established herself as a professional before com-ing to the institute, as many of the other Radcliffe Scholars had not. But she was the only one that year who held no college degree; most of the others had advanced degrees. "I used to go around saying 'I didn't go to college — I don't know anything — I'm very dumb and have a big mouth,' " she told White. "Now I say, 'I'm at the Radcliffe Institute.' It's just like I'd graduated." This made some difference to her standing in the Boston literary world. Sometimes it eased her relations with the people she met at social gatherings before and after her readings at various colleges, and in 1961 it inspired her to raise her speaking fees to $250, when $100 was regarded as pretty good. (Louis Untermeyer commented with admiration, "Only a few poets can obtain higher fees than that — and after many years of publishing and barnstorming.")

But her Radcliffe fellowship made the biggest difference, Sexton claimed, in her relations with her family. "It's a status symbol," she observed. "It immediately made what I was doing more respectable, to my husband. I wasn't taking so much from my family; I gave more back. You see, you always have a guilty feeling that it's selfish, because everyone says 'Why isn't it enough to be a wife and mother?' I still remember my mother-in-law saying 'Why aren't your husband and children enough — why don't you make it a hobby?' You have this guilt. But if you get this amount of money, then everyone immediately thinks you're respected, and beyond that, you're contributing." Years later, when she saw these remarks, Linda Sexton contested her mother's representation of family attitudes. She pointed out that Kayo and Billie had collaborated to give Anne time for writing poetry, even though they were baffled by it: Billie because she regarded the poetry as an invasion of family privacy, Kayo because it deprived him of Anne's company. Their resentment, she noted, did not make them ungenerous with help, and she doubted that the money Sexton received influenced their views of her career.

In any case, Sexton's comments about the impact of the Radcliffe grant on her family life do not reveal some of the urgent problems that were circulating under her optimism at the time. Nineteen sixty-one was to be the year she finally confronted one of the major difficulties in her daily life: the amount of authority she had delegated to her mother-in-law. Billie had mixed feelings about Anne's mounting success, and recognized that the Radcliffe grant would mean continuing sacrifices on the children's part. "She begged me to let her come to our house for two days a week," Sexton told Dr. Orne. "She's going to be crying over those poor kids whose mother has left and doesn't care about them; they aren't being loved. . . . Billie is hovering; I don't want to be selfish but there's no way to stop her — she's like a tide that comes in a little more each day."

Billie had a point. Sexton's illness had been extremely hard on Linda and Joy. Linda recalled being told by Billie from a young age that she must be very careful of her mother's feelings and never do anything that might unbalance her and make her sick. "I *always* lived on that brink of fear that she was going to fall apart and really kill herself," Linda said. Even at eight and six years old, the children felt enormously responsible for Anne's well-being, and Billie was worried about the pressures such a home life put them under. Joy remembered that her grandmother would come to their house at least three times a week, letting herself in with her own key to drop off shopping or clothes she had picked up from the cleaners, or sometimes just to bring a treat — a box of fresh jelly doughnuts from Hazel's Bakery or a carton of ice cream. Billie had the children overnight on many weekends, and, of course, they stayed with her whenever Anne needed a babysitter. Anne's ongoing rebellion against Billie's presence in their lives ignored the happiness and security Billie gave them. And it naturally occurred to Billie that Anne might spend more time with them

Anne Sexton with Joy.

and less on poetry now that she seemed to be feeling so much more stable.

Anne tended to handle the problem by sniping at her mother-in-law through Kayo. The tensions boiled over into a violent fight one Saturday night shortly after one of Kayo's long trips, and Sexton hobbled into Dr. Orne's office the next Tuesday wearing a neck brace. "It's just like Jekyll and Hyde," she explained to him. "There he is, my wonderful Kayo, so nice, then suddenly a terrifying monster. He completely loses control."

Anne and Kayo's fights had been a subject in her therapy for several years — at least since the occasion back in May 1958 when Kayo had become violently angry over Anne's involvement with poets and Anne had ripped up her manuscripts and thrown her typewriter across the room. Usually — as often as once a month — they fought after the cocktail hour had delayed dinner for several hours. Anne would be complaining, working up a grievance, badgering. Kayo would begin making dinner. Anne would taunt him from the sidelines, and he would fly into a rage and begin pummeling her. The children, who had been banished to their rooms so the adults could drink in peace, would fly down the stairs and push between them. As emotions ebbed, Kayo would return to his senses and be overwhelmed by remorse. Anne understood this pattern very well, and recognized the ways in which it fulfilled some of her deepest needs. "Oh my God, he loves me so after he beats me up, he's so sorry. It's so hard not to fall for this, he loves me so, and all the anger he's had for weeks, that has been coming out in small ways, comes out in a big way. Then, no matter how I hurt, it's gone, and he loves me."

Quite often they could not remember what got them started, but one time the outcome was different, Sexton told Dr. Orne, because there had been witnesses to help reconstruct the events. They had invited their neighbors Rita and Karl Ernst over for dinner. After they had all drunk numerous martinis, Kayo fixed steak and baked beans. Some remark by one of the guests elicited a dig from Anne: "Kayo always agrees with his mother — they are just alike." Kayo got red in the face and Anne ran from the room, slamming the door; Kayo went after her, threw her to the floor, and started choking her. The Ernsts separated them, and Joy rushed down from her room. It took a while for Anne to comfort her daughter and put her back to bed. When she rejoined the group, crying, Kayo was complaining about her. "So I started shrieking at the top of my lungs, 'You can get out of here! I own this house, you don't!' — and he ran back at me and the whole thing started over."

So far, this sorry incident had followed a familiar script. But after their friends left and they had calmed down, Kayo and Anne talked over what had happened; according to her, this was unusual. She described the conversation to Dr. Orne. Kayo had told her about how differently he felt on the road, where he "was somebody," and at home, where he felt like a nobody. He resented making breakfast for everyone and then dragging her out of bed; he hated the way she let the house go to hell. The pills were making it all worse, he said. But he was always afraid to tell her what he really felt, as he never knew how she would take his criticism.

Sexton told Dr. Orne that this recital gave her a new insight: the ideal wife Kayo was describing was actually his mother. Listening to him, she realized that he didn't remember what had started this fight: her crack about Kayo and Billie, which had touched a nerve in both herself and her husband. "You wouldn't kill your wife for not keeping the house clean enough; you would kill her for not being like your mother. When we married he thought I was going to be like his mother; and I used to be more like that, to keep a nice house. Now I'm kind of like a comrade — kind of amiable about disorder, where his mother isn't at all. The thing that really crushes me inside is that he thinks his mother is a better *mother* than I am. . . . It's one of the central issues of our marriage. If he wants to be married to me and wants me to be the mother of those children, then he's got to get rid of his mother in his mind."

Sexton prided herself both on hearing out Kayo's grievances and on resisting the role that she usually played in the aftermath of violence. Just as Kayo had been unusually searching and forthcoming about his feelings, so she too saw an opening for communication. "I took a piece of chalk and drew it across the kitchen floor. I said, 'That stands for divorce. Either you go into therapy or that's it.' " She told Dr. Orne that she felt she was relinquishing a valuable resource by making this suggestion: Kayo's willingness to play the role of the good parent for her. Each night before they went to sleep in their twin beds, he would sit beside her and smooth her hair, repeating, "Yes, you are my good girl" until she drifted to sleep. He was Nana then. At other times he was Daddy: returning from work, greeting the wife and children, he arranged around himself a recognizable family, where Anne was supposed to be the mommy and the wife — until he tied on an apron and became Mommy himself. In this and a score of other ways, he endowed her life with continuity and identity. She knew well how psychotherapy could disrupt this neurotic ecology by submitting the precious rituals to analysis and regressing their practitioner. "He's going to get confused, transferred, anxious," Sexton predicted. "I don't want that! I want him to be stable, sane. I don't want him to grow in a way, any more than I want to grow! I don't want these fights though. He's gotten worse as I've gotten better. . . . But this time I didn't crawl back to him to be loved when I was hurt. I separated us with a thought decision rather than an emotional decision."

Kayo did enter therapy, with Dr. Herbert Leiderman, a psychiatrist who had overseen Anne's treatment during Dr. Orne's absence in the summer of 1960. He saw Dr. Leiderman regularly for the next twenty-one months. As an immediate outcome, he brought his violence under control. Seven months after this episode, Sexton told Dr. Orne about dreams of being tied up in chains and otherwise wishing to be punished, and commented, "I can no longer act it out with Kayo — he no longer beats me. Therefore I start dreaming about it and it's clearer to me: when I feel depressed I keep wanting to hurt myself, but he no longer does it. I need to be punished, then forgiven. Never realized he was actually doing this for me."

By the time of Sexton's interviews with the Radcliffe Institute researchers, she had come to a certain appreciation of Kayo's point of view on the enormous changes they had both undergone in the past few years. "My husband can't see what good being a poet is. And I can't blame him. He's a businessman, and he didn't marry a poet. He just married a girl and wanted to make a home." Once she had started educating herself, however, there had been no turning back. "It opened a whole new world. I'd been all alone and I didn't know why. . . . Society isn't set up for somebody realizing yourself at twenty-eight. I really only started to live when I was twenty-nine. . . . But I couldn't have lived this long without being married. I mean, this is for me. To be married and have children. There's one more thing I have asked of life. That is, they've got to let me off to be a writer. And that's asking quite a bit of them."

Sexton referred to her children frequently in this interview as a source of "fulfillment." It might be thought, from the evidence, that she was merely paying lip service to one of the dominant conventions in her community, but by 1961 the four Sextons had begun to enjoy simply being together. When the Charles River froze solid near the golf course, they would all take out their toboggan or skates (Anne was pretty good on ice skates, her daughters recalled) and join the neighborhood in winter sports. In summer, the pool kept the children cool and became a neighborhood gathering place. Maxine Kumin came every day with her brood of three, and now and then the two women perched a typewriter at the pool's edge and brainstormed children's stories in a scheme to make their literary talents profitable. Kayo would come home after a hot day and take a plunge before lighting the barbecue; after dark, they liked to skinny-dip before bedtime.

This new strength was a source of happiness in Sexton's daily life; as she told Dr. Orne that year, "The only thing I'm sure of is that I wouldn't have gotten well if I hadn't had the kids, because they love me. They need me and make me feel like I am me, that they want me." Her confidence trickled to the reaches of her psyche where her oldest knowledge of love was stored, emerging in some of her strongest poems during the next few years. One, addressed to Linda and titled "The Fortress," was the poem she presented in her seminar for the Radcliffe Scholars.

The Scholars had decided to hold afternoon meetings at which they would present work in progress, and Sexton and Kumin were scheduled to open the series in February. Their status as artists rather awed the other women, one of whom recalled how they arrived at the first meeting like "exotic birds, both dressed in red, with black hair and shining eyes." A recording of their seminar shows better than any testimonial the complementarity of the public personae they had developed as poets. Kumin approached the occasion with self-professed stage fright but a firm pedagogical manner. In her reading she dovetailed poems from her children's books and her adult books, emphasizing technique. She supplied epigraphs and cited intellectual sources from Thoreau to Sartre and poetic models from Belloc to Starbuck. Despite her emphatic intellectualism and formality, the effect was warm and gracious — but Kumin gave the impression of not wanting to waste anyone's time.

Sexton, in contrast, opened with a claim that she was not very well prepared, that she usually gave formal readings to an audience seated at a distance, that she had simply thrown together some pages of notes "torn from a couple of readings." Between poems she apologized that her work was "so serious." Yet planted among her nervous and effusive comments were astute observations about the relations her poems seek with readers. "One of my secret instructions to myself as a poet is 'Whatever you do, don't be boring.' " Her purpose in a poem was to catch up the audience in an emotional attitude. Every poem owns itself, has its own voice, she claimed; the poet is like an actor, producing a character out of words. Many people confuse the personal voice of a poem with the poet who wrote it; however, Sexton pointed out, "I can be deeply personal, but often I'm not being personal about myself." As an example, she read "In the Deep Museum," in which she had adopted the voice of Christ in the tomb.

She ended by describing the way she had written a poem about a mother taking a lie-down with her daughter, making images from what they can see out the window.

> Outside, the bittersweet turns orange.
> Before she died, my mother and I picked those fat
> branches, finding orange nipples
> on the gray wire strands.
> We weeded the forest, curing trees like cripples.

The bittersweet of memory colors the poem, for "The Fortress" has to do with dangerous hidden connections between mother and daughter:

> I press down my index finger —
> half in jest, half in dread —
> on the brown mole
> under your left eye, inherited
> from my right cheek: a spot of danger
> where a bewitched worm ate its way through our soul.

In this poem, the disease that is dreaded is not madness, as in "The Double Image," but inevitable death. Breeding images serves as a defense, and also becomes a kind of cure.

> I cannot promise very much.
> I give you the images I know.
> Lie still with me and watch.
> A pheasant moves
> by like a seal, pulled through the mulch
> by his thick white collar. He's on show

like a clown. He drags a beige feather that he removed,
one time, from an old lady's hat.
We laugh and we touch.
I promise you love. Time will not take away that.

Sexton both tells about and shows the healing power of art, in the
language of finding the bittersweet fruit as "orange nipples." The dead
mother who haunts the poem, deprived of her breast by cancer, glows
along the fence in a radiant afterimage, feeding the daughter's hunger.
"Fat arm" was a term of disgust Mary Gray connected to her mutilation by surgery. "Fat" occurs at the end of the line in the poem's
fourth stanza, a gun not fired again, so to speak, until the last stanza
(fat-hat-that), where plumage is restored to a bird by the poet's witty

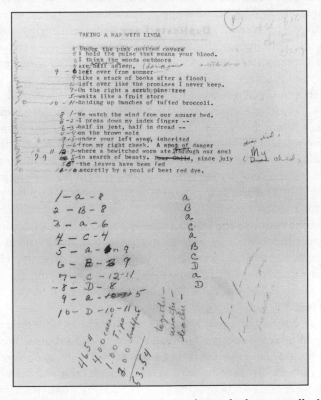

*Manuscript of "Taking a Nap with Linda," which eventually became
"The Fortress."*

assemblage of rhymes (much-watch-mulch-touch). Time will not take away that.

"You could say that Radcliffe was an approving mother," Sexton said of her years at the institute. In the work she presented at the seminar, one of her most accomplished poems on the subject of motherhood, she wrote for the first time (probably the only time) about her affiliation as a writer to her mother and to image-making as a form of mothering. Significantly, "The Fortress" is addressed to Linda Gray: to the legacy of writer in the family, the "gray . . . strand" that weaves through the generations from Arthur Gray Staples through Mary to Anne and on to Linda. Language, the writer's magic power, "cures" with names and images that undo the work of the worm.

Sexton wrote "The Fortress" in a phase of creative exhilaration during her first weeks at Radcliffe. But she hadn't abandoned her goal of finding someone to oversee her progress as a writer of short stories. She read avidly, looking for models. Shirley Jackson appealed to her: she had read somewhere that Jackson wrote " 'like a witch with a broomstick dipped in adder's blood,' " and felt "God damn it, that's what I want them to say about me. I want to scare people." She read Henry Miller's *Tropic of Cancer,* and liked it "because it's not so much a novel as a spit in the eye." J. D. Salinger's *Franny and Zooey* came out to enormous fanfare and immediate best sellerdom; Sexton seized on it. Reading it made her feel sad and wise, she said, but the morning she finished it she received a fan letter from a girl who was having an illegitimate baby and was turning to her for advice because in her poetry she seemed so mature and so wise. This coincidence made Sexton rethink her enthusiasm for Salinger's book. "Writers are such phonies: they sometimes have wise insights but they don't live by them at all. That's what writers are like. When you read what they write, whether it's their poems or their letters, you think they know something, but usually they are just messes. I think about this girl, and feel sentimental and lost."

Yet she envied Salinger's reputation. His were exactly the readers she hoped to reach: people numbed by life in the suburbs, nostalgic for childhood. No poet could hope for sales at Salinger's level, but Sexton thought she could probably write prose on a par with his. "I think you can move people more with a story than with poems. *Catcher in the Rye* speaks for its time, to many people," she observed. "And I have a best-seller mind, I'm really rather ordinary. I am popular with the masses: I have the common touch, I write about the middle class!"

As it happened, shortly after *Newsweek* featured Sexton as a star of the Radcliffe Institute, *The New Yorker* offered her a coveted "first reading" agreement. Though she spoke cynically about the literary taste of the magazine's editors, she shared the view that Sylvia Plath had confided to her journal back in 1959: for a certain class of writer, professional success could be measured by the thinness of the acceptance letters and the fatness of the checks mailed by *The New Yorker* to its lucky contributors. More important to the progress of her career, the *New Yorker* contract made her a peer of the very writers she hoped to be compared with. Shirley Jackson and J. D. Salinger were *New Yorker* writers; so was John Updike, whom she read with great interest. While Sexton had been prowling for models, the magazine had printed several poems by Updike, plus a couple of first-person stories that read more like autobiography than fiction. Four years younger than Sexton, Updike had not yet produced the prose that by the mid-1960s would establish him as an important writer. But he had taken the stride Sexton was in training for: it seemed *The New Yorker* would publish anything he wrote. That fall the magazine's slick pages of Christmas advertising were punctuated by witty cartoons about the Russians and fallout shelters and astronauts and the Chinese and psychiatrists and the Bomb; through these pages ribboned Updike's clever, ravishing, family-haunted prose. This was Sexton territory. Impulsively, she wrote asking him to give her a private tutorial on the short story. Updike replied graciously that he didn't wish to "pose as having any useful information" about writing. He advised her to trust her gifts, work out her stories as best she could, and let editors at magazines supply the criticism. This was good advice for somebody else, but Sexton's method of composition required a dialogue with her critic — indeed, required the critical equivalent of a countertransference.

Actually, Sexton knew very well who she wanted to work with, but he was not in Boston. "If Saul Bellow was teaching around here I'd be in his class," she told Dr. Orne. "You have to be careful who you study with. I have to be great, I want my work to last. I don't have time to start over — I want to leave the imprint of my personality carved in marble." Bellow's *Henderson the Rain King* remained for her a talismanic, dangerous book which she reread every time she grew restless with life in the suburbs. She called Bellow "the grown-up's Salinger,"

with a gift for comedy she wished she could emulate. Sexton considered *Henderson* "the greatest American novel written since Faulkner," and she told Dr. Orne that she thought Bellow had summarized
in one line what all of psychotherapy was about: " 'All my decay has
taken place upon a child.' " She worked up the courage to write Bellow a fan letter, and was overjoyed by his reply, a warm acknowledgment that "we seem to have entered into each other's minds." Sexton
said, "It was like getting a letter from Shakespeare — for me he is the
greatest living writer. My copy of this damn book *Henderson* is all
underlined: that is the way *I* feel, that is it!" Bellow had circled two
sentences from his novel in progress, *Herzog,* and labeled them "MES-
SAGE": "With one long breath, caught and held in his chest, he
fought his sadness over his solitary life. 'Don't cry, you idiot! Live or
die, but don't poison everything.' " Five years later, Sexton was to
adopt this message as the title of her third book, *Live or Die.*

Right after Thanksgiving, during several days of anxiety while Kayo
was away, Sexton found herself unexpectedly in just the frame of
mind to try her hand at fiction. Normally she could not write while
Kayo was out of town; as often as possible, she would put her energy
into a brief love affair. But during this particular absence she har-
nessed the energy in a short story titled "Cigarettes and Butternut
Squash," which she wrote for Linda, who was home with the flu.
Reading current magazines that published writers she knew personally, Sexton noticed how factual the stories were under the disguise of
fiction. "I had been reading *The New Yorker* — I decided I would just
use my exact life!" Nor was it necessary to have much of a plot; a
story was often based on what she described as a "seizure of awareness," a sudden deepening of ordinary life by irrational conviction: "I
have such seizures of awareness! Maybe that's what makes me a
writer: once in a while I take that seizure and write it. Then it won't
go away."

"Cigarettes and Butternut Squash" had a clever structure that
embedded a child's story in an autobiographical frame which captured the strangeness of Sexton's mood at day's end. She apparently
never revised it or sent it out for publication, but the momentum of
writing it carried over into another prose piece she wrote rapidly at
the beginning of December, "The Last Believer." This dealt with
memories of Christmas morning, when the head of the household
would stage a dawn performance as Saint Nick, assisted by all the
women in the family. Now that Ralph and Mary Gray were dead,

Anne and Blanche and Jane perpetuated this ritual. Linda and Joy remembered how their mother would come to their room while it was still dark on Christmas morning to wake them; all three would sit on the toybox at the window, straining to see through the branches of the trees. Then Anne would say thrillingly, "There he is, there he is!" pointing to the sky, "and we would say 'Oh, there he is!' convinced we had seen him," Linda recalled. "And then we would hear his voice below, calling 'Ho! Ho! Ho!' " In "The Last Believer," Sexton beautifully captured the thrill of illusion this charade produced in her own childish self, the family warmth it kindled, and the complex emotions she felt as a teenager permitted behind the scenes. The story evokes the problem of what Christmas was *about* for her in 1961; it manages to convey, inexplicitly, a parent's guilty struggle with unresolved religious belief when confronted by a child's thoughtful questions.

Talking to Linda was like talking to her own soul, Sexton remarked to Dr. Orne. Like other work she was writing that fall, "The Last Believer" was inspired by a jolt of identification with the daughter's position, with the eight-year-old in herself, and with an acute sense of having arrived at a midpoint in her life. The ninth of November brought Sexton's thirty-third birthday, and around that time, conscious of other important anniversaries, she began arranging poems in the manuscript of her second book, to be titled *All My Pretty Ones*. James Wright had suggested the title, derived from MacDuff's speech in Shakespeare's *Macbeth,* upon learning of the slaughter of his wife and children: "All my pretty ones? / Did you say all?"

The era of her parents' death returned to mind often as Sexton sorted her new poems into five sections and pored over discarded manuscripts for work worthy of revision. The book had a tight structure. Section I was thematically elegiac, revealing Sexton's deep identification with the dead. Section II contained religious poetry. Section III contained only one poem, "The Fortress," which she intended to dedicate to Dr. Orne (he dissuaded her, quoting wisdom he had learned from his own mentor, Elvin Semrad: "Unlike other doctors, psychiatrists are entitled to only one form of currency: money. Everything else costs the patient too much"). Section IV consisted of an assortment of poems she couldn't fit elsewhere, while Section V was inscribed to James Wright in the guise of "Comfort, who was actually my grandfather." So the end of the book looked back to its opening: the dead live again in projections onto the living, which makes both the living and the dead infinitely losable.

While working out this final arrangement for the book, Sexton became acutely suicidal. Kayo usually traveled a lot in November, adding a hunting excursion with "the boys" at the opening of deer season to his usual round of business trips. This year his hunting trip coincided with a professional meeting that took Dr. Orne out of town for the weekend. These trips were arranged and confirmed weeks in advance, but no amount of discussion prepared Sexton for the panic she felt when Saturday came. Terrified, she phoned Kayo's therapist, Dr. Leiderman. She knew she was breaking a lot of rules by consulting her husband's doctor, "but not knowing what to do precipitated me into an emergency," she explained.

He "helped me wait [for Kayo's return], not kill myself," she later told Dr. Orne. "I was asking to be put in the hospital, but what he did was keep me going hour by hour — I really wanted to go to Westwood but he said, 'I would like you to wait. If you can't wait, call me.' " She phoned him frequently that day, and that evening she left the children with Sandy Robart's family and went to his office to see him in person. The reassurance she received, however, evaporated the minute she left the office. She drove to a restaurant, ordered a glass of beer, and began taking what she intended to be an overdose of pills. She had brought her manuscript, so while she sipped the beer and washed down pills, she madly scribbled notes for Maxine Kumin, indicating changes she wanted made before the book was published. "It was a senseless kind of thing," she said lamely to Dr. Orne; she had brought the wrong pills. Eventually she drove home, vomited, and asked Sandy Robart to spend the night with her.

Sexton faltered through the following day, making almost hourly telephone calls to Dr. Leiderman, but by evening she felt she simply must go to the hospital. "I had everything all set up. I was so nervous I scooted the kids to bed at six o'clock; knew Kayo would be home around eight; I couldn't stand them any longer. . . . Sat at my typewriter, and I had the glass of milk and I had the pills. I was very nervous — if the cat moved in the house I would start to sweat. Finally I turned off the light. It was almost too late to run; I was afraid he'd catch me in the driveway. So I did something rather practical. Instead of taking the pills that would kill me I took Deprol [sleeping pills]. Finally they calmed me down; then he came home."

In retrospect, she was shocked and puzzled at the vehemence of her panic. She had not been invaded by such emotions for a year or more, and had come to believe that this kind of incident was behind her. Yet she also recognized — "intellectually," as she put it — that neither of these pill-taking sessions had been a real suicide attempt. "It was a *substitute:* it's the same symbolic act, but there's a difference between taking something that will kill you and something that will kill you momentarily. The 'kill me' pills are very special — I stole them from my parents and I have no way of getting any more." These were Nembutal, the fast-acting barbiturate, which is lethal in relatively small doses. Sexton had taken them from her mother and father's medicine chest after their deaths: "I raided the poisons." She told Dr. Orne she usually carried them in her pocketbook, in order to be prepared to kill herself anytime she was in the mood. "If I didn't have Deprol and Nodular as substitutes I'm sure I'd be dead by now — get rid of that girl out in the suburbs!"

Sexton staggered through the process of preparing *All My Pretty Ones* for publication, and at last sent it to Houghton Mifflin at the end of November. She told Dr. Orne, "You said to me one time, if you kill yourself you won't live (though it's one of my ideas that I'll be reborn). But you see, I've taken care of that 'live' part by writing my poems. I don't have time to learn to write short stories that will live — but I've made it with the poems now, I've hung on all those times! That was going to be the reason why I lived, anyway." She knew the new book was a very good one, and to Dr. Orne she confided her hope that it might even set her among the great: "Kafka, Dostoevsky are great because of the effect of their work. It's still going on; they are dead but it's still going on with the same impact as if they were alive. Their lives were messes but it doesn't make any difference — what they *did* was more important than a good life." Neither mental health nor the world's acclaim was necessary to the production of great work, she concluded. "I might kill myself tomorrow even if I had all the acclaim of a Salinger — matter of fact acclaim might be difficult to handle." The only source of greatness was the writer's ability "to go down deep" into the unconscious. "You can call it craft; it doesn't matter how you get there, but it has to dive down. That's what I try to do in a poem, though I don't always succeed. I have ambition I can grab, I can touch it."

9

POETRY AND THE
UNCONSCIOUS
1962

BY THE TIME *All My Pretty Ones* was in press, cultivation of her recently discovered talent had literally remade Anne Sexton as a person, turning her into someone self-created in the first-person voice of her poetry. Audiences encountered that vivid speaker on the printed page or in Sexton's marvelous, throaty vocalization at readings. Yet the published version of herself was no longer the "I" of the poet's living pursuit of words and rhythms. This conundrum of identity lay vividly before Sexton in the new year, while she spent hours smoking and twirling her hair with a forefinger, steering between the rock — trying to write poems — and the hard place — trying to write poems that didn't sound like poems she had already written. In retrospect, two important influences can be detected in the direction her art was to take: a six-month crisis in her therapy, which focused on problems of intimacy, especially intimacy with women, and a growing ambition to write for the stage.

The therapeutic crisis developed innocently enough out of Dr. Orne's advance notice that he planned to spend two weeks in Mexico at the beginning of February. "If Kayo would take me to Florida for two weeks I wouldn't mind so much, I could pretend *I* left *you*," Sexton joked. Faced with the prospect of desertion — that's how it felt — by both her doctor and her husband (who was away on business), she spent much of her therapy time in trance during the early weeks of 1962, weeping harshly. Waking at the end of the session, she would be shocked and embarrassed. "The feeling is so violent — I wanted to cry like this when my mother was dying, and I couldn't. . . . My father used to go on trips, just like Kayo. I was brought up on this same cycle; Kayo calls on the same customers as my father did, Kayo is now where my father used to go."

Her father was frequently in her thoughts that winter. Reviewing some of her old therapy tapes renewed her painful recollection of those events she had described to Dr. Orne: how her father had come into her room, and what Nana saw when she peered through the door, and how Nana then went crazy and said Anne wasn't Anne anymore. In trance, her accounts of this episode grew increasingly detailed. But the particulars varied significantly from her previous accounts; increasingly, they focused on Nana.

Sexton discovered that in some way Dr. Orne (and Kayo, and James Wright) played "Nana" when she was in the grip of that "fierce unreasonable emotion" of loss which only one person could undo: Nana, or, now, her substitutes. "It must be Nana who leaves, then everything is disorganized, then Nana who returns and everything is organized." Sexton acted out Nana's "return" by retreating into girlhood. In the doctor's office, this often took the form of wanting "to curl up and sigh 'Don't leave me.' " At home, the emotional dynamic she yearned for was captured in the refrain she demanded nightly from Kayo while he stroked her head: "Yes, Anne, you are a good girl." She believed that these safe feelings of dependency on Nana had been disrupted by sexual feelings for her father.

A.S.: I never want to go beyond that moment, I want to lie on the couch and be with Nana, where I was loved. . . . I wouldn't have stayed married to Kayo for all these years: what he means to me is that he's like Nana. Therefore you must be Nana.

Dr.: And if you became aware of sexual feelings about me?

A.S.: I must have seemed more awful to Nana than I ever was to my father. . . . I passed out all the time with Jim because those two feelings kept colliding: I fell in love with Jim through his letters, he was my Nana, my soul; but he was a man, so what did I offer him? He had all the skills, all the feelings of my father, part sexy and part prude.

Sexton worked on very little of this material with Dr. Orne in January, and she made a point of not taking notes when she listened to the tapes afterward. But after Dr. Orne had been away for a week, she made an appointment with his mother. Sexton told Dr. Brunner-Orne about the material that had been coming up, saying that her most intense feelings revolved around the process of leave-and-return and that she recognized that she associated this with Nana before and after the "discovery scene" she returned to in trances. She thought the consultation with Dr. Brunner-Orne helped her get through Dr. Orne's absence. "She is very good for my ego," Sexton reported to Dr. Orne when he returned. "Maybe she gave me permission to love you? I told her, 'I guess I have more of an Oedipal conflict than I thought,' and she said 'Oh yes.' "

During this time, Sexton was letting the energy of these themes feed her creativity. In the weeks before Dr. Orne's departure she began attending a playwriting workshop with her neighbor Eleanor Boylan, who staged puppet shows through Boston's Children's Theater and was also affiliated with the Charles Playhouse, which sponsored the workshop. After attending only a couple of meetings, Sexton was hooked. She splurged on "forty dollars' worth of avant-garde plays in paperback" and began reviewing her 1961 journal of therapy notes for ideas. Once she hit on a plot, she drafted a first version in two weeks. "Four scenes, three characters," she reported to Robert Lowell. "I was seized with it completely."

Titled *The Cure,* the play developed some of the religious questions Sexton raised in *All My Pretty Ones.* A suicidal woman named Daisy cannot rid herself of a guilty memory that as a child she killed her whole family by running away from home on the night of a fire that destroyed them all. She has begun consulting a psychiatrist, Dr. Alex. As the play opens, Daisy is telling Dr. Alex that she has been visited by Christ. She thinks that Christ has come to challenge the psychiatrist's "psychological explanations" for her fears and to offer salvation from her guilty existence. "I'm no more a woman than . . . than Christ was a man!" Daisy cries. After consulting a priest, only to receive the same unbelieving attitude toward her visions, Daisy kills herself.

Eleanor Boylan made an enthusiastic collaborator: "I'll do the priest, you do the psychiatrist!" Boylan had cheerfully low expectations of priestly behavior, and the character she wrote helped lighten the play's grim action. *The Cure* was given a staged reading by repertory actors associated with the Charles Playhouse, but their reactions were not favorable: "Very interesting, but not a play," said the director, Michael Murray. Discouraged, Sexton stuffed her copy into the glove compartment of her VW bug and forgot about it for three years — or so she claimed when she told the story later. But the effort to make creative use of the experience of transference burgeoned powerfully in the poems of her next book, *Live or Die* (1966), and in *Mercy Street,* the play that emerged eventually from *The Cure.*

Meanwhile, Sexton was also beginning to develop skills as a teacher. As Radcliffe Scholars were expected to contribute to the education of undergraduates, Sexton proposed an informal poetry workshop that would meet weekly (on Thursdays, after her appointment with her hairdresser) in a student lounge and be open to women and men. The class got going in the fall semester, then picked up again after the Christmas break. About fifteen students showed up, half of them from Harvard. Among these was Jeffrey Moussaieff Masson, who later gained considerable notoriety with his book *Assault on Truth: Freud's Suppression of the Seduction Theory* (1984). In 1962 he was in his second year at Harvard, trying to become a poet. He eagerly joined Sexton's workshop at its first meeting, and later recalled that she was already an effective teacher.

After the first student presented his poem I brashly raised my hand, thinking I would impress her. I said, "This poem has the naiveté of a picture of a puppy dog with its head out the window, tail wagging." I was a terribly young nineteen — an awful combination of arrogance and ignorance. She took me down very quickly. She was not cruel, but she told me that she did not want people hurting each other's feelings. She went on to make extensive criticism of the poem, and I realized that I was completely outclassed and outdistanced. I was struck at how good she was at that; very personal. This I found impressive — everything at Harvard had been terribly *im*personal, patrician. I'd found what I came for, a place where people talked about their feelings. At the same time I realized I had no talent at that kind of subjectivity. I was not a good poet, and would never thrive in that world.

Masson dropped out of the class after only a few sessions. Sexton continued meeting with the group through May, with mixed feelings about its success. Students told her that she seemed to be trying too hard, but her own view was that *they* didn't try hard enough.

Continually satisfying to her, though, was John Holmes's ongoing workshop, the model on which she based her own teaching. The group had teetered on the brink of disintegration when George Starbuck departed for Rome the previous September. Then Holmes learned that Theodore and Renée Weiss were visiting at MIT in Cambridge for the academic year, and invited them to take Starbuck's place. A literary couple — she a translator, he a scholar-poet — the

Weisses had founded *The Quarterly Review of Literature,* a little magazine that reflected the cosmopolitan scope of their taste. They tipped the balance toward the conservative elements in the workshop, represented by the Yankee sobriety of John Holmes and the intellectuality of Maxine Kumin. But together they turned out to be a great replacement for Starbuck, keeping the quotient of joking ebullience high and technical questions constantly in the foreground. Ted Weiss noted that Sexton, trained in the workshop and dependent on the literary marketplace for criticism, rarely used literary points of reference in either her poetry or her critique of other poets, but relied a good deal on Kumin for instruction.

The whole group celebrated when Holmes's *The Fortune Teller* was nominated for the National Book Award that year. Holmes felt that he had finally come into his own as a poet, and he was particularly proud of having created this intimate little institution that had sponsored so much good writing over the three-plus years of its existence. That winter he embarked on "The Five," a long poem in praise of workshops, especially the workshop that he had attended back in the 1940s with John Ciardi, Richard Eberhart, May Sarton, and Richard Wilbur, all of whom then lived in or near Boston. He was deeply disappointed when the National Book Award went to Alan Dugan's *Poems* rather than to his own collection, which had been so long in the making. He seemed to feel the disappointment with his whole body, as he suffered a lot of pain from undiagnosable complaints that winter. In March he turned an ache in his throat into a metaphor for poetry: "He looks across his audience, / Hearing the lines come to him as he wants them, bare, true, / Real as an ache in the bones or the throat. He is a poem's voice." In May, this ache was diagnosed as cancer. By the middle of June, Holmes was dead.

Sexton and Kumin were shocked by his rapid decline and terrible death. "We were so sure it was psychological — he's only in his fifties," Sexton told Dr. Orne. She felt sad that she had never found a satisfactory way to communicate either her anger or her gratitude to Holmes. "I learned to write from John, not Robert Lowell," she reflected. "That he wouldn't approve of me was something I couldn't bear."

Of course Sexton had brought all her transference poems to the workshop that winter and spring ("The Wallflower," "And One for My Dame," "Consorting with Angels," "Mother and Jack and the Rain," "The Sun") — fittingly, typed on stationery salvaged from her

father's business, under the letterhead "R. C. Harvey Company Du-
plicate Copy." John Holmes's death slipped neatly into place in her
imagination as the loss of yet another father, and the elegy she wrote
for him, "Somewhere in Africa," bore the imprint of literary values
that the workshop fostered and that she had long felt devalued her.

Must you leave, John Holmes, with the prayers and psalms
you never said, said over you? Death with no rage
to weigh you down? Praised by the mild God, his arm
over the pulpit, leaving you timid, with no real age,

whitewashed by belief, as dull as the windy preacher!
Dead of a dark thing, John Holmes, you've been lost
in the college chapel, mourned as father and teacher,
mourned with piety and grace under the University Cross.

Your last book unsung, your last hard words unknown,
abandoned by science, cancer blossomed in your throat,
rooted like bougainvillea into your gray backbone,
ruptured your pores until you wore it like a coat.

The thick petals, the exotic reds, the purples and whites
covered up your nakedness and bore you up with all
their blind power. I think of your last June nights
in Boston, your body swollen but light, your eyes small

as you let the nurses carry you into a strange land.
. . . If this is death and God is necessary let him be hidden
from the missionary, the well-wisher and the glad hand.
Let God be some tribal female who is known but forbidden.

Let there be this God who is a woman who will place you
upon her shallow boat, who is a woman naked to the waist,
moist with palm oil and sweat, a woman of some virtue
and wild breasts, her limbs excellent, unbruised and chaste.

Let her take you. She will put twelve strong men at the oars
for you are stronger than mahogany and your bones fill
the boat high with fruit and bark from the interior.
She will have you now, you whom the funeral cannot kill.

John Holmes, cut from a single tree, lie heavy in her hold
and go down that river with the ivory, the copra and the gold.

The decor of this poem owed a good deal to Saul Bellow's *Henderson the Rain King,* set in a mythical Africa. The poem also tapped

Sexton's ambivalent love for the fatherly Holmes. It praised his integrity ("cut from a single tree") and claimed for him the paradise allocated to the tribe of poets. Yet it also distinguished the censor from the artist in him. Criticizing her work, Holmes had invariably used the words "childish" and "selfish"; he saw her poems only as referential to the person, whom he deplored. Holmes thought poetry should take a moral stance toward feelings, but Sexton used feelings, rhymes, and rhythms to generate imagery. She relied on the poem's dramatic situation to give coherence to sometimes hallucinatory combinations. This made Holmes and Sexton very different poets, he sententious where she was imagistic.

Yet Holmes's gentlemanly disapproval had forced Sexton to clarify this difference for herself; in defying him, she had acquired perspective on herself as a poet of the unconscious, the "known but forbidden." By the time she wrote "Somewhere in Africa," she had achieved genuine separation from all her early mentors — De Snodgrass, Robert Lowell, James Wright — who were also, of course, censors. She had acquired a public persona and a voice distinctively her own. In "Somewhere in Africa," the poet carried her censors and teachers to their final resting place on her terms.

The self-conscious thematic use of the "tribal female" in the elegy for Holmes was probably stimulated by an invitation Sexton had received earlier that spring from the editor of Harper's to contribute to a special issue on "the American Female," although he wasn't really sure what he was after. Should the work be by the American female or for the American female? Harper's accepted "Mother and Jack and the Rain." Perhaps the editor recognized Sexton's allusion in this poem to Virginia Woolf's feminist essay A Room of One's Own, but most likely he did not. In 1962 there was no "feminist criticism" that celebrated "women's poetry."

Yet by 1962 Sexton had begun to experience the interesting social role of contemporary American woman poet as an identity with a life of its own, being shaped for her by the reception of her work. When All My Pretty Ones came out in October, it was her direct treatment of the female body in such poems as "The Operation" that attracted the interest of reviewers. The most positive notice came from Charles Simmons in The Saturday Review. He observed thematic similarities in the work of Sexton and Simone de Beauvoir, whose ground-breaking feminist treatise The Second Sex had recently been published in

English: "Mrs. Sexton sings with frightening intensity the feelings Simone de Beauvoir discusses dispassionately." Regarding "The Operation," Simmons noted, "Until recently neither women nor men made literature from this kind of experience. Now that it is possible, women have used the option more than men. Some of them, in fact, seem to have been waiting in the wings, to talk at last about the untalked about. Not everyone enjoys this kind of writing, although often, as in 'The Operation,' it is clear, touching and human — qualities one might think guaranteed good writing."

James Dickey, however, considered *All My Pretty Ones* "contrived" and worse. Reviewing the book for the *New York Times Book Review,* he lambasted Sexton: "It would be hard to find a writer who dwells more insistently on the pathetic and disgusting aspects of bodily experience, as if this made the writing more real, and it would also be difficult to find a more hopelessly mechanical approach to reporting those matters than the one she employs." His strong distaste perhaps masked a morbid fascination; his own work, culminating in the novel *Deliverance* (1970), was shortly to reveal similar obsessions.

Sexton's own attitudes toward "the woman question" had at first been strongly influenced by Robert Lowell's seminar, where the "lady poets" were consistently distinguished from the "greats." Perhaps she detected a bit of defensiveness in Lowell's concern to keep his distance from the ladies; to Alice Ryerson, the Radcliffe interviewer, she expressed the view that poetry was *essentially* feminine, so a female writer had to compensate by avoiding subjects too identified with women. The best compliment a female poet could receive, she said in 1962, "is 'she writes like a man.' " By 1969, however, she had changed her mind; asked to comment on the goals of a feminist journal, she wrote to the editor, "My comment is this: 'As long as it can be said about a woman writer, "She writes like a man" and that woman takes it as a compliment, we are in trouble.' " Potent influences on this change occurred during Sexton's years at the Radcliffe Institute, which introduced her to feminist ideas, and in her daily dialogues with Maxine Kumin: in private they could tailor feminist insights to the particularities of their situations as writers who were women, as women who were much alike, and as women raising daughters to have high expectations of life.

Sexton also responded gratefully to the praise of other women poets with whom she had much in common; from them, notice of the specially female aspects of her work didn't seem compromising. She sent an advance copy of *Pretty Ones* to Sylvia Plath, whose thank-you note was more than polite: "I was absolutely stunned and delighted with the new book. It is superbly masterful, womanly in the greatest sense, and so blessedly *un-literary*." Sexton was also grateful when May Swenson sent Houghton Mifflin a strong letter in response to the publisher's request for a blurb. Elizabeth Bishop was also asked for a blurb, but she wrote to Sexton instead. In *Bedlam*, she said, "You began right off [. . .] speaking in an authentic voice of your own; this is very rare and has saved you a great deal of time!" Tactfully suppressing reservations she had earlier expressed to Lowell, Bishop found the poems of *Pretty Ones* equally authentic, "harrowing, awful, very real — and very good." The poet Denise Levertov echoed this theme: "Your new book is full of such wild and beautiful things; it's really exciting."

All during the winter and spring of 1962, Sexton's work with Dr. Orne was building toward a big explosion, as he pressured her to take a more analytical role in treatment. During January — the anniversary of their taping routine — he asked her to go over her notes from the preceding year's tapes and select a couple of important sessions to review with him. She did her homework but returned protesting that just as at Brandeis in 1960, when she had been reading novels under Philip Rahv's direction, "all I can do is be emotional about it, the unconscious material overwhelms me — I don't have this kind of mind, I don't know how to be objective." The process of reviewing her notes on old tapes did send her into a flight of free association on her typewriter, however, and she captured the core problem in a very few phrases:

I would like to lie down beside you and go to sleep, and you will never leave me because I am a good girl. But I can't have sex with you because I can't have sex with Nana. My father was a king. The king can have sex with anyone. Don't say anything that will scare me or I will run away. I want to run but I am scared. Don't move because I am scared of things changing. I am so scared that my fingers hurt, my arm hurts, my stomach hurts. I pass out, for one thing, to get rid of my body. I'm myself, I tell you, that means my body is itself, that my soul has left it alone. I am going out of my mind, is there no place that is calm, a pool of milk. I want my mother, I hate my mother. Nana was safe. Nana was crazy. Daddy was drunk. I am a little bitch.

To "lie down and go to sleep" alongside an unchanging "you" was a goal Sexton accomplished with increasing frequency by passing out in therapy sessions in April, May, and early June. Increasingly Dr. Orne's calm edged into exasperation, and increasingly the closure of such appointments took place out of hearing: the tape would run out before the session ended, leaving Sexton with "no tape to go back to as a reality." The doctor's objective stance became a red flag as he pushed her to resume taking notes on her therapy tapes (her note-taking had languished after the flurry of reviewing old tapes) as part of the task of integrating and mixing aspects of herself. Sexton resisted this chore until he became very insistent.

A climax in the struggle occurred in the middle of June. Sexton went in for her regular Thursday evening appointment. At the beginning of the hour she told Dr. Orne she was going to have trouble leaving. Later she went into a trance. Her inability to waken made Dr. Orne impatient, and he slammed a book down on his desk; this gesture woke her, and she left his office.

Then she took her car to a drive-in restaurant (she had never done this before) and ordered a carton of milk from the carhop. She returned to the empty office Dr. Brunner-Orne usually occupied, since Dr. Orne was at work upstairs in another office. Stretching on the couch, she drank the milk, then passed out. "There I was curled up like a little girl, right back in the womb, on your mother's couch!" When Dr. Orne came into the room, he found her unconscious and impossible to rouse by saying her name, counting, or clapping his hands, the usual methods of waking her. He then slapped her cheek, and she woke. Very angry, he scolded her for leaving him "no room." She burst into tears and cried bitterly. As she sobbed, he explained that he had obligations that her behavior interfered with: to other patients, and to his home life.

It was late. Sexton went home, but she felt "shattered" and couldn't stop crying. Fishing in her pockets for tissues, she found a slip of paper on which she had transcribed a few lines from a poem by Rimbaud: "*Ma faim, Anne, Anne, / Fuis sur ton âne.*" "My publisher sent Rimbaud to me in prose translation, I don't read French, but all of a sudden saw my name — 'Anne, Anne' just hopped out of the French, my name — and the rest of the poem is about hunger." "Flee on your donkey": the message seemed to have arrived in her pocket as a direct gift from another mad poet who turned degradation into art. Around midnight she called Westwood Lodge and asked to be admitted; Dr.

Orne agreed, and Sexton drove herself to the hospital, where she rapidly grew calmer. She stayed only a day and a half, spending most of the time writing up the experience in a new poem she titled "Flee on Your Donkey."

During their next appointment, Dr. Orne told her he faulted himself for producing this crisis by pushing her to get well and by failing to inform her of the constraints his other obligations placed on his response to her symptoms. "I have liabilities as a therapist at this point in the relationship," he owned. "I expect you to try to work all the time. Might be better if I didn't make this demand." In the next few weeks they renegotiated some of the terms of treatment, with Sexton occasionally claiming that she was contemplating a change of doctors, still considering a psychoanalysis. She felt stalled in the same old symptoms. "I haven't even gone to the library in years now!" she complained. "I have Maxine — I've just found more people to use, probably." Throughout July she drifted in the doldrums of waiting for Dr. Orne to take his summer leave, and then to return; only when that problem was solved could she begin to work, maybe, on getting well. "Will you leave it up to me whether I get well or not?" she asked. "I know that if I push you, it won't work," he answered.

The poem that emerged from this crisis was in many ways a direct response to the unresolved issues of Sexton's therapy. This is the way it begins:

FLEE ON YOUR DONKEY
Ma faim, Anne, Anne,
Fuis sur ton âne . . . Rimbaud

Because there was no other place
to flee to,
I came back to the scene of the disordered senses,
came back last night at midnight,
arriving in the thick June night
without luggage or defenses,
giving up my car keys and my cash,
keeping only a pack of Salem cigarettes
the way a child holds on to a toy.
I signed myself in where a stranger
puts the inked-in X's —
for this is a mental hospital,
not a child's game.

Today an intern knocks my knees,
testing for reflexes.
Once I would have winked and begged for dope.
Today I am terribly patient.
Today crows play black-jack
on the stethoscope.

Everyone has left me
except my muse,
that good nurse.
She stays in my hand,
a mild white mouse.

A long, ambitious poem — 240 lines in its final version — "Flee on
Your Donkey" is a parable about the way Sexton channeled unconscious processes into artistic forms. It can be seen as a watershed in
her art, first, because it acknowledges that Anne Sexton the person
does not expect to get "well" in any ordinary sense — treatment can
educate but not cure her, it says — and second, because it shows Anne
Sexton the poet working out a new poetics, a distinctive way of "writing from the unconscious." To summarize the action: "Anne," settled
into yet another hospitalization, reflects on the repetitiousness of her
problems; like the other patients, she is acting out the same conflicts
that put her there before. The doctor, "better than Christ," has
"promised me another world." Yet despite years of treatment, nothing
has changed, except that "disorder is not what it was. / I have lost the
trick of it!" This discovery precipitates a decision. "Turn, my hungers!" she exhorts herself, paraphrasing Rimbaud; "flee this sad
hotel, / ride out on some hairy beast [. . .] Ride out / any old way you
please!" Otherwise she is bound to die in the hospital, still trapped in
"the fool's disease."

Illness is figured in the poem as entrapment in symptoms that appear again and again: "I came back" is a keynote line. Wellness is the
muse / nurse capacity that Anne holds "in my hand." The rhyme associates the writer's power with femaleness and with the domain of
cure, representing the muse as the doctor's assistant. For closure, the
poem hitches a ride on a metaphor that combines Christ (riding to
Jerusalem astride a donkey) with Rimbaud.

The reference "my hand" contains a range of meanings drawn from
Sexton's therapy. She had reluctantly come to recognize that Nana's
"mild white" hands had aroused sexual feelings she didn't wish to ac-

knowledge, and that desire to return to Nana was her most neurotic symptom, which she acted out by asking Dr. Orne to "be Nana" and hold her hand. To go "without luggage or defenses" would mean to live by the insight that her hunger for Nana must find more benign gratifications than she had been seeking. The regression muse / nurse / mouse conveys that she has accepted as "healthy" just such a sublimation or transfer of emotional satisfaction along a chain of substitutions, all of which evoke Nana. Moreover, vivid in the poem's confidence and wit is the female authoritativeness of Mary Gray, whose strengths are, through the magic compression of metaphor, what Anne holds on to after relinquishing all else: the pack of cigarettes (mentholated Salems, at that, to represent the cool and witchlike powers of the poet's mother). Mary Gray was a smoker, as was Dr. Orne. The muse / nurse is, among other things, the "good mother" that has been enlivened in Sexton's psyche by Dr. Orne's encouragement of her writing.

But another set of associations identifies the hand with punishment. This theme enters the poem at its fifth stanza:

> Hornets have been sent.
> They cluster like floral arrangements on the screen.
> Hornets, dragging their thin stingers,
> hover outside, all knowing,
> hissing: *the hornet knows*.
> I heard it as a child
> but what was it that he meant?

Hornets and bees were Sexton's symbols for "some terrible evil, some truth, that's always around even when everything's all right." Like Daddy when he was drunk and angry, the hornets knew about Anne's sexiness: when she tuned her bedside radio to "The Green Hornet" and "The Shadow," the man inside the radio could see her masturbating. These lines foreshadow all the bad things "he" — God, Daddy, the analyst — can tell about you as he "hover[s] outside, all knowing." Yet this omniscient figure is transformed in the course of the poem from a threat to a partner, as her "bachelor analyst" becomes the helpful *âne* onto whom she loads the burden of her dreams:

> I stared at [my dreams],
> concentrating on the abyss

the way one looks down into a rock quarry,
uncountable miles down,
my hands swinging down like hooks
to pull dreams up out of their cage.
O my hunger! My hunger!

Six years earlier Anne's hunger had brought her to an analyst as to a redeemer. Now she has reached a crisis: the fantasy of rescue must be approached as a code — "disorder is not what it was." The only satisfaction that seems to be on offer, however, is an ascent from the transference relationship into an "objectifying" analytical relationship. The poem's metaphors convey that this is an impossible position, an alignment with deadly forces of judgment, the masculine Shadow. The poem chooses art over analysis, which protects the madwoman's powers of magical thinking. Anne chooses to keep intact the uses of the fugue state as a source of poetry. Having internalized the power of the analyst (Orne-âne-Anne) insofar as it supported the production of poetry (on the model of Christ and Rimbaud rather than God or Daddy), she can let herself run (run-Brunner-Orne).

Sexton commented that "Flee on Your Donkey" had too much truth that it didn't explain. Yet she continued to work at it off and on for four years — partly, one assumes, for psychological reasons, as it attached an ambitious new artistic project to her therapy with Dr. Orne. By mid-1962 she had reached a crisis not only in her therapy but in her creativity. In her first two books, the speaking voice calmly narrates experiences the persona has lived beyond, extending to readers moral insights summarized in the refrain "I have been her kind." Now, with *All My Pretty Ones* in press, Sexton, though still a mental patient, was also experienced in the ways that the "I" of poetry is yet another kind of fraud, or con, as she liked to say. The authoritative, first-person center of her earlier poetry had been, among other things, an artistic device, a side effect of word choice and syntax.

"Flee on Your Donkey" represented a conscious effort at a new style. Sexton filled it with echoes of earlier poems about being in a mental hospital, but for Dr. Orne she made a distinction between writing in rhymed stanzas such as she had used in "The Double Image" and the structure she was struggling to achieve in "Flee on Your Donkey." When writing formal verse, she explained, "your ego and your unconscious are working at the same time. When you write the other way, your unconscious writes and your ego comes in and destroys. It's got to: there's too much, it's got to select. Nevertheless, if you let it all come out unconsciously, you've shaped it, right then, your ego didn't shape it, your unconscious shaped it, and that's what makes the difference."

Sexton's technique in reworking spontaneous poems like "Flee on Your Donkey" was, first, to take "what my unconscious offers me." Writing, she pointed out in an interview, was not at all like verbalizing in a therapy session. "Writing is much more unconscious. Even though therapy itself should be, should have a whole lot of unconscious stuff, you're aware of [your thoughts] — they become conscious. Not all my poems become conscious. Yet every book is an attempt — or every poem is an attempt — to master those things which aren't quite mastered." Once the lines were on the page, the ego could "go back over them," she explained. "For example, if I was talking about a love affair: that was an ego, conscious meaning [i.e., subject matter]. When I write without that vehicle, I don't have that conscious meaning, I have the unconscious going everywhere." One piece of work for the ego, then, was to find the story that lay somewhere in the imagery; she was sure that the unconscious had shaped it, that there was method in the madness. In "Flee on Your Donkey," she eventually produced a circular story line that spirals outward in a flight at the end: "Turn, my hungers! / For once make a deliberate decision. / [. . .] Anne, Anne, / flee on your donkey . . ."

Another mode of ego was supplied by the end rhymes or half-rhymes (such as "X's" and "reflexes," "muse" and "mouse," "sent" and "meant") and the internal rhymes ("inked-in" with "winked and," "donkey" with "car-keys"), which occur at frequent but irregular intervals. Irregularity underscores the point that to the disordered senses, random things and sounds can seem comically, ominously alike. And rhyme, Sexton commented, "adds a sound effect, a clang in your mind." The disorderly clang of the rhymes enhances the theme of struggle for insight that carries "Flee on Your Donkey" to its breakthrough ending. Needless to say, it is the ego that writes such an ending: willfulness is one of the ego's languages, and endings are one of the places where it likes to make a stand.

Sexton was aware of the kinds of criticism she would get for poetry produced by this process. One day, just before meeting Robert Lowell for lunch, she mused to Dr. Orne, "I know it's not written for the world, for regular people, probably not even for you. So I don't know who I'm communicating with." Lowell, who was unfailingly gracious

when Sexton asked him for an opinion, was always candid and sometimes severe. He had recognized her stylistic departure into the unconscious method as early as her much-admired "Letter Written on a
Ferry While Crossing Long Island Sound," which also had "spontaneous" origins in an extreme phase of a transference. Sexton recalled,
"Lowell said why do you write this [unconscious] way when you can
write the other way? I knew what he meant — it *is* a different way of
writing. Of course what's fashionable now may not be fashionable in
years to come." So she was not very surprised when he offered her
gentle discouragement after reading "Flee on Your Donkey."

This was important, because she counted on Lowell to serve as one
of her "superegos," as she put it. ("An editor works as a superego,"
she explained to Dr. Orne. "There aren't a lot of them around, except
for Lowell; and I have to catch him between his insanities.") She reported their discussion to Dr. Orne:

A.S.: Lowell said it ought to be a short story. That's bad for me: I want
to write a poem. He was talking about all my work since the new
book [*All My Pretty Ones*]; but he doesn't think it's successful, this
one, and it's the one I cared about. He likes other things, like the one
about "The Sun." But that's a very well-imagined poem: I'll always
be able to write a poem like that, *that* will never make me a great
poet! That's just "essence of poetry," but not that distinctive, it's just
a real poem, crystallized. I know it works, but you can't write a
bunch of lyrics like that. You have to be more daring. . . . I don't
want to be just a poet, writing essence of poetry. I want more content, story, more of the stamp of the individual. "The Double Image"
is daring, though a lot of people say it's bad. There's truth, a story in
"Flee on Your Donkey."
Dr.: Truth you don't own.
A.S.: I don't understand what you mean.
Dr.: Things that you don't want to own yourself, like an oyster building a pearl around something to isolate it.
A.S..: This poem is about all my acting out: I'm reliving what happened.

Building pearls out of whatever materials her unconscious discharged:
in 1962 that was exactly what she intended to go on doing as an artist,
working her way slowly toward another book of poems.

·   ·   ·

John Holmes's death ended the workshop era in Sexton's literary education. Every couple of weeks for the past four years she had been reaping the advantages of regular critical attention to her new work. Now she was stuck for a critical audience. She and Kumin continued to spend at least an hour working on the phone each day; that never changed, but it didn't supplant the need for more detached evaluation. George Starbuck had been particularly good at weeding out echoes of other poets and guiding Sexton toward technical subtleties, but he was now at the American Academy in Rome, so Sexton turned to Arthur Freeman. Now a Harvard tutor, Freeman was expected to encourage an intellectual seriousness of purpose among the young, and to this end he kept a steady stream of poets passing through Adams House, including Sexton.

"So I became Anne Sexton's designated adviser," Freeman explained later. "Designated victim, rather. She couldn't cross the street without getting advice. Typically, she would bring me ten poems at a time; I remember seeing versions of 'Flee on Your Donkey' and other pieces that went into *Live or Die*. Now, I knew what poetry was, and I didn't like what Sexton was doing. I would see ten poems and hate every single one! I praised 'Flee on Your Donkey,' I remember, because I saw it as the best of the lot. I thought of her as a beginner; but you never get those things quite right. Oh, what George had to go through — he saw every single version of every poem." Freeman didn't much like any confessional poetry, thought it was just the fashion in Boston, but he did like Sexton's sense of fun. He remembers her as very sociable. The Sextons invited him once or twice to their home for dinner; more often, Freeman and Sexton met at parties at the *Harvard Advocate* offices after readings, where her beauty and gaiety made a strong impression. "You could be excused for thinking Anne was a lot less crazy than she claimed," Freeman commented. "The cadre around Lowell romanticized madness; many people thought Anne in her poetry was aggressively dramatizing her mental states."

To Freeman, Sexton seemed lonely after Starbuck left Boston. She was. She began writing to a monk named Brother Dennis Farrell, who had sent her a fan letter after stumbling across *Bedlam*. He told her that poetry had liberated in him feelings long suppressed by excessive rationality, and he took great delight both in her letters and in Rilke's *Letters to a Young Poet*, to which she directed him. "Grace is working in you," he wrote thankfully.

After the blowup with Dr. Orne, Sexton reached out to Brother Dennis, asking for spiritual assurance: "I'm in trouble NOW. Write me anything . . . just words . . . I need a friend." (She sent a similar message to James Wright: "I need you — Please write me — please be my friend for a little while — I am in great inner distress — I need your deep good words.") Brother Dennis comforted her in a compassionate letter that ended with a reference to the "Song of Songs": "I am black but beautiful, O daughters of Jerusalem; therefore has the King loved me, and brought me into his chamber . . ." Of course he did not know how succinctly this imagery meshed with the imagery of Sexton's inner voice at the time ("My father was a king. The king can have sex with anyone").

As summer took Dr. Orne away from Boston, the friendship deepened. Poet and monk exchanged long, intense letters; Brother Dennis thought an uncomprehending reader might mistake them for the legendary Eloise and Abelard. It did seem that a faint whiff of scandal excited virtuoso performances on both sides of the correspondence. Sexton enjoyed exposing herself to young men she could keep at a distance. Brother Dennis did not flirt back, but he poured out the feelings of self-discovery her poems invited. This emboldened her to bring forward religious questions trenchant to her play, which she was working on again in her therapist's absence.

In *The Cure*, Daisy thinks of Christ as beyond gender. Sexton was developing this perspective in a monologue, later published as the poem "Consorting with Angels," which begins, "I was tired of being a woman." Brother Dennis objected vehemently to her representation of Christ as sexless, and Sexton concluded ruefully that he didn't really understand Daisy's longing "for a destiny that has nothing to do with gender." She thought he missed the point of her poem: "a rather naive desire to be absorbed in the great embrace." Shrewdly, she argued that a truthful poetic image captured a complex feeling even if the feeling was associated with neurosis. But a *desire* wasn't, couldn't be, neurotic. It was a testimony to a lost connection, a poignant universal in human life, and art was one of the vehicles of its communication.

Yet Sexton wasn't sure about the status, in her own complex of feelings, of that "desire to be absorbed in the great embrace." Was this fundamentally a spiritual longing, as Brother Dennis assured her? Or was it just another neurotic symptom? "I am so rather hysterical that I have a feeling that if I did believe I'd lose all grip on reality . . . but then, it wouldn't be the same reality." Transferring the struggle over these questions into art, as she had done in writing and revising *The Cure,* was (as she thought) an operationally productive use of conflicts that she still found irreconcilable in her life.

Religion was only one of the topics that straggled across many pages of letters that Sexton took days to write, yet the religious thought that infused Brother Dennis's letters was what nourished her most (and, as she was aware, associated him with James Wright in her mind). No detail she confided caused him to swerve from an attitude of voracious attention, though months might pass between her letter and his antiphon. But in March 1963, after a hiatus of two months, he wrote to say goodbye. His letters to her had been part of a larger movement toward ideals that were not commensurate with life in a monastery. Though he emphasized that his deep feeling for her had nothing to do with his choice to leave the priesthood, Sexton thought that it must. In a long letter (to which Brother Dennis did not reply) she distinguished between "a human relationship" and "a letter relationship between humans," in which "words can fly out of your heart (via the fingers) and no one really need live up to them."

As always, Sexton's measure of "a human relationship" was the sisterhood she shared with Maxine Kumin. That summer she persuaded Kumin to collaborate on a new version of *The Cure,* and they negotiated their way jointly to a plot that, as Sexton put it, could accommodate her friend's neurosis as well as her own. "It totally suits both of us, this girl, how she feels and what she does. It's amazing that you can write a play and meet two different women's needs!" They junked the first version almost completely, keeping only what Sexton considered its emotional centerpiece: suicide. In the new plot, Daisy kills herself as before, but is sent to the afterlife, where she is interrogated by angels and then forced to return to the living. It was Kumin, of course, who insisted that Daisy revive; but this turn of events suited Sexton too. "It's what kept me alive all summer. Killing myself, being judged and sent back is my ideal fantasy." The project also offered interesting formal problems, which they couldn't solve in six weeks: the play still contained too many flashbacks, too little action. In addition, "the new version of the play has seven poems in it. One of my original ideas is that poems can be spoken. It doesn't work." In one way the collaboration was a success, though: it gave Sexton a structure that assured the return of the one who went away every day. "I had Maxine's ego to keep me going even when I was despairing inside — she had to keep going, and I had another person to rely on."

Their friendship continued to deepen as their children grew up. When they broke from work in the afternoon to swim, the children would join them in the delicious cool of the Sextons' shady pool. Jane, Max's oldest, was everybody's big sister. Judy Kumin, two years older than Linda Sexton, formed a special friendship with Anne, who later tutored her in poetry and turned to her for advice in handling Linda's teenage rebellions. Danny and Linda were the same age, and Danny later set some of Sexton's poems to music for her chamber rock group. Joy was everybody's little sister, and needed minding. A jaunty, adventurous child, she repeatedly terrorized the adults by walking on the narrow train trestle that crossed the Charles River nearby. (The trestle was wide enough only for a train, but it led to a shopping center. "I'd be on my way to get a forbidden treat," Joy recalled. "I realized that these legs would take me wherever I wanted to go — I was mobilized!")

Anne and Max shared the children as they shared everything else. Remembering the days when they were neighbors in Newton, Jane Kumin felt wistful about that closeness: "Anne was really our mother's favorite child."

Sexton received galleys of *All My Pretty Ones* in July and was elated to learn that the book was scheduled to appear simultaneously in cloth and paper. She wanted to see her books widely available; *Bedlam* had so far appeared only in cloth, and she had been pressing Houghton Mifflin for a year to bring out a paperback edition combining *Bedlam* with *Pretty Ones*. When Paul Brooks, her editor, asked her for names of writers who might supply blurbs for advertising copy, Sexton screwed up her courage to ask Robert Lowell whether she might excerpt for publicity some comments he had written in a private letter to her just before she delivered the manuscript to Houghton Mifflin. As usual, Lowell had put his finger easily on the best and worst traits of the book. He told her that like Edgar Lee Masters's *Spoon River Anthology,* her collection seemed to him an integrated work in which "little moments prop the big moments."

Faults? I don't think they matter. Or perhaps they are unavoidable human limitations — yours! There are loose edges, a certain monotony of tone, a way of writing that sometimes seems to let everything in too easily, bald spots, uninspired moments that roll off disguised by the same certainty of voice, poems that all one can say about is that they are Sexton and therefore precious.

Though Sexton's request probably made him squirm a little, he assented. Perhaps he regarded it as fair exchange for the pains she had taken the previous year over "Classroom at Boston University," a short piece she wrote about his teaching for the *Harvard Advocate*'s special issue on Lowell.

Working up the book jacket just before *All My Pretty Ones* went to press, Sexton revised Lowell's friendly "you" into a formal "she" and drew a veil of ellipses across the negative comments so that the compunction suggested praise. She found this particular kind of self-promotion highly distasteful and phony, and once she had written up the back jacket considered withdrawing her version of Lowell's words. But business sense prevailed. She wrote to Paul Brooks, "Leave the Lowell quote as I sent it to you. My vanity is greater than my conscience."

Blurbs are not assessments; they are more like thumbtacks that fasten a new title to a notice board. But after *All My Pretty Ones* was published on 15 October, reviews in the major periodicals only reinforced the glowing advance notices — James Dickey's slashing review in the *New York Times* proved to be an exception. Some readers, especially poets, still think it is Sexton's best book. In November, *Poetry* magazine conferred on her a great honor by awarding its Levinson Prize to the seven poems that had appeared in its August issue. Sexton was in grand company: the first recipient had been Carl Sandburg (1914), and others had been Wallace Stevens, Robert Frost, Marianne Moore, H. D., Dylan Thomas, and Muriel Rukeyser — forty-seven in all, before Sexton. (Lowell received the Levinson Prize the following year.)

What poets found to admire in Sexton's recent work was nicely captured in a letter in which Denise Levertov explained that she planned to draw on *Pretty Ones* for a lecture on poetic technique at Indiana University: "I'm calling the lecture 'Ask the Fact for the Form.' As one of my illustrations I'm going to read a poem of yours — probably 'Flight' — that's a wonderful poem. Or maybe 'The Starry Night.' I hope you won't mind." Poet Richard Howard's review of *Pretty Ones* emphasized the handling of concrete experience: "[Sexton] has, in Mr. Lowell's choppy wake, restored to our poetry not only the lyric of self-dramatization that had hidden out in the novel, but an unmistakable notation of events — not witty but always grim, and without more music than mere accuracy allows." Howard found her "strong, colloquial diction" a "lucid obstruction to sentimentality."

Sexton's second book eventually found a much wider audience than the poet-peers and literary academics who were most likely to read it in the course of keeping up with the field; by the time of her death, 18,000 copies had been sold, and by the end of the 1980s, twice that many. (Sales figures for prizewinning books in the prestigious Yale Series of Younger Poets offer a yardstick; according to Peter Davison, now an editor at Houghton Mifflin, George Starbuck's *Bone Thoughts* [1960] sold about 4000 copies, and Davison's *The Breaking of the Day* [1964] sold 2500.) Not only poets but the elusive "general reader" valued *All My Pretty Ones* for its startling, canny imagery. "You don't write for an *audience*," Sexton said on a radio show in 1962; "you write for some *one* who'll understand." Sales figures conceal this fact, but one by one letters arrived at Sexton's door, each from a reader who felt spoken to directly, almost spookily, by her book. Some were inspired to send their own work for evaluation.

And many, many of these readers sought personal contact with Sexton as someone who spoke for the mentally ill. She handled gently those who identified with her as a model of recovery, but she knew how to be direct. Returning a manuscript that was apparently accompanied by a five-dollar bill, she told the hopeful author, "Frankly I do not feel there is any market for your work. You're wasting your time trying to sell your poetry. However, since you have been ill, your poetry may be a wonderful outlet and I suggest that you continue it in this capacity. [. . .] May I suggest you spend the five dollars on Rilke's *Letters to a Young Poet* published by Norton. He will say more to you than I ever could."

Of course Sexton welcomed all this recognition. Ebullient over the good reviews, she accepted several invitations to share a platform with critics that fall. In October she appeared with Peter Davison on a television interview show hosted by P. Albert Duhamel, literary critic on the *Boston Herald,* and in November she participated in a panel on "The Poet and Extra-literary Criticism" at a meeting of the New England College English Association. Normally Sexton detested writing talks for academic audiences, but she wrote this one in a mood of confidence. She could now speak with authority about criticism, from the point of view of someone on the receiving end.

"It seems to me that to have a live poet on this panel is an after-thought," she said. "I would like to change the title of our discussion from 'The Poet and Extra-literary Criticism' to Extra-literary Criticism AND THE POET,' for I am the mechanical cuckoo who sticks its neck into the hierarchy of literary labelists and calls out AND THE POET . . . AND THE POET . . . For I am the one who creates, not thinks . . . and if by mistake I should think — it is in symbols and met-aphors . . . and I must remind you that I am not responsible for what they mean . . . the critic would explain it better." The "real" critic, Sexton observed, "is usually concerned with dead or nearly dead writers." What the living writer needs from the critic is "in a word . . . praise! After that I can afford to be more particular. I can say that I need to be understood, and what is worse . . . to be ex-plained to myself." Yet the poet must *work* unconsciously, Sexton claimed, "must continue to be startled by life . . . if we should start to be reasonable, to understand why we write or just what we write, if we understood ourselves we might stop writing poems and become critics."

By the end of 1962 Sexton's artistic apprenticeship was complete. *All My Pretty Ones* was the work of a mature artist, and displayed as well the full range of subjects she was ever to write about: mental ill-ness, sexual love, spiritual anguish. Her apprenticeship had seen two phases of development. Under Lowell's guidance she had learned what to leave out. Under Kumin and Starbuck and Snodgrass and Wright she had learned how to let almost anything in, either by using "tricks" that permitted unconscious materials to ripple up and flash through grids of meter and rhyme, or — following Wright's exam-ple — by trusting the gangs of images that appeared in the poem when the poet was in a creative trance.

Furthermore, despite periodic setbacks in her therapy, Sexton felt she was at last on the road to getting better, if not being well. She was coping more successfully with her symptoms: remembering more, finding ways into feelings that she had previously escaped by trance. She had also regained confidence as a mother; her children had no doubts about who she was, and this too helped her, especially when Kayo was away. Now entering her thirty-fifth year, she had not only survived a mental breakdown, she had used it to acquire an education, and by channeling her insights into art had arrived on the American cultural scene as an important new poet.

A snapshot of Sexton taken by Oscar Williams that summer captures the moment wonderfully. The setting, Sexton noted on the photo, is Oscar's roof garden in Manhattan, "first time I met Saul Bellow." Only Sexton is in focus, her angular face and bare shoulders lit by the evening sun; she is poised and glamorous as she leans into conversation with another poet. It is Sexton who sheds celebrity on the party. She was entering her prime.

THE PRIZEWINNER
1963–1967

Anne Sexton

Anne Wilder

Maxine Kumin

Self-portrait

Four portraits by Barbara Swan

10

CIRCLE OF
WOMEN ARTISTS
1963

By 1963, Anne Sexton was established on the American scene as an important new poet. During the next decade she would receive most of the prizes, honors, awards, and fellowships available to American poets, and following publication by Oxford University Press of a *Selected Poems*, her work would achieve gratifying recognition in Britain as well. Rumors of prizes regularly began arriving in the mailbox at 40 Clearwater Road early in January, when Sexton's editor at Houghton Mifflin sent her the good news that *All My Pretty Ones* had made it onto the short list for the National Book Award. In March, she learned that she had been proposed for a Ford Foundation grant to work in the theater; Robert Lowell and Anthony Hecht had previously held such grants. ("My heart started going boom boom boom — it's a lot of money," she said.)

The most important recognition that followed in the wake of *Pretty Ones*, however, was a traveling fellowship sponsored by the American Academy of Arts and Letters: $6500 to pay the costs of spending a year abroad. Sexton was to be the first recipient of this new award, which would not be announced until May. Would she accept?

The committee offering the prize probably knew that Sexton's background included little formal education and even less travel, and probably also considered the award especially appropriate for these reasons. Its members could not have guessed Sexton's first, private reaction to the news: she felt cornered. She could not possibly go so far away from her home, not even for a tenth of that amount of time. Yet turning down such an honor would expose her to ridicule. She worried aloud to Kayo, and he astounded her by saying that he thought it was the chance of a lifetime and that she shouldn't pass it up. Gradually a plan evolved: Anne would split the money with Sandy Robart, who would take a leave of absence from her work with retarded children. Anne could tour as a poet, and Sandy would visit mental health clinics abroad. They could leave at the end of summer.

By May, *All My Pretty Ones* had been widely, enthusiastically reviewed, and Sexton was being interviewed in the local press and on radio and television. The American Academy of Arts and Letters was throwing a big party in New York to announce the award of the traveling fellowship, given "for [Sexton's] singular, idiomatic, and original work, in which passionate clarity of word and concept is set to uncommon music." Robert Lowell and Elizabeth Hardwick planned a small dinner to follow, with guests from the New York literary establishment, including Lillian Hellman, Stanley Kunitz, Marianne Moore, and others. Sexton joked to her publicity agent at Houghton Mifflin that since she was handing out copies of the book like chocolates to the rich and famous, they might as well send one to Jacqueline Kennedy at the White House: "She *is* cultural; she is a woman; she is a mother; doesn't she have a dead father? And her husband comes from Massachusetts."

The prospect of the award ceremony threw Sexton into a tailspin, though. "I'll have to go up onstage where the citation will be read," she said to Dr. Orne. "Reading a poem, I can sweep onto the stage, and before I'm done I can own them. But just to stand there! And afterward a big cocktail party!" ("What difference does it make if you shake?" Dr. Orne wondered. "Are they giving you a prize for adjustment?") Sexton felt that she had to choose between two very different public personalities, the little girl and the vamp. The child would do very well for interviews at home: "I was dressed like a little girl when the guy from the *Boston Globe* came — no shoes, and a shift, he couldn't tell if I had a figure." But for New York she had chosen a costume she would have to live up to: an orchid tweed suit with a halter top, "purplish, very low-cut and shocking. I'll have to wear a strapless bra; the top comes down low in the back. I have it all planned. I'll leave the jacket on until I'm high, then take it off." If she had any intention of letting people get to know her, Sexton claimed, she would have to dress like a child, in flat shoes. "When I'm that little girl I don't *have* my body! I can't explain that, but it's true."

A number of psychological reinforcements were helping Sexton put "that little girl" behind her at the time, however, chiefly the strengths she drew from her colleagues at the Radcliffe Institute. She and Kumin had both been appointed for a second term, 1962–1963. The preceding September a new buttress had arrived in the person of the San Francisco writer Tillie Olsen, whom Sexton had met in print when Olsen's novella *Tell Me a Riddle* shared the pages of *New World Writing* with Sexton's "Dancing the Jig" in 1960. *Tell Me a Riddle* immediately became another of Sexton's sacred texts. Olsen had been equally drawn to Sexton's work, and had cut Sexton's picture from the back cover of *Bedlam* and mounted it on the wall over her desk along with the faces of Tolstoy, Hardy, Whitman, Kollwitz, and "others who sustain and judge me."

At fifty, Olsen was older than most of the other women at Radcliffe. She had also lived in an utterly different social world. She found that like characters in a John Cheever novel, almost every one of the Radcliffe Scholars had spent some time in psychoanalysis and held theories about women that came straight out of Freud and other male-oriented models of human motivation. Maxine Kumin in particular was attracted to Freudian ideas; she was discussing Freud in a course and wanted her friends to share her excitement over *Civilization and Its Discontents* and *The Ego and the Id*. But when Betty Friedan's *The Feminine Mystique* came out that year, it stimulated great discussion at the institute, and Friedan's criticism of psychoanalysis revolutionized Kumin's attitudes, as she later wrote to Sexton: "Have been all but unable to put down FEM MYSTIQUE. Am mad for the message. Yes yes yes [. . .] it seemed all too true looking back over 3 yrs of college freshmen I taught, the apathy, the disinterest in any kind of abstract idea, the singleminded female goal to snag a man & make babies. But the best chunk of the whole book is THE SEXUAL SOLIPSISM OF SIGMUND FREUD [. . .] I'm rebelling against Freudianism in general."

Olsen added her personal perspectives to the bracing criticism of women's situation that was circulating at the institute. The wife of a printer and a working mother with four daughters, she looked to her "upbringing as a socialist daughter" for an understanding of family dynamics and the situation of women, she recalled. Her politics came strongly to the fore when she was told about the psychological profiles that were being gathered by Radcliffe. The Scholars were expected to take a battery of psychological tests as well as to be interviewed by social scientists, one of whose working hypotheses included the idea that the Scholars' high achievements reflected the influence of strong fathers. "This method, this 'study' of us, seemed to me to be both an unproductive and, indeed, an insulting way of trying to understand why we were 'exceptional,' seemingly different in motivation and achievement from other women," Olsen explained. "As I said to Connie Smith [the institute's director], 'We have intellects, powers of observation, life experiences. The best thing the institute could do would be to get us together to discuss *that* why.' I was asking for a shared, conscious process of coming to comprehension, which came into being seven years later. It is called 'consciousness-raising.' " Olsen refused to be interviewed by Dr. Ryerson. "And I could not understand, then, how Anne, Max, others could allow such an invasion."

Like Sexton, Tillie Olsen held no college degree, though she had been a writing fellow at Stanford University, working under the novelist Richard Scowcroft. She and Sexton found that they also shared a taste for certain unfashionable poets. "We were walking along the Charles River, under the sycamores changing to their fall colors; it was my first fall in New England," Olsen recalled. "I quoted Sara Teasdale and Anne said, 'Oh, so you love her poems too! But you must never, never admit it to anyone.' I said, 'What do you mean?' She told me once she had let it slip in that Holmes group that she liked Sara Teasdale, and discovered that Sara Teasdale was the lowest of the low. . . . From the outset we talked about writers who were life to us. We never needed to be guarded or dissemble. Our love of Sara Teasdale or Edna St. Vincent Millay didn't shame us, with each other."

Sexton's friendship with Tillie Olsen was one of several important changes the Radcliffe Institute had caused in her life. By the time she met Olsen, she was an "old girl" at the institute. Though she still felt the social liabilities of her bad memory, couldn't face the prospect of mingling with people unless Kumin was there to anchor her, hated to incur social debts for fear of having to repay them with invitations to her home, and had to have several drinks before appearing at the institute even just to sit and listen to a Scholar's seminar, she was gradually building into her life a circle of professional women who shared her ambitions to make a difference in the world.

Sexton formed an exceptionally close bond with Barbara Swan, one of the pair of painters appointed among what Swan dubbed "the Premier Cru," the first group of Radcliffe Scholars. Swan got acquainted with the others by sketching them. "Anne was a beauty and the challenge was to go beyond that beautiful face to what lay beneath," she recalled. "There is nothing like sitting for a portrait to make people open up and reveal themselves. In a funny way it's like sitting with your shrink. I'll ask questions and the sitters often reveal things to me that I don't expect and they don't expect, all from realizing they are being observed." Eventually, as their friendship developed, Swan made portraits of Sexton in several media, and in Tillie Olsen's view, she found her way into the essential Anne. "Barbara and Anne had one of the most beautiful relationships between women that I've seen," Olsen said. "With Barbara, Anne was her most natural, the way she must have been with her children. Barbara dwells in a special universe."

While they were both at Radcliffe, Sexton bought one of Swan's first lithographs, "The Musicians," and hung it in her study. The picture shows two figures playing wind instruments "and a great deal of background murk that could be anything," Swan joked. "Frankly, I was experimenting with possibilities of texture in lithography." Sexton based a poem on it, projecting onto the indistinct forms a fantasy of rebirth through a mouth-hole — possibly a metaphor for therapy, Kumin speculated. Swan was gratifyingly awed — "astonished!" — by what Sexton had done. "Anne moved into my world like a tornado. She shook it up, rattled it, possessed it like a demon. Naturally, I adored the poem." In Barbara Swan, Sexton had found another "two-way radio," to recall Mary Gray's term. The two artists collaborated on many projects over the years, including broadsides, jackets for *Live or Die, The Book of Folly,* and *The Death Notebooks,* and illustrations for *Transformations.*

Tillie Olsen, and then the sculptor Marianna Pineda, joined Swan, Kumin, and Sexton as a tightly knit cohort at the Radcliffe Institute in 1963. They joked about being "the Equivalents" — the artists President Bunting wanted to mix in with scholars who held advanced degrees. (Kumin, who held a master's degree, was the exception, but she was being resocialized by Sexton.) That was the year Olsen got her hands on Virginia Woolf's *A Room of One's Own,* which Sexton read too, calling it "health."

And that was the year Olsen gave a talk based on material that she eventually developed into her influential book *Silences.* Since girlhood, she had copied out treasured passages from library books and annotated them with her own thoughts. She brought with her to Radcliffe an enormous collection of loose pages gathered over the years and put into bundles of all shapes and sizes. When it was her turn to conduct the regularly scheduled Tuesday seminar, Olsen selected passages from these bundles and her own writing about "the circumstances which obstruct or silence writers, with some attention to the special circumstances of women," she remembered. "For the first time there was an occasion to put my material and thoughts together in some organized way."

When Sexton looked back over her two years at the Radcliffe Institute, she singled out Olsen's presentation as the high point. A passage Olsen read from "The Snows of Kilimanjaro" in particular roused her never-dormant worries about her own self-destructive tendencies. "What kills the creative instinct — what blunts the axe? Liquor and other devices. Of course they blunt my pain, too. . . . Maybe I'll have to do without my crutches." She told Martha White that "Tillie's seminar probably changed my writing as much as anything. She put in a theory of failure, how you can waste yourself. At that moment I was so worried about failure. Artists always are. You're looking for this wonderful thing that you may never get. Tillie rededicates you. That's what she did for me; I couldn't speak afterward, I was in a state of shock. Tillie's seminar went way overtime, but if anyone had stopped her, I would have chopped their head off."

In Tillie Olsen, Sexton found a unique mentor. An excruciatingly deliberate writer who hoarded words and knew how to be patient, Olsen tutored the younger woman in taking the long view. After the seminar Sexton borrowed her copy-outs and personal notes and spent many hours typing sixty-three pages of these precious distillations to keep in her own files. Olsen's stash seemed to her at once comic and magical, an eccentric and authentic kind of spirituality. She sought Olsen's company very parsimoniously ("Tillie is so harassed," she told another member of the institute; "I try not to bother her"), but with the same intensity she usually brought to her religious advisers. Olsen recognized such hungers, and thinking back on those days remembered Sexton with sadness, anguish, and deep love.

American newspapers briefly reported on 12 February 1963 that the poet Sylvia Plath had died in London. In the Boston area it was a local story, and it agitated the Boston poetry circle deeply. Though the cause of death was first claimed to be pneumonia, few doubted it was suicide, and it was: Plath had died of asphyxiation, her head in the gas oven. Some had heard rumors about Ted Hughes and another woman, and most saw the suicide as a particularly female revenge wrought on the model of a Greek tragedy, pathetic and terrifying. For those familiar with Plath's most recent writing, the shock was intensified by awareness that she had just found herself as a poet of immense, distinctive gifts.

Sexton's shock was personal, for Plath's rare but friendly letters had radiated contentment: "I am bedded in the country with Frieda [her daughter] and a very fine 6 months son Nicholas, keeping bees and raising potatoes and doing broadcasts off and on for the BBC." By 1963 Plath appeared to have realized fully the ambition she had confided to Sexton exactly four years earlier, over drinks at the Ritz after Lowell's class: a life in England blending motherhood, housewifery, and a writer's career. Fulfilling such ambition would require stable health of anyone, but of Plath it also required recovery from a powerful attraction — Sexton called it a lust — for suicide. The news of her death plunged Sexton into reverie about their conversations all those years ago, which she distilled into a poem titled "Sylvia's Death" and later expanded into a memoir.

As more rumors drifted across the Atlantic, Sexton's feeling of identification deepened. She imagined Plath abandoned and lonely, struggling to maintain the brisk, cheerful persona everyone in Boston knew so well. When the minister of the Unitarian church in Wellesley called requesting her assistance in putting together a memorial ceremony for Plath, she was glad to help select the poetry. But, she told Dr. Orne, she and the minister didn't see eye to eye about the person being memorialized.

I began to worry about what her funeral should consist of. Her husband was sleeping with someone else: why didn't Sylvia come home? Then I realized, she *has* come home. I explained this to her minister and I don't think he liked it very much. I said, you have to realize I look at it from a sick point of view — though he's very psychiatrically oriented — but that is my explanation. Why didn't she come home and stay with her mother? Well, she'd already come home to her mother once [when she married Hughes and they moved for two years to Massachusetts]. She couldn't do it again. By killing herself, she did. I don't think this should be left out of her funeral — I think this is an important way to die.

Plath's death saddened Sexton, but it also roused her own death wish, never far below the surface. Suicide, she decided, was like a drug: "The person who takes drugs can't explain why they want to do it, there's no reality reason," she said to Dr. Orne. He demurred:

"There always is: drugs are addicting." "Suicide is addicting too," Sexton observed. As she put it to a friend, Sylvia Plath "had the suicide inside her. As I do. As many of us do. But, if we're lucky, we don't get away with it and something or someone forces us to live." While the healthy aspects of Sexton's personality were being strengthened by her mingling happily with other women artists at the Radcliffe Institute, taking new paths in her own art, and feeling her powers as a performer work on ever-increasing audiences, Plath's suicide pulled her toward the stagnant pond of her old obsession with ritualized self-destruction. "Sylvia Plath's death disturbs me," she told Dr. Orne. "Makes me want it too. She took something that was mine, *that* death was mine! Of course it was hers too. But we both swore off it, the way you swear off smoking."

This rivalrous attitude made its way into Sexton's writings about Plath. A refrain of "me, me too" gives "Sylvia's Death" a spurious tone, saturated with self-pity posing as grief — though Sexton liked the poem and defended it to critics. Howard Moss turned it down for *The New Yorker*. Robert Lowell wrote that he thought it got "too much push from the pathos." Sending the poem to George Starbuck, Sexton said, "It's really good. You may paste it on your wall." To Galway Kinnell's criticism she responded, "I listened and let [the poem] go its own way, a little flawed, perhaps a little overwritten, but belonging more to itself than to me."

When, in July, Sexton finally received the copy of *The Bell Jar* she had ordered from a London bookstore back in March, she read it in a sitting, stretched out on the couch she had inherited from her mother. Reading Plath's novel aggravated her fiercely (and permanently: several years later, when she saw Linda avidly reading it, she said scathingly, "It's nothing but a potboiler!"). She wrote Dr. Orne a letter about the feelings it roused: Plath had written prose, as Kumin was now doing (the novel *Through Dooms of Love*) and as Dr. Orne had been encouraging Sexton to do, yet Plath was also a poet — "a great poet, with great potential." She had written a book about killing herself — a "very touching" book with a happy ending — and then she really had killed herself. "I keep reading it . . . have to read it, take myself back to her death like salt," Sexton said.

Muddled feelings come squirming into the letter at this point — emanations from the pea-green couch, no doubt. Feelings of rivalry toward Plath evoke Sexton's fury at Mary Gray for ignoring her; moreover, she now understands that her whole career as a writer has been based on an illusion, the "big cheat" of transference. "Now I see it! I existed to mean something to you, to matter to you and then to belong to you. I made up a whole person, a poet, Anne Sexton, who would be worth something to you. [. . .] All those people who write to me and believe in me. God! I don't even exist."

This was decidedly a familiar feeling to Sexton, but Plath's death gave it a new twist. To the attraction of death as a way of coming home to Mother, finally getting her attention, was added the attraction of death as splitting off the poet once and for all, releasing her into the immortality of her words. As early as May 1963, Sexton began plotting her posthumous reputation, telling Dr. Orne, "I've been thinking I'll write a book and leave it, so when I die it can be published posthumously." It was as if Sylvia Plath, the savvy rival, had leapfrogged right over Sexton's project of becoming famous, in which the fantasied finale was to be a well-publicized suicide. By this singular move Plath had once and for all reversed their positions as senior and junior in the ranks of poetry.

Despite brooding over Plath, Sexton looked forward to her trip abroad and hoped it would have good effects on her progress in therapy. "Now is the time to get well! No more delaying tactics!" When she wasn't bedeviled by fears about coping with strangers in Europe or about finding places to go to the bathroom in complete privacy (she worried a lot about this), she was thrilled at the prospect of traveling. She and Sandy Robart decided to sail rather than fly, so she could take all her "identity things": books, typewriter, and the big bound volume of letters Nana had written home from Europe, which would provide a kind of script for her own journey. Robart put herself in charge of arrangements and committed the pair to routine frugality based on Arthur Frommer's guidebook *Europe on Five Dollars a Day*.

As 22 August, the departure date, drew nearer, Sexton's brave facade began to crack. She had committed herself to the trip by an act of will; now aspects of herself that hadn't been consulted began to make trouble. On the last day of July she had an especially dramatic session in her doctor's office. Before her appointment, she passed out in the lavatory; the nurse had to help her upstairs. Once in Dr. Orne's office, Sexton went directly to the air conditioner and began cradling it in her arms, then collapsed on the floor, where she spent the entire appointment curled up in a trance, ignoring Dr. Orne's voice, praying, and calling him Nana. The next day she wrote a poem, "For the Year of the Insane," based on her inner experience of that hour.

Was she really strong enough to go? Dr. Orne thought so, for several reasons. First, he believed that she had made important progress toward integration in the past couple of years. From the day she announced her intention to travel until her departure, he spent a good deal of time spelling out just what progress he did observe. Right before she left, he pointed out, "You have undercut the mechanism of forgetting. Fact is, your memory, ability to keep things in mind, has improved. . . . I don't think it would have been possible for you to do this in a shorter time. Keep at it as long as it takes." (To this Sexton retorted, "I'm going to spend my whole life getting well, then it will be over!") Second, he believed that her stability could be supported by judicious use of medication. Third, he thought they could devise a way of staying in touch through letters: she would write to him weekly, and he would reply at appointed times. Before she left, Sexton took a Polaroid snapshot of him in his office, which she called "a charm to ward off evil."

But the most important guarantor of Sexton's health would be sturdy, sensible, cheerful, resourceful Sandy Robart. Though Sandy had been highly amused when Anne and Kayo first proposed the deal to her — "I had a family and three kids and had to keep the debts paid in a loose kind of way" — things just somehow fell into place. From years of depending on Sandy, Anne had a very practical knowledge of her virtues. "Nothing in the world frightens Sandy," she claimed. "She likes disturbed children, and they are worse than disturbed adults: they run around more, for one thing." Sandy would help her stay unconfused, help her through the brief periods of dissociation that were her most troublesome symptom.

The greatest problem Sexton faced was leaving the two anchor points of her sanity, Linda and Joy, for whom there was no magical substitute. She spent hours talking with them about where she would be when she was thinking about them and writing to them in care of Daddy. She worried that they were too young to understand such a separation. In spite of this, she also worried that Linda, who would turn ten just before her departure, might begin to menstruate while she was away, so she bought a box of sanitary napkins, told Linda how to use them, and stored them on the top shelf of Linda's closet just in case.

Sexton now found her children delightful companions. She had grown to depend on their ready warmth and concern for her, and she felt able to offer them the sort of intimacy her own mother had never been able to give. Expressing her newfound strength in numerous small ways, she made a point of teaching them to use the kitchen, surprising them when they arrived home from school by announcing it was a baking day. They made popovers, brownies, muffins, ginger snaps — and ate them right away, still warm. "Mother would lean back in her chair, *directing*," Joy remembered. Sexton also shared with them her delight in music, putting on a record so that all three could dance, Joy and Linda making stumbling efforts to imitate her graceful movements. "She would go off, sort of lifting her arms to the music — she was long and lean and graceful when she was young," Linda recalled. "She really loved music: could be anything, Andy Williams to Beethoven — she'd dance around, trying to sing along. We used to make fun of her then; she was tone deaf, couldn't sing a note." In 1963, Linda played the leading role in a school production of Frances Hodgson Burnett's *Sara Crewe,* and Anne encouraged her to take it seriously. "Mother would stand me at one end of the house, then she'd go to the opposite end, stand in the breezeway, and tell me to 'belt it out.' She patiently helped me to learn the part, made me feel it was awfully important to her."

The children have less happy memories of another game Sexton

The Sextons before Anne's trip to Europe.

liked to play, one that she called "being nine." She described this game to Dr. Orne: "Linda got in bed with me Sunday, and we spent about an hour pretending I was nine. She'd talk to me and I'd tell her everything just as it used to be. I was cuddling her, down lower in the bed than she was with my head on her chest, with her arms around me. I want to be nine!" Joy had been a little bit jealous, Sexton said, but she had found it impossible to pretend to be seven. The game went on and on, until finally Linda tired of it. "She really wanted me to be thirty-four; and I'd say 'Oh, I want to be nine,' I wouldn't do it. She started crying — both of them started trying to say some magic thing, like 'I want *you* back.' I really liked it, was acting out for about an hour and a half." Apparently she felt equally justified in climbing into Linda's bed now and then when she couldn't sleep. "Her body wants my body; she loves to cuddle," Sexton told Dr. Orne. "Kayo gets annoyed by my moving around, and Joy would bounce awake and immediately begin chatting. I probably relate to Linda as a child would to a mother, crawl up next to her as a child would, and she's receptive. I could feel her feet tapping on my leg just as mine do when I'm in bed with Kayo, half-awake. It put me back to sleep."

In later life, Linda Sexton remembered these as some of the most disturbing experiences she ever had of her mother: the image lingered of a giant head pressing against her chest, insisting on being the baby, making her the mommy; and the sense lingered of being asked for too much physical intimacy. As she grew older, these problems deepened into profound conflicts with her mother. But Sexton, ignoring the fraught memories of Nana's cuddling, claimed that she saw no harm in her need to have Linda and Joy mother her. "I can save myself through my children because there's a bond," she told Dr. Orne.

The night before she left for Europe, Sexton wrote each of her daughters a letter and placed them under their pillows to find and keep after she was gone. When the S.S. *France* pulled out of New York Harbor on the twenty-second of August, Sexton and Robart stood at the rail a long time, waving wand after wand of soap bubbles so their children could keep them in sight until the ship was entirely lost to view.

Sexton took a typewriter with her to Europe, expecting to write poetry and hoping to write a novel (she intended to base one of the characters on Sandy Robart), but mainly in order to keep a steady stream of letters flowing to her loved ones. She and Maxine Kumin vowed to pursue a version of their telephone workshop by sending manuscripts back and forth (with unexpectedly useful results: rhythmic flaws became more obvious when unmediated by the poet's voice). Max was also the reliable narrator of family life at the Sextons'. Following periodic check-ins, she would report to Anne how relaxed Kayo seemed with the household routines and how Linda was finding her way around the kitchen. Billie, too, sent frequent notes, all with stories about the children, especially about Joy. And with reassurances: "Wring every drop of happiness out you can, and know I'll try my utmost to do things the way you want them done."

Sexton wrote frequent letters home, travelogues that reveal her abundant capacity for pleasure. With beguiling openness she relayed happy discoveries of the commonplace. She and Robart traveled at a leisurely pace, stopping frequently and taking numerous photographs to send home. They tried to save money by doing their own hair and laundry and carrying numerous supplies, such as toilet paper, immersion heaters, picnic gear, and heating pads. Sexton said their dark blue VW looked like "the Grapes of Wrath," it was so loaded with stuff.

In Belgium their car was broken into and most of the luggage was stolen. They lost all their best clothes, of course, and Sexton's rhyming dictionary, and — irreplaceable — the bound volume of Nana's letters, Sexton's portable magic. They also lost Grandfather Staples's letters from Europe, which she had put in her luggage along with Nana's. "To lose your Europe lares & penates is almost to lose all!" sympathized Kumin when she heard the news. "OH HOW WE WISH we could have selected what to be stolen," Sexton wrote home. "How will thief even sell bathing suits, let alone ten copies of each of my books. [. . .] I didn't lose new poems in manuscript for they [were] in briefcase I brought to room." (The new poems were "Crossing the Atlantic" and "Walking in Paris"; in both, imagery of being a virgin suggests that one of Sexton's coping strategies was the fantasy of starting life over on this trip.) Zestily, she and Robart set out for the local flea market, on advice from the concierge, who told them it was common knowledge that thieves would immediately take stolen clothes to one particular corner of the square. They failed as detectives but triumphed as shoppers, returning with a classy new hound's-tooth suit that Robart bought for about two dollars. When they got back to their small hotel, tired and sweaty, Madame offered them a free bubble bath (a real concession), cooked them a meal, and invited them to stay over and celebrate her birthday. "Life is indeed, happening to us, over here," Sexton conceded. A week later, when Robart's wallet was stolen on a streetcar, Sexton wasn't fazed.

She was maybe a little surprised herself at the way she took such shocks in stride. "I don't have the time or energy to get depressed or anxious," she wrote to Kayo. "If anxious I seem to have four miles of walking ahead of me and that takes care of THAT." She grew cross about never hearing from the children — they complained that it was too hard to sit down and spell. But despite her regrets about being so far away, after two and a half weeks she wrote to Kayo, "I'm stubborn and stay I will." She wrote to Dr. Orne, "I am proud of my funny awkward strength that prevents me from getting sick in order to come home. [. . .] Action does a lot to forestall anxiety."

Sexton's spirits soared when they reached Amsterdam and found not only scads of letters from family and friends but an envelope forwarded from the Ford Foundation announcing that she had been awarded the grant to spend 1964–1965 in residence with a working

Anne at a flea market in Brussels, replacing stolen clothes.

theater company. Yet she found that she didn't need writing or its rewards to know who she was; she leaned on Robart when she couldn't
lean into her own curiosity and joy. To have moods sweep through her
without paying exorbitant attention to them was a new experience for
her. She took special pride in driving their "bloo jool" over the Alps
(heights were another of her phobias), and she wrote an ecstatic letter
to the family about Alpine scenery and the descent to Italy, "where the
sound of the Opera sprang up out of Switzerland."

Sexton's chattiest letters were addressed to the whole family, including her mother-in-law, but she often wrote only to Kayo about her
discoveries. One of these was the beauty and eloquence of his letters
to her. He wrote to her several times a week, long typed letters over-
flowing with love and news. He wrote easily, with the flair of a natural
writer, about moods, the weather, the pets, the neighbors, the yard,
and the children, and about how he missed her and what he was learning from it. Mutual longing made both of them deeply receptive, and
each observed in the other's letters dispositions neither had found
words for in the past. "Oh, dear love," Anne wrote, "I love what I
know — but how much more of you is there really???? What you has
spoken? And how well and fully may I speak back . . . love, love,
love." Their separation, she felt, was drawing them closer by restoring
to her, and to him, "the part of me you first fell in love with [at the
Charles River Country Club] . . . the girl who kept swinging the club
even when she couldn't hit the ball." At her best times she felt that her
venture was "the biggest joint project we ever undertook." But she
didn't want him to think of her anymore as Princess Anne, the girl of
his dreams. "I want to say a plain say of love, of my love. [. . .] You
are not the man of my dreams. You are my life."

I think perhaps you worry that I will change or "outgrow" you
(over here or in therapy) . . . But that change has taken place (even
if I'm not all well) and I have made the pick. It would have been a
little redundant to tell you . . . for after all we were married. But
there came a time when I picked you and knew it to be my happiness.
[. . .]

We never had this before. We have come through the Navy, three
major deaths, growth and my sickness. We have made it, stronger
than ever in our love. Without this I would give up the trip. [. . .] I
have always your confidence in me. That is the thing that drives me
to stay. How can I say it and make sense? I will never leave you,

not from a lack of choice, but from a decision. I want to become MORE than Princess Anne. [. . .] I must learn to be a woman, not a child.

Kayo affirmed his own sense of this growth. "Princess" was his word for the magic her love held for him, he told her, the love that continually filled up a perpetual doubt, "almost an incapability to believe and accept what is so very true. [. . .] Each time I read a new letter [. . .] my heart leaps all over again just as if it were the very first time you had ever said it" — as in the fairy tale, when Beauty's "I love you" transformed the Beast. "Words don't change me . . . words don't change my feeling for you as a Princess, or age change the feeling. My heart is still so heavy with love that I have not told you about — and I shall probably die without the full telling! [. . .] Believe that to you my whole soul gives one cry and writing, I write more than you receive — I'm sending you kisses through my finger tips — Princess, read this letter with your lips!"

Sexton wrote many of her love letters to her husband from Venice, in a state of enchantment with the commotion and beauty of that city. She and Robart spent much of the time in the Piazza San Marco, sunning and people-watching by day, drinking apéritifs at sidewalk tables or martinis at Harry's Bar after dark. One night they skated arm in arm in a kind of dance to the waltzes pouring onto the piazza from the outdoor cafés, while the great clocktower solemnly boomed the hours far into the night. Worksheets of unpublished poetry show that Sexton was nurturing her fertile identification with Nana.

In Venice, too, she received the first chapters of Kumin's novel in progress, *Through Dooms of Love*. Industrious research into leftist politics of the 1930s on both sides of the Atlantic provided background for the ambitious plot, which revolved around a struggle between a union organizer and his spunky, too idealistic daughter. Sexton returned a long, careful critique. As always, she felt deeply engaged by her friend's writing, and at some level the engagement was partly rivalrous. What kind of a story would *she* pluck from the Old World?

Then the weather changed, and Sexton's inner weather shifted precipitously. They drove to Florence to escape driving rain, which was flooding Venice. Sexton wrote to Dr. Orne that she felt she was shrinking, "dividing and re-dividing and each time the Me that is gets smaller." As "the thrall of new places" passed, she began to lose her balance. She lost it completely in Rome, in October, when a romantic Yugoslavian barber named Louis began to pursue her. They met on a beach; at a café the next warm evening they listened to violins play "Arrivederci Roma." They danced; they flirted; they bedded. A day later she and Robart took a train for Naples and Capri — they had smashed up the Volkswagen in Rome — and Louis followed, smitten.

Now Sexton went into panic mode. Louis hadn't used a safe when they made love; could she be pregnant? She wrote a dejected letter to Kayo, without, of course, mentioning Louis. ("I am just not well. Let's face it.") She also made a $180 phone call to Dr. Orne in Boston to discuss her plight. Then she went back to the beach for more sweet-talk with Louis. Then back to the telephone, to reserve a flight home to Boston, and back to the beach for a final rendezvous. "Capri is out of this world — Sun! Water! (Sex!)" she wrote to Dr. Orne. "I desire him frantically. [. . .] When I'm with him I am a happy, manic flirt. No! I haven't slept with him again (something he, of course, cannot understand — & I hardly — dying to do it with him — 'I want! I want! I want!') [. . .] So now I have both moods at once, pulling me like a yo-yo! [. . .] To be desired totally changes me." To Kayo she wired, "ARRIVING BOSTON SUNDAY OCT 27."

Sexton reached Newton Lower Falls chagrined and defiant, yet silenced by her secret. When her menstrual period started, one of the most worrying inner voices let up; but nine days after returning from Europe, four days before her thirty-fifth birthday, she was admitted again to Westwood Lodge, fleeing from the strain of keeping up pretenses at home. "I wrote such perfect letters!" she wailed. It was the old problem of the way words could con.

She was suicidal when she arrived in Dr. Orne's office on 5 November, carrying Nana's picture in her purse along with the "kill me" pills and her own favorite knockout pills, and, for good measure, a razor. On the tape Dr. Orne made that night, a thin, listless voice sighs from what sounds like a shrunken version of Anne Sexton. The doctor did not keep her in the office very long. "There's a simple rule in psychiatry," he told her gently. "You've got to have a patient." He called Westwood Lodge to arrange for her admission — she plugged for McLean — then called Kayo to tell him that she was not coming home.

At Westwood Lodge, Sexton was under the care of Dr. Brunner-Orne; once she had been admitted, Dr. Orne did not influence her treatment. Dr. Brunner-Orne decided to change her medication, which infuriated Sexton, who believed that Dr. Orne had abandoned her. She thought that he might have intervened with his mother on her behalf and explained her psychological and physical need for her customary sleeping pills. She knew he wanted her to confront this addiction, and she accused him of seizing this opportunity to wean her.

Sexton claimed that she didn't believe her pill-taking was dangerous, and the swift oblivion the sleeping pills provided was treasured bliss. Yet as early as 1961 she had begun wondering about the seriousness of her addictions to pills and alcohol. "Can't you be addicted in a calm way that doesn't hurt anyone?" she had asked Dr. Orne. At that time he told her, quite severely, that she was kidding herself: "It's a question of wanting to [deal with it]; you don't have any motivation." He added that he couldn't treat the problem until she recognized that it was a problem on its own, not a symptom of some other problem. ("Most psychiatrists get absolutely no results with alcoholics," he observed.) Earlier in 1963 she had returned to the question. "I ought to stop taking these pills, but I'd be in a state of panic. It's not that I'm killing myself but that I'm controlling myself. Also when I drink. I'd really be a mess if I quit. I use all these things to control my fear — when I have the fear, I shake. But I wouldn't even be safe at home if I didn't take my pills, my liquor; it would involve my marriage." Now, stuck in Westwood Lodge with neither alcohol nor sleeping pills, Sexton did indeed panic. She couldn't eat or sleep or rest; worse, she thought that the new medications would induce hallucinations. And it was all Dr. Orne's fault.

However, Sexton was manipulating another issue through her conflict with Dr. Orne over the withdrawal of her pills: Kayo's jealousy. Kayo felt duped and despairing that the person who had returned from Europe was not the "princess" he had been writing to but the depressed and washed-out woman he had hoped was gone forever. According to Sexton, he had yelled at her departing back as she left for her appointment with Dr. Orne the night she went to Westwood, "You've been in a swamp so many years, I'm tired of you!" She feared his violence at this point, not so much because he was out of control as because she was itching for punishment and knew how to goad him into providing it. Kayo was especially angry over the renewed intensity of her dependence, and he believed it was Dr. Orne's control of her that kept her whining and helpless. And he *wanted* her to drink with him during the cocktail hour, and to take her pills so they both could sleep. Dr. Orne was pursuing a hard line on this subject. "Alcoholism is happening at the level of tissue, not just at the level of psychology," he had warned — and neither Anne nor Kayo liked that. In fact, Kayo often viewed Dr. Orne's advice as unmitigated meddling.

So Sexton's perceived mistreatment at Westwood provided an opening for Kayo to press his own case against Dr. Orne. After Anne had been in the hospital for three days, Kayo went to see her. For privacy they went outside and sat in his car in the dark. It was raining hard. Close together in the stormy night, they had a long conversation, during which Kayo broke down and wept; he told her he couldn't go on. "He asked me, still crying, what I wanted," Sexton wrote later in a long letter to Dr. Orne.

> He said I could have anything in the world, McLean, Austen Riggs Center, or any doctor or any thing, divorce, or anything to make me happy. I was silent. He waited. I thought of all those things. [. . .] I really wanted to get well and for him to want me to get well. Knowing I can't do it, almost, in opposition toward him. It has become a war between us. [. . .] He has never experienced a rival before (he thinks) except you. [. . .] My answer was finally after five minutes of silence with rain pelting on the car, "I want *you* to go back into therapy so we can learn how to talk, so you can help me to help myself." He was shocked [. . .] asked me to give him a month. He loathes therapy. Not Doctor Leiderman, but therapy itself, the type of analytic thinking and questions.

"Our therapy is over," Sexton announced. "I am not quitting therapy as your patient but as a wife." Kayo helped her check out of Westwood Lodge on 8 November, the day before her birthday, against the advice of the staff, who thought she should stay at least another night.

Of course Sexton didn't leave therapy with Dr. Orne. Alliance with Kayo was not so much evidence of a resolve to reconstruct her marriage as it was an act of rebellion against Dr. Orne and Dr. Brunner-Orne, a scantily disguised Father and Mother. The whole episode appears to have been based on the need Sexton always felt near her birthday to struggle through a drama of separation and reunion, death and rebirth.

Muddle on this scale was fertile ground for Sexton the writer, whatever turbulence it created in her family life. She used her sleepless stay at Westwood to draft a new poem based on the episode with Louis and her regret over its sordid outcome. Originally titled "Menstruation at Thirty-five," it identifies suicidal wishes with an unwelcome menstrual period, which coincides with the speaker's birthday. The speaker fantasizes that her womb has briefly sheltered a real "survivor" bred of peasant stock, "Slavic and determined, [. . .] my carrot, my cabbage." The vigor of a life that might have been bleeds away, and the woman who might have been invigorated by this life shrinks back into a self-imposed darkness.

As with "Sylvia's Death," Sexton was too attached personally to some of the more pathetic or disheveled images to sacrifice them to an artistic superego. The images of cabbage and carrot (for girl and boy, and peasant hardiness) served as a private shorthand to refer to the way in which Louis had come through a horrible imprisonment during the war. In Capri, Louis had told her the story of how he had been shut in a cellar by the Fascists with ten other men and women who were also Yugoslav partisans. In water up to their chests, they took turns sleeping on the cellar steps. After several weeks they were offered release on the condition that two of the men would submit two of the women to torture, and they had complied. Sexton found Louis's survival a compelling testimony to human powers of recovery. She kept in her files a sheaf of notes about the rooms where they had lain and talked after love, the sounds of water and insects, the pitted rocks and the brilliant light of Capri — details that could be counted on to arouse that slumbering beauty the unconscious, if she ever found a way to tell a fuller version of this story.

Sexton had been abroad for only two of the twelve months awarded by her grant. But two months is a long time, and despite the shadow cast by the manner of her return, she felt that she had been stretched and deepened by her encounters with foreignness, with history, with other lives. "Everywhere my eyes and sense were stimulated and excited," she wrote to Felicia Geffen at the American Academy of Arts and Letters, offering to refund the remainder of the grant. She was delighted to receive the reply that the academy wished her to keep the money, which she and Kayo used the next June to follow an updated version of her original itinerary: London, Venice, Rome, and Capri.

11

THE NANA-HEX
1964

AFTER SEXTON RETURNED from Europe in October, Dr. Orne broke the news that he was going to leave Boston to accept an attractive research and teaching opportunity at the University of Pennsylvania Medical School and the Institute of Pennsylvania Hospital in Philadelphia. The appointment would begin in September 1964. After more than seven years, his and Sexton's work together was drawing to an end.

Sexton was unprepared for this kind of change. In her fantasies, Dr. Orne *died* when she (or he) left town; he didn't do anything so prosaic and treacherous as take another job. Yet the long termination process gave her a useful period of summing up. Despite her grief at separating from this fatherly, motherly man, she shared his confidence that the gains of therapy were real and permanent.

It would have been harder for her to hang on to such a belief without the lucky coincidence of finding a new soulmate. Just before she had left for Europe, she had met a psychiatrist named Anne Wilder, a friend of Tillie Olsen's. Wilder was sophisticated, high-spirited, full of jokes, warm, a few years older than Sexton, and fascinated by writers. "I'm in love with you already!" Sexton whispered dramatically when Olsen introduced them.

Home from Europe and grounded in Newton Lower Falls, Sexton kept in touch with Wilder, who had returned to her home in San Francisco. They wrote to each other often and phoned several times a month to talk for an hour or more at a stretch. Once Dr. Orne had declared his intention to leave Boston, Sexton began recruiting Wilder for the new team. Because her friend was a psychiatrist, Sexton felt that no revelation of her own mental states could alienate her.

She indulged in very comprehensive revelations indeed, about her life and about her therapy. Going back over her three-year collection of therapy notebooks, she condensed the details for Wilder into a tight narrative of two single-spaced typed pages, of which the theme was childhood trauma ("Of course not trusting goes back to parents . . ."). There she ironed out and fit together the torn, wrinkled, sometimes illegible fragments that had surfaced, usually in trances, during nearly eight years of treatment, making a concise account of little Anne's subjection by Mother, Nana, and Daddy to bodily humiliations and spirit-killing rejection. Never before had she put the story together so coherently, snapping effect into cause as if setting pieces into a jigsaw puzzle. The story of her transformation was now complete. In this letter to Wilder may be glimpsed the seeds of the most fully achieved, ambitious works of Sexton's artistic maturity: the plot of *Mercy Street,* the genesis of *Transformations,* and the inspiration for *O Ye Tongues.* Assembling this version of her personal history appears to have been one of the gains of her termination with Dr. Orne.

For Sexton, writing to and receiving letters from Anne Wilder restored an opportunity for intimacy that had been missing in her life since Jim Wright and Brother Dennis Farrell had dropped out. Even phone calls with Kumin did not give so much scope to the desire for exposure, the delight of receiving unflagging attention from a "twin." This one had everything — even Sexton's name. Another Nana! Of course Wilder recognized this aspect of Sexton's ardor as the tug of transference. "I'll be glad if in the course of our relationship the fact of my being a psychiatrist becomes less and less important to you," she wrote after receiving Sexton's nutshell version of issues from childhood. "The less our relationship is a 'transference' relationship, the more it is a real one, *in both directions,* the more deeply rewarding, lasting, etc. it will be." She pointed out that since the two of them had not entered into a professional relationship, they should be on the lookout for the transference effect and its power to produce "disillusion, disappointment, recrimination and bitterness."

Easier said than done. On her side, Wilder recognized her attraction to Sexton as in part a fascination with writers — she was a second cousin of Thornton Wilder's and hoped that writing might be found to run in the family. Suffering from lupus, an incurable degenerative disease that made it necessary to curtail her practice, she told Sexton that she wanted to spend her new-found time writing fiction. This message distressed Sexton very much, and she wrote a long reply that can be summarized in one sentence: In the time you have left, "stick to your trade."

Wilder gathered that Sexton thought she was dying of lupus, and they spent some time untangling the misunderstanding. But now that the theme of death had been engaged, Wilder — knowing of Sexton's persistent suicidal thoughts — raised a question that almost anyone might have wished to ask Anne Sexton in 1964. Here she was, a prizewinning poet, the mother of two darling children, a beautiful woman with a comfortable life. So what was the big attraction in suicide? "This may sound shallow as hell to you," Wilder wrote, "but at my worst, deepest despair I've thought [. . .] that to take my own life is so silly. Because it's going to be taken from me soon enough anyway. [. . .] I love living and the things and objects that are available here on Earth. Like blades of grass, for example." What was the big attraction?

At the moment that Wilder asked this question, Sexton was not thinking about killing herself; she was thinking, once again, of writing about it. *Life* and the *Saturday Evening Post* had just published big spreads on Arthur Miller's new play, *After the Fall,* which *Life* implied drew one of its main characters from Marilyn Monroe. Sexton read avidly about the play, since both its theme of suicide and its structure — confession to a silent listener (read psychoanalyst) — provocatively resembled those of *The Cure.* She wrote enthusiastically to Wilder, "Miller's play really gets me . . . the suicide stuff, etc. It *is* too confessional . . . but me, I likes confession . . . mostly I liked the method he used . . . one that I have been fooling with . . . a method that kicks time in the face. I have a big interest (don't know why) in kicking time in the face, shuttling it up like a pack of cards & reordering it to suit my style." Wilder's question about suicide was therefore well timed, and triggered a "morbid free association" that Sexton appended to a letter: "We live at such contrasts . . . you and me . . . me lapping the edges . . . me testing death . . . me raging at the fruit, the plump moon, the arthritic hands, thick with pleasure, the old corpse, the bread that I took for a kiss, the love, an infection. [. . .] It will be very ugly, but it was always very ugly and this time I will be part of it . . . I'll be its other children."

A few days later Sexton sent Wilder the poem "Wanting to Die," which organized much of this material into lucid statements about the obsession that sets the suicide apart from others:

But suicides have a special language.
Like carpenters they want to know *which tools*.
They never ask *why build*.

She also acknowledged that she had avoided discussing her suicidal obsessions with Wilder or working on them in therapy until she had "gotten" the poem.

Sexton's thoughts about suicide were pretty well established by 1964, and so were her practices. Which tools? She would combine alcohol with an overdose of pills, which she considered "the woman's way out," she told Dr. Orne. "For Ernest Hemingway to shoot himself with a gun in the mouth is the greatest act of courage I can think of," she said. "I worry about the minutes before you die, that fear of death. I don't have it with the pills, but with a gun there'd be a minute when you'd know, a terrible fear. I'd do anything to escape that fear; death would be a friend, then." Plath's death by asphyxiation offered another model she recognized as "the woman's way." As she put it in her therapy notebook at the time of Plath's death, "I don't want to die in some hospital — or on a bridge that will collapse — I don't want to die of something I'm afraid of." Around the time she was writing "Wanting to Die," she expanded on this theme to Dr. Orne. "I'm so fascinated with Sylvia's death: the idea of dying perfect, certainly not mutilated. . . . To lose your virginity is to be mutilated; virginity is unopen, not yet spoiled. . . . I'd rather die than have a breast removed — talk about mutilation! By the time they were done with my mother — or life was done with my mother or Nana! My father had this thing about perfection, physical perfection that is — Sleeping Beauty remained perfect."

Dying perfect was what Sexton did every night when she took her sleeping pills, making herself a Sleeping Beauty. (As Linda Sexton later noted, the contrast with having a breast removed conveys Sexton's horror of undergoing a death like her mother's, invaded by cancer, out of control.) Taking her "kill me" pills was another kind of action: punishment of a self she hated. Like rousing her therapist's anger or her husband's physical violence, the suicide attempts would, from the point of view of her neurosis, settle some accounts. "He'd have punished me — like killing yourself is punishment — and when Nana looked at me and said I wasn't Anne." What is it you strive for? Dr. Orne asked. Someone to look at me and tell me I'm all right — or to hit me, she answered. Being hit is like taking pills, "destroying a part of me, squashing it — I've killed part of me." This killed part is the notion behind Sexton's image of a split-off aspect of herself as a "rat" who in death could find its own "star," and of the metaphor in her letter to Wilder of being one of the children of ugliness. Diminutive and helplessly evil, this inner creature had a life of its own that Sexton longed to destroy. That did not mean, in 1964, that she wanted to die.

The question of suicide was raised from another direction by news of the death of Sexton's old friend Ruth Soter. There were conflicting rumors: some thought that Soter had died of a heart attack (she had a severe heart ailment), and others thought that she had committed suicide (she had made attempts on her life in the past). Sexton wrote to one of Soter's friends, "I would rather that she had killed herself (which seems a matter of free will) than to have died of a heart attack (which seems a matter of being put through a terrifying machine). This doesn't make any sense to anyone when I try to explain it. Ruth would have understood it. She had a special language all her own and my life is much emptier now that she has left it."

By the time she got around to intellectualizing about suicide, Sexton had achieved some control over the impulses that had once possessed her; unsentimental clarity gives "Waiting to Die" force and beauty. Yet the poem puts into memorable imagery the state of mind that makes sense of Sexton's terse declaration to Dr. Orne, following Plath's death, that "suicide is addicting too."

The spring of 1964 was completely devoted to working out a satisfactory routine with a new therapist. Dr. Orne did a preliminary search, Sexton made a number of visits to different doctors, and then she settled on Dr. Ollie Zweizung. She began seeing Dr. Zweizung once a week while she remained in therapy with Dr. Orne twice a week. Not surprisingly, all of the poems she wrote during these months were addressed to a doctor — either Anne Wilder or Dr. Orne — in her psyche. Three of these appeared in *Live or Die*: "KE 6-8018" (Dr. Orne's office phone number), "Wanting to Die," and "The Wedding Night." Sexton consigned two others to a manuscript of therapy poems, which was eventually published as *Words for Dr. Y.*: "I remember my mother dying" and "I put some daisies in a bowl."

In mid-May, Anne and Kayo left for the month's vacation made possible by her award from the American Academy of Arts and

Letters. It was a romantic trip. They revisited Anne's favorite spots in Italy. They visited friends in Zurich and drove through the Black Forest. From France, Sexton wrote to Wilder about an unbuttoned moment in their Paris hotel when a room-service waiter arrived with champagne cocktails while Kayo was drawing a bath. Naked, Kayo joined Anne to sip the drinks before bathing. She decided to take a photo of him as Bacchus, and after he had been posing and she shooting, she glanced out their window and found herself looking into the amused faces of other tourists seated in the dining room across the courtyard. They had fun together, yet Anne was eager to get home; she complained to Dr. Orne and to Wilder that her ego had once again "sprung a leak" about halfway through the trip, and though she struggled to conceal her grim feelings from Kayo, she counted the days till their return, and was glad she didn't fall apart before they made it back.

In midsummer Sexton returned to work on her long-abandoned play, *The Cure.* Her Ford Foundation grant would underwrite workshop development and production costs at the Charles Playhouse in Boston when the season opened in September. She expected this experience to be something like the poetry workshops she had found so productive for creative revision, and she wanted to be ready with a draft hot off the typewriter. She gave the play a new title, *Tell Me Your Answer True,* and a new plot: "A girl who has committed suicide finds herself in death as a character in a circus sideshow looking for Christ. She is hounded by morality figures with names like Backbiter, Barker, Flesh, and Charity." Inspired by Arthur Miller's handling of flashbacks in *After the Fall,* she put the secondary characters onstage, seated on bleachers, awaiting their cue from the Barker. The framing device for Daisy's harrowing assault by guilty memories was now a circuslike purgatory into which her scenes with doctor, priest, and family — lifted straight from *The Cure* — were nested. As in Miller's play, the action built toward the revelation of a crushing secret from which the main character's guilt flowed. In *Tell Me Your Answer True,* that secret is an incestuous episode between Daisy and her father, Arthur (nicknamed Ace), which is witnessed by Daisy's maiden great-aunt, who goes crazy as a result. Daisy has committed suicide in expiation. The play begins and ends in the afterlife, a limbo Sexton calls The Place.

Sexton wrote much of this new version in a frenzy during the six weeks that her children were away at camp. Additional motivation to lose herself in work was provided by the rapidly approaching departure of Dr. Orne, who would be moving to Philadelphia by the first of August. Work was an effective distraction from this painful loss, for it gave Sexton the consoling sense of a return to an earlier period of her relationship with him. Back in 1958, while Joy was still living full-time with Billie, she had worked just this demonically on early drafts of "The Double Image." Then she had been losing her mother. Now she was losing the one who had literally stood in for *all* her pretty ones. As she wrote to Anne Wilder, "I'm not okay, but maybe I'll survive the mourning period for MY BEST FRIEND — DOC ORNE, Nana, Mommy, Daddy — & Love & Growth & Understanding." The termination of therapy with Dr. Orne was bringing very intense and very old feelings sharply into focus; writing the play licensed Sexton to plunder these feelings, particularly the clamorous guilts over Nana.

At the worst periods of her sickness, Sexton often felt possessed by Nana's vengeful spirit, which haunted her in the form of voices only she could hear. In one of her late poems she called this "the Nana-hex"; in therapy, she traced its origin to the memory or fantasy of hearing Nana say, "You're not Anne!" During one of her spells of anxiety in 1958 she had written notes to Dr. Orne about the voices that attacked her. "I am looking for Nana — I know she is here — everyone who dies becomes a voice that follows me. [. . .] The voices are small in my ear — they are tiny because they are shouting from so far away. Sometimes the voice is a stranger's — but he is dead — I do not know him. The dead people control me — they don't comfort me — they say awful things — I am afraid — they laugh at me — they can see through me. [. . .] Nana, how can I let go. Oh why won't you let go of me Nana, with your voice in my head?"

In her play, Sexton drew on these voices to create the Witnesses. The new setting freed her comic gifts, and she wrote witty, raunchy doggerel for the three Barkers and four Witnesses:

BARKER TWO

Hark ye! Gather round, pull up your chair, to see the universe in its underwear. Hark ye! Give me your sentiments please. Don't push for places like rats on cheese. [. . .] Pregnant nuns and crooked financiers, the hairy, the horny, the gouty in this arena, arrive for your eyes without subpoena. Forget about shawls and chains and chow, we have our victim ready now.

BACKBITER
My name is Backbiter. I ride on a horse.
This is my hobby — a lobby of sorts.
Being the devil, I take none by force.
                With death on his tongue
                And a dart in his heart
                Everyman here is a fool and a fart.

CHARITY
My name is Charity and I live with my daughter.
Her name is Mercy but she's gone insane.
We live without beef, we live without water.
Life is our portion, but most of it's pain.

Sexton imagined the Barkers as wooden figures with tape-recorded voices. For contrast, the Witnesses would caper about the stage, while the Manager served as ringmaster and director, setting a rapid pace at the opening of each act. The carnival atmosphere was meant to diminish the proportion of static, or ecstatic, recollection that Daisy's role demanded.

Writing the play required Sexton to bring Daisy's point of view into tension with that of the other characters, which she managed with great skill. The family scenes might have been lifted directly out of her therapy notebooks, but the play fits the pieces into a design much larger than Anne Sexton's life history. All the characters except the doctor are like damaged children, trying to conjure happiness by magical thinking. Daisy's mother is hooked on nostalgia for the romantic past. Her father is a salesman (did Sexton borrow his name from Arthur Miller?) who keeps up a bold front by staying drunk. He is thinking of his erection, not his daughter, while he tipples and jokes, and despite the horror created by the scene of incest, Sexton makes him a touching figure. His tone is tender at first: "Lie back now and I'll give you a back rub like Aunt Amy does." Then his hands move between Daisy's legs.

The play endows with definitive importance for Daisy not the father's act but the great-aunt's response to witnessing it. Aunt Amy goes crazy before Daisy's eyes, expressing madness through a torrent of associations (she calls it "doubling off"): "Who put the hex into Texas! Ha! You make a double, a conversation that goes on between your two selves and then it starts . . . starts to scream obscene things and then it rolls down the hill and the other joins in, howling with laughter, calling off its own words, own signals, little plaything, away from itself . . . then these two are over, are dead . . . They are cast off, double trouble." She idealizes Daisy's childish innocence and cannot bear the discovery that her niece experiences desire. The play shows us, further, that Aunt Amy is psychologically fused with Daisy, so that what contaminates Daisy destroys her.

But everyone in the play wants Daisy to remain a child, an object of projection and fantasy. "I'm half crazy over the love of you," as the song goes. Growing conscious of the motivations behind this infantilizing love is what maddens Daisy, makes her fear for her own children and yearn for a return through insanity to the point in childhood before the incestuous episode, and at last leads her to Christ. His death calls to her: As Christ sacrificed his life to undo original sin, so Daisy thinks death will both end the progress of disease through the generations and restore her to the state of childhood idealized in her family relations, "no more a woman than Christ was a man." When Sexton was first formulating the play, back in 1962, she told Dr. Orne that she saw Daisy's pathology — and her own — in religious terms: "This girl is *me*, a different idea of Christ!" But the psychiatrist in the play, Dr. Alex, sees no difference between Daisy's vision of Christ and her other delusions. He sternly requests commitment to "things of this world," and when she resists his skepticism, he medicates her and sends her back to the hospital, where she commits suicide.

The play's action is on the doctor's side: No Christ, no forgiveness, awaits Daisy after death. Neither medical nor religious institutions could address the problem of her guilt, which lay in the power of her body to arouse sexual desire in those with power over her life. Daisy's dilemma invites feminist political analysis in every scene — analysis that Sexton was in no way prepared to make. Nonetheless, the play exposes Sexton's resistance to the reductive Freudian interpretations of women's sexuality current in her day. Daisy's erotic feelings flow first toward a woman, Aunt Amy, who is too repressed to acknowledge them, then toward a father who identifies manhood with an erection. Finally they fix on an image of a Christ redeemed from a phallocentric psychology. In the aspiration to be "no more a woman than Christ was a man," Sexton articulated the psychological conflict from which the play's action unfolded in each of its many versions, from *The Cure* in 1961 through *Tell Me Your Answer True* in 1964–1965 and on to *Mercy Street* in 1969. The possibility of establishing a relationship between Christ's suffering and that of a "hysteric" remained for Sexton a compelling spiritual issue of productive importance to her work.

It is always disappointing to find that a work of art is wiser than its maker, but Anne Sexton's play was both wiser and more compassionate than Anne Sexton the person. That summer, Sexton's complex relationship with Linda, who celebrated her eleventh birthday on 21 July, was drawn powerfully into the play's vortex. In many ways Linda *was* Daisy: a child whose body was changing in front of everyone's eyes, awakening in her mother old memories and new pride. Sexton reported to Anne Wilder that she had noticed three hairs under her daughter's arm: "I say to her with obvious delight, 'Linda, you're like a garden! Something new every day!' [. . .] It's so lovely and it breaks me up."

When Sexton wasn't working on the play that month, she was writing a birthday poem for Linda, "Little Girl, My String Bean, My Lovely Woman." Tender and celebratory, the poem nonetheless bears

Kayo with Linda on Halloween.

the bruise of Sexton's preoccupation with Daisy. For Daisy, the onset of womanhood precipitates the disaster of seduction by her father and reveals a guilty eroticism behind her great-aunt's cuddling. The same threat haunts the poem, in the mother's fantasy about her daughter's sexual awakening.

> and someday they will come to you,
> someday, men bare to the waist, young Romans
> at noon where they belong,
> with ladders and hammers
> while no one sleeps.

> But before they enter
> I will have said,
> *Your bones are lovely,*
> and before their strange hands
> there was always this hand that formed.

The odd emphases "where they belong," "while no one sleeps," "their hands . . . this hand" hold at bay the shame of incest that occupied neighboring circuitry in the poet's brain: incestuous actions taken by the hands of both Ace and Amy. Writing "Little Girl" seems to have enabled Sexton to make artistic use of her confused erotic feelings toward Linda, converting them into a poem of celebration that she read proudly in public whenever Linda traveled with her. Many readers found this poem touching and successful, partly because of its theme of a mother's protective pride in a daughter's sexual budding. It may be the best example in all of Sexton's writing of the way she resolved in one work feelings that she was permitting rampant license in another.

Unfortunately, the artistic resolution of these feelings did not have its counterpart in life. For many years, when Sexton couldn't sleep — especially when Kayo was away — she had been going to Linda's bed for comfort. Now her cuddling began to feel different to Linda: clingy and furtive. Only later did Linda realize that her mother must have been masturbating as she lay beside her. She recalled, "I would be turned on my side, and I would lie there like a stone, pretending to be asleep, waiting for something to be over. I don't think I wanted to know what it was."

Sexton never acknowledged to her daughter that she was conscious of transgression, but how could she have failed to see how wrong this was? The most generous interpretation is that she may have been very dissociated when she made sexual use of Linda. Sexton identified deeply with this daughter, through whom she relived her own psychological development. For her, losing Dr. Orne was much like losing Nana. Sexton was eleven years old when Nana moved into the Harvey household. It may be that in trance, reversing the position of mother and child as she always did in her "games" with the children, she sought from Linda the "safe" feelings, never acknowledged by Nana or herself as sexual, that Nana had provided so abundantly. Linda concurs with this view of her behavior; as she put it later, "The compulsion to repeat and to *recast* her own history was just too strong." Sexton turned to Linda whenever she was feeling particularly fragile, and Linda bore this as one of the costs of her mother's instability.

As Dr. Orne's departure loomed closer, Sexton got shakier. Toward the end of July, after a month of zealous work rewriting Daisy's story, she began to suffer from more and more of Aunt Amy's symptoms. She was pushing herself hard, eating very little and sleeping only a few hours each night, and she was calling upon some of her most ravaging memories to create voices for the Witnesses and the Barkers and Aunt Amy and Ace. Eventually, her "left hand" took over, she wrote to Anne Wilder. "I'm not (overtly) depressed . . . oh no. MANIC. [. . .] That is what was driving the machine that drove the play that drove me (when over — note the large EGO of the writer — won't break down until play is over — play being more important than any plans to get sick). . . . nuts!"

When Sexton did break down, in late July, Dr. Orne was in the last stages of preparation for departure and was no longer formally treating her, but Dr. Zweizung was away on a research trip. Dr. Orne decided that Sexton should be hospitalized and put her under the care of a doctor she dubbed "Jack Frost" at Massachusetts General Hospital in Boston. In a long letter to Wilder, she reported details of interviews with this new doctor, as if she and he were characters in a play.

> *Doc.* Did anyone ever tell you what yr illness was, Mrs. Sexton?
> *Me.* Yes. I'm an hysteric.
> *Doc.* And what does that mean?
> *Me.* Well, it means I'm not psychotic!
> *Doc.* Are you so sure?
> [Here Sexton inserted stage directions: "fear of being psychotic.

fear of being out of control. fear." At the next appointment, "Jack Frost" returned to the question of diagnosis of her illness.]

    Doc. So what if you are psychotic. There isn't such a wall between neurotic and psychotic, such a difference?

    Me. Fear. Fear of being out of control. Fear. My grandfather died in a straight jacket. Nana died crazy. Fear of psychotic. To be neurotic is, to me, fairly normal.

    Doc. And this rhyming that you keep doing?

    Me. I know it's silly. And I keep laughing. I can't seem to feel anything but silly. I keep talking LANGUAGE.

The symptoms she dramatized were actual at that point. Bedeviled by "a constant rhyming inside my head," Sexton sought relief in a flow of babble with another patient who shared her symptom: "We laugh for ten minutes at a group of rhymes . . . At night I dream in jokes," she told Wilder. "And Dr. Orne talks about the underlying depression and the mania mounting as I wrote play that deals so brilliantly with madness (guess why? cuz it's authentic . . . the clang words are Mine and not from a textbook or a guess. fished them up out of my own machine even!)."

After her release from the hospital, she had the manuscript of *Tell Me Your Answer True* retyped and presented one of the carbon copies to Dr. Orne as a farewell gift. It was a remarkably layered and eloquent testimony to the bond between them. By "abandoning" Sexton, Dr. Orne had triggered a replay of the loss of Nana, in all its dimensions, for through the miraculous economy of transference he had helped her relive and sort out the complicated splitting off by which she had protected the deep love she felt for her parents and for the great-aunt tragically lost in psychic pain of her own. The play rationalized these insights into a story, and was more economical and successful than a dream in fulfilling many of Sexton's wishes. It restored Dr. Orne in all the characters opposite Daisy: Amy, Ace, Dr. Alex, and the priest. Moreover, it made Daisy and Amy into heroines of language, very like Freud's famous hysterics. Anne / Orne were authors of this story, and Dr. Orne its ideal reader, for it was he who had authorized the emergence of the poet by validating Sexton's special gifts of language.

Sexton was hospitalized in the psychiatric ward at Mass. General for two weeks — much longer than her usual stay at Westwood — apparently so that she could be established on a course of medication. She provided Anne Wilder with a detailed commentary on her treatment, which indicates that she was tried first on an antidepressant, Tofranil (imipramine). When this proved ineffectual, she was put on Thorazine (chlorpromazine), which by 1964 was widely used to treat people with psychoses such as schizophrenia, to relieve hallucinations and delusions, and to quell mania of the kind Sexton displayed in her "doubling off." She joked to Wilder, "Thorazine, they say, is supposed to make the rhymer go away." Not much was yet known about its neurological side effects after long usage, which Sexton probably did experience: tremors, which made her handwriting difficult to read; facial distortions, which strongly emphasized the asymmetry of her features; involuntary movements of mouth, lips, and tongue, which bothered her children. Thorazine was known to produce discomfort, however: it was highly sedating, caused weight gain, and made the user's skin extremely sensitive to sunlight. Sexton would curse and struggle with all of these for the next eight years.

She not only resisted the drug's side effects, she resisted its frontal attack on the linguistic powers she referred to as "Language," often capitalized — the name for her inspiration that most acknowledged its alliance with her illness. As she told Wilder, "Language has nothing to do with rational thought. I think that's why I get so horribly furious and disturbed with rational thought. [. . .] I mumble language to the trees by the pool as if they knew and am fiercely resenting anyone who doesn't talk language (and now it's an obsession). Well, nevermind. I think language is beautiful. I even think insanity is beautiful (surely the root of language), except that it is painful." After her release from the hospital, she took a brief trip to New York, accompanied by Sandy Robart, to see several plays. By then she had been on Thorazine for three weeks and reported that "manic me is under control thanks to Thorazine . . . except for one day in New York when I forgot to take it and went out and bought a four feet high stuffed DOG (for myself). He is very funny — looks great in bar at the Waldorf and the Sheraton." During this brief holiday from the drug, she wrote to Dr. Orne, "Quite manic. Very. Sandy likes me manic. She laughs at me all the time. I also laugh. If I can pick, I pick this illness (if it is one)."

Sexton had experienced the brilliant verbal and emotional energies of mania in July as a pure gift, one she had used to attain a new level of art. She wrote to Kayo, who was away on a business trip the day of their sixteenth anniversary, that she knew the play had taken her away from him that summer and she was sorry. But "if the magic only comes around every 5 or 6 years, I've got to use it, just got to." *Was* insanity the root of "Language"? Would Thorazine eliminate the magic?

By the time September rolled around, Sexton had put *Tell Me Your Answer True* through enough drafting that she felt able to step into her new apprenticeship at the Charles Playhouse, where with funding from the Ford Foundation it was slated for workshop development, possibly for production. Her project was assigned to Ben Shaktman, a diminutive, curly-headed wise guy, twenty-six years old and exuding confidence. Shaktman joined the Charles Playhouse that month as head of the new Musical Theater for Children and the theater's high school touring program. He was also placed in charge of the Experimental Theater, where Sexton was to be installed as playwright in residence.

Shaktman and Sexton met for lunch in Boston, to get acquainted. He later remembered her arrival at the restaurant — she was as glamorous as a fashion model, breezy, enthusiastic, with a big shoebox under her arm. They seemed to hit it off at once, but she kept excusing herself from the table; later, when they had become good friends, she confessed that she had been so nervous she had run to the ladies' room again and again to throw up. Shaktman told her that he hoped she would get started immediately: "Write a scene a day for our experimental group, and force us to play it." Little did he know. She opened the shoebox and brought out the fat, scissored-and-taped copy of *Tell Me Your Answer True*. Shaktman delighted her a week later by announcing to the press at a reception, "Sexton's play is a blockbuster!"

Sexton began spending long hours at the Charles Playhouse, watching plays go into production under the different directorial styles of Shaktman and Michael Murray. Mondays and Thursdays, when her housekeeper replaced her at home, she went into Boston for appointments with her psychiatrist and sessions at the Charles. Back at her typewriter, she would rewrite a scene and send it to Shaktman special delivery. Next day he would phone and pick it to pieces; by evening another rewrite would be on its way to him. Every so often the actors would read a scene for her, and she would be mortified to find Shaktman disputing what she thought sounded great.

Shaktman knew what drama he was after: the tragic failure of family love at the core of the play. "Anne Sexton taught me what it was like to be a daughter — a daughter with an Ace at the center of her life. In many ways, the character of Aunt Amy was the juiciest in the play because it most clearly dramatized the deformation of the daughter's role." He thought Daisy's most significant characteristic was not her craziness but her sweetness; Sexton's vision of a child-becoming-woman seemed to him "extravagantly interesting," but it needed to be rescued from both the maniacal frenzy of its framing device in the afterlife and from heavy-handed exposition through the monologues of psychotherapy. "Facts sound much better in an actor's mouth than does imagery," he commented on one of her drafts. "Any encumbrances such as additional POETRY, additional references, additional characters easily unbalance the basic weight of the whole work." Shaktman advised Sexton to cut the Witnesses entirely and focus the drama wholly on Daisy. ("Why, Daisy is a Joan of Arc for health!" he later commented.) "Daisy is just as crazy as I am," Sexton retorted. "And as for God, he now has an answering service that informs us, like the weather girl, that he is out."

Their close collaboration ended early in March 1965, when Shaktman was invited to direct a play in New York and resigned from his position at the Charles. Perhaps, in any case, he had reached the limits of his usefulness to her. Sexton agreed that the play's main problem was its structure, but she never agreed to abandon the theme of Daisy's struggle for religious belief. Shaktman wanted to ground the play in psychological realities, but Sexton wanted to probe the conflict between psychological explanations and the mysteries of meaning that cannot be approached through reasonableness. Throughout her apprenticeship at the Charles, she was frustrated by her inability to express this conflict artistically in a way that made sense to the theater people whose professional advice she needed. As she wrote to her agent, "Right now I'm beginning to doubt the whole basis of the play (One, that the inaccuracy of memory fools us all forever; two, that the idea of Christ fools us all, twisting life into little jigsaw patterns, leaving us all at the ever-resurrection terror of 'The Place.')" She concluded that she just needed to be "more stubborn about getting a good play out of Daisy. I think she has a story to tell."

Now that Sexton's career was prospering, she wanted more freedom to be away from home. The children, aged eleven and nine, still needed someone to look after them. Sexton claimed to enjoy being a mother very much, and her daughters were devoted companions who relished her swooping good humor and her vibrancy, when she had it to offer them. This made her happy. More, they were her inspiration. Closeness to them put her in touch with joys and sorrows buried deep in her own nerves. She resonated with their animal presence, their developing intelligence; they made her own unconscious life as available as a fountain.

But she had never liked and never would like the responsibility of managing a household, and of course she needed undisturbed time to work. Billie Sexton was happy to take the children on the days when the housekeeper wasn't there, but Anne thought the problem might be solved best by hiring an *au pair* girl to live in. She and Kayo advertised in a Stockholm newspaper for a mature woman. As Sexton told Anne Wilder "What I need is a mother! WANTED . . . A RENTED MOTHER!! U.S.A. . . . That is how the ad ought to read. No answers as yet." But if they were to bring another adult into the house, they would have to move.

More and more, Kayo pressed for this. His father's death in 1960 had provided a legacy that he was saving with an eye on pursuing a new career, perhaps going to medical school. But now the family's discomfort pressured him. There was no spare room in the house; even the back yard was full, since the Sextons had built Anne's study and the pool.

When they had moved to Newton Lower Falls in 1953, Anne had hated the house and the neighborhood, which she referred to scathingly as "the asshole of Newton." Over the years, though, she had made wonderful friends on Clearwater Road. Sandy Robart, Rita Ernst, and Eleanor Boylan all lived within a short half-block, and Anne, who still panicked when she had to walk alone on a city sidewalk, liked being able to run across the lawns to see them. The Sextons shared drinks and meals almost every week with one or another of their neighbors.

But by 1964 they were ready to move to a better neighborhood, with better schools nearby. As autumn came on, Anne and Kayo began house-hunting. The search took them to Weston, where Billie lived and where Anne had grown up. There the houses were spacious, often grand, set on hills or beside meandering roads. The Sextons spotted the house they finally bought, at 14 Black Oak Road, on a beautiful day in October, when the New England foliage was at its zenith. Tall swamp maples flanked the olive green house, and woods bordered the lot at the back. A two-story modern colonial, brand new, the house was roomy and light, with a sunny kitchen that looked out on the perfect site for a swimming pool. Adjacent to the kitchen was a paneled room with a dark brick fireplace, which Anne could use as a study. In the large sunken living room, two steps down, Kayo could install the huge stereo system he wanted. They chose bright wallpaper, and installed a brilliant orange carpet in the living room and a brilliant gold carpet through the front hall and up the stairs. "I meant to pick things that were dramatic," Sexton wrote to Wilder. They moved just after Christmas.

12

"ICARUS CATCH"
1965

BACK IN THE DAYS of the John Holmes workshop, someone introduced Anne Sexton to one of the few classical literary allusions that she adopted as personal shorthand. This was Ovid's story of how Daedalus and his son Icarus fled from Crete by fastening on wings made of wax and feathers; Daedalus escaped, but Icarus soared too near the sun, so that the wax melted and he fell to his death in the sea. W. H. Auden had popularized this theme for contemporary audiences in a much-anthologized poem on Brueghel's painting of the subject, "Musée des Beaux-Arts," and this may have been Sexton's source. In any case, when W. D. Snodgrass's *Heart's Needle* won the Pulitzer Prize in 1960, she referred to the story in her poem "To a Friend Whose Work Has Come to Triumph."

> [Icarus] glances up and is caught, wondrously tunneling
> into that hot eye. Who cares that he fell back to the sea?
> See him acclaiming the sun and come plunging down
> while his sensible daddy goes straight into town.

The tribute suggests a comparison between types of poets: the Daedalus, whose know-how gains him practical advantages, and the Icarus, whose craziness carries him very high.

The identification of her poet-self with Icarus took on new meaning while Sexton was on Thorazine, which interfered both with her creative manias and with her devotion to the sun. During her first six months taking the drug, she felt that her creativity had entirely dried up. She wrote to Tillie Olsen around Valentine's Day 1965, "The g.d. tranquilizers I started to take at M.G.H. this summer have completely stoppered any original idea. I haven't had one since the first madness of the play took over (and that was before M.G.H.). [. . .] I haven't written a poem since this summer, since M.G.H. . . . (have I been, unwittingly, lobotomized?)"

Sexton discounted all the rewriting of *Tell Me Your Answer True,* which she had recently finished; that seemed like a mere exercise. Mornings now, in her new house, she spent hours just sitting at the kitchen table, feeling "woolly." A flood of cheerful sunlight poured into the room through the east-facing windows, which looked across the large back yard into the woods, but it could touch neither her heart nor her skin. Before Thorazine, on days like this she would have wrapped herself in her mother's fur coat for the trip outdoors to catch the first vernal rays of February on her face. "All my life I have been in love with the sun," she said. "I looked at it as the great lover, the great seizure. Somehow, letting the sun wash over you, letting its heat adore you, was like having intercourse with God." Now she had to protect her skin from any exposure to ultraviolet light: "Just a spot of sun on my arm as I drive along and it is like bees stinging me." This side effect felt like daily evidence that the drug was blocking her inspiration.

Sexton stayed with the treatment, though, in the hope that adapting to Thorazine was a way of assisting her "right hand," her rationality, her Daedalus side. She saw Dr. Zweizung, a psychiatrist who had also been through psychoanalytic training, twice every week, and thought that her therapy with him was at last going well. She had felt very proud in December when he suggested that she move to the couch, since she considered that a sign of progress. As she wrote to Anne Wilder, "For years I heard I was too sick for couch, but I feel okay right now. [. . .] I'm in a little flurry about having been 'on the couch,' à la Maxine, à la analysis, à la what I never did before."

She continued to communicate to Wilder many details of her treatment, although Wilder disowned the therapist's role, keeping the tone of her long, frequent letters light and friendly. When she commented on Sexton's progress, she did so from the perspective of common sense and avoided using medical jargon. Nonetheless, she spoke to Sexton with the authority of a psychiatrist.

Inevitably, the relationship between Sexton and Wilder had become an issue in Sexton's therapy, first with Dr. Orne and then with Dr. Zweizung — not only because Wilder was a psychiatrist, but more because of the component of sexual attraction in the intensity the two had felt toward each other from their first meeting. They encapsulated the quality of this attachment in a myth: they called each other "Icarus catcher," a name Wilder gave them — never having read Sexton's poem about Icarus, not knowing about Sexton's private mythology — on the day Tillie Olsen introduced them. Wilder recalled this meeting in one of her first letters to Sexton: "It was like Icarus plummeting not to destruction in the sea, but into a haven, my lap (maybe heart would be better)." Sexton agreed.

> As an image between us it worked both ways. [. . .] In ways you can't know, the time when I met you I too was hungry and really awfully afraid . . . and you did much for me and so, you see, I felt you had made up the image. You said 'and I caught you like Icarus.' [. . .] To be caught is not to fall. [. . .] I guess I didn't think you knew you were catching me but when you used the Icarus image, that you did. Well one thing for sure. I did fall in there out of the sky and that was love and you did catch me and that was love. And let Icarus be our image.

Wilder assented. "Yes, we are highly combustible as a pair," she wrote. "Low combustion level and high flame."

It was the beautiful, driven, foolhardy Icarus in Sexton that had first attracted Wilder's affection, and it was the "Icarus catcher" in Wilder that Sexton returned to, as to a mother's lap, whenever she was in trouble. For Anne Wilder the myth may have been about romance; for Anne Sexton it was about rescue. The difference in their emotional investments didn't matter much as long as these were displaced into classical imagery, but Sexton became aware that the intensity that was so exciting in letters and phone calls turned awkward when they met.

After Wilder made a brief visit to Boston during the summer of 1964, Sexton confessed in a letter that she had been trying to back away a little. Reluctantly, she acknowledged the erotic feelings that her friend aroused: "Out of love I was about to, was afraid, was confused, was . . . about to respond. Get it? Can I be plainer." What she wanted to keep, she insisted, was "my own warm open quick response" to Wilder's presence. She had brought the problem to therapy and received support for the view that "acting upon anyone's sexual desires (yours or mine)" wouldn't be "benign." Sexton did not mention making, in the context of her psychotherapy, the obvious connections between her feelings for her other "twin," Nana, and this new "twin," Anne, nor the feelings toward Linda she had been acting out.

She only said, cryptically, "It's not the kind of experience I could have and ever get over and return to heterosexual life. So, it's better repressed."

Wilder was stung by what seemed to be a reproof, not only from Sexton but from Sexton's doctors, her professional peers.

Dear, I appreciated your honesty [. . .] about how both your doctors were warning you about giving in to your impulses toward me. [. . .] I'm pretty sure in the face-saving sessions, it came out as against *me*. [. . .] Not only am I primarily your friend and person-who-loves you, but in truth, it was you, dear Icarus, who made the first [. . .] overtures to *me!* [. . .] which you had conveniently forgotten.

Wilder had strong heterosexual attachments herself. The young husband she had married while still in medical school had been killed in the war, and she had not remarried, but she still thought she might do so. Nonetheless, she recognized that the tensions between herself

Anne Wilder and Anne Sexton.

and Sexton carried an erotic charge that should be acknowledged rather than denied.

> I think both docs were right in warning that you could not swim in these particular waters at this time, or, perhaps, ever. [. . .] Do you think that for a moment knowing that situation-tinder-box that existed in your life, also knowing your supreme carelessness and naiveté about privacy, etc. I would actually have risked not only myself, but more importantly, you, in the situation? Really? Do you?

Sexton vigorously disputed the claim that her impulses had been *seductive*; Wilder's use of the word "overtures" made her very angry. "I don't agree with a lot you say," she replied.

> I LOVE LINDA (is that strange?) I LOVE MAXINE (is that?) I LOVE DOC ORNE (is that?) not strange, I mean, is it sexual? Is it?? for christsakes, is it?? I mean I can tell all of them this, with those words, and it's not an overture to anything but a mutual admiration. It isn't interpreted in a sexual light. Well, it ISN'T. So I don't think it's fair for you to see it in that light. Love covers a lot of ground. [. . .]
> ICARUS was pure. So who questions it? I mean if I listened to you I'd have to start in questioning. [. . .]
> (Why am I mad? I don't know? I don't!) But let's not change the poetic truth. It meant something different to both of us.

What bothered her most in this exchange, apparently, was Wilder's matter-of-fact statement that their ardor had been erotic all along. Sexton had a lot at stake in denying this interpretation of their intimacy. Over a week later, she was still contesting the point, in the same terms she had used to Dr. Orne when he had suggested that her relationship to Nana had a sexual component. In her emotional economy, being loved by the world's Nanas (Linda, Maxine, Dr. Orne) required keeping sex out of the picture: Icarus was pure. "For you to see it as sexual was to deny the life it had," she sulked to Wilder. "That's why the anger. I felt that you were *forcing* me to reject you and 'us' by saying everything had always been seen in a sexual light. I will tell you frankly that I see sex with *anyone* as contaminating the purity of a relationship. You probably have guessed that. I don't completely but in my little dwarf heart self I do. It's a labyrinth of meanings then and no way out but to slam doors and get sarcastic."

Commenting that they were both behaving like twelve-year-olds, Sexton tried for two days to let go of this letter, but couldn't bring herself to mail it. Every time she thought about Wilder's last letters she felt more outraged. She added her final remarks under the dryer at the hairdresser's. "We are important, & it's worth protecting & fighting about & understanding," she scrawled. "Please write soon — Kayo goes away next week — I'm trying to get off Thorazine so we can go to Florida on March 15 (when Zweizung is away)."

Sexton was anxious to heal this breach, because withdrawal from the drug, in combination with Kayo's absence, left her emotionally vulnerable. The next letter she wrote to Wilder offered terms of peace in her favorite metaphor for intimacy, "I HAVE ROOM" — a phrase Dr. Orne had used during her first year of treatment. It answered in an image the question that for Sexton underlay all relationships: Is it possible to come and go? A room was permanent space for an occupant; it stayed in place, waiting for the absent one to return. It was inside; private; home.

Oh dear one! Even if the room is small. Still, dear Anne-one, the room is full! (is that too cryptic?) Oh. Tell me it's plain!!! Tell me! It seems I'd rather die than think it wasn't plain and just the way it is, it is, it is . . . IT IS. A small plain old fashioned room, rather small, not convenient or modern, pretty simple, pretty ordinary, old-used furniture . . . with room to sit, to sprawl, to talk, to BE . . . with a blast of love in it.

She had found a way to rest in the labyrinth of feelings rather than seek a way out, slamming the door — for the time being.

Despite the tight financial squeeze that buying their new house had put the Sextons in, Anne wanted a winter getaway to Florida with Karl and Rita Ernst. Kayo resisted. He didn't enjoy sunbathing and thought it was foolish to squander money on a trip. And he worried about Anne's going off Thorazine just to get a suntan — and to get manic enough to begin writing again (as she was candid enough to admit: "I am not going to take anymore thorazine. I want to write poems!"). His attitude enraged her. "I was so mad with Kayo for not wanting to go that I almost cut up all his suits . . . or I also thought of turning on the faucet in the sink and plugging the drain and letting it run all night and spoil and flood the entire downstairs of this glorious hotel." When Rita Ernst commented that Sexton had changed under Thorazine, grown "more childlike," she had to agree.

Then she had a brainstorm: She could arrange a reading tour that would pay back the cost of a trip to Florida. Through her agency she received frequent invitations to read at colleges. A number of these could be combined into a package that would cover travel expenses and produce a profit. Currently she had a number of inquiries from the Midwest that she might follow up.

There was always a hitch, though: She couldn't bear to travel alone. On the phone, she talked to Anne Wilder about the logistics of getting together on a spring tour. They settled on Michigan as a place to rendezvous. Sexton had the Redpath Agency set up a reading at Wayne State University in Detroit, where Wilder would join her; then they would drive to colleges in Ypsilanti, Rochester, East Lansing, Mt. Pleasant, Kalamazoo, and Ann Arbor. The trip was to last almost two weeks in the beginning of May.

When Wilder arrived in Detroit, she spent several hours in their hotel room making a long entry in her journal. "I look forward to Anne's coming, but with wings clipped," she commented.

> The main and iron limitation on it on A's part is the usual human failure to be able to match action with words, with feelings, vows, promises. Or to be psychiatric about it, the good old hysterical discrepancy between what is felt and what is admissible, admitted. [. . .] It occurs to me that in our friendship Anne and I, psychologically, are, have been, coming toward each other from exactly *opposite* directions. I, from the direction, the position, of being freer to let my feelings express themselves, after years of strangulation; and Anne from her newly won and very precious position of discovering some reliable control within herself, a control that in truth must be preserved and strengthened and respected by me, of all people. [. . .] So here I am, in a Detroit hotel room, waiting for Anne, with an appropriately muffled, somewhat sagging heart.

Sexton arrived with little time to spare before her appearance at Wayne State, and gave a splendid reading. Wilder, who had never seen her friend perform, commented later in her journal about the disparities she observed — as many of Sexton's close friends did — between the woman and the actress. "I am only mildly amazed sitting in the audience at her poetry readings, hearing her tell the TRUTH about the human condition, the possibility of human feeling and experience, and then realizing with the good old blinding [in]sight that in real life she can no more put this wisdom into action, into realization than fly to the moon." Sexton was a real trouper, too. The pay wasn't very good (a hundred dollars a reading), the campus lodgings tended to be cinder-block dormitories without air conditioning or food service, and audiences were often rude. She reported to Wilder that in Indianapolis, one of the faculty members in the audience had risen to request "a little less Phyllis Diller, if you please, and a little more Anne Sexton."

But Sexton had developed a set of rituals to get her through such a tour. Arriving in any hotel room, she followed an inviolable proce-dure, going directly to the bathroom to turn on the shower full blast and hang her performance clothes in the steam, then to the ice ma-chine for supplies to chill the first of many glasses of vodka tipped from the stash in her suitcase. Juiced, she was manic, an absolute ne-cessity for performing. At every stage of preparation she required the service of as many attendants as she could corral, to drive, to set up her podium (she couldn't read without smoking and sipping water), and to deliver food and drink (she disliked eating in public). After each performance she called Kayo to say goodnight; Wilder was taken aback by the change in her personality while she spoke to him. " 'This is your princess . . .' — like a china doll on a music box." At bedtime Sexton always swallowed her sleeping pills in ritual order, with milk. She was also beset by fears of constipation. When she arrived at their hotel in Detroit after her reading and the requisite party, she discov-ered that she was out of the laxative she always carried. Stretching out on the bathroom floor, she spent about ten minutes not moving. When Wilder asked what was the matter, Sexton begged her to go find an all-night drugstore and buy her a laxative. Wilder thought this was absurd. "It won't hurt you to wait until tomorrow," she told her in her best professional manner. Mightily offended, Sexton got up and put on her coat. "Will you at least come with me?" "No." Sexton took a cab and scouted Detroit at midnight for the remedy.

In Ann Arbor, Wilder saw another side of Sexton she had only heard about: Anne in trance. They were picked up by Professor Allan Seager and one of his colleagues to be driven to the reading. At a stop-light, another driver rear-ended the car, tossing Wilder, seated in the back, up against Sexton, in the passenger seat. Wilder's cigarette burned a hole in her friend's white coat, but no one was injured. "Sex-ton gave a wonderful reading that afternoon, despite the shaking-up she got — and despite the fact that the university band was practicing outside the open windows of the packed auditorium," Wilder recalled. But while Seager was driving them back to their lodgings afterward, Sexton went into a fugue state. "She grew silent and rigid, and responded to no stimuli," Wilder said. "Seager was worried. I said, 'I'm sure she can hear everything we say, and she will cooperate when we help her out of the car.' We staggered with her between us up to the room, and Seager left his phone number in case she needed further help. I sat with her and talked quietly. Gradually she emerged from the trance. She couldn't figure out why she kept remembering band music!"

The drive through Michigan gave them plenty of time for the meandering, jokey talk that the threat of long-distance charges usually curtailed before either was satiated. They discovered that they shared a passion for Laurindo Almeida's guitar rendition of Villa-Lobos's "Bachianas Brasileiras." For years afterward, the fluting voice of Salli Terri on that recording expressed for Sexton an epitome of feeling, a purity that poetry could never reach; its wordless rapture stood for the liberty of those days with Anne Wilder. The more distance she put between herself and New England, the more room there seemed to be for feelings and actions long denied or deferred. "I really am in love with you," she told Wilder. "I know," Wilder answered. At last, emboldened by privacy, they went to bed. "Love twists me, a Spanish flute plays in my blood," Sexton wrote in the poem that memorialized this adventure ("Your Face on the Dog's Neck") — though her readers thought that the lover was a husband.

Upon returning home, Sexton flooded Wilder with shy, triumphant letters. "I'm still bi-sexual as of a week or two ago," she wrote — apparently she really did worry that forming a sexual attachment to a woman would extinguish her heterosexuality — "but meanwhile, I often think of what it is like kissing you." Her imagination had been roused from its year-long torpor; she felt refreshed, grateful. That she had finally crossed this frontier with Wilder delighted her. "It was my need, my overture," she wrote. "Later we'll go into why the need to sexualize the tenderness (the never-had tenderness for me) of mother. O Mary, little mother . . . [. . .] I play that side of THE RECORD constantly." And the feeling was returned. "I adore the poem, have it almost memorized," Wilder wrote from San Francisco, "but I'm like you. I need to be told. [. . .] In our private, dear house, where I am and want to be naked-me, I always need to know again and again, it's true.

You're with me. As I tritely remarked, but truly, this is a miracle, a once-in-a-lifetime thing. [. . .] It has no relation, in my mind, at least, to whether it's with man, woman, dog, cat, or giraffe. Once in a very great while, it does happen, and it's happened."

Sexton stayed off Thorazine for another month, with her doctor's permission, even though her high spirits disturbed Kayo. "He is scared as hell about me, thinks I'm totally psychotic," she reported to Wilder. "I try to play it very cool in front of Kayo but he says I am manic anyhow. He says I am going to smother him just as his mother did. Poor guy. I'm trying damn hard to shut up, know nothing, and not smother ANYONE."

Gradually her feelings for Wilder subsided into their old channels. Later that summer, when Wilder visited Boston, Sexton hurt her deeply by arranging a dinner party in her honor, then ignoring her and finally making cutting remarks about her in front of the guests. She apologized the next day, but Wilder recognized that she meant to establish distance. The friendship never regained its freewheeling openness, though they continued to exchange letters and numerous phone calls.

But the getaway in May did release Sexton's creative energy. She began pulling out files of poems written since the publication of *All My Pretty Ones* and "fixing up old ones that didn't quite make the show." Finding a poem called "Suicide Note," which she had started on a paper napkin, she transferred it to the typewriter and put it through several drafts. "If it were a real suicide note, there would have been one draft, I imagine," she joked. "One does not perfect at gunpoint." She rewrote "A Little Uncomplicated Hymn," which she had begun in March and set aside when depression overtook her but which she intended to be as celebratory for Joy as "Little Girl . . . ," written the previous year, had been for Linda. "I wanted to write it, and I couldn't, perhaps because of my own guilt," she acknowledged. "You can't always write the way you want to. You've got to tell it true."

Going back into even older files, Sexton discovered "Self in 1958," written the summer before she had met Snodgrass and consigned to her "bone pile" in the old days of profligate creativity, which seemed so far behind her now. It was written in a form she liked and rarely used anymore, each stanza rhyming emphatically but irregularly, adding "a sound effect, a clang in your mind."

By mid-June she had assembled the preliminary version of a book she decided to call *Live or Die,* a title that had been waiting in the wings for years. The manuscript now contained twenty-seven poems, some of them quite long, arranged by date of composition. Actually, Sexton fudged that date when convenient, but on the whole the book conveyed the twists and turns her life had taken during the momentous three years since *All My Pretty Ones* had been published. The advantage of chronological order, she thought, was the feeling of urgency it conveyed. She briefly considered opening with "For the Year of the Insane," which had just come out in *Harper's* and which had close affinities with *Tell Me Your Answer True,* but keynoting the theme of suicidal anguish might negatively influence the book's reception. "In a literary way, if the choice is 'Die' it will be a bad book and so considered," she mused to Anne Wilder. "If it's 'Live' it might be a better book. Can't tell. Haven't written the 'Live' poems . . . not the ones I had in mind when I returned all hutzpah-ie from Detroit."

As the manuscript stood, "Flee on Your Donkey," "Wanting to Die," and "For the Year of the Insane" were its strongest poems, and all were despairing. In her writing life and in real life, Sexton's theme was completely expressed in the ending of "For the Year": "O little mother, / I am in my own mind. / I am locked in the wrong house." Yet her literary hero Henderson had also been a "monster of despair," and Bellow had been able to end his story with regeneration. She decided to put the manuscript aside until she had some new poems to tip the balance toward "Live."

Many of Sexton's admirers would have disagreed that an emphasis on madness or dying made a bad book, though. She was hearing from several such readers during the same months she was revising poems for *Live or Die.* Aspiring poets continued to write to her about their own psychiatric treatment, enclosing their writing and asking for advice. She almost always answered such letters, if only with a postcard, because she remembered her own hunger for response when she had first been ill and trying to use poetry for therapy. If she observed real talent, she sometimes wrote a thoughtful letter about her own career — a legacy, perhaps, of her friendship with James Wright and his gift of *Letters to a Young Poet.* Sometimes her advice was tough. "Stop writing letters to the top poets in America," she reprimanded one young man. "Fight for the poem. Put your energy into it. Force discipline upon madness."

In addition to worrying about producing new work, Sexton was pressured that summer by dread of Dr. Zweizung's August vacation — dread that began appearing in her letters to Anne Wilder as early as June. "He says my job is to get with it and stop denying he is going, denying my despair, etc. He says it is pretty angry of me to wait until he leaves to collapse, and then he won't be here to pick me up. [. . .] 'Sexton get on the emotional ball and break the frozen sea' [. . .] when I write those true but breaking-up things it's done with my left hand, so my right hand won't perceive and feel the crack!"

Sexton couldn't dissuade Dr. Zweizung from abandoning her, but she did ask Linda to come home from summer riding camp to keep her company during his absence. Linda, twelve years old that July, had settled happily into the camp routines at Highlawn Farm in Warner, New Hampshire, near the Kumins' farm, their summer home. She had written asking to extend her stay by another month, through August. Sexton replied that she simply wasn't ready to face the empty nest; one month of separation from Linda was all she could stand. "Please give me another year to grow up myself so that I can let you go longer. Meanwhile try to put up with me the way I am."

Sexton caused her family great distress by insisting on the priority, at all times, of her needs, and this did not change. Sometimes these were needs for care, sometimes for allowances; she wanted to be able to ignore the family at will in order to tend to the management of a now-mature professional career. Significant new awards continued to arrive that summer, and she found ways to accept them on her own terms — which meant arranging to be accompanied by a friend. Scheduling a number of readings on the New York poetry circuit for that fall, she indicated that she would not be available for socializing as part of the deal. Gatherings disturbed her, she explained. "I work better under the 'buddy system' . . . meaning a chaperone, someone to eat breakfast with, someone to keep me more or less stable."

In August she received news that the International Congress of Cultural Freedom was to bestow on her its first Literary Magazine Travel Grant of $5000, to be spread over several months. She had been nominated by Frederick Morgan, of the *Hudson Review*. Sexton was grateful but amused, and reminded him that as he well knew from her visits, "I can hardly cross the street alone in The Big City." To George Lanning of Kenyon College, who administered the prize, she wrote candidly, "I cannot work the grant in the exact manner in which it is given. First of all I am not (from some previous experience) good at traveling without my husband thus we must plan this as a mutual trip. Also, and beyond and before, he can't leave this country for more than two months a year. Thus we (I!) could accept the grant if I could take it in two sessions (two years)." She proposed traveling to Africa in 1966 and to Asia or Latin America ("where I love the poetry") the following year.

Another welcome surprise was news from London of her election as an overseas Fellow of the Royal Society of Literature. In 1964 Sexton had been approached by Jon Stallworthy of Oxford University Press. "At the time, there was really only one publisher of poetry in England, namely, Faber and Faber," Stallworthy recalled. "How to get our own list moving fast, how to challenge Faber, was the problem. It struck me that in America there were a lot of very good poets who had not been published in England." He liked Sexton's work. Oxford's *Selected Poems* by Anne Sexton, which combined the author's choices from *Bedlam* and *Pretty Ones*, was singled out for recognition by the Poetry Book Society, touted in the society's autumn list of recommendations in 1964, and quickly found its audience. The thousand copies Oxford printed sold out quickly, "in eight or nine months, which was very, very rare then," said Stallworthy. "Most poets sold only about fifty copies of a book in a year." This successful debut culminated rather grandly in Sexton's election to the Royal Society of Literature — a delightful name to drop, she found.

In the spring following Sexton's English publication, Faber and Faber issued Sylvia Plath's *Ariel*, which had been significantly introduced by the discussion in the press of Plath's suicide and by serial publication of many poems. Ted Hughes wrote notes on the content and background of poems in *Ariel*, and these appeared in the *Poetry Society Bulletin* for February. A cascade of reviews began in March.

The book was dazzling. Across the Atlantic, its success raised a question in many minds: Why was Sylvia Plath being treated as an English poet? One person who took up this issue was Lois Ames, who had known Plath in school in Wellesley and who now lived in Chicago, where she practiced as a psychiatric social worker. The news of Plath's death in 1963 had stirred her at many levels, and she had decided to undertake a biography of the poet. Finding Sexton's poem "Sylvia's Death" in a current issue of *Poetry*, she wrote to inquire further about the Wellesley connection. Sexton replied cordially, though she felt she had little to offer a biographer: "[Sylvia] wrote me a few times from England — but always about her life. About her death she was silent. Damn it."

In the summer of 1965, Ames was accepted at the Bread Loaf Writers' Conference in Vermont to work on the book, and she decided to stop off in Weston to follow up Sexton's friendly letter. The two women took an instant liking to each other. Ames was warm, high-spirited, brisk, and rather in awe of Sexton. Impressed by Ames's energy and spunk, Sexton kept in close touch during ensuing months. When the editor Charles Newman wrote that autumn asking her to contribute to a forthcoming issue of *TriQuarterly* dedicated to Plath, she put him in touch with Ames (both women wrote widely reprinted pieces for this collection, which was later expanded into a book).

The following year, when Ames received a contract from Harper & Row for her biography, Sexton decided it was time to appoint her own official chronicler. Quite possibly because Ames was already committed to writing about Plath, Sexton asked her to become *her* biographer. As Ames told the story, on Christmas Eve 1966, Sexton "telephoned me and with her usual exuberance said, 'My Christmas gift to you is to make you my biographer.' I replied only half-jokingly, 'I'm not sure this is a present.' "

From then on, Lois Ames accompanied Sexton on important trips and shared all of her adventures, either in person or over the telephone. Within a short time she had slipped neatly into the psychological space emptied by Anne Wilder. Like Wilder, Ames was a trained clinician and a good listener, willing to become another long-distance confidante, another "twin."

13

"A SEDUCING SORT OF WOMAN"
1966

AS THE NEW YEAR opened Sexton was impatient to finish the manuscript that had been sitting for years in the folder labeled *Live or Die*. Her impatience was fueled by the desire to work on a novel, as she had what she thought was a great subject: sex in the suburbs. But before she could get to it, *Live or Die* needed an ending. Life helped her out: in mid-January the Sextons' pet Dalmatian, Penny, gave birth to a big litter of puppies fathered by the Kumins' Dalmatian, Caesar. The whole family gathered around, thrilled, as eight feeble creatures struggled free and began nursing. Shortly afterward, Sexton wrote the programmatic ending for her book:

> I say *Live, Live* because of the sun,
> the dream, the excitable gift.

The poem came "straight from God," she told a friend happily. Now, at last, she could get on with a novel, like all the other poets.

Sexton drew on current frustrations with her marriage for the emotional dynamics of this book, which she planned to title *Marriage — USA*, or maybe *Women — USA, The Marriage Bed,* or *Out of Adam's Rib*. The protagonist, Vicci, was a thirty-seven-year-old woman dreading menopause, whose husband, Oscar, no longer made love to her. As in *Tell Me Your Answer True*, priests and psychiatrists were to be important figures. "I seem to have lots of info on the strange goings on behind suburban houses, priests who make love to married women and fail — can't get an erection. Analysts who ACTUALLY make love to their patients and then the normal (?) variety of infidelity of any neighborhood," Sexton wrote enthusiastically to her agent.

Marriage — USA was to be a comic novel made up of the wry insights Vicci gained in therapy as she contended with her husband's coldness and her body's defections by trying to sublimate her frustrated sexuality in art (Sexton couldn't decide whether to make her a painter or a violinist). Sexton drew Vicci's internal monologues on menopause from a current issue of *Look* magazine. But her literary model was probably (again) Bellow's *Henderson the Rain King,* whose protagonist is a middle-aged upper-crust suburbanite whose decaying teeth and high blood pressure generate important turns of plot, and who expresses his raging spiritual desire by playing themes from Handel's *Messiah* on his father's violin.

When Lois Ames visited for a week at the end of February, Sexton showed her the chapters she had drafted and was encouraged by her enthusiasm. Burdened by the effects of Thorazine, however, Sexton could work only sporadically. "Every letter, every syllable is a strain," she told a friend. "I feel botched up." Her mental health continued to fluctuate distressingly, with many "downers" in January and February and more in May — though as she wrote to Jon Stallworthy in April, "I act rather well for someone who is crazy."

But her depressions also reflected real problems in family life. There was strife between Anne and Kayo, and they were both worried about Joy, now ten years old. At the time of the move from Newton to Weston, Joy had been put back into the third grade because she couldn't multiply or write cursive script. ("I hadn't 'earned my ink,' as they put it in school," Joy said with a laugh, remembering this later.) Now she was in the fourth grade, but flailing; it seemed, as Sexton put it, that she was in the way of becoming "as bad an underachiever as I was." After numerous discussions with teachers and school counselors, Anne and Kayo decided that Joy should begin treatment with a psychiatrist, which meant that everyone in the family but Linda was undergoing regular psychotherapy. And Joy caught up; being a little older than the other children in her class, she became a social ringleader, as Anne had been.

Sexton was at work on her novel when she was contacted by a team from National Educational Television to be interviewed for a series called *USA: Poetry.* After a crew spent two days in early March filming her at home, a thirty-minute film was made and distributed nationwide.

The seamless version edited for national consumption emphasizes the enviable integration of work and love in Sexton's life: the suburban comfort of her surroundings; her steady intelligence as she frowns over the typewriter keys or comments on the autobiographical background of such poems as "Her Kind," "Ringing the Bells," "Those Times," and "The Addict." She seems very healthy and calm as she reads affectingly from the manuscript of *Live or Die*. In another scene, dogs and children swarm into the room and Kayo's car noses into sight through the study window; handsome and a bit shy, he enters in raincoat and business suit for a husbandly kiss. Anne Sexton looks quite literally the model housewife. Indoors she wears an elegant sleeveless white shift that hovers above the knee; outdoors she strolls beside the swimming pool in casual clothes and Roman sandals. (Linda Sexton recalled shopping with her mother for these clothes: "They were from her bargain basement stage!" Sexton could make clothes look classy.) The film ends with Sexton reading her brand-new, mostly upbeat poem "Live."

The film was edited from an abundance of footage, and shortly after Sexton's death the outtakes were spliced into a second film, ninety minutes long. These disclose Sexton's interactions with the director and cameraman and show how the final narrative emerged from a set of quite diverse options. As the outtake film opens, Sexton rummages through worksheets, rambling about how she wrote "Live" and doubting that the poem is really finished yet. She fetches a bottle of beer, "just to keep my voice wet," and frequently licks and compresses her lips — her mouth is dry, probably a side effect of the Thorazine. The beer loosens her up; she chats about mental hospitals and occupational therapy ("I assume we'll cut judiciously so that I won't sound like a total nut"), then turns to the subject of ancestry. Maybe way back she was related to Shakespeare? More likely Grimm, she jokes: "Good witch or bad witch, right from Grimm's fairy tales. Wish I could find I was related to him — *or* to a witch."

They were leading up to a reading of "Her Kind," but the duality "good witch / bad witch" organized her self-commentary throughout this first day's interview with Richard Moore, the director. Perhaps she hoped he would permit "Her Kind" to keynote the film in the way it prefaced each of her readings. In any case, their discussion of witchery set up the most provocative scene in the outtake film, where Sexton explains the role of background music in her process of composing poems: "I want you to understand how emotionally based some of my poems are in music." She puts on a Chopin ballade, opus 23, to make a point. "I'll tell you what poem I wrote to this: 'Your Face on the Dog's Neck.' . . . This song is like making love." She cocks her head. "It's not yet that it really turns me on, but it comes in a minute." She listens some more.

Wait, here comes the woman. Hesitant but there. [Laughs] But *so* there. [Whispers] This is it. Right here. Right in here, I love it. I think that's the most sensual thing I ever heard. I wouldn't want to have an orgasm in front of you, but no, that is it. Listen! [Cries out] Ahhhh, it's beautiful! You hear how that is like sex? I mean, it's like the most beautiful . . .
I guess I listen for my melody. When it comes, I just turn . . . Like a little dancer. And here, hear it? God. I can't write like that.

While Sexton speaks the camera zooms, intimate, catching the blissful clench of her hand at her throat, the pregnant pauses, the ecstatic lift of her eyes. When the scene ends she is unembarrassed, self-possessed. She has made her point. To invoke the line from Kafka she often quoted, "Art should serve as the axe for the frozen sea within us," and it has.

But what about that allusion to her poem for Anne Wilder? Sexton does not tell the camera that she is thinking of a woman lover; it seems that, like a method actor, she has been using this memory as a path to the emotions she expresses so irrepressibly on camera. She does say that performing gives her "a sense of extension, of power, that you've reached somebody. . . . Even depressed I can act, I can still be me." How do you handle this? asks Moore. Do you fake it? "I fake it up with the truth; I'm always doing that, though."

Midway through the interview, Moore expresses his puzzlement at all the contradictions he is witnessing: "Here you are, this puritanical, beautiful chick in I. Magnin clothes; how do we handle that?" "I don't know how you handle that," Sexton replies. "That's going to be your problem, 'cause underneath it, the bad witch writes her poems." The way Moore solved the problem for his thirty-minute film on NET was slightly to sentimentalize Sexton's libidinal relationship to art and the making of art, and to leave on the cutting room floor most of her exhibitions of inspired, disturbing, associational looseness.

As the unpublished drafts of her novel show, in early 1966 Sexton was groping her way toward expressing discoveries about her sexuality. At midlife, she was undergoing a reeducation in sexual pleasure, and the experiences she embarked upon that year would inspire the themes of her most widely read book, *Love Poems*.

The sexual tensions Sexton wrote into the marriage of Vicci and Oscar Hammersmith had their counterparts in her relation to Kayo. In the past she had told Dr. Orne that the other men she slept with "never meant anything to me" in comparison with her husband. "Kayo and I have wonderful sex if I can get sexy. . . . Lots of acting out on my part. Wouldn't be anyone I'd rather have sex with, even though everything's wrong with the marriage. . . . He never knows who I'm going to be, hysteric that I am. . . . With him I'm free to act out any part I want, and so is he — it's *fine*." But by 1966 this had

Anne in her pool.

changed, according to Sexton, and increasingly she had fantasies of getting a divorce and starting over with another man.

In any case, her satisfaction with Kayo, when she was satisfied, had never foreclosed her desire for sexual intrigue or sexual display. In an interview, the poet Allen Grossman recalled this aspect of her personality. He and Sexton met rarely, but on several occasions during the 1960s he drove her to gatherings of poets involved in the peace movement. "One was always being solicited to do such things for her," he recalled. "She was delightful company. Yet she was a seducing sort of woman, constantly talking about her body and its mutilations. I remember one time driving her somewhere, when we had a long conversation about the Blue Grotto, in Capri, about her swimming there — naturally without any clothes on. It was a curiously displaced reference, juxtaposed to conversation about how some organ of hers had been liberated from her body. One was not interested in her body, under the circumstances — at the same time one was being invited into her blue grotto!"

During the winter and spring of 1966 Sexton was conducting just such a seducing sort of dialogue, by mail, with several poets. One was James Dickey, under whose critical lash she had winced every time one of her books appeared. He had given *To Bedlam and Part Way Back* a condescending review in *Poetry* in 1961, when she was an apprentice poet and glad to be reviewed in prestigious journals. But in 1963, when he lambasted *All My Pretty Ones* in the *New York Times Book Review*, she was hurt, then outraged. She felt that he was using her for target practice, the desired target being that chimerical beast confessional poetry ("a new kind of orthodoxy," Dickey called it, "as tedious as the garden-and-picture-gallery school of the forties and fifties"). From then on she nursed a grievance and watched for an opportunity to work on him what she called her "female con."

The occasion arose when they finally met at a literary gathering at Syracuse University, sometime in December 1965. Dickey remembered the occasion: "I had given a reading and then gone to bed, staying clear of the almost obligatory party that follows such affairs. I was stopping at the home of the college president, Dr. Piskor, and Anne woke me up over the phone to see if we could not meet for at least a little while. I got up and she came by, in a big black coat that looked like it had come from a gorilla, and we walked up and down the suburban road a few times, during which, as I remember, she told me about various episodes of her childhood."

Dickey apparently asked her in a loose moment, "Do you sleep around?" Afterward he wrote a couple of gallant letters, apologizing. "You have opened a new tenderness in me," he said. "I hope there will always be a good strong man-woman response between us." Sexton responded that the last thing she wanted was a love affair: "I would avoid one if it looked me in the face. I would run to the end of town to avoid it." He replied in kind. "Believe me, I am not trying for any relationship with you other than the tenderness you describe. We should go no deeper. [. . .] That is where the Demons are likely to get stirred up."

The Demons did get stirred up late one night in February, when Dickey called Sexton from wintry Wisconsin, where he held a temporary appointment at the state university. He was lonely and drunk and excitable. Sexton wrote to him the next day that his insistence on being told she loved him had gotten her in trouble with Kayo, who overheard her half of the surprising dialogue. "I'm ready to love you as a dear friend and fellow poet. [. . .] Will you throw it away because I can't be all woman — all whore — all that your momentary desire might wish to call forth?" Dickey's apology was philosophical. "It must be shocking and saddening and bewildering to hear your wife tell another man over the phone that she loves him not one but fifteen times. [. . .] It's just one of the sadnesses of husbands that things like this sometimes happen to them. I hope I haven't done any permanent damage to your marriage; I can't believe I have, really. But I *am* sorry, and I hope that, if you won't forgive me, you will at least not fret any more about it."

In fact, Kayo's considered opinion by that time was that most poets were "jerks," so he may not have taken much notice of the midnight melodrama. Sexton, of course, was sympathetic, as she had made her own drunken phone calls to fellow poets. Her reply suggests that she hoped for something like her old communion with Jim Wright to spring up with Jim Dickey. "If there is such a thing as a soul — and I think there is a 'Soul in Space' — then I know my soul loves you. I think such tenderness is my specialty. There are lots of girls to sleep with — but not hardly any for tender and lasting feeling. Am I wrong?" They sealed the understanding with a date to meet chastely for lunch in Towson, Maryland, when their respective reading circuits overlapped in April.

Sexton's trip, which included visits to several colleges in Pennsylvania, Maryland, and Virginia, was arranged by Philip Legler, a young faculty member in the English Department at Sweet Briar College, in Virginia, who was an ardent fan of her work. Although Sexton disliked traveling so far from home, she succumbed to the contract after Legler wangled a high fee (five hundred dollars), helped contact English Departments at other colleges, and promised her copious martinis on arrival. (She had written, "If Virginia is a 'dry' state [this is] to prepare you for my need of a semi-wet state before dinner and a reading.") The trip was scheduled for mid-April, and Sexton decided to take thirteen-year-old Linda along for company. "Linda's never flown, stayed at a hotel or a motel or ridden in a taxi," she observed to a friend. "It's about time she got a ride somewhere except in my VW or Kayo's Batman Buick or on a horse. Besides, we could talk and girl talk it up and get to know each other out of here for a change."

Traveling with Anne Sexton, however, meant taking care of Anne Sexton: holding on to airline tickets, keeping an eye on her pocketbook, managing itineraries, remembering people's names. Linda's youthfulness had no influence on Sexton's behavior on this trip; on tour, she was the star. Though the reading at Sweet Briar went beautifully, she had to be carried from the party afterward. As she wrote apologetically to her host, "I feel kind of awful about the way I acted at Sweet Briar taking my pills. I mean, I waited too long to get to that motel. The pills aren't kidding, or rather I'm not, they just knock me out." The pills, she said, "are a mother but better. [. . .] God! What must you have thought? Well, I guess you just thought crazy Annie baby." Usually, she added, "I try to keep my illness ways a secret (except for printing it for the world to read) still I don't want the world to *see*."

But Linda saw. The pills were a mother, Anne was a baby, and that was the bond that counted when Anne was needy — so Linda was on her own or, worse, responsible for looking after her mother. "Throughout my childhood I always felt that I was loved, but I always felt insecure, too — that bad things could happen at any time," she recalled. "On that trip, I began to feel there was a way out of my insecurity: If I could just take care of it *all,* then things would be okay."

Sexton was not intentionally callous toward Linda, and she did make time for special moments with her. They stayed at the Williamsburg Inn; Linda remembered their lunch in the spring sun, sitting on the terrace, as the occasion when she felt she had "been received into the tribe." Sent away when very young, Linda "felt more deeply than she knew all the separations we'd been through — her hospitalizations, her long trips away. Now she could take me with her." Yet she also felt the increased burden this change brought in its wake. Sitting that summer by the swimming pool, she told Maxine Kumin about trying to fill her mother's needs. "Maxine said to me, 'Linda, you're only thirteen. Don't try to be an adult. Let the weight of the world off your shoulders.' " Linda remembered this advice gratefully — though she couldn't follow it.

Returning from Sweet Briar, Sexton wanted to fan, a bit, the sparks struck between herself and Philip Legler. The night Legler helped carry her to her motel, he wrote her a long passionate letter; the next morning he checked into a psychiatric hospital in Richmond. "You have no idea how much seeing you shook me up, and I don't mean just because of the poems. You live at such a screaming intensity, it's almost too painfully beautiful to bear. [. . .] You've got both a lifetime fan of your work and a mad mad mad mad lover to cope with." Sexton reveled in his extravagance, which wakened echoes of Jim Wright in her psyche. "I liked your love letter. [. . .] Well, maybe it's a love letter . . . . . poets are always writing each other love letters — sometimes it's hard for wifes and husbands of same to understand this. Still, I was right about the weird abundance (if you know that poem, The Black Art)."

Legler's emotional troubles could not bear the strain of this pressure, however; he begged her not to write (though he continued to flood her with letters), so she began phoning, and he begged her not to phone. Contrite, she tried to explain her vision of the soulmating of poets, with its basis in transference, and the conditions that led to her own excesses. Her letter captures some of the frustration and a good deal of the self-pity she was feeling in her marriage.

I talked about it with my doctor-daddy who, by the way, is the only other ABUNDANCE person I know. But he has training. He says I'm not doing you any favor, letting you fill my needs when you probably ought to be concentrating on yours. [. . .]

My husband is short, good looking, stern, moral, nice, strict, square, hates poetry, hates my abundance, hates my sickness, almost always for years doesn't desire me as a woman. [. . .] The door is slammed in my face and he has continually informed me that I don't attract him any longer. I have wrung my hands and cried over no love all winter long. So your fullness, your flower, your acceptance came like a shock. Except for my daughters, my doctor, there is no love here and I was lonely. I have constant fantasies of a divorce but can't do it. He says I should wait for him as he waited for me, says he loves me (then tells me I'm ugly, he hates my hair, my voice, etc.) Yet we are a family. I've hung on for 18 years. [. . .]

I just went a bit haywire over getting some love — having been this whole last year on a starvation diet. [. . .] I don't call because you asked me not to and because it is a sign of my own manic person-sick that I have to call people, can't wait, must be in touch, instant touch. Crazy Anne-ie.

Sexton played with the idea of divorcing Kayo a good deal now. She knew she depended on him for the stable home life that insured whatever psychological health she possessed and made her work possible. For the past ten years he had shouldered most of the burdens for which she had no strength, or no inclination, and she recognized how much support this had given the children as well as herself. Yet she also thought that Kayo resisted the kinds of changes that age, professional success, and ongoing psychotherapy made possible for her. The splitting she acted out with Philip Legler — body anchored in marriage to a "square," soul in "space," the white sheet of paper rolled into a typewriter — was regressive. Divorce began to seem like an answer to this problem.

Meanwhile, throughout the spring she went on planning the trip abroad that she and Kayo might take. With her grant from the International Congress of Cultural Freedom, she had decided to buy Kayo a first-class safari. It was a costly enterprise, but this was to be her poetry's gift to him, a thank-you for his support during the long years when her development as a writer taxed the family resources in every way.

Africa for Kayo; maybe South America for her. At an early stage in the planning, she wrote to Elizabeth Bishop for advice about visiting Brazil. She knew Robert Lowell had held a similar grant and had been Bishop's guest in Rio; it seemed to be a place where poets gathered. Bishop pleasantly corrected this false impression. Lowell had given a few readings, she told Sexton, but he had lounged more than he had lectured. "There are so few 'tourist attractions' in these parts, and it is so hard to get about, that a traveler would have to have something in mind, like entomology or Indians or Portuguese baroque or the race question, etc. — to keep him happy under trying or boring circumstances. After Italy, it is just one vast, ungarnished, unswept room, with so very little in it — and the distances are great."

Nonetheless, Bishop encouraged Sexton to visit and offered to make reservations and advise her and show her around. Sexton was enthusiastic. "I am interested in how people live and eat and dance and sing and fish and get along with life," she replied. "Both my husband and I are interested in new places. If it weren't for the snakes, I think I would get him up the Amazon." She planned to arrive in August and spend winter in the southern hemisphere.

But in mid-May she wrote to Bishop about a change in plans. "There is a question of health . . . I may need an operation which would veto the summer trip." Excessive bleeding during her menstrual periods suggested cysts or tumors in her uterus (Sexton suspected cancer). One gynecologist proposed a hysterectomy, but she was appalled at the prospect of the early loss of her fertility. A second opinion led to a biopsy in late May. Eventually Sexton's doctors decided to address the problem with "the pill," which would prevent ovulation and control bleeding. She was in the hospital only a couple of days, but the dread lingered to take root in her writing: first in her novel, and later in the poem "In Celebration of My Uterus."

Meanwhile, she became interested in obtaining a position teaching creative writing. The seminar she had taught at Radcliffe and her post-reading classroom visits at college campuses indicated that she had a flair for teaching. Furthermore, when Robert Clawson, a young teacher at Weston High School, had invited her to read for his English class the previous year, he had mentioned his idea of having a poet in residence in the school. The idea had sunk its hook; "I'm a resident! Invite me!" Sexton told him, and she let it be known at other local schools and mental hospitals that she would like to become a resident poet.

In June she was invited to a conference in East Hampton on Long Island, "to explore possibilities for revitalizing the teaching of English in elementary and secondary schools through the close collaboration of teachers and writers." Herbert Kohl was organizing the project, which eventually blossomed into a nationwide program in the public schools. Accepting her invitation, Sexton thought of asking to bring Bob Clawson as one of the cohort of teachers. Perhaps Weston High would be one of the schools chosen for "revitalization" with project financing, and she would end up as its poet in residence after all.

So on the morning of 22 June, Clawson picked her up in his little black Mercedes convertible. "Before we left, I remember Kayo and the kids saying, 'Now, take care of Mom,' " Clawson recalled. "Anne had said a couple of times to me that she'd had problems. I told the family, 'Don't worry, I'll take care of her,' thinking, 'Why does she need taking care of?' " Sexton brought a six-pack and cracked a beer as soon as they were on the road; she was in high spirits. They stopped in New London for lunch. "On a jukebox we listened to Ray Charles sing 'We're Together Again.' This turned out to be significant," Clawson said. "Remember, I didn't really know her very well. This was turning into a lark, right? I was married and had kids; here I was, going off with this libidinous creature."

When they arrived in East Hampton, the conference was just getting under way. Clawson was impressed by the group of writers and teachers Kohl had brought together: "Nelson Aldrich and John Holt were there. Jonathan Baumbach, Jeremy Larner, Mark Mirsky. The guy who publishes the *New York Review of Books* — Robert Silvers. Grace Paley. Mitchell Goodman and Denise Levertov. John Hollander, Benjamin DeMott — and Muriel Rukeyser. That's where Sexton met Rukeyser. Then there were also some hard-working teachers from the New York schools." On their first evening the writers went out for a big Italian meal at a local restaurant. "Muriel Rukeyser was at the heart of it all, like an earth mother. People obviously had great admiration for her. She and Anne got on famously."

After dinner, Clawson and Sexton were about to return to their lodgings when Clawson remembered he had left something behind in the restaurant. "I came back out, and Anne was sitting in the car — the top was down — just looking up into the trees. She was in some kind of hypnotic trance. She was mumbling, incoherent, and her eyes were very strange. I brought her out of the trance by kissing her. She didn't want to go back to the hotel, so I drove down to the beach for some fresh air. She seemed to come around. She told me, 'You know what the waves say? They say I am, I am.' And we made some poetry jokes about iambic pentameter." When she seemed more herself, Clawson took her back to the hotel and put her to bed, then sat with her through the night.

Sexton and Clawson became lovers for the seven days they lived in this other world. She emerged completely from the withdrawn state that disturbed him so greatly, and was a lively contributor to the discussions of teaching and writing. On the last evening, some of the writers lingered late at the bar, and Sexton was disappointed when Clawson wanted to stay on rather than go upstairs with her. He watched her leave. Later, when he went to join her, he thought he heard someone else in her room; jealous, he went outside and stood for a long time looking at her lighted window. At lunch in Baron Cove the following day she chastised him for abandoning her, and he confessed his suspicions. "Look," she told him, "I stayed up all night writing these poems for you." She pulled from her bag a handful of love poems: "The Kiss," "The Touch," "The Breast." Reading them, he began to weep. "It was the most romantic moment of my life," he remembered. " 'Bob,' she said, 'let's not go home, let's run away to Mexico. Right now. We can both get divorces, and marry, and live there and write.' The realist in me had already returned. 'We don't have any money, for one thing.' 'Money!' she said. "I don't care about money.' She dug in her purse for a lighter, took out a twenty-dollar bill, and set it on fire in front of an amazed waitress."

They left the restaurant and headed home. All during the long drive back to Weston, Sexton's behavior was "spooky," Clawson recalled. When he stopped for gas, she climbed out of the car and ran into a nearby field. "On the ferry, she was frantic — kept trying to jump off the back of it. I was literally going into the women's room with her, to be near her all the time."

Sexton didn't tell Clawson about the last time she had been on this ferry, returning from Montauk after a week with James Wright, but it seems likely that he was witnessing a dramatization of feelings connected with that other painful separation. When they debarked at New London, they returned to the restaurant where they had eaten lunch the week before. "I was trying to re-establish things in some way," Clawson remembered. "I played Ray Charles singing 'We're Together Again' on the jukebox again, and she came out of the trance. On the drive back to Weston she fell asleep, and I kept thinking about that phrase 'Take care of Mom.' "

Home again, Clawson wrote Sexton letters flowing with gratitude for the work of love's axe on the frozen sea, enclosing poems he had written to her. "You crept inside of me, got at the fine feelings I've been storing, threatened to display them, displayed them, made them rich proud things, made me have to grow." Now, though, he wanted to establish a relationship more brotherly than romantic.

What Clawson didn't know — and what Sexton never told him — was that the love poems she had laid on the restaurant table during lunch on Long Island had been written in Weston a week or so earlier, to another man. By mid-June she had embarked on a passionate love affair with her psychiatrist, Dr. Zweizung. She later explained that the deterioration of her marriage led her to seek sexual intimacy in her therapy, but at the time she ascribed it flippantly to "the old summer madness" — "I have a theory about the sun being the life force, sex too, but life mostly," she wrote to him. A folder of letters and poems she kept among her papers indicates that the folly was mutual. Dr. Zweizung too began writing poems and giving carbons of them to her (Dr. Z., she rejoiced, was "a word magic guy"), and the dialogue his poems establish with her own writings of the period convey a tender, earnest, audacious sexual love. In one of his verses he quoted back to her her favorite paradox: "In poetry, truth is a lie is a truth." But in plain language, his behavior toward her was a breach of professional ethics. As early as 1931, Freud had criticized the younger analyst Sándor Ferenczi for attempting to introduce physical intimacy into psychoanalytic technique; patients "are to be denied erotic gratifications," Freud insisted. This view was made explicit in the code of conduct regulating the practice of psychiatry, which explains that "the necessary intensity of the therapeutic relationship may tend to activate sexual and other needs and fantasies on the part of both patient and therapist, while weakening the objectivity necessary for control. Sexual activity with a patient is unethical." If Dr. Zweizung had indeed fallen in love with Sexton, he was under professional obligation to discontinue the therapy and to seek counseling himself.

Sexton, however, rejoiced in the surge of sexual feelings for both Bob Clawson, who continued to resist them, and the man she called her "doctor-daddy," who did not. From day to day these loves alternated in her heart; as she later told Dr. Zweizung, "I wondered, once in a while this summer, which one of you I loved. I did wonder a little. There's no doubt in my mind now. I lived with Bob for a week. I haven't lived with you for a week. [. . .] Christ! Ollie, do you hear me? I love you very much. Hear! Get it? Yes, yes, yes. Just like that and no question about it. You untied my feet. You untied my heart (the kids untied my heart before) but in all truth you're the first man to untie it just this way."

One outcome of this conquest was an outpouring of love poems. Sexton drafted several in June; one that started out with the title "Love Gone" and struggled for completion as "Divorce" ended up being called "Woman at the Window" before being discarded as unfit for print. None of this new work went into *Live or Die,* which Houghton Mifflin was readying for publication in September. Instead, Sexton started a new file for these love poems, tentatively titled *Rats Live on No Evil Star.* She was glad to be launched into another book, yet her desires in this case were greatly opposed to her real-life interests, and she knew it. Wishes like hers were what she was paying a doctor to treat, and the doctor had to be trusted not to act on them, no matter how clever the patient. Sexton's coy phrase "doctor-daddy" conveys how conscious she was of her own transgression in this relationship. Small wonder that she began suffering from an acute sense of unreality as she crossed and recrossed Long Island Sound with Bob Clawson near the anniversary of her escapade with James Wright.

When Maxine Kumin returned from a vacation in Europe, Sexton confided in her about the new development with Dr. Zweizung. Kumin, who had just completed a psychoanalysis, was indignant. Years later, she was still indignant: "Imagine paying to get laid twice a week!" Why did Sexton persist in the affair? "Anne always had the notion she was the most underloved person in the universe," Kumin said. "There could never be enough proof that she was loved."

Kumin urged Sexton to consult other professionals about the situation, so she turned to Lois Ames, who as a psychiatric social worker was well positioned to give her an insider's perspective. They held a marathon long-distance call one night, which Ames followed up the next day with a letter summarizing her advice on the matter. She was sympathetic to both parties, but strongly reinforced Kumin's message. "In this particular setup the structures of orthodoxy make sense," she told Sexton. "The rules are a safeguard, not that violation is not often therapeutic or desirable for a number of excellent reasons, but orthodoxy protects the potential victim and the potential perpetrator, however innocent his intentions, however deep the swamp in which he unintentionally mires himself — but you know all this." Ames suggested that the break during Sexton's trip to Africa, scheduled to begin on 6 August, would form a natural point of separation, following which Sexton might consider finding a new therapist. Then it might just be possible, she ventured, for Sexton and her doctor to construct a life together. In closing, though, she advanced the reality principle: "Remember, in love as in everything, especially sex, someone has done it — accomplished the impossible, and so may you, but more likely you will not."

This was not what Sexton wanted to hear. Give up the solace of "cuddling"? Or undergo another termination of her treatment? No, no, never! A week or so after her talk with Ames, she took an overdose of pills and was hospitalized for forty-eight hours; as a consequence, she missed an appointment with Dr. Orne, who continued to follow several of his Boston patients on a monthly basis. Learning from Sexton about the turn her therapy had taken, Dr. Orne had given her the same advice as Kumin and Ames had. She acknowledged in a letter to him that she was ashamed to face him, since she had not accepted his advice. "I didn't want to tell you how it was — & I felt disloyal to both of you — To him if I talked & to you if I didn't. Nevermind that. At least I didn't die. [. . .] Things are generally pretty bad and I don't know how to fix them. Sure, I know what ought to be done . . . but not how to do it. Nothing much has changed since I last saw you. The best I can say is that I'm not pregnant."

Writing to Lois Ames, Sexton treated the suicidal episode as an acting-out of her poem "The Addict":

> Sleepmonger,
> deathmonger,
> with capsules in my palms each
>   night,
> [. . .]
> Don't they know
> that I promised to die!
> I'm keeping in practice.
> I'm merely staying in shape.
> The pills are a mother, but better,
> every color and as good as sour balls.
> I'm on a diet from death.

This time "it wasn't a serious attempt or I would have succeeded," she said. "Part of me is live. But I forgot about the diet from death. I went on a binge. [. . .] Hell. If I'd died it would have been awful in light of my forthcoming book."

And what must have been the impact of all these erotic storms on Anne and Kayo's relationship from day to day? A beautiful letter from Kayo survives in Sexton's files, opening a window on a moment of sadness in the life of this long-married couple. Undated, it was probably written near their nineteenth wedding anniversary.

No matter what has been the matter, it is not like us to sleep in separate rooms. [. . .] Tonight you asked me to cuddle you. It was so hard even to say maybe, 'cuz the stings of the cactus yesterday and today had made me leery of getting close to the cactus bush. [. . .]

On the other side of the fence, [. . .] I am tired and short-tempered. I overly react to what you do or say. [. . .] I am asking you to let me cuddle you — I don't want to play the game and hit you and let you feel there is one more in the world against you. I am for you — yet I am afraid of you. I can't fight or equal the mad hitting words. I can only write and say, I'm still Boots — maybe I have spurs on — but then my Button still has the needle that sews her to me. [. . .]

I love you, want to make everything OK, but it's beyond my power. I'm just a jerk, tongue-tied, emotionally unable to keep up with you. Hear me — come to me — Kayo.

Looking back on that bitter time, Kayo recalled feeling a constant frustration. Aware of her infidelities — "Murder will out," he said, laughing ruefully — he felt constrained by her illness from confronting her with the pain they gave him; "I thought that if she ever got well, we could put that kind of thing behind us."

Anne and Kayo embarked for England, Africa, and Italy on schedule, just after Joy's eleventh birthday. Sexton's recent suicide attempt had left her shaky, so they added to their itinerary a brief rest stop in London before continuing on to Nairobi. Hoping to spend some comfortable time as a tourist, Sexton wrote ahead to Ruth Inglis, an old friend from high school days who had married an Englishman. She knew that Jon Stallworthy, her editor at Oxford University Press, would put her in touch with literary folk, but she dreaded this. What she wanted most was to arrive safely (always doubtful, to her mind) at Heathrow, find Brown's Hotel, sleep off the fear of flying, and get a tour of the "swinging London" that *Time* had hyped in a cover story that April. As luck would have it, Inglis had become a literary agent. Rather than a tour, she planned a luncheon for the Sextons and set up an interview with *Nova*, a slick new arts magazine. The Sextons were also invited to dinner at the home of George MacBeth, who produced poetry programming for the BBC.

Sexton and MacBeth had met earlier that year, while MacBeth was on a tour of the East Coast. At that time he had eight books of poetry in print and had recently won the Faber Memorial Award. As he later explained, his work for the BBC required a good deal of scouting: "I went over as a BBC literary man with a chance to go anywhere and meet anybody. I asked to meet numbers of American poets. She was one." Sexton had picked him up at the train station on Route 128 and driven him to Weston. "Things warmed up when she realized that I actually read her poems. (I don't think she had read my stuff then.) We got talking much more freely and became much more at ease." MacBeth thought that seeing Sexton at home gave him an insight into her art. "It was apparent she saw sincerity as a *technique,* the style that happened to fit what she wanted to say. She could've faked any career for herself and written well about it, once she found out a way to do it." He also liked the "risk-taking" in her poetry: "Reminded me of Hemingway, a hero of exploration, of adventure. I'm sure I said that to her and that she responded very favorably to that assessment. Especially from a male reader."

That agreeable meeting was in the background when Anne and Kayo went out to Richmond for dinner with MacBeth and his wife, Elizabeth, on the Sunday after their arrival. MacBeth recalled, "I learned that Anne had never read *The Green Hills of Africa,* so I lent her my copy — a fantastic book! What better time to discover it? I gave it to her but never got it back — it's in Anne's library somewhere. I know she was very caught up in the idea of Hemingway."

From London the Sextons flew to Nairobi for a three-week safari on which they crossed the Serengeti Plain, visited Ngorongoro Crater, and camped at Lake Manyara. "It was a very posh trip, like a safari out of a movie," Kayo remembered. "A great gift, Anne's last great gift to me — certainly not anything she was interested in." Once they were in the bush, hunting began early every day: They were wakened at 4:30 with cups of tea, had breakfast at 5:00, then got into the Land Rover for a drive of thirty miles or more. "It was pitch black and probably thirty-six degrees when we'd set off. We'd get up on the high land and look around with binoculars. If you were looking for, let's say an impala, there'd be countless thousands, but you would try to find a good impala with the horns, or a zebra — you'd try to find one that wasn't all scarred up. When you finally found one, you'd mark the herd, then come back the next day and start stalking him."

Anne would wait in the Land Rover, Kayo recalled, "reading old copies of the *Reader's Digest.* When the wind would shift, the buffalo would spook and run, and one time they came down over the hill where the Land Rover was parked. She just sat there as this great herd came running. And it split and ran around her. The Land Rover was shaking and the dust was flying — and the roaring! She was awfully brave. . . . I had a super time. It was a culmination for me, as a hunter."

Sexton brought her little portable Olivetti and wrote a few letters on the trip. To Ollie Zweizung she poured out the disgust she kept from Kayo: "I am thinking about you constantly. True, I haven't written every day as I said I would. True. But I couldn't; it was too terrible; heat, sweat, flies, death, guns, miles of driving like a tractor over rough, rocky, barren land, blazing sun, blood running in bucketfulls out of the car, meat, blood, death, decay, vultures, danger, elephant charging right up to five feet from you, then shot — [. . .] At night we eat the game I watch die slowly."

When Kayo and Anne emerged from the bush they took a plane to Mombasa, "so Anne could get the red dust of Africa out of her pores" by swimming in the Indian Ocean and basking on the beach. She had

Kayo on safari.

deliberately stopped taking Thorazine in order to enjoy the seacoast at Mombasa and at Capri, where they headed next. All her joy returned as they swam again in the Blue Grotto. Capri "is my spiritual home and like being born again," she wrote to Lois Ames. "Capri is like a beautiful mother. The water holds you up like a float and is so clear. Capri is the mother we never had, young, beautiful, exotic, accepting and loving arms."

Shortly after their return in September, *Live or Die* was published, with a drawing by Barbara Swan ("Gothic Heads") on the front, and on the back a portrait taken at Sexton's interview with NET for *USA: Poetry*. It was a dramatic photograph, Sexton perched on the end of her desk, eyes left, unsmiling and intense, shot from below so that she seems very tall. It filled the back jacket. There were no blurbs on this book, for by now Sexton had high name recognition.

Many of the favorable reviews took their cue from the "Author's Note" that stood in place of an introduction in *Live or Die*: "I have placed these poems (1962–1966) in the order in which they were written with all due apologies for the fact that they read like a fever chart for a bad case of melancholy." Joseph Slater (*The Saturday Review*), reading the book as if it were a novel, noted a "jagged and suspenseful" movement upward, and praised "the sure, dramatic movement of whole poems." Millen Brand (*Book Week*) thought that "the appeal, the pull of these poems may depend on the moment when they are read and on the strength and tolerance of the reader"; it was Sexton's candor that appealed to him. It was Sexton's candor that other reviewers disliked. Her prickly friend Louis Simpson wrote a painful attack for *Harper's* ("Her previous books were interesting, but now mere self-dramatization has grown a habit. A poem titled 'Menstruation at Forty' was the straw that broke this camel's back"). "MEANY," Sexton wrote to Simpson when he sent her a copy of the review. "The poems are children of mine, unattractive but mine."

Unfavorable reviews tended, à la Simpson, to compare Sexton to herself and find her wanting; readers missed the canny formal effects more common in the previous volumes and tended to dislike the looseness of the new poems. The tendency to compare Sexton unfavorably with Sylvia Plath (encouraged by the publication of the bathetic "Sylvia's Death" in *Live or Die*) was already full-blown, and thus a critical perspective joining these two reputations began to seem inevitable. And many critics took the occasion of reviewing Sexton to deplore, once again, the pernicious spread of confessionalism in contemporary writing. Of these, Charles Gullans produced the most dehydrated assessment: "The Romantic stereotype says that the poet is sensitive and suffers; the neo-Romantic stereotype says that anyone who is sensitive and suffers is a poet." These poems of Sexton's are not poems, Gullans decided; "they are documents of modern psychiatry and their publication is a result of the confusion of critical standards in the general mind."

Sexton went back to her novel that fall. Hoping for reappointment, she wrote to the Radcliffe Institute, arguing that to produce a novel she needed both a housekeeper and a secretary. "A novel seems so big, so 'full time.' I cannot hold it in my arms like a poem, though one may have to hold a poem in his arms for a week or even for years." To her agent Cindy Degener she wrote that the part she had written was so inept she was considering turning the book into "a forthright pornographic novel, with no humor (I am NOT a humorist) that I could bring out under a pseudonym. [. . .] True confession style only a bit better and of course really vulgar."

Sexton also went back to her lover that fall. From Capri she had written to Lois Ames, "Maybe the summer break will have changed things with my doctor. The trouble is that he is the best doctor I ever had . . . it just got too intense . . ." Once she was home again, the love affair surged back full force, leaving ghostly traces in the poetry he wrote for her. New work mounted in her file of love poems: "The Interrogation of the Man of Many Hearts," "That Day," "In Celebration of My Uterus," "The Nude Swim," "Song for a Red Nightgown," "Loving the Killer" — all written in October.

But the pressures of continuing adultery were forcing changes on both of the men Sexton looked to as lovers. Clawson continued to frustrate her efforts to revive their affair, and Ollie Zweizung now began to pull back too. The romance between patient and doctor collapsed in early November, when, according to Maxine Kumin, Dr. Zweizung told Sexton that his wife had discovered their love poems among his private papers and become very angry. He resolved to reform. They must break off the affair. A poem he gave Sexton dated merely "October 1966" elegizes a stolen autumn holiday that left a legacy of images: feeding each other halved cherrystones to make them littleneck clams; hair curling like smoke out a car window. Another, dated 29 October, sounds a theme of sad purposefulness: It is time, not the end of desire, that guides him away from her.

Though the end of the affair cannot have been unexpected, it was still a shock to Sexton. On her birthday — often a day she chose to punish herself — she tumbled down the stairs at home and broke her hip. Family lore explained that she wanted a replay of her birthday in 1965, when a major power failure darkened the eastern seaboard and the Sextons had celebrated by roasting hot dogs in the fireplace by candlelight. In 1966, at dusk on 9 November, Sexton set out candles and turned off all the lights. She was called upstairs by Joy to relight a candle, and in the dark at the top of the stairs she caught her heel. She fell all the way down.

In the hospital she revenged herself mildly on Dr. Zweizung by writing two poems: "The Break" and "For My Lover, Returning to His Wife," which pillaged images from Zweizung's autumn lyric:

> Let's face it, I have been momentary.
> A luxury. A bright red sloop in the harbor.
> My hair rising like smoke from the car window.
> Littleneck clams out of season.

The accident may have been symbolic (in "The Break," Sexton called it "a feat sailing queerly like Icarus"), but the pain was intense and of long duration. She exaggerated a bit when she wrote to Lois Ames about the prognosis — "I'm flat on my back & WILL BE FOR A YEAR — [. . .] If I step on right leg my hip will be permanently crippled" — but the fracture was closed with screws, a treatment that required ten days of hospitalization.

Returning home to Black Oak Road, Sexton settled in for a long convalescence. Icarus was really grounded now. Cheerfully she involved her friends in prose-writing schemes. She told Ben Shaktman that she had begun work on a movie script that was starting out very comic. "Maybe with a broken hip the joker in me is coming out. It will have a cast of about 100 . . . and everyone in it seems to have sexual fantasies." And she returned once again to the novel she had been taking up and laying aside since January. Ames offered her a suggestion: Sexton might build in the turns of plot that life had handed her. "It should begin with the crash down the stairs, down the gold carpet, the broken hip, the pain, then the hospital, the doctor coming with the circles under his eyes to talk about his wife having read his poems, the broken hip, the broken heart, all foreshadowed and then back, back, back. [. . .] It's only how I would write that if I were you. [. . .] Like sex and love and family and trouble we all see how the other fellows should do it, and it all seems so easy, crystal clear, a great work."

But Sexton was never to finish that novel.

14

MONEY AND FAME
1967

THE SLOW HEALING of her injury confined Sexton to the lower floor of her house for several months that winter. Much of the time she kept to a bed set up in her study, adjacent to the kitchen. One brick wall held a cheery fireplace, and two others were lined with bookshelves; Mary Gray's old desk stood in the corner, and a radio like hers, tuned low to an FM station, played music continuously. The crowded study now became the center of Sexton's world. From her bed she looked out through a pair of windows across deep snow into the woods bordering Black Oak Road. She could watch for the daily pause of the mailman's car, bringing galleys of her work coming into print, letters, and the journals she subscribed to — her literary lifeline.

Sexton wrote little during December and January. She couldn't hold a typewriter on her lap and couldn't sit at the desk. Her energy went into recovering. Fortunately, she usually had the companionship of a nurse who had become a fan of her poetry long before meeting her and who was to become a loyal, steadying friend until the day of her death: Joan Smith, a neighbor of Maxine Kumin's in Newton Highlands. Sexton and Smith had met a year earlier, at the Kumins' farm in New Hampshire. One September afternoon the Kumins and Smiths were trudging back to the farmhouse, hot and sticky from picking blackberries, when they spotted the Sextons waiting in the shade. Joan Smith remembered, "I was madly in love with the book *All My Pretty Ones* — had worn out a copy, practically. As we walked down the hill to the pond we saw a perfectly glamorous woman sitting on a chaise and Max said, 'Oh, good, Annie's here,' and I thought, 'Oh my God' — I was wearing a shirt and dungarees and remember feeling very shy, monosyllabic." Sexton remembered the meeting too, and when she learned that her medical insurance would pay for home nursing, she called Smith from the hospital. " 'Joan, I've broken my hip, I need a nurse at home, will you save my life?' Very dramatic," Smith recalled. "And I said yes. And then I began to think, 'What have I done!' "

Sexton had been home from the hospital only a few hours when Smith paid her first visit. "Kayo was there, Anne's mother-in-law, Billie, was there, the housekeeper, Mary, was there, the telephone kept ringing, the doorbell kept ringing — it was one of the most confusing, hair-raising days I have ever spent," she said. "I had to make a few rules about routines."

For the next nine months Smith was at the Sextons' for eight hours a day, five days a week. After the first couple of months she was not really nursing Sexton. As she put it, "Anne needed an authoritative person around to keep some sanity and to adhere to a schedule." Joan would arrive just as Kayo was leaving in the morning after making breakfast for the children and seeing them off to school; Anne was usually still asleep. Immediately upon waking, she would call Joan to tell her her dreams. Joan would bring breakfast on a tray; then Anne would phone Maxine Kumin to discuss Kumin's progress on her new novel, *The Passions of Uxport*. She was full of bright ideas about the main character, Sukey — "Anne wrote whole speeches for Sukey," Kumin remembered. Overhearing them, Joan mistook the workshop for a gossip session: "It was days later that I learned these were fictional characters."

After bathing Anne, Joan would help her do the painful exercises that were crucial to the repair of her broken hip. She taught Anne how to use crutches to get to her desk, and she shared her happiness the day she was finally able to begin writing. As the physical care became less arduous, Joan took on other tasks. At one point she helped Anne sort the papers mounded in her study, and she was thrilled to receive in the process the galleys for *Bedlam* and *Pretty Ones*. She also became Anne's chauffeur, taking her to appointments with her psychiatrist or on other errands; Sexton was again regularly seeing Dr. Zweizung, trying to reinstate a therapeutic relationship in the wreckage of the romance ("am trying to work instead of lounge in a kiss," as she put it to Lois Ames). On the housekeeper's days off, Joan did some of the cooking as well. "Anne encouraged that; at Christmas she gave me a cookbook," she remarked dryly.

Another addition to the household that year was a secretary, Jean Moulton, who also worked for Sexton off and on until her death.

Moulton made an ideal counterpart to Joan Smith; an admirer of Sexton's work who enjoyed sharing the excitement of Sexton's professional life, and a discreet, competent professional who was able to organize chaos, she valued her own privacy and knew how to keep Sexton's dominating personality at a comfortable distance.

"Anne's files were inimitably chaotic," she recalled. "She kept everything. Of course, *she* could always lay hands on things she wanted. I remember that she kept her very private papers along with business papers in an old-fashioned filing cabinet with a lift-up top. Anne's private papers were off limits to me in the early days. After I started working for her, we retired that filing cabinet, made it into a telephone stand. We got a new one, and I took over the correspondence and record-keeping."

With Moulton on hand to perform the typing, Sexton began dictating her letters. "It worked out best when she dictated to me directly at the typewriter. That made the process more spontaneous," Moulton recalled. "At first I was nervous and made a lot of typos. She liked that — said it made her letters look more as if she'd written them. Her thoughts would come in a rush, and she wouldn't want to change or fiddle with them." Later Sexton bought a transcribing machine, and Moulton also worked from dictation on tape. "I was a morning person and Anne was not," Moulton explained. "When I arrived at her home, I'd often find a tape she'd dictated: could be minor revisions in poetry to retype and send out, could be letters or other kinds of notes."

The addition of Joan Smith and Jean Moulton to the household gave Sexton a real staff, the sort Mary Gray had always leaned on. Its third, most durable member was the housekeeper, Mary LaCrosse, or Meme. Nearing eighty, Meme had been attached to Anne's family before Anne was born, keeping house for Mary Gray and Ralph Harvey in Wellesley, then Weston, then Boston, then Annisquam. Mary Gray had made a gift of her services twice a week back in 1957, after Anne's first breakdown, and after the Harveys' deaths Meme had stayed on as an important contributor to the Sextons' comfort. A big-boned, gruff woman who radiated a sour body odor, she didn't actually clean the house (in Linda's and Joy's memories, the house was never clean), but she had a deft touch at tidying; just passing through a room, she could set it to rights in a minute, imprinting it with her care. She put fresh flowers about, she washed and ironed, and she cooked plain food the children loved.

No matter how many paid assistants Sexton acquired, however, the key to the smooth running of her life was still her mother-in-law. At thirteen and eleven, the children needed to be chauffeured to lessons and appointments and helped with their shopping. With Anne out of commission, Billie dropped by almost every day to pick them up or drop them off, or to run errands. Joan Smith remembered her as "wonderful about pitching in. She spent a lot of time with the girls; I think she was a great stabilizing influence on them. Her manner was gracious, very nice."

By February, able to sit up at her desk, Sexton was feeling like a poet again. In just a few weeks she wrote three new pieces: "Moon Song, Woman Song," "You All Know the Story of the Other Woman," and "It Is a Spring Afternoon." A few months later these were followed by two more love poems: "The Ballad of the Lonely Masturbator" and "Barefoot" — the latter possibly an anniversary poem, looking back to the week at Easthampton with Bob Clawson. Thoughts of spring were bolstered by good reports from the surgeon — her bones were knitting rapidly, and it seemed likely that by summer she would be able to trade her crutches for a cane.

In March she and Kayo bought a king-size bed — a sign, maybe, of another kind of recovery. After her chaste little rented hospital bed, the new bed seemed huge; she called it "the passion pad." She wrote to Lois Ames, "Kayo likes it. We haven't made love in it but did twice before it got here (as if to prepare?)."

Rested and well tended, Sexton experienced the New England spring in 1967 quite personally, as a force lifting her to a new peak in her career. Within the space of three weeks she received news of two major awards: the Shelley Memorial Prize, awarded annually by the Poetry Society of America "for the excellence of the body of a poet's work," and the Pulitzer Prize, awarded annually by Columbia University for the best book of poems published during the preceding year.

Sexton had aspired to the Pulitzer Prize for years; she had confided to Dr. Orne that she had plans "to write a book and leave it, so when I die it can be published, and of course it will get the Pulitzer Prize. — I want it just as much for when I'm dead as when I'm alive!" She was overjoyed by the news. Kayo too was terribly proud, Joy remembered: "Daddy brought her great champagne, and flowers — it was one of the triumphs he really shared." Max arrived, and Joan Smith, and Sandy and Les Robart and Rita and Karl Ernst, and other well-wishers whose feelings were all the deeper for having known the shaky beginnings of this fairy-tale transformation of a suburban housewife into a famous poet. Even Anne's sister Jane, in a rare fit of cordiality, sent greetings: "After numerous attempts at foning we decided your deserved popularity and publicity made you available only via Western Union. Generous congratulations from us both it is great to be related to a celebrity."

Although the Pulitzer Prize did not carry a large cash award (five hundred dollars; the Shelley Prize was over three times larger), it did indeed bestow, or confirm, celebrity status. Immediately after the prize was announced, Sexton began receiving inquiries from lecture agencies. Within two weeks she notified Redpath, her previous lecture agency, that she was upping her fees and would not accept any booking that didn't net seven hundred dollars per reading for herself. She also reported that she was being handled by a second lecture agency as well, the American Program Bureau. Actually, the Redpath Agency had done little for her in the four years since she had engaged it, and she had been serving successfully as her own booking office, handling correspondence with colleges and universities personally and receiving steadily increasing honoraria. By the end of her life she was among the best-paid poetry performers in America, setting her fees by monitoring the fees offered to James Dickey.

Both the Pulitzer and the Shelley were awarded to Sexton partly because she had just published *Live or Die*, but they also acknowledged the success of her whole career. During the decade since she had begun writing poems, her work had acquired major importance in the eyes of peers, institutions, and many readers. These honors did not have much immediate impact on sales — 6640 copies of Anne Sexton's books were sold the year she received the Pulitzer Prize — but they did confirm the new direction her art had taken.

Reviewers of *Live or Die* had been complaining about the looseness of Sexton's versification, looking for the careful formal effects of her first two books and speculating that the poet had become too self-absorbed. Reviewers, however, were not privy to the artistic goals that guided the change. In such poems as "Flee on Your Donkey," "Consorting with Angels," "Wanting to Die," and "The Addict," Sexton had begun to take great pains over poetry as a spoken art. Increasingly, the medium she worked in was the voice, and she strove to transfer feeling into word association as her fingers played over the typewriter keys, setting words to emotional rhythms (as she had indicated in her remarks to the NET interviewers a year earlier about her practice of writing to music). The result was in effect a monologue. What nonplussed poetry reviewers when they encountered it between the covers of a book might not have surprised them in a published script for performance, with voice cues and pauses added.

Sexton's own performance was the intended vehicle of this art. Onstage she projected a commanding, confident, glamorous physical presence; from her husky voice issued a hint of vulnerability, reinforced throughout the reading by rehearsed breaks and catches. Repeated showings of the NET film on public television that year ("Channel 2 is rerunning me like an advertisement," she said) expanded the audience for these performances, and fame itself drew letters from would-be poets. Among the most amusing letters Sexton kept was a request from the celebrity lawyer Melvin Belli, who enclosed two poems he had typed himself (apologizing for typos) and requested comments. "I can only appreciate your poems, I cannot possibly criticize them" was her usual gracious reply.

Readers, who encountered Sexton only on the page, had to supply the voice themselves. The peculiar power of the lyric poem has always been its ability to enlist a reader's empathic identification; Sexton understood this very well, and it helped focus her as an artist. As she told Anne Wilder, "I get letters daily from the so-called 'transference' feelings of readers . . . they all think of me as 'well,' as having 'solved' what I wrote about. Ha! So I know all about being on a so-called pedestal. A fake one that the reader creates (perhaps to separate them from the actual suffering of the writing) or else to reassure themselves about such suffering that they themselves have."

Many of Sexton's readers identified with her mental illness. She particularly treasured a letter from a psychiatrist who told her, "Your poems I find unusually *paleological,* even physiological. [. . .] Understanding the language of psychiatric patients, or of anyone, for that matter, is advanced by sympathy, I think, more than any acumen for recognition of the *mot juste* or the *bon mot.*" People who were in treatment themselves, or who had been, or who were close to others in treatment, drew encouragement from her candid representations of their very common condition. Her talent as a storyteller and her courage in acknowledging what could happen to ordinary people had drawn such readers in the past, and the publicity surrounding her Pulitzer Prize caught the attention of more.

But Sexton's audiences were not limited to those who identified one way or another with "illness" in her work. Her poetry is imbued with the era of her coming-of-age as a wife and mother, under the Eisenhower presidency and the conformity it exacted in the middle classes: gray flannel for men and compulsory domesticity for women, the cold war, nuclear politics. Sexton's work offered the mental hospital as a metaphorical space in which to articulate the crazy-making pressures of middle-class life, particularly for women. The home, the mental hospital, the body: These are woman's places in the social order that apportions different roles to the sexes; and woman herself is the very scene of mutilation, according to the theory of penis envy, which had great currency in Sexton's milieu. Yet as Sexton put it in her challenging poem to John Holmes, this "woman's space" is not restricted to women, for

> sometimes in private,
> my kitchen, your kitchen,
> my face, your face.

Sexton's poetry, in forcing discipline upon madness, fed opposite types of cultural appetite: for truth about the feel of illness, and for somewhat more disturbing truth about shifting ground between the sexes. She accomplished this goal by entrusting her voice to the understanding of the ideal listener — a space of understanding where a woman's version of things could get a new kind of hearing.

By June, Sexton's hip was strong enough to permit a trip to New York to attend a meeting of the board of directors of the Teachers and Writers Collaborative, which had evolved out of the conference on Long Island. Herbert Kohl had received one-year funding from the U.S. Office of Education to construct pilot projects, which would begin that September at selected schools in New York City, Philadelphia, and — with Sexton and Clawson in charge — Wayland, Massachusetts. "Why should such a good project be restricted to inner-city schools?" Sexton had asked Kohl on Long Island. "None of the public schools have writers in residence. Why don't we go into white, WASP North America and see what happens there, too?"

By the time the grant came through, Clawson had quit his job at Weston High, disgusted by ongoing conflicts with the administration, and carried the proposal to the superintendent in Wayland, where he and his family lived. As he explained, "It was a potent package to present to any public school. I had a reputation as a teacher, and by then, Anne had won the Pulitzer Prize. Here we are offering ourselves free" — that is, with funding from Kohl's project.

After the board meeting in New York, Sexton and Clawson made the rounds of Sexton's literary friends. They visited with Tony Hecht, and they met Howard Moss for drinks at the Algonquin Hotel. Moss recalled this as his first encounter with Sexton in person. "It was a beautiful spring day; the doors to the Algonquin were open onto the street. We all had a lot of Bloody Marys, and chatted for some time. They walked me to the bank. . . . It was one of those lovely occasions hard to put into words later. I was enchanted with her." The feeling was mutual. Sexton was particularly happy with Moss at that point because *The New Yorker* had been accepting her new love poems at a rapid rate; "Moon Song, Woman Song," "For My Lover, Returning to His Wife," and "It Is a Spring Afternoon" had found instant favor. "You were utterly charming and distinguished, and I would have liked a third Bloody Mary and more laughter," she wrote in her thank-you note.

Sexton also met her literary agent, Cindy Degener, face to face for the first time. Degener had taken over Sexton's work at the Sterling Lord Agency in 1964, and their business relationship had blossomed into a friendship when they had learned they had much in common. One was a fear of flying. Another was Boston. Degener (born Sweeney) was Boston Irish, and though she had had a classy education at Radcliffe, she could call Sexton's bluff: Sexton could forget the Plantagenets in the genealogy she loved to quote. Degener's jokes, in combination with her great track record as a literary agent, put Sexton at ease, though she thought Degener took the lace curtain caricature a bit too far ("I love you, dear," she wrote after their meeting, "and there's no bad side of Boston. There's just a windward and leeward.")

On this occasion she hand-delivered a copy of her play, *Tell Me Your Answer True,* long ignored, and asked Degener for suggestions about revising and marketing it. The producer of the NET documentary had expressed interest in it, and Sexton had been in touch with Ben Shaktman about renewing their collaboration. Now the Pulitzer Prize had stirred her name to the top. She wanted to seize the moment.

Degener was a pro, and she thought Sexton really could write for the stage, if opportunities were put her way. That day she gave Sexton some advice: Write more plays, Anne, and leave the marketing to Cindy. Sexton followed it, working up perhaps three plays over the next several years, and she also mailed Degener several stories which Degener was never able to place.

In fact, as Degener knew, Sexton worried about the opinion of New York intellectuals. One of the members of the board of the Teachers and Writers Collaborative was Robert Silvers, a founding editor of the *New York Review of Books*. Home from New York with a sense that she had successfully exercised her charisma, and with her prizes still fresh in everyone's mind, Sexton decided the time had come to submit some poems to this publication. She enclosed the best of the love poems that Howard Moss had recently turned down, after exercising his first reading rights, telling Silvers that the *New York Review* might find "The Man of Many Hearts" too long, but that since it was "the most widely-read newspaper-magazine among the intelligentsia [. . .] quite naturally I would like to appear in it." (Silvers declined.)

She also used momentum from winning the Pulitzer Prize to carry her through the process of applying for a fellowship from the National Endowment for the Arts, with references from Dudley Fitts, Robert Lowell, and Louis Untermeyer. She requested $20,000 to support work on a new book of poems. Interestingly, she claimed to fellow poets *not* to be working on poetry. "God, I wish I could write something," she wrote to Philip Legler later that year. "Have been blocked for so long . . . nothing but one poem since the hip." In fact she had written seven poems since breaking her hip, all dealing with clandestine love affairs; many of them were about to be published in *The New Yorker*. But she had begun trying to overcome her reputation as a crazy lady, and "the hip" was henceforth to provide her with a socially acceptable rationale for being unable to do something inconvenient. It never mended fully; she limped for the rest of her life.

Sexton's application to the NEA did not receive funding, but at least she was on the move again. Anticipating the teaching that she and Clawson would begin in September, she started keeping a journal. This was a departure for her, as she commented self-consciously in her first entry, dated 16 June. "I don't like the idea of a journal. I'm afraid it will show all my weakness. It is not disciplined enough. A poem has more rules, either inner or outer. [. . .] I, who reportedly write so truthfully about myself, so openly, am not that open." Deciding that she needed a bit of practice with an assignment she would be giving to students, Sexton kept the journal fitfully that summer. Extra motivation came from knowing that it would have other readers, as Herbert Kohl planned to collect journals from all the teachers and students.

.   .   .

A few months after *Live or Die* came out in the United States, it was published in England. Sexton was disappointed when it failed to become a Poetry Book Society recommendation and shocked by its bad notices in the English press. Jon Stallworthy, her British editor, played down the negatives. "I know how you must feel about those cruel reviews and, if I hadn't lost my voice (at a reading versus Kingsley Amis), I would dictate a letter explaining why certain poetry reviewers on this side of the Atlantic are so tigerish at present," he wrote soothingly. "It should comfort you to know that only 50 copies of our first printing of your *Selected Poems* remain." Even more comforting was the excellent review by Alan Ross that had just appeared in *London Magazine,* which Stallworthy clipped and tucked into the letter. "Anyone experiencing the process of breakdown knows the impossibility of describing it," Ross began. "Once you can find the words you are halfway cured and it is another situation altogether." His review focused thoughtfully on Sexton's exploration, as an artist, of neurotic mood-states with chiefly histrionic qualities. "Yet for all their burden, these poems rarely sink, for they carry the weight of their own conviction without poetic strain," he commented. "The rewards of these poems are many, for they are the products of a tough original mind, of an engaging poetic personality."

Sexton was grateful for the praise. *Live or Die* had been scheduled to appear in time for promotion at the five-day Poetry International Festival sponsored annually in London by the Poetry Book Society and the Arts Council of Great Britain, and she had been invited to present her work by Ted Hughes, who was one of the organizers. She had been delighted to accept; here was a chance to position her work in an international forum. But as she lamented to George MacBeth, "My reviews in London are not to be mentioned. How will I ever hold my head up?"

Nonetheless, she departed for England on 11 July, accompanied by much gear, including a wheelchair. She had managed to patch together travel expenses from a number of sources and to schedule herself and Lois Ames, her companion for this trip, on the same flight with Anthony Hecht. The three of them were chatting in the departure lounge, Sexton in her wheelchair, when the public address system began blaring Sexton's name. A photographer was paging her; he wanted publicity shots. She beckoned for Hecht to join the session, which made quite a stir among the passengers. "Only later did it occur to me that Sexton had set this up herself!" Hecht recalled. "I challenged her about this episode, and she never actually denied it. Anne,

I think, never quite recovered from getting the Pulitzer Prize; she thought it meant everyone should notice her from then on."

Rooms for the festival poets had been booked at the 69 Hotel, not far from Queen Elizabeth Hall. Sexton found this hilarious. "What does one do in such a hotel and being the only woman at the conference? 69 Hotel! Don't they know I have a broken hip?" In fact, she wasn't the only woman. Bella Akmadulina, the Russian poet, was supposed to read on one evening with Sexton (at the last moment she was denied permission to travel), and the Austrian poet Ingeborg Bachmann was also on the program.

Sexton was originally slated to read at Poetry International only once, but when John Berryman failed to show up on the day of his scheduled reading, last-minute rearrangements put her in his place on the opening-night program, with Pablo Neruda and W. H. Auden. She made a second appearance three nights later. She scrawled Kayo the gossip from under the dryer at a hairdresser's shop: "Tony [Hecht] and I are crushed into tiny speaking spots (10 minutes) — I guess we're not very important," she reported. "My reading (13 minutes) the other night was not as good as usual. Not up to par. Auden was glowering behind me, furious at foreign poets who were on first and took up so much time. It's a hell of a trip for a lousy 13 or 10 minutes."

Sexton's first reading may have been short, but many found it memorable. "Auden was very cross with Anne, because she went way over her allotted time," Jon Stallworthy recalled. "He was a real pro and thought we should recite accurately *without* books and finish pretty much on the second. She went way over, and he kept taking off his dark glasses and swinging them around and gesturing in irritation and mounting fury." Stallworthy too was disconcerted by Sexton's stage manner. "I suspect she was taking some kind of medication. She was also drinking too much." He remembered her whole approach to the English audience as "ill-judged": "When Anne had finished, she laid down her book, threw wide her arms like a pop singer embracing her audience, and blew them a fat kiss. It was in a hall that held about two thousand people, I should think, and they looked at her in disbelief and horror. It was the most grotesquely ill-judged gesture I've ever seen at a poetry reading." Hecht also recalled the stir Sexton made. "Well, yes, she was sensational, and she was highly criticized for it in the press the next day. Nonetheless, she was the *only* poet the press paid any attention to. For all the complaints, she made the headlines."

Sexton was surrounded by stars of the poetry world that week. In addition to Neruda — her hero since James Wright had introduced her to his work — there were Allen Ginsberg and John Berryman, whom she had wanted to meet, and Stephen Spender, whom she had not seen since 1960, at Brandeis. Since almost everyone was staying in one hotel, she must have made many new acquaintances. But Sexton didn't have much to say — in letters, anyway — about "all those egos cluttered together in one hall," as she put it. The only poets with whom she maintained a little correspondence later were Nathaniel Tarn, George MacBeth, and Israeli poet Yehuda Amichai.

While she was in London, Sexton recorded an interview with MacBeth for later radio play on the BBC. On the air, she rewrote history a bit in accounting for her development as an artist, probably hoping to correct certain British misconceptions about her debt to Robert Lowell: She omitted all references to her years in the John Holmes workshop and claimed she had joined Lowell's seminar after completing *Bedlam*. Strategic untruthfulness was, of course, an element of her poetry, so perhaps she regarded it as a legitimate characteristic of her self-representation before an audience interested in poems. (Reading a transcript of the interview later, Sexton commented to D. M. Thomas, "It's fascinating to read though in places highly inaccurate. I am known to lie, and I never let myself down.") "Facts," she said to MacBeth, "are very unimportant things, there to make you believe in the emotional content in a poem. . . . I can feel any feeling," she added sensibly, "and write about it. I don't have to be autobiographical."

MacBeth asked her to read a poem from *Live or Die* that he admired, "The Addict," which ends,

> What a lay me down this is
> with two pink, two orange,
> two green, two white goodnights.
> Fee-fi-fo-fum —
> Now I'm borrowed.
> Now I'm numb.

This one, she said, proved her point exactly. "My friends say it's a cruel poem, because addiction is so self-destructive: 'You are so flamboyant about your addiction!' I say, 'Wait a minute — isn't any addict flamboyant about addiction? They show it off, and say, Look I'm an addict.' " She repeated the point: "I'm trying to say, 'Hello, everyone. Here's what I do. Now watch it. Take part.' Which is rather exhibitionistic of me, but remember, I don't make too much fuss about the whole bit. 'I'm very little trouble' is what I'm trying to say — even about my whole illness. After all, I *am* crazy."

Seeking to give Sexton as much credit as possible, MacBeth made an interesting inference here. "It seems to me your poetry isn't so much autobiographical as moral. That is to say, you are dealing with extreme situations, but you are suggesting a way in which one ought to behave in them. In this poem, what you're saying is that the important thing is not to cause too much trouble." Sexton accepted this benevolent interpretation, but in fact her own point was quite different. Her poetry is the *voice* of the extreme situation, and in "The Addict" this includes the tactics by which the addiction seeks to perpetuate itself in the face of moral censure. MacBeth played the role, so to speak, of "codependent": Addiction is okay if the addict doesn't make too many waves. Sexton's poem offers a stronger dose than that: The addict will say anything to make you go along with her. But after all, she is crazy.

MacBeth and Sexton enjoyed this interview. Afterward they drifted out into the London streets together, went to a pub to unwind, stayed on, drifted to dinner, drifted back to Sexton's hotel and into each other's arms. They arrived at Sexton's room to find Lois Ames asleep in the second bed. Undeterred, or only slightly, they made love. "This added an eccentric dimension," MacBeth remembered with a laugh.

> Lois Ames was like Anne's shadow at the time; it seemed essential to Anne that at all times there be a recording angel present. The biographer sleeping in the next bed! Though when I look back on it, there was nothing particularly louche or Sixties about it, no crowds of people sitting about smoking pot. But then, she was always anxious to be seen as striking, to exhibit a characteristic that other people might exhibit in a smaller hall, if you see what I mean. I feel this in myself — that's probably why we responded to each other. This extravagance: you know you're going too far, but you do it or say it anyway.

MacBeth acknowledged being very stirred by Sexton. "I subsequently wrote a poem about Anne flying back to America — somewhat ritualistic, perhaps in a certain sense not a personal love poem, perhaps about a state of mind. When *Love Poems* came out, she remarked there was one for me in it, but she didn't say which one. I've been through the book and I've never been able to discover which one it was. It occurred to me very often that she might have been lying."

Excess was equally the keynote of Sexton's meetings with Michael Bearpark, her old friend from junior high school, who was now a psychiatrist with a practice in York. He drove down from the north for a night on the town with her, and they dined at Rules, a restaurant near Covent Garden that had been patronized by the Prince of Wales and his friends in the 1890s. "Anne was in an emotionally labile state," he remembered. "She went on to question me about my sexual preference as we drank our soup. [. . .] This was all a little traumatic to me and the hovering waiter." After dinner they moved on to a pub in Chelsea; "we kissed in the back of the taxi, and the slightly acrid taste of her lips recalled the play kisses of years before." The warm reunion ended on a disturbing note, however. Back at the hotel, Sexton asked Bearpark to remain "until she got into bed and took her near-annihilating sedation," which roused him to professional horror. It was "excessive in dose, and an unorthodox mixture of major and minor tranquilizers, antidepressants and barbiturates," he noted. "She seemed to take them indiscriminately."

The following day Sexton and Lois Ames were to drive to Herefordshire to meet D. M. Thomas, a young poet with whom Sexton had been exchanging letters. Unused to driving on the "wrong" side of the road, they went hopelessly astray, so Michael Bearpark, who had agreed to meet them there, arrived at Thomas's home two or three hours before they did. "It may have been indiscreet but I primed him ahead of time to buy her some gin; I knew she would expect several stiff shots."

Thomas was an "exuberant, curly-haired bear of a man," Ames remembered. A young writer with "a third of a book" of poems in print, he taught at a college for women; later he was to achieve praise and notoriety for his novel *The White Hotel.* Writing to Sexton in 1966, he had told her how affected his students were by such poems as "Unknown Girl in the Maternity Ward" and "The Fortress," and added — music to her ears — "There is no poet in the world, not Graves, not Auden, not Lowell, whose future work I look forward to with as much excitement as I do yours."

Once Sexton and Ames arrived and the cap had come off the gin bottle, the evening went very pleasantly. Sexton read some of her poems. "I admired her courage as an artist: not being timid about using the material of your own life," Thomas remembered. "This went so much against the English conventions of decorum and good taste. I thought this was an ideal one should aim for. I was much more aware of the sanity in her writing than of madness. In those early poems I connected the voice with Robert Frost — that sort of calmness, a New England quality they had in common. Wit with an underlying seriousness."

After Bearpark departed, Thomas drove the women "out to a little black-and-white village called Woebly, to the Unicorn Inn," where, as he had promised, he had booked them the room he thought (erroneously) that Rilke had occupied the year before Sexton's birth. Sexton invited him up. "She asked me to turn away while she undressed and got into her nightdress, then I was allowed to turn around and look. It was splendid — she said, 'I bought this with my Pulitzer Prize.' " They chatted for a few minutes; then she counted out her pills. "She said, 'Please stay, in thirty seconds I'll be asleep.' And in thirty seconds she was asleep. What struck me," he added, "was the theatricality of that goodnight, a very subdued eroticism about it. She was going to be Sleeping Beauty."

The next day Thomas's colleague Tony Riding drove Sexton and Ames around the border country. At a castle in Shropshire they stopped to have a look around, but Sexton felt too lame for a walk. She said to Thomas, " 'Better than stones and castles are my bones.' Then, 'I'll give that to you,' said she — she tore out a sheet of paper and wrote it down. I've kept it ever since, and used it later as a point of departure for an elegy." In the evening they stopped at a country pub, where Sexton "played the fruit machines, and generally wowed it up. And talked about death and poetry. And was generous and kind, encouraging to a young writer," Thomas recalled. "The whole time I was with her, she was in high spirits, fun to be with. 'Live or die, but don't poison everything': that's what she lived by." Riding drove them back to the Unicorn, with Ames in the front seat. "I was in the back with Anne and we exchanged one passionate kiss," Thomas said. "I thought, Wow! I've kissed Sexton!"

Thomas couldn't accompany them on the final leg of their journey, to Devon, "where Lois has baronial relatives," Anne reported to Kayo, and where they had a dinner engagement with Ted Hughes. Ames would have a chance to see Court Green, the home and surroundings Plath had absorbed into so many poems. She must have comported herself with consummate tact, because Hughes later wrote to Sexton that their visit "completely redeemed the general unease I felt about Mrs. Ames." In turn, he hoped to redeem Sexton from the disappointments of her critical reception in England. Knowing that she was smarting over the bad reviews, he wrote her consolingly, saying don't worry, good reviews are bad for poets. He went on to compile a catalogue of the harms produced by favorable reviews: "They tend to confirm one in one's own conceit — unless they praise what you yourself don't like. Also they make you self-conscious about your virtues — just as when you praise a child for some natural charm. Also they create an underground opposition: applause is the beginning of abuse. Also they deprive you of your own anarchic liberties — by electing you into the government. Also, they separate you from your devil, which hates being observed and only works happily incognito." Although Sexton posted this good advice over her desk, it was, unfortunately, to grow more and more pertinent.

Reverberations of these colloquies with British poets followed Sexton back across the Atlantic. D. M. Thomas reaffirmed his devotion by quoting her back to herself in a letter he signed with "temporary adulation": "Crazy, you're 'as nice as a chocolate bar,' apart from being, in my view, one of the finest poets in the world, and fated to be a great one." George MacBeth sent her a love letter written while she was on the plane and a few days later a poem inspired by this letter, "A Threnody, for Nefertiti in the Caravelle." (Jon Stallworthy had referred publicly to Sexton as "the Nefertiti of New England"). Sexton adored being adored, but the trip left a slightly sour taste in her mouth, which ardent testimonials did not dissolve. She had been in pain; she had been more put out by bad press than she liked to show; she felt "humbled" by the atmosphere of seriousness in which many of the festival poets worked; and she had been drunk a little too often. Her dejection spilled over into a letter she wrote to a young admirer shortly after returning, scolding her for being so needy of praise. "[I am] full of self-doubts at this time, having returned from England & hearing more poets who write far better than I. I do not write to them and ask them to tell me that someday I will be good. It is something you do alone — *all the way alone.*"

Anne and Kayo ended the summer by taking weekend trips to visit friends on Cape Cod and to visit Joy at riding camp in New Hampshire. Linda had returned from a different camp the same day Anne returned from England, at her mother's insistence. Though Anne adjusted easily to Joy's absences, it pained her deeply each time Linda left home. "I cried in daddy's arms last night," she had written to Linda in July. "He says he misses you too, and very much, but that I have to get used to you going away. You are so much a part of this house and my life that it feels as if a big hole had been cut out of life."

Anne and Kayo rarely traveled during the summer; since Kayo was constantly on the road, he found it more relaxing to stay in Weston and play golf. Anne spent most of the summer days outdoors, and when her women friends dropped by, which they often did, informal workshops took place in the shade by the pool. She and Max tried to keep some time free just for each other, however, not only in morning phone calls but in almost daily visits.

Friends noticed around this time how much alike Kumin and Sexton looked in the fashions just coming in. They were about the same height and build, broad-shouldered, and had the same dark skin that quickly took a tan. Both had sleek haircuts, and wonderful long legs to show off with short skirts. Kumin remembered fondly that "one of the joys of our relationship was the ease with which we traded dresses back and forth, and shoes, and pocketbooks, and coats. We really only needed one outfit between the two of us. I remember a navy-and-white-striped wool that I just loved, and so did Anne, and we had to take turns. Then, at one point, we both had the same dress and wore them together like little Bobbsey twins!" (The striking ways in which they doubled each other left a strong impression; today, many people remember them as going everywhere together, though in fact they only rarely gave joint poetry readings and almost never traveled together.)

But Sexton noticed that summer that her clothes no longer fit very well; as she wrote to Anne Wilder, "It all comes from lying around drinking eggnogs and not walking." She should probably get a girdle, "but I protest the discomfort and the idea and so I have just plain grown. Three sizes larger and a lot in the pot, quite a bit in the breasts and a lot in the round face. [. . .] I wear shifts and hope no one notices." Kumin remembered her friend's surprise at these changes: "She had no sense of herself as heavy. She probably put on thirty pounds or more. We used to just howl about this — that she was always the thin girl inside the fat girl and I was always the fat child inside the thin adult. I mean when I looked in the mirror I saw another outline: Mine was a balloon. When she looked in the mirror, she didn't see the balloon she had become, she saw the slim outline of her former self."

In the best of times, Kumin recalled, Sexton avoided exercise. She liked to skinny-dip, but in Kumin's view (Kumin having been a competitive swimmer), this was not exercise. "I would wheedle and beg, cajole and bully her into taking a very small walk; I could never get her on a bike or a horse, although she did once sit on my horse Taboo to have her picture taken — just to prove she could do it. Of course, after she broke her hip she had the perfect excuse: She couldn't walk." And that summer, since she would be starting a job that required regular commuting, Kayo decided she needed a new car; her VW bug — the "bloo jool" she had been driving since its retrieval from Rome in 1965 — seemed to him too dangerous for daily use. They bought her a new red Cougar.

On the opening day of school at Wayland High, local journalists filed into class with the students, since it was news that a working writer would be teaching a writing course. The group was limited to twenty students, who would meet for one hour every day but would follow no set curriculum and receive no grades. Sexton and Clawson planned the writing exercises one day at a time, over lunch at his house in Wayland. "After class we'd go to the Red Coach Grill and have a few drinks and talk about the next day. So that was the way we did our planning — it was like an indulgence, luxurious."

Sexton didn't get over her nervousness about being in the classroom, and she made Clawson promise that he wouldn't abandon her for an instant. After the class had been meeting for a couple of months, he once stepped out of the room for a moment. "Anne was holding forth, doing a splendid job — all the questions were going to her and she was really working like a good teacher when I left the room. I came back in, and there she was, sitting there — in a trance. When she heard me come in, she snapped out of it. The kids were tense. Afterwards she said, 'I told you — don't ever leave the classroom. Don't leave me alone.' I said, 'Anne, for Christ's sake, you've got to learn to be alone sometime.' She said, 'We're in this together.'"

Homework for the class pushed Sexton's own writing in a new direction. As a way to get going on their own writing, the students were to read and discuss short stories and novels, such as Ralph Ellison's *The Invisible Man* and Sherwood Anderson's *Winesburg, Ohio.* Anderson's example stimulated Sexton to write about Kayo's adventure with a charging elephant in Tanzania and the way it had changed him. "The story of Wing Biddlebaum is the story of hands," she told the students. "The Story of Kayo Sexton is the story of an elephant bracelet." More often, though, her work emerged from dialogue with the students; a poem titled "The Papa and Mama Dance" got started in class and ended up in *Love Poems*. (In her journal she observed that it was about incest, "but the students didn't get it.") When she gave an assignment to write a prayer, she wrote one herself, titled "Turning God Back On," and then another, "Man with a Prayer." Violence, sex, religion: strong stuff. But Sexton's goal was not to shock, it was to stir associations. She meditated on the problem in her journal. "I'm not sure when to talk about images. I'm afraid to frighten the kids. I just write fantastic on their papers when they use them. I think images come from the unconscious and you can't force them. I expose them to poems with images and hope that in this way they will catch on to the value of them. [. . .] The naughtiest kids are the ones with the most intelligence and the most creativity. They're creating a scene in class and they can create a scene on paper just as well."

The school's administration regarded the experiment as a success, and funding was renewed for a second semester. Sexton continued to collaborate with Clawson throughout the year, but after the first six weeks she became disillusioned, as she began to take in that these were not just young writers banding together against the world, they were public school students whose parents entertained anxious hopes of upward mobility as an outcome of education. As the content of the course grew more literary, Sexton grew apathetic. "I have now come to a passive position where I let the class happen. The discussion of *The Invisible Man* has put me off my stride because it is beyond me, and I am incapable of discussing it intelligently. I experience the book, but I can't discuss it."

Still, teaching the course was to have two important consequences for Sexton. One was an enhancement of confidence in her teaching abilities. She knew now what she couldn't do (teach literature), but, more to the point, what she could do — encourage teenagers to write by adapting the workshop model from which she had learned the tricks of the trade herself.

Another outcome, less predictable, was the formation of a group of young musicians to serve as backup for her poetry performances. Sexton's journal records the origin of this interesting development. The class had read Edward Arlington Robinson's "Richard Cory" and listened to the musical adaptation of this poem by Simon and Garfunkel.

Then Sexton had read her poem "Johnny Pole on the Forgotten Beach." One of the students, Steve Rizzo, borrowed *To Bedlam and Part Way Back* after class. Three weeks later, he invited Sexton and Clawson to hear his guitar settings of "Johnny Pole," "Music Swims Back to Me," and "Ringing the Bells." Clawson remembered, "Steve was a big, good-looking kid, probably one of the best football players that school ever had, but he didn't have the football attitude. A lot of kids were putting bands together in those days. But musically, Steve was a primitive — he didn't read notes." Clawson invited a friend who was a professional pianist, Bill Davies, to listen to Sexton read while Steve strummed the songs. Davies liked it, and agreed to help work out the musical ideas. "We went back to my house and recorded a little — began to put a sound together." Eventually, this classroom project developed into a touring chamber rock group dubbed Anne Sexton and Her Kind.

But that was later. In the autumn of 1967 Sexton was as fully booked as she wanted to be on the poetry circuits in the Northeast, in readings carefully chosen to give her the best returns on the investment of her precious and limited human capital. She had kidded with George MacBeth about her fees, and in October he reported on his own itinerary: "I've been touring the English petty-cash circuits, reading my old (boring) poems at a penny a second and dreaming of you and your five hundred dollarses." Most schools and universities in the U.S.A. worked out of petty-cash accounts, too, and offered Sexton honoraria in the range of fifty to a hundred dollars, which she usually turned down. Sometimes, though, she felt well enough reimbursed by the venue itself to read for a small fee or none at all, as when she appeared for the Academy of American Poets at the Guggenheim Museum in New York in November, two days before her birthday.

No matter how often she performed in public, Sexton underwent the same monumental anxiety beforehand and took several days at home to recover. Though readings offered her a chance to meet people who interested her, and even more chances for people interested in her to arrange a personal exchange, it didn't work that way. Before her appearance at the Guggenheim Museum, for instance, Sexton wrote to a young poet who wanted very much to meet her, "If I seem to be ignoring you, please know that I'm very disturbed before and after a reading." As she had told Dr. Orne at the outset of her career, onstage facing an audience she knew who she was; surrounded by these same strangers afterward, she hadn't a clue.

By mid-November, Sexton was so depleted by teaching and travel that she canceled a long-scheduled engagement at the University of Arkansas in Fayetteville. As it happened, the space opened in her calendar by this prudent move became time for creative work. Dr. Zweizung left with his family at the beginning of December for a three-week vacation, and "gone" was the rhyme word that gonged over and over in the first poem of a series called "Eighteen Days Without You":

> I hibernated under the covers
> last night, not sleeping until dawn
> came up like twilight and the oak leaves
> whispered like money, those hangers on.
> The hemlocks are the only
> young thing left. You are gone.

It is apparent from many sources that Sexton's therapeutic alliance with Dr. Zweizung had become a sexual relationship once again at

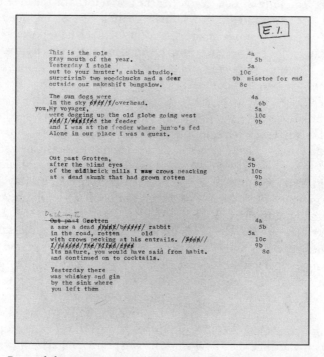

Part of the manuscript of "Eighteen Days Without You."

some point following her convalescence from the broken hip. The specific scenes that give "Eighteen Days" the feel of narrative must be regarded as the products of the fantasy process underlying all imaginative writing, perhaps Sexton's writing in particular. Nonetheless, Sexton's comments in letters and elsewhere indicate that she deliberately planted coded references to this romance in the poem. However, it was not passion but the prospect of loss — even before Dr. Zweizung actually left town — that gave impetus to her countermove to her desk.

Sexton continued to teach with Bob Clawson and brought manuscripts of "Eighteen Days" to share after class, when they were often joined by John Clark, another teacher Sexton liked at Wayland High. Clawson remembered the excitement of watching the poems take shape. "She was writing *Love Poems* then. She'd say 'Her hip cracked like — like — like —' 'Like a pistol' we'd say. 'Wow, that's a great metaphor,' she'd say. Just a cliché, but she put it in anyway."

Once she returned home to her typewriter, Sexton lost herself for hours at a time every day. To the poet Richard Eberhart she wrote happily, "I have had a spurt of creativity that quite makes up for a bad year." To another friend she reported, "I'm in the middle of the longest poem of my life, and I'm so excited about it that I stay up 'til three in the morning typing my heart out. The poem has nothing to do with hospitals but is a pastoral love poem. Someday I will send you a copy if I ever finish it." She did finish it. "Eighteen Days Without You" became the finial on the bedpost of *Love Poems*.

IV

THE PERFORMER
1968–1974

15

ANNE SEXTON AND
HER KIND
1968

"EIGHTEEN DAYS WITHOUT YOU" was not only the final poem, it was the best poem in a book that accompanied another change of direction in Sexton's professional life. *Love Poems* was the first of her books produced in the atmosphere of celebrity, and "Sexton" was now an established brand name. Certain effects were trademarks of the product, very much on display in Sexton's own all-time favorite among these poems, "The Touch":

> For months my hand had been sealed off
> in a tin box. Nothing was there but subway railings.
> Perhaps it is bruised, I thought,
> and that is why they have locked it up.
> But when I looked in it lay there quietly.
> You could tell time by this, I thought,
> like a clock, by its five knuckles
> and the thin underground veins.
> It lay there like an unconscious woman
> fed by tubes she knew not of.

One Sexton trademark is the frequent use of simile ("like . . ."). Another is the repetitious structure, a set of associational forays that do not develop into thoughts but terminate in surreal images, as "I" stares obsessively at her own body, atomizing it with her look. ("Nothing was there but subway railings" — fingerbones? raised veins?) Another is the pool of metaphors from which the poem draws: "bruise" in this stanza, hunger, food, death, blood in the others. Still another is the tone, blending pathos with black humor. Finally, there is the Sexton signature of "clang," the knock and jangle of assonance:

off-box-locked-looked-clock-knuckles-not of, to follow just one pathway in this sonic maze.

Sexton had already produced a number of just such poems, including the last poem ("Live") of *Live or Die*, which she had knocked out to meet a deadline. Was this bad writing? Well, as Robert Lowell put it tactfully at an earlier moment, "all one can say is that they are Sexton and therefore precious." A poem like "Live" worked, for some people, when Sexton performed it at a reading, and many people quoted its ending sentiments as evidence that her outlook was healthy after all. If you were "into" Sexton, you would like "Live."

But "Eighteen Days Without You" was a return to an earlier mode. Each day in the series has its own scheme of end rhymes that continually, comfortingly close up the lines of the stanzas on one another, coupling and trebling the sounds. "Word magic," Sexton called it; the speaker plays a word game like the "Fort! Da!" game Freud ascribed to his grandson in *Beyond the Pleasure Principle,* casting a spool and reeling it back over and over and over to make the beloved come home. "December 11th" is a good, brief example of the technique at its best.

> Then I think of you in bed,
> your tongue half chocolate, half ocean,
> of the houses that you swing into,
> of the steel wool hair on your head,
> of your persistent hands and then
> how we gnaw at the barrier because we are two.
>
> How you come and take my blood cup
> and link me together and take my brine.
> We are bare. We are stripped to the bone
> and we swim in tandem and go up and up
> the river, the identical river called Mine
> and we enter together. No one's alone.

Sexton also gave "Eighteen Days" a broad range of references. From the private rooms and trysting places of the poem's opening sections, these widen to the dates of political assassinations and military battles and to the state school for retarded children. The clever use of anniversaries makes intimacy ironic. Disaster is all around the parted lovers in the poem, but do they glimpse its scale? The Vietnam War, for them, is the size of a TV set, and the march on Washington is a carnival. In "Eighteen Days," the female ego-center is not a fountain of associations but a person with a history; as in a work of fiction, we witness her acting in an integrated circuit of significance that is greater than she knows but that the poem fathoms.

The surge of creative energy that went into "Eighteen Days Without You" produced other new work that winter. Sexton added a few quite lovely lyrics ("Us," "Just Once") to *Love Poems,* and then — a complete change of focus — wrote a poem based on a newspaper photograph, "The Firebombers." This new subject had two sources. One was Sexton's daily teaching, which made her take more active possession of her thoughts about the social function of poetry. The other was her participation in protest against the Vietnam War as a member of a community of artists.

The notion that there *was* a community of artists, whose views on war and peace might be worth hearing, gathered in the wake of escalating U.S. bombings of North Vietnam in 1965, in the action the military called Operation Rolling Thunder. There were actual bombs, and then there were idealizing terms that justified dropping them. It was the second, rhetorical or poetic power that artists addressed: what you call what you are doing. Justin Kaplan evoked this sense of community when he announced that he would turn over the money he won from the Pulitzer Prize for *Mr. Clemens and Mark Twain* to the American Friends Service Committee to support opposition to the war. He wished "to honor the American tradition of constructive dissent Mark Twain served so nobly," he said, "to voice my distress over the course we are following in Vietnam, and to express my faith and hope that we are capable of devising positive alternatives to that course." Among the forms of constructive dissent undertaken by intellectuals and artists was the public scrutiny of propaganda during "teach-ins" at colleges and universities all over the country.

Sexton did not participate in the demonstrations in Washington, nor was she among hundreds of thousands who marched down Fifth Avenue in New York, led by Martin Luther King, Jr. But she was drawn into the waves of protest that convulsed the East Coast in those days. Beginning in 1966, she read at several antiwar meetings. Her participation aroused some conflict with Kayo, as she told a fellow poet: "Tonight I take part in a vast Anti-Vietnam read-in [at Harvard's Sanders Theater]. I expect they will throw eggs, or my husband (the republican who hates my pink — he calls it — politics) says they may throw hand-grenades." She summarized her own views in the journal she kept for her class: "I hate killing of any kind, and protest the war in every way, and my husband thinks we ought to 'win' the war. I live a lie. [. . .] We just don't talk about the war. A lie."

Sexton's friend Allen Grossman, a poet and professor at Brandeis, was one of the organizers of several of the "read-ins" in which she took part. Brandeis had long been a site of ardent political debate, and the student population was full of "red diaper" babies, many of whom went on to become the most radical leaders of antiwar action. Grossman was not a political theorist but he had strong convictions about the political functions of poetry. He was also a pragmatist. "We wanted participation by well-known writers, to get these readings going, and Sexton was well known," he commented.

At the read-in at Sanders Theater, she was, as always, strikingly well groomed, in a sleek white dress and spike heels. Robert Bly and Galway Kinnell were on the program as well. Adrienne Rich, another of the organizers, recalled that Sexton's poetry made a strong impression. "She read 'Little Girl, My String Bean, My Lovely Woman,' and you cannot imagine the impact that poem had. Bly and others were reading poems describing various people in the government; there were poems about napalmed babies and so on. Then Anne got up and read this poem for her daughter — so out of kilter with the occasion in one sense, and in another sense so completely the right thing. It was about life and surviving. It made people rather uncomfortable, but she was completely self-possessed."

In 1968 Sexton wrote a few poems influenced by the example of Rich, Grossman, Muriel Rukeyser, Denise Levertov, and Robert Lowell — poets who were able to bring into their art their outrage as the war increased in ferocity. In January she typed out "The Firebombers" for Rukeyser.

> The woman is bathing her heart.
> It has been torn out of her
> and because it is burnt
> and as a last act
> she is rinsing it off in the river.
> This is the death market.
>
> America,
> where are your credentials?

Sexton was diffident about this poem, which she told Howard Moss she had written "for a local mimeographed-stop-the-war newspaper — so if you could return it as fast as possible (I don't see you wanting it) I will give it to them for the encouragement they ask of me." Later in the year, when *Look* ran a story on her, she told Lois Ames that the magazine might be printing "The Firebombers" alongside the article, "to show I care about the world, the war and all that contemporary crap. I do care," she added, "but I don't think caring is the same as good writing." One of several differences between "Eighteen Days" and "The Firebombers" is the speaker's censoriousness in the latter poem; Sexton's outlook was too psychoanalytic to render censoriousness authentic. At her best, she localized emotions in situations, not in big symbols like "America." So "Little Girl, My String Bean" became her antiwar poem: not a protest, but a statement about the obligations that older generations bear to the young.

In February, Sexton was asked for another kind of contribution: a manuscript to be auctioned in New York by the Fifth Avenue Vietnam Peace Parade Committee, to support actions against the war. She was having trouble placing her poem "The Touch" in a magazine and had sent it to Theodore Solotaroff, editor of *New American Review* and also a sponsor of this "Literary and Art Auction for Peace," so she wrote to the committee that they could keep it. "I would be glad to sign it, though I don't wish to inscribe it. I can't think of anything else that I have on hand that would be appropriate, but am glad to release that manuscript to you." Though she continued to take part in readings for peace, by 1970 Sexton was prepared to describe herself as "not a political poet . . . not even a very social one. I just do my thing and it's very personal."

Sexton's love poems were gradually coming into print that spring. *The Hudson Review* spread over several pages of its special twentieth anniversary issue "The Interrogation of the Man of Many Hearts," "The Break," and "The Ballad of the Lonely Masturbator," and the twenty-fifth anniversary issue of *The Quarterly Review of Literature* carried "The Kiss," "In Celebration of My Uterus," and "Song for a Red Nightgown." *The New Yorker* brought out "For My Lover, Returning to His Wife" as well as several more traditional romantic lyrics: "It Is a Spring Afternoon," "Moon Song, Woman Song," and "Us." These poems had a surprising freshness. Women hadn't published such sexually explicit poems in English for a couple of centuries. Many of them were quite evidently about adultery, but with a new twist: a wife interfered in the triangle, leading a man back to Mother and leaving the narrator in the position of abandoned daughter.

At about the same time, *Time* magazine featured John Updike, whose novel *Couples* had just climbed rapidly to best sellerdom, in a cover story on "The Adulterous Society." Sexton sent Updike a note congratulating him on the new book. Nobody suspected *him* of being a confessional writer — though he might have said, as Sexton did, "My stuff is always just what is actually going on" — but the success of *Couples* no doubt seemed a bit of well-timed preparation for Sexton's own new work, which might gather momentum in its slipstream.

For a while, finding a good title gave her trouble. She had been keeping the poems in a file labeled *Rats Live on No Evil Star,* but by 1968 the manuscript had outgrown this title. She wrote to Paul Brooks at Houghton Mifflin, "This is the first time I have been stuck. I could call it THE TOUCH. I could call it THE MAN OF MANY HEARTS. I was going to call it MANY A BELOVED and although that's pretty sounding, it just doesn't fit the book. Do you mind a simple title such as LOVE POEMS?"

Just after she sent off the manuscript, she was interviewed by Brigitte Weeks, a former editor at Houghton Mifflin who had recently joined the editorial staff of *Boston Magazine.* Weeks had read Sexton's work enthusiastically, and as she said, "It occurred to me that many Bostonians would be most interested in learning a little more about such a distinguished local resident." Foremost in Sexton's mind during the interview was the sense that once again her secret work had been pulled together in one place and would soon be an object held in the hands of strangers. She tried to characterize it for Weeks. "I do think this is a happier book than the others," she said. "The love poems are all a celebration of touch [. . .] physical and emotional touch. It is a very physical book." Do you learn about yourself from truths revealed unconsciously? Can you analyze "the magic"? Weeks asked. "I can't, but then I'm not sure that I want to. Obviously it is *your* job to try to analyze, but in a way it is *mine* to try to hide. I don't really know what the magic is — as I said before it begins with a kind of heightened awareness."

If it is our job to analyze, we can note that in assembling this book Sexton did not put dates on poems to provide documentary interest, as she did in organizing *Live or Die.* Instead, she gave *Love Poems* a quasi-narrative structure. "The Touch" leads to "The Kiss," then to "The Breast" — and to hesitations: What manner of man is this "Man of Many Hearts"? Consummations follow. The plot takes a downward turn with "For My Lover, Returning to His Wife." This is the era of "The Break," the "Again and Again and Again" of pain, the "Ballad of the Lonely Masturbator." Then another cycle opens: "Barefoot," "Now," "Us," "Mr. Mine," and another separation, "Eighteen Days Without You."

"The Touch" establishes the theme as a resurrection of the middle-aged body through sex. Through sex, the body reconnects to its own secret history of pleasure; sex regresses the practitioner, as a way of linking the severed chapters of desire back into a living whole:

> My nerves are turned on. I hear them like
> musical instruments. Where there was silence
> the drums, the strings are incurably playing. You did this.
> Pure genius at work. Darling, the composer has stepped
> into fire.

The infantile origins of sexual gratification return at the opening of *Love Poems*: fingers, tongue, lips, nipples, thighs, grip and are gripped in alternating currents, while pleasure investigates apertures and protuberances. These poems celebrate zones of intense responsiveness in weirdly dissociated imagery. Later in the book the zones are attached to people and problems. The people are female and male. The problems are, on the one hand, adult conflicts between duty and pleasure, and on the other, something more like disappointment, the failure of desire summarized at the end of "The Interrogation of the Man of Many Hearts":

> and every bed has been condemned
> not by morality or law,
> but by time

Lovers grow bored in time. But the poem has a deeper insight, too: Desire seeks what has been lost forever, the unsymbolic experience of infant intimacy with a maternal body. The lovers are conscious of playing roles that legitimate the forms satisfaction may take; more sobering, they are conscious that the roles they choose signal the return of the repressed. In Sexton's case, this was the again and again and again of losing Mother, or the guilty joy of attracting Mother's man or of desiring Mother herself. The center of gravity in these love poems is a mother carrying heavy, sleepy children up to bed. *She* is the true rival, and she stands at the origin even of the joy a man gives a woman.

> Loving me with my shoes off
> means loving my long brown legs,
> sweet dears, as good as spoons;
> and my feet, those two children
> let out to play naked. [. . .]
> Long brown legs and long brown toes.
> Further up, my darling, the woman
> is calling her secrets, little houses,
> little tongues that tell you.

With the armory of information available in Sexton's literary archives, we could attach names and addresses to the houses in *Love Poems*. But factual information leads interpretation in the wrong direction. The architecture of the book is repetitious not only because Sexton had numerous affairs, or even because she stopped and started and stopped the same affairs, but because as one of love's poets she had news to bring. *Love Poems* was yet another book about the work of transference, the immortality of the love burned into the circuits of the body from its first hours of awareness of the body of another. Sexton was no sociologist, but she had her own way of putting details on record about some differences between men and women in this regard — men and women in love, that is, in middle age, in her world, in her time.

As a matter of course, Sexton offered the manuscript of *Love Poems* to her editor at Oxford University Press, Jon Stallworthy, as soon as it had been accepted at Houghton Mifflin. She was joking, probably, when she told Stallworthy she felt "a certain uncharacteristic shyness" in sending it, because of the bad reviews *Live or Die* had received in Britain. A rather long silence fell. It was not until early November that Paul Brooks forwarded a letter Houghton Mifflin had received some time earlier from Stallworthy expressing serious reservations about the manuscript. Could Sexton be persuaded to undertake some judicious pruning? Brooks, embarrassed for Sexton, had procrastinated until he had received some favorable advance notices for *Love Poems* in which he could wrap the bitter pill of Stallworthy's letter before sending it on to her.

Sexton was shocked, all right, but what appears to have irritated her most was Brooks's procrastination. She was almost always glad to undergo "judicious pruning" by editors; Howard Moss had long ago endeared himself through editorial tinkering. But by November it was too late to tinker with the American edition of *Love Poems*. A bit stiffly, Sexton told Stallworthy that she would be amenable to changes in the British edition. "Quite frankly, Jon, I do not like to think of you printing a book you don't believe in."

Stallworthy did accept *Love Poems*, and the difficulties between author and publisher subsided. However, he remembered that manuscript as a definitive turn for the worse in Sexton's art. "I liked the poems less and less and less; they weren't as carefully worked as before. She had learned to write, with Robert Lowell, with such fluency in a compact metrical structure; now the poetry began to get looser and more inflammatory, and I found it harder and harder to hear any sort of musical structure. We were still and always remained on good terms, she was a good friend, but she can't have been pleased by my diminishing enthusiasm for the books."

Another problem soon arose — this time over Maxine Kumin's work. In the spring, Kumin's second novel was about to appear — the novel Joan Smith had heard Kumin and Sexton dissecting over the phone for months the preceding year. Titled *The Passions of Uxport,* it was set in the Boston suburbs, and to those who knew its author, certain real-life stimulants could be detected in the plot and characters. One was Kumin's friendship with Anne Sexton, discernible in the sisterly attachment of two of the main characters, Hallie and Sukey. Another was Sukey's suicidal depressions, deeply probed in the novel. Sukey was not based very closely on Sexton, but when Kumin's publisher sent galleys to Tillie Olsen, requesting a blurb for the cover, Olsen made the connection and was disturbed by it. Not only the representation of Sukey but the psychoanalytic values she saw as permeating the whole novel bothered her a good deal.

Sexton was baffled by Olsen's dislike of the novel, and hurt by the rumor she had heard that Olsen blamed her for its shallowness. "It was like a knife in the back," she wrote to Olsen later. "No, Tillie, I never understood what you meant. If you would ever care to tell me, I would surely listen and listen hard. [. . .] One of Maxine's favorite writers is John Cheever. Maybe *he* shallowized her book." The three women did meet once again, for lunch in Boston, when Olsen flew in for a reading, but the wound left a scar. What upset Sexton most, it seems, was the fierce importance Olsen attached to ideas, a loyalty Sexton felt only toward people.

In spite of this brouhaha, the spring of 1968 brought Sexton a good deal of satisfaction. Late in the preceding fall, she had been notified by the Harvard chapter of Phi Beta Kappa that she had been selected for the honor of reading at the annual induction of new members, a ceremony that took place during commencement week at Harvard. She told the chapter president she would not be writing a poem for the occasion, but she thought a fifteen-minute reading from "Eighteen Days Without You" would make a fitting contribution. Selection as Phi Beta Kappa poet brought with it an honorary membership in Phi Beta Kappa — at Harvard, no less; and as the chapter president later informed her, Sexton was the first woman ever to become a member of that chapter. She was thrilled, but worried too, being unaccustomed to academic protocol. "I think you had better make arrangements for a cap and gown for me," she wrote to Harvard. "When I read, do I keep the cap on? (I am more nervous about wearing a cap and gown than I am about giving a reading. As usual, it's the unfamiliar that's disquieting.)" She declined the invitation to make a little speech at the luncheon following the ceremony. "I have no message except 'thanks for the honor.'"

Sexton arranged for Kayo to join her in the academic procession and at the luncheon afterward. She was happy to share with him any honors her poetry brought to the family, and she knew he would be especially proud of this one. Paul Brooks was proud, too, and hurried back from a business trip to San Francisco to be present. "It should be the most memorable occasion since Emerson had his say from the same platform," he rejoiced in advance.

The members assembled on the morning of 11 June to be gowned and then walked in formal ranks to Sanders Theater while a light rain fell. Pictures show a somber face on Anne Sexton as she took her place among the scholars and later rose to read her poems. Only a week earlier Robert Kennedy, a Harvard man, had been assassinated in Los Angeles, and his death followed by exactly two months the assassination of Martin Luther King. These deaths gave ironic timeliness to Sexton's choice of "Eighteen Days Without You," and she dedicated the reading to Kennedy's memory.

Of course she ordered the Phi Beta Kappa key to which she was entitled, writing to the chapter president, "Yes, I think I'd like to purchase a key — I'm not sure why as it isn't honestly earned but in memory of such an honor. I would like my name to appear 'Anne Sexton.'" A year later she received a second honorary membership in Phi Beta Kappa, from the Radcliffe chapter — not bad for the former goof-off of Rogers Hall. But that was another Anne, before the "rebirth at twenty-nine" that gave the world "Anne Sexton."

Meanwhile, as the end of the school year approached at Wayland High, Sexton hoped very much that she and Bob Clawson would be invited to teach their writing course again the following September. It didn't help their case that one of the star students had dropped out after the first semester, saying that the course "was just too disorganized and murky." As Clawson said, "She wasn't going to hurt her chances for college." In his view the student had been overcautious: "All she had to do was put down that she'd had a class with Anne Sexton, she could have gotten into any college, probably." Despite much good publicity about the course and a strong write-up by Herbert Kohl, the contract was not renewed.

But Clawson had another idea. What about developing the little classroom project Steve Rizzo had undertaken — setting Sexton's poems to music — into a business venture? It was a good time for a poet to address the audiences for popular music. Rizzo's inspiration, Simon and Garfunkel, was only one of many groups working imaginatively with poetic language, intending the words to be heard; the Byrds, the Beatles, and the Doors too had poetic aims. In comparison with these stylish groups, the group Clawson built around Sexton had simple goals. The musicians were to write backup rhythms and song motifs to already-existing poems, preferably those whose images and associational structures lent themselves to rock arrangements. Sexton learned to deliver words in an acoustical envelope formed by the instruments. They called themselves Anne Sexton and Her Kind.

In addition to Sexton, Her Kind had four, sometimes five members, a changing cast as the group developed artistically. Steve Rizzo, on acoustic guitar, was the only amateur; he was joined by Teddy Casher, later by Gerald Oshita, on flute and saxophone; Bill Davies, who played electric keyboards; and drummer Harvey Simons, later replaced by Doug Senibaldi. Bass players were added as the group coalesced: Mark Levinson and later "Hank" Hankinson. They started rehearsing seriously in the spring of 1968, and by summer they had worked out much of a seventeen-song repertoire.

Anne Sexton and Her Kind gave its first performance in July at a benefit in Boston for Eugene McCarthy, the night before a big rally in Fenway Park, while McCarthy's bid for the presidency was still lively.

Sexton wrote about the performance to Lois Ames: "No one could hear us, people drank and talked, the cash register bonged, the glasses clinked, but a few people (the important ones) liked it a lot." It was fitting that the group should have volunteered its services to McCarthy, the only published poet in the U.S. Senate. Cambridge was a home base for his campaign; it was his daughter Mary, a Radcliffe antiwar activist, who had persuaded him to oppose Lyndon Johnson in the Democratic primaries and to mobilize the affluent liberal students deferred by college enrollment from serving in Vietnam. Sexton could have expected some members of this audience to have read her poetry.

She regarded the benefit as a rehearsal for the group's first paid ap-

Anne Sexton and Her Kind rehearsing. Left to right: *Steve Rizzo, Sexton, Theodore Casher, Bill Davies, and Robert Clawson.*

pearance, scheduled for September at the De Cordova Museum in Lincoln. Although she exulted to Ames that this was "a very swinging place [. . .] where I first heard [W. S.] Merwin (my first reading ever)," she went into panic mode as the date grew near. Off Thorazine (probably because it slurred her speech), she reeled wildly among her various other antidotes to anxiety, mainly booze and sleeping pills, reporting to Ames that she was heading for trouble, overdosing dangerously on her nightly knockout mixture: "I'm in such a panic that I won't sleep that even drugged I think I'm not sleeping. Lois, I don't *think* I want to die by mistake!"

The performance was held outdoors under a tent; as the weather was rather chilly, Sexton put on long underwear beneath her evening dress. She decided afterward that Her Kind had been "pretty good. I mean it was a little great!" The concert pleased at least one other person — Paul Brooks, who wrote her a warm note: "Last week at the De Cordova I realized why your readings have been such a wild success. As you well know, you are something of an enchantress. And I am still under your spell. In earlier times you would probably have been either worshipped or hanged — or perhaps both, in that order."

Sexton hoped that performances by Her Kind would expand her audiences. As she told an interviewer that summer, the music "opens up my poems in a new way, by involving them in the sound of rock music." Whereas traditional poets seemed to be losing touch with audiences, she observed, "people flock to Bob Dylan, Janis Joplin, the Beatles — these are the popular poets of the English-speaking world." Working up a program with Her Kind cut a new path through the poems, even for her. She let the musicians take the lead, and they made surprising choices. "Cripples and Other Stories" accommodated a Nashville beat. "Woman with Girdle" received a slow, sensuous treatment that enhanced the poem's strengths, revealing the immanence of a goddess archetype in the imagery. "The Sun" and "The Addict" were similarly "opened up," as Sexton put it, by musical scoring.

From the outset, Sexton wanted to maintain artistic control of the group. But to attract the anticipated new audiences, publicity for Her Kind plucked the string of anti-intellectualism vibrating in the counterculture. "The 1967 Pulitzer Prize [. . .] freed her to do what she wants," commented the *Boston Sunday Globe*. "And what she most wants to do seems to be to relax from the rituals which surround our major contemporary poets: rounds of seminars and readings, seas of students' eager faces and poised pencils. [. . .] Her Kind aims to enhance the poetic message with music; its members are concerned with getting things down for audiences, not theses." Exactly such emphases bothered Maxine Kumin a good deal. "I hated her readings," Kumin said flatly. "They were so melodramatic and stagey. I felt they took away from the marvelous texture of the poems by making them into performances. I hated the way Annie pandered to an audience. I felt that way especially about the chamber rock group — even though it was my own darling son who wrote the music for 'The Little Peasant.' " Linda Sexton and Danny Kumin and their friends, high school sophomores in 1968, loved Her Kind, though, right from the start, and they were the kind Anne Sexton had in mind.

Maxine Kumin's attitude is worth pausing over, however, since she loved Sexton and wanted to see her flourish. Celebrity holds well-known disadvantages for an artist, and Sexton was to experience all of them. By giving excess value to the signature style, fame pressures an artist to repeat herself. More important for someone like Sexton, fame alters the relation between the artist and the peers on whom she relies for honest evaluation. As we have seen, Sexton was accustomed to circulating her work among critical-minded friends. From the outset, she tried everything on Kumin, and she continued to do this throughout her life; it was a mutually productive exchange, and Kumin never failed to give her truthful encouragement. Sexton wore other people out. De Snodgrass had fallen away before *All My Pretty Ones* was finished; James Wright had grown elusive while *Live or Die* was under way. Robert Lowell was now preoccupied with questions of translation. George Starbuck was in Iowa and hardly ever answered letters. Anthony Hecht, too, kept his distance, though he continued to render valuable judgments about her work through *Love Poems* (Sexton was proud to mention his approval of "The Interrogation of the Man of Many Hearts" to Fred Morgan when she sent the poem to *The Hudson Review*).

Fortunately, by mid-1968 Sexton had attracted the attention of a few younger poets capable of replacing the exacting former mentors she cherished. Among these, by far the most important was to be C. K. Williams, with whom she hit it off when they met at her reading at Temple University in the spring of 1968. Sexton invited him to send her his manuscript of poems, *Lies,* then pleased him by suggesting he submit it to Shannon Ravenel at Houghton Mifflin.

Sexton's respectful attention released new energy in Williams, as he wrote her a month later; he saw his own direction as converging with hers. "I think I have been trying to understand stillness in poetry, that is, when everything in poems stops, waits, glares, and simply goes on, and yours has so many of these moments that they are a way in to that." She had entered the picture at just the right moment. First, she helped to get *Lies* published. When Houghton Mifflin expressed some squeamishness about the subject matter of some of the poems, she sent a strong defense. "The point isn't whether the poems are negative or positive but how alive they are. Subject matter itself is not as important as the genius inherent in a great metaphor," she said. "In these so-called 'unpleasant poems' he is being a Fellini of the word."

For once, her good word worked. Houghton Mifflin accepted *Lies,* and Williams accepted Sexton's offer to come to Weston to give the manuscript a final working-over. He remembered the occasion vividly.

I got there early in the morning. We sat down and went over every poem. She was just astounding, she was just terrific. She knew every line. She knew every line that I hadn't been quite sure about, she could pick them out. And there were a few poems that she picked out as being really not right. It wasn't that she did much work, but that everything she did was right. I always felt — and this is sort of a digression — that the role that she played in poetry, as the suffering soul of the universe, did injustice to her. Technically, she was very, very astute, marvelous. So much of her poetry seems effortless — it doesn't really show that gift. Well, it does show in the early books, but when she became more a figure of suffering, people began to forget what a marvelous technician she was.

Sexton was drawn to Williams. A tall, quiet, well mannered man, just over thirty when they met, he was self-possessed and deferential. He did not hang on her; nor did she attempt to sexualize this relationship, apparently. His work was taking a turn that interested her. Moreover, he had a semiprofessional interest in psychiatry. He had established a poetry workshop for emotionally disturbed patients at the Institute of the Pennsylvania Hospital in Philadelphia, and he also worked as a group therapist for disturbed adolescents. Sexton occasionally discussed her own therapy with him. "I used to get an uneasy feeling of how big a part her shrink was playing in her life," he remembered. "Maybe I was just surprised by how much she would talk about her therapy when our relationship was not very intimate. But then, it wasn't a very intimate subject to her."

By late 1968, though, Sexton was hoping to step into the therapist's position herself by developing a program for McLean Hospital like the one Williams offered in Philadelphia. So, after they went over his manuscript that morning, it was Williams's turn to listen and counsel. Sexton played the tape of Anne Sexton and Her Kind recorded at De Cordova in September. Williams had a friend who produced records; could he help the group get to the next level of sophisticated production? Could he help arrange a concert at Temple? And what about those poetry workshops in mental institutions? She was full of plans. They went on to lunch, where Sexton drank a stupendous amount. "We both got a little tipsy, but I was impressed by the quantity that she drank rather than how drunk she was," Williams remembered. Next day he sent her a thank-you note accompanied by a little pen-and-ink drawing of himself as a reeling owl. "I guess I owe you another whole universe of thanks — the last layer of laziness was scraped off some poems, the last haze of self-deception from others," he said. "Anne, it was a wonderful day for me. I wish I'd stayed a little soberer so that my words didn't desert me so."

The idea of running a course for the mentally ill was not just a momentary enthusiasm for Sexton. Everyone knew the story of how Dr. Orne had instigated her writing a decade earlier. That experience was in the back of her mind when she proposed and then designed a weekly poetry workshop for patients at McLean. She had never been a patient there, but it had always held an odd glamour for her as the hospital of choice for the occasionally mad artists of Boston.

Sexton's class met for a couple of hours on Tuesday evenings, for a shifting population of about a dozen patients with widely varying talents. At least two of them had published poems; others were more in need of occupational therapy than artistic guidance. Sexton tried to provide structure and continuity by devising homework exercises in writing and reading. In organizing and conducting the group, she had the assistance of Lois Ames, who had recently separated from her husband and moved with her children to nearby Sudbury. Ames tape-recorded all the sessions and made useful written comments on class dynamics.

Spasmodically during these months, Sexton kept a workshop journal. Some of the participants were too intellectual, she thought; for these, she prescribed Diane Wakoski, Frederick Seidel, Robert Bagg, and Aliki Barnstone. Most of them didn't need loosening, though. Sexton's practiced eye could distinguish the genuine manic types from their look-alikes who had been taking LSD. In generational conflicts, which were common, she tended to stick up for the younger people, defending "the hippie offbeat word play elements" in their poems.

Sexton was alarmed at how angry the workshop made her when students responded to each other with hostility. At one point Lois Ames noted that a certain class was like a party of liberals where you can point out the one Republican. Ames's sense of humor helped keep such problems in scale. Sexton wasn't there as a psychotherapist, after all, yet she remembered the days when a mental hospital had been a place of personal development, when its validation of wordplay had been a liberating experience. When one of the talented members of the workshop chastised her for not being critical, Sexton responded from the heart: "You are right. I don't like to discourage anyone at Mc-Lean. I feel that everyone has something to say and will perhaps, in time, have more important things to say. Poetry led me by the hand out of madness. I am hoping I can show others that route."

When her schedule permitted, Sexton offered the workshop at McLean off and on through 1969. Another attractive teaching opportunity surfaced in 1968 when she received a request from Steven Whitney, a student at Oberlin College in Ohio, to lead a workshop for a half-dozen students who would be home in Massachusetts during the winter intersession. In accepting, Sexton confidently spelled out her expectations of the course: "listening for the half-spoken image" and "look[ing] for the stories in poetry in the sense of life lived in the poet we may be discussing." She proposed meeting at her home. (In one letter she offered to serve tea, but in the next letter she took it back; she was embarrassed by the Thorazine-induced shakiness of her hands.)

The students wrote a poem every day for a month, kept journals, and read steadily. Every evening Steve Whitney delivered the day's poems, and twice a week the students gathered for an afternoon of passionate discussion. Sexton read and criticized their poems and journals, exhorting and encouraging them. At the end of the month she said she had taught them all her tricks. They scattered, but they kept in touch. Sexton had launched yet another phase of her career, as a college teacher.

On 9 November 1968 Sexton marked her fortieth birthday. A few months earlier, on 16 August, she and Kayo had celebrated their twentieth wedding anniversary by blowing her advance for *Love Poems* on a trip to Bermuda. By then they had spent half their lives married to each other. For about half their married life, Anne had been in treatment for depression; for about half their married life, she had been a poet. Anne's successes often brought wonderful rewards she could share with him, such as European holidays and African safaris and honors at Harvard commencement and trips to Bermuda. Yet day-to-day life was ruled by her demands to be taken care of, on some days because she was ill, on others because she was famous. The whole family had rallied to make this brilliant career possible, and Kayo had shouldered most of the responsibility for managing the household. As her star had risen, he was increasingly cast in the role of celebrity spouse: Mr. Anne Sexton.

This was a role he played very well. At forty, he was still boyishly handsome, with a wide smile and a warm, gracious modesty that won the admiration of many of Sexton's friends. Kayo knew how to partner his wife in public. An interview run by an English magazine the preceding fall had represented him as being a good sport about the journalist's intrusive questions and Anne's unbuttoned answers. For Anne's interview with *Look,* he had posed nose-to-nose and provided quotable quotes: " 'I learned,' he said, 'her sickness was like a flood — all I could do was take to high ground.' " Yet Anne felt a gulf of estrangement in him that his good nature concealed from outsiders. As they packed for their anniversary trip to Bermuda, she confided to Lois Ames, "We are renting motor bikes, sailboats, fishing, I hope making love, eat, swim, read. I HOPE Kayo will talk to me and like me. What a pitiful wish, really . . ." He could not share the things she loved most, and they had worn out the old rituals.

Still, she had much to celebrate as she stepped across the threshold of another decade. The week of her birthday, as so often that year, she was on the road, in Cleveland this time. But really she had been feted all year: at Harvard commencement; in two interviews and a feature story in *Look*; in Chicago at Poetry Day, the annual black-tie gala in honor of *Poetry Magazine,* where she shared a podium with the elegant Kenneth Koch; in Manhattan as a featured reader at the Poetry Center's celebration of *The Hudson Review*'s twentieth anniversary. The week she turned forty, Dr. Zweizung presented her with a cupcake set with a burning candle ("for the child in me") and a bottle of Arpège ("for the woman"); flowers, cards, telegrams, and messages awaited her everywhere she went. She got the message. As she wrote melodramatically to a friend, she felt she had "solved" that year "for the first time since I was 14 the terrible things that happened once on my birthday."

In a spirit of having arrived on a plateau of joy and achievement, Sexton wrote a letter to Linda expressing her recognition that this sense of womanly fulfillment was a legacy from her own mother, Mary Gray. Sexton was aloft, heading for St. Louis. Like her father and like Linda's father, she had become a traveling salesman of sorts. The plane trip put her in touch with all the lives she carried inside her. "I was reading a *New Yorker* story that made me think of my mother and all alone in the seat I whispered to her, 'I know, Mother, I know,' " she wrote. "I thought of you — someday flying somewhere all alone and me dead perhaps and you wishing to speak to me. And I want to speak back. [. . .] This is my message to the 40-year old Linda. No matter what happens you were always my bobolink, my special Linda Gray. Life is not easy. It is awfully lonely. *I* know that. Now you too know it — wherever you are, Linda, talking to me. But I've had a good life — I wrote unhappy — but I lived to the hilt. You too, Linda — Live to the HILT!"

16

OFF-BROADWAY WITH
MERCY STREET
1969

IN 1969, IMPORTANT DEVELOPMENTS in Sexton's art emerged from an the opportunity to collaborate in the production of her play. Working with theater people helped bring together two contradictory energies: self-display and spirituality. Over the years she had made herself into a good businesswoman, pushing herself to give performances for which she could require exceptionally high fees, for a poet. In so doing, she had also made herself into an actress, a woman whose body was the vehicle of sense that came from somewhere beyond her. Indeed, as one interviewer noted, Sexton gave an *interview* as if on-stage: "Often, her answers sounded like incantations, repetitious chants. [. . .] Even when replying from written notes, she read with all the inflections and intonations of — as she describes her readings — 'an actress in her own autobiographical play.' "

For the past three years Sexton's literary agent, Cindy Degener, had been patiently trawling to get *Tell Me Your Answer True* noticed in New York. In 1969, a young director, Charles Maryan, approached her with the news that he had (he thought) a "live one" interested in bankrolling a play off-Broadway. Did Degener have anything good in hand? The agent sent manuscripts, including Sexton's, and Maryan was hooked. "I brought it to Wynn Handman, director of the American Place Theater, the home base of a project to attract American poets and novelists to writing for the stage." Degener had showed the play to Handman in 1967, but he had turned it down. "I told Handman, 'Read it again!' " Maryan recalled. "Anne was a hot enough writer at that point to get their attention. Taking writers from other disciplines and putting them in the theater was what the American Place was all about."

Everything came together in April, when Handman invited Sexton down to New York to discuss the play and she received a grant from the Guggenheim Foundation that put a platform of funding under her work. Both Handman and Maryan recognized that the play would need plenty of revision before it was viable for the stage. When the three of them met, Handman explained the deal he had in mind: a two-week revision and rehearsal period under the American Place Theater writers' development program, leading to a staged reading for a small group of evaluators; then, if the results were good, production for the fall season.

Sexton quickly discovered that she and Chuck Maryan were on the same wavelength. He had done his homework on her poems, and he was excited by the richness of the material in her play. "That first meeting established that we could talk," he explained. "Anne would listen; she listened as well as anyone I've ever known and permitted me to say whatever I needed to say and responded simply and directly." So by the end of lunch, the agreement was struck: she and Maryan would work on the play with a group of actors for two weeks, beginning in May.

Even before meeting with Sexton, Maryan had been mentally casting the play. He saw its structure as an "odyssey" through Daisy's recollections, focused by "an essential issue in everybody's life — whether to live or to die." His choice for leading lady was Marian Seldes. "Poetry is a big part of her life. When I called her up and said I had this play by Anne Sexton, she immediately said 'I'll do it.' That was it." Moreover, as he noticed on first meeting Sexton, the poet and the actress looked enough alike to be sisters.

Home from New York, Sexton went straight to work on *Tell Me Your Answer True.* She got out the copy she had retyped back in 1965, at the end of her association with the Charles Playhouse in Boston, and attacked it again with scissors and tape.

The play had evolved its present structure during Sexton's termination of her therapy with Dr. Orne. History repeated itself in 1969, when she renamed the play *Mercy Street* and rewrote it during her termination from Dr. Zweizung.

Sexton had freely acknowledged to her closest confidants that she and her therapist were conducting a sexual affair during her treatment hours. She loved to tell the story of how she would tuck her sexy red nightie into her big purse, like Grace Kelly in *Rear Window,* before heading off to her sessions on the couch. Maxine Kumin and Lois Ames knew of the liaison: "Puritanical Yankees, what we couldn't stand was her *paying* him!" Ames remembered. Barbara Swan, Sexton's artist friend from her Radcliffe Institute days, heard jokes about the goings-on, as did Bob Clawson. Sexton also confided in two women who were little more than acquaintances: Barbara Kevles, who had interviewed her for the *Paris Review,* and Alice Smith, whom she had met at a reading in New York and with whom she carried on an active correspondence. Quite clearly, she did not attempt to keep the relationship itself a secret. Nor did it *appear* to be doing her any harm; during the years Dr. Zweizung was her therapist, her suicidal thoughts and attempts abated, she underwent fewer hospitalizations, and she seemed far more stable to her family.

Some of those privy to the affair regarded it as deeply problematic on ethical grounds, however. Anne Wilder was one friend to whom it was most disturbing. She felt that she had a professional responsibility to report Dr. Zweizung's misconduct to the licensing board, for the physicians' code of conduct required that colleagues "expose those physicians deficient in character or competence, or who engage in fraud or deception." Wilder realized this, and together with Kumin worried over the question of whether they should intervene. According to Wilder, several considerations prevailed against their taking action. To bring official charges against Dr. Zweizung might prove ruinous to his professional reputation, and Wilder was squeamish about this; she also had reason to think that he had been critical of the erotic aspects of her own relationship with Sexton. More important, in her view, was Sexton's decidedly provocative role in the situation. Sexton knew full well that sex during the therapy hour violated medical ethics and, according to well-established theories, was damaging to psychotherapy. But she was a strong-willed person who would certainly object to interference by her friends, even if they considered themselves to be doing what was best for her.

Another person who was concerned about the situation was Dr. Orne. "I saw Sexton almost every month, though I was not her primary therapist. I maintained a relationship more like that of a parent or friend," he commented later. "Thus, when she was in trouble, real trouble, she'd call on me." In Dr. Orne's view, Dr. Zweizung had been a very effective therapist at the outset, with attributes that Dr. Orne didn't bring to the alliance. "She was able to develop a kind of closeness which she really needed," he said in retrospect. "I am a fairly formal person, which was probably necessary for her when she entered treatment; she would not have trusted me otherwise. But I think by 1964 she was at the point where someone like Zweizung was important for her. She found him a most understanding and giving person, before the countertransference problem set in." Dr. Orne was particularly critical that Dr. Zweizung had undermined Sexton's relationship with Kayo, whom Sexton needed absolutely, in his view. "There is no doubt, by the way, that Anne wanted to, tried to, and succeeded in seducing Dr. Zweizung," added Dr. Orne. "After all, I sat with her for eleven years, I know how she could be! But this in no way excuses the behavior of Dr. Zweizung."

Sexton had called on Dr. Orne to adjudicate the first round of countertransference, back in the summer of 1966.

Anne told me what was happening, and I said to her, "All right, you've got to stop this." She said, "I can't." And I said, "Okay, I'll be in Boston, I want to see you and Dr. Zweizung together in my office."

Dr. Zweizung wasn't eager to come but I asked whether he'd prefer me to go to an ethics committee. He came, and we talked. I told him, very straightforwardly, "Well, therapists are people too, and these things happen. But it isn't something which is good for Anne. And you know you have no right to charge her: you use her, that's destructive." I said, "Look, if you want to continue to treat her, you go back to your analysis, and if you don't want to go back into analysis, then you can't treat her."

Dr. Orne felt that Sexton had realized "incalculable gains" in treatment with Dr. Zweizung, and that it was particularly important that she not lose yet another significant figure from her past, one of her "anchors," if she could be spared the loss. Even though there were risks in continuing, he believed that Dr. Zweizung understood his responsibilities and could be trusted to reestablish the therapeutic relationship on firm ground, as he had explicitly promised. But, Dr. Orne said, "his behavior later indicated that he hadn't done what was necessary, however, whatever, with whomever. Instead, he became more careful, and Anne withheld from me the information that they were still having sexual relations during the therapy hour. Ultimately the relationship became so complex that when he wanted to try to control things with Anne, he would leak to his wife that he was having an affair. Pushing Anne away poisoned the benefits she had received from her work with him."

This is apparently what happened again in January 1969, as Sexton wrote urgently to Dr. Orne.

[Dr. Zweizung] went to Washington last week and I met him there for an evening together. Without restrictions and time worries we were just great together. Still, in my mind it was a hell of a trip for one evening. Nevertheless I'm glad I went. We were real lovers. I didn't once act like a patient and he didn't once act like my doctor. Still I have the feeling it was the last time. Since then a lot has happened that makes it the last time. He talked with another doctor all about it. He determined to work on his marriage. [. . .] I suggested (and quite honestly) that we turn off the love, the sex and concentrate on therapy. Frankly, I don't think I could bear to lose him as a therapist. I suppose you think, "what the hell, she lost me and she lived through it." But you know it wasn't easy losing you and further I didn't lose you all the way. You do come back month after month and I trust you always will. Trust! . . . . I don't trust him. He promised he'd never leave me but now he tells me it depends on how he works things out with his wife. I told him if we worked together we could keep it just therapy (after all we'd had our fling in Washington) . . . . . . I pled with him. But he just said he'd see. I told him that when he and I saw you on March 8th that you'd be talking us into just therapy. He said he'd see you with an open mind.

Sexton described this consultation to Barbara Kevles afterward. "It was kind of like a fantasy coming to life. [. . .] Dr. Orne saying, 'You did what I could never do. Anne has gotten much better with you.' [Dr. Zweizung] saying, 'You did what I could never do. Anne came so far with you.' And on and on. All I can say is, they were very nice to each other." As Dr. Orne later explained, "Anne was annoyed, but I tried to emphasize the positive aspects of the situation, to be as affirming as possible, because this was going to be a catastrophic change for her. I hoped that she could retain him in her mind as a positive figure. I expected to assist in her transition to a new therapist and to remain a resource to her."

In the end, Dr. Zweizung helped find Sexton a new therapist. Within a couple of months — by May — she was settled with Dr.

Constance Chase, who made it a condition of treatment that Sexton not see Dr. Orne for therapy again.

So Sexton was again working on her play in the unlucky month of March, the anniversary of her mother's death, during a phase of separation from one of the people who stood in for her parents; and once again writing gave her a way to maintain precious aspects of the connection that was being severed in reality. "I wrote this play four years ago," she told Alice Smith. "I was losing my old doctor and going crazy and the playwriting was saving my sanity. This time I'm losing a doctor and going a little crazy (the difference is this time I have the right tranquilizer to take so I don't expect to end up in the hospital)."

By 15 April, right on schedule, she sent a revised, shortened manuscript to Wynn Handman, and at the end of the month she went to New York again. Chuck Maryan had now assembled a cast: along with Marian Seldes as Daisy were Rosemary Murphy as Aunt Amy, William Prince as Ace, and Virginia Downing as Daisy's mother, Judith. They gathered at the New Dramatists, Handman's studio near City Center. "It wasn't casual," Seldes remembered. "No one just came in and read the play. Everyone had been affected by it and read it beautifully." Sexton was elated. "Until she heard the actors, especially Marian Seldes, she thought she read her own work very well," Maryan recalled. "She was excited and concerned and totally open to what the actors said." Although they liked it scene by scene, they were having trouble grasping it as a whole, so it was agreed that Sexton should come down to New York to collaborate with them in making her revisions rather than mailing changes from Boston.

The following week Sexton returned to New York, this time with Lois Ames ("as companion and advisor," Sexton explained to Handman. "New York frightens me to death"). They stayed at the Algonquin Hotel, which was close to Handman's studio and which Sexton associated fondly with Howard Moss and other writers. She brought her typewriter and put in long days, making notes while the actors rehearsed and typing changes in the evening. More and more it seemed to everyone that the climax of the play came too soon, in the first act. "Anne and I were discussing the scene and the problem of where it was placed," Maryan said, "when Marian looked at us from the stage and said, 'Why don't you just reverse the acts?' Neither Anne nor I had thought of the solution, but we agreed with Marian and that began the form of the play that we finally presented."

While in New York that spring, Sexton was hunted down by one of her fans, an Australian named Brian Sweeney. A tall, handsome, rich, extroverted businessman just a few years older than Sexton, he was also, improbably, a dabbler in poetry and a deeply religious man. He told her how, arriving in San Francisco, he had asked the customs agent, "Is Anne Sexton still alive?" During the five days of her stay in New York he kept her hotel room filled with yellow roses and pampered her with meals at La Côte Basque. He went from bookstore to bookstore buying all the Sextons, to stimulate the market.

What luck for Anne Sexton — to have the Ace of Daisy's nightmares show up in benignly flamboyant flesh, just when she needed him most! For Brian Sweeney outshone all of Sexton's previous father-substitutes. Unlike her doctors and lovers, he had a refreshingly direct interest in her religious beliefs, particularly her beliefs about Christ. He described himself as "the last link in a production line of Catholic iron chain; wracked and wrenched with the human faith divine, limned and charred since before the Celtic domination." Appearing at Sexton's side, summoned only by his passion for her words, he loved her for her spirit alone, and this was indeed exactly what the doctor ordered. What she called her womanly con was unnecessary to win him and useless against his exuberant chastity.

Sexton's working idyll was interrupted on 8 May when she received a phone call from Kayo: his sister, Joan, had been killed in a car accident on her honeymoon. Billie was devastated. Married only six days earlier, Joan was thirty-eight years old and had been Billie's closest companion since George Sexton died in a similar accident. Linda and Joy, who had been her bridesmaids, were deeply shaken by her death and drew closer than ever to Billie, who took to saying "Joanie" when she meant "Joy" — a slip of the tongue that stayed with her for the rest of her life.

While Sexton was back in Massachusetts with her family, Handman struggled with making a final decision about producing *Mercy Street*. Even after a good deal of revision with assistance from a committed group of actors, it was very loosely structured. The problem, he told Maryan, was where and how to situate the action. The play was now composed of numerous scenes in numerous locations (in the afterlife, in the doctor's office, in Daisy's family home); how could it be tied together in time and place? Finally Handman and Maryan hit on a concept. Since the play had a religious theme, the action might be staged within the framework of an Episcopal Mass. "Daisy could come to this church to decide whether to live or die — the priest could be transformed into the psychiatrist." This was an ingeniously cost-effective solution, because the American Place Theater was housed in St. Clement's Episcopal Church. At last, on 26 May, Sexton received a telegram from Cindy Degener: "HOORAY SHOW BIZ HERE YOU COME." Sexton was to revise the play over the summer and return in September to New York. *Mercy Street* would open the new season at the American Place Theater in October.

Sexton was already involved in show business, though, in the minor leagues. She spent the month of May rehearsing intensively with Her Kind for a big performance at Boston's Jordan Hall. With Clawson's encouragement, she was devoting serious attention to this project; a letter she wrote to Jon Stallworthy that spring mentions the possibility of producing a record. When she received inquiries about giving readings, she now sent a copy of the tape of Her Kind made at the De Cordova Museum and proposed a concert instead.

But she was also heavily booked for readings. Before receiving the Guggenheim grant, she had scheduled engagements at colleges in Houston, Texas, and Marietta, Ohio, in February; Binghamton, New York, and Salem, Massachusetts, in March; and Baltimore, Maryland, in April. These trips exhausted her, especially when she had to travel alone. *Love Poems* had been published near Valentine's Day and had sold four thousand copies the first month. When the grant came through and it looked as if Sexton would be working full-time on the play, she decided to test the market by raising her reading fees again (from $750 to $1000), in the hope that she could reduce the number of readings she gave in a year, especially if she could replace them with concerts.

Sexton's idea of a poetry reading differed from that of her peers in any case. Most poets appearing on the college circuits deported themselves as teachers, rather diffidently submitting to expectations that they would answer questions and offer a workshop or teach a class. Sexton would have none of this. She brought to the task the charisma of the *artiste,* dressing in beautiful clothes and, as often as possible, traveling with an entourage. Moreover, her readings were carefully rehearsed — as she confessed with a bit of chagrin after one of her academic admirers wrote up one of them for a literary journal. "All the things you quote from the reading, my little introductory notes, are, I hate to tell you, not in the least spontaneous with the exception of one or two sentences," she said, asking him to remove these from his article. "I hate to admit I am so studied, but there it is." As Marian Seldes remembered her, "There was a great deal of what people think of as an actress about Anne. She was a dramatic-looking person; her behavior was interesting; her laugh, people would say if she was an actress, was a theatrical laugh. Oh yes, her reactions were spontaneous and full, not guarded. She fit in with actors instantly."

The most improbable outcome of Sexton's current celebrity was a number of requests to contribute to celebrations of the historic landing of *Apollo 11* on the moon on 20 July 1969. The American press waxed fantastical, and the more highbrow publications asked well-known writers for their views. Sexton's poem "Moon Song, Woman Song" (from *Love Poems*) was reprinted in a special supplement of the *New York Times* for 17 July. The cover of *Esquire* asked, "What words should the first man on the moon utter that will ring through the ages?" The answer, headed "Fifty Helpful Hints," pictured Anne Sexton (among others) in a space helmet; *Esquire* too reprinted "Moon Song, Woman Song." When *Harper's Bazaar* asked a number of famous people what they would place in a time capsule on the moon, Joyce Carol Oates replied, "The confessional poems of Anne Sexton, Sylvia Plath, Robert Lowell, and W. D. Snodgrass."

However, the big work of the summer for Sexton was a thorough reconstruction of *Mercy Street*. Chuck Maryan made field trips to Boston so they could attend a church service together and work their insights into the play. Sexton decided that Maryan should learn the Mass — that was the director's problem, she thought — while she took charge of fitting liturgical language into appropriate scenes. She had her churchgoing friends snitch hymnals from various Protestant churches, and she began combing them for suitable excerpts. "I seek unity in the play and want a hymn that follows the theology of the sacrament," she explained. In the hymn she chose, "one is supposed to feel cleansed of sin, the one thing Daisy can't be."

During July and August, Maryan went several times to Weston, where he and Sexton worked throughout a long day, sitting at the kitchen table. (Sexton's dog, Penny, wouldn't let him into the study, Maryan remembered: "I love dogs and I understand dogs, and that dog was Anne's dog.") The gears would shift in the late afternoon, when Max usually dropped by and they would all often take a swim. Kayo would come home, they would have drinks, and Kayo would cook dinner on the barbecue. During July the children were away at riding camp, but in August they returned. Maryan was impressed by the way Kayo and the girls took charge of the things Anne couldn't do, and by Anne's matter-of-factness about the way illness influenced the management of her life. "I was struck by how adjusted everybody was, how Anne had made everything work for her, being as sick as she was," he commented. "Anne never projected herself as being anything but disabled. I never doubted her. But she accommodated her craziness so that she could function. . . . Kayo was a terrific guy; I give him a lot of points for making it work." They often discussed what Maryan called "Anne's reality" — "the way you would talk to someone who was adjusting to the fact that they have a short limb," he explained. "I couldn't pretend that her illness wasn't there, because she wrote about it. I couldn't pretend that she wasn't writing from her own experience. And she was marvelous, on a one-to-one basis, in talking about it. She didn't have any shyness with me at all."

Maryan thought the family was on its best behavior in his honor. He was right. Behind the scenes that summer stirred a good deal of turbulence, agitated by the rebelliousness of the Sextons' maturing daughters. As Maryan observed, Anne was worried about Joy, who was a daredevil, just as she had been. Joy had been truant, and she had been caught smoking pot. As she loved horses, Kayo decided to build a stable at the back of the house so both girls could bring horses down from Highlawn Farm, the riding camp, to winter over; perhaps Joy would gain maturity from the discipline of caring for animals. Problems between Anne and Linda also heated up around the time of Linda's sixteenth birthday on 21 July. Anne and Kayo took a transistor radio as a birthday present to Linda at Highlawn Farm, where she was a counselor-in-training, and when they got home, Anne wrote her a perturbed letter: "I'm so worried about you . . . sex, drugs, boys, cigarettes." Especially drugs. "Your attitude towards drugs 'oh everyone is in drug trouble' for instance. Really, Linda!!!"

In 1969 it seemed harder than ever to be parents of teenagers. Suddenly, even in the suburbs, everyone *was* in drug trouble, if marijuana was the drug in question (letters indicate that Anne too sneaked a joint now and then during Kayo's absence; he loudly disapproved of pot). The point wasn't so much the drugs, though, as the "drug culture," which made parents lose their bearings. Nineteen sixty-nine was the summer of Woodstock; albums by Janis Joplin, the Jefferson Airplane, and the Doors, prescribing sex, drugs, and rock-and-roll, were hard to get away from. These new media stars were white, middleclass young people with good educations who had seemingly evolved in a single generation into sleek, charismatic animals of a new breed. Their music surged into suburban homes and, like a tide lifting all the boats, made parents worry about what their own children were up to. Sexton reported to Brian Sweeney that Linda had "fallen in love with a hippy with long, long hair. What do I say? I'm kind of a hippy myself." Should Linda go on the pill? If she smoked, shouldn't she pay for her own cigarettes? Sexton phrased such inquiries carefully in letters to Linda at camp, because she hoped to retain her daughter's confidence. She also turned for help to Max's daughter Judy, whom she was tutoring in poetry. Linda trusted Judy, and might listen to her advice.

At the end of August Charles Maryan began casting for the production of *Mercy Street*. He was often on the phone to Sexton, reporting progress, and she passed the news on to Sweeney, who was greatly interested in the details. Three of the rehearsal actors — Virginia Downing, William Prince, and Marian Seldes — were to stay on. But Maryan had trouble casting Aunt Amy. In one scene, this character stalks about the stage flourishing a riding crop and reciting a litany she calls her "garbage bible." The scene is powerful and disturbing, and Sexton worried about casting an older woman in the part in case she might have a heart attack or a stroke, Lois Ames recalled. (Ames doubted that this would be a problem.) Eventually Maryan cast a young actress, M'el Dowd, as Aunt Amy.

From Sexton's point of view, *Mercy Street* was now "more about Aunt Amy; more her story." She had finally found a fully imaginative use for her complicated childhood relationship with Nana. In *Mercy Street* she came to terms with a reality her own guilty emotions usually denied: that Nana had been a real woman with a life separate from that of the needy girl to whom she was such a powerful force for good and ill. Though all the characters in the play are dramatically achieved, the most complex is Aunt Amy, who is based not only on Sexton's memories but on details she had learned since Nana's death: importantly, that Nana had had money and that she had paid for her own keep while living in Ralph Harvey's home. Aunt Amy is a hard-headed realist who has seen through Daisy's ineffectual, charming father, yet she too has a flaw — the frustrated sexuality that erupts into her relationship with Daisy.

At the center of the action of *Mercy Street* is Daisy's seduction by Ace, which Sexton called "the remembrance scene." Ace forces whis-

key on Daisy, praises her "little peachy breasts," begins rubbing her
back, then slides his hands between her legs. During this drama of seduction, the scene contains another figure, stage left: Aunt Amy, shut
away in her own room, pacing and twisting her hands in an obsessive
private ritual, chanting and raving, cracking a small riding whip. Her
self-castigating "garbage bible," a psalmlike litany modeled on the poetry of the mad eighteenth-century British writer Christopher Smart
and on the Bible's "Song of Songs," weaves like a chorus through the
lines exchanged between Ace and Daisy.

Ace: Here, we'll make a woman of you yet. (Holds bottle to her lips.)
Take some. No. Three swallows.
Daisy: I don't like it.
Ace: A few more swallows. You will. It's good for you, prewar Scotch,
like medicine. Here, have another swig.
Amy: Once I was a shedder of blood and the great eagle took me in his
claws and came into my mouth and ate thereof. He traded me for figs
and oil and wine. He drank of me and caused me shame.

This split action prepares for and explains the way Aunt Amy inhabits
Daisy's consciousness. What Daisy brings to the Mass at the play's
opening is defilement by sin inherent in the female body, because it
attracts the parents' lust.

These disturbing themes did not bother the actors or the director,
who approached the material as artists. Just as Sexton had felt the releasing recognition "These are my people!" when she entered the
mental hospital those many years ago, and again when she began her
first poetry workshop, she now felt liberated and stimulated by the
world of the theater. After rehearsals were well under way she said as
much to Ollie Zweizung. "I have never been so happy. If only I could
be with you to share it with you and bubble up about it! Damn it all, I
feel you deserve to see me so happy after so many sad times . . . God,
it's great, the theater. I just adore it. Everyone in it is so intuitive
and warm. They aren't boxed in [. . .], such a fine sense of using the
unconscious."

It was ironic, or worse, that Sexton felt so celebratory about the development of this play, for it did disturb her family life. Behind her ordinary parental worries lay her very specific difficulty with Linda, with
whom she continued to act out the complex intimacy scripted in her

relationship with Nana. Her deepest difficulties as a mother arose from her need to occupy the position of needy little girl, the need she had brought to Nana. That relationship had been severely disrupted by Nana's breakdown when Anne was thirteen and making her first tentative romantic friendships with boys. Now that Sexton's children were developing into women themselves, their physical maturity, in combination with her work on her play, seems to have carried her back into her own pubertal struggles and her guilty attachment to Nana. Beneath her loving concern and motherly pride, she remained more identified with her daughters, particularly with Linda, than was good for everybody: invasive of their privacy, a little too interested in their bodies, a little too interested in talking about sex.

As Linda had neared puberty, she had begun to dislike her mother's intrusiveness more than ever. For several years she had been pretending to be asleep when her mother got into bed with her and clung to her. But one night, when Linda was around fifteen, Anne had insisted that she come to the big bed and spend the night. Kayo was away on a

Marian Seldes and M'el Dowd in Mercy Street.

trip, and Anne didn't want to be alone. They watched television for a while; then Linda fell asleep. In the middle of the night she woke, feeling that she couldn't breathe. It was dark, but she realized that her mother was lying astride her, rubbing against her and kissing her on the mouth. "I felt suffocated. I remember pulling out of bed and throwing up. Mother followed me into the bathroom, and soothed my head."

Linda felt deeply humiliated and pulled in two directions. She wanted to feel close to her mother, but she was disgusted and frightened by the pressure for a clearly sexual intimacy. Shortly after this event, she asked to begin seeing a psychiatrist. "I had gotten awfully depressed," she remembered.

After all those years of saying to Mother, "Love me! Hold me! Don't leave me, don't be crazy," now I had to find a way to separate from too much closeness. I would talk in code to the doctor about all this. She wasn't interested in delving into what was going on. Nobody believes there *is* such a thing as mother-daughter incest: it's not in Freud, it's not in the theories. But the doctor helped me draw a line that Mother couldn't cross; she told Mother not to insist on being so close. After the conversation Mother went into my closet and stood there crying, hanging on to my clothes! At least the doctor helped drive a wedge between Mother and me, helped me take the first steps away.

Sexton resisted the changes, though, and reported to Linda that *her* psychiatrist said there could never be too much love between parent and child. She no longer came to Linda's bed, but she now began confiding in Linda about her sexual escapades. Thinking back on her mother's behavior, Linda speculated, "It was as if she now needed to cast me in the role of the disapproving parent — Nana at the doorway — because it was inevitable that I would be hurt and disgusted, for my father's sake, by her philandering." Although *Mercy Street* illuminated a warped double bond — father with daughter, great-aunt with great-niece — that deformed a family through several generations, its author was reproducing and amplifying the situation in her own family.

During the entire month of rehearsal, Sexton stayed four out of seven days in New York. She would sit at the back of the muggy theater with her feet propped up (Marian Seldes gave her a pair of gold slippers to wear), sipping beer, watching the scenes develop, and making notes. Evenings she spent rewriting dialogue as needed. Just such collaboration provided the context in which Sexton worked best, always. Throughout its revisions, the play had retained many characteristics of its origins in the unconscious; now Sexton had a ring of critical "superegos" to shape the material. The actors' questions helped clarify the conflict between Aunt Amy and Daisy, and the Mass helped structure the theme of Daisy's quest for expiation. ("The sections I stole from the Mass are great theater," Sexton crowed, "but wasn't it always so? We have incense and gregorian chanting and the works!")

Throughout September Sexton flew back to Boston on Saturdays and returned to New York on Tuesday mornings. "God . . . the money I'm spending," she said. "I don't eat much . . . just a little caviar for dinner or maybe caviar and a slice of melon." With Brian Sweeney's help she had arranged a special rate for herself and Lois Ames at the Algonquin Hotel (Sweeney was pals with Andrew Anspach, the manager). Because she still hobbled, almost three years after injuring her hip, she and Ames took taxis from the Algonquin (on West 44th Street) to St. Clement's (at West 46th). Sexton was receiving air fare from the American Place Theater and planned to spend all her Guggenheim fellowship on this project, but she worried that it wouldn't be enough. "Enough" was a vague estimate, for she avoided getting an accurate grasp of such matters as how much something would actually cost; one of the roles she assigned to Ames was calculating the tips for meals and taxis.

Emboldened by Sweeney's past generosity, Sexton suggested that he underwrite some of these expenses. "Did you mean it when you said I could ask for one thousand dollars (but only once a year)? If you did mean it I'd like to ask." She told him that her Guggenheim grant would cover Ames's expenses, "but I can't pay her a salary." Sweeney responded with a check (which Ames says she never saw); his promise had been to share any ill-gotten gains from betting on horses, and he had gotten lucky on a trip to Ireland. What with all the beer and immobility, Sexton gained five more pounds and swelled up to a size 16 dress, she reported. She had never been happier.

As opening day grew near, however, it became clear that problems with the play's dramatic structure were increasingly troublesome to the actors and director. Suggestions about cuts and alterations sometimes became arguments, and Sexton's confidence began to slide. One contest she didn't win was her effort to keep the Witnesses in the play.

As Chuck Maryan recalled, "They were difficult to integrate into the play due to the new concept of the Mass, but I loved them. [. . .] Wynn wanted them out; I wanted them in; Anne had to decide." Sexton felt that the manic Witnesses were crucial to the representation of Daisy's torment. For one thing, they were quite literally real to her: they were a dramatization of the voices in her head. (Since Nana's breakdown, Sexton had been dwelling in the presence of acoustical ghosts.) In Daisy's story, they had the interesting artistic function of conveying the feel of possession familiar to artists and thinkers. Their speeches, which were wild riffs of "doubling off," added comic energy to the play, and they disrupted the atmosphere of realism that prevailed in the "remembrance scene."

In her conviction that these surreal elements were essential, Sexton found an ally in Virginia Downing, who played Daisy's mother. "The man Witness was cruel, the woman was overmotherly," Downing recalled, "and Sexton put in their mouths some of the most original writing she ever did. These characters appeared to Daisy only when she was alone; their dialogue was wonderfully actable and playable. It showed Sexton's intuitive stagecraft." For Downing, the Witnesses made sense of Daisy's malady; they "were there to undo what the doctor was trying to do. And they were irresistible. The male Witness's cruelty was sexual — Anne was trying to write about what happened to a mind possessed by such irresistible beings."

Yet as the Witnesses made less and less sense to the producer and the director, Sexton was at a loss to defend them. Maryan remembered one occasion when she broke down under such a conflict. "Wynn was pressing her, asking 'What's the great-aunt *doing* there?' And it was at that point that Anne started to go. Anne had told me some very interesting things about madness, about what she called doubling off — that was a sign, for her, of her own instability. So there she sat saying over and over, 'The aunt is like Job doing her job.' Well, if someone repeats that often enough, it gets pretty funny. Especially when you have somebody there like me — when she would say something really crazy, I would break up, I'd just laugh. It was never meant with any anger. The way that meeting ended was I said, 'Anne, you're getting nutty. Enough, you're not making any connections. You're not here anymore. Let me take you home.' God, it's funny even now."

The actors noted Sexton's mood swings, too. Downing recalled her surprise, after working with "this vivid, blue-eyed woman," to see her appear one day "gray-eyed, dull — a completely different person." For Marian Seldes the contradiction was a source of pain. "Anne was not like an amateur, just as her performing was nothing amateur. Something about her was just first-class. Distinguished. And that's why if you saw her when she wasn't at her best, it was so upsetting. You thought, 'I don't want anyone else to see this.' She was suffering."

Seldes was especially attentive to Sexton, in whom she found cues to Daisy. "To me, the *work* is what you have of the person. The Anne I have is in *Mercy Street*. And it's a wonderful one: a productive one, a creative one, and an exciting one. Nothing can change that. Because of the way she wrote the play, I felt that I could pray, that I could talk about God, that I could do things which in my life I cannot do or will not do, refuse to do. I so believed the torment that she got into the play." Seldes also admired Sexton's physical presence. "She was an enormously sexual, sensual person, and that is thrilling to feel about a poet, about an American poet. If she'd been European, we wouldn't be quite so surprised. She exuded it. The way certain wonderful cats, or other animals, make you want to touch them, and be near them. She had that. It was partly her beauty; how people look has a great deal to do with how new people respond to them. But it was more than that — something inside saying 'I'm alive, I'm alive, I'm seething, I'm burning' — that's the word I'm looking for. 'I'm burning, if you come too close, you'll get burned.' She really had it."

Sexton felt the full weight of the actors' confidence; for her, drifting in and out of mental pain was business as usual. In fact, to many people she seemed healthier than ever, a feeling she communicated to Dr. Zweizung. "The actors turn to me for interpretations, the director practically holds my hand, and the producer, Wynn Handman, hugs me," she wrote. "Lois is being a fine friend and we did a 20 page interview about the play for the Boston *Herald*'s new literary supplement to be published October 5. We are the lead article for their first magazine."

The play opened on Friday, 3 October, for previews. It was scheduled to run six weeks, but was extended after favorable reviews began to appear. "Miss Sexton has written a play to be considered rather than dismissed," said Clive Barnes in the *New York Times* after opening night. Walter Kerr, in the Sunday *Times,* praised the use of ritual, the actors (especially Marian Seldes and William Prince), and the one-line images that were Sexton's poetic strengths, but found the play shapeless, "impotent to complete itself." Charles Maryan assessed these reviews as "positive, for the most part, but no 'money' notices."

In his view, Sexton didn't understand this critical milieu. "Four weeks in a row we were page one in the *New York Times* entertainment section," he observed, "but the acceptance of her play was not like that of her books and she was more convinced than ever that she was not a playwright." The worst reviews — by Stanley Kauffmann in *The New Republic* and John Simon in *New York* — were printed after the play had closed.

Sexton made several trips to watch the play; she was gauging its success by the reaction of audiences, which was overwhelmingly favorable. However, shortly after opening night she gave an interview to the *New York Times,* which ran a story under the headline " 'Oh, I Was Very Sick.' " Some of her friends felt she had been duped by the interviewer into saying more than she should have about her private life, and later she expressed regret about this. But in the interview itself she stated the position she usually acted on. "I can invade my own [privacy]," she insisted. "That's my right. It's very embarrassing for someone to expose their body to you. You don't learn anything from it. But if they expose their soul, you learn something. That's true of great writers."

One family member who did not share Sexton's view of the artist's right to public confession was her niece Lisa Taylor, Blanche's daughter, who had graduated from college in June and was working at a television station in New York. She took flowers around to the stage door before the performance on opening night, but Sexton was so nervous that they spoke for only a moment. The play distressed Taylor. She had vivid personal memories of Ralph and Mary Gray Harvey, which were greatly at odds with the characters portrayed in *Mercy Street.* "Anne's family was her gimmick. She wrote about them harshly and cruelly, selfishly and subjectively," she said later. "When she was presenting the material, it was marvelous to listen to — dramatic and daring. But for those who suffered at the expense of her success, the impact can never be measured."

Mercy Street closed on 21 November, to make way for the next production at the American Place. Marian Seldes and Charles Maryan both thought it would be produced again soon, and often, and Sexton expected Houghton Mifflin to bring it into print. Gradually, however, Sexton's feelings about the play soured, and though she perked up whenever Shaktman, Maryan, or Handman contacted her about rumors of interest, she let the manuscript languish unpublished in the halfway house of her files.

·   ·   ·

The momentum of collaboration on *Mercy Street* carried over into Sexton's collaboration with the musicians of Her Kind, who planned an important concert in December at Ursinus College in Pennsylvania. Shortly after Thanksgiving the group assembled for five days of solid work on their repertoire. Flutist Teddy Casher was replaced by Gerald Oshita, who drove east from California on the invitation of bass player Mark Levinson, with whom he had been working on what Oshita called "audio images." "We were not trying to *set* Anne Sexton's poetry to music, we were trying to embellish it," Oshita emphasized. "Music is so mathematical; fitting the poem into music, you make it keep musical time. We were trying to produce an acoustic package in which hearing her read was the artistic goal." Sexton's capacity for hard work impressed Oshita. "Her demeanor was that of a conventional New England housewife," he recalled. "But she was actually a burning-the-candle-at-both-ends type of artist." Maybe people didn't understand the experimental nature of her project, he speculated. "She wanted the music to help bring the audience closer to her poetry." That differentiated their chamber rock music from rock-and-roll, with its driving beat. "As a soloist, Anne needed leeway, needed time to change her mind in performance, to stretch out a syllable."

The band had been together long enough now to have established a style. For performances, they avoided the costumed look of rock stars; Sexton wore a long dress, and the musicians wore coats and ties. By the time of the concert at Ursinus College, "we really had a product," Oshita said. "Now it was time to see whether it would take off as a business." For the group to become really profitable, they would have to accept a large number of bookings. But "Anne didn't have a burning desire to travel," Oshita noticed. Under Bob Clawson's active management, the group eventually went to upstate New York, to Michigan, and as far west as Fargo, North Dakota. But even though Sexton was always happy to rehearse, she was never happy to get on a plane, and so Her Kind was grounded too. When the group disbanded in 1971, she was relieved as much as disappointed.

At the year's end, Sexton wrote Anne Wilder a chatty letter to catch her up on family news. "I don't drink martinis anymore. Jack Daniels, Canadian Club or rot-gut bourbon. Time passes . . . I smoke more and I cough more. I am size 14–16 . . . big belly. [. . .] Kayo is well, overworked, underpaid and unfulfilled — but he is still funny. He is getting quite gray. I am too, only I get my hair tinted so you can't tell." The real news, as it happened, was buried in a couple of questions: "Have you read *Slaughterhouse Five* by Kurt Vonnegut? And *Mother Night* by same? He is my this year's favorite. Very funny. His style is so simple." Nineteen sixty-nine had been a drought year for poems, as Sexton told Wilder; almost everything she had written had gone silently into a file titled *Words for Dr. Y.*, which was to remain unpublished until after her death. But by the year's end she had tapped a new inspiration. Bob Clawson had led her to Vonnegut, and Linda had led her to the Brothers Grimm. Her next book would be *Transformations,* a book of reconstructed fairy tales.

17

"A MIDDLE-AGED WITCH"
1970

ANNE SEXTON'S LIFE took a neat, decisive turn as the decade turned. She had been a poet in the world's eyes for exactly ten years, from her professional debut in *To Bedlam and Part Way Back*. She now had four books in print, selling well: in 1969 alone they sold over 20,000 copies, with *Love Poems* leading the pack — 14,147 in the United States since its release in February. Sexton had achieved what Maxine Kumin a decade earlier called the "vertical audience" of peers living and dead, measurable in the tables of contents of influential anthologies, on lists of "major" contemporaries gathered at congresses of writers, and on the mastheads of literary journals. Sexton had her detractors, but she could not be ignored.

The decisive turn was away from peers and toward her audiences. Her success in reaching large numbers of people through the theater and on the concert circuit seems to have consolidated her confidence as an artist. In 1970 she experienced a surge of creative energy comparable to the one that had carried her through the completion of *Bedlam* and the writing of *All My Pretty Ones*. Within eight months she wrote the seventeen long poems comprising *Transformations,* and within the year she made headway with two other volumes, *The Book of Folly* and *The Death Notebooks*. All three were written simultaneously and were planned with specific audiences in mind. *Transformations* was to be a popular book, narrated by

> a middle-aged witch, me —
> tangled on my two great arms,
> my face in a book
> and my mouth wide,
> ready to tell you a story or two.

The Book of Folly was for work more typically "Sexton"; it should appeal to readers who had grasped the associational method she employed in some poems of *Live or Die*. *The Death Notebooks* was intended for posthumous publication.

At forty-one, then, Sexton was projecting the completion of her career. This is not to say she was planning her death, merely that she was thinking about it differently, positioning it in her work. In 1970 she wrote several poems that illuminate her thoughts: "Godfather Death," which she placed in *Transformations*; "The Death of the Fathers," a sequence published in *The Book of Folly*; "For Mr. Death Who Stands with His Door Open" and the sequence "The Death Baby," which she saved for *The Death Notebooks*. These poems are not much alike, but they have one thing in common: for the first time Sexton naturalizes death, permits mortality its place in the passing of the generations.

The work that occupied her chiefly that year was *Transformations,* a book of "black humor," she said, which might take its place among the works of experimental fiction that college students were trading among themselves. Novels such as Vonnegut's *Slaughterhouse-Five* and Donald Barthelme's *Snow White,* which ran in *The New Yorker* in February 1967, suggested to Sexton that there was space in literature for the sadistic spin she could give a children's story. She thanked Linda for sparking the "magic in the head" that produced this book. As Linda remembered, "Every day when I came home from school I would heat a can of soup and sit down to read in the kitchen while eating it — slopping soup all over myself and the book. I was underweight in those years; I was always hungry. One day Mother came into the kitchen and found me reading my Grimm's fairy-tale book that I'd had since 1961. It had an introduction by W. H. Auden. She asked me which stories I liked, and wrote the titles down on a napkin."

A major source of symbolism in *Transformations* was eating. From Linda's point of view, the book captured a disturbed side of family life: family dynamics around meals. "Joy and I would be banished during the cocktail hour, while Daddy and Mother absorbed their martinis or whatever. By the time dinner was served at eight or nine o'clock they would be sloshed. The meal was full of tension. And there was just never enough food! Daddy would open one small package of frozen peas, maybe bake those small boiling potatoes, one apiece — no salad, no dessert. Mother would gag down a drumstick. She was hardly able to swallow anything solid; she'd often get up from the table and vomit her food."

The dearth of food had nothing to do with the Sextons' financial situation, as during those same years they ordered champagne by the case. It was a combination of Anne's queasiness toward food and neurotic fear of markets — she placed exactly the same order every week by telephone — and Kayo's efforts to cover the bases both at home and at work. There was also the need to maintain a ritual in the midst of disorder. "I think we felt required, as a family, to do things the same way every day as far as possible," Linda remembered. "The evening meal became a pivotal point, rimmed and edged with tension. At the table, Mother was so often crazed; we had to contain it somehow. She'd talk gibberish, she'd stare at the wall, her eyes traveling mechanically up then down in a way my father called 'headlighting' — it drove him wild. We'd have to put her to bed. One night she fell

From Anne Sexton's modeling portfolio.

straight forward and her face landed in the mashed potatoes! My father would say, 'Anne, stop it, you're frightening the children.' "

During this time, however, Sexton was successful in keeping her disorders private. Linda recalled that family rules preserved strict boundaries around home life. Kayo closed the door behind him when he returned from work in the evening, and that was that. He and Anne rarely entertained their neighbors in Weston, and the children were discouraged from having friends over and visiting their friends' homes. So the family kept up a front of normality, and behind the olive green facade of their handsome two-story house, all that winter the witch wrote her poems at an enchanted kitchen table, "mouth wide, / ready to tell you a story or two." As Sexton noted to friends,

Anne Sexton at her desk.

fairy tales — both the originals and her own — were full of food imagery and mouth imagery, and the theme is keynoted in the dedication of *Transformations*: "To Linda, who reads Hesse and drinks clam chowder."

Another hidden influence on the book was Sexton's new psychiatrist, Constance Chase, who received a deep curtsy in "The Frog Prince":

> Frau Doktor
> Mama Brundig,
> Take out your contacts,
> remove your wig.
> I write for you.
> I entertain.

Sexton's letters speak of her therapy at this time in only the most general terms, but it is clear she liked and respected Dr. Chase, and *Transformations* can be looked on as in part a courtship offering. This was a moment ripe with possibility in Sexton's life, with a new "mama" and two adolescent daughters battling toward womanhood to inspire her. As she told Linda, the fairy tales had a lot to say about human behavior, if you looked at them with a twisted mind.

Once she formed the plan of writing a whole book of them, the poems of *Transformations* rushed easily through her fingers. (Wrote Maxine Kumin, "I must immodestly state that I urged and bullied her to go on after the first few.") They seemed strong enough, and her psyche sturdy enough, to risk putting under the scrutiny of James Wright, who was now contentedly remarried (he and his wife, Annie, had invited Sexton to dinner in New York during the run of *Mercy Street*), and whom Sexton hoped to reenlist in her circle of sharers. She was even back in touch with George Starbuck, who was about to leave the University of Iowa and become the director of the creative writing program at Boston University. Immediately after finishing the first two poems for the new book, she fired them off to Starbuck with a plea: "If you could pick them apart, I will buy you a drink when you get here."

By May Sexton had written over half the book. She explained the genre to Brian Sweeney: "I take the fairy tale and transform it into a poem of my own, following the story line, exceeding the story line and adding my own pzazz. They are very wry and cruel and sadistic and funny." Though she often compared the poems favorably, invidiously, to *Mercy Street,* these two works had more in common than she acknowledged. Fairy tales deal with the struggle of children to overcome giants, ogres, and witches, often to satisfy the wishes of kings and queens by undergoing terrible ordeals. In *Mercy Street* she had transferred to dramatic narrative her personal struggle with the living dead, which had fueled her work from the beginning. The story lines of *Transformations* further distanced the same struggle, placing it in legend rather than personal history, and the distance permitted her to play freely in this old terrain. Embedded in *Transformations* are newly disguised versions of Judith the cold mother ("Snow White"), Aunt Amy the witch of libido ("Rapunzel"), and Ace the seducing father ("Briar Rose/Sleeping Beauty"):

> Daddy?
> That's another kind of prison.
> It's not the prince at all,
> but my father
> drunkenly bent over my bed,
> circling the abyss like a shark,
> my father thick upon me
> like some sleeping jellyfish.
> What voyage this, little girl?
> This coming out of prison?
> God help —
> this life after death?

As usual, the poems went out as soon as Sexton thought they were finished. She hoped to hook a fat check or two from *The New Yorker,* which was currently paying her over four dollars per line. Howard Moss rejected them tactfully, but Cindy Degener was able to place a few in sophisticated "adult" magazines such as *Playboy* and *Cosmopolitan.* Still hoping that Sexton would write a novel, Degener rejoiced in this new departure. "Anne Sexton in the Popular Culture — Whoopee," she wrote. "Look at this enclosed letter from *Playboy* and remember that *Cosmo* is paying you $500 for two poems and desperate for more and we are waiting word from *Vogue* where they love you. You are 'in.' [. . .] I can see you glaring at this paper and cursing that I am weak and vulgar, but the money is good and it will be good for the book when you bring it out."

By September, Sexton was ready to show the collection to Paul Brooks at Houghton Mifflin. "They are full of charm and original images," he responded soothingly. "On the other hand, they do of course lack the terrific force and directness of your more serious poetry." Brooks's criticism came as a shock. Defending her fairy tales, Sexton offered a rare and interesting perspective on her entire career. "I look at my work in stages," she told him. "Now that I've almost finished *Transformations* I see it as part of my life's work . . . a kind of dalliance on the way. After this, and I have already begun, I would like to do a book of very surreal, unconscious poems called *The Book of Folly*. At the same time I plan to start another book called *The Death Notebooks,* where the poems will be very Sexton . . . intense, personal, perhaps religious in places. I will work on the *Death Notebooks* until I die." With *Transformations,* she observed, she had moved as far as possible from confessionalism; she wanted him to see that as a stride.

Her confidence in these poems was justified: *Transformations* proved to be her second most popular book, second only to *Love Poems.* To her delight, Kurt Vonnegut agreed to write a foreword, and Houghton Mifflin agreed to illustrations by Barbara Swan.

Such issues as sales figures, royalties, and fees were very much on Sexton's mind during 1970. For the past year the R. C. Harvey Company, along with the rest of the textile industry, had been in the doldrums. In January, Kayo's salary was halved; in February, he was fired. This was "a scary time" in family life, Linda Sexton remembered. A junior in high school, thinking about applying to colleges, Linda was in regular psychotherapy, as was her mother; Anne had a secretary; Joy boarded a horse. Everyone had grown accustomed to the affluence that made such middle-class luxuries feel like necessities. Sexton took pride in the steady rise in her income from royalties and readings, which alleviated some of the worry about coping with their uncertain financial situation. She was invited to teach her January seminar to Oberlin students again that year, and had begun tutoring a few student poets privately. Best of all, she had been hired as a lecturer in creative writing at Boston University, beginning in January. When Kayo's career faltered, she was able to assume some of the burden. With five thousand dollars of her savings, she helped him form a wool partnership with an associate.

The challenge of a new business venture was bracing to Kayo. "He's out there all by himself, and he's got to make it," Sexton reported. "Often when he comes home he is manic and enthusiastic." The marriage took on new life, Linda Sexton recalled; "the two of them began functioning, for the first time, as a team." By early March the financial picture was again bright enough to allow Anne and Kayo a week of sunshine in Bermuda, during the semester break at Boston University. As always, Billie Sexton stepped in to manage the household in their absence. While waiting at a self-service dry cleaners' for draperies and children's clothes to finish a cycle, she wrote a note to them: "Have been thinking of you both and all the job problems and had a brilliant idea. What would you think, Kayo, of looking for a position in California and we all move there? [. . .] Anne's work would probably find even greater reception in California than stuffy New England, and think of the opportunity of starting fresh in a warm sunshiny climate!!" Really, anything seemed possible in the new decade.

Probably for the sake of making money, Sexton dovetailed a number of readings into her schedule that spring. Her friend from Sweet Briar College, Philip Legler, was now teaching at Northern Michigan University and helped arrange a well-paid performance in April. He hoped she could stay on an extra day, but she told him ruefully, "I can't miss class as I'm missing it the following week and then two weeks before also. I just can't afford to get fired." Her one-semester contract at Boston University, which she hoped would be renewed for the following year, had been arranged by Arthur Freeman, now a professor of English there. "I liked her, and I was probably interested in making trouble when I proposed her for the job," he recalled. "Anne was one of my privileges; I didn't want to teach poetry myself."

When George Starbuck came out to interview for the position as head of creative writing, Freeman arranged a celebratory re-creation of their reading at the Poets' Theater in Cambridge back in 1959. Sexton was elated to have Starbuck in Boston again. Moreover, she hoped he would "see to it that I continue to be hired" at Boston University, as she told him rather wistfully. She probably realized that the faculty was skeptical about her credentials. As Freeman recalled, "It mattered a lot that she had absolutely no education — that outraged people." She probably would have been let go, he thought, except that she kept getting prestigious awards. In June, she received an honorary doctorate from Tufts University — "something like having a baby without having had intercourse," she joked. The award was well timed: her contract as lecturer for the next academic year was renewed in August, and she always claimed that the honorary degree had saved her job. Then Starbuck arrived, to head the creative writing program and become another important ally.

But by all accounts, Sexton was a marvelous teacher for a certain type of student. Not necessarily for the well-read in literature: if someone floated an allusion to Yeats or Hardy, Eliot or Pound, she often had to bluff. But her ear for a good phrase, her patience, her openness, and above all her hard work paid off in the classroom. Determined to overcome the mistrust of her colleagues, she gave the student writers what they valued most: generous amounts of individual attention. A graduate student who worked with Sexton later described this aspect of her teaching: "At some point during the semester, she would have you out to her house for a private discussion. You'd give her your work in advance, and she would go through it quite carefully and gently. I so wanted some kind of parental thing there — I wanted to be taken up. Then she would show you her stuff, in manuscript. She would actually sit there with this black manuscript binder, with these onionskin, thin pages, very carefully typed — a lot of them obviously retyped and redone and retyped. So we got this little peek, a great, generous, equalizing gift — 'Here, I want you to see what I've done.' "

Moreover, Sexton had absorbed from her experience in workshops a method for eliciting productive interchange among class members. One of her students in 1970 was Ellen Bass, who went on to make a successful career as a poet and editor. At the end of the semester Bass rated Sexton's course the best of six such classes she had taken previously, at Goucher College and Boston University, commenting, "Mrs. Sexton has turned a class of individuals into a group which can work together. She leads the discussion, but [. . .] treats us as poets, beginning poets, but serious ones." Another member of the class had a poem accepted at *The New Yorker* that spring; "it made me feel like a happy grandmother," Sexton said.

Linda Sexton had begun writing poetry too. She regularly went to Maxine Kumin for tutorials, just as Judy Kumin went to Anne Sexton. As Linda's skill developed, her mother began making her a sounding board for new work, trying out *Transformations* and then other poems on her. If an image wasn't clear to her, Sexton would go back to work on it. She also taught Linda the tricks she had learned herself and was now passing on to students at Boston University. "That was a wonderful thing to share with her," Linda remembered. Occasionally, Sexton took Linda along to class; as she wrote to a friend, "I'm determined that she get an education, and not a mediocre one. I know so little, just barely enough to write."

In August, Sexton had a bizarre attack of some kind. "Everything had strange colors and sounds were either very loud or very far away," as she put it. After meeting as usual with Dr. Chase, who (according to Sexton) did not regard the symptoms as very significant, she drove to Joan Smith's house, where she made crazed phone calls to Dr. Chase and to Maxine Kumin. Then she went home and took an overdose of sleeping pills. Max called, and when she heard how disoriented Sexton was, she reached Joy by screaming into the phone. By then Anne was comatose. Joy called the psychiatrist, who called Billie, who was giving Linda a permanent wave. Leaving the rollers in Linda's hair, Billie rushed to the scene and dragged Anne down the stairs. As soon as Kayo got home, they put her in the back seat of the car and headed for Massachusetts General Hospital in Boston. Anne's breathing grew shallower and shallower while they idled along in rush-hour traffic. Sexton recounted the horrific episode in a long letter to Alice Smith. "Poor Joy," she said. "How could I have left her with that."

This was the first of what proved to be a throng of health crises in which the whole family, including its youngest member, was increasingly caught up. Sexton's letter to Alice Smith indicates that she was deeply frightened by this attack, which resembled an involuntary hallucinogenic drug trip. Significantly, her account differs in several details from those of family members, who recall the episode more as a melodrama than as a medical emergency. Hardened by Sexton's self-absorption and perpetual exaggerations, they had grown increasingly unsympathetic. "I thought Mother took a certain pride in this kind of behavior," Linda later commented icily. "It began to seem very self-indulgent to me."

18

THE PROFESSOR
OF POETRY
1970-1972

DURING THE HOLIDAY SEASON in 1970, Sexton received a shocking piece of news from an old family friend, Azel Mack. He and his wife had been very close to Ralph and Mary Gray and were the godparents of Anne's children. Mack decided it was now time to tell Anne a secret he had kept for over forty years: he and her mother had been lovers, and he believed that Anne was his daughter. He brought "proof": a lock of her baby hair and a fancy studio portrait taken when she was sixteen (Mary Gray had covertly ordered an extra print for him). "I don't want to die with this proof on me," he told her. Sexton was dumbfounded. Could it be true that her "real" father was still alive? Or was this tale the product of an old man's fantasy?

Mack persisted. He took Sexton on a trip to show her the place where, supposedly, she had been conceived, and chatted freely about his clandestine meetings with Mary Gray, telling Sexton how he and her mother had sneaked out the back doors of their neighboring homes to meet for brief, passionate embraces and whispered talk — or so Sexton reported. Mack claimed that the affair had continued right up to the time of Mary Gray's death, saying that he had comforted her after her mastectomy, when her husband turned away, repulsed by her "imperfections."

Azel Mack eventually succeeded in convincing Sexton that he was in fact her biological father, but he made these disclosures more than a decade after the deaths of Ralph and Mary Gray, and many members of her family remain convinced that the story is false. Nevertheless, it touched Sexton's deepest vulnerabilities, jarring loose a flood of memories and longings that she channeled that winter into a sequence of six poems titled "The Death of the Fathers."

This extraordinary group of poems returns to the scene of the crime

342

explored in *Mercy Street*: the erotic dynamics of family life viewed through the experience of a daughter. The first four of the six, "Oysters," "How We Danced," "The Boat," and "Santa," are snapshots of family celebrations. The nostalgically evoked father resembles the masculine type Sexton created in Ace of *Mercy Street*, always drinking; he is wickedly titillating in "Oysters," a daredevil in "The Boat," and in "How We Danced" high on champagne, covertly making sexual use of his daughter's body.

> Mother was a belle and danced with twenty men.
> You danced with me never saying a word.
> Instead the serpent spoke as you held me close.
> The serpent, that mocker, woke up and pressed against me
> like a great god and we bent together like two lonely swans.

In the last two poems in the sequence, "Friends" and "Begat," the sensual father is supplanted by a strangely aggressive, strangely tolerated family "friend" who roughly fondles and playfully beats the little girl.

> I was stained with his red fingers
> and I cried out for you
> and Mother said you had gone on a trip.
> You had sunk like a cat in the snow,
> not a paw left to clasp for luck.

The emotional dynamic in "The Death of the Fathers" is complex and radically interesting. The series asserts the reality of various kinds of incestuous wishes in two kinds of fathers, one treacherously fixated by instinct, the other domineering, asserting rough sex play as his father-right. But Sexton had fantasized in her poems, and acted out in her life, seduction of and by mothers as well, most recently in "Rapunzel," in *Transformations* ("A woman / who loves a woman / is forever young, / [. . .] Old breast against young breast . . ."). In "The Death of the Fathers," the early-wakened sexuality of the daughter looks in two directions, toward the fathers she is thrilled and terrified to arouse and toward the elusive woman whose desire can never be secured. Sexton's imagery suggests that Mother's absence creates the vortex of desire that both ignites and distances them all. Perhaps it took her work with a female psychotherapist to sharpen the focus of this insight. The broken taboo, signified by the color of blood and love, drenches both mother and father by the end of the series.

> red, red, Mother, you are blood red.
> He scoops her up in his arms
> all red shivers and silks.
> He cries to her:
> How dare I hold this princess?
> A mere man such as I
> with a shark's nose and ten tar-fingers?
> [. . .]
> Those times I smelled the Vitalis on his pajamas.
> Those times I mussed his curly black hair
> and touched his ten tar-fingers
> and swallowed down his whiskey breath.
> Red. Red. Father, you are blood red.
> Father,
> we are two birds on fire.

Sexton's poetic sequence casts another revisionary look over her past. As in a dream, she herself occupies all the positions in the fantasy that shapes it. She has been the daughter incestuously aroused by a father who split himself in two: one day the handsome salesman who could charm your pants off, the next a raging stranger on a binge. She has been the seductive parent too, aroused by a daughter's body and making surreptitious use of it. And she has been abandoned, like her mother's lovers, those two lonely swans, those two birds on fire. At the end sit just Azel Mack and herself, tending the hearth still warmed by that old passion.

Overwhelmed by the alterations life had inscribed on her oldest memories, Sexton wasn't sure "The Death of the Fathers" worked as a sequence, so she sent it to her friend C. K. Williams for help with the task of clarifying the internal relation of image with image. She had tried out a number of her *Transformations* on him and had found his judgment to be shrewd.

Williams was made uneasy by these poems. "I know how close the poem must be to you," he acknowledged, "but something happened so that the craft of your poetry (which always astonishes me by the way) turned against you, so that you used it, or some part of you used it, to prevent what truly profound thing was happening from really happening." He went on,

There isn't enough *dumbness* in the poem, enough of that language that floats just above incoherency, the incoherency of those mysteries of time and love that fatherhood and childhood embody . . . I remember when I heard you read, that long silence you had in the poem about your mother ["The Double Image"], and how utterly important that silence was, as though it *was* the poem, and the rest framed it, allowed it, created it. That isn't in this one, anywhere, and the poem seems to know it, and almost is ashamed by it, so that even the metaphors have often a kind of silly grin on their faces, saying, Well I don't really mean it this way, but you understand.

It may be that Williams, the father of a little girl, was unprepared to respond deeply to the emotions cycling in "The Death of the Fathers," but his letter put into words a principle of evaluation that Sexton could bring to the poem and to others like it. What he sentimentalized as "mysteries of time and love that fatherhood and childhood embody," Sexton did not. "Dumbness," "silence," was precisely what had to be given up as the daughter groped back along the branching path of Daddy's-girl memories and fantasies to the enigma of Mother's desire. And once the poem was in print, Williams changed his mind "completely" about it: "I think it's really fine. I don't know whether you've changed it or I've changed or what, but it seems to me now one of your most powerful poems."

In addition to working on two books that winter and teaching her seminar on Thursday afternoons at Boston University, Sexton was on the road several times with Her Kind. But the pace exhausted her; in February she collapsed. She was admitted to Westwood Lodge on a Thursday evening and stayed through the weekend, canceling a reading engagement in Philadelphia, where she had looked forward to staying with Williams. She then left the hospital under the care of Joan Smith, who had nursed her when she broke her hip.

Sexton felt that she needed a caretaker for a while, as her heart seemed to be acting up: she had had a frightening blackout while driving. A week after her release from Westwood Lodge, she reported to Cindy Degener that her physical problems were probably psychosomatic; nonetheless, she was in a deep depression and was being sent to Florida "on doctor's orders." However, she told Anne Wilder that the depression was probably triggered by going off Thorazine so she could get a suntan in Florida. "Thorazine isn't an anti-depressant and

yet it keeps me sane," she said. "Dr. Chase says it's a major tranquilizer. [. . .] I'm not aware that I need to be that tranquil." Wilder replied sensibly, "If Thorazine works for you [. . .] why not resign
yourself to taking the stuff?"

Sexton didn't answer this question, but it was trenchant. Just six
months earlier, a suicide attempt, the first since 1966. Now a brief stay
at Westwood Lodge, her first hospitalization for psychological problems since 1964. In retrospect, this pair of events seems to have ush-
ered in the final era of her disorder. From then on the spans of health
shortened, the crises deepened.

Why was it that Sexton began to deteriorate again at just this period
of her life, when she claimed never to have been happier? One place to
look for an answer is in her losses. Learning Azel Mack's secret made
her lose her past again; those charming, cruel parents had forced their
ambiguities on her yet once more. At the same time, a significant attrition was occurring steadily in her relationship with her daughters.

Finding ways to mother her children had been at least as important
to the restoration of Sexton's mental stability as writing poetry. Their
infancy had made intolerable demands on her psyche, and breaking
down had relieved her of their presence but intensified her self-hatred.
Then they had grown up a little. The charm and vitality of children at
four and six — the ages of Joy and Linda in 1959, when Sexton
emerged as a poet — must have supported her feeling of a fresh beginning. Because she so identified with her daughters *as* daughters, they
gave her renewed access to unconscious materials that nurtured her
art. And once she had readjusted to their presence, they surrounded
her with a magic circle of care, mothering her as much as she moth-
ered them. Equally, they collaborated in the management of her sickness through family rituals designed to contain it.

Now Linda and Joy were young women. Joy, now fifteen, had developed the "big boobs" Sexton envied and had started running with
what her parents regarded as a fast crowd, and Linda, at seventeen,
was bringing home lovely boys. The timing of Sexton's breakdown in
February 1971 invites interpretation in the context of their growing
sexuality, particularly because the annual winter vacation to seek the
sun was one Sexton had labeled "a great ritual of the body."

Both Sexton's daughters had begun keeping secrets from her, secrets about their bodies: what they ate and smoked, whom they touched
and where. They found their mother emphatically censorious about
such secrecy. "Little Girl, My String Bean, My Lovely Woman"
had proudly imagined the mother as an "old tree in the background"

of the daughter's developing sexual maturity, assuming that it was a mother's prerogative to witness the changes and commend them. "Snow White," written six years later, acknowledged other, harder emotions. The mirror cannot lie when the queen poses her famous question, "Who is fairest?" and the queen — "eaten, of course, by age" — is doomed to assert herself through witchlike strategies against that "dumb bunny" who has only youth and beauty.

At forty-two, Anne Sexton still had arresting looks. Many people remember her as a beauty at that time. She had glamour, the power to enchant the gaze and inflame the imagination. Interviewers always mentioned the intensity of her gaze, though some described her eyes as intensely blue while others remarked that they blazed green. Moreover, because of her olive complexion she was often perceived as deeply tanned, though Thorazine kept her mainly out of the sun. Published interviews always described her as "slender," despite the steady weight gain registered in her letters and medical records. (Her children said that Thorazine gave her a "spider body": slim arms and legs with a ballooning middle.)

But despite her captivating aura and genuine good looks, Sexton had begun to feel the effects of age, and in 1971 something like the drama of "Snow White" was unfolding in the Sexton household. Linda began taking the pill, ostensibly to regulate her menstrual cycle. Her mother expected that this development would lead to sexual experiments, and she expected to be kept informed. "When I finally did lose my virginity at age eighteen, after all the hoopla, I did it when she was away for a weekend," Linda explained. "I confided in Lois, but not in Mother; it was too complicated. Then she began saying things like, 'I can smell the sex between you! I know you've done it!' I'd say, 'I don't know what you're talking about.' Finally I accused Lois: '*You've* told her — she knows too much.' Lois said, 'She's read your journal.' I hadn't exactly been hiding my journal; it was in my desk. Knowing her as I did, I think this must have fulfilled an unconscious wish. A part of me wanted to give her the gift of it. Another side of me knew it wasn't appropriate."

More and more, Linda was learning how to protect herself from her mother's invasiveness. Now she had broken the family rule that said that Anne mustn't be opposed or she would collapse. And Anne was enraged by what seemed like Linda's callous betrayal, withholding from her such important information. She blamed Linda's psychiatrist for conspiring against her, and she channeled her anger into an extremely confrontational poem, "Mother and Daughter." In this painful fantasy, an insouciant maiden confronts a destitute crone and banishes her.

> Linda, you are leaving
> your old body now.
> You've picked my pocket clean
> and you've racked up all my
> poker chips and left me empty
> and, as the river between us
> narrows, you do calisthenics,
> that womanly leggy semaphore.
> Question you about this
> and you will sew me a shroud
> and hold up Monday's broiler
> and thumb out the chicken gut.
> Question you about this
> and you will see my death
> drooling at these gray lips
> while you, my burglar, will eat
> fruit and pass the time of day.

Anne with Linda.

These were the only terms, in Sexton's psyche, on which a daughter could separate from the wicked queen: little Anne from elderly Nana (as in *Mercy Street*), Anne Sexton from Mary Gray (as in "The Double Image," where mother wilts while daughter waits); now Linda from Anne.

Sexton did collapse, in February; that she called in Joan Smith to care for her was probably a sign of defeat. She had begun giving in to steady pressure from both Linda and Linda's psychiatrist, and also, apparently, from Dr. Chase, who must have rebuked her for showing Linda "Mother and Daughter." Sexton wrote hotly to her therapist,

> I don't like you telling me what I can write poems about, what is a good subject. [. . .] I felt manipulated. Much as my mother manipulated me. [. . .] At any rate, Linda does not feel that way. She thinks of course that I must write poems about her if I want to — just as she writes poems about me on occasions. She is a writer. She understands. I strongly resent the fact that you feel I am using Linda. [. . .] You so winningly said, "People come first" meaning before the writing. You forced me to say the truth. The writing comes first. [. . .] This is my way of mastering experience.

Writing had always come first, though. What was new, and increasingly important, was Linda's and Joy's growing independence — and in her own way Sexton welcomed this. No one was happier when Linda was admitted to Harvard: "Me who never went to college with a daughter flying upward," she crowed to a friend. It was in just such a spirit of pride that, wrapping up the manuscript of *Transformations* that spring, she dedicated the book to Linda.

And though in the deepest recesses of her psyche Sexton resisted the process of letting Linda go, she also began to let it work in another way on her imagination, by preparing spiritually for her own death. "The Death of the Fathers" was matched in her new work in 1971 by three other sequences that were ambitious in both form and theme: "Angels of the Love Affair," written in May and June, "The Jesus Papers" in July, and "O Ye Tongues" at the year's end. These poems, which can legitimately be regarded as Anne Sexton's "last" poems (though they were not the last she wrote), are religious works that associate a specifically female form of spiritual grace with the breast.

Much has been written about Sexton as a religious writer who, slightly ahead of her time, intuited the need for a feminist revision of patriarchal monotheism. The poetry and correspondence of 1971 validates such a view. Nominated to be commencement speaker at Regis College, where she was to receive an honorary doctorate, Sexton proposed the topic "God Is a Woman." She said she would "make a few comments," then read three very short poems. "Despite the provocative title," she added, "I will endeavor to be tasteful and meaningful." After worrying about this speech for a month, she canceled, saying that her doctor had advised abandoning all speaking engagements. Regis found another commencement speaker and made Sexton a doctor *honoris causa* anyway, but she didn't leave us her comments on her proposed subject. Instead, she went on to write ambitious sequences of religious verse.

"Angels of the Love Affair," a series of sonnets, came in a rush at the end of May and the first days of June and seems to have been stimulated by an invitation to help celebrate the centennial of Squirrel Island; Sexton was to be a guest of honor in July at this charmingly provincial fete. She had visited Squirrel Island only once since the property had been sold after her grandfather's death in 1940. Her impending visit, like Azel Mack's intrusion, made her oldest "love affair," the family romance, available to fresh imagining.

The poems of "Angels of the Love Affair" are prayers to the spirit of paradox. In each of the six sonnets the speaker sets her madness in simple language before an "Angel" of reversal. Etymologically, "angels" are "messengers," but Sexton's angels are more like the charged poles in an electrical circuit. Polarized herself by despair, fear, or disgust, or even by joy, Sexton summons the messenger of its opposite. To the Angel of Fire and Genitals she shows slime; to Flight and Sleigh Bells she shows paralysis; but to the fearsome angel of Blizzards and Blackouts she shows raspberries gathered on a July morning. Her associations zap swiftly into stanzas, tightly rhymed.

> Angel of fire and genitals, do you know slime,
> that green mama who first forced me to sing,
> who put me first in the latrine, that pantomime
> of brown where I was beggar and she was king?
> I said, "The devil is down that festering hole."
> Then he bit me in the buttocks and took over my soul.
>
> Fire woman, you of the ancient flame, you
> of the Bunsen burner, you of the candle,

you of the blast furnace, you of the barbecue,
you of the fierce solar energy, Mademoiselle,
take some ice, take some snow, take a month of rain
and you would gutter in the dark, cracking up your brain.

Mother of fire, let me stand at your devouring gate
as the sun dies in your arms and you loosen its terrible weight.

"Angels of the Love Affair" can be designated "religious" poems
because they show the speaker entrusting ego to Logos: the principle
Sexton had called "Language," the power of words to communicate
more meanings than can be grasped from any insistently exclusive —
call it "mad" — point of view. Reverence for this spiritual power was
what gave talismanic status, for Sexton, to the palindrome, "rats live
on no evil star." As she had explained in 1960, writing "With Mercy
for the Greedy," if God exists, the despised must have their place in
the order of things, "owning a star [. . .] without the stain of evil."
Now she began trying to accommodate the female principle to a spiritual vision, using "star" as a key term. Sexton applied this word repeatedly to her mother, in letters written during Mary Gray's
treatment for breast cancer. By substitution, "star" became "breast"
in later images, where an aroused woman's nipple is a "starberry" and
breasts released from a brassiere have "nipples as uninvolved as warm
starfish."

Sexton had grouped "Mercy for the Greedy" with two other poems
about religious belief in *All My Pretty Ones*. "Need is not quite belief," she had stated ruefully in that poem, resigning herself to need. In
1971 she was ready to think again about the question of belief and its
availability to a woman. The poems of "The Jesus Papers" question
urgently the meaning of Jesus as the meeting-ground of divine with
human. Revisionary parables about life in a body and in a family, the
nine poems in the sequence are based on stories most children know.
As in *Transformations*, Sexton requires these old stories to answer
Freudian questions. What were the infant fantasies of the baby Jesus?

You give me milk
and we are the same
and I am glad.
No. No.
All lies.
I am a truck. I run everything.
I own you.

How did the son of God experience his Oedipal conflict?

> In His dream
> He desired Mary.
> His penis sang like a dog,
> but He turned sharply away from that play
> like a door slamming.

Did he really work miracles? No; they were tricks easily played on those who cannot distinguish need from belief ("Jesus Raises Up the Harlot," "Jesus Cooks," and "Jesus Summons Forth").

These poems confront the reader with a Jesus who in fact resembles Anne Sexton, an often very disagreeable person, disgustingly fixated on the female body, neurotically self-absorbed, terrified of the death for which s/he has been singled out. *This* Jesus must be imagined before we can believe in him, because as Sexton knew well, suffering reduces any human being to humiliating neediness. Her purpose was not to mock but to pose at its human extreme the question "What use to others can individual suffering conceivably be?"

In reducing Jesus to suffering in a body, however, Sexton again and again ran up against a theological problem: Jesus had the body of a man. Thus in "The Jesus Papers" she also investigated the question of Mary's role in the Incarnation. Mary's transformation from maid to mother is the subject of "Jesus Unborn," in which Mary is approached by the angel of the Annunciation.

> a strange being leans over her
> and lifts her chin firmly
> and gazes at her with executioner's eyes.
> Nine clocks spring open
> and smash themselves against the sun.
> [. . .]
> Now we will have a Christ.

History will have a Christ, and Mary will have milk in her breasts. For Sexton, this is the principle by which the Incarnation is manifest in the female body. Christ sacrifices his blood at the crucifixion; Mary's sacrifice is the blood-sacrifice of female chemistry, which makes body fluids into milk. In the last poem of the sequence, Sexton brings the example of Mary's sacrifice into the present, when "The Author of the Jesus Papers Speaks":

I went to the well and drew a baby
out of the hollow water.
Then God spoke to me and said:
Here. Take this gingerbread lady
and put her in your oven.
When the cow gives blood
and the Christ is born
we must all eat sacrifices.
We must all eat beautiful women.

Sexton's ambitions for this sequence seem oddly served, though, by the ironies on which the poem limps to this ending. Was she unnerved by the outcome of her rigorous questions about what import Christianity held for women? For herself in particular, a woman with a mother named Mary? The poem implies more interesting insights than it pursues, possibly because Sexton was not really interested in theological issues. After "The Jesus Papers" she abandoned the effort to identify with Christ (the symbol of redemption) or Jesus (the man who sacrificed himself), but she retained her fascination with the religious connotations of milk. Milk became her personal sign for the grace that could flow from her and toward her — for the reversal of "rats" (the horrible and disgusting body) into "star" (the transcendent mother-principle). This is the theme of Sexton's beautifully sustained sequence of ten psalms titled "O Ye Tongues."

Sexton borrowed the form of this poem from "Jubilate Agno," written by the eighteenth-century poet Christopher Smart, who was considered insane and was hospitalized for extensive periods because of a compulsion to public prayer. A masterful poet schooled in Latin, Greek, and Hebrew prosody, Smart adapted the antiphonal structure of Hebrew psalms for "Jubilate Agno," alternating sections of verse beginning "Let" and "For": "Let Jael rejoice with the Plover, who whistles for his live, and foils the marksmen and their guns. [. . .] For I will consider my Cat Jeoffry. [. . .] For he rolls upon prank to work it in. [. . .] For in his morning orisons he loves the sun and the sun loves him." Sexton preserved this structure. Her "Let" sections celebrate God's abundance: "Let there be a God as large as a sunlamp to laugh his heat at you," the poem begins ("First Psalm"). The "For" sections find mirroring abundance in Sexton's life: "For I pray that Emily King, whom I do not know except to say *good morning,* will observe my legs and fanny with good will" ("Second Psalm"), which extends the implication of the sunlamp to a backyard sunbath smiled upon by a neighbor.

Through such loose but ingenious linkages, Sexton draws the ten psalms into an autobiographical narrative that culminates in the letting-go of a daughter:

> For the child grows to a woman, her breasts coming up like the moon while Anne rubs the peace stone.
>
> For the child starts up her own mountain (not being locked in) and reaches the coastline of grapes.
>
> For Anne and her daughter master the mountain and again and again. Then the child finds a man who opens like the sea.

The simplicity of the story line is enriched by the gravity and gaiety of images along which it unspools toward death, ending where it began ("Tenth Psalm"):

> For Anne walked up and up and finally over the years until she was old as the moon and with its naggy voice.
>
> For Anne had climbed over eight mountains and saw the children washing the tiny statues in the square.
>
> For Anne sat down with the blood of a hammer and built a tombstone for herself and Christopher sat beside her and was well pleased with their red shadow.
>
> For they hung up a picture of a rat and the rat smiled and held out his hand.
>
> For the rat was blessed on that mountain. He was given a white bath.
>
> For the milk in the skies sank down upon them and tucked them in.
>
> For God did not forsake them but put the blood angel to look after them until such time as they would enter their star.
>
> For the sky dogs jumped and shoveled snow upon us and we lay in our quiet blood.
>
> For God was as large as a sunlamp and laughed his heat at us and therefore we did not cringe at the death hole.

Along with the form, Sexton absorbed Smart's theological assumptions in "Jubilate Agno." Primary was the example of the way in which a holy madness licensed the poet to speak of the body without shame ("For I shat and Christopher smiled and said let the air be sweet with your soil"). "Jubilate Agno" inspired Sexton to explore the one area of trust she had ever developed: the certainty that for every work of the human tongue, there was an auditor. In "O Ye Tongues" she calls the knowing hearer God, a blend of all the parents, lovers, friends, children, doctors, readers, listeners, and imaginary brothers in the universe. Like a nursing mother's face, God's face bends over the world; and as the infant's tongue connects with the mother's breast, the poet's tongue connects with the uninterruptable attention of this Other, the milk of the skies.

Information is tantalizingly scarce about who led Sexton to Christopher Smart's catalyzing text, under what circumstances she wrote "O Ye Tongues," and whose advice she sought as she revised it; her worksheets provide little of the usual overlay of dates and comments. The sequence appears to have been the product of a sustained inspiration, undertaken at Christmas 1971 and completed near Easter 1972. After finishing it, she told a friend, "It's 18 pages long and is (perhaps) a major poem."

Just as baffling is the source of the ever-strengthening religious impulse in Sexton's work, for the spiritual preoccupations she condensed into her "last" poems remained largely invisible to her family and colleagues (although she did enjoy dialogue with Catholic priests about these topics). In the notes Sexton made toward her never-finished novel, in 1966, the main character jokes about her religious indecision: "Last year I was almost a Catholic by choice, but decided it would be too flashy a move and perhaps Jesus would understand my feelings for him although I was not a member of His Church." But Sexton tended to turn away direct questions about her beliefs. Asked about the religious feeling a reader found in "For the Year of the Insane," written after an extreme trance experience in Dr. Orne's office back in 1963, she responded, "Whoever God is I keep making telephone calls to him. I'm not sure that's religion. More desperation than faith in such things."

She did share her spiritual concerns with a very few friends, including Cindy Degener, who said, "Why, we chatted away about Jesus all the time, as if he were just in the other room!" Degener thought "The Jesus Papers" showed Sexton's fascination with the *True Confessions* version of life; "there was a lot of melodrama in his story, and a lot of exchanges with women. Anne really tried to trust the connections she felt with that Jesus, the ordinary man." Sexton's Australian fan Brian Sweeney was another of her spiritual confidants. Theological mysteries delighted him; he liked, for example, the thesis "God Is a Woman," and wrote to Sexton, "If man and woman are really one, is not God as man's brother (through Jesus Christ) also man's sister? [. . .] Oh dear, kick it around; I will write again in an hour or so when I have time to consider." Both Degener and Sweeney were Catholic, more or less, and Irish fantasists too, so perhaps they could not be shocked by the magic thinking by which Sexton found milk in blood or "star" in "rats" or "live" in "evil."

Around the time Sexton was putting the finishing touches on "The Jesus Papers" in the late summer of 1971, the reviewers were receiving *Transformations*. Houghton Mifflin threw a lavish party at Sardi's at the end of September to inaugurate the book, and Sexton pulled together a grand invitation list, including her champions Louis Untermeyer and Howard Moss; Fred Morgan, Paula Dietz, and Irene Skolnick from *The Hudson Review,* which she credited with discovering her; Tony Hecht and his new wife; Ben Shaktman and his new wife; the loyal Alice Smith; Gloria Steinem (whom Sexton hadn't met but adored at a distance); and a gaggle of other New York poets and editors who had welcomed her work. The director, producer, and cast of *Mercy Street* held a reunion at the party, too. It was altogether a happy occasion for her.

She returned to New York a week later to read from *Transformations* at the YMHA, on a program with Tony Hecht, which drew a large crowd. Shortly afterward she was delighted to learn that the Saturday Review Book Club was buying the book for sale to subscribers ("Never did I think I was writing poems for a book club," she told Howard Moss).

Reviewers praised the book as "delightfully accessible" and observed that the poems invited reading aloud. *The Radcliffe Quarterly* printed an admiring interview, dubbing Sexton "a contemporary witch." Demurrers mentioned the tediousness of "hip allusions" and the dilution of authentic terror by a Disneyland effect, "the flashing of the strobe lights and the piped-in bonging of the vibes." Since Sexton hoped for a popular success, even these negative reviews said the right things. The book quickly found its audience, and after only a month in print *Transformations* had earned Sexton $6400 in royalties, or $1400 over and above Houghton Mifflin's advance of $5000 — a record for her on both counts.

These were good earnings from a book of poems, but Sexton had her eye on another prize: a permanent position at Boston University. She was still on a one-year contract as a special lecturer, half-time, in the creative writing program. While George Starbuck appreciated her talents as a teacher, the more influential English professors remained skeptical. Sexton heard rumors that students were being warned by senior faculty members not to take her course. Moreover, the university was having financial difficulties. She was relieved when her contract was finally renewed — in August, for the semester beginning in September — even though faculty salaries had been frozen.

Good luck came her way that autumn, however, when she received another honorary degree, this one from Fairfield University, a small liberal arts college in Connecticut. Sexton shared the award with Senator Margaret Chase Smith, Sarah Caldwell, director of the Boston Opera, and actress Ruby Dee. Under pressure from the women's movement, colleges all over the country were seeking "role models" to set before women students. Around the same time, Colgate University — Kayo's college — offered her the Crashaw Chair in Literature for the spring semester in 1972, February through May. The appointment would carry the rank of full professor and a salary of $13,000.

When Sexton updated her professional résumé for Boston University's files that fall, she was able to list a new book of poems (her fifth), another honorary doctorate (her third), and appointment as a distinguished visiting professor at another institution. She thought these items might provide some leverage with the English Department, where her salary had been set at $7000 for the same number of courses she would be teaching at Colgate the following spring. She wrote a polite letter to the chairman of the department, mentioning her Colgate salary and suggesting that he do something for her: "There is money to think about and some sort of permanence to think about." Hinting got no results; the following year she was more direct. "If John Barth doesn't come back next year and you pay his replacement four grand per course more than I am getting I'm going to wonder if a woman's fist shouldn't be painted on my classroom door," she warned Starbuck. In September 1972, Sexton was appointed a half-time full professor, with a salary of $10,000 for a semester's work and a five-year contract.

The Sextons were still quite strapped for money; otherwise it seems likely that she would have turned down the Crashaw Chair at Colgate. The position required a long weekly journey so she could teach two days of classes back to back. Moreover, she was expected to teach a lecture course on poetry in the afternoon as well as a writing work-shop for ten or so students in the evening. It was the lecture course she worried about — she had never even attended such a course, let alone prepared one. With the help of Bruce Berlind, the chairman of Col-gate's English Department, she worked out a syllabus: she would offer a series of eleven lectures titled "Anne on Anne," for delivery to a small group of English majors. The students would participate by en-gaging imaginatively with the life of the writer, "a total immersion." They too would write poems, sometimes the continuation of a poem by Anne Sexton. They would study her worksheets, watching a poem clamber from false starts into published form. They would also write an "interview," fabricating a person from details in her poems and lectures. All along they would be discussing the transformation of a living human being into the persona of a poem.

Sexton worked diligently on her lectures. While from one point of view the course had a scandalously egotistical agenda, from another it could — and did — enable a skilled crafter of poems to show students how she achieved her effects. Since Sexton never published book re-views or essays on poetics, these lecture notes provide unique access to her view of contemporary poetry and her place in it.

She comments efficiently, for example, on the "lyric instances" that flow from empathy. These need not be blissful, she asserts. "Ugliness, sin, depravity, wretchedness, wickedness are equally orthodox and useful subjects for a lyric poem." Empathy requires projection of one's inner life onto another person; the resulting persona should sound au-tobiographical, and that requires deep identification. "The rapist. What moment of his life would you pick to tell about? While he's hav-ing a cup of coffee at Howard Johnson's? [. . .] Perhaps he eats a clam roll. I myself like clam rolls but I have more than a clam roll in com-mon with the rapist. What have I ever wanted to take? When have I ever wanted to scare and terrify? [. . .] If you will look around you with eyes stripped you will hear voices calling from the crowd. Each has his own love song. Each has a moment of violence. Each has a moment of despair." But, she observes, identification or empathy is an imaginative state, different from truth-telling. "Sometimes the soul takes pictures of things it has wished for but never seen." Denying one critic's claim that her own work was always related "intimately and painfully" to her life, Sexton commented, "I use the personal when I am applying a mask to my face [. . .] like a rubber mask that the robber wears."

Surely Sexton also was nurtured by this process of review and evaluation, which licensed her to survey her own creation and find it good. She was working on the Crashaw lectures during the months she was writing the celebratory poems of "O Ye Tongues," and it seems likely that these two activities encouraged each other. In fact, in this period Sexton had at hand nearly all the poetry she was ever to write. *The Book of Folly* was complete; she was only waiting a decent interval before selling it to Houghton Mifflin. Ambitious about being seen someday as a fiction writer, she feared that her stories would be lost to posterity if she didn't smuggle them into a book of poems, so she considered including some in *Folly*: "The Letting Down of the Hair" (which she described as "an allegory for my devotion to poetry"), written in the early 1960s, and the more recent "Ballet of the Buffoon" and "All God's Children Need Radios." These, she claimed to Brian Sweeney, were actually "prose poems that I call stories."

At the same time Sexton had two additional book manuscripts in process: *The Death Notebooks,* which she would complete in June 1972 with a centerpiece sequence titled "The Furies," and a sequence titled "Letters to Dr. Y.," which C. K. Williams persuaded her to leave unpublished until she could find an appropriate artistic context. *The Death Notebooks* was to be the last book published during her lifetime, and "O Ye Tongues" the last poem in it. Though Sexton went on writing poems until the week of her death, nothing after "O Ye Tongues" was so full of her peculiar artistic daring and yet so formally controlled. And while she referred to it in letters as a "major work," she did not include it in public readings. Perhaps she too regarded this sequence as a culmination, a transformation of her entire career into legend.

19

AWFUL ROWING
1972–1973

DURING A SPRING BREAK from Colgate, Sexton spent a week on a Florida beach, shaded from the sun by a big umbrella and peacefully watching the waves roll in. These waves, or their twins farther up the Atlantic coast, recurred in the poems she wrote during the next two years, whenever she sought an image for serenity, as in "The Consecrating Mother."

> I stand before the sea
> and it rolls and rolls in its green blood
> saying, "Do not give up one god
> for I have a handful."
> The trade winds blew
> in their twelve-fingered reversal
> and I simply stood on the beach
> while the ocean made a cross of salt
> and hung up its drowned
> and they cried *Deo Deo*.

Sexton was tired. Kayo's new business had been very slow getting started, and financial worries dogged them. She was holding up her end by teaching, but the Colgate commute made her so anxious that she complained constantly of nausea and was finding it hard to keep down her meals. She lived on what she called "mother food": hot chocolate and scrambled eggs and thick milkshakes. Again her weight was rising. "I had to buy a size 18 bathing suit," she admitted with chagrin. She and Kayo had decided it would be worth it to blow some money by staying at the Beach Club in Fort Lauderdale, where they could relax together and splurge a bit on wine and food. Kayo played golf all day while Anne snoozed and read on the beach. "If I could do just what I wanted, I'd live in the ocean," she liked to say.

At the end of the Colgate term, Sexton went into the hospital for minor surgery, during which the screws were removed at long last from her mended hip. Hospitalizations always opened a mother lode of imagery. During her recuperation Sexton began a sequence of poems on animals, later collected in her posthumous volume *45 Mercy Street* as "Bestiary U.S.A.," and another sequence she titled "The Furies." Its opening poem ("The Fury of Beautiful Bones") recalled her old romance with George Starbuck, into whose arms she had escaped from the horror of hospital visits to her dying mother in 1959. "I was the fury of your bones," the poem remembers, inviting a reading of Starbuck's cryptic dedication of *Bone Thoughts*. The poems coded Sexton's relationship to Sylvia Plath as well, in imagery and pared-down lines redolent of Plath's *Ariel*. For all that, the sequence unfolded along an arc of feeling that was authentically Sexton's, anchored in relief at her own survival:

> breakfast like a dream
> and the whole day to live through,
> steadfast, deep, interior.
> After the death,
> after the black of black,
> this lightness —
> not to die, not to die —
> that God begot.

She worked on a third sequence that summer as well, poems on child abuse that she collected under the title "The Children's Crusade" and sent to the editor of *Harper's*, with a note saying she felt that taken together, the group had "the strength of a novel." These, like "The Furies," she planned to save for book publication in her posthumous volume *The Death Notebooks*, but, chronically short of cash, she also wanted immediate serial publication of all new work the instant she thought it was ready for print. (A year later she explained to J. D. McClatchy that she had decided to bring out *The Death Notebooks* before her death because "I fell in love with the fury poems and decided 'oh foo to that idea.' Anyhow, I'm not going to die for a long time.")

Many of the poems Sexton wrote in 1972 reflect her contentment with suburban life. She loved the mornings in her house. Climbing out of bed, she would shiver her way to the bathroom, her chirping "Br-r-r-rt! Brrrrt!" announcing to the world that she was awake. In a fancy peignoir she would make her way to the sunny kitchen for scrambled eggs, flip the radio to soft music, sip coffee, and read awhile in the sun. The kitchen was a mother-place, whereas in the study, the darker currents of family life flowed into the lines her fingers released from the typewriter.

Released herself from many of the stresses of family life, in the 1970s Sexton worked with more social awareness than before. Students arrived at her door, and so did loads of mail, affirming daily that her work bound her to others and anchored her at many points of connection. Sequences she wrote in 1972, such as "The Children's Crusade" and another, never published, on "Dog-God," show her trying to fit her own experiences into frameworks of cultural critiques she absorbed from her reading and from circulating in academic environments. Never a critic herself, Sexton knew her strengths lay in the indirect ways in which new ideas filtered into her consciousness through layers of association she could tap only by turning inward. Poems of "The Children's Crusade" were precipitated by a touching story she heard from her secretary, Jean Moulton, but drew their power from her own guilts, while the "Dog-God" poems showed what satire she could make from being a poet in secular America, "fighting the dollars." She started calling herself "Ms. Dog."

Now that the manuscript of *The Book of Folly* was ready for publication by Houghton Mifflin, Sexton had to confront head on the problems that had been gathering with her English publisher. Jon Stallworthy had been dubious about both of her last two books. *Love Poems*, he told her, "we find less persuasive than those of 'The Song of Solomon,' say, or Marvell's 'To His Coy Mistress,' or Donne's 'The Anniversarie.' You do not always convince us that the cause of celebration justifies the fireworks." Stallworthy's view was seconded in print by reviewer Ian Hamilton's dismissal of *Love Poems* as "a dead end," though other reviews were favorable; for example, the *Guardian*'s Christopher Driver acknowledged faults but allowed Sexton's voice the power to inject "whole phrases and stanzas into the memory without one noticing it." *Love Poems* sold out its first British edition of a thousand copies in two years. That was a respectable rate of sales for a book of poetry, but Oxford did not reprint it, and when Stallworthy accepted *Transformations* for publication in 1972, he was forthright about his misgivings. "We will be happy to do our very best for *Transformations* [. . .] but I think we both have to accept that the direction you are taking — and good luck to you — is not the direction our list is taking." He added, "If our lines were with your next book to converge again, no-one would be more delighted." As Stallworthy predicted, British reviewers were unkind to *Transformations*; the poems "might be expected to appeal to a fairly sophisticated but undemanding American adolescent," sniffed the *Times Literary Supplement*.

With these exchanges in the background, Sexton decided in August to feel Stallworthy out before she had Cindy Degener send him the manuscript of *The Book of Folly,* due to be published by Houghton Mifflin in November. Would Oxford continue to publish her in Britain? *Transformations* had been a "departure," she claimed, "just as one might look up from the page and have his husband tell them a joke and smile for a moment and then return to the written word." It was Stallworthy's criticism of *Love Poems* that needed clarification. "Perhaps I'm getting too loose, leaving the strict poems behind me, the intricate forms, all those wild animals in their cage. Do you think that?" No, Stallworthy replied. "Not because you were moving away from 'form' — some of the best poets now writing have done that — but because [. . .] you were perhaps becoming too much aware of your audience."

His letter must have settled the question in Sexton's mind. She sent him a gay little note that he didn't recognize as a goodbye, then she followed up a lead with Chatto & Windus, sending *Folly* to poetry editor D. J. Enright. When Stallworthy heard the rumor that one of Oxford's authors had submitted a manuscript to Chatto, he recalled, "My immediate reaction was fury. Enright said it was Anne Sexton. Then I understood. With wonderful tact she had written me an extremely nice letter in which she hadn't mentioned a book, gave no indication — and made her move. Great delicacy on the part of Anne."

Looking back on that turning point, Stallworthy thought the problem was that Sexton misjudged the British audience, just as she had done at the Poetry International Festival in London five years earlier. He noted that the change in her poetry's quality did not seem to affect her American reputation. "The media in America are always looking for a new boxer and a new film star and a new poet. The intense spotlight of celebrity in which the Lowells and Sextons are put is difficult for a poet."

From this point of view, Sexton's continuing popularity, as measured in sales of her books, was less significant than the negative critical responses published in influential journals in defining her value as an artist for the British audience. *The Book of Folly* did receive some respectful notices in Britain along with the scathing ones, but all reviewers found Sexton's confessional style derivative of Plath, and less interesting. (American reviewers tended to claim defensively that Sexton had been composing poems of psychic torment "before Sylvia Plath, and with as much violence.") Moreover, there was no equivalent in Britain of the women's poetry movement in America, which was making writers into scouts at a new cultural frontier. Stallworthy reduced Sexton's popularity to the category of mere "celebrity" like that surrounding Lowell, missing the salience of age and gender. The poet and critic Anne Stevenson, however, put these together in an ambitious, disapproving overview of the American poetry scene published shortly after Sexton's death. "Perhaps a serious fault of creative-writing classes is that they have failed, in America, to make this distinction between art and life," she wrote. "Sensitive students, seeking a meaning in life, or a justification of their own abnormality in American society, turn to poetry as an alternative to reality — and a way of redeeming themselves, at the same time, from social insignificance."

Stevenson was right. It was the accepted notion of the "abnormality" or "social insignificance" of women's experience as a subject for art that made Plath's themes of rage and vengeance so heady a model for young writers, especially women, and in America, at least, this insight fueled a social movement in which grassroots feminism was the theory, grassroots poetry the practice. Among students and among women readers, Plath and Sexton were necessary aids to understanding hysteria as resistance to social programming. Consequently, writing poetry in the manner of Plath and Sexton became a mode of consciousness-raising. Thus what a poetry reviewer might dismiss as morbid self-preoccupation, another interested reader might welcome as liberating candor. Women poets and critics, of course, had the most at stake in deciding which kind of reader to be, for gender would always be perceived as salient in their case.

But Sexton worked outside the arena of public debate. She neither reviewed books nor commented on the social purposes of art. Her attitude to such questions is probably best captured in an observation she made to a Japanese translator of her work around the time she was readying *The Death Notebooks* for publication. Trying to classify her work, Yorifumi Yaguchi asked whether she had been an "academic" or a "beatnik" writer at the outset. "I think I belong to the academics by coincidence," she replied. Was she in fact a confessional writer? "Not everything I document is factual." Was she a feminist? "I suppose there is social criticism in my poems. I don't know. I try to write true to life."

The question of whether she was a feminist bothered Sexton, possibly because of the word's associations with anger. When a woman on the faculty of the University of California at Santa Cruz wrote asking for advice about a women's studies course, she chided, "Just remember that women are human first." To another scholar she wrote, "I have always first tried to be human but the voice is a woman's and was from the beginning, intimate and female." Later, when she was invited by the painter Miriam Schapiro to contribute a note to a catalogue for a Seven-Day Women's Art Festival at Cal Arts in Los Angeles, Sexton took some pains with the assignment, yet gave no emphasis whatever to the question of gender; indeed, she sounded very much like Rilke in *Letters to a Young Poet*: "The most important thing is to find the deep underground voice of your own self. [. . .] Remember at all times to honor the work of other writers [. . .] keep their books around and let those books love you in your honest endeavor to tell it true."

Still, she was pleased by letters she received from young women writers such as Susan Fromberg, Mary Gordon, and Cynthia Macdonald, as well as Erica Jong, who warmly acknowledged the crucial support she received from Sexton's example and then Sexton's friendship just when her own career was taking off. Jong's letters, written in big loopy handwriting in purple ink on mauve stationery, arrived in Weston like blasts of energy. At the time she first wrote to Sexton, she had one book of poems in print and another on the way, and was working on *Fear of Flying,* the novel that established her reputation as a fantasist of sex. Sexton's blend of sexual and spiritual themes attracted Jong's lasting admiration. "If Anne had stuck around another ten years, the world might have caught up with her," she later remarked.

Sexton retained her interest in writing for the theater, and now and then pressed Cindy Degener to circulate the script of *Mercy Street*. So Degener was delighted to contact her with some unexpected news:

Wesley Balk, director of the University of Minnesota's Chamber Theater, had decided to develop an opera based on *Transformations*. The commission was offered to Conrad Susa, a young composer who had written music for Broadway shows and for the Globe Shakespeare Festival in San Diego.

In mid-September Balk and Susa began assigning lines to voices, searching for the "visual poetry or physical metaphors" that would bring the words to life as spectacle. Aiming for a performance of ninety minutes, they winnowed the work to ten poems. By the end of two weeks' rehearsal, the cast had questions about the meanings of lines and images. It seemed time to involve the poet, so Susa flew to Boston. "I had my own agenda, too," he recalled. "I wanted to expose myself like a Petri dish to Anne Sexton — take in the sound of her voice, the rhythm of her speech, hear the way *she* would read these texts. I knew I would have to have that voice inside me in order to become Anne Sexton, demons and all."

They met at Joseph's, Sexton's favorite Boston restaurant, for lunch. Sexton was a very good customer and could count on getting the table she liked best, in a quiet corner two steps up from the main room. When Susa arrived she was already seated, looking every inch the businesswoman. "I felt like a supplicant, approaching those stairs," Susa remembered. He found Sexton cordial about the plans to abridge her work for performance and reassuring about the problems of interpretation that the cast was undergoing. Feeling that he had her blessing on the project, Susa went home to San Francisco and, as he put it, "began pouring colored sand around Anne Sexton's pebbles." Once or twice he wrote to her about the work, but mainly he let the words lead him inward. "One morning I went in to brush my teeth," he recalled, "and the mirror greeted me: 'Good day, Mama.' I recognized that the demons were going to take care of themselves."

But Sexton's demons were pursuing her full force. Between 10 and 30 January 1973 she wrote — "with two days out for despair and three days out in a mental hospital" — thirty-nine poems, a whole volume: *The Awful Rowing Toward God*. She framed the book in two poems that provided beginning and end, as of a narrative: "Rowing" and "The Rowing Endeth." The poems between were short, loosely organized explosions of imagery; the theme, if it can be generalized, was self-disgust. Yet the poems flowed from a seizure of energy that felt to her like hope, and the resulting imagery had the urgency of exploration. Every day at five P.M. she would phone Maxine Kumin, who was writer-in-residence at Centre College in Kentucky for six weeks that winter, and go over the day's work. Kumin remembered being worried about how agitated Sexton seemed — "She was writing like a fugitive one length ahead of the posse" — and thought it had been a mistake for Sexton to go off Thorazine; her friend's manic energy reminded her uncomfortably of the stories told about Sylvia Plath writing *Ariel* at white heat.

In early February Sexton gave the manuscript to Cindy Degener, who would negotiate the contract with Houghton Mifflin, and began doling out several pages at a time to Howard Moss at *The New Yorker*, who rarely accepted poems from her these days. She also sent the whole manuscript to colleagues at Boston University, hoping for detailed criticism; she knew the work was still fairly raw. Her next-door officemate, John Malcolm Brinnin, wrote encouragingly without giving specific advice: "That's a fairly astonishing twenty-day sea harvest & I should think you could spend months selecting & examining what your net has hauled in." George Starbuck more or less ignored his copy, and later regretted it. "When you were close enough — courtin' distance — she did exhaust all of us," he said ruefully. But he recognized that "she was trying out new ways to shape a poem," and he knew how much she could profit from the rigorous criticism the manuscript cried out for.

Sexton did find one critic willing to give her manuscript a working-over just as he had in the old days: James Wright. She had decided to dedicate the volume to him and to Brother Dennis Farrell, perhaps because they had been sources of religious insights. She wrote an affectionate letter to Wright, enclosing the manuscript, and signed it with his old name of endearment, Bee. He returned the poems promptly, but not the sentiment. "I have no intention of excusing your bad verse and your bad prose," he scrawled at the bottom of her letter to him. "There are some poems here that I think are fine. There are some that I think are junk. The choice between them is yours. — C[omfort]." Down the righthand margins of the pages Wright's pedantic, impassioned marginalia argued with both Sexton's craft and her theology. "Leave God his own poems, and cut these lines out. God damn it Bee, stop trying to be a saint. Be a poet, and get rid of the junk." On "The Earth Falls Down" he commanded, "Delete this poem. For Christ's sake, Bee, read Jung's analysis of *Job*." He urged her to abandon all but three lines of "After Auschwitz," adding, "Bee, what I ask is a terrible sacrifice. But *listen, listen*; trust your own strange voice."

Sexton reacted with chagrin to these exhortations, sometimes scratching deep black X's through the pages he disliked. Then she passed along the manuscript to Kumin, who patiently defended much that Wright had attacked. "The Fallen Angels" elicited a typical tug-of-war. Wright had turned the right margin into a niggle of dispute over the nature of heaven, culminating in the advice "Bee, stop making stupid cute remarks about angels. We don't even know enough about each other." Sexton had X'ed the poem, but Kumin came to its defense in the left margin: "I like this poem — it isn't intended as a deep theological investigation but a way of hoarding up the good signs, or omens to keep going." Sexton readmitted the poem to the book, along with other poems, stanzas, and images that Wright disputed. Undoubtedly, she should have given his advice more weight; reviewers later echoed his criticisms. Nonetheless, the final version of *The Awful Rowing* reflected his intervention. Imploring her to "*listen, listen*" and to "strip the language and shackle accidents," he had guided Sexton's attention to arbitrary similes and rhythmically wooden passages, which she was sometimes able to revise. But it was to Maxine Kumin that Sexton owed the completion of the book. As always, Kumin encouraged more than she disparaged, keeping the channels open and helping Sexton recognize the shaping principles in her own work, not proposing different ones.

Sexton continued to play the same role in the development of Kumin's work, helping the externalization of an inner voice. It happened that Sexton was invited to serve as a juror for the 1973 Pulitzer Prize, the year Harper published Maxine Kumin's *Up Country: Poems of New England*. Sixty-nine books of poetry were nominated that year, including several by poets Sexton knew well — her protégé C. K. Williams, among others. When the jury — William Alfred, Louis Simpson, and Sexton — awarded the prize to Kumin, Sexton confided to a friend that she had argued passionately for *Up Country* yet dreaded to get her way, since she was aware that Kumin's receiving the prize would "work to my own detriment — I was going to lose her." As Sexton foresaw, the prize consolidated Kumin's reputation as an important writer and changed her life. From then on she traveled more, spending whole semesters teaching in faraway places, and when she returned, she retreated "up country" to the farm in New Hampshire as soon as possible. Sexton and Kumin still talked at length on the phone every day, from wherever they happened to be, and they still oversaw the progress of each poem, without exception, that either of

them wrote. But gone were the old days of easy dropping-by, the summers spent in Sexton's back yard, where they took turns standing in
the shallow end of the pool at the typewriter balanced on the ledge,
giggling and plotting the next pages of the children's books they wrote
for money.

On 3 February, Anne and Kayo held a reception at 14 Black Oak
Road for Billie, who had remarried after a long courtship. In her late
sixties, Billie was still a handsome, active woman. Her daughter's
death four years earlier had left her very lonely, and Anne supported
her decision: "Catch your chance to be really happy!" she advised.
The timing was ironic, however, for by the date of the wedding, Anne
had decided to divorce Kayo. She waved her mother-in-law off on a
honeymoon and began devising the end of her own marriage.

Divorce had sometimes appealed as a solution to their problems
earlier, but Sexton had always come back to the recognition that Kayo

Maxine Kumin and her dog, Caesar.

filled deep needs. Now the balance seemed to have shifted. During the years that her network of friends and colleagues had spread and strengthened, Kayo had grown increasingly distant and again prone to explosions of violent rage.

At two separate times in the marriage, when prodded, Kayo had entered treatment to address these problems. During one particularly frightening episode in 1969, Anne had begged Linda to phone the police. The officers called to the scene reported that "Mr. Sexton admitted to the story as told by Mrs. Sexton. He stated that he can only take it so far, then he loses his head and physically attacks her." The report added that the Sextons "have two such fights each year." The daughters remembered, though, that explosions occurred more frequently than this, perhaps monthly; they formed part of the routine of family life. "Daddy didn't seem to know how to be tender," Joy recalled, "didn't know how to give a gentle hug. He expressed affection in little slaps." Then, in 1971, what seemed to Anne an ominous new development in the pattern occurred when Kayo blew up and hit Joy. Though the blow was never repeated, his verbal assaults on Joy continued, especially at the dinner table. This put Anne in mind of her own father's nastiness at the dinner table in years past; she was well aware of the emotional damage this could do an adolescent daughter.

Thinking back on the marriage, Kayo Sexton acknowledged his tension and his intemperance. His consultations with Dr. Leiderman hadn't helped much, in his view, because they didn't get to the root of the problem, which was partly the way he and Anne used drinking to license their worst abuses of each other. "It always happened when we'd had two or three drinks before dinner," he recalled. "Anne had a mouth like the needle on a Singer sewing machine. She'd start in on me and I'd blow up. Afterward she would walk around with a hurt look — it was always all my fault. She had a way of making me the goat." The changes brought about in their lives by Sexton's therapy burdened him in many ways, he felt. "From the time she started seeing Martin Orne, I became the unwanted third party. From then on, I felt that if I interfered between her and her doctors, I'd have to pay the price of her breaking down." In time, Kayo had grown aware of his wife's intimate relationships with other men, including Dr. Zweizung. "I would overhear her talking on the phone. She wasn't particularly careful." Never addressing her directly about the pressures her illness and her fame laid on him, he let his fury explode from time to time. "Somebody was always paying the price of living with her. Always, it was me."

The turning point came in mid-January, during Sexton's seizure of productivity. Joy recalled that she had been "plotting and planning her escape," preparing Joy for some months. "I felt as if I were being seduced into some *caper* of hers," Joy recalled. Upon returning from Westwood Lodge, Sexton told Kayo, "Our marriage is on the rocks," a phrase she often used, according to Joy; but this time she added that she wanted a divorce. To her lawyer — for whom she was trying to establish a strong case against Kayo — Sexton claimed that the primary cause was the attrition in their sexual relationship. She attributed the timing of this decision to her newly established independence from Thorazine, which gave her a feeling that she might make other, equally health-giving choices about her life. "I went off [Thorazine] very, very slowly," Sexton told her lawyer, "and all my feelings rushed out over the fall and winter. It was obvious my husband could not stand me this way. I was beginning to get more independent, less drugged, a little bit angrier (naturally not striking anyone) and more talkative." In a statement written for the lawyer, Dr. Chase seconded the view that Sexton had recently shown significant gains and that the decision to seek a divorce was reasonable.

Once she had resolved to leave Kayo, Sexton laid plans. On a predetermined Sunday, she sent Joy to stay with Louise and Loring Conant, good friends who lived nearby, in Wellesley. Then she slipped over to a neighbor's — the home of Kayo's best friend — and asked him to stand by her while she informed Kayo of her decision. The neighbor had seen a lot of the Sextons' ups and downs and agreed to let her phone Kayo to meet her there. Sexton later told her lawyer that she had hoped she could explain herself gently and lengthily to him, but that the encounter had been very brief. As she described it, Kayo had simply told her, "You are crazy. You don't know what you're doing." Then he had turned on his heel and gone home. Expecting a violent reaction (which never materialized), Sexton hired a bodyguard.

Many years later, Kayo was still baffled by Anne's decision to leave him. "The Sunday afternoon when she said, 'Get out of the house, I want a divorce,' I didn't know what the hell was going on," he recalled. "I have wondered, was it brought about by her meteoric rise, by having too much money, too much of a sense of power? Her head was turned by adulation and all that business. I suppose I tried to build a shell around myself — just do this, keep the family going, and don't inquire, don't think about it. That probably didn't help Anne at all. But I honestly don't know, never have known, what her real, driving motive was in the divorce. Which is another reason why it absolutely drove me into the floor like a nail when she did it."

For the next few weeks, Sexton's life was thoroughly disrupted. She camped like a Gypsy in the homes of sympathetic friends, to whom the separation didn't come as a surprise. Most shared the view of Barbara Swan: "Kayo was a sweet man in his way . . . he tried. But his mind was tuned to a different wavelength." Others saw it as ominous; Lois Ames, who had been through a divorce, tried to talk Sexton out of this decision. Both daughters were angry at the way their mother was treating their father, who seemed hurt and bewildered, and they refused to side with her against him.

Whatever their views, Sexton's friends rallied to insure that she was not alone. Maintaining a parody of home life (but with her bodyguard in tow), she stayed first with the Kumins, then with her old friend Rita Ernst in Newton. On weekends she joined Joy at Louise and Loring Conant's. "Anne ran the spectrum from endearing to infuriating," Loring Conant recalled, laughing. "We were literally invaded." Her constant smoking afflicted him, and her incessant drinking worried him. Yet both Conants found her a source of spiritual nurturing. As an example, Loring remembered how Sexton brought him a bottle of wonderful German wine for his birthday. "She toasted me with it, and then she began to free-associate, transforming the palate into all sorts of visual and auditory images. A profusion of images would just pour forth from her. She created an atmosphere of freedom around her that seemed marvelous to me. And she called forth Louise's creativity — Louise's poetry simply caught fire." From Louise's point of view, the advent of Sexton in her existence was like a miracle: difficult to integrate with normal life, but a blessing nonetheless. "Anyone on whom Anne turned her full attention felt cherished and exalted," she wrote in her diary. "Her warmth was like having the sun turned on full."

Sexton's women friends made the break from Kayo feel like an exciting new start, not a calamity. Max and Lois were mainstays, but she also had new friends to share the burden of rearranging her life. Particularly helpful was her Weston neighbor Maryel Locke, a handsome, businesslike woman who was studying for a law degree. When the Sextons separated, Locke's loyalty went to Anne, as she identified with the suburban housewife who had broken the rules and won a Pulitzer Prize. She helped Anne find a lawyer and pull together documents that would make a favorable case if Kayo challenged her mental health.

Louise Conant was drawn to Sexton for similar reasons. Sexton fascinated her, both as a person and as a poet. Later, as Sexton had more and more financial worries, the Conants paid Linda's tuition at Harvard, and at crucial junctures Louise stepped into the role of a mother for Joy. "I loved staying with the Conants," Joy recalled. "They were the real-life examples of my ideal, the station-wagon family. When I was a kid and talk of a new car would come up, I always wanted us to buy a station wagon. I thought that would make us a normal family. The Conants were that kind of family."

Lois Ames, 1970.

Finally, after a court hearing in March, Kayo moved out of 14 Black Oak Road and Anne reclaimed the house, which would be hers from then on. The family Dalmatians, Penny and Daisy, became her constant companions, moving from room to room with her as she worked or visited with guests. She also advertised for a live-in couple, to help with expenses and to keep the house from feeling too empty at night. By early April Sexton wrote with satisfaction to Alice Smith that she had found a delightful pair, Simon and Sandra Fahey: "He's very kind to dogs and people. His wife, quiet, I adore . . . she is very wise. They are doing most of the cooking and he is paying for ground work and going to run the pool." The Faheys remained until Thanksgiving, when the relationship became burdensome on all sides.

One of the major casualties of Sexton's divorce was her relationship with Billie, who learned the unwelcome news on her honeymoon. Not surprisingly, this action and its timing plunged her into abiding bitterness. Years later, she spoke to Linda about the cascades of unhappiness that had poured into her life from the day of her son's elopement to the day of his divorce. Linda, taken aback, drew from her grandmother's outburst the insight that for Billie, Anne's illness and her poetry were the same; from Billie's point of view, Anne "was getting rewarded for writing about an illness which had brought her family to its knees." Success had allowed her to spend whatever health she regained on art, keeping Billie in bondage all the years the children were growing up; moreover, Anne wrote about things that in Billie's view ought to remain utterly private. For Billie, Anne's desertion of Kayo was the last, and the unforgivable, outrage.

Despite the domestic turbulence, Sexton kept up a full professional schedule that winter and spring. Accompanied by Lois Ames, she flew to Minneapolis in May for the preview performance of *Transformations*. Conrad Susa had written several times for help in working out the implications of imagery, and they had arranged to meet privately for a celebratory drink before the performance. Sexton looked smashing in a floor-length dress printed with giant red hibiscuses. "She wore clothes like a professional beauty," Susa recalled. "Yet I marked about her appearance something wildly asymmetrical — at once sleek and clumsy." She told him that she was very nervous about the opera. "Trying to be helpful, I offered her one of my tranquilizers. This cracked her up. She opened her big purse and showed me an enormous stock of pills — bottles and bottles of pills."

Sexton was quite explicit about the source of her nervousness: she was concerned about the way he had staged the Rapunzel scene, perhaps her most radical departure from the tale she had found in Grimm. The story of an erotic relationship between an older woman and a teenage girl, Sexton's "Rapunzel" was to Susa an emotional high point in the opera, "a dome of vocal exaltation." His model was Monteverdi's *Orfeo,* he explained, in which stunning theatrical effects and frequent use of recitative give a privileged place to language. Keeping Sexton's text intact, Susa had evolved what he labeled "a musical entertainment" for eight singers and eight instrumentalists.

Much of the rest of the opera was set in *parlando* style, in which measures were meant to be sung with the rhythm of speech: "The singers should remember that they are telling stories, not indulging themselves," Susa cautioned. The opera accentuates the carnival daring of Sexton's work and makes the river of fear running through *Transformations* fully accessible. "Those familiar with Anne Sexton's poetry will know that she can be entertaining without necessarily being funny," Susa observed in a program note.

Not sure what Sexton's reactions would be, Susa hung back from her during the intermission. "But while I was sneaking back to my seat as the houselights dimmed, she spotted me and shouted across the aisle, 'Conrad, you're a genius!' She hugged and kissed me, to a smattering of applause, quite dramatic. I was thrilled." At the end of the performance, Susa led Sexton to the stage for a curtain call, and as the audience rose to its feet she embraced each singer in turn. It was a high moment for her poetry.

The opera went on to be produced in Madison, Boston, Houston, Amsterdam, and San Francisco, and a performance telecast by PBS reached large audiences. Following the New York première, music critic Andrew Porter called it "one of the brightest and best of recent American operas. [. . .] A cunning theater piece." He ranked Susa's witty, allusive score with Stravinsky's *Renard* and Kurt Weill's *Mahagonny* in scale and tunefulness: "a delightful entertainment that is not trivial." Susa was satisfied, too, with the collaboration. "I didn't make over *Transformations,* I gave Anne Sexton an opera," is the way he put it. "Sexton wrote the poems, but I wrote a libretto."

In spite of this triumph, by early summer the loneliness of divorce was setting in. Sexton's friends were bored, Linda was away for the summer, and Joy was trying to live her own life. Sexton wanted a companion, so she began probing her old friendships for possibilities. She spent an evening with Ben Shaktman and several evenings with Philip Rahv. By chance, her ardent fan Phil Legler had dropped her a line in March; when he heard the news of her impending divorce, he immediately began arranging for her to give another reading at Northern Michigan University. All his old feeling for her surged back. "Oh Crazy Annie Baby," he wrote in May, "my whole being has been responding to you these days. It's the disease — the abundance, the intensity. Wow." They exchanged several letters, then they began holding long conversations, Legler phoning from his office or making excursions from home late in the evening to call from pay phones. By June, as Sexton wrote to a friend, he was "sending flowers every day, four letters a day, daily phone calls, and is married. He is a very sweet guy, but has no sense of proportion."

In early July, Sexton spent a week in Michigan with Legler, who more or less moved into the lodge where the university put her up for the week. They sat late in the bar or by the big stone fireplace, talking with the locals as if their other lives didn't exist. During this trip Sexton began suffering with her teeth and developed a bad sinus infection; then, at the airport just before departure for Boston, she went into a trance state that frightened Legler so much he decided to accompany her home. They spent another week together in Weston.

By the time Legler left Boston to return to his family, Sexton was deeply in love with him. They began scheming about ways to get together secretly. Sexton wrote to some friends about arranging, or faking, invitations that would bring him to Boston. They were equally desperate for each other's company, but Sexton wanted to have Legler around full-time, not only because she was anguished by being alone, though she certainly was, but also because, as she wrote him, "you gave me back my body." Making love with him surprised her with the deepest sexual and sensual fulfillment she had ever known.

They managed to spend another ten days together in mid-August by finagling residencies at the Bread Loaf Writers' Conference, where they dubbed each other "Camp Director" and played at being married. When Legler returned to Michigan to resume his teaching duties, Sexton was miserable. Though her psychiatrist apparently cautioned that she needed "an old-fashioned courtship" before making any new commitments, she threw this advice to the winds and flooded Legler with long erotic letters urging him to leave his marriage, to marry her.

His state of mind may be imagined. After years of erratic employment, he now had a good academic appointment; he had a family to support, and owed much of his current well-being to his wife's loyalty. Despite his enduring passion for Sexton, he was aware that they had dangerously resonant weaknesses and might well destroy each other. He wanted to marry her, yes, but he did not want to abandon his family. She tormented him with letters projecting a future together: "There must be, or one hopes there can be, life shared, a love combining, weaving, rooting together." Little by little Legler began to unweave and uproot himself from her, with sorrowful, vacillating hardheadedness. She resisted; "I refuse — now that I know what real love is — to be a watercolor and wash off," she countered. In a shrewd move, he returned to psychotherapy and let his doctor's advice do the work of disentangling him from this complicated alliance.

While the drama with Legler was unfolding, Sexton's psychiatrist was taking a three-month vacation, leaving Sexton with what she described scathingly as a series of "babysitter" doctors. Linda was in Seattle, working in the mental health department of a children's hospital and living with a boyfriend. These absences placed an unwelcome burden on Joy, who at seventeen was a cheerful, earthy, self-possessed young woman but not up to the task of holding her mother's psyche together. She too went away as much as possible, spending the month of July with the Conants in Maine.

Shortly after Legler returned to Michigan, Joy arrived home to find her mother in an awful state. Sexton had begun having fugues again, falling suddenly into trancelike states from which it was hard to rouse her. Moreover, what she thought to be a sinus infection turned out to be an abscess surrounding two teeth and reaching deep into the nasal cavity. Her eyesight was affected (and it never fully returned to normal; she began wearing bifocals). For weeks she was sleepless, anxious, and in pain, constantly nauseated from the penicillin she took for the abscess and frequently drunk. Max, Lois, and Louise kept an eye on her, but Joy took the brunt. Finally, encouraged by a phone conversation with Linda, Joy began pulling back from her mother's demands, and after one especially horrible evening she gave up trying to cope and drove Sexton to a hospital.

Sexton's temporary psychiatrist arranged for her to enter McLean, where she stayed for five days to undergo extensive examinations. These included an electroencephalogram to check for temporal lobe epilepsy, a condition that would explain the fugue states she was experiencing. These episodes would begin with visual distortions; the walls and floor seemed to shift and heave while her fear mounted into panic. Her eyes would close as she sank deeply inward. To an on-looker, Sexton would seem to be asleep; to a cynical onlooker, she would seem to be faking some kind of attack. The EEG revealed nor-mal brain functioning.

Dr. Chase returned at the end of August, around the time Joy grate-fully went back to boarding school in Maine. Shortly after this, Philip Legler informed Sexton, sorrowfully but finally, that he had decided to remain in his marriage. Sexton took an overdose of what she called her usual bedtime cocktail of sleeping pills on top of quite a lot of vodka, and was treated overnight at Newton-Wellesley Emergency Room, then released in the afternoon. The next evening she took an-other overdose, this time mixing in a dozen or so quinidine pills, which she took for cardiac arrhythmia. She was taken to Westwood Lodge, where she spent two nights. At this point Dr. Chase decided that she should be hospitalized for lengthier treatment, so on 3 Octo-ber, Max accompanied her to the Human Resource Institute of Bos-ton, where she remained for the rest of the month.

Sexton entered the hospital very much against her wishes. For one thing, she was worried about keeping her job at Boston University. She received Dr. Chase's permission to continue meeting her seminar each Thursday afternoon and with the help of friends concealed her hospitalization from colleagues, but she went to class disheveled and disoriented, and the students wondered what was going on with her. Friends who visited were shocked at her chalky, haggard appearance. She had been losing weight steadily since going off Thorazine and now weighted 110 pounds, the same as Joy, who was five feet tall. She looked thin and drawn, her face strangely asymmetrical. The Kumins and Barbara Swan and her husband, Alan Fink, took turns having brief dinners with her early in the evening, since she was expected to return to the hospital for "community meetings," which she detested, each night.

She was in fact miserable much of the time. She disliked the mode of treatment at the HRI, which featured a good deal of group therapy. "This might be okay for a young person going through her first break-down," she told Louise Conant, "but for me it makes no sense." To-ward the end of her first week she was permitted a dinner date with Robert Abzug, a young literature scholar she and Lois Ames had met on a bumpy airplane ride home from a reading engagement at the Li-brary of Congress. They had been at the restaurant for about forty-five minutes when Abzug left the table briefly; when he returned, he found that Sexton had fled. Frantic phone calls located her in Weston. She had grabbed a taxi and gone home "to sleep in her own bed," she told the hospital authorities.

One person who did not visit her at the Human Resource Institute was Linda. Sexton called Linda's room at her Harvard dormitory one evening very tearful, begging her to come for "family night," but Linda refused. Linda remembered this as a hard decision, but she felt that her own independence was at stake. "I didn't want to support the *sickness* anymore. I was angry with her for all the years of hysteria, but I was ambivalent as well. I painted daisies for her on a card, I told her I loved her and believed in her, but I couldn't bear to see her in there."

Sexton was discharged on 29 October. She was to live less than a year afterward, eventually choosing suicide over what she suspected was the looming alternative, permanent hospitalization. She had always feared that her life would end as Nana's had: that she would lose her family home and be permanently hospitalized; that she would lose her mind and reside in the infantile twilight zone of social life reserved for the aged and ill.

During that last year she spent most of her time keeping up appearances. Her live-in companions departed in dismay after the upheavals of the late summer and fall, and although she replaced them with another couple, she increasingly found she needed the services of a paid attendant (often Joan Smith). She managed to meet her classes regularly, because Lois Ames or one of her students would accompany her, and she managed to keep reading engagements by taking friends along. For a time Louise Conant traveled with her, but as her health deteriorated, she more often paid Joan Smith to do so.

Nonetheless, most of the time now Anne Sexton felt truly alone. Joy was out of reach; "Mother," Joy had said to her in exasperation, "you've overloaded my circuits." So was Linda, who avoided the phone calls she was receiving from her mother that year, often several times a day. Sexton made a vow to herself, on one of the many lists she kept at the time, to "stop worrying friends." By the time of her divorce hearing on 5 November, she wished she had never undertaken the separation: broken by losses, she recognized how the routines of family life had upheld a sense of security that she had confused with inward strength.

Worse, her gift was deserting her. Sexton wasn't writing poems anymore; she was writing anguished appeals for attention. With *Awful Rowing* and after, poetry became her principal therapy, as it had been when she first began writing. For a long time she had stimulated herself to creativity by free-associating on the typewriter. The sheer act of moving the inward turmoil onto the page, observing the order inherent in phrase and syntax, told her that she belonged to an order greater than herself that waited everywhere around her, ready to receive her spirit, connect her to others. "God is in your typewriter," she was assured by a priest. Her poems still sounded like Anne Sexton, for she retained the ability to spill words into lines. Crucially missing, though, was the empowering urgency of a new artistic goal.

One reason was her drinking. Alcohol was now Sexton's chief, self-prescribed medication, taken morning, noon, and night. In combination with loneliness, it was lethal to her art. Alcohol helped generate the curves of feeling on which her poetry lifted its wings, but it dropped her too, into depression, remorse, sleeplessness, paranoia — the normal host of furies that pursue alcoholics. More serious for her poetry, it deprived her of "the little critic" in her head that she had formerly summoned to the task of cut, cut, cut, expand, expand, expand, cut, cut, cut. She had the drunk's fluency but not the artist's cunning.

Loneliness was the other killer. Few of her friends enjoyed Sexton's company after she had been drinking; alcohol made her imperious, paranoid, and sensitive to slights, given to quarreling and tantrums. In search of companionship, during the last year of her life she spent hours on the phone late at night, her voice following the westward pace of the moon. The poet William Stafford, who lived in Oregon, remembered receiving warm, slurry calls at what would have been three A.M. in Weston. Sexton's poems of that era were the artistic equivalent of a boozy phone call — addressed to specific auditors, whose forbearance if not affection she could elicit by a pathetic appeal.

Even the friends who loved her couldn't help much now. As Louise Conant put it despairingly in a letter to Sexton, "Love as big as [mine] ought to make a difference — a fundamental difference in *your* life — and it doesn't, not when it really matters." Knowing this, they did what they could and hoped for the best. The best probably would have been treatment for multiple addictions, in combination with a strong relationship with a loving, emotionally solid partner at home — a new mother for another rebirth, at forty-five; an entirely new hand in the card game, and the wits to play it. But who was left to intervene on behalf of such monumental changes?

Not surprisingly, Sexton's anguish put an immense burden on her medical caretakers. In late 1973, Dr. Chase abruptly terminated therapy. By all reports, trouble between doctor and patient had been evolving steadily since Sexton's separation from Kayo. Sexton had taken Dr. Chase's summer absence very hard, and apparently Dr. Chase had taken a dim view of Sexton's untruthfulness concerning her financial situation (the fact that she was not as hard up as she claimed had slipped out during the divorce). Other problems apparently developed in the treatment as well. At the end of December, Dr. Chase informed Sexton that she could no longer continue as her doctor. Writing to one of the Boston "matchmaker" therapists, Sexton claimed, "This is no termination of any sort but an amputation, and I feel pretty damned desperate." Whether she could have been successfully transferred to another doctor's care at that moment in her life does seem doubtful. But losing Dr. Chase was one loss too many. Hindsight makes the nine months remaining in her life seem like a time-lapse photograph of a house collapsing in an earthquake.

More and more often now, Sexton thought about suicide. On 29 December she typed out a "confessional statement" suggesting that what kept her going was the ability, still, to write.

> I am afraid to die. Yet I think it might do a few favors. If I COULD I'd just die inside, let the heart-soul shrink like a prune, and only to this typewriter, let out the truth. I feel awfully alone — crying in the bathroom so no one need hear — crying over these keys, where they sit as patient as an old granny . . . . Can I save myself? I can try . . . I can keep right on trying. Granny, you electric Smith Corona heart, you buzz back at me, and I pray you do not break. I keep forgetting, these last weeks, to thank God each day for something, anything. I do [not?] ask either. But let me right now thank God for friends, many, many who like my love, swim in it[,] and for this granny machine.

But hindsight is deceptive. Sexton didn't kill herself impulsively. Instead, she found a new healer to mother her and set about winding up her affairs.

Sexton's last therapist was not a psychiatrist but a psychiatric social worker with a reputation for a warm manner and a cool head. Barbara Schwartz accepted Sexton against the time a "real" psychiatrist could be found for her, since Sexton was angling for a psychoanalytically trained therapist who could also prescribe medication. Sexton always called Schwartz by her first name, at first as a kind of snub, but soon as an acknowledgment of friendship.

At least as important as Barbara Schwartz in keeping Sexton alive after her divorce was attention from her admirers in the poetry world, who were keeping her poems alive. She particularly enjoyed being interviewed by Steven Axelrod, a young professor at the University of California at Riverside, and his wife, Rise, who were planning a book on contemporary poetry. Sexton told them that she thought of herself as the *only* confessional poet. Yet, she pointed out, the poet does not find herself by looking at old poems; "Live," for example, did not stand in Sexton's life as an article of faith. "The poems stand for the moment they were written and make no promises," she told them. "I guess of all my old poems, 'The Truth the Dead Know' and the two last stanzas of 'The Touch' have the most meaning for me to this day, although that is just a passing thought and I could change my mind in five minutes."

Sexton was contacted by another scholar that year: J. D. McClatchy, a Ph.D. candidate at Yale who was completing a dissertation on confessional poetry. McClatchy drove up from New Haven twice to interview Sexton in Weston. He found her alert, lively, thoughtful, and helpful. "I always liked her vitality — I didn't sense how frail she really was."

For Sexton these inquiries from scholars and critics were well timed. Perhaps because of her experience as a university teacher, she was now interested in trying to define for an academic audience what place in literature her work might be destined to occupy. Though she bravely claimed to McClatchy that she expected to live a long while yet, she spoke of her work as if in retrospect. Sexton hoped she would be seen as a witness to life. "Wouldn't that be worth something? I don't mean a testimony exactly, but just one life, ordinary not extraordinary really — except maybe madness, but hell, that's common. I say to my students, sometimes, that we're all writing one big poem, one great big poem. [. . .] It's a poem of our time." And yet a poem addresses just one person, not a group, not an era. "Through [speaking of] inner life, you reach other people's inner life."

Sexton enjoyed her meetings with McClatchy, who was fun-loving, intelligent, a wonderful reader, and also savvy about the practical side of a career in art. When she asked him to replace Maxine Kumin as the literary executor named in her will — Kumin had had second thoughts about this prospectively burdensome honor — he refused, but he gave her excellent advice about this problem, which (from an academic's point of view) writers sometimes handled in an unbusinesslike way. He also helped her revise the pertinent clauses in her will. Sexton decided to make Linda her literary executor, a decision she announced to Linda on her twenty-first birthday.

In the city of poets that Boston was, Sexton held a senior rank, and she kept up her connections, managing to avoid disclosing the depth of her difficulties. Elizabeth Bishop was now in Cambridge, teaching at Harvard, and Sexton finally met her in person, over lunch. Bishop was professionally an opposite type to Sexton: she abhorred making public appearances, and took teaching positions only when she needed the money. But in private she liked to joke and to drink. At lunch, they talked — according to Sexton — about money. Hearing from John Brinnin that Sexton was in the dumps following her divorce, Bishop sent her an amusing postcard of a dog smoking, with the message, "At John's I always see two fine photographs of you, taken in that sun-room, and I shd. think you would find it very cheering to *look* so poetic!"

Robert Lowell was back, too, teaching at Harvard. His arrival followed a summer of scandalized reviews of *The Dolphin*, a book of poems dedicated to his third wife, Lady Caroline Blackwood, which quoted liberally from letters Elizabeth Hardwick had written to him during the breakup of their marriage. Sexton arranged to meet him for lunch — as it happened, on the day that the death of W. H. Auden was announced — and worried to Arthur Freeman about how to steer the conversation tactfully around the subject of divorce. "Just tell him he's the greatest English poet, now that Auden is dead!" Freeman said.

Just before Christmas, Sexton's old mentor Philip Rahv, who was also getting a divorce, committed suicide. This was a blow to her. Shortly after her separation from Kayo, she and Rahv had begun meeting for dinner almost once a week, but in early September Rahv's addiction to tranquilizers had begun to unnerve her and she had stopped seeing him. Sexton was asked to read a eulogy at his memorial service. When Linda came home for the Christmas break, she found her mother struggling with heaps of scribbled notes, which Linda helped her shape for delivery. Working together over these words for a dead friend brought mother and daughter closer than they had been for months.

Anne Sexton at her kitchen table.

20

POSTHUMOUS PERFORMANCES
1974

THE DEATH NOTEBOOKS, which Sexton jokingly called her post-humous book, was published on 21 February 1974. Following close on the heels of *The Book of Folly,* it stimulated many invitations for personal appearances, and that year Sexton made trips to Maryland, Pennsylvania, New Jersey (three times), New York, Connecticut, Texas, and Maine and gave numerous readings in the Boston area. Flying still terrified her, which was one reason she requested such large fees for out-of-town trips ($2000 by 1974, though she usually settled for $1500). She had dedicated *The Death Notebooks* to Louise and Loring Conant, who had offered her and Joy refuge so often in the past year, and Louise sometimes accompanied her on these flights, good-naturedly putting up with Sexton's demands to be waited on. Louise recalled, "I must pack everything in a bag small enough to carry on (no waiting for baggage, which would surely be lost anyway), join her in a taxi to the airport, arriving at least an hour early to allow time for getting her a seat in the smoking section on an aisle, so she could stretch out her bad leg." The grande dame also required that "I must carry her briefcase (such a long walk, with a bad leg), must keep track of tickets, have a black felt-tipped pen handy for autographs."

For a while, Conant found the value of intimacy with Sexton well worth the costs. They had a standing engagement every Monday morning: Conant would let herself into Sexton's house while Sexton was still asleep, then chat or read while Sexton breakfasted and tended to the mail. Often they would go to the study for uninterrupted conversation about religion or writing. Sexton was frequently self-absorbed and aloof, but in her own way she was a generous friend. Conant remembered how, one morning in January, she put together a "poetry kit": a pile of the bright yellow-orange "lucky paper" that she used in drafting poems, a pile of three-by-five cards for scribbling notes at odd moments, and a yellow legal pad. Then Sexton dramatically instructed Conant in its use. " 'On the front page of the yellow pad,' she said, 'write CHERISH.' I did. 'Now write three or four things you cherish.' I did. 'Turn the page. Now write CAMERA. What can the camera cherish?' I did. 'Turn the page. Write LIES. Then write three lies that hurt you most.' I did." The tutorial went on until many pages had been labeled with topics. Finally Sexton told her with satisfaction, "That ought to give you something to start on."

Conant thought these inventions were wholly spontaneous. Perhaps they were, but Sexton had been taking just such performance-oriented approaches with all her students that winter. Hoping to become a full-time professor at Boston University, she was attempting to systematize her teaching methods and adapt them for broader application. She wanted to offer some undergraduate courses, if she could develop a syllabus out of the workshop techniques she used with graduate students. She was also offering workshops in her home for hourly fees. These had begun as poolside chats with mature students she looked on as friends, but Sexton now hoped that a more businesslike version would become a source of income.

Anne Sexton, 1974.

Teaching was now Sexton's real work. Assisted by Lois Ames, who tape-recorded every class that she taught at Boston University, she was usually able to meet her classes no matter how bad she felt. Her courses were popular, and some students returned semester after semester. One of these was Eric Edwards, a Quaker who was serving his term as a conscientious objector by working as an orderly at Mass. General Hospital. He was older than many of the other members of the seminar, and one of the few men. Edwards thought Sexton was looking for a protégé, someone brilliant, as C. K. Williams had been brilliant, whose career she might foster. Betting on him was a misjudgment, he later said, laughing. He did not aspire to be a protégé, and when Sexton appointed him to lead the class during her increasingly frequent absences, the students' morale would plummet.

Sexton's students did not know that many of her absences were due to hospitalizations following suicide attempts — two during the semester straddling the winter and spring. But Edwards recalled a conversation during those months about methods of suicide, to which Sexton seemed to be devoting a good deal of thought. "She told me that the way to kill yourself would be in the garage with the car engine running. This brought me up short; I was not interested personally in suicide. I asked, 'Why is that the best way?' And she said, 'It's painless, it's quick, it's sure.' " Even students who were not privy to Sexton's thoughts recognized how fragile she was. Those who stayed with the course, Edwards reflected, became a "sort of class-beast that surrounded her, great, loving and focused, attentive."

Edwards was also taking courses from John Malcolm Brinnin, and he found the two teachers usefully complementary. "Brinnin was such a measured man, elegant and beautifully articulate. He directed students to internalize the critic — internalize. He was the opposite of Anne; he didn't want you to get too close. Anne was unmeasured, but also less distanced." Edwards observed that it was the women in the class who brought the most passion to their work with Sexton. "A lot of her students wrote what you might call standard adolescent poetry, but for the women in my generation, that kind of expression was more than just emotional business that you work your way through — for them it was a determination of identity, one that the world didn't want them to have. That was before the rise of feminism as a workable social concept. These women had to do it on their own."

Women students often responded to what they interpreted as the anger in Sexton's work: the drive for self-definition and independent psychological strength. One of these was Robin Becker, now an established teacher of creative writing and the author of several books of poems. As a young woman coming to terms with feminism and lesbian identity, Becker found Sexton encouraging. But looking back at the poetry course, she observed that Sexton could not really serve as a mentor that year, partly because she was too unstable to provide a productive environment in which to practice the techniques she had developed for helping students let go of inhibitions. As an example, Becker recalled a session when Sexton decided to "unrepress" the class by putting them through an exercise in association, using a procedure she called the "storming" of images. Edwards remembered it too: "Her image-mongering technique was a way to develop, more or less communally, whole passels, whole columns of them." On this memorable occasion, Sexton set a Coke can on the table and directed the students to make up an unconscious for this little being. They gave it a name and began rapidly associating, one student outshouting the next, spewing a torrent of imagery that no one even tried to write down, some of it raunchy. Sexton, at first the facilitator of the process, succumbed to its power too: she went wild. Her behavior probably violated most students' expectations of a teacher, and some of them did not reenroll in her class after that semester. Who knew what demons within Sexton might wriggle out for good, once released by such witchcraft?

However, Sexton believed she had stumbled on a teaching technique that could be put to excellent use in dislodging students from conventions that were impeding their artistic development. In April she wrote a proposal for a new undergraduate course called "Creative Writing of Poetry: Raising of the Unconscious," and suggested that Eric Edwards team-teach it with her. He recalled her enthusiastic plans: they would set up the process with directives (very like the ones Sexton gave Louise Conant) that would teach students how to liberate poems trapped in the too-easy mechanics of metaphor. Edwards explained, "We would both have been up there, doing this little image thing, getting the students to do it. But I was never a good disciple; I think I was still too buried to come to grips with the process freely." Of course, Sexton herself had not fully come to grips with the process; it was the "image-mongering" that made reviewers of *Awful Rowing* dubious about its finish. As one critic put it, "She continues to go over the top with words, letting them fill her pages like breeder piles. Having set up the situation in a poem, she lets a network of associations do the rest."

Did instability diminish Sexton's powers as a teacher that year? What some found inappropriate, others found charismatic. As Edwards put it, "Her presence was really wonderful to be with, when it was functioning; and even when it wasn't functioning, it was kind of wonderful — it was just dark. It was as if she would take you down into hell with her. Since I was such a little innocent abroad, I would just go along and see how bad it was. 'Oh, this is pretty bad. But shucks.' Later on, I might go 'Aargh, where have I been? What is going on here?' But Anne for me was a godawful miracle. She was so productive, writing not the way I would write, but with an intensity and focus, an always-present energy." George Starbuck, who heard informal reports about faculty in the program, concurred in this judgment. "Her kind of teaching demanded what a great actor puts out every evening, immense presence and energy and alertness. The fact that she was doing that well didn't necessarily mean that she was 'safe' mentally, any more than it did for John Berryman." (Berryman, who taught at the University of Minnesota, had committed suicide in 1972.)

The high point of the winter for Sexton was the reading arranged for her at Sanders Theater on 7 March by the Harvard Literary Club. Since this reading was to serve as the Boston debut of *The Death Notebooks,* she was ambitious for a big turnout. When she saw the mimeographed flyer — with a typo in the book title — produced by the Literary Club, she went into high gear. Bob Clawson now owned an advertising agency, so she hired him to produce a poster, using the photograph by Gwendolyn Stewart she had wanted Houghton Mifflin to print on the dustjacket of *The Death Notebooks*. This was inserted into both the Harvard *Crimson* and the Boston *Phoenix* as a flyer, and was also distributed around greater Boston by a flying wedge of friends. Sexton sent copies of the book to local radio stations, provocatively requesting announcements of the event: "I dare you to read on your station page 31, 'The Fury of Guitars and Sopranos' or would you prefer p. 37, 'The Fury of Cocks'? At any rate, I think both have a wide appeal in a very sexual, sensual way." She wrote personal invitations to several of the psychiatrists who had treated her and her daughters.

The stress of anticipation took its toll; on the morning of the reading Sexton arrived for her regular appointment with Barbara Schwartz only to slump to the floor in one of her fugue states, from which Schwartz could not rouse her for two and a half hours. By evening, no one could have guessed it. Beautifully groomed, she arrived at the prereading dinner at Ferdinand's restaurant in Cambridge on the arm of her current man and greeted the other guests cordially. Her new editor, Richard McAdoo, and his wife hosted the party, which included the Conants, the poet Celia Gilbert, and the novelist Dan Wakefield, who was to introduce Sexton. The reading was scheduled for eight, but Sexton liked to enter five or ten minutes after the appointed time. When she arrived at Sanders with the McAdoos, the doors were closed and the building looked deserted. They knocked, and the door was cracked: "Sorry, there's no more room." The hall was filled to the rafters: every seat, every aisle was crammed; some people were sitting in the windowframes, and others were stationed on the fire escapes. The fire warden had appeared earlier and threatened to clear the floor, but had withdrawn after a special university intervention.

Sexton paced slowly to the stage with Dan Wakefield. While he made a warm introduction, she stood leaning against the wall behind him, stunning in a black jersey top that wrapped her body and a long black-and-white skirt slit to the knee. (The poster did its work so well that later, people who had been in the audience thought she had been wearing the dress in the photograph, which one person remembered as red.)

Among the audience receiving Sexton's gaze that night were some to whom she had sent those personal invitations. Most dear, perhaps, was Dr. Martha Brunner-Orne, who beamed approvingly from her seat and later sent Sexton a motherly note complimenting her on looking so well. Barbara Schwartz was there, relieved to see her patient in command of herself. Past and present students and current lovers and former lovers and the widening circle of Sexton's women friends were there too. Others, like Christina Robb, later a reporter for the *Boston Globe,* came just out of curiosity. "It was the most publicized event I'd ever heard in Boston! Advertised far and wide. I heard about it in my little tenement down in Riverside and went with my sister, just for something to do."

Linda Sexton, sitting in the audience with friends, felt a thrill of nerves as her mother moved to the podium. Her opening words sounded slurred and thick: "I would like to dedicate this reading to a nameless woman. There are many kinds of love — woman to man, mother to child, woman to woman, man to man, God to us . . ." The words seemed like a public gesture of forgiveness for Linda's earlier refusal to visit Sexton in the hospital. (Linda was not the only person who believed these words were a message directed to her or him. Barbara Schwartz recalled that after Sexton's death, a number of friends told her in confidence, "You remember Anne's reading at Sanders Theater? It was dedicated to me . . .") But worry invaded Linda's pleasure: "Watching her readings I always had the fear that she would fall apart right in front of all these people, and oh how embarrassing."

Just when it looked as if Sexton were going to lose coherence, her posture gathered confidence and her voice deepened and took hold. She joked, as usual now, that she was reading that night from her "posthumous work," *The Death Notebooks,* newly published, and *The Awful Rowing Toward God,* still in manuscript. This was in a way true, for the person who wrote those poems existed no more; the poet had been survived by the performer. Sexton gave a very upbeat reading, bantering with the audience. She made cracks about *The New Yorker;* she made "a bow to the madness" with a reading of "Music Swims Back to Me"; she touched heartstrings with a reading of "Old," telling how her physician friend Loring Conant had kept a clipping of it in his wallet to remind him what it felt like to be an old lady. Her easy manner emboldened a poker player in the crowd to put her on notice that the winning poker hand in "The Rowing Endeth" required either two wild cards or a deck with five aces. He was right, but Sexton never revised the poem: it was finished, from her point of view. Nor did she lose her stride. Back in 1961 she had commented to Dr. Orne about this facility she had for switching into performance mode: "I could perform just before I die, I think, but it's a performance of the poems. I know the lines — it's a practiced emotion, one I've felt before — when I'm caught in a poem someone doesn't suddenly interject something and say *this* is reality." Sexton ended with a reading of "The Touch," and the audience rose to its feet and applauded for a long, long time.

The many friends who rejoiced in Sexton's triumph that night were her substitute for the family she so sorely missed. Joy and Linda, living at school, were also emotionally distant, absorbed as much as possible in their own lives. Sexton's friends more or less knew how dependent she was on them to be the caretakers her children and husband had been. But as the months following her divorce wore on, she sank more deeply into her addictions; now what she seemed to need was not a group of buddies but a nursing service. From this, her friends backed off. When Sexton took an overdose of Thorazine and other pills in

February, she wasn't discovered for more than a day; brain damage was feared. Lois Ames, alerted by a worried phone call from another friend, found her comatose and called an ambulance. When Sexton regained consciousness, she said to Ames, "You won't get another chance to save me," a phrase that Maxine Kumin heard later that year, when she interrupted Sexton in the act of taking pills. Realizing that Sexton's support structure had broken down — no one could substitute for Kayo, who had always come home to her, had always been there to pick up the pieces — Ames thought of a plan to have Sexton's closest friends take turns being "on call," to ease the pressure on some of them some of the time. She proposed that they hold a meeting at her home to discuss it, but Sexton got wind of this plan and was very unhappy. "Anne called us a witches' coven and insisted we stop talking about her," Louise Conant recalled. So they did. Nonetheless, Sexton received the same message from all of them: It was hard to be candid with her, because resistance to her demands was likely to trigger a suicide attempt.

Even Maxine Kumin was getting worn down by her deterioration, and finally they came to bitter words. Invited jointly to read at Douglass College in New Jersey, they traveled together, and were later interviewed together by two young professors on the faculty, Elaine Showalter and Carol Smith. Sexton, who was tired, insisted on holding the interview in bed at their motel and punctuated it with phone calls, trying to track down a recent lover. Kumin was a good sport about the shenanigans, but later, in private, blew up and told Sexton she had been impossibly selfish and needy. From Kumin's point of view, that was that; she trusted that her friend would see the justice of her point. She left shortly afterward on a trip to Europe and wrote Sexton long, gossipy, affectionate letters. But Sexton felt wholly betrayed and abandoned, as she said in a three-page letter to Kumin. "True. I am selfish as many of us are and far too needy. [. . .] I can only tell you that it's been breaking my heart that we've been so far apart this last half year, and yet I've realized that you love your 'up country' and that it feeds you." She told Louise Conant that she felt she had lost her dearest friend for good.

The evening after they returned from New Jersey, Sexton put on a fancy red dress — one she wore for readings — and told her current tenant that she was going dancing. She took a cab to Cambridge and got out a short distance from Linda's dormitory, then strolled down to the Charles River and danced her way along the embankment, wading in and out of the water, until she was across from Barbara Schwartz's office, where Schwartz always left a light burning, at Sexton's request. Then she began taking handfuls of pills, washing them down with milk from a Thermos bottle she had taken along. A good samaritan came along and asked if he could help. He took her to the emergency room at Mount Auburn Hospital. Lois Ames was called, and spent the rest of the night by her side.

Yet no act of concern overrode Sexton's belief that her old friends were "melting away." She thus responded all the more readily to the many strangers her poetry had made to feel intimate with her, and to the young women who regarded her as a pathbreaker. Among these, Erica Jong became a great favorite. When Sexton went down to New York at the end of May for two nights to read for a Caedmon recording, Jong spent many hours keeping her company at the Algonquin one evening, and on another evening held a party in her honor — a visit Jong later memorialized in an episode of her novel *How to Save Your Own Life.*

As summer approached, Sexton felt increasingly shaky about living alone. At one point she called Dr. Brunner-Orne, inquiring whether she could return to therapy; she was gently refused, on professional grounds. She hired Joan Smith full-time as her nurse, but since the tenants who occupied her house with her were moving out, she would be on her own at night, and the nights terrified her. Often she would call Barbara Schwartz at bedtime — sometimes very late at night — to be "lullabied" while her sleeping pills took hold. At last she persuaded Joy to live at home that summer by promising to be considerate. She bought Joy a camera and paid for her to study with the Boston photographer Arthur Furst, and she encouraged her to invite friends home whenever she wanted.

Mother and daughter lived together as roommates for three months, much like the characters in John Updike's melancholy novel *Rabbit Redux,* about the splintering and reconfiguring of a family. Joy dug up a sunny spot on the back lawn and put in a plot of marijuana. Watered twice a day by the automatic sprinkler system Kayo had installed several years back, protected from wind and spies, the plants flourished and produced a magnificent crop of high-quality weed. Joy and her friends shared joints around the pool. Anne didn't join the skinny-dipping, but she did often spend long afternoons with Joy's friends, drinking wine and talking about life. "Everybody thought Mother was so hip," Joy said. "I regret to say I couldn't enjoy her as much as others did. I still wanted your basic station-wagon family life."

Sexton didn't keep her word about being considerate, either. Several times she commandeered the house for herself and various lovers, ordering Joy to stay with friends for the night. When frustrated, she would throw tantrums, stamping and screaming "like a three-year-old," Joy remembered, and it was this behavior that made Joy angriest. "Without my dad she was incapable of being a parent. We went from having rigid family routines to no rules at all." Joy took to spending more time at her father's apartment, and when September arrived, she escaped back to boarding school. Sexton found another young couple to live in the house with her.

"I think I spoke to Mother only once on the telephone before her death," Joy remembered, "though on that occasion she was quite upbeat, laughing because she couldn't figure out why her pocketbook was so heavy. She emptied it while we were talking, and found fifty-five Bic lighters." When Joy thought about the legacies of life with her mother, she felt forgiving. "What she couldn't give me, she made sure I got from someone else," she mused. "I also think of Mother as a survivor, a fighter. She wasn't self-sufficient — I departed from her in that. It's because of her that I've taught myself how to plumb and wire a house, how to fix things. But she taught my soul about books. And she was an emotional survivor, and so am I."

As Sexton grew more isolated from her family and as old friends responded with aversion, she took up more often with strangers. Anyone who would share a drink and a smoke at a nearby bar was a welcome companion. She took out personal ads in newspapers and followed up promising notes from fans, but she stayed lonely, although she found a soulmate that fall in John Cheever, who joined the Boston University faculty as a writing instructor. John Malcolm Brinnin remembered the evening Sexton and Cheever met, when all the writing faculty joined the dean for dinner at the Athens Olympia, a hangout in the theater district of Boston. "At the restaurant the two of them acted deliberately very naughty, outdoing each other in outrageousness," Brinnin recalled. "George Starbuck and I tried to occupy the dean and his wife at the other end of the table, both of us wondering, Did they overhear *that*?" Like Sexton, Cheever had driven away his family in order to drink full-time, and Sexton obliged him during faculty meetings by pouring into his coffee cup nips of the whiskey she carried in her bag.

During the last six months of her life, she was also regularly receiving religious instruction from a young seminarian at the Episcopal Divinity School, Pattie Handloss. Sexton contemplated being baptized in the Episcopal church, but, never a joiner, she continued to claim that "Saint Mattress is just as appropriate a place to find the unknown, doubtful, ever-possible, joyous 'God' " as any church service. Her religious inquiry at that time seems to have been infused with a sense that she was approaching the end. When Sexton imagined that end, however, it was not as a turning to God but as a return to the arms of what she called a "consecrating mother"; in one of her last poems, addressed to Barbara Schwartz, she imagined death as a walk into the sea: "I wish to enter her like a dream, [. . .] sink into the great mother arms / I never had."

"Worse than dying in many ways is feeling that one is hurting people," Sexton wrote in 1974 to a young man who had confided his suicidal thoughts to her. She was hurting people, and she was hurting. She turned almost daily to her typewriter, tapping words into lines as she had now done for eighteen years. Deep down, Sexton knew these were no more poems than the senile ravings of an old woman were conversation. She could easily summon the memory of Nana's helplessness the day she was carried off to the nursing home where her freedom ended. Sexton believed — she always had believed — that death was better than the life Nana had chronicled with the same phrase day after day: "No one came."

Anne Sexton ended her life on Friday, 4 October. She chose the day and the method very deliberately. On Thursday the third of October she returned triumphantly from a well-paid reading at Goucher College, in time to teach her poetry workshop at Boston University. As a surprise, the whole class went to meet her plane. Sexton regaled them all the way into Boston with an account of how she managed the buttons on the long red dress she wore for readings, which would open from both top and bottom as if by accident. She conducted the class in high spirits.

She was in bed the next morning when Louise Conant arrived to be given a birthday present, a recording of a flute being played in the Taj Mahal. They breakfasted in the kitchen, and as Sexton sipped her coffee, she kept breaking off sentences to look at the chickadees visiting the window feeder, which always delighted her. At ten she was due in Cambridge for her regular appointment with Barbara Schwartz. She and Louise parted tenderly.

Into her purse Sexton folded a copy of a new poem, "The Green

Room," written for Schwartz. The fourth of October was an important anniversary: their first appointment had been nine months ago to the day. The poem's title alluded to a book Sexton wanted Schwartz to read, *Autobiography of a Schizophrenic Girl,* which was an account of a remarkable therapy during which a female psychoanalyst took a young woman through a symbolic gestation and rebirth. Sexton felt a similar gratitude to Schwartz for the mothering Schwartz had given without stint during those nine months: "Lady, lady of the sea/in your womb my heart beats like a junkie./Never tear me out." Sexton was so calm that morning that Schwartz did not intuit a goodbye, but after she left, Schwartz found her cigarettes and lighter tucked behind the bowl of daisies in her office and grew somewhat apprehensive. The gesture seemed deliberate, and Anne Sexton without cigarettes was unthinkable.

Sexton had a lunch date with Maxine Kumin; they were to correct galleys of *The Awful Rowing Toward God,* scheduled for publication in March 1975. She took "The Green Room" to show Kumin. *Awful Rowing* had been written before the watershed of the divorce, but Sexton's poetry since that time had had a quality of agitated appeal. Many of the poems were addressed to a specific auditor, as was "The Green Room." What did Max think? Was it any good? Kumin remembers telling her that it was always a good thing to keep writing poems — you could never predict when you would hit pay dirt. Now *The Awful Rowing* — those were good poems.

"We had a wonderfully gay and silly lunch together, and I remember thinking how much better she seemed," Kumin recalled. By 1:30 they had finished with the galleys. Kumin had an appointment that afternoon to pick up her passport, as she was shortly to leave on a long trip with her husband to Europe, Israel, and Iran. She knew Sexton dreaded her departure, which would take place before Sexton's birthday, always a time when Sexton needed support. "Yes, she was very demanding," Kumin said later. "But I never felt manipulated by her. I guess that I loved her so much that I couldn't have felt any manipulation. There were times when I felt the pressures of the demands, but you know, Annie gave as good as she got. She was extremely generous and giving, loving. And when she was ready [to kill herself], she kept it a deep dark secret." Kumin walked Sexton to her car and watched her pull away. Sexton rolled down the window and called something, but Kumin didn't quite catch it. It was a most considerate farewell — a receiver never set back on the hook.

Sexton drove home through beautiful Indian summer weather, the trees of Weston already in what she called their sourball colors, vivid as candy. In the peace of her airy kitchen she poured another glass of vodka to sip while she phoned her date for the evening and changed the hour of their meeting. She seems to have talked to no one else, and she wrote no notes.

She stripped her fingers of rings, dropping them into her big purse, and from the coat closet she took her mother's old fur coat. Though it was a sunny afternoon, a chill was in the air. The worn satin lining must have warmed quickly against her flesh; death was going to feel something like an embrace, like falling asleep in familiar arms. Long ago she had told Dr. Orne, "Every time I put it on I feel like my mother. A genuine fur coat. Only she wasn't big, my mother was very small." ("She was big," said Dr. Orne.) Fresh glass of vodka in hand, Sexton let herself into the garage and closed the doors behind her. She climbed into the driver's seat of her old red Cougar, bought in 1967, the year she started teaching. She turned on the ignition and turned on the radio.

No one who knew Anne Sexton well was surprised by her suicide, but it was shocking all the same. During visiting hours, friends and relatives crowded the mortuary in Wellesley where her casket lay covered in a blanket of daisies, to pay respects to the family. The funeral, with Pattie Handloss's help, was held at the Episcopal church in Dedham. On 15 October a memorial service was held at Boston University's Marsh Chapel, where Sexton's colleagues and students spoke and read poems and Bob Clawson played tapes of Her Kind in memory of the woman who "lived to the hilt."

Sexton had been scheduled to read on 30 October at Town Hall in New York, and that occasion became a memorial service too. For some who offered eulogies, it seemed important to segregate the suicide from the poetry that was Sexton's bequest. Adrienne Rich put the problem bluntly: "We have had enough suicidal women poets, enough suicidal women, enough self-destructiveness as the sole form of violence permitted to women." Denise Levertov echoed this theme in a thoughtful obituary she wrote for a Boston paper. "Anne Sexton's tragedy will not be without influence in the tragedies of other lives," she foresaw. "We who are alive must make clear, as she could not, the distinction between creativity and self-destruction. The tendency to confuse the two has claimed too many victims. [. . .] To recognize that for a few years of her life Anne Sexton was an artist *even though* she had so hard a struggle against her desire for death is to fittingly honor her memory."

For her family, dispersed by the divorce, Sexton's death felt like the end of a siege. They returned stunned and awkward to Black Oak Road: Linda arrived from Harvard, Kayo fetched Joy from boarding school, and as in the old days, Billie made herself quietly useful to them all. It was Linda, with Kayo and Joy's support, who arranged for cremation and brought Anne Sexton's ashes home.

Shortly afterward, Kayo moved back into the house, and three years later he remarried. Joy finished boarding school and then enrolled at the School of the Museum of Fine Arts; eventually she earned a nursing degree at Simmons College. Linda completed college and went on to become a writer of fiction.

It was two years before Sexton's ashes were interred, and by then the pain had mellowed into sadness. On a warm August afternoon in 1976, Kayo, Billie, Linda, and Joy gathered at the Sexton family plot at Forest Hills Cemetery, which had been opened again to receive Anne Sexton. They placed the heavy box in the earth, and Linda and Joy scattered pansies from the garden at Black Oak Road over it. Weeping, the four of them linked hands around the grave. Looking at the reunited family, Linda said, "I think Mother would be proud of us."

CODA

CODA

ANNE SEXTON HAD BEEN RIGHT, back in 1961, when she told Dr. Orne, "I've taken care of that 'live' part by writing my poems." It was through writing that she survived for another thirteen years as a human being, and it would be through writing that she might retain her place in the poets' afterlife, the vertical columns of high school and college literature anthologies. Nevertheless, from early on in her career, she seems to have understood that her magical transformation from housewife into poet would itself attract the broader interest of social and literary historians. She anticipated a biography that would clarify the relationship between her life, her illness, and her work, and she took an active role in making sure that her biographer would draw from very full documentation, including collections of audiotapes, videotapes, photographs, and film, to which others have added since her death. Because she was a performer, and a beauty with a marvelous speaking voice, her physical presence had exceptional charge for audiences, and something of that legacy has marked her afterlife, through the agency of electronic records on which her presence is inscribed, and through the potent ambiguity of her medical records.

The most unusual of these records is the collection of therapy tapes made by Dr. Orne for Sexton's use in treatment. Cocooned in the vaults of his clinical archives for more than twenty years on hundreds of spools of high-quality polyester tape, Sexton's voice when she was thirty-three, thirty-four, and thirty-five years old retains a compelling liveliness. Most psychiatric records represent the person as a "patient," a word that descends from Latin *patior*: to suffer, to put up with. The tapes restore to the record an *im*patient Sexton: active, impious, resourceful, witty, intelligent, deeply needy of medical treatment from time to time, but also engaged, through treatment, in exciting discoveries about herself and her art, "Language."

While this biography was circulating to reviewers in bound page proofs, information about the use of the tapes became sensational news: "Poet Told All; Therapist Provides the Record" was the headline on the story that ran on page one of *The New York Times*. Sexton sprang to life again as a celebrity, the center of extreme controversy within the profession of psychiatry. Before the book was even published, medical ethicists went on the record to charge Dr. Orne with professional misconduct for his perceived violation of doctor-patient privilege. "A patient's right to confidentiality survives death," said one, "only the patient can give that release. What the family wants does not matter a whit." Following publication, opinions based on fuller evidence focused on potential damage to current and future therapeutic relationships: "Anne Sexton is dead and beyond harm," said one commentator. "The legions of other patients who will learn of Dr. Orne's action are not, and erosion of trust in the profession is irreversible."

Sexton's biography was not the first to use psychiatric records — Nancy Milford's biography of Zelda Fitzgerald (1970), Scott Donaldson's of John Cheever (1988), and Peter Ostwald's of Vaslav Nijinsky (1990) rely on extensive access to notes and interviews with psychiatrists who treated their subjects, to name only a few — but it was the first to use audiotapes of treatment, and that seems to have mattered most in shaping the critical opinions of commentators on the biographical use of these materials. Feelings ran high, partly because challenges to doctor-patient confidentiality have grown increasingly common during the last decade, and controversy roused by the Sexton case provided an occasion for airing firm opinions. As the medical ethicist Alan Stone observed, "Any radical break with traditional practice is seen as unethical. But in fact the whole last twenty years of medical ethics has been devoted to giving patients more autonomy and more control." Stone noted that "it is now widely accepted as a matter of both ethics and law that patients should have access to all their medical records and can also choose to relieve their physicians of the obligation to preserve confidentiality." Had he been Anne Sexton's psychiatrist, he would have urged her to allow destruction of the tapes, he added, "but if she had refused I hope I would have used them according to her wishes." Orne replied to such critics that though he did not follow procedures in 1964 that he or other psychiatrists would follow today in deciding on the disposition of patient records, in 1964 written releases were not pro forma, and that Anne Sexton *had* explicitly made her wishes known. "When I left Massachusetts I offered to return all of the therapy tapes to Anne. She asked that I keep them to use as I saw fit to help others, though she retained a few for herself."

Debate within the medical profession largely ignored the question of the cultural importance of Sexton's case history, but publication of her biography polarized other kinds of discussion as well, which gained force from the brief but significant historical distance that separates Sexton's treatment from contemporary psychiatric theory and practice. The period of Sexton's therapy (1956–1974) coincided with vast, ongoing changes in the understanding of mental illness, including the evolution of psychopharmacology and the development of political analysis in the field of diagnosis. The use of "hysteric" as a diagnostic term applied almost exclusively to women, for example, was discarded as the name for a clinical disorder during Sexton's lifetime. These shifts in the practice of psychiatry at large are reflected in the treatment Sexton received, and the fullness of Sexton's medical documentation therefore licenses wide speculation. Researchers in the field of biologically-based psychiatric problems have proposed that current diagnostic methods might have revealed a manic-depressive illness at the base of Sexton's disturbances. Others found in the case decisive evidence that Sexton was the largely unacknowledged victim of abuse: substance abuse, family violence, incest. Recovery programs for victims of abuse have made popular a simple diagnosis focused on a short list of symptoms, many of which are the sort Sexton possessed in abundance; readers who identify passionately with Sexton as a fellow-sufferer view her early death as the outcome of therapeutic ignorance about diagnosis and treatment of these psychodynamic issues. Sexton's only living sister, Blanche Harvey Taylor, took the opposite position, contending that Sexton's acknowledged predilection for "truth crimes" should have precluded from the biography any references to her memories or fantasies about her father's sexual interest in her body, or of her own confused sexual feelings for Nana, that could be derived from her medical records. For all therapeutically oriented readers, Sexton lives on in the enigma of the haunting question, intensified by her suicide: What was really wrong with her?

Quite another kind of fascination with Sexton is roused by contact with her voice. Students of acting adapt monologues from Sexton's poems for auditions; theater and dance performances inspired by her work — especially her fairy tales — resurrect the body that was Sexton's peculiar gift to articulate. She survives, too, as a body of light, a twentieth century American ghost captured forever on film, repeating herself with overwhelming immediacy. And perhaps, if she is destined for immortality — a permanent spot in that "vertical" axis of history — it will be as an initiator of the performance art by which women artists in the late twentieth century made new space for their work as women.

The tape archives of Sexton's performances permit valuable insights into her development of this second art. A studio recording made for Harvard's Lamont Library poetry room in 1959 indicates that Sexton's early reading style was self-consciously formal: her voice is high, her intonations New England proper. But by the time Sexton published *To Bedlam and Part Way Back,* in 1960, she had developed the performance style that typified her public appearances from 1960 on. Sexton's — any poet's — reading style lifts words from a printed page into the intimate, ephemeral medium of the speaking voice. But Sexton's performance style converted the voice into a role; at the speaker's podium she became "an actress in her own autobiographical play." Her onstage manipulation of female charisma, the manner in which she separated herself as speaker from the first-person pronoun in the text, and the way she capitalized on elements of style in her poetry — all lent themselves to effective delivery in performance.

Eyewitness accounts of Sexton's readings often emphasize her physical appearance: "She glided on stage with a cigarette and a rueful smile. Her black and white costume was striking: black jersey top wrapping the lithe body with just the hint of a straitjacket; long skirt slit to the knee. There was, somehow, an opening night atmosphere. . . . Hard to say why . . . possibly the back-tilting Lauren Bacall stance, the sidelong cast of eye. . . . Her words drifted out on the blue smoke of the perpetual cigarette. . . . " The word "costume" is telling; Sexton usually wore a long dress with significant apertures that promised a display of the body they never delivered: slit skirt, deep armholes, unbuttoned bodice. Whereas there was nothing at all indecent about her dress, it conveyed to onlookers that she assumed she would be regarded as a sex object: self-exposure was part of the act. Moreover, Sexton the actress delivers the lines as lines. The poet who wrote them would make a brief appearance on stage — thanking her host, getting things right — but then the actress would step forward: "I have gone out, a possessed witch. . . ." Even to an audience unfamiliar with her work, Sexton's lines would convey an apparently firm referentiality: this poetry seemed to be about real life, a real person. Yet the performer had a way of making it seem personal about somebody else.

In using herself publicly this way, Sexton was quite different from women poets around her between 1960 and 1974, including writers whose poetry reflected a political consciousness such as June Jordan, Denise Levertov, Audre Lorde, Adrienne Rich, and Muriel Rukeyser. Political consciousness places the poet in an authoritatively critical relation to the culture. Sexton's authority did not convey criticism; it conveyed knowingness. In the powerful presence she impressed upon audiences, Sexton was most comparable to the generation of performance artists who came to prominence during the seventies and eighties: Laurie Anderson, Eleanor Antin, Lynn Hershman, Poppy Johnson, Grace Jones, Annie Lennox, Ntozake Shange, Patti Smith, Faith Wilding, and Madonna (who tells interviewers that in college she "devoured the dark poetry of Sylvia Plath and Anne Sexton"). Each has evolved a self-possessed artistic persona who is not a vamp, a floozie, a bimbo, or a self-consuming artifact. The voice is a role for which they write their own material, and for which a fairly elaborate performance, not publication, is the necessary medium of circulation — though technical expertise places these feminist artists of the seventies and eighties at a definitive distance from the performance art of Anne Sexton. Sex, violence, derangement, humor, and passionate spirituality are all themes of their performance art, as they were of Sexton's. And like them, Sexton delivered her lines as lines, opening a space between the poet and her text which revealed she was not confessing but acting. Her gestures said to the audience: what you seem to see is a woman. What you actually *see* is a role.

The woman is gone, but the scripts remain.

APPENDIX

SOURCES AND NOTES

BIBLIOGRAPHY

ACKNOWLEDGMENTS

INDEX

APPENDIX: THERAPY TAPE

THURSDAY, 21 SEPTEMBER 1961

This excerpt from the transcript of one of Sexton's therapy tapes was chosen to convey the flow of exchange, insight, and association typical of an active session between Anne Sexton and Dr. Martin Orne on one of Sexton's better days, when she did not go into a trance. The excerpt begins thirty minutes into the session. Small omissions in the transcript are signified with a dash (—); lengthier omissions are signified with bracketed ellipses ([. . .]).

A.S.: Why did I want to kill Nana?

Dr.: Isn't this the business of power?

A.S.: How could I feel powerful? At this stage in my life I never felt powerful — It seems to me that my whole childhood was powerless, and feeling angry about it. Wasn't it?

Dr.: We still have yet to get to your childhood fantasies.

A.S.: I was a nothing crouching in the closet!

Dr.: Never see "The Secret Life of Walter Mitty"?

A.S.: I didn't think anything; I read fairy tales. That was power, magic power. Probably masturbating is powerful — thinking today — so depressed — lay down on the bed, halfway masturbating, halfway going to sleep — this has nothing to do with power, but I'm associating, maybe it does have something to do with power: thought, masturbating is just like being sick, the same type of thing leads me into doing one or the other; it's something like hiding — But in a sudden flash of inspiration before I went to sleep I thought this is the very same thing as being sick — by being sick I mean living sick, in the hospital. [. . .]

    Now I keep thinking back: why would I have wanted to kill Nana? That's pretty distressing.

Dr.: Is that so difficult?

A.S.: Hmmnn?

Dr.: Nobody can stand to see someone they love suffer.

A.S.: But I didn't know she was suffering.

Dr.: Didn't?

A.S.: I don't think so.

Dr.: A child of five would know.

A.S.: But I needed her too much to think of her like that. It was so dreadful, it was like something that couldn't be true! Like a nightmare, it couldn't be true! I kept trying to find out it wasn't true, and it kept being true!

Dr.: Not quite true. You had discovered boys by then.

A.S.: So?

Dr.: You had others to love you now.

A.S.: — Oh no, that didn't matter.

Dr.: It did.

A.S.: — It mattered the minute I found out something had happened to her; if I'd known, I wouldn't have gone out with the boys.

Dr.: She'd still have gotten sick, but you don't believe that.

A.S.: I guess I probably don't. — That's why I think I'm powerful.

Dr.: Kind of hard to separate your feelings from hers.

A.S.: Yes, but it had been all right.

Dr.: You mixed them up very nicely for a long time, and Nana would say, "It's all right, it's all right."

A.S.: Then when she stopped saying "It's all right," as a matter of fact, she started saying "It's all awful."

Dr.: It's been that way ever since.

A.S.: All awful, unless someone were in love with me to tell me every two minutes, and then it's never enough — I'd really rather be dead! I don't like my personality and there's no getting away from it —

Dr.: Is it your personality?

A.S.: Yes, it's the way I'm made!

Dr.: Or is it Nana's, sick Nana?

A.S.: That's what my mother said when I went into Westwood. I didn't tell her I was going; she didn't even know I was going to a doctor. She called me up my first night there and I was really rather depressed, I was depressed before I went in. I was talking to her on the phone; she was furious and said, "I hope they give you lots of shock treatments like Nana and you get just as sick as she did." [Long pause.] I don't remember what I said. I didn't get mad.

Dr.: She made the association for you.

A.S.: Well, I said to Kayo, "Please don't let them give me any shock treatments." — Because she just got better, then she got sicker; they didn't do her any good — Maybe I'm like Nana: she really just wanted Mother. I think that something very [?] was hard for me, you know, because she had been my mother in many ways — She got sick and just wanted to be my mother's *child*: she kept saying my mother's name under her breath, "Mary, Mary Gray," every single minute. Every time she said it, it meant "You're not my child, I'm your mother's child." And actually, as you said, I got sick when my mother went away. — When Nana died I was pregnant with Joy; after that, when Joy was six months old, Mother went away — it was a combination of things — probably I *am* just like Nana.

Dr.: But you are not Nana.

A.S.: Why would I try to become Nana? That doesn't make any sense: I try to become Nana in order to kill her?

Dr.: In order not to lose her. It's what we do when we can't let people die.

A.S.: I become the Nana I didn't want, which I suppose I thought was better than nothing, after she died. — Maybe I come from a morbid — just inherited this. My father was really rather depressed, even though he didn't seem it, he was depressed. — And Nana, who was so active and intelligent and warm, that's what happened to her —

Dr.: Nana led a pretty empty life.

A.S.: Just because she didn't get married? For someone who didn't get married she had a very full life —

Dr.: Mmm. A function of a woman is to have children.

A.S.: Well, I have them.

Dr.: Mmm-hmmn.

A.S.: I don't like to remember —

Dr.: Mmm-hmmn.

A.S.: Nana did have children, she had me.

Dr.: No she didn't. You forget that.

A.S.: The thing that I forget is that she really had my mother — that was certainly more her child — That's one of my troubles with Billie and Joan, aside from all the troubles they present. I call Billie "Nana" because she picked up the name; then there's Joan hovering over my family.

Dr.: We have to stop shortly. Will I see you Saturday at our regular time?

A.S.: What is that?

Dr.: One o'clock.

A.S.: Am I ever going to work my way through this?

Dr.: That's what you're doing.

A.S.: That's what I'm doing?

Dr.: It will be important for you to listen to this. There's a lot there.

A.S.: Hmm?

SOURCES AND NOTES

SOURCES

Virtually all of Anne Sexton's papers are housed in the Harry Ransom Humanities Research Center at the University of Texas in Austin, cited as HRHRC.

The psychiatric records made available to the author contain the following kinds of material:

Hospital records

Notes made by Dr. Martin Orne during Sexton's therapy sessions over a period of thirteen months, from November 1957 through December 1958, with a break from June to August 1958 — cited as "doctor's notes"

Audiotapes of therapy sessions from 1961 to 1964 — cited as "therapy tape"

Notes on these tapes that Sexton made for her own use, which have been placed under restriction at HRHRC — cited as "therapy notebook"

Letters that Sexton wrote or typed to therapists, especially to Dr. Orne, dealing with issues in treatment

Manuscripts of unpublished poems that Sexton brought to therapy sessions with Dr. Orne and with Barbara Schwartz.

Works frequently cited are abbreviated as follows:

CP: Anne Sexton, *The Complete Poems* (Boston: Houghton Mifflin, 1981)

Letters: *Anne Sexton: A Self-Portrait in Letters,* ed. Linda Gray Sexton and Lois Ames (Boston: Houghton Mifflin, 1977)

McClatchy: *Anne Sexton, The Artist and Her Critics,* ed. J. D. McClatchy (Bloomington: Indiana University Press, 1978)

NES: No Evil Star: Selected Essays, Interviews and Prose, ed. Steven E. Colburn (Ann Arbor: University of Michigan Press, 1985).

NOTES

I. BEGINNINGS

3   After she became famous: See Barbara Kevles, "The Art of Poetry XV: Anne Sexton," *Paris Review*, 52 (Summer 1971): 159–91. Reprinted in *NES*, pp. 83–111.

3   "rebirth at twenty-nine": Patricia Marx, "Interview with Anne Sexton," *Hudson Review*, 18, no. 4 (Winter 1965–1966): 560–70. Reprinted in *NES*, pp. 70–82.

3   "When I'm writing": A.S., interview with Barbara Kevles, *NES*, p. 103.

4   seeds of her identity: Much of the following information about Sexton's childhood and adolescence comes from interviews with family members who requested not to be identified.

7   "Blanche was all fired up": A.S., interview with Alice Ryerson, January 1962, Radcliffe College Archives.

7   Blanche was the only: Anne's sister Jane died in January 1983, at age fifty-nine, of an overdose of sleeping pills after a period of despondency.

8   "I was a nothing": A.S. to Dr. Orne, therapy tape, 21 September 1961.

8   "locked in": "For the Year of the Insane," *CP*, p. 133.

9   "When Mother and Daddy": Quoted by A.S. to Dr. Orne, therapy tape, 17 January 1963.

11   "the end of the flapper era": Alison Johnson to D.M., 29 July 1990.

12   "glorious pulchritude": Arthur Gray Staples to Blanche Harvey, 8 May 1933.

13   "Hands around the table!": A.S. to Dr. Orne, therapy tapes, 24 May 1962 and 18 April 1963.

13   "Daddy was either drunk": Reported by A.S. to Dr. Orne, therapy tape, 17 January 1963.

13   "could drink anytime": A.S. to Dr. Orne, therapy tape, 13 June 1963.

14   "Fuck the heirs!": Alfred M. Sexton, interview with D.M., 21 February 1983.

14   "He would just": Doctor's notes, 21 December 1957.

15   Apparently the Harveys: Editorial note, Linda Sexton and Lois Ames, *Letters*, pp. 5–6.

15   "Down here": A.S. to Frances Harvey ("Franny"), n.d., HRHRC.

15 "Nana had been": A.S. to Dr. Orne, therapy tape, 21 September 1961.

16 "She wasn't like": A.S., therapy notebook, 21 September 1961, restricted collection, HRHRC.

16 "My father was drinking": A.S. to Dr. Orne, therapy tape, 3 August 1963.

16 "tiny voice": A.S., typed notes to Dr. Orne, n.d. [probably 1958].

16 "[I] should never": A.S., therapy notebook, 3 August 1961, restricted collection, HRHRC.

16 "I'd much rather": A.S. to Dr. Orne, therapy tape, 3 August 1961.

2. ROMANCE AND MARRIAGE

17 "party preceding 1st kiss": A.S., annotation dated 20 March 1943, vertical file, HRHRC.

17 "never having recovered": Michael Bearpark to A.S., 1 February 1964, HRHRC.

17 "I should have": A.S. to Michael Bearpark, 21 February 1964, HRHRC.

18 "beautifully furnished" and "Anne stole": Richard M. Sherwood to D.M., 20 February 1983.

18 "His father worked": Michael Bearpark, "A Memoir of Anne Sexton," unpublished typescript, n.d.

18 "did things first rate": John McCarthy, interview with D.M., 24 February 1984.

19 "Anne's best friend": Ibid.

19 "bleak, depressed": A.S. to Dr. Orne, therapy tape, 9 February 1961.

20 "Evil": *Letters*, p. 10. Sexton's cinquains loosely follow the five-line stanza form invented by Adelaide Crapsey, which has lines of two, four, six, eight, and two syllables.

20 "elegant excuses": A.S., therapy notebook, 12 June 1962, restricted collection, HRHRC.

20 "We ought": A.S. to Dr. Orne, doctor's notes, 1 May 1958.

21 In fact, poems by Sara Teasdale: "On the Dunes" and "Spirit's House," *Letters*, pp. 9 and 12, are from *The Collected Poems of Sara Teasdale* (New York: Macmillan, 1937), pp. 195 and 121.

21 "top billing": A.S., interview with Barbara Kevles, *NES*, p. 85.

21 "Have fallen": A.S. to Mary Jane Filer, 27 March 1947, HRHRC.

21 Alfred Muller Sexton II: Unless otherwise indicated, information about the Sexton family is drawn from an interview with Alfred M. Sexton, 21 February 1983.

22 "a woman of mystery": A.S. to Alfred M. Sexton, 4 June 1948, scrapbook, vertical files, HRHRC.

22 "a riot!": A.S., scrapbook, vertical files, HRHRC.

22 Invited to Sunday dinner: Editorial note by Linda Sexton and Lois Ames, Letters, p. 13.

23 "We eloped": Manuscript of untitled, unfinished novel, HRHRC.

23 "After a short time": Richard M. Sherwood to D.M., 20 February 1983.

23 "later on": Ralph Harvey to A.S., 26 August 1948, scrapbook, vertical files, HRHRC.

23 "We lived": A.S. to Marian Blanchard, 17 November 1971, HRHRC.

23 "Before I was married": A.S. typed notes to Dr. Orne, 25 May 1958.

24 "dedicated to the development": A.S. blue scrapbook, graduation certificate, 11 June 1949, vertical files, HRHRC.

24 "dreadful lies": A.S., interview with Alice Ryerson, January 1962, Radcliffe College Archives.

25 Billie also noticed: Editorial note by Linda Sexton and Lois Ames, Letters, p. 22.

26 She later recalled: A.S. to Dr. Orne, therapy tape, 29 February 1964.

26 "I took the pills": A.S., typed ms., "Sunday April 5" [1959?], doctor's files.

26 "difficulty controlling": Westwood Lodge medical records, 13 July 1956.

26 "When he's gone": A.S. to Dr. Orne, 16 November 1961. D.M. condensed material from the tape with notes Sexton entered for this session in her therapy notebook, which give slightly more emphasis to the sense of being out of control.

27 "I had given": A.S. to Dr. Orne, therapy tape, 11 March 1961.

27 "All of my mother's": A.S. interview with Alice Ryerson, January 1962, Radcliffe College Archives.

27 "first stirrings": Anna Ladd Dingley, diary, 20 February 1953, miscellaneous collection, HRHRC.

27 "Wheel collapsed": Anna Ladd Dingley, diary, 7 February 1953, miscellaneous collection, HRHRC.

28 "Nana, forgive me": A.S., in Anna Ladd Dingley, diary, miscellaneous collection, HRHRC.

28 "I hope to see": Ralph Harvey to A.S., miscellaneous collection, HRHRC.

29   "I was under his thumb": Alfred M. Sexton, interview with D.M., 21 February 1983.

29   "One of my presents": Ibid.

30   "Anne always dropped": Sandy Robart, interview with D.M., 11 November 1982.

30   "hanging over me": A.S., interview with Alice Ryerson, January 1962, Radcliffe College Archives.

3. BREAKING DOWN

31   "terrible spells of depression": A.S. to Dr. Orne, therapy tape, 10 March 1962.

31   "I came home": A.S. to Dr. Orne, therapy tape, 10 March 1962.

32   It was several days: Alfred M. Sexton, interview with D.M., 11 September 1989.

33   In later life: Editorial note, Linda Sexton and Lois Ames, *Letters*, p. 22; years later Sexton evoked this incident in the poem "Red Roses." Sexton's mother-in-law also recalled incidents of Anne's outbursts in an interview with D.M., 17 March 1983.

33   They called her psychiatrist: A.S. to Dr. Orne, therapy tape, 23 September 1961.

33   "I want to curl up": A.S. to Dr. Orne, 6 April 1961, doctor's files.

33   At the time, Dr. Brunner-Orne: A.S. to Dr. Orne, therapy tape, 28 April 1964.

33   "has no sympathy": Westwood Lodge medical record, 26 July 1956.

34   "rather prevalent psychoneurotic features": Westwood Lodge medical record, 13 July 1956.

34   When the effects: "Her routine would be, 'I took the pills, now save me.' " Alfred M. Sexton, interview with D.M., 11 September 1989.

34   "Her family was not": Martin Orne, interview with D.M., 4 December 1990.

35   "I was trying": A.S., interview with Barbara Kevles, *NES,* p. 84.

35   "Went to Billie's": A.S. diary, restricted collection, HRHRC.

35   "She wouldn't even": Wilhelmine Sexton Knight, interview with D.M., 17 March 1983.

35   "I just pretended": A.S., interview with Alice Ryerson, January 1962, Radcliffe College Archives.

36   "I used to leave": Alfred M. Sexton, interview with D.M., 21 February 1983.

36 "I am so alone": Handwritten notes dated "February 16th or so" [probably 1957], Dr. Orne file, restricted collection, HRHRC. Sexton's punctuation, except where bracketed.

37 An overview of her case: For assistance in formulating this overview of Sexton's disorders, I am grateful to Drs. Richard Almond, Ellen Bassuk, and Norman Dishotsky, as well as to Dr. Orne.

37 "I know I was dependent": A.S. to Dr. Orne, therapy tape, 9 May 1961.

37 "My mother": A.S., interview with Barbara Kevles, *NES*, p. 85.

37 "dancing the jig": "Dancing the Jig," *The Book of Folly* (Boston: Houghton Mifflin, 1972), pp. 65–71.

37 "a masculine Nana!": A.S. to Dr. Orne, therapy tape, 18 July 1961.

38 Even though Anne: In 1961, Sexton told Dr. Orne that her sister Jane had said that Nana's purchase of the picture of her "pretend brother" coincided with Nana's earliest symptoms of mental disorder. A.S. to Dr. Orne, therapy tape, 23 September 1961.

39 "I want to be a child": A.S., typed notes for Dr. Orne, 18 March 1957, restricted collection, HRHRC.

39 "She was very, very sick": Martin Orne, interview with D.M., 9 January 1991.

40 "I wanted to get married": A.S., interview with Alice Ryerson, January 1962, Radcliffe College Archives.

4. "THESE ARE MY PEOPLE"

41 "We had a relationship": Martin Orne, interview with D.M., 8 September 1989. Unless otherwise noted, all comments by Dr. Orne cited in this chapter are drawn from interviews with D.M. on 26 August 1985 and 8 September 1989, and by telephone in January 1991.

42 Dr. Orne's judgment: A.S. to Dr. Orne, therapy tape, 8 March 1962.

42 "I thought": A.S., interviews with Alice Ryerson, January 1962, and with Martha White, July 1963, Radcliffe College Archives.

42 "You can't kill yourself": A.S., interview with Alice Ryerson, January 1962, Radcliffe College Archives.

43 "I had found": A.S., interview with Barbara Kevles, *NES*, p. 85.

44 "All your life": Dr. Orne to A.S., therapy tape, 5 December 1963.

46   "No! Why should I?": A.S. notes, n.d. [February 1957], restricted collection, HRHRC.

46   "Mother makes me sick": A.S. diary, 10 February 1957, restricted collection, HRHRC.

47   " 'Mother sort of' ": Doctor's notes, 26 December 1957 and 21 November 1957.

47   "We have always been": Mary Gray Harvey, undated holograph letter, miscellaneous file, HRHRC.

47   "I will die": "A Small Journal," Ms., November 1973. Reprinted as "All God's Children Need Radios," NES, pp. 23–32.

47   "It matters not": Undated holograph manuscripts of poems by Mary Gray Harvey in miscellaneous file, HRHRC.

48   "I sit upon": A.S., "A Birthday," 1 September 1957, HRHRC.

48   "Mother probably": Adapted from doctor's notes [D.M. completed syntax], 24 April 1958.

49   "I always thought": A.S. to Dr. Orne, therapy tape, 11 July 1961.

49   "She had retreated": Sandy Robart, interview with D.M., 11 November 1982.

50   "all intimidating sophistication": Maxine Kumin, "How It Was," foreword to The Complete Poems of Anne Sexton, p. xix.

50   "The most important aspect": A.S., interview with Barbara Kevles, NES, p. 87.

51   "prayed that our poems": Maxine Kumin, "Reminiscence Delivered at Memorial Service for Anne Sexton in Marsh Chapel, Boston University," To Make a Prairie (Ann Arbor: University of Michigan Press, 1979), p. 79.

51   "unlike college": A.S. to a fan, R.S., 18 July 1963, HRHRC.

51   "Although I lie": "Traveler's Wife," in Letters, p. 25.

52   "I'd rather be doing": Adapted from doctor's notes [D.M. completed syntax], 29 November 1957.

52   "Some of them": Doctor's notes, 21 December 1957.

53   "implication of a psychosis": Doctor's notes, 6 March 1958.

53   "I had been with you": Adapted from doctor's notes [D.M. completed syntax], 15 December 1957.

53   "to learn what": Doctor's notes, 26 April 1958.

53   She appears: Doctor's notes, 14, 24, 26 April 1958, and in A.S., typed notes, circa 15 May 1958.

53   "Someone asked me": Doctor's notes, 12 February 1957.

54   "Well Doctor": A.S., "Real Love in Imaginary Wagon," doctor's files, 7 February 1957.

54   "More Than All the Rest": 8 February 1957; "The Poems I Gave You," 24 February 1957; doctor's files.

55 "Looked (for some reason)": A.S., typed notes, n.d. [probably mid-May 1958], doctor's files.

55 "Help me somehow": A.S., typed letter, 18 September [probably 1957], doctor's files.

55 "If you give": Ibid.

56 "Only sometimes": A.S., typed ms., n.d. [probably May 1958], doctor's files.

56 "Father comes in drunk": Doctor's notes, 13 May 1958.

56 "I couldn't make": A.S. to Dr. Orne, therapy tape, 18 April 1961.

58 "I could never believe": Lois Ames, phone conversation with D.M., 15 December 1990.

59 "looking at me": Sexton found references to this surgery in a book of her grandfather's letters that Mary Gray had bound and placed in the family library; when she asked about it, Mary Gray confirmed it. Doctor's notes, 22 May 1958.

59 "I have frozen": A.S. to Dr. Orne, therapy tape, 27 July 1963.

60 During the same months: Doctor's notes, 16 November 1957. "Jerry" is a pseudonym.

60 "With Jerry": Doctor's notes, 23 December 1957; "Jerry is vital": Doctor's notes, 18 November 1957.

60 "Problem of Jerry": Doctor's notes, 2 December 1957.

60 "I think it's me": Doctor's notes, 2 December 1957.

60 "I suppose": A.S., typed notes, n.d. [probably May 1958], doctor's files.

60 "It was helpful": Dr. Orne, phone conversation with D.M., 18 February 1991.

61 " 'Elizabeth' expresses": Dr. Orne to A.S., quoted by A.S. in therapy notebook, 27 February 1964, restricted collection, HRHRC.

61 "I feel like": Doctor's notes, 8 February 1958.

61 As early as November: Doctor's notes, 6 November 1957.

61 "can't be determined": Doctor's notes, 1 May 1957.

61 "Poems don't lie": Adapted from doctor's notes [D.M. completed syntax], 1 May 1958.

62 "I am nothing": A.S., typed notes, 29 April 1958, doctor's files.

62 "truth crimes": A.S., typed notes, n.d. [probably May 1958], doctor's files.

63 Actually, Sexton had confessed: Doctor's notes, 16 November 1957.

63 "I realize, with guilt": A.S., typed notes, n.d. [circa 15 May 1958], doctor's files.

63   "Only in that funny": A.S., typed notes, n.d. [probably early May 1958], doctor's files.

63   "Think I am a poet?": Doctor's notes, 24 April 1958.

63   "My goals": A.S., typed notes, 30 May [1958], doctor's files.

64   "I was thrilled": A.S. to Anne Wilder, 3 July 1964, *Letters*, pp. 244–45. "Anne Clark," the name used in *Letters*, is a pseudonym.

64   "It is the split self": A.S., "Lecture Nine," Crashaw Lectures at Colgate University, 1972, HRHRC.

64   "Not all language": A.S. to Anne Wilder, 3 July 1964, *Letters*, p. 245.

65   "The surface cracked": A.S., interview with Barbara Kevles, *NES*, p. 84.

65   "I found I belonged": Ibid.

65   "By God, I don't": A.S. to Dr. Orne, therapy tape, 9 May 1961.

65   "Here are some": A.S. to Mary Gray Harvey, Christmas Day 1957, *Letters*, pp. 31, 33.

66   "NEVER TO BE SEEN": After considerable deliberation, Linda Sexton decided to place this manuscript with Sexton's other papers in the Sexton Archive at the HRHRC, with the understanding that the poems would not be published, but would be available to scholars interested in studying Sexton's development as an artist. They are currently in the restricted collection, HRHRC. Among these are the more than sixty poems that Sexton had also been bringing to therapy.

5. FROM *RATS* TO *STAR*

69   "the most frump": Anne Sexton and Maxine Kumin, joint interview with Elaine Showalter and Carol Smith, 15 April 1974. See "A Nurturing Relationship," *Women's Studies*, 4 (1976): 116, reprinted in *NES*, pp. 158–79.

69   "Music Swims Back to Me": *CP*, pp. 6–7. A draft of this poem in Dr. Orne's files is dated 29 September 1957.

71   "almost whole": Maxine Kumin, interview with D.M., 11 November 1982.

71   Born in 1925: Information condensed from Maxine Kumin, interview with D.M., 18 June 1983; from Kumin's interview with Joan Norris, in Kumin, *To Make a Prairie* (Ann Arbor: University of Michigan Press, 1979), pp. 12–18; and from Kumin's brief memoir "Blessed Be the Tie that Binds," *The Harvard Gazette*, 3 June 1983, p. 14.

72   "I made a pact": Maxine Kumin, interview with D.M., 11 November 1982.
73   "Max is Jewish": Doctor's notes, 8 December 1957.
73   "I think Max": Doctor's notes, 17 and 21 December 1957.
73   "It is my personal belief": George E. Sexton to Dr. Orne, 8 April 1957.
73   "take half an hour": Doctor's notes, 8 February 1958.
73   "If I didn't have [Linda]": Doctor's notes, 18 November 1957.
73   "I've loved Joy": Doctor's notes, 17 December 1957.
73   "I *think* a different": A.S., typed notes, 13 April 1958, doctor's files.
75   "My father was terribly proud": A.S., interview with Alice Ryerson, January 1962, Radcliffe College Archives.
75   "I really have the feeling": Doctor's notes, 24 April 1958.
76   "yet here I am": Doctor's notes, 20 April 1958.
76   "gray flannel poetry": Arthur Freeman, interview with D.M., London, 8 August 1987.
77   "I ran up": A.S., interview with Barbara Kevles, *NES,* p. 89.
78   "Other poems": Robert Lowell, interview with Frederick Seidel, *Paris Review* 25 (Winter–Spring 1961), pp. 56–95.
78   "When I read": A.S. to W. D. Snodgrass, 11 March 1959, *Letters,* p. 66.
78   "Unknown Girl in the Maternity Ward": *CP,* pp. 24–25.
79   "furious — purple with rage": Doctor's notes, 19 April 1958.
79   "In a physical way": Doctor's notes, 20 April 1958.
80   "He said that": Adapted from doctor's notes [D.M. completed syntax], 3 May 1958.
80   "As Ruth advised": A.S. to W. D. Snodgrass, 31 August 1958.
81   "by a considerable margin," "Everything she wrote": W. D. Snodgrass, audiotaped comments for D.M., September 1985.
81   "Here I am": Nolan Miller to D.M., 9 September 1985.
81   "Bawdy and funny": Jack Matthews to D.M., 16 November 1988.
81   "Dashing": Nolan Miller to D.M., 9 September 1985.
81   "simply marvelous": W. D. Snodgrass, audiotaped comments for D.M., September 1985.
81   "terribly exciting": Ibid.
82   "If I write RATS": A.S., typed notes, 29 September 1958, doctor's files.
84   "The Double Image": *CP,* p. 27.
84   "Dear passionflower": A.S. to W. D. Snodgrass, 28 November 1958, *Letters,* p. 45.
84   "I am always saved": A.S. to W. D. Snodgrass, 15 November 1958, *Letters,* p. 41.

85   "the unconscious area": A.S. to W. D. Snodgrass, 31 August 1958, *Letters*, pp. 35–38.

87   "the 'sealed hotel' ": A.S. to W. D. Snodgrass, n.d. [circa 26 November 1958], *Letters*, pp. 43–44.

87   "The mother-daughter": A.S. on Florence Lennon's "Enjoyment of Poetry," 9 April 1961 (Library of Congress T 3993).

88   "What the poem does": Ibid.

89   "Mother wasn't a Puritan": A.S. to Dr. Orne, therapy tape, 24 May 1962.

89   "You have 'discovered' me": A.S. to Russell Lynes, 29 October 1958, HRHRC.

89   "You have real power": Frederick Morgan to A.S., 16 December 1958, HRHRC.

6. MENTORS

91   "Of course": Robert Lowell to A.S., 11 September 1958, HRHRC.

91   Lowell's writing courses: See Judith Baumel, "Robert Lowell: The Teacher," and Alan Williamson, "Robert Lowell: A Reminiscence," *Harvard Advocate* 13, nos. 1 and 2 (November 1979), 32, 38.

92   "I shall never": A.S. to W. D. Snodgrass, 6 October 1958, *Letters*, p. 40.

93   "Cal had to be": Quoted in Ian Hamilton, *Robert Lowell: A Biography* (New York: Random House, 1982), p. 241.

93   After Lowell was appointed: Kathleen Spivack, "Lear in Boston: Robert Lowell as Teacher and Friend," *Ironwood* 25 (1985): 90.

93   "soft dangerous voice": A.S. to W. D. Snodgrass, 26 November 1958, *Letters*, p. 43.

93   "almost perfect": Celia Gilbert, "The Sacred Fire," *Working It Out*, ed. Sara Ruddick and Pamela Daniels (New York: Pantheon Books, 1977), p. 313.

93   "I am very bitchy": A.S. to W. D. Snodgrass, 11 January 1959, *Letters*, p. 49.

93   "Lowell can not": A.S. to W. D. Snodgrass, 1 February 1959, *Letters*, p. 53.

93   "I am learning leaps": A.S. to W. D. Snodgrass, 11 January 1959, *Letters*, p. 48.

93   "He taught me great": A.S. to W. D. Snodgrass, 9 June 1959, *Letters*, pp. 79–80.

94   "Jesus God!": W. D. Snodgrass to A.S., 2 December 1958, HRHRC.

94 "Lowell is really helping": A.S. to W. D. Snodgrass, 1 February 1959, *Letters*, pp. 51–52.

94 She "would willingly": Maxine Kumin, "How It Was," *CP*, p. xxv.

95 "Despite many successes": A.S. to Howard Moss, 13 February 1959, *Letters*, p. 60.

95 "It is politics": A.S. to W. D. Snodgrass, 24 February 1959, *Letters*, p. 64.

95 "Anne struck me": Frederick Morgan, interview with D.M., 19 November 1982.

96 "I might have axed": A.S. to W. D. Snodgrass, 1 February 1959, *Letters*, p. 50.

96 "Most of the really": A.S. to W. D. Snodgrass, 11 March 1959, *Letters*, p. 65.

96 When the workshop met: Doris Holmes Eyges, interview with D.M., 9 October 1982.

97 "held court for us": Joseph DeRoche, journal entry, 16 November 1960.

98 "None of us": George Starbuck, interview with D.M., 13 September 1983.

98 There are no: "For God While Sleeping," worksheets, HRHRC.

98 "It's a book": John Holmes to A.S., 8 February 1959, HRHRC.

100 "I tapped my own head": *CP*, pp. 34–35. Earlier stanzas of the poem echo phrases from Holmes's letter.

100 "ragged with horrors": Doris Holmes Eyges, interview with D.M., 9 October 1982.

100 "John never got over it": Maxine Kumin, interview with D.M., 9 October 1980.

101 "He acts about ten": A.S. to W. D. Snodgrass, 8 February 1959, *Letters*, p. 51.

101 "blown up": A.S., typed notes, n.d. ["Sat p.m."], doctor's files.

101 "I feel as if": A.S. to W. D. Snodgrass, 8 February 1959, *Letters*, p. 51.

101 "I go in today": A.S., typed notes, n.d. ["Sat p.m."], doctor's files.

101 "if I don't watch out": A.S. to W. D. Snodgrass, 8 February 1959, *Letters*, p. 51.

102 Mary Gray had seen: A.S., interview with Barbara Kevles, *NES*, p. 88.

102 "didn't pick it apart": A.S. to W. D. Snodgrass, 11 March 1959, *Letters*, p. 65.

102 "I know it's crazy": A.S. to W. D. Snodgrass, 8 February 1959, *Letters*, p. 51.

102   "I wanted to hold": A.S. to Anne Wilder, 22 January 1964, *Letters,* pp. 229–30.

102   "The Division of Parts": *CP,* pp. 42–46.

103   "who also wrote": Adrienne Rich, interview with D.M., 18 May 1983.

103   "I shall go better": *The Journals of Sylvia Plath,* ed. Ted Hughes and Frances McCullough (New York: Dial, 1982), p. 164.

104   "tough, knotty": Ibid., p. 222.

104   "an objective structure": Ibid., p. 263.

104   "laziness": Ibid., p. 293.

104   "the quiet righteous": Ibid., p. 186.

104   "Arrogant, I think": Ibid., pp. 211–12.

105   " 'Reminds me of Empson' ": Kathleen Spivack, "Lear in Boston," op. cit., p. 81; and "Poets and Friends," *Boston Globe Magazine,* August 9, 1981, p. 11.

105   "peculiar private and taboo": Quoted in A. Alvarez, "Sylvia Plath," *The Art of Sylvia Plath,* ed. Charles Newman (Bloomington: Indiana University Press, 1970), p. 62.

105   "eight years later": Kathleen Spivack, "Robert Lowell: A Memoir," *The Antioch Review,* p. 188.

105   "We orbited": A.S., "The Bar Fly Ought to Sing," *The Art of Sylvia Plath,* p. 174; reprinted in *NES,* pp. 6–13.

105   "might rub off": Robert Lowell, interview with Ian Hamilton, *American Poetry Review* (September/October 1978): 27.

105   For example, Sexton's: Heather Cam rediscovered "My Friend, My Friend" and comments on its influence in " 'Daddy': Sylvia Plath's Debt to Anne Sexton," *American Literature* 59, no. 3 (1987): 429–32. The poem is reprinted in *Selected Poems of Anne Sexton,* ed. Diane Wood Middlebrook and Diana Hume George (Boston: Houghton Mifflin, 1988), p. 5.

106   "I cry at everything": *Journals of Sylvia Plath,* op. cit., pp. 300–301.

106   "We would pile": "The Bar Fly Ought to Sing," op. cit., pp. 174–75.

107   "I guess that's as close": George Starbuck, interview with D.M., 13 September 1983.

108   "I should be turning": *Journals of Sylvia Plath,* op. cit., p. 302.

108   "An insufferable woman": Ibid., p. 311.

108   "The cooked": Quoted in Hamilton, op. cit., p. 277.

109   During his convalescence: Ibid., pp. 227–38, 253–68.

109   "The diagnosed manic-depressive": Ibid., p. 257.

109 "There's a strange fact": Ibid., p. 337.

110 "(shhh secret)": A.S. to W. D. Snodgrass, "April in Wednesday" [1959], HRHRC.

110 "Lowell has shifted": A.S. to W. D. Snodgrass, 1 May 1959, private collection of W.D.S.

110 "In the thin classroom": "Elegy in the Classroom," *CP*, p. 32.

110 "I remember feeling": Adrienne Rich, interview with D.M., 18 May 1983.

111 "I answered something": Ibid.

111 in the women's poetry: Sylvia Plath, "The Disquieting Muses," *The Colossus* (London: William Heinemann, 1960), pp. 58–60; Adrienne Rich, "Snapshots of a Daughter-in-Law," *Snapshots of a Daughter-in-Law* (New York: Norton, 1967), pp. 21–25.

113 "real situations": *Journals of Sylvia Plath*, op. cit., p. 298.

113 "not a love lyric": A.S. to W. D. Snodgrass, 9 June 1959, *Letters*, p. 80.

114 "Who see me here": Worksheets, *To Bedlam and Part Way Back*, HRHRC.

114 "I have gone out": "Her Kind," *CP*, pp. 15–16.

7. DEATHS, DISPLACEMENTS, AND SUBSTITUTIONS

116 "almost nil": A.S., interview with J. D. McClatchy, 23 September 1973, private collection.

116 "His personality changed": A.S. to Dr. Orne, therapy tape, 13 April 1961.

117 Astounded by the bad news: Linda Sexton, interview with D.M., 13 October 1980.

117 "The trouble": A.S. to W. D. Snodgrass, 9 June 1959, *Letters*, p. 81.

118 "the big ones": Arthur Freeman, interview with D.M., 1 August 1987.

118 "To the one": *Bone Thoughts* (New Haven: Yale University Press, 1960), p. vi.

118 "Doors, Doors, Doors": *CP*, p. 80. Sexton enclosed an early version of this poem in a letter to Snodgrass (23 September 1959) that included the lines "We do not say that my mother and father are really dead. / We do not explain doom. We make house. Love is the only leaven." HRHRC.

119 That fall, one of her readings: A.S. to Frederick Morgan, 16 October 1959, *Letters*, p. 89. This recording apparently was never pressed for the series.

119   At the party: Herbert Gold to D.M., 1 January 1989.

120   "I soar": *CP*, p. 58.

121   "Kayo's father": A.S. to W. D. Snodgrass, 25 March 1960, *Letters*, p. 100.

122   "I have, indeed": "Notebooks Started May 25th, 1960, Anne Sexton," 1960–1965, HRHRC.

122   "The life of poetry": A.S. to W. D. Snodgrass, 10 or 11 May 1960, *Letters*, p. 107.

122   "I certainly don't believe": A.S. to W. D. Snodgrass, 1 February 1960, *Letters*, p. 98.

122   "I wish religion": A.S. to W. D. Snodgrass, 25 March 1960.

122   "For my friend": "With Mercy for the Greedy," *CP*, pp. 61–63.

123   "I think Maxine": George Starbuck, interview with D.M., 9 September 1983.

124   "An Obsessive Combination": In *Voices: A Journal of Poetry*, no. 169 (1959): 34; reprinted in *SP*, p. 4.

124   "In the Deep Museum": Sexton later acknowledged James Wright's influence on this poem. A.S. to Thomas Victor, 12 May 1971, HRHRC.

124   "Of course I KNOW": A.S., typed notes, 29 September 1958, doctor's files.

125   "a natural": Thomas Lask, "Books of the Times," *New York Times*, 18 July 1960, p. 25.

125   "Irving Howe said": Allen Grossman, interview with D.M., 13 October 1982.

125   "seem to me": Allen Grossman to A.S., 24 June 1960, HRHRC. His review, "The Point of View of the Survivor: Anne Sexton," was published in *The Justice*, 11 June 1960, p. 7.

125   "John Holmes saw it": A.S. to Dr. Orne, 26 June 1960, doctor's files.

125   "She *is* good": Elizabeth Bishop to Robert Lowell, 19 May 1960, Houghton Library; quoted in D.M., "Anne Sexton and Robert Lowell," *Original Essays on the Poetry of Anne Sexton*, ed. Frances Bixler (Conway: University of Central Arkansas Press, 1988), pp. 18–19.

126   "the luckiest poet": Elizabeth Bishop to Robert Lowell, 14 December 1957; quoted in Hamilton, *Robert Lowell*, op. cit., p. 233.

126   "from the other side": Allen Grossman, interview with D.M., 13 October 1982. Grossman's term *dérèglement* refers to Rimbaud's dictum, "Le Poète se fait voyant par un long, immense et raisonné dérèglement de tous les sens."

126   The review Sexton took: James Dickey, "Five First Books," *Poetry*, February 1961; reprinted in McClatchy, pp. 117–18.

126   "But you've just started": A.S. to Dr. Orne, therapy tape, 14 February 1961.

126   "As a poet": A.S. to Nolan Miller, 11 May 1959, HRHRC.

127   "Howe had written": A.S. to W. D. Snodgrass, 11 October 1960, *Letters*, p. 114.

127   "a wonderful pair": George Starbuck, interview with D.M., 9 September 1983.

127   "It is amazing": A.S. to Dr. Orne, 1 June 1960, doctor's files.

127   "Walking into places": A.S., typed notes, n.d. [probably 1957], doctor's files.

127   "It's very important": A.S. to Dr. Orne, 26 June 1960, doctor's files.

127   "Rahv asked me": A.S. to W. D. Snodgrass, 11 October 1960, *Letters*, p. 114.

128   "After two hours": A.S., eulogy for Philip Rahv, 24 December 1973, HRHRC.

128   "Anne kept on": George Starbuck, interview with D.M., 9 September 1983.

128   "several hundred": A.S. to Brother Dennis Farrell, 22 January 1963, restricted collection, HRHRC. "Brother Dennis Farrell" is the pseudonym used in *Letters*.

129   "I wasn't poor": A.S. to James Wright, 21 March 1962, Kenyon College Archive.

129   "Be glad of": James Wright, "A Fit against the Country," *The Green Wall* (New Haven: Yale University Press, 1957), p. 3.

129   "I knew that": A.S. to James Wright, 21 March 1962, Kenyon College Archive.

130   "Blessing": James Wright, "A Blessing," *Collected Poems* (Middletown, Conn.: Wesleyan University Press, 1971), p. 135.

130   "My beautiful kind": James Wright to A.S., 12 August 1960, HRHRC.

130   "is a South American": Ibid.

130   "narrower and less powerful": James Wright to A.S., 16 August 1960, HRHRC.

131   "To Anne Sexton": Anne Sexton Archive, HRHRC.

131   "I just left": A.S. to Dr. Orne, therapy tape, 9 September 1961.

131   "like a king": A.S. to Dr. Orne, therapy tape, 21 April 1962.

132   "I was afraid": James Wright to Dr. Orne, 14 September 1960.

133   "as is my habit": Ibid.

133   "The gray world": Ibid.

133   "You people don't understand": Quoted by A.S., therapy note-book, 19 April 1962, restricted collection, HRHRC.

133   "I kept paying": Ibid.

133   "Lazy on a Saturday Morning": Anne Sexton Archive, miscellaneous file, James Wright, page dated 8 Sept 1960, HRHRC.

134   "My dear Bee": James Wright to A.S., 11 July 1962, HRHRC.

134   "It makes transference": A.S., therapy notebook, 11 July 1961, restricted collection, HRHRC.

135   "I've never known": Dr. Orne to A.S., therapy tape, 23 April 1964.

135   "safe": Joy Sexton, phone conversation with D.M., 24 January 1991.

136   "I used to tease": Joy Sexton, interview with D.M., 13 September 1989.

8. GETTING A HEARING

137   "Anne was so busy": Dr. Orne, conversation with D.M., 28 January 1989.

138   "symptoms that some part": Dr. Orne to A.S., therapy tape, 5 December 1963.

138   "It allowed Anne": Dr. Orne, conversation with D.M., 28 January 1989.

138   "I hate to go": A.S. to Dr. Orne, therapy tape, 9 March 1961.

138   "Somebody sees me": A.S. to Dr. Orne, therapy tape, 2 January 1962.

139   "I feel as if": A.S. to Dr. Orne, therapy tape, 21 February 1961.

139   "Right now": A.S., therapy notebook, 19 January 1961, restricted collection, HRHRC.

139   "The time has": Dr. Orne to A.S., therapy tape, 21 February 1961.

139   "This is the audience": Quoted by A.S. to Dr. Orne, therapy tape, 9 February 1961.

139   "I have felt": A.S. to Louis Untermeyer, 8 February 1961, HRHRC.

139   "a mess of father substitutes": A.S. to Dr. Orne, therapy tape, 27 April 1961.

139   The resulting talk: A.S. to Dr. Orne, therapy tape, 29 April 1961.

140   "Anne read splendidly": Peter Davison, interview with D.M., 6 June 1983.

140   "I was scared": A.S. to Dr. Orne, therapy tape, 25 April 1961.

140   "Why do we stand": John Holmes to Maxine Kumin, 6 August 1961, private collection.

141   "You gave Sam": John Holmes to Anne Sexton, 25 January 1961, HRHRC.

141   "What kind of workshop": A.S. to John Holmes, 30 January 1961, *Letters*, pp. 118–19.

141   "This perfect voice": A.S. and Dr. Orne, therapy tape, 7 February 1961.

142   "Max and I": A.S. to Dr. Orne, therapy tape, 17 June 1961.

142   "We sometimes connected": Maxine Kumin, "A Friendship Remembered," in McClatchy, p. 103.

142   "milk[ing] the unconscious": A.S., interview with Barbara Kevles, *NES*, p. 85.

142   "All poets": A.S., interview with Brigitte Weeks, *NES*, p. 114.

143   "ongoing, complete encouragement": Maxine Kumin, interview with D.M., 9 October 1980.

143   "I said way back": John Holmes to Maxine Kumin, 16 August 1961, private collection.

143   "wrote openly about": Maxine Kumin, "How It Was," *CP*, p. xxxiv.

144   "harness the talents": Fred M. Hechinger, "Radcliffe Pioneers in Plan for Gifted Women's Study," *New York Times*, 20 November 1960, p. 1.

144   "climate of unexpectation": Dr. Mary Ingraham Bunting, interview with D.M., 2 December 1982.

145   "I know my academic background": Application to the Radcliffe Institute, 7 March 1961, Radcliffe College Archives.

145   "unusually keen": Ibid.

145   "Wow!": Ibid.

145   "running into": A.S., interview with Alice Ryerson, January 1962, Radcliffe College Archives.

145   "Hark Hark": A.S. to Dr. Orne, 29 May 1961, HRHRC.

145   "This is something": A.S to Dr. Orne, therapy tape, 30 May 1961.

145   "was a real coup": A.S. to Dr. Orne, therapy tape, 27 April 1961.

147   "And now, what do I say": Anthony Hecht to A.S., 14 April 1961, HRHRC.

147   "I have come to think": Anthony Hecht to A.S., 23 May 1961, HRHRC.

147   "It's not that I want": A.S. to Dr. Orne, therapy tape, 15 June 1961.

147   "It's not that I'm beautiful": A.S. to Dr. Orne, therapy tape, 20 June 1961.

148   "As though Oedipus": James Wright, holograph notes on manuscript filed in A.S. Works, *All My Pretty Ones*, HRHRC.

148   "A woman who writes": *CP*, p. 88.

149   "A warm-to-hot": Roger Hecht to D.M., 25 November 1986.

149   "No matter what": A.S. to James Wright, 6 February 1964,
HRHRC.

149   "Letter Written During a January Northeaster": *CP*, pp. 91–92.

150   "sent her willing children": "Women of Talent," *Newsweek*, 23
October 1961, p. 97.

150   hated the clutter: A.S., interview with Alice Ryerson, January
1962, Radcliffe College Archives.

151   "I can meet my goals": A.S., interview with Martha White, July
1963, Radcliffe College Archives.

151   The long window: A.S. to Brother Dennis Farrell, 21 July 1962,
Letters, p. 143.

151   "My books make me happy": A.S., interview with Alice Ryerson,
January 1962, Radcliffe College Archives.

151   "That's a very big subject": Ibid.

152   "I used to go around": A.S., interview with Martha White, July
1963, Radcliffe College Archives.

152   "Only a few poets": Louis Untermeyer to A.S., 10 January 1962,
HRHRC.

152   "It's a status symbol": A.S., interview with Alice Ryerson, January 1962, Radcliffe College Archives.

152   Years later: Linda Sexton to D.M., 17 July 1989.

152   "She begged me": A.S. to Dr. Orne, therapy tape, 17 June 1961.

153   "I *always* lived": Linda Sexton, interview with D.M., 13 October
1980.

153   Joy remembered: Joy Sexton, interview with D.M., 24 September
1986.

154   "It's just like Jekyll and Hyde": A.S. to Dr. Orne, therapy tape,
27 June 1961.

154   "Oh my God": All details of the following account of the quarrel
are from A.S.'s description to Dr. Orne, therapy tape, 27 June
1961.

156   "I can no longer act": A.S. to Dr. Orne, therapy tape, 17 February
1962.

156   "My husband can't see": A.S., condensed from interview with
Martha White, July 1963, Radcliffe College Archives.

157   "The only thing": A.S. to Dr. Orne, therapy tape, 29 June 1961.

157   "exotic birds": "On the Edge of Women's Liberation," Brita
Stendahl, *Radcliffe Quarterly*, June 1986, p. 16.

157 "torn from a couple": Audiotape recording of presentations by Maxine Kumin and Anne Sexton at the Radcliffe Institute, 13 February 1962, Radcliffe College Archives.

158 "The Fortress": *CP*, pp. 66–68.

160 "You could say": A.S., interview with Martha White, July 1963, Radcliffe College Archives.

160 " 'like a witch' ": A.S. to Dr. Orne, therapy tape, 11 July 1961.

160 "because it's not so much": A.S. to Dr. Orne, therapy tape, 6 July 1961.

160 "Writers are such phonies": A.S. to Dr. Orne, therapy tape, 21 September 1961.

160 "I think you can move": A.S. to Dr. Orne, therapy tape, 30 November 1961.

160 "And I have a best-seller": A.S. to Dr. Orne, therapy tape, 25 July 1961.

161 "pose as having": John Updike to A.S., 8 December 1961, HRHRC.

161 "If Saul Bellow": A.S., therapy notebook, 30 November 1961, restricted collection, HRHRC.

161 "the grown-up's Salinger": A.S. to Dr. Orne, therapy tape, 25 November 1961.

162 "the greatest American": A.S. to Dr. Orne, therapy tape, 15 June 1961.

162 "All my decay": A.S. to Dr. Orne, therapy tape, 14 October 1961.

162 "we seem to have entered": Saul Bellow to A.S., n.d. [November 1961], HRHRC.

162 "It was like getting a letter": A.S. to Dr. Orne, therapy tape, 25 November 1961.

162 "I had been reading": Ibid.

163 Linda and Joy remembered: Linda and Joy Sexton, interview with D.M., 6 October 1989.

163 Talking to Linda: A.S. to Dr. Orne, therapy tape, 31 August 1961.

163 "Unlike other doctors": Dr. Orne to A.S., therapy tape, 28 November 1961, and conversation with D.M., 28 January 1989.

164 "but not knowing": A.S. to Dr. Orne, therapy tape, 21 November 1961. This tape is the source of Sexton's entire narrative about this episode.

165 "I raided the poisons": A.S. to Dr. Orne, n.d., written while awaiting Kayo's return from his hunting trip 19 November 1961, doctor's files.

165   "If I didn't have Deprol": A.S. to Dr. Orne, therapy tape, 25 November 1961.

165   "You said to me": A.S. to Dr. Orne, therapy tape, 30 November 1961.

9. POETRY AND THE UNCONSCIOUS

166   "If Kayo would take": A.S. to Dr. Orne, therapy tape, 6 January 1962.

166   "The feeling": A.S. to Dr. Orne, therapy tapes, 4 and 9 January 1962.

167   "fierce unreasonable emotion": A.S. to Dr. Orne, 6 April 1961, doctor's files.

167   "I never want to go beyond": A.S. and Dr. Orne, therapy tape, 25 January 1962.

168   "She is very good": A.S. to Dr. Orne, therapy tape, 17 February 1962.

168   "forty dollars' worth": A.S. to Dr. Orne, therapy tape, 25 January 1962.

168   "Four scenes": A.S. to Robert Lowell, 25 January 1962, *Letters,* p. 134.

168   "I'm no more a woman": The play contains lines that Sexton eventually built into the poem "Consorting with Angels," published in *Carleton Miscellany* 4 (Spring 1963): 41–44, and reprinted in *Live or Die* (1966).

168   "I'll do the priest": Quoted by A.S. to Dr. Orne, therapy tape, 23 January 1962.

168   "Very interesting": Audiotape of reading and discussion at Charles Playhouse, n.d. [January 1962], HRHRC; quoted by A.S., "Author in Residence in a Little Town Called Boston," unpublished ms., HRHRC.

169   "After the first student": Jeffrey Moussaieff Masson, interview with D.M., 10 May 1989.

170   Ted Weiss noted that Sexton: Ted Weiss, interview with D.M., 3 February 1984.

170   "He looks across": John Holmes, stanzas appended to "The Five," in a letter to Maxine Kumin, 26 February 1962, private collection.

170   "We were so sure": A.S. to Dr. Orne, therapy tape, 17 May 1962.

171   "Must you leave": *CP,* pp. 106–7.

173   "Mrs. Sexton sings": Charles Simmons, *Saturday Review of Literature,* 30 March 1963, p. 47.

173 "It would be hard": James Dickey, "Dialogues with Themselves," *New York Times Book Review*, 28 April 1963, p. 50.

173 "is 'she writes' ": A.S., interview with Alice Ryerson, January 1962, Radcliffe College Archives.

173 "My comment is this": A.S. to APHRA [Elizabeth Fisher], 2 July 1969, HRHRC.

174 "I was absolutely": Sylvia Plath to Anne Sexton, 21 August 1962, HRHRC.

174 "You began right off": Elizabeth Bishop to A.S., 14 September 1962, HRHRC.

174 "Your new book": Denise Levertov to A.S., 29 November 1962, HRHRC.

174 "all I can do": A.S. to Dr. Orne, therapy tape, 16 January 1962.

174 "I would like": A.S., typed notes, 13 January 1962, restricted collection, HRHRC.

175 "no tape": A.S. to Dr. Orne, therapy tape, 23 June 1962.

175 Sexton went in: The tape for this session is missing. This account is reconstructed from Sexton's therapy notebook, from Dr. Orne's summary of it at the beginning of their next session, and from references made to it in subsequent sessions.

175 "There I was": A.S. to Dr. Orne, therapy tape, 26 February 1963.

175 "My publisher sent": A.S. to Dr. Orne, therapy tapes, 23 June 1962 and 26 February 1963. The poem is "Fêtes de la faim." Discussing the background to "Flee on Your Donkey" later, Sexton slightly rewrote the episode: see Lecture Seven, Crashaw Lectures, HRHRC.

176 "I have liabilities": Dr. Orne to A.S., therapy tape 2 (of 2), 19 June 1962.

176 "I haven't even gone": A.S. to Dr. Orne, therapy tape, 21 June 1962.

176 "Will you leave": A.S. and Dr. Orne, therapy tape, 20 September 1962.

176 "Flee on Your Donkey": *CP*, pp. 97–98.

178 "some terrible evil": A.S. to Dr. Orne, therapy tape, 14 November 1961.

178 Like Daddy: A.S. to Dr. Orne, therapy tape, 26 February 1963.

179 Sexton commented: A.S. to Dr. Orne, therapy tape, 28 February 1963.

179 "your ego and your unconscious": A.S. to Dr. Orne, therapy tape, 10 January 1963.

180 "what my unconscious": Ibid.

180   "Writing is much more": A.S., interview with J. D. McClatchy, 23 September 1973, private collection.
180   "For example": A.S. to Dr. Orne, therapy tape, 10 January 1963.
180   "adds a sound": Lecture Three, Crashaw Lectures, HRHRC.
180   "I know it's not": A.S. to Dr. Orne, therapy tape, 10 January 1963.
181   "An editor works": A.S. to Dr. Orne, therapy tape, 11 April 1961.
181   "Lowell said it ought": A.S. and Dr. Orne, therapy tape, 28 February 1963.
182   "So I became": Arthur Freeman, interview with D.M., 8 August 1987.
182   She began writing: Brother Dennis Farrell to A.S., 26 June 1961, HRHRC. "Dennis Farrell," the name used in *Letters,* is a pseudonym.
182   "Grace is working": Brother Dennis Farrell to A.S., 5 February 1962, restricted collection, HRHRC.
183   "I'm in trouble": A.S. to Brother Dennis Farrell, 21 June 1962, *Letters,* p. 141.
183   "I need you — ": A.S. to James Wright, 18 June 1962, Kenyon College Archive.
183   "I am black": Brother Dennis Farrell to A.S., 1 July 1962, restricted collection, HRHRC.
183   "for a destiny": A.S. to Brother Dennis Farrell, 5 January 1963, HRHRC.
183   "I am so rather hysterical": A.S. to Brother Dennis Farrell, 19 November 1962, *Letters,* pp. 148–49.
184   "a human relationship": A.S. to Brother Dennis Farrell, 28 March 1963, *Letters,* p. 159.
184   "It totally suits": A.S. to Dr. Orne, therapy tape, 20 September 1962.
185   "I'd be on my way": Joy Sexton, interview with D.M., 24 September 1986.
185   "Anne was really": Jane Kumin, conversation with D.M., 10 May 1986.
185   Sexton received galleys: A.S. to Paul Brooks, 8 August 1962, HRHRC.
185   "little moments": Robert Lowell to A.S., 1 December 1961, HRHRC.
186   "Leave the Lowell quote": A.S. to Paul Brooks, 13 April 1962, HRHRC.
186   "I'm calling the lecture": Denise Levertov to A.S., 29 November 1962, HRHRC. This lecture evolved into Levertov's influential

essay "Some Notes on Organic Form," first published in *Poetry,*
September 1965.

186   "[Sexton] has, in Mr. Lowell's": Richard Howard, "Five Poets,"
Poetry, March 1963, pp. 413–14.

187   "You don't write": A.S., "Program P.M.," WBZ Boston, 18
February 1962, audiotape, HRHRC.

187   "Frankly I do not": A.S. to R.R.R., 26 February 1963, "Fan
Mail" file, HRHRC.

188   "It seems to me": A.S., typed manuscript, no title, holograph
note "B.C., Nov 4th, 1962," HRHRC.

10. CIRCLE OF WOMEN ARTISTS

193   "My heart started": A.S. to Dr. Orne, therapy tape, 12 March
1963.

194   "for [Sexton's] singular": Citation dated 22 May 1963, signed
by Lewis Mumford, President, American Academy of Arts and
Letters, HRHRC.

194   "She *is* cultural": A.S. to Anne Ford, 29 May 1963, HRHRC.

194   "I'll have to go up": A.S. and Dr. Orne, therapy tape, 18 May
1963.

194   "When I'm that": A.S. to Dr. Orne, therapy tape, 27 July
1963.

195   "others who sustain": Tillie Olsen to A.S., postcard, 7 November
1960, HRHRC.

195   "Have been all": Maxine Kumin to A.S., 23 August 1963,
HRHRC.

195   "upbringing": Tillie Olsen, interview with D.M., 12 June
1987.

196   "We were walking": Ibid.

196   "the Premier Cru": Barbara Swan, "Premier Cru," *Radcliffe
Quarterly,* June 1986, pp. 17–18. The other visual artist at the
Radcliffe Institute in 1961–1962 was Lois Swirnoff.

196   "Anne was a beauty": Barbara Swan, "A Reminiscence," in
McClatchy, p. 83.

196   "There is nothing": Barbara Swan, interview with D.M., 4 December 1982.

197   "Barbara and Anne": Tillie Olsen, interview with D.M., 12 June
1987.

197   Sexton based: A.S. to Dr. Orne, therapy tapes, 10 January and
28 February 1963.

197   "Anne moved into": Swan, "A Reminiscence," p. 82.
197   That was the year: A.S. to Dr. Orne, therapy tape, 21 March 1963.
197   "the circumstances": Tillie Olsen, interview with D.M., 12 June 1987.
198   "What kills": A.S. to Dr. Orne, therapy tape, 21 March 1963.
198   "Tillie's seminar": A.S., interview with Martha White, July 1963, Radcliffe College Archives.
198   "Tillie is so harassed": A.S., Ibid.
199   "I am bedded": Sylvia Plath to A.S., 21 August 1962, HRHRC.
199   "I began to worry": A.S. to Dr. Orne, therapy tape, 7 March 1963.
199   "The person who": Ibid.
200   "had the suicide": A.S. to Lois Ames, 4 June 1965, Letters, p. 261.
200   "Sylvia Plath's death": A.S. to Dr. Orne, therapy tape, 5 March 1963.
200   "too much push": Robert Lowell to A.S., 25 June 1963, HRHRC.
200   "It's really good": A.S. to George Starbuck, 17 June 1963, HRHRC.
200   "I listened and let": A.S. to Galway Kinnell, 20 February 1964, Letters, p. 233.
200   "It's nothing": Linda Sexton to D.M., September 1990.
200   "a great poet": A.S. to Dr. Orne, 20 July 1963, doctor's files.
200   "Now I see it": Ibid.
201   "I've been thinking": A.S. to Dr. Orne, therapy tape, 23 May 1963.
201   "Now is the time": A.S. to Dr. Orne, therapy tapes, 5 and 21 March 1963.
201   "identity things": A.S. to Dr. Orne, therapy tape, 28 February 1963.
202   "You have undercut": A.S. and Dr. Orne, therapy tape, 10 August 1963.
202   "a charm to ward": A.S. to Dr. Orne, therapy tape, 16 August 1963.
202   "I had a family": Sandy Robart, interview with D.M., 11 November 1982.
202   "Nothing in the world": A.S. to Dr. Orne, therapy tape, 12 August 1963.
203   "Mother would lean": Joy and Linda Sexton, interview with D.M., 6 October 1989.

203   "Mother would stand": Linda Sexton, interview with D.M., 14 October 1980.

204   "Linda got in bed": A.S. to Dr. Orne, therapy tape, 21 February 1963.

204   "Her body wants": A.S. to Dr. Orne, therapy tape, 11 June 1963.

204   "I can save": A.S. to Dr. Orne, therapy tape, 13 June 1963.

205   "Wring every drop": Wilhelmine Sexton to A.S., 26 August 1963, HRHRC.

205   "the Grapes of Wrath": A.S. to the Sexton family, 4 September 1963, *Letters,* p. 179.

205   "To lose your Europe": Maxine Kumin to A.S., 10 September 1963, HRHRC.

205   "OH HOW WE WISH": A.S. to the Sexton family, 4 September 1963, *Letters,* pp. 184–85.

205   "Life is indeed": A.S. to the Sexton family, 5 September 1963, *Letters,* p. 189.

206   "I don't have the time": A.S. to Alfred M. Sexton, 7 September 1963, *Letters,* p. 192.

206   "I'm stubborn": A.S. to Alfred M. Sexton, 19 September 1963, *Letters,* p. 194.

206   "I am proud": A.S. to Dr. Orne, 19 September 1963, doctor's files.

207   "where the sound": A.S. to the Sexton family, 25 September 1963, *Letters,* p. 203.

207   "Oh, dear love": A.S. to Alfred M. Sexton, 27 September 1963, *Letters,* p. 206.

207   "the part of me": A.S. to Alfred M. Sexton, 2 October 1963, *Letters,* pp. 210–11.

207   "I want to say": A.S. to Alfred M. Sexton, 6 October 1963, *Letters,* pp. 212–14.

208   "almost an incapability": Alfred M. Sexton to A.S., 8 October 1963, HRHRC.

208   "dividing and re-dividing": A.S. to Dr. Orne, 6 October 1963, doctor's files.

208   "the thrall of new places": A.S. to Alfred M. Sexton, 11–12 September, *Letters,* p. 197.

209   They met on a beach: A.S. to Dr. Orne, n.d. [circa 23 October] 1963, doctor's files.

209   "I am just not well": A.S. to Alfred M. Sexton, 18 October 1963, *Letters,* p. 219.

209   "Capri is out": A.S. to Dr. Orne, 22 October 1963, doctor's files.

209   "ARRIVING BOSTON": A.S. to Alfred M. Sexton, 22 October 1963, *Letters*, p. 221.

209   "I wrote such": A.S. to Dr. Orne, therapy tape, 7 November 1963.

209   "There's a simple rule": Dr. Orne to A.S., therapy tape, 5 November 1963.

210   "Can't you be addicted": A.S. and Dr. Orne, therapy tape, 21 October 1961.

210   "I ought to stop": A.S. to Dr. Orne, therapy tape, 19 March 1963.

210   "You've been in a swamp": Quoted by A.S. to Dr. Orne, therapy tape, 5 November 1963.

211   "Alcoholism is happening": Dr. Orne to A.S., therapy tape, 21 October 1961.

211   "He asked me": A.S. to Dr. Orne, 9 November 1963, doctor's files.

211   Kayo helped her: Westwood Lodge record, 8 November 1963.

212   "Slavic and determined": "Menstruation at Forty," *CP*, pp. 137–38.

212   In Capri: A.S., letter to Dr. Orne, 9 November 1963, doctor's files.

212   She kept in her files: A.S., Works, "Arevederchi," holograph manuscript, HRHRC.

212   "Everywhere my eyes": A.S. to Felicia Geffen, 5 November 1963, *Letters*, p. 226.

11. THE NANA-HEX

213   "I'm in love": Quoted back to A.S. by Wilder, 31 January 1964, restricted collection, HRHRC.

214   "Of course not trusting": A.S. to Anne Wilder, 13 November 1963, private collection.

214   "I'll be glad": Anne Wilder to A.S., 15 November 1963, restricted collection, HRHRC.

214   Thornton Wilder: Anne Wilder, interview with D.M., 15 July 1981. Wilder referred to this relation in a letter to A.S., 5 April 1964.

215   "stick to your trade": A.S. to Anne Wilder, 2 January 1964, restricted collection, HRHRC.

215   "This may sound": Anne Wilder to A.S., 31 January 1964, private collection.

215   "Miller's play": A.S. to Anne Wilder, 29 January 1964, restricted collection, HRHRC.

215 "morbid free association": A.S. to Anne Wilder, n.d. [mid-January 1964], private collection.

216 "But suicides have": "Wanting to Die" is dated 3 February 1964, *CP*, pp. 142–43.

216 "the woman's way out": A.S. to Dr. Orne, therapy tape, 14 March 1963.

216 "I don't want to die": A.S., therapy notebook, restricted collection, HRHRC.

216 "I'm so fascinated": A.S. to Dr. Orne, therapy tape, 25 April 1964.

216 "He'd have punished": A.S. and Dr. Orne, therapy tape, 16 January 1962.

217 "I would rather": A.S. to Joyce Lebra, 17 August 1964, HRHRC. Lebra had written Sexton about Soter's death from an overdose of sleeping pills, 13 August 1964, HRHRC.

217 "suicide is addicting": A.S. to Dr. Orne, therapy tape, 7 March 1963.

217 Dr. Orne did: Ollie Zweizung is a pseudonym. Details have been suppressed to protect the doctor's anonymity.

218 From France: A.S. to Anne Wilder, n.d. [June 1964], private collection.

218 "sprung a leak": A.S. to Dr. Orne, 6 June 1964, doctor's files; to Anne Wilder, 6 June 1964, private collection.

218 "A girl who has committed": A.S., interview with Lois Ames, *Boston Sunday Herald Traveler Book Guide,* October 12, 1969. Reprinted in *NES,* p. 121.

219 "I'm not okay": A.S. to Anne Wilder, 31 July 1964, private collection.

219 "the Nana-hex": "The Hex," *CP,* p. 313.

219 "I am looking for Nana": A.S., typed notes to Dr. Orne, n.d. [probably 1958], doctor's files.

219 "Hark ye!": A.S., *Tell Me Your Answer True,* Act One, unpublished ms., p. 4. All quotations and references are to Dr. Orne's copy.

221 "This girl": A.S. to Dr. Orne, therapy tape, 23 January 1962.

222 "I say to her": A.S. to Anne Wilder, 3 July 1964, *Letters,* p. 243.

222 "Little Girl, My Stringbean, My Lovely Woman": *CP,* p. 147. Sexton's poem makes Linda twelve, not eleven, on this birthday.

223 "I would be turned": Linda Sexton, interview with D.M., 19 July 1989.

224 "The compulsion to repeat": Linda Sexton to D.M., September 1990.

224 "left hand": A.S. to Anne Wilder, 4 August 1964, private collection.

224 "*Doc*. Did anyone": A.S to Anne Wilder, 6 August 1964, private collection. Spelling and punctuation are Sexton's.

225 "a constant rhyming": Ibid.

226 "Thorazine, they say": Ibid.

226 "Language has nothing": A.S. to Anne Wilder, 3 July 1964, *Letters*, p. 245.

226 "manic me": A.S. to Anne Wilder, 25 August 1964, *Letters*, p. 249.

226 "Quite manic": A.S. to Dr. Orne, 22 August 1964, doctor's file.

227 "if the magic": A.S. to Alfred M. Sexton, 17 August 1964, *Letters*, p. 248.

227 He later remembered: Ben Shaktman, interview with D.M., 23 April 1983.

227 "Anne Sexton taught me": Ibid.

228 "Facts sound much better": Ben Shaktman to A.S., 2 July 1965, HRHRC.

228 "Why, Daisy is": Ben Shaktman, interview with D.M., 23 April 1983.

228 "Daisy is just as crazy": A.S. to Ben Shaktman, 6 July 1965, HRHRC.

228 "Right now": A.S to Claire Degener, 16 November 1964, *Letters*, p. 253.

229 "What I need": A.S. to Anne Wilder, 10 December 1964, *Letters*, p. 255.

229 "the asshole": A.S. to Dr. Orne, therapy notebook, 2 May 1964, restricted collection, HRHRC.

230 "I meant to pick": A.S. to Anne Wilder, 10 December 1964, *Letters*, p. 255.

12. "ICARUS CATCH"

231 "[Icarus] glances": "To a Friend Whose Work Has Come to Triumph," *CP*, p. 53.

231 "The g.d. tranquilizers": A.S. to Tillie Olsen, 14 February 1965, *Letters*, pp. 256–58.

232 "All my life": A.S., Lecture Six, Crashaw Lectures, HRHRC.

232 "For years I heard": A.S. to Anne Wilder, 10 December 1964, *Letters*, p. 255.

233 "It was like Icarus": Anne Wilder to A.S., 22 August 1963, restricted collection, HRHRC.

233 "As an image": A.S. to Anne Wilder, 1 September 1963, private collection.

233 "Yes, we are": Anne Wilder to A.S., 6 November 1963, private collection.

233 "Out of love": A.S. to Anne Wilder, 24 December 1964, restricted collection, HRHRC.

234 "Dear, I appreciated": Anne Wilder to A.S., 23 January 1965, restricted collection, HRHRC.

235 "I think both docs": Ibid.

235 "I don't agree": A.S. to Anne Wilder, 27 January 1965, restricted collection, HRHRC.

235 "For you to see": A.S. to Anne Wilder, 8 February 1965, restricted collection, HRHRC.

236 "We are important": Ibid.

236 "I HAVE ROOM!": A.S. to Anne Wilder, 15 February 1965, *Letters*, p. 260.

236 "I am not going": Ibid., p. 259.

236 "I was so mad": A.S. to Anne Wilder, 29 January 1965, private collection.

237 "more childlike": A.S. to Anne Wilder, 15 February 1965, *Letters*, p. 259.

237 "I look forward": Anne Wilder, journal entry, 5 May 1965, private collection.

237 "I am only mildly amazed": Anne Wilder, journal entry, 6 May 1965, private collection.

238 "a little less": Anne Wilder, interview with D.M., 28 June 1989.

238 " 'This is your princess' ": Ibid.

238 "Sexton gave a wonderful": Ibid.

239 "I really am in love": Ibid.

239 "Love twists me": "Your Face on the Dog's Neck," *CP*, p. 153.

239 "I'm still bi-sexual": A.S. to Anne Wilder, 4 June 1965, private collection.

239 "It was my need": A.S. to Anne Wilder, 17 May 1965, private collection.

239 "I adore the poem": Anne Wilder to A.S., n.d. ["Tuesday"], restricted collection, HRHRC.

240 "He is scared": A.S. to Anne Wilder, 17 May 1965, private collection.

240 "fixing up old ones": A.S. to Anne Wilder, 9 June 1965, private collection.

240 "If it were a real": A.S., Lecture Ten, Crashaw Lectures, HRHRC.

240   "I wanted to write": Ibid.

240   "a sound effect": A.S., Lecture Three, Crashaw Lectures, HRHRC.

241   "In a literary way": A.S. to Anne Wilder, 9 June 1965, private collection.

241   "O little mother": "For the Year of the Insane," *CP*, p. 133.

241   "monster of despair": A phrase Sexton used, apparently, in her fan letter to Saul Bellow, who quoted it back to her. Saul Bellow to A.S., n.d., HRHRC.

241   "Stop writing letters": A.S. to Jonathan Korso, 12 August 1965, *Letters*, p. 267. "Jonathan Korso" is the pseudonym used in *Letters*.

242   "He says my job": A.S. to Anne Wilder, 9 June 1965, private collection.

242   "Please give me": A.S. to Linda Sexton, 8 July 1965, *Letters*, p. 266.

242   "I work better": A.S. to Syracuse University, 6 August 1965, HRHRC.

242   "I can hardly": A.S. to Frederick Morgan, 12 August 1965, HRHRC.

242   "I cannot work": A.S. to Kenyon College (George Lanning), 23 August 1965, HRHRC.

243   "At the time": Jon Stallworthy, interview with D.M., 15 May 1983.

243   "[Sylvia] wrote me": A.S. to Lois Ames, 4 June 1965, *Letters*, p. 262.

244   "telephoned me": Lois Ames, "Remembering Anne," in McClatchy, p. 111.

13. "A SEDUCING SORT OF WOMAN"

245   "Live": *CP*, p. 170.

245   "straight from God": A.S. to Ben Shaktman, 5 March 1966, HRHRC.

245   "I seem to have": A.S. to Claire Degener, 25 September 1966, HRHRC.

246   "Every letter": A.S. to Philip Legler, 26 May 1966, HRHRC.

246   "I act rather well": A.S. to Jon Stallworthy, 5 April 1966, HRHRC.

246   "I hadn't 'earned' ": Joy Sexton, interview with D.M., 6 October 1989.

246   "as bad an underachiever": A.S. to Joseph Gauld, 17 May 1967, HRHRC.

246 The seamless version: "Anne Sexton," *USA: Poetry,* produced and directed by Richard Moore of the KQED Film Unit, San Francisco, California, for National Educational Television, 1966.

247 "They were from her bargain": Linda Sexton to D.M., 19 July 1989.

247 The film was edited: "Sexton," a film based on *USA: Poetry* outtakes, produced by the American Poetry Archive Film Unit, Poetry Center, San Francisco State University, San Francisco, California, 1975. All quotes in the following passage are taken from this film.

249 "never meant anything": A.S. to Dr. Orne, therapy tapes, 10 December 1963 and 3 March 1964.

250 "One was always": Allen Grossman, interview with D.M., 13 October 1982.

250 "a new kind of orthodoxy": James Dickey, "Dialogues with Themselves," *New York Times Book Review,* 28 April 1963. Reprinted in *Anne Sexton: Telling the Tale,* ed. Steven E. Colburn (Ann Arbor: University of Michigan Press, 1988), p. 106.

260 "I had given": James Dickey to D.M., 24 July 1989.

251 "Do you sleep": A.S. to James Dickey, 12 December 1965, HRHRC. "I fear a letter relationship. When you met me you asked me 'Do you sleep around?' or something like that. My answer was negative, as I recall, but I'll tell you this: I once made the mistake of believing in a letter-relationship — I 'wrote around.' " Phrases omitted from *Letters,* p. 276.

251 "You have opened": James Dickey to A.S., 27 December 1965, HRHRC.

251 "I would avoid": A.S. to James Dickey, "the end of December 1965," *Letters,* p. 275.

251 "Believe me": James Dickey to A.S., 1 February 1966, HRHRC.

251 "I'm ready to love": A.S. to James Dickey, n.d. [circa 14 February 1966], HRHRC.

251 "It must be shocking": James Dickey to A.S., 17 February 1966, HRHRC.

251 "jerks": Alfred M. Sexton, interview with D.M., 21 February 1983.

251 "If there is": A.S. to James Dickey, n.d. [circa 14 February 1966], HRHRC.

252 "If Virginia": A.S. to Philip Legler, 26 January 1966, HRHRC.

252 "Linda's never flown": A.S. to Anne Wilder, 2 April 1966, private collection.

252 "I feel kind of awful": A.S. to Philip Legler, 27 April 1966, HRHRC.

252 "Throughout my childhood": Linda Sexton, interview with D.M., 13 October 1980.

252 "been received into": Linda Sexton, interview with D.M., 19 July 1989.

253 "Maxine said to me": Linda Sexton, interview with D.M., 13 October 1980.

253 "You have no idea": Philip Legler to A.S., 25 April 1966, HRHRC.

253 "I liked your love letter": A.S. to Philip Legler, 27 April 1966, HRHRC.

253 "I talked about it": A.S. to Philip Legler, 6 May 1966, HRHRC.

254 "There are so few": Elizabeth Bishop to A.S., 10 November 1965, HRHRC.

255 "I am interested": A.S. to Elizabeth Bishop, 10 May 1966, HRHRC.

255 "There is a question": A.S. to Elizabeth Bishop, 23 May 1966, HRHRC.

255 "I'm a resident!": Robert Clawson, interview with D.M., 16 March 1983.

255 "to explore possibilities": Tinka Topping to A.S., 23 February 1966, HRHRC.

256 "Before we left": Robert Clawson, interview with D.M., 16 March 1983. All quotes in the following passage are drawn from this interview unless otherwise noted.

257 "You crept inside": Robert Clawson to A.S., 3 July 1966, restricted collection, HRHRC.

258 "the old summer madness": A.S. to Ollie Zweizung, 2 August 1966, restricted collection, HRHRC.

258 "a word magic guy": A.S. to H. Harris, 17 May 1966, HRHRC.

258 "are to be denied": Sigmund Freud to Sándor Ferenczi, 13 December 1931, Freud-Ferenczi Correspondence, Library of Congress; quoted in Peter Gay, *Freud: A Life for Our Time* (New York: Norton, 1988), p. 578.

258 "the necessary intensity": *The Principles of Medical Ethics, With Annotations Especially Applicable to Psychiatry* (Washington, D.C.: American Psychiatric Association, 1981), p. 4.

258 "I wondered": A.S. to Ollie Zweizung, 22 August 1966, restricted collection, HRHRC.

259 "Imagine paying": Maxine Kumin, interviews with D.M., 9 October 1980 and 11 November 1982.

259 "In this particular setup": Lois Ames to A.S., 18 July 1966, restricted collection, HRHRC.

260 "I didn't want": A.S. to Dr. Orne, 4 August 1966, doctor's file.

260 "Sleepmonger, deathmonger": "The Addict": *CP*, pp. 165–66.

260 "it wasn't a serious": A.S. to Lois Ames, 2 August 1966, *Letters*, p. 298.

261 "No matter what": Alfred M. Sexton to A.S, n.d., HRHRC.

261 "Murder will out": Alfred M. Sexton, interview with D.M., 11 September 1989.

262 "I went over": George MacBeth, interview with D.M., 14 August 1987.

262 "I learned that Anne": Ibid.

262 "It was a very posh trip": Alfred M. Sexton, interview with D.M., 21 February 1983. All quotations in the following passage are drawn from this interview unless otherwise noted.

263 "I am thinking": A.S. to Ollie Zweizung, 22 August 1966, restricted collection, HRHRC.

263 "so Anne could get": Alfred M. Sexton, interview with D.M., 21 February 1983.

264 "is my spiritual home": A.S. to Lois Ames, 7 September 1966, *Letters*, pp. 299–300.

264 "jagged and suspenseful": Joseph Slater, "Immortal Bard and Others," *Saturday Review*, 31 December 1966, p. 25.

264 "the appeal, the pull": Millen Brand, "A Dark Time," *Book Week*, 25 September 1966, p. 13.

264 "Her previous books": Louis Simpson, "The New Books," *Harper's*, August 1967, pp. 90–91.

264 "MEANY": A.S. to Louis Simpson, 17 August 1967, HRHRC.

265 "The Romantic stereotype": Charles Gullans, "Poetry and Subject Matter: From Hart Crane to Turner Cassity," *Southern Review*, Spring 1970, pp. 497–98; reprinted in McClatchy, pp. 131–32.

265 "A novel seems": A.S. to Constance Smith, Radcliffe Institute, 9 November 1966, *Letters*, p. 304.

265 "a forthright pornographic": A.S. to Claire Degener, 25 September 1966, HRHRC.

265 "Maybe the summer": A.S. to Lois Ames, 7 September 1966, *Letters*, p. 299.

265 A poem he gave: restricted collection, HRHRC.

266 Family lore: Editorial note, Linda Sexton and Lois Ames, *Letters*, p. 304.

266 "Let's face it": "For My Lover, Returning to His Wife," *CP*, p. 188.

266 "I'm flat": A.S. to Lois Ames, 19 November 1966, *Letters*, p. 305.

266   "Maybe with a broken hip": A.S. to Ben Shaktman, 10 December 1966, HRHRC.

266   "It should begin": Lois Ames to A.S., 27 December 1966, restricted collection, HRHRC.

14. MONEY AND FAME

268   "I was madly": Joan Smith, interview with D.M., 9 March 1983. Quotations in the following passage are drawn from this interview.

269   "Anne wrote": Maxine Kumin, interview with D.M., 9 October 1980.

269   "am trying to work": A.S. to Lois Ames, 8 March 1967, restricted collection, HRHRC.

270   "Anne's files": Jean Moulton, interview with D.M., 12 September 1983. Quotations in the following passages are drawn from this interview.

271   "the passion pad": Linda Sexton to D.M., September 1990.

271   "Kayo likes it": A.S. to Lois Ames, 8 March 1967, restricted collection, HRHRC.

271   "to write a book": A.S. to Dr. Orne, therapy tape, 23 May 1963.

271   "Daddy brought": Joy Sexton, interview with D.M., 24 September 1986.

272   "After numerous": Jane Harvey Jealous to A.S., telegram, 3 May 1967, HRHRC.

273   "Channel 2": A.S. to Mrs. Willard P. Fuller, 31 May 1967, HRHRC.

273   Among the most amusing: Melvin Belli to A.S., 6 May 1967, HRHRC.

273   "I can only appreciate": A.S. to Melvin Belli, 31 May 1967, HRHRC.

273   "I get letters": A.S. to Anne Wilder, 18 November 1963, restricted collection, HRHRC.

273   "Your poems I find": David Forrest, M.D., to A.S., 13 December 1965, HRHRC.

274   "sometimes in private": "For John, Who Begs Me Not to Enquire Further": *CP*, p. 35.

274   "Why should such": Robert Clawson, interview with D.M., 16 March 1983.

274   "It was a potent": Ibid.

275   "It was a beautiful": Howard Moss, interview with D.M., 16 November 1982.

275 "You were utterly": A.S. to Howard Moss, 15 June 1967, HRHRC.

275 "I love you, dear": A.S. to Claire Degener, 21 June 1967, *Letters*, p. 317.

276 "the most widely-read": A.S. to Robert B. Silvers, 28 June 1967, HRHRC.

276 "God, I wish": A.S. to Philip Legler, 6 September 1967, *Letters*, p. 319.

276 "I don't like": "Journal of a Living Experiment," 16 June 1967 (typed ms.), HRHRC. An edited version was later published in *The Whole Word Catalogue*, ed. Rosellen Brown et al. (New York: Teachers and Writers Collaborative, 1972), and reprinted in *Journal of a Living Experiment: A Documentary History of the First Ten Years of Teachers and Writers Collaborative*, ed. Phillip Lopate (New York: Teachers and Writers Collaborative, 1979).

277 A few months after: A.S. to Jon Stallworthy, 15 May 1967, HRHRC.

277 "I know how": Jon Stallworthy to A.S., 4 July 1967, HRHRC.

277 "Anyone experiencing": Alan Ross, review of *Live or Die*, in *London Magazine*, July 1967, pp. 102–3.

277 Sexton was grateful: Ted Hughes to A.S., n.d. [January 1967], HRHRC.

277 "My reviews": A.S. to George MacBeth, 28 June 1967, HRHRC.

277 "Only later did": Anthony Hecht, interview with D.M., 28 December 1989.

278 "What does one do": A.S. to Jon Stallworthy, 28 June 1967, *Letters*, p. 318.

278 "Tony [Hecht] and I": A.S. to Alfred M. Sexton, 15 July 1967, HRHRC.

278 "Auden was very cross": Jon Stallworthy, interview with D.M., 15 May 1983.

278 "Well, yes": Anthony Hecht, interview with D.M., 28 December 1989.

279 "all those egos": A.S. to Donald Junkins, 18 October 1967, HRHRC.

279 "It's fascinating": A.S. to D. M. Thomas, 21 January 1970, HRHRC.

279 "Facts," she said: A.S., interview taped on 17 July 1967, HRHRC. Quotations in the following passage are drawn from this interview.

279 "What a lay me down": "The Addict," *CP*, p. 166.

280 "This added": George MacBeth, interview with D.M., 14 August 1987.

281 "Anne was in": Michael Bearpark, "A Memoir of Anne Sexton," unpublished, n.d.

281 "It may have been": Ibid.

281 "exuberant, curly-haired": Lois Ames, conversation with D.M., 9 December 1990.

281 "There is no poet": D. M. Thomas to A.S., 12 October 1966, HRHRC.

282 "I admired": D. M. Thomas, interview with D.M., 12 August 1987. Quotations in the following passages are drawn from this interview.

283 "completely redeemed": Ted Hughes to A.S., 9 August 1967, HRHRC.

283 "temporary adulation": D. M. Thomas to A.S., 24 July 1967, HRHRC.

283 "the Nefertiti": Jon Stallworthy, "Poets of the World Unite," *The Sunday Times* [London], 16 July 1967.

283 "humbled": A.S. to Jon Stallworthy, 3 August 1967, HRHRC.

283 "[I am] full": A.S. to Dorianne Goetz, 3 August 1967, HRHRC.

284 "I cried": A.S. to Linda Sexton ("Stringbean"), 1 July 1967 [misdated 1976], HRHRC.

284 "one of the joys": Maxine Kumin, interview with D.M., 9 October 1980. Kumin drew on this memory for a poem, "How It Is," reprinted in *Our Ground Time Here Will Be Brief* (New York: Penguin, 1982), p. 68.

284 "It all comes": A.S. to Anne Wilder, 21 September 1967, *Letters,* pp. 320–21.

284 "She had no sense": Maxine Kumin, interview with D.M., 9 October 1980.

285 "I would wheedle": Ibid.

285 "After class we'd go": Robert Clawson, interview with D.M., 16 March 1983.

285 "Anne was holding": Ibid.

286 "The story": A.S., "Journal of a Living Experiment," 17 September 1967, HRHRC. "The Story of Kayo Sexton," dated 12 September 1967, is in the restricted collection, HRHRC.

286 "Turning God Back On": A.S., "Journal of a Living Experiment," 3 and 20 October 1967, HRHRC.

286 "I'm not sure": Ibid.

286 "I have now come": Ibid.

287 "Steve was a big": Robert Clawson, interview with D.M., 16 March 1983.

287 "I've been touring": George MacBeth to A.S., 14 October [1967], HRHRC.

287 "If I seem": A.S. to Dorianne Goetz, 18 October 1967, HRHRC.

288 "I hibernated": "Eighteen Days Without You," *CP,* p. 206.

288 It is apparent: Sexton referred to this liaison in letters to Barbara Kevles and to Alice Smith, HRHRC, as well as in letters to Dr. Zweizung, restricted collection, HRHRC. Additional commentary was offered by Robert Clawson, Claire Degener (now Derway), Maxine Kumin, Martin Orne, Barbara Swan, and Anne Wilder, during interviews.

289 "She was writing": Robert Clawson, interview with D.M., 16 March 1983. The poems referred to are "The Break," *CP,* pp. 190–93, and "December 13th," *CP,* p. 216.

289 "I have had a spurt": A.S. to Richard Eberhart, 12 December 1967, HRHRC.

289 "I'm in the middle": A.S. to Dorianne Goetz, 5 November 1967, HRHRC.

15. ANNE SEXTON AND HER KIND

293 "For months": "The Touch, *CP,* p. 173.

294 "Then I think": "December 11th": *CP,* p. 214.

295 "to honor the American": "Boston Area Residents Win 5 of 15 Pulitzer Prizes," *Boston Globe,* 2 May 1967, pp. 1, 5.

295 "Tonight I take part": A.S. to Philip Legler, 2 May 1966, *Letters,* p. 290.

296 "I hate killing": "Journal of a Living Experiment," typed ms., 16 June 1967, HRHRC.

296 "We wanted participation": Allen Grossman, interview with D.M., 13 October 1982.

296 "She read": Adrienne Rich, interview with D.M., 18 May 1983.

296 "The woman is bathing": "The Firebombers," *CP,* p. 308.

296 "for a local": A.S. to Howard Moss, 24 June 1968, HRHRC.

297 "to show I care": A.S. to Lois Ames, 30 July 1968, *Letters,* p. 327. *Look* did not print the poem.

297 "I would be glad": A.S. to Ron Wolin, Fifth Avenue Vietnam Peace Parade Committee, 6 March 1968, HRHRC.

297 "not a political poet": A.S. to Joshua Stoller, 25 March 1970, HRHRC.

298 "My stuff is always": A.S. to W. D. Snodgrass, 1 February 1959, *Letters,* p. 54.

298 "This is the first time": A.S. to Paul Brooks, 1 May 1968, HRHRC.

298 "It occurred to me": Brigitte Weeks to A.S., 25 October 1967, HRHRC.

298 "I do think": Quoted in Brigitte Weeks, "The Excitable Gift: The Art of Anne Sexton," *Boston Magazine* (August 1968), pp. 30–32; reprinted in *NES*, pp. 112–18.

298 "I can't": Ibid., p. 116.

299 "My nerves": "The Kiss," *CP*, p. 175.

299 "and every bed": "The Interrogation of the Man of Many Hearts," *CP*, p. 180.

300 "Loving me": "Barefoot," *CP*, pp. 199–200.

300 "a certain uncharacteristic": A.S. to Jon Stallworthy, 3 July 1968, HRHRC.

300 It was not until early November: Paul Brooks to A.S., 6 November 1968, HRHRC.

301 "Quite frankly": A.S. to Jon Stallworthy, 13 November 1968, HRHRC.

301 "I liked the poems": Jon Stallworthy, interview with D.M., 15 May 1983.

301 "It was like": A.S. to Tillie Olsen, 21 July 1960, *Letters*, pp. 355–56.

302 "I think you": A.S. to Mason Hammond, 8 May 1968, HRHRC.

302 "It should be": Paul Brooks to A.S., 20 May 1968, HRHRC.

302 "Yes, I think": A.S. to John B. Radner, 12 June 1968, HRHRC.

303 "She wasn't going": Robert Clawson, interview with D.M., 16 March 1983.

304 "No one could hear": A.S. to Lois Ames, 30 July 1968, *Letters*, p. 326.

305 "a very swinging": A.S. to Lois Ames, 30 July 1968, *Letters*, p. 326.

305 "I'm in such a panic": A.S. to Lois Ames, 25 September 1968, *Letters*, p. 332.

305 "pretty good": Ibid.

305 "Last week": Paul Brooks to A.S., n.d. [September 1968], HRHRC.

305 "opens up my poems": Quoted in Kevles, *NES*, p. 108.

305 "The 1967 Pulitzer": Bill Kirtz, "Anne Sexton and Her Kind," *Boston Sunday Globe,* 20 April 1969, p. 27.

306 "I hated her readings": Maxine Kumin, interview with D.M., 9 October 1980.

307 "I think I have": C. K. Williams to A.S., 29 July 1968, HRHRC.

307   "The point": A.S. to Houghton Mifflin Company, 17 September
       1968, HRHRC.

307   "I got there": C. K. Williams, interview with D.M., 15 February
       1984.

307   "I used to get": Ibid.

308   "We both got": Ibid.

308   "I guess I owe you": C. K. Williams to A.S., 5 November 1968,
       HRHRC.

309   "the hippie offbeat": A.S., McLean notebook, 7 January 1969,
       HRHRC.

309   "You are right": A.S. to J.P., 15 January 1969, HRHRC.

309   "listening for": A.S. to Steven Whitney, 30 October 1968,
       HRHRC.

310   " 'I learned' ": Barbara Kevles, "Through Bedlam's Door,"
       Look, 10 December 1968, p. T40.

310   "We are renting": A.S. to Lois Ames, 30 July 1968, Letters, p.
       327.

311   "solved": A.S. to Alice Smith, 4 December 1968, HRHRC.

311   "I was reading": A.S. to Linda Sexton, n.d. [April 1969], Letters,
       p. 424.

16. OFF-BROADWAY WITH MERCY STREET

312   "Often, her answers": Barbara Kevles, interview with A.S., NES,
       pp. 83–84.

312   "I brought it": Charles Maryan, interview with D.M., 10 May
       1983.

313   "That first meeting": Charles Maryan, "The Poet on Stage," in
       McClatchy, p. 90

313   "an 'odyssey' ": Ibid.

313   "an essential issue": Charles Maryan, interview with D.M., 10
       May 1983.

314   "Puritanical Yankees": Lois Ames, conversation with D.M., 4
       December 1990.

314   "expose those physicians": The Principles of Medical Ethics,
       With Annotations Especially Applicable to Psychiatry (Wash-
       ington, D.C.: American Psychiatric Association, 1981), p. 2.
       Though not codified explicitly for psychiatry until 1973, similar
       written guidelines formulated by the American Medical Asso-
       ciation would have applied in this case.

314   According to Wilder: Anne Wilder, interview with D.M., 29 June
       1989.

314 "I saw Sexton": Martin Orne, interview with D.M., 26 August 1985. Quotations in the following passages are drawn from this interview.

315 "his behavior": Ibid. and interview on 4 December 1990.

316 "[Dr. Zweizung]": A.S. to Dr. Orne, 4 February 1969, restricted collection, HRHRC.

316 "It was kind": A.S. to Barbara Kevles, 17 March 1969, HRHRC.

316 "Anne was annoyed": Martin Orne, interview with D.M., 4 December 1990.

316- Within a couple: "Dr. Constance Chase" is a pseudonym. The
17 doctor declined to be interviewed for this biography.

317 "I wrote this play": A.S. to Alice Smith, 9 April 1969, HRHRC.

317 "It wasn't casual": Marian Seldes, interview with D.M., 11 April 1983.

317 "Until she heard": "The Poet on Stage," op. cit., p. 91.

317 "as companion": A.S. to Wynn Handman, 15 April 1969, Letters, p. 337.

317 "Anne and I": "The Poet on Stage," op. cit., p. 91.

318 He told her: Linda Sexton and Lois Ames, editorial notes, Letters, p. 338.

318 "the last link": Brian Sweeney to A.S., 8 December 1969, HRHRC.

318- "Daisy could come": "The Poet on Stage," op. cit., p. 92.
19

319 "All the things": A.S. to John Mood, 21 July 1970, HRHRC.

320 "There was a great deal": Marian Seldes, interview with D.M., 11 April 1983.

320 "I seek unity": A.S. to Claire Degener, 13 August 1969, HRHRC.

320 "I love dogs": Charles Maryan, interview with D.M., 10 May 1983.

321 "I'm so worried": A.S. to Linda Sexton, 23 July 1969, Letters, p. 342.

322 "fallen in love": A.S. to Brian Sweeney, 12 August 1969, HRHRC.

322 "more about": A.S. to Ollie Zweizung, 29 August 1969, restricted collection, HRHRC.

323 "little peachy breasts": Mercy Street, unpublished ms., HRHRC. Quotations in the following passages are from this source.

323 "I have never": A.S. to Ollie Zweizung, n.d. [September 1969], restricted collection, HRHRC.

325 "I felt suffocated": Linda Sexton, interview with D.M., 19 July 1989.

325 "I had gotten": Linda Sexton, interviews with D.M., 13 October 1980 and 19 July 1989.

325 "It was as if": Linda Sexton to D.M., September 1990.

326 "The sections I stole": A.S. to Ollie Zweizung, n.d. [September 1969], restricted collection, HRHRC.

326 "God . . . the money": Ibid.

326 "Did you mean": A.S. to Brian Sweeney, 21 June 1969, HRHRC.

327 "They were difficult": Charles Maryan, "The Poet on Stage," op. cit., p. 94.

327 "The man Witness": Virginia Downing, interview with D.M., 11 May 1983.

327 "Wynn was pressing": Charles Maryan, interview with D.M., 10 May 1983.

327 "this vivid": Virginia Downing, interview with D.M., 11 May 1983.

328 "Anne was not": Marian Seldes, interview with D.M., 11 April 1983.

328 "To me": Ibid.

328 "The actors turn": A.S. to Ollie Zweizung, n.d. [September 1969], restricted collection, HRHRC.

328 "Miss Sexton": Clive Barnes, "Theater: Seeking Either a Priest or a Psychiatrist," *New York Times,* 28 October 1969, p. 43.

328 "impotent": Walter Kerr, "A Woman Upon the Altar," *New York Times,* 2 November 1969, Section II, p. 1.

328 "positive, for": "The Poet on Stage," op. cit., p. 95.

329 "I can invade": Beatrice Berg, " 'Oh, I Was Very Sick,' " *New York Times,* 9 November 1969, p. D7.

329 "Anne's family"; Lisa Taylor Tompson, letter to D.M., 25 September 1983.

330 "audio images": Gerald Oshita, interview with D.M., 1 August 1989.

330 "I don't drink": A.S. to Anne Wilder, 26 December 1969, *Letters,* p. 349.

331 "Have you read": Ibid.

17. "A MIDDLE-AGED WITCH"

322 "a middle-aged witch": "The Gold Key," *CP,* p. 223.

333 "magic in the head": Daphne Abeel Ehrlich, "Anne Sexton: A Contemporary Witch," *Radcliffe Quarterly,* December 1971, pp. 6–7.

333   "Every day": Linda Sexton, interviews with D.M., 14 October 1980 and 24 August 1989.

333   "Joy and I": Linda Sexton, interview with D.M., 15 October 1980.

334   "I think we felt": Ibid.

336   "Frau Doktor": "The Frog Prince," *CP*, p. 281.

336   "I must immodestly": Maxine Kumin, "A Friendship Remembered," in McClatchy, p. 108.

336   "If you could": A.S. to George Starbuck, 28 January 1970, *Letters*, p. 350.

336   "I take the fairy tale": A.S. to Brian Sweeney, 26 May 1970, HRHRC.

337   "Daddy?": "Briar Rose (Sleeping Beauty)," *CP*, pp. 294–95.

337   "Anne Sexton in the Popular Culture": Claire Degener to A.S., 24 July 1970, HRHRC.

338   "They are full": Paul Brooks to A.S., 17 September 1970, HRHRC.

338   "I look at my work": A.S. to Paul Brooks, 14 October 1970, *Letters*, pp. 362–63.

338   "a scary time": Linda Sexton, interview with D.M., 21 August 1989.

338-   "He's out there": A.S. to Anne Wilder, 17 November 1970,
39   *Letters*, p. 366.

339   "the two of them": Linda Sexton, interview with D.M., 21 August 1989.

339   "Have been thinking": Wilhemine Sexton to Mr. and Mrs. A. M. Sexton, 4 March 1970, HRHRC.

339   "I can't miss class": A.S. to Philip Legler, 27 February 1970, HRHRC.

339   "I liked her": Arthur Freeman, interview with D.M., 1 August 1987.

339   "see to it": A.S. to George Starbuck, 11 March 1970, *Letters*, p. 351.

339   "It mattered a lot": Arthur Freeman, interview with D.M., 1 August 1987.

339   "something like having a baby": A.S. to Hollis Summers, 21 July 1970, HRHRC.

340   "At some point": Eric Edwards, interview with D.M., 26 April 1982.

340   "Mrs. Sexton": Ellen Bass, photocopy of written evaluation, 4 April 1970, HRHRC.

340   "it made me feel": A.S. to Hollis Summers, 21 July 1970, HRHRC.

340   "That was a wonderful thing": Linda Sexton, interview with
       D.M., 13 October 1980.

340-   "I'm determined": A.S. to Michael Dennis Browne, 17 July 1970,
41   HRHRC.

341   "Everything had strange colors": A.S. to Alice Smith, 19 August
       1970, *Letters*, pp. 357–59.

341   "I thought Mother": Linda Sexton, interview with D.M., 15
       October 1980.

18. THE PROFESSOR OF POETRY

342   "I don't want": Quoted by A.S., interview with J. D. McClatchy,
       23 September 1973.

342   "imperfections": Ibid.

343   "Mother was a belle": "How We Danced," *CP*, p. 324.

343   "I was stained": "Friends," *CP*, p. 328.

343   "A woman/who loves": "Rapunzel," *CP*, pp. 244–45.

344   "red, red": "Begat," *CP*, pp. 331–32.

344   "I know how close": C. K. Williams to A.S., 19 January 1971,
       HRHRC.

345   "I think it's really fine": C. K. Williams to A.S., 28 October
       1971, HRHRC.

345   "on doctor's orders": A.S. to Claire Degener, 3 March 1971,
       HRHRC.

345   "Thorazine isn't an anti-depressant": A.S. to Anne Wilder, 4
       May 1971, HRHRC.

346   "If Thorazine works": Anne Wilder to A.S., 16 May 1971, pri-
       vate collection.

346   "a great ritual": A.S. to Dr. Orne, therapy tape, 8 March 1962.

347   "eaten, of course": "Snow White," *CP*, pp. 225–28.

347   "When I finally": Linda Sexton, interview with D.M., 19 July
       1989.

348   "Linda, you are leaving": "Mother and Daughter," *CP*, pp. 306–
       7.

349   "I don't like you telling": A.S. to Dr. Chase, 20 September 1971,
       restricted collection, HRHRC.

349   "Me who never": A.S. to Joseph Murphy, 10 June 1971,
       HRHRC.

350   "make a few comments": A.S. to Regis College, 11 February
       1971, HRHRC.

350   "Angel of fire": *CP*, pp. 332–33.

351   "owning a star": A.S. to Brother Chvala, 25 August 1970,
       HRHRC.

351   "starberry": "O Ye Tongues," *CP,* p. 397, and "Woman with Girdle," *CP,* p. 70.

351   "You gave me milk": "Jesus Suckles," *CP,* pp. 337–38.

352   "In His dream": "Jesus Asleep," *CP,* pp. 338–39.

352   "a strange being": "Jesus Unborn," *CP,* p. 344.

353   "I went to the well": "The Author of the Jesus Papers Speaks," *CP,* p. 345.

353   "Let there be a God": "O Ye Tongues," *CP,* pp. 396–413. All quotations in the following passage are drawn from this sequence.

355   "It's 18 pages long": A.S. to Alice Smith, 29 March 1972, HRHRC.

355   "Last year": A.S., untitled novel, ms. dated 26 January 1966, HRHRC.

355   "Whoever God is": A.S. to Dorianne Goetz, June 1965, HRHRC.

355   "Why, we chatted": Claire Degener, interview with D.M., 6 October 1985.

356   "If man and woman": Brian Sweeney to A.S., 18 February 1971, HRHRC.

356   "Never did I think": A.S. to Howard Moss, 20 October 1971, HRHRC.

356   "delightfully accessible": Christopher Lehmann-Haupt, "Grimm's Fairy Tales Retold," *New York Times,* 27 September 1971, p. 33.

356   "a contemporary witch": Daphne Abeel Ehrlich, "Anne Sexton: A Contemporary Witch," *Radcliffe Quarterly,* December 1971, pp. 6–7.

356   "hip allusions": Louis Coxe, "Verse: A Muchness of Modernity," *New Republic,* 16 October 1971, pp. 26, 29–30.

356   "the flashing": Victor Howes, "One Poet's Freud: Getting Grimm," *Christian Science Monitor,* 23 September 1971, p. 21.

357   "There is money": A.S. to Morton Berman, 17 November 1971, *Letters,* p. 377.

357   "If John Barth": A.S. to George Starbuck, December 1972, *Letters,* pp. 384–85.

358   "a total immersion": A.S., "Preface," Crashaw Lectures at Colgate University, 1972, HRHRC. All quotations in the following passages are from this unpublished ms. of lectures.

359   "an allegory": A.S. to Brian Sweeney, 11 February 1971, HRHRC.

19. AWFUL ROWING

360 "I stand before": "The Consecrating Mother," *CP,* p. 554.

360 "I had to buy": A.S. to Alice Smith, 29 March 1972, HRHRC.

361 "If I could do": A.S., interview with J. D. McClatchy, 3 July 1973, private collection.

361 "breakfast like a dream": "The Fury of Sunrises," *CP,* p. 378.

361 "the strength of a novel": A.S. to Robert Shnayerson, 8 August 1972, HRHRC.

361 "I fell in love": A.S., interview with J. D. McClatchy, 3 July 1973.

362 "fighting the dollars": "Dog-God Fights the Dollars," unpublished ms., HRHRC.

362 "we find less": Jon Stallworthy to A.S., 20 November 1968, HRHRC.

362 "a dead end": Ian Hamilton, "Loads of Heavy Thinking," *London Observer,* 18 January 1970, p. 34.

362 "whole phrases and stanzas": Christopher Driver, "Woman in Love," *Guardian Weekly,* 10 January 1970, p. 18.

363 "We will be happy": Jon Stallworthy to A.S., 10 September 1971, HRHRC.

363 "might be expected": "Bedtime Initiations," *Times Literary Supplement,* 28 July 1972, p. 873.

363 "departure": A.S. to Jon Stallworthy, 29 August 1972, HRHRC.

363 "Not because you were moving": Jon Stallworthy to A.S., 9 October 1972, HRHRC.

363 "My immediate reaction": Jon Stallworthy, interview with D.M., 15 May 1983.

363 "The media in America": Ibid.

364 "before Sylvia Plath": Seldan Rodman, "Petrified by Gorgon Egos," *New Leader,* 22 January 1973, p. 20.

365 "Perhaps a serious fault": Anne Stevenson, "Is the Emperor of Ice Cream Wearing Clothes?" *New Review,* 17 August 1975, p. 43.

365 "I think I belong": A.S. to Yorifumi Yaguchi, 19 January 1972, HRHRC.

365 "Just remember": A.S. to Nancy Taylor, 8 November 1972, HRHRC.

365 "I have always": A.S to Steve Neilly, 13 December 1973, HRHRC.

365 "The most important thing": A.S. to "Dear All," 6 March 1974, HRHRC.

365 "If Anne had stuck around": Erica Jong to D.M., 5 January 1991.

366 "visual poetry": H. Wesley Balk, "Chamber Theater Opera," *Transformations: An Entertainment in Two Acts from the Book of Anne Sexton* (Boston: E. C. Schirmer, 1976), p. x.

366 "I had my own agenda": Conrad Susa, interview with D.M., 7 November 1989.

366 "I felt like": Ibid.

366 "with two days": A.S., "To you few who will read these first drafts," typed cover sheet for worksheets of *The Awful Rowing Toward God*, 31 January 1973, HRHRC.

367 "She was writing": Maxine Kumin, "Sexton's *The Awful Rowing Toward God*," in *To Make a Prairie* (Ann Arbor: The University of Michigan Press, 1979), p. 82.

367 "That's a fairly astonishing": John Malcolm Brinnin to A.S., n.d. [February 1973], HRHRC.

367 "When you were close": George Starbuck, interview with D.M., 13 September 1983.

367 "I have no intention": James Wright, holograph annotations on A.S. letter dated 31 January 1973, HRHRC.

368 "work to my own detriment": A.S., interview with J. D. McClatchy, 3 July 1973.

369 "Catch your chance": Quoted by A.S. to Louise Conant, in unpublished memoir of A.S.

370 "Mr. Sexton admitted": Officer's Report, Police Department, Town of Weston, 27 April 1969, 7:54 P.M.

370 "Daddy didn't seem": Joy Sexton, interview with D.M., 26 May 1983.

370 "It always happened": Alfred M. Sexton, interview with D.M., 11 September 1989.

371 "plotting and planning": Joy Sexton, interview with D.M., 26 May 1983.

371 "I went off": A.S. to Paul Sugarman, 21 February 1973, private collection.

371 " 'You are crazy' ": Ibid.

371 "The Sunday afternoon": Alfred M. Sexton, interview with D.M., 21 February 1983.

372 "Kayo was a sweet man": Barbara Swan, interview with D.M., 4 December 1982.

372 "Anne ran the spectrum": Loring Conant, interview with D.M., 28 October 1984.

372 "Anyone on whom": Louise Conant, unpublished memoir of A.S.

373 "I loved staying": Joy Sexton, interview with D.M., 24 September 1986.

374 "He's very kind": A.S. to Alice Smith, 7 April 1973, HRHRC.

374 "was getting rewarded": Linda Sexton to D.M., 16 July 1989.

374 "She wore clothes": Conrad Susa, interview with D.M., 7 November 1989.

375 "a dome": Ibid.

375 "The singers should": Conrad Susa, "Introductory Notes," *Transformations: An Entertainment,* op. cit., p. ix.

375 "But while I was": Conrad Susa, interview with D.M., 7 November 1989.

375 "one of the brightest": Andrew Porter, "Household Tales," *The New Yorker,* 14 June 1976, pp. 97–99.

375 "I didn't make over": Conrad Susa, interview with D.M., 7 November 1989.

376 "Oh Crazy Annie": Philip Legler to A.S., 16 May 1973, restricted collection, HRHRC.

376 "sending flowers": A.S. to Alice Smith, 28 June 1973, HRHRC.

376 "you gave me back": A.S. to Philip Legler, 7 September 1973, restricted collection, HRHRC.

376 "an old-fashioned courtship": Quoted by Philip Legler to A.S., n.d. [late July 1973], restricted collection, HRHRC.

377 "There must be": A.S. to Philip Legler, 7 September 1973, restricted collection, HRHRC.

377 "I refuse": A.S. to Philip Legler, 9 September 1973, restricted collection, HRHRC.

377 "babysitter" doctors: Admission notes, McLean Hospital record, 2 August 1973.

378 "This might be okay": Louise Conant, unpublished memoir of A.S.

379 "to sleep in her own bed": "Discharge Summary," Human Resource Institute of Boston, 29 October 1973.

379 "I didn't want": Linda Sexton to D.M., September 1990.

379 "Mother": Joy Sexton, interview with D.M., 24 September 1986.

379 "stop worrying friends": A.S., miscellaneous handwritten notes, 21 October [1973], HRHRC.

380 "God is in": Maxine Kumin, "How It Was," *CP,* p. xxiii.

380 "Love as big": Louise Conant to A.S., n.d. [probably 1974], HRHRC.

381 Sexton had taken: Editorial note, Linda Sexton and Lois Ames, *Letters,* p. 400.

381 "This is no termination": A.S. to Dr. Ed Daniels, 2 January 1974, HRHRC.

381 "I am afraid to die": A.S., "Confessional Statement," 29 December 1973, HRHRC.

382 "The poems stand": A.S. to Rise and Steven Axelrod, 10 September 1974, HRHRC.

382 "I always liked": J. D. McClatchy, interview with D.M., 17 November 1982.

382 "Wouldn't that be worth": A.S., interview with J. D. McClatchy, 3 July 1973.

382 "Through [speaking]": A.S., interview with J. D. McClatchy, 23 September 1973.

383 "At John's": Elizabeth Bishop to A.S., 14 November 1973, HRHRC.

383 "Just tell him": Arthur Freeman, interview with D.M., 8 August 1987.

20. POSTHUMOUS PERFORMANCES

385 "I must pack": Louise Conant, unpublished memoir of A.S.

386 " 'On the front page' ": Ibid.

387 "She told me": Eric Edwards, interview with D.M., 26 April 1983.

388 As an example: Robin Becker, interview with D.M., February 1983.

388 "Her image-mongering": Eric Edwards, interview with D.M., 26 April 1983.

388 "We would both": Ibid.

388 "She continues": Peter Porter, "Journey into English," *London Observer,* 27 February 1977, p. 25.

389 "Her presence": Eric Edwards, interview with D.M., 26 April 1983.

389 "Her kind of teaching": George Starbuck, interview with D.M., 13 September 1983.

389 "I dare you": A.S. to "Charles," 21 February 1974, HRHRC.

390 "It was the most publicized": Christina Robb, interview with D.M., 28 April 1983.

390 "I would like": A.S., "Dedication," n.d.; also audiotape, HRHRC.

391 "You remember Anne's reading": Quoted by Barbara Schwartz, interview with D.M., 14 March 1983.

391 "Watching her readings": Linda Sexton, interview with D.M., 13 October 1980.

391 "I could perform": A.S. to Dr. Orne, therapy tape, 11 April 1961.

392 "You won't get another chance": Lois Ames, conversation with D.M., 15 December 1990, and Maxine Kumin, interview with D.M., 9 October 1980.

392 "Anne called us": Louise Conant, unpublished memoir of A.S.

392 "True. I am selfish": A.S. to Maxine Kumin, 25 April 1974, HRHRC.

393 "melting away": Quoted by Barbara Schwartz, interview with D.M., 14 March 1983.

393 "Everybody thought": Joy Sexton, interview with D.M., 24 September 1986.

394 "like a three-year-old": Ibid.

394 "I think I spoke": Joy Sexton, interview with D.M., 26 May 1983.

394 "At the restaurant": John Malcolm Brinnin, interview with D.M., 17 February 1990.

395 "Saint Mattress": A.S. to John Silber, 30 January 1974, HRHRC.

395 "I wish to enter": "In Excelsis," CP, pp. 609–10.

395 "Worse than dying": A.S. to M.D., 26 February 1974, HRHRC.

396 The poem's title: Autobiography of a Schizophrenic Girl, with analytic interpretation by Marguerite Sechehaye, translated by Grace Rubin-Rabson (New York: New American Library, 1970).

396 "Lady, lady": "The Green Room," unpublished ms., HRHRC.

396 "We had a wonderfully gay": Maxine Kumin, interview with D.M., 9 October 1980.

397 "Every time I put it on": A.S. and Dr. Orne, therapy tape, 28 November 1961.

397 "We have had enough": Adrienne Rich, "Anne Sexton: 1928–1974," On Lies, Secrets and Silence (New York: Norton, 1979), p. 122.

397 "Anne Sexton's tragedy": Denise Levertov, "Anne Sexton: Light Up the Cave," Light Up the Cave (New York: New Directions, 1981) p. 80.

398 "I think Mother": Linda Sexton, interview with D.M., 15 October 1980.

CODA

401 "I've taken care": A.S. to Dr. Orne, therapy tape, 30 November 1961.

402   "Poet Told All": Alessandra Stanley, *The New York Times*, 15 July 1991, pp. A1, B2.

402   "A patient's right": Jeremy A. Lazarus, M.D., quoted in Stanley, *op. cit.*, p. A1.

402   "Anne Sexton is dead": Carola Eisenberg, M.D., "Confidentiality in Psychotherapy — The Case of Anne Sexton," *The New England Journal of Medicine*, 14 November 1991, p. 1451.

402   "Any radical break": Alan A. Stone, quoted in Samuel M. Hughes, "The Sexton Tapes," *The Pennsylvania Gazette*, December 1991, p. 28.

402   "it is now widely accepted": Alan A. Stone, M.D., "Confidentiality in Psychotherapy — the Case of Anne Sexton," *op. cit.*, pp. 1450, 1451.

403   "When I left Massachusetts": Martin Orne, "The Sexton Tapes," *The New York Times*, 23 July 1991, p. A19.

404   "an actress in her own": quoted in Barbara Kevles, *op. cit.*, p. 3.

404   "She glided on stage": Dorothy H. Kelso, "Poetry and Performance: Anne Sexton's Particular Appreciation of Life," *The Patriot Ledger*, undated clipping from Anne Sexton Vertical File, HRHRC.

BIBLIOGRAPHY

WORKS BY ANNE SEXTON

To Bedlam and Part Way Back. Boston: Houghton Mifflin, 1960.

"Dancing the Jig." *New World Writing* 16 (1960).

"Classroom at Boston University." *Harvard Advocate* 145, special supplement (November 1961).

"On 'Some Foreign Letters.' " *Poet's Choice*, ed. Paul Engle and Joseph Langland. New York: Dial Press, 1962.

All My Pretty Ones. Boston: Houghton Mifflin, 1962.

"The Last Believer," *Vogue* (15 November 1963).

Eggs of Things (with Maxine Kumin). New York: Putnam, 1963.

More Eggs of Things (with Maxine Kumin). New York: Putnam, 1964.

Selected Poems. London: Oxford University Press, 1964.

"The Barfly Ought to Sing." *TriQuarterly* 7 (Fall 1966).

Live or Die. Boston: Houghton Mifflin, 1966.

"For the Year of the Insane." Boston: Impressions Workshop, 1967. [Broadside illustrated by Barbara Swan]

Foreword to *The Real Tin Flower: Poems About the World at Nine*, by Aliki Barnstone. New York: Collier-Crowell, 1968.

Poems by Thomas Kinsella, Douglas Livingstone and Anne Sexton. London: Oxford University Press, 1968. [Previously published poems]

Love Poems. Boston: Houghton Mifflin, 1969.

Joey and the Birthday Present (with Maxine Kumin). New York: McGraw-Hill, 1971.

Transformations. Boston: Houghton Mifflin, 1971.

"The Letting Down of the Hair." *The Atlantic Monthly* (March 1972).

The Book of Folly. Boston: Houghton Mifflin, 1972. [Includes an unpublished story, "The Ballet of the Buffoon"]

"The Freak Show." *American Poetry Review* 2, no. 3 (May/June 1973).

"A Small Journal" ("All God's Children Need Radios"). *Ms.* (November 1973).

The Death Notebooks. Boston: Houghton Mifflin, 1974.

The Awful Rowing Toward God. Boston: Houghton Mifflin, 1975.

45 Mercy Street. Edited by Linda Gray Sexton. Boston: Houghton Mifflin, 1975.

The Wizard's Tears (with Maxine Kumin). New York: McGraw-Hill, 1975.

Anne Sexton: A Self-Portrait in Letters. Edited by Linda Gray Sexton and Lois Ames. Boston: Houghton Mifflin, 1977.

Words for Dr. Y.: Uncollected Poems with Three Stories. Boston: Houghton Mifflin, 1978. [Includes "The Ghost," "Vampire," "The Bat or To Remember, To Remember"]

"Journal of a Living Experiment." In *Journal of a Living Experiment: A Documentary History of the First Ten Years of Teachers and Writers Collaborative,* ed. Phillip Lopate, pp. 44–75. New York: Teachers and Writers Collaborative, 1979.

The Complete Poems. Boston: Houghton Mifflin, 1981.

No Evil Star: Selected Essays, Interviews and Prose. Edited by Steven E. Colburn. Ann Arbor: University of Michigan Press, 1985.

Selected Poems of Anne Sexton. Edited by Diane Wood Middlebrook and Diana Hume George. Boston: Houghton Mifflin, 1988.

SELECTED BIBLIOGRAPHIES, COMMENTARIES, AND ESSAYS

Bixler, Francis, ed. *Original Essays on the Poetry of Anne Sexton.* Conway: University of Central Arkansas Press, 1988.

Colburn, Steven E., ed. *Anne Sexton: Telling the Tale.* Ann Arbor: University of Michigan Press, 1988.

George, Diana Hume. *Oedipus Anne: The Poetry of Anne Sexton.* Champaign: University of Illinois Press, 1986.

———, ed. *Sexton: Selected Criticism.* Urbana: University of Illinois Press, 1988.

McClatchy, J. D., ed. *Anne Sexton: The Artist and Her Critics.* Bloomington: Indiana University Press, 1978.

Northouse, Cameron, and Thomas P. Walsh. *Sylvia Plath and Anne Sexton: A Reference Guide.* Boston: G. K. Hall, 1974.

Poulin, A., Jr., ed. "A Memorial for Anne Sexton," *American Poetry Review* 4, no. 3 (May/June 1975): 15–20. [Contributions by John Malcolm Brinnin, Maxine Kumin, Kathleen Spivack, Susan Fromberg Schaeffer, C. K. Williams, and others]

Wagner-Martin, Linda, ed. *Critical Essays on Anne Sexton.* Boston: G. K. Hall, 1989.

OTHER REFERENCES

Almond, Richard, *The Healing Community*. New York: Aronson, 1974.
Berman, Jeffrey. *The Talking Cure: Literary Representations of Psychoanalysis*. New York: New York University Press, 1985.
Bernheimer, Charles, and Claire Kahane, eds. *In Dora's Case: Freud — Hysteria — Feminism*. New York: Columbia University Press, 1985.
Bowlby, John. 'The Making and Breaking of Affectional Bonds." *British Journal of Psychiatry* 130 (1977): 201–10.
Cheever, Susan. *Home Before Dark*. Boston: Houghton Mifflin, 1984.
Chodorow, Nancy, *The Reproduction of Mothering: Psychoanalysis and the Sociology of Gender*. Berkeley: University of California Press, 1978.
David-Ménard, Monique. *Hysteria from Freud to Lacan: Body and Language in Psychoanalysis*. Translated by Catherine Porter. Ithaca, N.Y.: Cornell University Press, 1989.
Davison, Jane Truslow. *The Fall of a Doll's House: Three Generations of American Women and the Houses They Lived In*. New York: Holt, Rinehart and Winston, 1980.
Dickey, James. *Babel to Byzantium*. New York: Farrar, Straus and Giroux, 1968.
———. *The Suspect in Poetry*. Madison, Minn.: Sixties Press, 1964.
Dickstein, Morris. *Gates of Eden: American Culture in the Sixties*. New York: Basic Books, 1977.
Dinnerstein, Dorothy. *The Mermaid and the Minotaur: Sexual Arrangements and Human Malaise*. New York: Harper Colophon, 1976.
Fernald, Anne. "Meaningful Melodies in Mothers' Speech to Infants." In *Nonverbal Vocal Communication: Comparative and Developmental Approaches*, ed. H. Papousek, U. Jurgens, and M. Papousek. Cambridge: Cambridge University Press (forthcoming).
Friedan, Betty. *The Feminine Mystique*. New York: W. W. Norton, 1963.
Gallop, Jane. *The Daughter's Seduction: Feminism and Psychoanalysis*. Ithaca, N.Y.: Cornel University Press, 1982.
Gitlin, Todd. *The Sixties: Years of Hope, Days of Rage*. New York: Bantam, 1989.
Gross, Harvey. *Sound and Form in Modern Poetry: A Study of Prosody from Thomas Hardy to Robert Lowell*. Ann Arbor: University of Michigan Press, 1964.
Grossman, Allen. *Against Our Vanishing: Winter Conversations with*

Allen Grossman on the Theory and Practice of Poetry, ed. Mark Halliday. Boston: Rowan Tree Press, 1981.

Hall, Donald, Robert Pack, and Louis Simpson, eds. *New Poets of England and America.* New York: Meridian Books, 1958.

Hamilton, Ian. *Robert Lowell: A Biography.* New York: Random House, 1982.

Hardwick, Elizabeth. *A View of My Own: Essays on Literature and Society.* New York: Farrar, Straus, and Cudahy, 1962.

Herman, Judith. *Father-Daughter Incest.* Cambridge, Mass.: Harvard University Press, 1981.

Howard, Richard. *Alone with America: Essays on the Art of Poetry in the United States since 1950.* New York: Atheneum, 1971.

Johnson, Barbara. *A World of Difference.* Baltimore: Johns Hopkins University Press, 1989.

Kalstone, David. *Becoming a Poet: Elizabeth Bishop with Marianne Moore and Robert Lowell.* Edited by Robert Hemenway. New York: Farrar, Straus and Giroux, 1989.

Kohut, Heinz. "Beyond the Bounds of the Basic Rule: Some Recent Contributions to Applied Psychoanalysis." In *The Search for the Self,* vol. 1, ed. P. Ornstein. New York: International Universities Press, 1978.

———. *How Does Analysis Cure?* Chicago: University of Chicago Press, 1984.

Kramer, Peter D. *Moments of Engagement: Intimate Psychotherapy in a Technological Age.* New York: W. W. Norton, 1989.

Kumin, Maxine. *Our Ground Time Here Will Be Brief.* New York: Penguin, 1982.

———. *To Make a Prairie: Essays on Poets, Poetry and Country Living.* Ann Arbor: University of Michigan Press, 1979.

Lacan, Jacques. *Feminine Sexuality: Jacques Lacan and the école freudienne.* Edited and translated by Juliet Mitchell and Jacqueline Rose. New York: W. W. Norton, 1982.

Levertov, Denise. *Light Up the Cave.* New York: New Directions, 1981.

Mack, John. "Psychoanalysis and Biography: Aspects of a Developing Affinity." *Journal of the American Psychoanalytic Association* 28 (1980): 543–48.

Mahler, Margaret, et al. *The Psychological Birth of the Human Infant.* New York: Basic Books, 1975.

Malcolm, Janet. *Psychoanalysis: The Impossible Profession.* New York: Knopf, 1981.

Miller, Alice. *The Drama of the Gifted Child (Prisoners of Childhood).* Translated by Ruth Ward. New York: Harper and Row, 1981.

Olsen, Tillie. *Silences*. New York: Delacorte/Seymour Lawrence, 1978.

Ostriker, Alicia Suskin. *Stealing the Language: The Emergence of Women's Poetry in America*. Boston: Beacon Press, 1986.

———. *Writing Like a Woman*. Ann Arbor: University of Michigan Press, 1983.

Perloff, Marjorie. "*Poètes Maudits* of the Genteel Tradition." *American Poetry Review* 12, no. 6 (May/June 1983): 32–38.

Rich, Adrienne. *Of Woman Born: Motherhood as Experience and Institution*. New York: W. W. Norton, 1976.

———. *On Lies, Secrets, and Silences: Selected Prose, 1966–1978*. New York: W. W. Norton, 1979.

Rosenfield, Israel. *The Invention of Memory: A New View of the Brain*. New York: Basic Books, 1988.

Roth, Moira. *The Amazing Decade: Women and Performance Art in America, 1970–1980*. Los Angeles: Astro Artz, 1983.

Ruddick, Sara, and Pamela Daniels, eds. *Working It Out*. New York: Pantheon, 1977.

Sacks, Oliver. *The Man Who Mistook His Wife for a Hat, and Other Clinical Tales*. New York: Harper and Row, 1985.

Sayre, Henry. *The Object of Performance*. Chicago: University of Chicago Press, 1989.

Schafer, Roy. *The Analytic Attitude*. New York: Basic Books, 1983.

Schickel, Richard. *Intimate Strangers: The Culture of Celebrity*. New York: Doubleday, 1985.

Showalter, Elaine. *The Female Malady*. New York: Pantheon, 1985.

Simpson, Eileen. *Poets in Their Youth: A Memoir*. New York: Random House, 1982

Steinman, Louise. *The Knowing Body: Elements of Contemporary Performance and Dance*. Boston: Shambhala, 1986.

Stern, Daniel N. *The Interpersonal World of the Infant: A View from Psychoanalysis and Developmental Psychology*. New York: Basic Books, 1985.

Stevenson, Anne. *Bitter Fame: A Life of Sylvia Plath*. Boston: Houghton Mifflin, 1989.

Stone, Michael H., ed. *Essential Papers on Borderline Disorders*. New York: New York University Press, 1986.

Updike, John. *Couples*. New York: Knopf, 1968.

———. *Rabbit Redux*. New York: Knopf, 1971.

Wagner-Martin, Linda. *Sylvia Plath: A Biography*. New York: Simon and Schuster, 1987.

Warhol, Andy. *The Philosophy of Andy Warhol*. New York: Harcourt, Brace, Jovanovich, 1975.

Yalom, Marilyn. *Maternity, Morality, and the Literature of Madness.* University Park: Pennsylvania State University Press, 1985.

Young-Bruehl, Elisabeth. *Mind and the Body Politics: Lectures and Essays, 1975–1988.* New York: Routledge, Chapman and Hall, 1989.

Zetzel, Elizabeth. *The Capacity for Emotional Growth.* London: Hogarth Press, 1970.

Žižek, Slavoj. *The Sublime Object of Ideology.* London: Verso, 1989.

ACKNOWLEDGMENTS

Of the many debts to generous people I have incurred during the ten-year project of writing this book, the greatest is to Linda Gray Sexton, literary executor of Anne Sexton's estate, whose large-mindedness and gifts of insight as a daughter and as a writer will be evident to every reader. The contributions of Anne Sexton's other closest survivors, Alfred Muller Sexton II and Joyce Ladd Sexton, can only be adumbrated in these words of thanks. To Al Sexton, now remarried and rooted in a new life, my gratitude for exceptional kindness and cooperation. To Joy, an accomplished photographer and now a nurse, my gratitude for her unsparing candor and unflagging spirit of fun. To Joy's spouse, Stephen Wollmer, my appreciation for graciousness throughout a decade of invasions. To Linda's spouse, John Freund, great thanks for interventions deft and timely.

Other members of Sexton's family provided extensive help in early stages of research but were unwilling to be acknowledged by name. For their time and patience in helping me achieve accuracy and clarity, I owe them a great debt.

The bountiful cooperation of Anne Sexton's most influential therapist, Martin Orne, provided this book with a foundation of understanding that cannot be indicated even by the numerous footnotes that acknowledge him; for his time, his devotion, and his confidence in me, I owe him a very great debt. Sexton's last therapist, Barbara Schwartz, was also an indispensable source of insight. Another of my greatest debts is to Ellen Bassuk, M.D., an intellectual partner who shared every phase of work on this book and whose abundant affection gave me another sister. I want to acknowledge the generosity of other mental health professionals, too: for extensive commentary on versions of the manuscript, my special thanks to Barbara Almond, Richard Almond, Norman Dishotsky, and David Lake; and for other contributions, to Alfred Bochner, Stephanie Brown, Margy Cottle, George Hogle, Pierre Johannet, Marilynne Kanter, Patrick Lamb, P. Herbert Leiderman, Peter Ostwald, Benjamin Riggs, Stephen Schoonover, David Spiegel, Alan A. Stone, and Irvin Yalom.

Colleagues who have provided me with careful readings of the manuscript during its long gestation and to whom I owe particular thanks for repeated, extensive commentaries are poets Martha Collins, Maxine Kumin, and Alicia Ostriker; professors Barbara Babcock, John Bender, Terry Castle, Barbara Freeman, Diana Hume George, Barbara Johnson, Susan Krieger, Herbert Lindenberger, Ira Livingston, Joanne Martin, and Arnold Rampersad; and the members of the Stanford Biographer's Seminar, 1987–1990, and of the Seminar on Writing and Psychoanalysis, 1989–1990. At Houghton Mifflin, I owe special thanks to my editor, Peter Davison, for his encouragement through every difficulty; to my manuscript editor, Liz Duvall, for being able to read my mind; and to Barbara Williams, Esq., for clever applications of good sense.

Among librarians, I would like to thank above all the excellent staff of the Harry Ransom Humanities Research Center at the University of Texas at Austin, especially Ellen Dunlap, former research librarian, Cathy Henderson, its current research librarian, and Richard Oram. For additional assistance and permissions I am indebted to Stratis Haviaris, curator of the Poetry Room, Lamont Library; Ruth Mortimer, curator of rare books, Smith College; Jane Knowles, Radcliffe College archivist, Schlesinger Library; and members of the staff at the San Francisco Poetry Center and the Kenyon College Archive.

For their generosity in contributing memories, contacts, information, and correspondence to this project, I am glad to thank, at long last, Robert Abzug, Samuel Albert, Lois Ames, Deirdre Bair, Michael Bearpark (for an unpublished memoir), Robin Becker, Frank Bidart, Chana Bloch, John Malcolm Brinnin, Theodore Casher, Alan Cheuse, Robert Clawson, Steven Colburn, Loring Conant, Louise Conant (for an unpublished memoir), Peter Davison, Claire Degener (now Derway), Joseph DeRoche (for an unpublished journal), James Dickey, Virginia Downing, Eric Edwards, Doris Holmes Eyges, Arthur Freeman, Susan Stanford Friedman, Jonathan Galassi, Dana Gioia, Herb Gold, Linda Gregerson, Allen Grossman, Donald Hall, Wynn Handman, Anthony Hecht, the late Roger Hecht, the late Firman Houghton, Ted Hughes, Alison Johnson, the late David Kalstone, Freda Karpf, Larry Kessenich, Carolyn Kizer, the late Wilhelmine Sexton Knight, Jane Kumin, Maxine Kumin, Denise Levertov, Claire Lindenberger, Herbert Lindenberger, Maryel Locke, Melody Lothes, Victor Luftig, George MacBeth, John McCarthy, J. D. McClatchy, James McConkey, Peggy McIntosh, Charles Maryan, Jeffrey Moussaieff

Masson, Jack Matthews, Alice Methfessel, Nolan Miller, Frederick Morgan, the late Howard Moss, Jean Moulton, Karen Ocamb, Tillie Olsen, Emily Carota Orne, Gerald Oshita, Adrienne Rich, Sands Robart, Christina Robb, David Rosenhan, Mollie Rosenhan, Alice Ryerson, Marian Seldes, Ben Shaktman, Richard Sherwood, Elaine Showalter, the late Alice Lorenda Smith, Joan Smith, W. D. Snodgrass, William Stafford, Jon Stallworthy, George Starbuck, Peter Stitt, Conrad Susa, Barbara Swan, Brian Sweeney, D. M. Thomas, Helen Vendler, Linda Wagner-Martin, Dan Wakefield, Theodore Weiss, the late Anne Wilder (for unpublished correspondence and an unpublished journal), C. K. Williams, and Annie Wright.

In 1982–1983 I held a fellowship for independent study from the National Endowment for the Humanities and was also a fellow at the Mary Ingraham Bunting Institute at Radcliffe College, a women's institution that had more to do with the shaping of Sexton's life and of this biography than can easily be surmised. Explicit thanks here to the circle of Bunting Fellows, from whose intelligence and generosity I learned much that has stayed with me — especially to Ellen Bassuk, Martha Collins, Jorie Graham, Rachel Jacoff, Barbara Johnson, Joan Landes, Elinor Langer, Carolyn Williams, and Linda Williams; to the former director of the Bunting Institute, Margaret McKenna, and its present director, Florence Ladd; to the staff, especially Janice Randall; and to former presidents of Radcliffe College Mary Ingraham Bunting and Matina Horner.

Research on this biography received substantial institutional support from the Stanford University Academic Computing and Informations Systems (1982–1990), the Stanford Humanities Center (1983–1984), the Pew Memorial Trust (1985–1987), the John Simon Guggenheim Memorial Foundation (1988–1989), and the Rockefeller Study Center at Bellagio (1990), and research funds were made available by my appointment as the Howard H. and Jessie T. Watkins University Professor at Stanford University (1985–1990). Stanford deans Herant Katchadourian, Peter Stansky, and Norman Wessells deserve acknowledgment for timely support, as do successive chairs of the Department of English, especially Albert Gelpi and Martin Evans.

Special thanks for fundamental insights are also due to the graduate students with whom I worked in two Stanford University courses: the Seminar on Psychoanalysis and Feminism, 1984, and the Colloquium on Contemporary North American Poetics, 1990. To Joseph Conte, Jonathan Ivry, Maria Koundoura, Andrea Lerner, and Brett Millier, my thanks for careful work as research assistants; and to Tom Goodrich, David Hoggan, Inge Kuhn, Barbara Sawka, and Marcia Tanner, my thanks for technical assistance.

Invitations to contribute essays to journals and books helped clarify my thinking, as did the comments of their editors. My thanks for editorial assistance with early versions of parts of this book go to Linda Rhoads, *New England Quarterly* (1983); Diana Wilson, *Denver Quarterly,* special issue on feminist criticism (1984); Herb Leibowitz, *Parnassus,* special issue on women poets (1985); Mark Rudman, *Pequod,* special issue on autobiography/biography (1988); and Francis Bixler, editor of *Original Essays on Anne Sexton* (1988). From the outset of my research I was fortunate to collaborate with one of Sexton's most astute critics, Diana Hume George, whom I thank for the opportunity to contribute to her *Sexton: Selected Criticism* (1988) and for the many conversations that resulted in our joint editorship of *Selected Poems of Anne Sexton* (1988).

For involving me in theater productions of Anne Sexton's work, my thanks to Dean Seabrook, for the production *Anne Sexton's Transformations,* Portland, Oregon, 1985; to members of the Chamber Theatre Ensemble for a production of *The Room of My Life* at the Manhattan Theatre Club in 1986; to Wallis Annenberg and Salome Jens for a benefit performance of *About Anne,* American Film Institute, Los Angeles, 1988. For invitations to present work in progress, special thanks to Claire Sprague, Faculty Seminar in American Literature, Columbia University, 1984; Marilyn Yalom, deputy director of the Stanford Center for Research on Women, sponsor of a conference on "Autobiography, Biography, and Gender," 1986; Aileen Ward, founder of the NYU Biography Seminar, 1988; and David Wilbern, organizer of the Fifth International Conference on Psychoanalysis and Literature, Kirchberg-am-Wechsel, Austria, 1988.

For opportunities to discuss work in progress with mental health professionals, my thanks to Antonia Bercovicci and Murray Bilmis, who invited me to address annual meetings of the California Psychological Association, 1986 and 1987; to Randall Weingarten for my place on the program of the Northern California Psychiatric Association at Yosemite in 1988; to Margaret Brenman-Gibson and Peter Ostwald for opportunities to participate in discussions of psychoanalysis and the creative process at meetings of the American Psychoanalytic Association in New York in 1988 and San Francisco in 1989; to the Stanford Department of Psychiatry to present at Grand Rounds in

1981, 1989, and 1990; and to Diana Kirschner for the honor of sharing the podium with Martin Orne at the Sixth Annual Conference of the Society for the Exploration of Psychotherapy Integration, in Philadelphia in 1990.

For hospitality during these many expensive years of work, special thanks to Ellen Bassuk and Steve Schoonover for a room of my own in Chestnut Hill; to Joshua and Marguerite Lederberg for numerous residencies in the President's House at Rockefeller University; and to Vern McGee for a home in Austin, Texas.

Finally, immeasurable gratitude to my husband, Carl Djerassi, for his love, his companionship, and his marvelous wits. This book could not have been written without him.

INDEX

"Abortion, The" (Sexton), 122
Abzug, Robert, 378
Academy of American Poets, Sexton reads for, 287
Acrostic poems, 98, 99
"Addict, The" (Sexton), 247, 260, 272, 279–81, 305
Africa, AS and Kayo tour, 262–64
"After Auschwitz" (Sexton), 367
After the Fall (Miller), 215
"Again and Again and Again" (Sexton), 299
Aiken, Conrad, 131
Akmadulina, Bella, 278
Albert, Sam, 50, 96, 141
Alcohol and alcoholism: and AS's childhood, 13–14; of AS's father, 13–14, 15, 16, 18, 26, 33; of Kayo's father, 22; and AS's aunt Frances, 33; AS's dependence on, 139–40, 210, 238, 330, 380; and AS-Kayo fights, 370; and AS at dinner with Cheever, 394
Aldrich, Nelson, 256
Alfred, William, 94, 96, 368
"All God's Children Need Radios" (Sexton), 359
"All My Pretty Ones" (Sexton), 58, 117
All My Pretty Ones (Sexton), xxi, 163, 165, 172–74, 185–87, 188, 194, 332; and Wright, 133, 134, 163; and National Book Award, 140, 193; and *The Cure*, 168; Dickey on, 173, 250; and Joan Smith, 268; and religion, 351
Almeida, Laurindo, 239

American Academy of Arts and Letters, AS grant from, 193, 206–7, 212, 217–18
American Place Theater, 312–13, 319
Ames, Lois, 58, 243–44; as *Self-Portrait* editor, xxi; and AS's comic novel, 246, 266–67; and AS-Zweizung affair, 259–60, 265, 314; AS letters and remarks to, 266, 269, 271, 297, 304, 305; on London trip, 277, 280, 281; with McLean workshop, 308, 309; and *Mercy Street* in New York, 317, 322, 326, 328; as Linda Sexton's confidante, 347; and AS's divorce, 372; picture of, 373; on Minneapolis trip, 374; as companion (1973), 377, 379; and Robert Abzug, 378; B.U. classes recorded by, 387; and AS suicide attempts, 392, 393
Amichai, Yehuda, 279
Anderson, Elizabeth. *See* Harvey, Elizabeth
Anderson, Laurie, 405
Anderson, Sherwood, 285
"And One for My Dame" (Sexton), 58, 170
"Angels of the Love Affair" (Sexton), 349, 350–51
Anna O. (Freud patient), 55
Anne Sexton and Her Kind (music group), 286–87, 303–6, 319, 330, 345; and critical process, 143; and Dan Kumin, 185, 306; and McLean workshop,

Anne Sexton and Her Kind (*cont.*)
308; tapes of at funeral, 397
Anne Sexton: A Self-Portrait in Letters, xxi
Anspach, Andrew, 326
Antin, Eleanor, 405
Antioch College, Writers' Conference at, 79, 80–81, 83, 124
Antioch Review, 89
Apollo II landing, Sexton in celebration of, 320
"Appointment Hour" (Sexton), 52
Ariel (Plath), 113, 243, 361, 367
Auden, W. H., 72, 231, 278, 333, 383
Audience, AS receives prize from, 118–19
"Author of the Jesus Papers Speaks, The" (Sexton), 352–53
Autobiographical poetry. *See* Confessional poetry
Autobiography of a Schizophrenic Girl (Sechehaye), 396
Awful Rowing Toward God, The (Sexton), xxi, 150, 366–68; as therapy, 380; "image-mongering" in, 388; and Harvard reading, 391; AS and Kumin to proofread, 396
Axelrod, Rise, 382
Axelrod, Steven, 382

Bachmann, Ingeborg, 278
Bagg, Robert, 308
"Balance Wheel, The" (Sexton), 75
Balk, Wesley, 366
"Ballad of the Lonely Masturbator, The" (Sexton), 271, 297, 299
"Ballet of the Buffoon, The" (Sexton), 359
Barbiturates ("kill me" pills), 34, 165, 209, 216
"Barefoot" (Sexton), 271, 299
Barnes, Clive, 328
Barnstone, Aliki, 308
Barth, John, 357
Barthelme, Donald, 333

Bass, Ellen, 340
Baudelaire, Charles, 65
Baumbach, Jonathan, 256
Bearpark, Michael, 17, 18, 281, 282
Beauvoir, Simone de, 172–73
Becker, Robin, 388
Bedlam. See To Bedlam and Part Way Back
"Begat" (Sexton), 343
Belli, Melvin, 273
Bell Jar, The (Plath), 200
Belloc, Hilaire, 157
Bellow, Saul, 161–63, 171, 189, 241, 246
"Bells, The" (Sexton), 58, 75
Bennett, Joseph, 95, 119
Berlind, Bruce, 358
Bermuda, AS and Kayo vacation in, 309–10, 339
Berryman, John, 65, 81, 109, 278, 279, 389
"Bestiary U.S.A." (Sexton), 361
"Birthday, A" (Mary Gray Harvey), 48
Bishop, Elizabeth, 93, 109, 125–26, 174, 254–55, 383
"Black Art, The" (Sexton), 134, 148, 253
Blackwood, Lady Caroline, 383
Bly, Robert, 149, 296
"Boat, The" (Sexton), 343
Bobby Pressit, (AS's pretend brother), 12, 38
Bone Thoughts (Starbuck), 118, 140, 187, 361
Book of Folly, The (Sexton), xxi, 332, 333, 338, 359, 362; and Barbara Swan, 197; British publication of, 363
Booth, Philip, 95
Boston Center for Adult Education: AS enrolled in, 49–51, 69, 75, 76, 82, 140–41; Kumin enrolled in, 72
Boston University: AS considers attending, 46; AS in Lowell's class

at, 89, 91–94; AS teaches at, 338–40, 378, 386, 387–89
Boylan, Eleanor, 168, 229
Brand, Millen, 264
Brandeis University, AS studies at, 126–28
Bread Loaf Writers' Conference: 79; AS and Starbuck at, 118; AS and Legler at, 376
"Break, The" (Sexton), 266, 299
Breaking of the Day, The (Davison), 187
"Breast, The" (Sexton), 257, 298
Brecht, Bertolt, 127
"Briar Rose/Sleeping Beauty" (Sexton), 337
Brinnin, John Malcolm, 92, 95, 367, 383, 387, 394
Brooks, Jane, 92
Brooks, Paul, 185, 186, 298, 300, 302, 305, 338
Browning, Elizabeth Barrett, 104
Browning, Robert, 93
Brunner-Orne, Martha, 26, 31, 34, 167–68, 209–10; and AS's suicide attempt, 33; on AS's illness, 37; and AS accomplishments, 145; AS passes out in office of, 175; as mother, 211; at Harvard reading, 390; refusal by, 393
Bunting, Mary Ingraham, 144, 150, 197

Caedmon, Sexton records for, 393
Cairnie, Gordon, 117–18
Caldwell, Sarah, 357
Camus, Albert, 127
Capri, AS visits, 209, 212, 218, 250, 264
Casher, Theodore, 303, 304, 330
Centre College, Kumin at, 366–67
Charles Playhouse: AS in workshop at, 168; and *The Cure (Tell Me Your Answer True)*, 218, 227–28, 313
Chase, Constance, 316–17, 336, 341, 346, 349, 371; vacation

of, 377, 378; AS terminated by, 381
Chatto & Windus, xxi, 363
Cheever, John, 301, 394, 402
"Children's Crusade, The" (Sexton), 361, 362
Christian Science Monitor, 20, 75
Ciardi, John, 79, 170
"Cigarettes and Butternut Squash" (Sexton story), 162
"Cinquains" (Sexton), 20
Clark, John, 289
"Classroom at Boston University" (Sexton), 186
Clawson, Robert, 255–58, 274, 285, 286, 289, 303; and Her Kind music group, 287, 319, 330; picture of, 304; and Zweizung affair, 314; and Vonnegut, 331; and poster for Harvard reading, 389; and Her Kind tapes at funeral, 397
Coleridge, Samuel Taylor, 65
Colgate University: Kayo attends, 22, 23; AS teaches at, 357–58, 360
Collected Poems, The (Plath), 113
Colossus, The (Plath), 104
"Comfort" (term of endearment), 12, 128–29, 134, 163
Complete Poems, The (Sexton), xxi; Kumin introduction to, 143–44
Conant, Loring, 371, 372, 377, 385, 390, 391
Conant, Louise, 371, 372–73, 377, 379, 385; AS to on HRI therapy, 378; and "poetry kit," 385–86, 388; at prereading party, 390; on support efforts for AS, 392; and morning of AS's suicide, 395
Confessional poetry, 78, 83, 100, 112; "Double Image" as, 86; Dickey on, 250; Gullans on, 265; and Oates's time capsule, 320; AS's departure from, 338;

Confessional poetry (cont.)
and AS's relation to Plath, 364;
and AS's view of self, 365, 382
Conrad, Alfred, 110
Consciousness-raising, 196, 364
"Consecrating Mother, The" (Sexton), 360
"Consorting with Angels" (Sexton), 58, 170, 183, 272
Cornell University Arts Festival, AS reads at, 140
Counterculture: and Her Kind, 305; and drugs in suburbs, 321–22
Crane, Hart, 93
Crapsey, Adelaide, 93
"Cripples and Other Stories" (Sexton), 305
Critics: and AS dream, 141–42; Kumin as, 142, 182, 306; AS need for, 142–43, 146, 182, 306, 326; AS on, 188
"Crossing the Atlantic" (Sexton), 205
Cure, The (Sexton play), 168, 183, 218–22; and After the Fall, 215. See also Mercy Street; Tell Me Your Answer True
"Curse Against Elegies, A" (Sexton), 130

"Daddy" (Plath), 105
Daedalus-Icarus legend, 231, 232–33
"Dancing the jig" (AS expression), 37
"Dancing the Jig" (Sexton story), 103, 120, 145–46, 195
Davies, Bill, 287, 303, 304
Davison, Peter, 140, 187
Dealand, Helen, 9, 10, 18, 35
"Death Baby, The" (Sexton), 333
Death Notebooks, The (Sexton), xxi, 332, 333, 338, 359, 361, 385; and Barbara Swan, 197; and Harvard Literary Club reading, 389, 391

"Death of the Fathers, The," 58, 333, 342–45, 349
De Cordova Museum: Merwin reading at, 72; Her Kind concert in, 305, 319
Dee, Ruby, 357
Degener, Cindy, 275; and AS's plans for novel, 265, 337; and Tell Me Your Answer True/Mercy Street, 312, 319; and popular magazines, 337; AS to on physical problems, 345; and AS's spiritual concerns, 355, 356; and Book of Folly, 363; and Transformations opera, 365–66; and Awful Rowing, 367
DeMott, Benjamin, 256
Depression, and Sexton's illness, 34, 37, 39, 345. See also Sexton, Anne MENTAL ILLNESS OF
DeRoche, Joseph, 97–98
Dickey, James, 126, 173, 186, 250–51; and speaker's fees, 272
Dickinson, Emily, xix, 104
Dietz, Paula, 356
Dingley, Anna Ladd. See Nana
Dingley, Jane (grandmother of AS), 11
Dingley, Nelson, Jr., 5
"Disquieting Muses, The" (Plath), 111
Dissociative mechanisms. See Trances of AS
"Division of Parts, The" (Sexton) 102
"Divorce" (Sexton), 258
"Dog-God" (Sexton), 362
Dolphin, The (Lowell), 383
Donaldson, Scott, 402
"Doors, Doors, Doors" (Sexton), 118
Dostoevsky, Fyodor, 122, 127, 128, 165
"Double Image, The" (Sexton), 75, 84, 85–89, 94, 102, 158; and mother-daughter dynamic, 85–89, 102, 349; at Poets' Theater

reading, 96; and Plath, 105; and mother's illness, 120; AS to Orne on, 181; C. K. Williams on, 345
Douglass College, AS reads at, 392
Dowd, M'el, 322, 323
Downing, Virginia, 317, 322, 327
Driver, Christopher, 362
Drugs: "kill-me" pills, 34, 165, 209, 216; medication prescribed, 75–76, 78, 226–27, 317, 345–46 (see also Thorazine, AS's use of); pill supply, 252, 374; marijuana, 321, 393; quinidine overdose, 378; pill overdose (1974), 391–92; pills taken on Charles River stroll, 393. See also Alcohol and alcoholism; Sleeping pills, AS's use of
Dugan, Alan, 170
Duhamel, P. Albert, 187

"Earth Falls Down, The" (Sexton), 367
East Hampton, AS at conference in, 255–58
Eberhart, Richard, 170, 289
"Eden Revisited" (Sexton), 52
Edwards, Eric, 387, 388, 389
"Eighteen Days Without You" (Sexton), 288, 289, 293, 294–95, 299; vs. "The Firebombers," 297; at Phi Beta Kappa reading, 302
Eisenhower era, 274
"Electra on Azalea Path" (Plath), 104, 106
Eliot, T. S., 65, 83, 127
Elizabeth (AS persona), 55–56, 60–61, 63
"Elizabeth Gone" (Sexton), 75
Elliott, Mary Emma, 95
Ellison, Ralph, 285
"End of the Illusion, The" (Sexton), 52
Enright, D. J., 363
Ernst, Karl, 154, 236, 271

Ernst, Rita, 154, 229, 236, 237, 271, 372
"Exorcists, The" (Sexton), 75
"Eye-mote, The" (Plath), 104
Eyges, Doris Holmes, 96

Fahey, Simon and Sandra, 374, 379
Fairfield University, AS honorary degree from, 357
Fairy tales, in Transformations, 335–38
"Fallen Angels, The" (Sexton), 368
"Farmer's Wife, The" (Sexton), 82, 89, 114
Farrell, Brother Dennis, 182–84, 214, 367
Faulkner, William, 127
Feminism: AS's attitude toward, 151, 365; and "women's poetry" (1962), 172; in Tell Me Your Answer True, 221; and women's places, 274; and AS on religion, 350; and AS's appeal, 364, 387–88
Ferenczi, Sándor, 258
Ferry, David, 95
Fiddlehead Review, The, 52, 61
Fink, Alan, 378
"Firebombers, The" (Sexton), 295, 296–97
Fitts, Dudley, 145, 276
Fitzgerald, Zelda, 402
"Five, The" (Holmes), 170
"Flee on Your Donkey" (Sexton), 58, 176–80, 272; AS to Orne on, 181; Freeman on, 182; in Live or Die, 241
"Flight" (Sexton), 186
Florida, as AS-Kayo vacation spot, 236–37, 360–61
"Foggy Adjustment, A" (Sexton), 52
"For Anne at Passover" (Kumin), 143
Ford Foundation, AS grant from, 193, 206–7, 218, 227
"For God While Sleeping" (Sexton) 98, 122; manuscript of, 99

"For John, Who Begs Me Not to Enquire Further" (Sexton), 100, 101

"For Johnny Pole on the Forgotten Beach" (Sexton), 75, 79, 114, 287

"For Mr. Death Who Stands with His Door Open" (Sexton), 333

"For My Lover, Returning to His Wife" (Sexton), 266, 275, 297, 298

"Fortress, The" (Sexton), 157, 158–60, 281

Fortune Teller, The (Holmes), 140, 170

"For the Year of the Insane" (Sexton), 201, 241, 355

45 Mercy Street (Sexton), xxi, 361

Freeman, Arthur, 96, 117–18, 139, 182, 339, 383

Freud, Sigmund, and Freudianism: in AS's study of psychology, 53, 55; and AS's poetry, 61; and Kumin, 195; and *Tell Me Your Answer True*, 221, 225; and sex in psychotherapy, 258; and AS word games, 294; and mother-daughter incest, 325; and AS's revisionary religious parables, 351

Friedan, Betty, 195

"Friends" (Sexton), 343

Fromberg, Susan, 365

Frommer, Arthur, 201

"From the Garden" (Sexton), 134

"Frost, Jack" (MGH doctor), 22–25

Frost, Robert, 72, 76, 79, 186, 282

Frost Fellowship, AS receives, 118

Fugue states. *See* Trances of AS

"Funnel" (Sexton), 119

"Furies, The" (Sexton), 359, 361

Furst, Arthur, 393

"Fury of Beautiful Bones, The" (Sexton), 361

"Fury of Cocks, The" (Sexton), 389

"Fury of Guitars and Sopranos, The" (Sexton), 389

Gardner, Isabella, 95, 104

Garland School, AS attends, 21

Geffen, Felicia, 212

"Ghost of a Memo" (Sexton), 119

"Ghosts" (Sexton), 58, 122

Gide, André, 127

Gilbert, Celia, 390

Ginsberg, Allen, 108, 279

Glenside, AS hospitalized at, 34, 52

"Godfather Death" (Sexton), 333

"God Is a Woman" (AS proposed commencement topic), 350, 356

Gold, Herbert, 119

Goodman, Mitchell, 256

Gordon, Mary, 365

Goucher College, AS's reading at, 395

Graves, Robert, 72

"Green Room, The" (Sexton), 395–96

Green Wall, The (Wright), 129

Grossman, Allen, 118, 125, 126, 250, 296

Guggenheim Foundation, AS grant from, 313, 326

Guggenheim Museum, AS reads at, 287

Gullans, Charles, 265

Halfway (Kumin), 140

Hall, Donald, 118

Hamilton, Ian, 109, 362

Handloss, Pattie, 395, 397

Handman, Wynn, 312–13, 317, 318, 327, 328, 329

Hankinson, "Hank," 303

Hardwick, Elizabeth, 110, 194, 383

Hardy, Thomas, 126

Harper's, 75, 89, 264, 361

Harry Ransom Humanities Research Center (HRHRC), xxii

Harvard College, Lamont Library poetry room, recording of AS, 404; Linda at, 349, 373

Harvard Literary Club, AS reads for, 389–95

Harvey, Anne Gray. *See* Sexton, Anne

Harvey, Blanche (sister of AS), 4, 7; schooling of, 8–9, 10; childhood of, 9–10, 11–12; and AS's biography, 403; and AS's breakdown, 34; and father's funeral, 116–17; and Christmas morning, 162–63

Harvey, Elizabeth Anderson (grandmother of AS), 5, 55

Harvey, Frances (aunt of AS), 5, 15, 33, 116

Harvey, Jane (sister of AS), 4, 7, 16; schooling of, 8–9, 10; childhood life of, 9–10, 11, 12, 13; and father's death, 116–17; and Christmas morning, 162–63; Pulitzer Prize greetings from, 272

Harvey, Louis (grandfather of AS), 4–5, 10, 16

Harvey, Mary Gray Staples (mother of AS), 4, 5, 6–7; marriage and family life of, 9–10, 11, 13, 14, 18; drinking of, 13–14; and AS's bowel movements, 14–15, 59; and Jack McCarthy, 18, 19; as writer, 20, 113; and AS's elopement, 22; AS and Kayo live with, 25; and AS's mental illness, 26, 33, 34, 15, 102; and AS's marriage, 27; AS's relation to, 30, 37, 48–49, 89, 200–201; and Mary LaCrosse, 33, 270; and education for AS, 45–46; picture of, 46; mastectomy of, 46, 83–84, 216, 342; final illness and death of, 47, 84, 101, 102; poetry of, 47–48; on husband's behavior toward AS, 57; genital inspections by, 59; AS wears ring of, 117; and James Wright, 129; and "fat arm," 159; and Taylor on AS's work,

329; and legacy of womanly fulfillment, 311; Azel Mack as lover of, 342, 344

AND AS'S POETRY: suspicion toward, 20–21; suggestion for, 42; competition, 45; poems presented to (Christmas 1957), 45, 65–66; encouragement, 47, 48–49; "The Double Image," 85–86, 88–89, 102, 120; "Dancing the Jig," 103, 120; "The Operation," 120; "Flee on Your Donkey," 178; and "star," 351

Harvey, Ralph Churchill (father of AS), 4, 5, 6–7; business life of, 4, 5, 9, 13, 14; family life of, 7, 9–10, 11, 13, 18; house built by, 13; alcoholism of, 13–14, 15, 18, 26, 33; and Jack McCarthy, 19; and AS's poetry vs. Mary Gray's letters, 20; and AS's marriage, 23; AS and Kayo live with, 25; and AS's pregnancy, 28; Kayo works for, 29–30; and AS's breakdown, 33; AS's view of, 49; AS's sexual memories of, 56–59, 167, 178; stroke suffered by, 84, 89; and wife's dying, 101, 102; death and funeral of, 116–17; Kayo compared with, 166; in AS's free association, 174, 183

Hawk in the Rain, The (Hughes), 103

H.D. (Hilda Doolittle), 186

"Heart's Needle" (Snodgrass), 76–78, 85

Heart's Needle (Snodgrass), 119, 231

Hecht, Anthony, 146–48, 193, 275, 277, 278, 306, 356

Hecht, Roger, 148–49

Hellman, Lillian, 194

Hemingway, Ernest: suicide of, 216; and MacBeth on AS, 262

"Her Kind" (Sexton), 113–15, 126, 247

Her Kind (music group). *See* Anne Sexton and Her Kind
Hershman, Lynn, 405
Hitchens, Herbert, 103
Hollander, John, 118, 256
Holmes, John, 50, 100, 170; AS in workshop of, 50–52, 75, 76, 81, 82, 140–41, 169–70, 182; Kumin in workshop of, 72; writers' conference of, 79; parties at house of, 95; dislike of AS, 96, 140–41, 143, 172; and private workshop, 96–98; picture of, 97; on *Bedlam*, 98, 100, 125; at Boston College panel, 139; death of, 170; as AS's father, 171, 172; elegy to, 171–72; and "woman's space," 274; and AS broadcast on BBC, 279
Holt, John, 256
Hopkins, Gerard Manley, 93
Houghton, Firman, 118–19
Houghton Mifflin Company, xxi; and Starbuck, 106, 107; and Plath, 108; and *Bedlam*, 108, 125; and *All My Pretty Ones*, 165; *Bedlam–Pretty Ones* paperback proposed to, 185; and *Live or Die*, 259; and *Love Poems*, 300; and Williams's *Lies*, 306–7; and *Mercy Street*, 329; and *Transformations*, 338, 356; and *The Book of Folly*, 359, 362; and *The Awful Rowing Toward God*, 367; and *The Death Notebooks*, 389
"House, The," 58
Howard, Richard, 186–87
Howe, Irving, 125, 126, 127, 128
"Howl" (Ginsberg), 108
How to Save Your Own Life (Jong), 393
"How We Danced" (Sexton), 343
Hudson Review, The, 89, 95, 297, 306, 356
Hughes, Ted, 103, 113, 119, 198, 277, 282–83, 310

Human Resource Institute of Boston, AS patient in, 378–79
"Hutch" (Sexton), 75

Icarus-Daedalus legend, 231, 232–33
"In Celebration of My Uterus" (Sexton), 255, 265, 297
"Incest: and AS's memories of abuse, 57–60, 344; and AS-Linda, 223, 325; and "The Papa and Mama Dance," 286; mother-daughter, 325
"In Defense of Not Trying" (Sexton), 50
Inglis, Ruth, 261
Insanity. *See* Mental illness; Sexton, Anne MENTAL ILLNESS OF
International Congress of Cultural Freedom, AS grant from, 242–43, 254
"Interrogation of the Man of Many Hearts, The" (Sexton), 265, 276, 297, 298, 299, 306
"In the Beach House" (Sexton), 58
"In the Deep Museum" (Sexton), 122, 158
"I put some daisies in a bowl" (Sexton), 217
"I remember my mother dying" (Sexton), 217
"It Is a Spring Afternoon" (Sexton), 271, 275, 297

Jackson, Shirley, 160, 161
James, Henry, 127
Jarrell, Randall, 72, 81, 109
Jealous, Brad, 17, 29
Jerry (fellow student), 60
"Jesus Cooks" (Sexton), 352
"Jesus Papers, The" (Sexton), 349, 351–53, 355, 356
"Jesus Raises Up the Harlot" (Sexton), 352
"Jesus Summons Forth" (Sexton), 352
"Jesus Unborn" (Sexton), 352
Johnny (medical-student romance), 25–26, 27

Johnson, Poppy, 405
Jong, Erica, 365, 393
Jones, Grace, 405
Jordan, June, 405
Jordan Hall, Boston, Her Kind
    plays in, 319
"Jubilate Agno" (Smart), 353, 354
"Just Once" (Sexton), 295

Kafka, Franz, 128, 165, 248
Kaplan, Justin, 295
Kauffmann, Stanley, 329
Kayo. See Sexton, Alfred Muller II
Keats, John, 111
Kennedy, Jacqueline, 194
Kennedy, Robert, assassination of,
    302
Kerr, Walter, 328
"KE 6-8018" (Sexton), 217
Kevles, Barbara, 314, 316
King, Martin Luther, Jr., 295, 302
Kinnell, Galway, 200, 296
"Kiss, The" (Sexton), 257, 297, 298
"Kite, The" (Sexton), 75, 119
Kizer, Carolyn, 95, 119
Koch, Kenneth, 310
Kohl, Herbert, 255, 256, 274, 276,
    303
Kumin, Dan, 71–72, 185, 306
Kumin, Jane, 71, 185
Kumin, Judy, 71, 185, 322, 340
Kumin, Maxine, xxi, 40, 69, 70–
    73; in Holmes workshop, 50,
    71, 170; at party, 95; at poetry
    reading, 96; at private work-
    shop, 96, 97, 118; mother-
    daughter poetry of, 111–12; and
    Radcliffe Institute, 145, 157,
    194, 197; and feminism, 173,
    195; portrait of, 192; and
    Freudianism, 195; and Smith,
    268; and Passions of Uxport,
    269, 301; at Pulitzer Prize party,
    271; and swimming, 285; Pu-
    litzer Prize to, 368; pictures of,
    71, 369
AND AS AS FRIEND: on AS

memories of sexual abuse, 58;
    companion, 79, 117, 138, 176,
    196, 284; responsiveness of, 83;
    on AS and Wright, 130; as sis-
    ter, 142; at family activities,
    157, 185; and AS suicide at-
    tempts, 164, 341, 392; and AS-
    Zweizung affair, 259, 265, 314;
    and Linda on AS's needs, 253;
    as AS double, 284; neighborly
    visits, 284, 320; Linda tutored
    by, 340; away on travels, 368–
    69, 396; and AS divorce, 372;
    as caregiver (1973), 377; argues
    with AS on Douglass College
    trip, 392; and day of AS's sui-
    cide, 396
AND AS AS POET, 69–73, 78,
    113, 188, 306; on AS's writing
    process, 94; and Holmes-AS re-
    lation, 100, 140–41, 143; on
    AS's readings, 115, 306; daily
    phone conferences, 117, 142–
    43, 182, 269, 366–67; "My
    Friend, My Friend" addressed
    to, 123; on vertical audience,
    139, 332; on subjects of AS's
    poetry, 143–44; and The Cure,
    184–85; and Transformations,
    336, 338; and AS's Europe trip,
    204–5, 208; and literary execu-
    torship, 382–83
Kumin, Victor, 72
Kunitz, Stanley, 94, 95, 103, 194

LaCrosse, Mary, 33, 269, 270
Ladybug, Fly Away Home (Sexton
    play), 122
"Lament" (Sexton), 149
"Language," AS on, 225, 226–27,
    351
Lanning, George, 242
Larner, Jeremy, 256
"Last Believer, The" (Sexton story),
    162–63
"Lazy on a Saturday Morning"
    (Wright), 133

Legler, Philip, 251–53, 339, 376–77, 378; letter to, 276
Leiderman, Herbert, 156, 164, 211, 370
Lennox, Annie, 405
Letters to a Young Poet (Rilke), 131, 139, 182, 187, 241, "Letters to Dr. Y." (Sexton), 359
"Letter Written During a January Northeaster" (Sexton), 149–50
"Letter Written on a Ferry While Crossing Long Island Sound" (Sexton), 133–34, 148, 181
"Letting Down of the Hair, The" (Sexton), 359
Levertov, Denise, 40, 174, 186, 256, 296, 397, 405
Levinson, Mark, 303, 330
Levinson Prize, to AS, 186
Lévi-Strauss, Claude, 108
Library of Congress, AS reads at, 378
Lies (Williams), 306–7
"Life Again" (Sexton), 50
Life Studies (Lowell), 91, 108, 109, 111, 112; and *Bedlam*, 125; Bishop on, 126
Literary agent, of AS, 120, 275. *See also* Degener, Cindy; Lord, Sterling
"Little Girl, My String Bean, My Lovely Woman" (Sexton), 222–23, 240, 296, 297, 346
"Little Peasant, The" (Sexton), 306
"Little Uncomplicated Hymn, A" (Sexton), 240
"Live" (Sexton), 247, 294, 382
Live or Die (Sexton), xxi, 162, 168, 240–41, 245, 259, 264–65; and Barbara Swan, 197; and Pulitzer Prize, 271–72; and Shelley Prize, 271–72; British publication of, 277, 300; "Live" in, 294; and *The Book of Folly*, 333
Locke, Maryel, 372
Lord, Sterling, 120
Lorde, Audre, 405
Louis (Yugoslav met in Rome), 209, 211–12

"Love Gone" (Sexton), 258
Love Poems (Sexton), xxi, 249, 281, 298–300, 319, 332; "Papa and Mama Dance" in, 286; and Wayland High class, 289; "Eighteen Days Without You" in, 289, 293; and AS's celebrity, 293; British publication of, 300–301, 362, 363; and Hecht, 306
"Love Song for K. Owyne" (Sexton), 134
"Loving the Killer" (Sexton), 265
Lowell, Amy, 104
Lowell, Robert, xxi, 78, 108–10; as "mad" poet, 65; and Snodgrass on AS, 81; and poet's identity, 83; and Snodgrass reading, 84; AS in class of, 89, 91–94, 119, 126; *Life Studies*, 91, 108, 109, 111, 112, 125, 126; picture of, 92; as influence on AS, 93–94, 172, 181, 188, 296, 306; AS sees at parties, 95; on AS's poetry, 101, 294; and Plath, 10–5, 113; *Bedlam* cover blurb by, 119, 125; Bishop to on *Bedlam*, 125; and Untermeyer anthology, 139; AS to on *The Cure*, 168; and AS on Holmes, 170; and AS on "woman question," 173; on AS's unconscious style, 180–81; *Pretty Ones* blurb by, 185–86; Levinson Prize to, 186; Ford Foundation grant to, 193; award party for AS by 194; on "Sylvia's Death," 200; and trip to Brazil, 254; references from, 276; and AS broadcast on BBC, 279; and Stallworthy on AS, 301; in Oates's time capsule, 320; Stallworthy on celebrity of, 363, 364; return of (1973), 383
Lynes, Russell, 89

McAdoo, Richard, 390
MacBeth, George, 261–62, 277, 279–81, 283, 287

McCarthy, Eugene, Her Kind performance for, 303–4
McCarthy, Jack, 18–19; on Harvey family drinking, 13; on Boston College faculty, 139
McCarthy, Mary (daughter of Eugene McCarthy), 304
McClatchy, J. D., 361, 362
McConkey, James, 80
MacDonald, Cynthia, 365
McGinley, Phyllis, 104
Mack, Azel, 342, 344, 346, 350
McLean Hospital: Lowell at, 108–9; AS workshop at, 308–9; AS patient at, 377–78
MacNeice, Louis, 72
Madonna, 405
Mann, Thomas, 127
"Man with a Prayer" (Sexton), 286
Marijuana, 321, 393
Marriage — USA (planned novel), 245–46, 266
Maryan, Charles, 312–13, 317, 318, 320–21, 322, 327, 328, 329
Massachusetts General Hospital, AS at, 22–26
Masson, Jeffrey Moussaieff, 169
Masters, Edgar Lee, 185
Mathews, Blanche Dingley (great-aunt of AS), 11
Matthews, Jack, 80, 81
Mayo, Jean, 10
Medication. See under Drugs; Sleeping pills, AS's use of "Menstruation at Forty" (Sexton), 264
"Menstruation at Thirty-Five" (later "Menstruation at Forty") (Sexton), 211–12
Mental illness: of AS's grandfather, 4–5, 16; of great-aunt Nana, 15–16; of Lowell, 65, 78, 108–10; in poetic lineage, 65, 109; and religion (Mercy Street), 221–22. See also under Sexton, Anne
"Mercy for the Greedy." See "With Mercy for the Greedy"
Mercy Street (Sexton play), xix, xxi, 58, 59, 168, 221, 313, 317, 318–19, 320, 322–24, 325–29; and mother-daughter relationship, 59, 349; and therapy notebooks, 214; and Transformations, 337; and "Death of the Fathers," 343; cast reunion of, 356; attempts to circulate, 365. See also The Cure; Tell Me Your Answer True
Merwin, W. S., 72, 305
"Metaphors for a Pregnant Woman" (Plath), 106
Milford, Nancy, 402
Millay, Edna St. Vincent, 92, 93, 94, 104, 196
Miller, Arthur, 215, 220
Miller, Henry, 160
Miller, Nolan, 79, 80, 81, 89
Mirsky, Mark, 256
"Misery" (Mary Gray Harvey), 48
"Mr. Mine" (Sexton), 299
Montauk, N.Y.: AS and Wright together at, 131–33; in "Letter . . . ," 150
Moon landing, AS in celebration of, 320
"Moon Song, Woman Song" (Sexton), 271, 275, 297, 320
Moore, Marianne, 72, 104, 186, 194
Moore, Richard, 247, 248
"More Than All the Rest" (Sexton), 54
Morgan, Frederick, 89, 95, 242, 306, 356
Morgan, Rose, 95
Morris Gray reading, AS gives, 119
Moss, Howard, 95, 275, 300–301, 367; rejections by, 200, 276, 337; and "The Firebombers," 296; and Algonquin Hotel, 317; at party, 356
"Moss of His Skin, The" (Sexton) 58, 75, 114
"Mother and Daughter" (Sexton), 347–48, 349
"Mother and Jack and the Rain" (Sexton), 170, 172
Moulton, Jean, 269–70, 362

Muller, Wilhelmine. *See* Sexton, Wilhelmine Muller
Murray, Michael, 168, 227
Murphy, Rosemary, 317
"Music Swims Back to Me" (Sexton), 69–71, 72, 75, 287, 391
"My Friend, My Friend" (Sexton), 105, 123, 143

Nana (Anna Ladd Dingley, great-aunt of AS), 3, 12, 14, 15–16, 27–28, 37–38; AS's feelings for, 3, 15, 16, 28, 37–38, 43–44, 54, 135, 167, 174, 177–78, 403; in Harvey home, 12, 13; mental-institution reporting scheme of, 12, 52; volume of letters by, 12, 201, 205; and "You're not Anne," 16, 167, 216, 219; and AS's voices, 16, 219, 327; and AS's first kiss, 17; diary of, 27, 28, 29, 33, 48; death of, 29, 39; and AS suicide attempt, 33; Kayo in role of, 37–38, 155, 167; portrait of, 38; and sexual abuse memories, 57, 59, 167; fifth anniversary of death of, 117; and James Wright, 134, 167; and AS's retreat into girlhood, 167; Orne as, 167, 201, 224, 225; and AS's relation to daughters, 204, 224, 324, 325; AS's identification with in poetry, 208; and Anne Wilder, 233; vs. Icarus, 235; and *Mercy Street*, 322; and AS's fear of hospitalization, 379, 395; in therapy tape, 409–11
"Nana-hex," 219
National Educational Television, AS documentary by, 246–48, 273
National Endowment for the Arts, AS application to, 276
Neruda, Pablo, 279; Wright on, 130; at Poetry International Festival, 278, 279
New England Poetry Club, AS in, 50
Newman, Charles, 244

New Poets of England and America, AS reads, 76
New World Writing, 120
New Yorker, The: AS acceptances from, 75, 95, 275, 276, 297; AS first-reading agreement from, 161; rate of payment from, 337; AS student's poem in, 340; acceptances dwindled, 367. *See also* Moss, Howard
New York Times, The, and publication of therapy tapes, 402
New York YMHA, AS readings at, 119, 356
"Night Voice on a Broomstick" (later "Witch")(Sexton), 113
Nijinsky, Vaslav, 402
Northern Michigan University, AS readings at, 339, 376
"Now" (Sexton), 299
"Nude Swim, The" (Sexton), 265

Oates, Joyce Carol, 320
"Obsessive Combination of Ontological Inscape, Trickery and Love, An" (Sexton), 124
Oedipus and Oedipal relations, 53, 87, 88–89, 101, 168, 352
"Old" (Sexton), 391
"Old Dwarf Heart" (Sexton), 122
Olsen, Tillie, 195–96, 197–98; and Wilder, 213, 233; letter to, 231; and *Passions of Uxport*, 301
"One Life Asks the Question" (Sexton), 50
"One Patient Released Today" (Sexton), 52
"One Way of Avoiding the Issue" (Sexton), 52
"Operation, The" (Sexton), 74, 120, 140, 172–73
Orgel, Stephen, 118
Orne, Martin, xxii, 34, 38, 41, 213; AS's comments to, 37, 391, 397, 398, 401; on AS's diagnosis, 39; picture of, 43; on AS's sexual abuse memories, 58; on AS's writing, 126; and James Wright,

129, 134; Australia fellowship for, 134, 137; and AS acceptance at Radcliffe Institute, 145; Mexican vacation of, 166; as Nana, 167, 201, 224, 225; and AS's sleeping pills and alcohol, 210–11; as father, 211; termination of AS's therapy with, 213, 217, 219, 224, 225; and Zweizung affair, 260, 314–16; and writing for mentally ill, 308; and Chase as therapist, 317; and Kayo on AS, 370; tape of therapy with, 401, 402, 409–11

Oshita, Gerald, 303, 330

Ostwald, Peter, 402

Oxford University Press, xxi, 193, 243, 300, 363

O Ye Tongues (Sexton), 349, 353–55, 359; and therapy notebooks, 214; and Colgate lectures, 359

"Oysters" (Sexton), 343

Paley, Grace, 256

Palindrome of AS ("rats"/ "star"), 82, 124, 351, 353, 356

"Papa and Mama Dance, The" (Sexton), 286

Passions of Uxport, The (Kumin), 269, 301

Peace movement, AS involved in, 250, 295–97

Phi Beta Kappa, and AS, 301–2

Pineda, Marianna, 197

Pirandello, Luigi, 127, 312

Plath, Sylvia, 40, 65, 103–8, 113, 198; as confessional poet, 111–12; *Ariel*, 113, 243, 361, 367; on professional success, 161; and *Pretty Ones*, 174; death of, 198, 216–17; and Ames, 243; AS compared with, 264, 367, 405; in Oates's time capsule, 320; and "The Furies," 361; and *Book of Folly*, 364; and feminism, 364

Play(s) by Sexton. See *Cure, The; Mercy Street; Tell Me Your Answer True*

"Poems I Gave You, The" (Sexton), 52, 54

Poetry: confessional, 78, 83, 100, 112, 265 (*see also* Confessional poetry); "cooked" vs. "raw" (Lowell), 108; and dilemma of women's position, 144; and life (Stevenson), 364; AS's view of, 382. See *also* Sexton, Anne POETRY OF

Poetry Book Society: and Selected Poems, 243; and *Live or Die*, 277

Poetry International Festival, AS attends, 277–79, 363

"Poetry kit" by Sexton, 385–86

Poetry magazine: AS gets Levinson Prize from, 186; AS at gala for, 310

Poetry Society of America, Shelley Prize from, 271, 272

Poets' Theater, 96, 339

"Point Shirley" (Plath), 104

Popular culture, AS in (Degener), 337

Porter, Andrew, 375

"Portrait of an Old Woman on the College Tavern Wall" (Sexton), 82

Pound, Ezra, 65, 83

Pressit, Bobby (AS's pretend brother), 12, 38

Pretty Ones. See *All My Pretty Ones*

Prince, William, 317, 322, 328

Psychology, AS reads, 53, 54–55

"Psychosomatic Stomach" (Sexton), 52

Pulitzer Prize: AS receives, 271–72, 273, 276, 305; AS as juror for, 368

Punctuation, Sexton's use of, xxiii

Quarterly Review of Literature, The, AS printed in, 297

Rabbit Redux (Updike), 393

Radcliffe Institute: AS attends, 144–

Radcliffe Institute (*cont.*)
46, 150–52, 157–60, 169, 173,
194–98, 200; and Tillie Olsen,
195–96; AS applies to, 265
Radio: and AS-mother relation, 47;
and "Music Swims Back to
Me," 71
Rahv, Philip, 127, 145, 174, 376,
383
"Rapunzel" (Sexton), 337, 343,
375
"Rats live on no evil star" (Sexton
palindrome), 124, 217, 351,
353, 356
Rats Live on No Evil Star (tenta-
tive title), 259, 298
Ravenel, Shannon, 306
"Reading, The" (Sexton), 75
"Real Love in Imaginary Wagon"
(Sexton), 53
"Refusal" (Sexton), 130
"Refusal, The" (Wright), 130
Regis College, AS honorary degree
from, 350
Religion: and AS's poetry, xxi; and
AS's childhood, 8; in AS's self-
questioning, 122; and "With
Mercy for the Greedy," 122–23;
in *All My Pretty Ones*, 163,
351; in *The Cure*, 168; in corre-
spondence with Brother Dennis,
183, 184; in *Tell Me Your An-
swer True*, 221–22, 228; and
Brian Sweeney, 318, 356; and
AS's feminist views, 350; AS's
attitude toward, 355–56, 395;
AS instructed in (1974), 395
IN "LAST" POEMS, 349, 350–
51; "Jesus Papers," 351–53,
356; "O Ye Tongues," 353–56
Rhymes: AS on, 124; as breakdown symptom (1964), 225
Rich, Adrienne Cecile, 40, 110–11,
112–13, 405; and Plath, 104;
"Snapshots of a Daughter-in-Law,"
111; Freeman on, 118; at read-
in, 296; on AS's suicide, 397

Rich, Cynthia, 118
Richards, I. A., 42, 75, 90, 118,
119
Riding, Tony, 282
Rilke, Rainer Maria, 127, 128,
131, 134; *Letters to a Young
Poet*, 131, 139, 182, 187, 241,
365; AS in room of, 282
Rimbaud, Arthur, 65; and "Flee on
Your Donkey," 175–80
"Ringing the Bells" (Sexton), 102,
247, 287
Rizzo, Steve, 287, 303, 304
Robart, Les, 72, 271
Robart, Sandy, 30; on AS and
mother, 30; as neighbor, 49, 72,
164, 229; with AS on Europe
tour, 193–94, 201, 202, 204,
205–6, 207, 271
Robb, Christina, 390
Robert Frost fellowship, AS re-
ceives, 118
Robinson, Edward Arlington, 286
Rock music group. *See* Anne Sex-
ton and Her Kind
Roethke, Theodore, 65, 109
Rogers Hall, AS attends, 19–20,
21, 303
Rosenblatt, Roger, 105
Rosenthal, M. L., 112
Ross, Alan, 277
Rossetti, Christina, 104
"Rowing" (Sexton), 366
"Rowing Endeth, The" (Sexton),
150, 366, 391
Royal Society of Literature, AS
elected to, 243
Rukeyser, Muriel, 186, 256, 296, 405
Ryerson, Alice, 151, 173

"Said the Poet to the Analyst"
(Sexton), 75, 119
Saint Judas (Wright), 128
Salinger, J. D., 52–53, 160, 161,
165
Sandburg, Carl, 186
"Santa" (Sexton), 343

Sappho, 104
Sara Crewe (Burnett), 203
Sarton, May, 170
Sartre, Jean-Paul, 127, 157
Saturday Review Book Club, and
    Transformations, 356
Schapiro, Miriam, 365
Schwartz, Barbara, 381–82, 389,
    390, 393, 395
Schwartz, Delmore, 65, 109
Scott, Reg, 23
Scowcroft, Richard, 196
Seager, Allan, 238–39
Seidel, Frederick, 308
Seldes, Marian, 313, 317, 320,
    322, 323, 325–26, 328, 329
Selected Poems (Sexton) (Oxford,
    1964), xxi, 193, 243, 277
Selected Poems (Sexton) (1988), xxi

"Self in 1958" (Sexton), 240
Semrad, Elvin, 163
Senibaldi, Doug, 303
Sex: and AS as teenager, 18; by AS
    before marriage, 22, 23; in notes
    on breakdown, 36; in AS's
    memories of father, 56–59; with
    Jerry, 60; with Kayo, 60, 249,
    253; and need to have lover,
    148; and retreat to girlhood,
    167, 174; with Louis in Italy,
    209; and AS-Wilder relationship,
    232–35, 239–40; in *Marriage
    USA*, 245, 46, 266; and
    Chopin ballade, 248; AS's reed-
    ucation in, 248; and AS as se-
    ducing, 250; and "The Touch,"
    299; in *Mercy Street*, 322–23;
    and AS's relation to daughters,
    346–47; and AS with Legler,
    376. *See also* Incest
Sexton, Alfred Muller II (Kayo),
    21–22, 310; pictures of, 24,
    203, 222, 263; in father-in-law's
    business, 29–30; and Nana, 37–
    38, 155, 167; and AS's writing
    career, 74, 79–80, 152, 156,
310; and father-in-law's estate,
    117; therapy for, 155, 156, 211,
    246, 370; letters of to AS in Eu-
    rope, 207, 208; on poets and
    poetry, 251; opposed to mari-
    juana, 321; loss of job, 338;
    new business, 338–39; after
    death of AS, 398. *See also* Sex-
    ton, Anne MARRIED LIFE
Sexton, Anne, xix-xx; public per-
    sona of, xix, xx, 96, 157–58,
    194, 237–38, 273, 278, 312;
    documents saved by, xxi-xxii;
    will of, xxii, 382–83; birth of,
    4, 7; family background of, 4–
    7; pictures of, 8, 25, 32, 71, 87,
    153, 203, 206, 234, 249, 304,
    334, 335, 348, 384, 386; por-
    trait painted of, 45, 85, 117;
    door-to-door job of, 53, 129;
    physical illnesses of, 119–20,
    255, 345, 376, 377; abortion of,
    121, 122; replies to readers,
    189, 241, 273; portrait of
    (Swan), 192; biographer of
    (Ames), 244; broken hip of,
    266, 268–69, 276, 361; journal
    of, 276; and ideas vs. people,
    301; cremation and interment
    of, 398
EARLY LIFE OF, 7–11; and
    Nana, 3, 12, 14, 15–16, 27–28,
    37–38, 167 (*see also* Nana);
    schooling, 8–9, 14, 18, 19–20,
    302–3; and father's drinking,
    13, 14; acne, 14, 24, 57; consti-
    pation problem, 14–15; teenage
    social life, 17–18; Jack Mc-
    Carthy, 18–19; fake injury joke,
    19; memories of sexual abuse,
    56–59, 167; recollections of toi-
    let training and genital inspec-
    tion, 59; and father's death,
    116–17; desire to share with
    parents, 139, 142, 145; and
    Christmas morning, 162; and
    Azel Mack claim to be father,

Sexton, Anne (*cont.*)
342, 344, 346, 350. *See also individual family members*
MARRIED LIFE OF, 309–10; elopement and marriage, 21, 22–23, 24; at Colgate, 23; at parents', 23–25; Cochituate and Johnny, 25–26; Korean War and separation, 26–27; first pregnancy, 27–28; home in Newton, 28; Kayo in R. C. Harvey Company, 29–30; and mother/mother-in-law, 30; and AS's mental illness, 34–35, 334–35, 341, 370; and sociological perspective on breakdown, 40; and affair with Jerry, 60; "personal record" on, 63; and AS's writing, 65, 79–80, 156; violent disputes, 80, 154–55, 210, 370; tension (1960), 136; difficulties with everyday tasks, 138; and use of Radcliffe grant, 150–51; Kayo's roles, 155–56, 167; family activities (1961), 156–57; Christmas mornings, 162–63; Kayo compared with father, 166; letters from Europe, 207–8; alliance with Kayo after Westwood stay, 211; European trip with Kayo, 212, 217–18; *au pair* sought, 228–29; house in Weston, 229–30; and Florida, 236–37, 360–61; phoning to Kayo from speaking tour, 238; priority to AS's needs, 242; Europe-Africa trip, 242–43, 254–55, 261–64; in NET documentary, 246–48; satisfactions and dissatisfactions with Kayo, 249–50; divorce considered, 254, 257; letter from Kayo, 260–61; and AS's infidelities, 261, 370; new car bought, 285; Bermuda trips, 309–10, 339; Maryan's view of, 320–21; mealtimes, 333–34; Kayo's loss of job and

new business, 338; financial worries, 338, 357, 360; contented routine (1972), 361–62; divorce, 369–74, 379; post-divorce isolation, 380, 391–92, 394
RELATION TO DAUGHTERS, 39, 135, 202–4, 346; birth, 28–29; and AS's mental illness, 31–33, 34, 35, 39, 153, 224, 341, 379; feelings of rage and guilt, 32–33, 73; and Billie and Joan as caregivers, 35, 135–36, 152–54; vs. AS's writing career, 135, 152, 349; in family activities, 156–57; physical intimacy, 203–4, 223–24, 323–25; Joy's school trouble, 246; and counterculture rebelliousness, 321–22; and sexual maturity, 346–47; and Joy on station wagon, 373, 393; during last year, 379, 391, 393–94. *See also* Sexton, Joyce Ladd; Sexton, Linda Gray
PERSONAL CHARACTERISTICS OF: appearance, xix, 19, 96–97, 111, 140, 284–85, 331, 347, 374, 378; lack of reserve, xxii; meals carried off to room, 9; intensity, 81, 127; smoking, 91, 140, 330, 372; love of music, 203; height phobia, 207; drinking, 210, 330, 380, 394; constipation fear, 238; as good witch and bad witch, 247, 248; dislike of exercise, 285; and marijuana, 321, 393; physical presence (Selden), 328
MENTAL ILLNESS OF, xix–xx, 4, 37–40, 65; and childhood separation from mother, 15; and childhood experience with Nana, 16, 17, 33, 167, 219, 409–11 (*see also* Nana); voices, 16, 219, 327; sleeping pill overdoses, 26, 341, 378 (*see also* Sleeping pills, AS's use of); and separation

from husband, 26–27, 34, 36, 39, 138, 164; breakdown during daughter's infancy, 31–40; suicide attempts, 33, 34–35, 42, 45, 47, 63, 107, 260, 261, 346, 387, 391–92; tests at Westwood, 34; dissociation, 39, 44, 57, 137, 166, 175 (*see also* Trances of AS); aloneness and finding others, 50, 64; and creativity, 64–65; poetry and religion as help for, 122–23; use of in poetry, 125–26; anxiety over public situations, 127–28, 138, 139–40, 151, 176, 194, 196, 227, 242, 287, 334; Montauk episode, 133; alcohol use, 139–40, 210–11, 238, 330, 380; need to feel love from men, 147–48; wish for punishment, 156; suicidal urge (1961), 164–65; and European trip, 202, 206, 208–9; and split-off inner "rat," 216–17; breakdown at time of Orne's departure, 224–26; readers' identification with, 273; AS's openness about (Maryan), 321; and *Mercy Street* rehearsals, 327–28; behaviors at home, 334–35; bizarre attack and pill overdose, 341; February 1971 breakdown and final deepening, 345–47, 380; and 1973 EEG, 377–78; hopelessness in face of needed changes, 380, 391–92; Charles River and pill episode, 392–93

MAJOR RELATIONSHIPS OF: John Holmes, 50–52, 96, 100, 140–41, 143, 169–72; Maxine Kumin, 69–73, 78, 113, 142–43, 157, 182, 184–85; William DeWitt Snodgrass, 76–78, 80–82, 83, 84–85, 188; Robert Lowell, 89, 91–94, 108–10, 119, 172, 180–81, 188; George Starbuck, 96, 106–7, 117–18, 182, 188; James Wright, 128–

34, 146, 148–50, 167, 172, 188, 336, 367–68; Anthony Hecht, 146–48; Brother Dennis Farrell, 182–84; Tillie Olsen, 195–96, 197–98; Anne Wilder, 213–16, 217, 232–36, 237–40; Lois Ames, 243–44; James Dickey, 250–51; Philip Legler, 251–53, 276, 339, 376–77, 378; Robert Clawson, 255–58, 274, 285, 286, 287, 289, 303; C. K. Williams, 306–8, 344–45, 368, 387. *See also specific individuals*

POETRY OF, xx, 3; internal rhymes, 51; writing process, 74–75, 94; and radiation of meaning, 82, 124; and identity of poet, 82–83, 179, 401; and women's experience, 172–73, 364, 387–88; new spontaneous style, 179–81; as monologue, 272–73; facts and feelings in, 279; trademark features of, 293–94, 405; and AS as technician (Williams), 307; during last year, 379–80, 395, 396

POETRY OF (INFLUENCES AND CIRCUMSTANCES), 3, 64; and mother's crossword puzzle interest, 6; and childhood memories, 7–8; and mother, 20–21, 42, 65–66, 101, 103 (*see also under* Harvey, Mary Gray Staples); John Holmes and workshop, 50–52, 82, 140–41, 169–70; and lineage of psychotic poets, 65; Maxine Kumin, 69–73, 113, 142–44, 182, 188, 306 (*see also under* Kumin, Maxine); place of in home life, 73–74; Snodgrass, 76–78, 81–82, 83, 84–85, 188; Kayo's view, 79, 152, 156, 310; Lowell, 91–94, 110–11, 119, 126, 172, 181, 188, 306; private workshop, 96–98; Plath, 105–8; and critics, 142–43, 182,

Sexton, Anne (*cont.*)
306, 326; medication as blocking, 231–32, 246; in NET documentary, 247–48; family as
second to, 349; seizure of productivity (1973), 366–67, 371
POETIC DEVELOPMENT AND
CAREER OF, xxi, 3, 61, 63–64,
188; book sales, xix, 187, 272,
319, 332; first poems, 19, 20;
encouragement from Orne and
enrollment at Boston Center,
42–43, 47, 49–51; first publications, 52, 75, 89–90; renamed
as "Anne Sexton," 65, 303; Antioch Writers' Conference, 79,
80–81, 83; and poetry as business, 83, 95; *Bedlam* (first
book), 94, 98, 100–101, 102,
108, 113–15, 125–26 (*see also*
To Bedlam and Part Way Back);
celebrity, 110–11, 139–40, 166,
188–89, 272, 277–78, 293,
306, 320, 363; literary agent,
120, 275; speaking fees, 152,
272, 287, 319, 385; Her Kind
rock group, 286–87, 303–6 (*see
also* Anne Sexton and Her
Kind); royalties and advances,
356
PLAYS AND PROSE OF, xxi;
short stories, 52–53, 103, 120,
145–46, 160–63; and play-
wrighting, 168; *The Cure*, 168,
183, 218–22; *Tell Me Your Answer True*, 218–22, 227–28,
232; *Mercy Street*, 221, 313,
317, 318–19, 320, 322–23,
325–29; comic novel, 245–46,
249, 265, 266, 355; and Degener's encouragement, 275–76.
See also individual works
PSYCHOTHERAPY OF, 44, 135,
137, 174–76, 403; tapes of,
xxii, 43, 137–39, 175, 402,
409–11; first visit, 26; Dr.
Orne, 41; notes on, 41–42, 137,
138, 175, 214; third weekly session, 53; Elizabeth role, 55–56,
60–61, 63; and memories of
sexual abuse, 56–60, 167; and
personal record, 62–63; drugs,
75–76, 78, 226–27, 317, 345–
46 (*see also* Thorazine, AS's use
of); leave-and-return theme in,
166–68, 211; analytic role for
AS, 174, 179; session before Europe trip, 201; progress as of
Europe trip, 202; Orne termination, 213, 217, 219, 224, 225;
love affair with Zweizung, 258,
259–60, 265–66, 313–16;
Chase replaces Zweizung, 316–
17; Kayo's view of, 370; "babysitter" doctors, 377; at Human
Resource Institute, 378–79;
Chase terminates, 381; with Barbara Schwartz, 381–82, 389,
393; Brunner-Orne refusal, 393
PSYCHOTHERAPY-POETRY RE-
LATION, 3; encouragement and
turning point, 42–43, 47; in earliest poems, 52; and psychoanalytic concepts, 53–54; and sexual
abuse memories, 58–59; unconscious meanings, 61–62; and
language, 64; Holmes's comments on, 98, 100; and *Bedlam*,
100–101; and "confessional"
poetry, 112; and critical-estab-
lishment dream, 141–42; and
"Flee on Your Donkey," 176–
80; and "Death of Fathers," 343
ACADEMIC WORK AND POSI-
TIONS, xix; education sought,
45–46, 49, 53; in Holmes's
workshops, 49–51, 69, 75, 76,
82, 169–70, 182; Boston University course with Lowell, 89,
91–94, 119, 126; teaching style,
98, 169, 340; as Brandeis student, 126–28; Radcliffe Institute, 144–46, 150–52, 157–60,
194–98, 200; gives Radcliffe po-

etry workshop, 169; Wayland High School teaching, 274–75, 285–87, 303; McLean Hospital workshop, 308–9; workshop for Oberlin students, 309, 338; Boston University teaching, 338–40, 357, 386, 387–89; Colgate professorship, 357–58, 360; home workshops, 386

AWARDS AND HONORS: Frost Fellowship to Bread Loaf, 118; Morris Gray reading 119; Levinson Prize, 186; American Arts and Letters traveling fellowship, 193, 206–7, 212; Ford Foundation grant, 193, 206–7, 218, 227; Literary Magazine Travel Grant, 242–43, 254; Shelley Memorial Prize, 271, 272; Pulitzer Prize, 271–72, 273; Guggenheim Foundation grant, 313, 326; honorary degrees, 339, 350, 357

POETRY READINGS, 319–20, 404, 405; at New York YMHA, 119, 356; 1965 tour, 237–39; 1966 tour, 251–52; for Academy of American Poets, 287; 1969 engagements, 319; at Northern Michigan (1970), 339; at Northern Michigan (1973), 376; at Library of Congress, 378; after *Death Notebooks* publication, 385; at Harvard's Sanders Theater, 389–91; at Douglass College, 392; at Goucher College, 395

TRAVELS ABROAD; Europe, 12, 193–94, 201, 202, 204–9; Europe (with Kayo), 212, 217–18; Europe-Africa (with Kayo), 242–43, 254–55, 262–64; London, 277–83

SUICIDE OF, xix, xx, 395–97; and Frances Harvey, 5; and fear of hospitalization, 379; contemplation of, 381, 387; comment on, 397–98. *See also under* Suicide

Sexton, George (father of Alfred M. Sexton), 21–22; AS and Kayo live with, 23; move to Annisquam, 31; and AS's breakdown, 33, 121; Joy with, 73, 76; death of, 120–21; picture of, 121

Sexton, Joan (sister of Alfred M. Sexton), 22, 23–24, 25, 27; and AS's cosmetics selling, 53; and AS's children, 135–36; death of, 318; in therapy tape, 403

Sexton, Joyce Ladd (Joy) (daughter of AS), 29, 30; AS's feelings toward, 30, 73, 135; and AS's mental illness, 34, 35, 39, 153; remains with AS's inlaws, 73, 76; and AS's poetry, 78, 135; returns home with AS, 78–79; and "The Double Image," 85, 86, 88; pictures of, 87, 153, 203; and aunt Joan, 135, 318; and AS-Kayo fights, 154, 370; and Christmas morning, 162–63; adventurousness of (1962), 185; and AS's European trip, 202, 204, 205, 206; AS's intimacy with (1963), 202–4; school trouble and psychotherapy, 246; at riding camp, 283; rebelliousness of, 321; horse of, 338; and AS's sleeping pill overdose, 341; maturing and AS's reaction, 346–47, 349; Kayo's emotional abuse of, 370; and AS-Kayo divorce, 371, 372; and Conants, 373; and AS's 1973 summer, 377, 378; and AS's last year, 379, 391, 393–94; as self-sufficient, 394; after AS's death, 398

Sexton, Linda Gray (daughter of AS), xx, xxii; as literary executor, xx, 383; as *Self-Portrait* editor, xix; birth of, 28; and grandmother (Billie), 30; and

Sexton, Linda Gray (*cont.*)
AS's mental illness, 31, 32–33, 34, 39, 45, 153, 341, 379; pictures of, 32, 203, 222, 348; and AS vs. Billie, 35; and AS's poetry, 78; and aunt Joan, 135, 318; on AS's view of family, 152; and AS-Kayo fights, 154; and "The Fortress," 157, 160; and "Cigarettes and Butternut Squash," 162; and Christmas morning, 162–63; and Judy Kumin, 185; and *The Bell Jar*, 200; on AS and mother's cancer, 216; and Daisy in *Tell Me Your Answer True*, 222–23; call home from camp (1965), 242; and Her Kind, 306; on parents' marriage, 310; and "drug culture," 321–22; psychotherapy for, 325, 338, 347, 349; and Brothers Grimm, 331, 333; *Transformations* dedicated to, 336, 349; on father's losing job, 338; poetry written by, 340; at Harvard, 349, 373; and AS-Kayo divorce, 372; in Seattle, 377; and Rahv eulogy, 383; after AS's death, 398
AS's RELATION TO, 346; during childhood, 32–33, 73, 135; and AS's European trip, 202, 204, 205, 206; companionship, 202–3; intimacy, 203–4, 223–24, 324–25; maturing and AS's reaction, 222, 346–47, 349; on AS's reading tour, 252–53; AS lonely for, 242, 283–84; AS on womanly legacy, 311; Linda's desire for separation, 325; sharing in poetry writing, 340–41; and Linda at Harvard, 349; at Harvard Literary Club reading, 390–91; and AS's last year, 391
Sexton, Wilhelmine Muller (Billie, mother of Alfred M. Sexton), 21–22, 24; AS and Kayo live with, 23, 24–25; and AS's modeling, 24; and AS's relationship to, 30, 35; move to Annisquam, 31; and AS's breakdown, 34, 35; AS's daughters watched by, 34, 73, 76, 118, 131, 135, 136, 152–54, 229, 271, 339, 374; as AS abortion companion, 121; picture of, 121; as shopper for AS, 138; and AS's writing career, 152, 374; and AS-Kayo fights, 154, 155; and AS's Europe trip, 205; at AS's house during hip recovery, 269; and death of daughter Joan, 318; proposes California move, 339; and AS's sleeping pill overdose, 341; remarriage of, 369; and AS-Kayo divorce, 374; after AS's death, 398; in therapy tape, 411
Shaktman, Ben, 227–28, 266, 275, 329, 356, 376
Shange, Ntozake, 405
Shapiro, Karl, 72
Shaw, George Bernard, quote from, 131
Shelley Memorial Prize, AS receives, 271, 272
Sherwood, Richard, 18, 23
Showalter, Elaine, 392
Silences (Olsen), 197
Silvers, Robert, 256, 276
Simmons, Charles, 172
Simon, John, 329
Simon and Garfunkel, 286, 303
Simons, Harvey, 303
Simpson, Louis, 264, 368
Sitwell, Edith, 104
Skolnick, Irene, 356
Slater, Joseph, 264
Sleeping Beauty, 216, 282; "Briar Rose/Sleeping Beauty," 337
Sleeping pills, AS's use of, 210–11, 238, 252; overdose after love for Johnny, 26; as substitute for suicide, 33; Bearpark on, 281; and Her Kind performance, 305;

overdose (1970), 341; over-
dose (1973), 378
Smart, Christopher, 323, 353, 354,
355
Smith, Alice, 314, 317, 341, 346,
374
Smith, Carol, 392
Smith, Connie, 196
Smith, Joan, 268–69, 271, 341,
345, 349, 379, 393
Smith, Margaret Chase, 357
Smith, Patti, 405
"Snapshots of a Daughter-in-Law"
(Rich), 111
Snodgrass, William DeWitt, xxi,
76–78, 80–82, 84–85; and Antioch workshop, 79; and confes-
sional poetry, 83; and Lowell's
seminar, 91; AS remarks and let-
ters to, 92, 93, 94, 95–96, 101,
102, 109–10, 113, 122, 127; on
AS publication, 94; and AS
abortion, 122; at Boston College
panel, 139; separation from,
172; AS's writing influenced by,
188; Pulitzer Prize to, 231; as
critic, 306; in Oates's time cap-
sule, 320
"Snows of Kilimanjaro, The"
(Hemingway), 198
"Snow White," and AS's account
of life, 3
"Snow White" (Sexton), 337, 347
Sobiloff, Hy, 131–32, 133
Solotaroff, Theodore, 297
"Some Hope" (Sexton), 52
"Somewhere in Africa" (Sexton),
171, 172
"Song for a Red Nightgown" (Sex-
ton), 265, 297
"Song of Songs," 183, 323
Soter, Ruth, 50, 80, 81, 122–23,
217
Spender, Stephen, 72, 127, 279
Spivack, Kathleen, 105
Squirrel Island, 6–7; summer holi-
days on, 10–11, 13; in "Let-

ter . . . ," 150; AS and centennial
of, 350
Stafford, William, 380
Stallworthy, Jon, 243; letters to,
246, 319; and London trip, 261;
and Live or Die reviews, 277;
on AS at London festival, 278;
on AS as "Nefertiti," 283;
and Love Poems, 300, 301,
362; and Transformations,
362–63
Staples, Arthur Gray (grandfather
of AS), 5, 10–11; and Mary
Gray, 6, 18, 20; and Ralph
Harvey, 10; and Blanche
Harvey, 11; and "Comfort," 12,
129, 134, 163; death of, 13, 14;
books of essays by, 20; Jane
caught plagiarizing from, 21;
and AS's poetic efforts, 52; and
"Letter . . . ," 150; letters of lost
in Europe, 205
Staples, Jane Dingley (grandmother of AS), 5–6; death of,
10
Staples, Mary Gray. See Harvey,
Mary Gray
Starbuck, George, xxi, 96, 106; at
party, 95; at Holmes's workshop, 97, 169; AS praised by,
98; with AS and Plath, 106–7;
as AS lover and companion,
107, 117, 118, 182; Bone
Thoughts, 118, 140, 187, 361;
YMHA reading by, 119; on AS
and Jewishness, 123; on Sexton
and Howe, 127; on Sexton at
Brandeis, 128; at Cornell festival, 140; Kumin cites as source,
157; in Rome, 169, 182; AS's
writing influenced by, 188; "Sylvia's Death" sent to, 200; as
critic, 306; and Boston University, 336, 339–40, 357, 389;
and "Fury of Beautiful Bones,"
361; on Rowing, 367; at AS-
Cheever dinner, 394

"Starry Night, The" (Sexton), 122, 186

Steinem, Gloria, 356

Stevens, Wallace, 105, 127, 186

Stevenson, Anne, 364

Stone, Alan, 402

Suicide: and Frances Harvey, 5; of Jane Harvey, 7; AS's attempts at, 33, 34–35, 42, 45, 47, 63, 107, 260, 261, 346, 387, 391–92; and "kill me" pills, 34, 165, 209, 216; AS's thought of, 55, 381, 387; and "The Double Image," 85, 88; in conversation with Plath, 107; AS's urge toward (1961), 16–65; and The Cure (Tell Me Your Answer True), 184, 218, 221; of Plath, 198, 199, 200, 201; AS sees as addicting, 199–200, 217; and AS's plan for posthumous reputation, 201; AS's urge toward (1963), 209; Wilder questions why, 215; and After the Fall, 215; and "Wanting to Die," 215–16; AS on tools for, 216; AS's rationale for, 216–17; and Ruth Soter, 217; of Philip Rahv, 383; of John Berryman, 389; of AS, 395–97; and commentary on AS's life, 397–98

"Suicide Note, The" (Sexton), 50, 240

Summers, Hollis, 80

"Sun, The" (Sexton), 181, 305

Susa, Conrad, xxi, 366, 374, 375

Swan, Barbara, 196–97; self-portrait of, 192; Live or Die cover by, 197, 264; and AS's affair with Zweizung, 314; Transformations illustrations by, 197, 338; on Kayo, 372; and AS at HRI, 378

Sweeney, Brian, 318, 322, 326, 336, 356, 359

Sweeney, John L., 139, 145

Swenson, May, 104, 174

"Sylvia's Death" (Sexton), 199, 200, 212, 243, 264

"Taking a Nap with Linda" (later "The Fortress") (Sexton), 159

Tarn, Nathaniel, 279

Tate, Allen, 127, 131

Taylor, Lisa (daughter of Blanche Harvey), 329

Teachers and Writers Collaborative, AS at board meeting of, 274–75

Teach-ins, 295

Teasdale, Sara, 21, 93, 196

"Technique poems," 98

Tell Me a Riddle (Olsen), 195

Tell Me Your Answer True (Sexton play) 218–22, 227–28, 312–13; and Linda Sexton, 222–23; and AS's breakdown, 224; Orne given copy of, 225; rewriting of, 232; and "For the Year of the Insane," 241; and Degener, 275. See also The Cure; Mercy Street

"Tenth Psalm" (Sexton), 354

Terri, Salli, 239

"That Day" (Sexton), 265

Thomas, D. M., 279, 281–82, 283

Thomas, Dylan, 186

Thorazine, AS's use of, 226–27, 232, 345–46; adverse physical effects, 226, 232, 247, 309, 347; and poetical ability, 227, 231–32, 246; interruptions, 236, 263–64, 345; stops taking, 367, 371, 378; overdose, 391–92

Thoreau, Henry David, 157

"Those Times" (Sexton), 247

Through Dooms of Love (Kumin), 200, 208

"To a Friend Whose Work Has Come to Triumph" (Sexton), 231

To Bedlam and Part Way Back (Sexton), xx, xxi, 70, 94, 102, 113, 125–26, 404; Holmes on, 98, 100; epigraph of, 101; acceptance of, 108; poem added to, 110; and AS as celebrity, 110–11, 139; and "Her Kind," 113–15; Lowell cover blurb for, 119,

125; Dickey on, 126, 250; and National Book Award, 140; and Her Kind rock group, 287; as professional debut, 332

"Torn Down from Glory Daily" (Sexton), 75

"Touch, The" (Sexton), 257, 293, 297, 298, 299, 382, 391

Town Hall, New York, memorial services at, 397

Trances (dissociative or fugue states) of AS, 39, 44; during therapy sessions, 56, 57, 137, 166–67, 175; and sexual abuse memories, 57; and poetry, 63; and "Music Swims Back to Me," 70–71; at Montauk with Jim Wright, 133, 167; in Orne's office, 175, 355; and "Flee on Your Donkey," 179; and AS's improvement, 188; and European trip, 202; and intimacy with Linda, 224; at Ann Arbor, 238–39; at East Hampton with Clawson, 256; in Wayland High class, 285; with Legler in Michigan, 376; in 1973 summer, 377; with Barbara Schwartz, 389

Transformations (Sexton), xxi, 58, 331, 332, 333, 336–38, 356; and Barbara Swan, 197, and therapy notebooks, 214; and Linda Sexton, 336, 340, 349; "Rapunzel" in, 343; and C. K. Williams, 344–45; Freudian questions in, 351; British publication of, 362–63; opera from, 366, 374–75

"Traveler's Wife" (Sexton), 51

"Truth crimes," 62–63

"Truth the Dead Know, The" (Sexton), 58, 130, 382

Tufts University, AS honorary degree from, 339

"Turning God Back On" (Sexton), 286

University of Minnesota, Transformations performed at, 366, 374–75

University of Texas at Austin, Harry Ransom Humanities Research Center at, xxii

"Unknown Girl in the Maternity Ward" (Sexton), 75, 78, 114, 281

Untermeyer, Louis, 139, 145, 152, 276, 356

Up Country: Poems of New England (Kumin), 368

Updike, John, 161, 298, 393

"Us" (Sexton), 295, 297, 299

USA: Poetry (TV series), AS featured in, 246–48, 273

Vietnam War, AS protests against, 295–97

Vonnegut, Kurt, 331, 333, 338

Wakefield, Dan, 390

Wakoski, Diane, 308

"Walking in Paris" (Sexton), 205

"Wallflower" (Sexton) 58, 170

"Wanting to Die," 215–16, 217, 241, 272

Wayland, Massachusetts, AS teaches at, 274, 285–87, 303

"Wedding Night, The" (Sexton), 217

Weeks, Brigitte, 298

Weiss, René, 169–70

Weiss, Theodore, 169–70

West, Jessamyn, 80

West, Nathanael, 127

Weston: Harvey family house in, 13; AS and Kayo house in, 229

Weston High School, AS reads poetry at, 255

Westwood Lodge: Ralph Harvey at, 14; AS at, 33–34, 39, 42, 64, 84, 101–2, 116, 117, 175–76, 209–10, 211, 345–46, 410; and AS book plan, 52

"What's That" (Sexton), 75

"Where I Live in This Honorable House of the Laurel Tree" (Sexton), 82

White, Martha, 151, 195–96, 198
Whitney, Steven, 309
Wilbur, Richard, 95, 170
Wilder, Anne, 213–16, 217, 232–
    36; portrait of, 192; letters to,
    218, 219, 222, 224, 225, 226,
    229, 232, 239, 241–42, 273,
    330, 345–46; picture of, 234;
    contrasts self with AS, 237; on
    AS lecture tour, 237–39; and
    NET documentary, 248; and
    AS-Zweizung affair, 314
Wilding, Faith, 405
Williams, C. K., 306–8, 344–45,
    359, 368, 387
Williams, Oscar, 131, 188–89
Williams, William Carlos, 93
Williamson, Alan, 91
"Witch" (later "Her Kind") (Sex-
    ton), 113–14
"With Mercy for the Greedy" (Sex-
    ton), 122–25, 351
"Woman at the Window" (Sexton),
    258
"Woman with Girdle" (Sexton), 305
Women's liberation, and AS, 151.
    See also Feminism
"Women's poetry," 172
Woolf, Virginia, 172, 197
Words for Dr. Y. (Sexton), xxi,
    217, 331
Wright, Annie, 336
Wright, Franz, 129
Wright, James, xxi, 128–34, 146,
    148–50, 214, 241, 336; and All

My Pretty Ones, 133, 134, 163;
    as Nana, 134, 167; separation
    from, 172; distressed plea to,
    183; and Brother Dennis, 184;
    AS's writing influenced by, 188;
    and Dickey, 251; and Legler,
    253; and Clawson, 257; and
    Neruda, 279; as critic, 306; and
    The Awful Rowing Toward
    God, 367–68
Wright, Marshall, 129
Wyatt, Sir Thomas, 147

Yaguchi, Yorifumi, 365
Yale Series of Recorded Poets, AS
    recorded for, 119
Yale Series of Younger Poets, 187
YMHA, New York, AS readings at,
    119, 356
"You, Doctor Martin" (Sexton),
    75
"You All Know the Story of the
    Other Woman" (Sexton), 271
"Young" (Sexton), 58
"Your Face on the Dog's Neck"
    (Sexton), 239, 248

Zweizung, Ollie, 217, 224, 232,
    241–42; AS's love affair with,
    258, 259–60, 265–66, 269,
    288–89, 313–16, 370; letter to
    from Africa, 263; and AS's for-
    tieth birthday, 310–11; termina-
    tion with, 313, 316; AS to on
    theater, 323, 328